*Reprints of Economic Classics*

# SCARCE AND VALUABLE TRACTS
# ON THE NATIONAL DEBT & THE SINKING FUND

## Reprints of Economic Classics

Also published in this series of

Select Collections of Scarce and Valuable Tracts

Edited by John R. McCulloch

COMMERCE [1859]
ECONOMICAL TRACTS [1859]
MONEY [1856]
PAPER CURRENCY & BANKING [1857]

# A SELECT COLLECTION OF SCARCE AND VALUABLE TRACTS

And Other Publications

ON

# THE NATIONAL DEBT AND THE SINKING FUND

Edited with a Preface, Notes and Index

By John R. McCulloch

[1857]

REPRINTS OF ECONOMIC CLASSICS

AUGUSTUS M. KELLEY · PUBLISHERS
NEW YORK · 1966

Original edition 1857

LIBRARY OF CONGRESS CATALOGUE CARD NUMBER
65-16989

PRINTED IN THE UNITED STATES OF AMERICA
*by* SENTRY PRESS, NEW YORK, N. Y. 10019

# SCARCE AND VALUABLE TRACTS, &c.,

ON THE

# NATIONAL DEBT

AND

# THE SINKING FUND.

*** THIS volume has been printed by LORD OVERSTONE for distribution amongst his friends; the duty of editing it having been kindly undertaken by J. R. Mc Culloch, Esq.

A

# SELECT COLLECTION

OF

SCARCE AND VALUABLE TRACTS AND OTHER PUBLICATIONS,

ON

# THE NATIONAL DEBT

AND

# THE SINKING FUND,

FROM THE ORIGINALS OF

HARLEY, GOULD, PULTENEY, WALPOLE, HUME, PRICE, HAMILTON, AND OTHERS.

WITH A PREFACE, NOTES, AND INDEX.

---

LONDON:
MDCCCLVII.

# PREFACE.

THIS volume includes the principal tracts that have been published relating to the progress of the National Debt of Great Britain, its influence, and the more prominent plans that have been formed for its extinction. They are for the most part so very scarce that, for a lengthened period, they have been known only to a few curious inquirers. But the principles which they embody, and the powerful influence they have had over financial measures, make an acquaintance with them indispensable to those who would accurately trace the economical history and policy of the country. And we flatter ourselves that in rescuing several of these tracts from oblivion, and making them readily accessible, we have rendered a considerable service to the cause of historical and financial inquiry.

Though of gigantic dimensions, the National Debt of Great Britain has been all but wholly contracted since the Revolution. That great event involved us in hostilities with Louis XIV, the most powerful monarch of his time, who espoused the cause of the Stuarts. And while

while the danger from without was great and imminent, it was probably inferior to the danger from within. A large proportion of the population being either openly or secretly attached to the exiled family, the imposition of such an amount of new taxes as would have been required to defray the heavy cost of the war which it was necessary to wage in defence of our newly acquired liberties, became all but impossible. And though it had been possible it would have been highly impolitic, inasmuch as it would have supplied the Jacobites with the means of inflaming the popular discontents, and of traducing and, perhaps, overturning the new government. The contraction of debt was then not a matter of choice but of necessity; and to it we are, in great measure, indebted for our liberties. But having once been introduced, the practice of funding was found to be so very convenient a means of obtaining supplies that it has since been resorted to on all occasions whether it were really required or not. And hence the rapid growth and vast magnitude of the debt.

In the infancy of the funding system loans were generally raised either upon annuities for terms of years or for lives. But the inconvenience resulting from this practice soon became obvious, and since the reign of Anne very little money has been raised otherwise than upon perpetual annuities, that is, upon annuities redeemable only on payment of the principal.

Owing to the supposed insecurity of the revolutionary establishment, the interest paid on the money

borrowed

borrowed in the reigns of William and Mary, William III, and the earlier years of Anne, was comparatively high. And according as confidence in the new order of things gained ground, and loans were obtained on more favourable terms, the high interest paid on the previous loans began to form a topic of complaint. Instead, however, of attempting to reduce it by offering the creditors payment of their debts in the event of their declining to accept a lower rate of interest, it was proposed, both in Parliament and out of doors, to effect the end in view by laying a tax on the funds. But this proposal, which involved a flagrant breach of the public faith, was happily defeated. This result was in no inconsiderable degree owing to the influence of the first two tracts reprinted in this volume, in which the mischievous operation and dishonest character of the scheme for taxing the funds is set in the clearest light. The first of these tracts, an "Essay upon Publick Credit," believed to be the production of Harley, Earl of Oxford, was referred to in terms of high commendation in 1786 by the first Marquis of Lansdowne, in the debates on Mr. Pitt's Sinking Fund. But the second tract—"A Letter on the Inviolable Nature of Publick Securities"—is the more able of the two, and deserves the special attention of the reader.

The first sinking fund for the extinction of the public debt was formed in 1716. It consisted of various surpluses of revenue arising from the saving that was then effected by reducing the interest of the debt, and other sources. Nothing was said when this fund was organised

about

about the supposed influence of compound interest in increasing its efficiency. That idea seems to have been first brought forward in the Tract No. III, in this volume, entitled "An Essay on the Publick Debts of this Kingdom," published in 1726. It was written by Sir Nathaniel Gould, M.P., an eminent merchant and a director of the Bank of England. It contains tables and statements showing the rapid growth of funds laid out at compound interest; and demonstrating, among other things, that a million sterling, accumulated at 4 per cent. compound interest, would amount in 105 years to 1575 millions! But, in addition to these visionary calculations, which were afterwards reproduced with so much effect by Price, Gould's tract contains various statements, intended to show that the debt existing in 1716 had been materially reduced in the interval. This, however, was stoutly denied by many; and among others by Mr. Pulteney, afterwards Earl of Bath, then leader of the opposition in the House of Commons. He, indeed, is believed, and apparently on good grounds, to be the author of the "State of the National Debt as it stood December 24th, 1716," published in 1727, and reprinted (No. IV,) in this volume; in which it is endeavoured to be shown, in opposition to Gould, that instead of being diminished, the debt had been considerably increased in the interval referred to by the latter. But Gould, who was a skilful accountant, and not to be easily vanquished on a question of this sort, replied to Pulteney, and repeated his statements in "A Defence of an Essay on the Publick Debts," which we have also reprinted.

This

This controversy occasioned a good deal of interest at the time, and was alluded to as follows in the House of Commons—"On the 23rd February, 1727-28, the Committee of Supply resolved to raise £1,750,000 on the coal duty. Hereupon Mr. Pulteney observed that the shifting of funds was but perpetuating taxes, and putting off the evil day: and that notwithstanding the great merit that some had built on the sinking fund, it appeared that the National Debt had been increased since the setting up of that pompous project. On which Sir Nathaniel Gould said he apprehended that Hon. Gentleman had his notions out of a Treatise entitled a 'State of the National Debt,' supposed to be written by that very gentleman. But that if he (Sir N. G.) understood anything it was numbers, and he durst pawn his credit to prove that author's calculations and inferences to be false. To this Mr. Pulteney replied that he took them to be right, and he would likewise pawn his credit to make good his assertion. Upon this Sir Robert Walpole took up the cudgels, and said he would maintain what Sir Nathaniel Gould had advanced. Several warm expressions having followed on both sides, Mr. Hungerford interposed in a jocular speech that put the House in good humour, and so the dispute ended."*

There can, however, be no doubt that the statements of Gould and Walpole on this occasion were well founded, and that the debt was considerably diminished during the ten years

* History and Proceedings of House of Commons, vol. v, date referred to.

years ending with 1726. This is established beyond all question in the Representation on the subject of the Debt addressed by the House of Commons, to George II, in 1728. This important document is here reprinted for (we believe) the first time from the Journals of the House.

The next treatise in this volume, the "Essay of Public Credit," by the celebrated David Hume, is of a very different character from those by which it is preceded and followed. We have inserted it partly that the beauty of its style might relieve the dryness of these discussions, and partly that the reader might see the sort of estimate which the ablest men of last century formed of the influence of the public debt when it did not amount to a twelfth part of its present magnitude. And it must be confessed that no estimate could be wider of the mark. But this does not really reflect so much discredit on the sagacity of Hume, and of Adam Smith and those by whom similar views were entertained, as has been supposed. Their error did not consist in their making a false estimate of the influence of the debt, but in their overlooking those circumstances by which that influence might be, and has been, countervailed. And this neglect on their part was not much to be wondered at. From the little progress that had previously been made in manufactures none could have anticipated in 1750, in 1760, or even in 1770, the extraordinary career of invention and discovery on which we were soon after to enter The creative genius of Watt, Arkwright, Crompton, Cartwright, Wedgwood

Wedgwood and others, by making immeasurable additions to our means and capacities of production, falsified all the predictions in regard to the sinister influence of the public debt. The latter has vastly increased; but the ability of the country to bear it having increased still more rapidly, its injurious operation, though by no means inconsiderable, is less at this moment than in the earlier part of the reign of George II, when it amounted to little more than 50 millions.

The Essay of Hume is followed by an extract from the Commentaries of Blackstone. It completely disposes of the extraordinary notion which was then entertained by numbers of people, that "the national debt was so much added to the public wealth by the magical influence of credit."

Hume and Blackstone appear to have been unacquainted with the tract of Sir Nathaniel Gould, and do not once refer, in treating of the reduction of the public debt, to the supposed influence of sinking funds operating at compound interest. Had they done so, the presumption is, they would have perceived and exposed its fallacy. But their statements, and more especially those of Hume, by representing the debt as at once an oppressive and an irremediable grievance, were well fitted to conciliate the public attention and favour to those of an opposite character. And such were speedily brought forward. Dr. Price's "Appeal to the Public on the Subject of the National Debt," published in 1771 and 1774, and reprinted in in this volume, shows that his views in regard to the efficiency of a sinking fund increasing at compound interest, were nearly identical with those of Gould. But he states them with incomparably greater force and earnestness; and with a confidence in their accuracy that was well calculated to make, and did make, a powerful impression. This was increased, partly by the theory of Price being one which most people were extremely desirous should prove to be well-founded, and partly from his calculations being deduced from hypotheses that were mathematically correct. The fact that they were at the same time practically impossible was conveniently forgotten or kept out of view; and it appears that for a lengthened period it was taken for granted that a penny laid out at 5 per cent. compound interest at the birth of Christ would have amounted in 1770 to above a hundred and fifty millions of globes of solid gold, each of the size of the earth! (See post, p. 325.) With such a power at command it is not surprising that it should have been deemed an easy matter to deal with the debt.

The delusion caused by Price's writings though very general was not universal. In this volume are two tracts, one by a Mr. Wimpey, published in 1772, in answer to Price's Appeal, and one by an anonymous author ("Considerations on the Annual Million Bill"), which show the entire fallacy of the views put forward by the Doctor and adopted by Mr. Pitt. But, how conclusive soever, these pamphlets appear to have fallen still-born from the press. They attracted no attention and had no effect.

The

The delusive nature of a sinking fund supposed to operate at compound interest may be shown in a few words. Suppose that a million sterling is put into the hands of commissioners to form such a fund: In the first place the commissioners would divest themselves of this million for an equivalent amount of stock, and would thereafter receive the dividends or interest on that stock which had previously been paid to the public creditor. If this dividend were 5 per cent., or £50,000, the commissioners would purchase stock with it, on which they would, of course, receive a corresponding dividend; so that at the end of the 1st year they would have £52,500 to invest in a new purchase; at the end of the 2nd year, £55,125; at the end of the 3rd year, £57,881, and so on. Now this is what Sir Nathaniel Gould, Dr. Price, and Mr. Pitt call paying off the public debt by a sinking fund increasing at compound interest. But it is plain that there is no such fund in existence; and that any diminution which may be effected in the public debt in the way now stated, is effected by applying a constantly increasing portion of the dividends on the debt, that is, of the taxes paid by the public, to the purchase of stock. No doubt it is true that by laying out any given sum in that way, and then laying out the dividends accruing on the purchased stock in the purchase of additional stock, a diminution of the debt will be effected in the same manner as if the funds employed were derived from a source increasing by an inherent energy of its own at compound interest. But though the results be the same, the means are altogether different. The debt is reduced because that portion of

the

the revenue required to pay the dividends or interest on the stock bought by the Commissioners is not remitted to the contributors, but continues to be taken from them and applied to the purchase of fresh stock. Compound interest has nothing whatever to do with the matter. In this case there is no fund to increase at compound interest; and if there were, neither money nor capital can increase in that ratio unless it be employed in industrious undertakings, and, unless the profits, instead of being spent as income, are regularly saved and added to the capital. But it is needless to say that no such sinking fund ever existed. Those that have been set on foot in this and other countries have all been supported either by loans or by the produce of taxes, and have never paid off a single shilling of debt by their own agency.

Neither must it be supposed that the notion of the wonder-working effects of sinking funds has been a mere harmless error. On the contrary, few delusions have been practically so mischievous. By making it be believed that the greatest amount of debt might be defrayed by a sort of hocus pocus machinery without loss to any one, it was one of the principal causes of the extravagance that characterised the early portion of the war with revolutionary France, and of the ruinous extent to which the system of funding was then carried. And independent of these, which may be considered its indirect effects, its direct influence was not less injurious.

Dr. Hamilton of Aberdeen has the merit of having dissipated the delusion in regard to the sinking fund. The work in which this valuable service was performed is the

last

last in this volume. It is entitled an "Inquiry into the Rise, Progress, &c., of the National Debt," and was first published in 1813, when the author was above 70 years of age. But it has all the vigour and condensation that are supposed to belong to works produced at an earlier period of life. He showed that, instead of reducing, the sinking fund had increased the debt. And he proved to demonstration that the excess of revenue over expenditure is the only fund by which any portion of the public debt can ever be discharged. Besides the elaborate inquiry into the real and imaginary properties of a sinking fund, the work contains a great many discussions with respect to other important matters, and gives a very complete account of the progress of the national debt from the Revolution down nearly to the end of the French war.

But since Dr. Hamilton's work appeared, more correct accounts have been obtained of the expenditure, loans, &c., during the great struggle terminated in 1815. And from these it may be easily shown that the sinking fund was not a clumsy only but a costly imposture. In proof of this we beg to state that the loans contracted in each year from 1794 to 1816, both inclusive, amounted in all to £584,874,557, at an annual charge to the public of £30,174,364. Of these loans the Commissioners of the Sinking Fund received £188,522,350, the proportional annual charge on such portion being, of course, £9,726,090.* But it farther

*584, 874,557 : 30,174,364 :: 188,522,350 : $9,726,089\frac{15817827}{584874557}$

farther appears from the accounts referred to, that the stock which the Commissioners purchased with this sum of £188,522,350, transferred to them out of the loans, only yielded an annual dividend of £9,168,232.* On the one hand, therefore, an annual charge of £9,726,090 was incurred to enable the Sinking Fund Commissioners to go to market; and, on the other, they bought stock which yielded £9,168,233 a year; so that, on the whole, their operations during the war occasioned a direct dead loss to the country of no less than £557,857 a year, equivalent to a 3 per cent. capital of £18,595,233, exclusive of the expenses of the office, which amounted to above £60,000. Such was the practical result of Mr. Pitt's famous sinking fund, so long regarded as the palladium of public credit, and the sheet anchor of the nation!

Notwithstanding Dr. Hamilton's book was published, as already stated, in 1813, the statute for the suppression of the sinking fund, the 10 Geo. IV, c. 27, was not passed till 1829. It enacted that in time to come the sum to be applied to the reduction of the National Debt should be the actual annual surplus of revenue over expenditure.

After these statements it might have been supposed that this generation would have heard no more of compulsory sinking funds. But financial errors appear to be endowed with

* See for a Table giving these statements in full, McCulloch's Treatise on Taxation, 2nd ed., p. 457.

with something approaching to immortality. No sooner has their fallacy been demonstrated than we frequently find them put forward as if their soundness neither had been nor could be questioned. Such, at all events, has been the case with regard to the sinking fund. In 1855 a loan of £16,000,000 was contracted under the 18 & 19 Vict., c. 18; and it enacts that, until an equivalent amount of the funded debt of the United Kingdom has been paid off, the sum of £1,000,000 shall be annually advanced to the Sinking Fund Commissioners, the first advance being made within a year after the signature of a definitive treaty of peace with Russia. Hence, should we be involved in a contest with any other great power, or with Russia herself, before the debt contracted in 1855 is paid off, or should any circumstance connected with our domestic or foreign policy make it impossible or unadvisable to maintain a clear surplus revenue of £1,000,000 a year, government, however disinclined, must borrow the money with which to make this annual payment. No condition could, in truth, be more uncalled for, or more opposed to sound principle. Whatever surplus might exist would have gone to the extinction of the debt under the Act of 1829; while if there be no surplus, or one that is insufficient, we shall be compelled to adopt what may be a most inexpedient course of policy.

It may be proper to adopt means for the reduction of the debt. But that grand object will never be effected by resorting to measures which tie up the hands of Parliament, and hinder our profiting either by changes of circumstances or the lessons of experience.

# CONTENTS.

# AN ESSAY UPON Publick Credit:

BEING

An ENQUIRY

How the PUBLICK CREDIT comes to depend upon the Change of the *Ministry*, or the Dissolutions of *Parliaments*; and whether it does so or no.

With an ARGUMENT,

Proving that the PUBLICK CREDIT may be upheld and maintain'd in this Nation; and perhaps brought to a greater Height than it ever yet arriv'd at; Tho' all the Changes or Dissolutions already Made, Pretended to, and now Discours'd of, shou'd come to pass in the World.

---

*LONDON*:

Printed, and Sold by the Book-sellers, MDCCX.

AN

# ESSAY

UPON

## *Publick Credit*, &c.

THE World being so full of Polititians, and so many Authors having of late turn'd Statesmen, it behoves me to lay every Thing down exceeding plain, as I go on; The Subject is nice, the Age abusive, the Town full of *Observers* and *Reviewers*, who Write to please and content the Notions of Men, who, directed by their Interest and Parties, differ even with themselves; Reason, it is true, is DICTATOR in the Society of Mankind; from her there ought to lye no Appeal; But here we want a Pope in our Philosophy, to be the infallible Judge of what *is* or *is not* Reason.

I am to speak of what all People are busie about, but not one in Forty understands: Every Man has a Concern in it, few know what it is, nor is it easy to define or describe it. If a Man goes about to explain it by Words, he rather struggles to lose himself *in the Wood*, than bring others out of it. It is best describ'd by it self; 'tis like the Wind that blows *where it lists*, we hear the *sound* thereof, but hardly know *whence it comes*, or *whither it goes*.

*Like the Soul* in the Body, it acts all Substance, yet is it self Immaterial; it gives Motion, yet it self cannot be



said

said to Exist; it creates *Forms,* yet has it self *no Form*; it is neither Quantity or Quality; it has no *Whereness,* or *Whenness, Scite* or *Habit.* If I should say it is the essential Shadow of something that is Not; should I not Puzzle the thing rather than Explain it, and leave you and my self more the Dark than we were before?

To come at a direct and clear Understanding of the Thing, the best Method will be to describe its *Operations,* rather than define its *Nature*; to show *how it Acts* rather than *how it Exists,* and *what it does,* rather than *what it is.*

TRADE, as the Author of the *Review* has told us, and who I can better submit to learn of on that subject, than some other he talks more about "was derived by Con-" venience from the profitable exchanging of Goods from " Nation to Nation, and from Place to Place, as People " encreasing, found their Neighbours possest of what they " wanted, and themselves having to spare of what their " Neighbouring Countries did not produce. *This we now call Barter,* and is not so much in Use as it was in the Infancy of Commerce in the World.

The *Brittains* Inhabiting this Island were found to Exchange their *Block Tin* with the *Phenician* Merchants for *Spices, Wines* and *Oyls,* even long before *Julius Cæsar* set his Foot upon this Island.

But as Trade increased, two Accidents *fell in,* as Effects; being the great *Mediums* of Universal Commerce, *the Vehicle* in which Trade is Preserv'd or Administred thro' the World; these were *Money* and *Credit.*

This thing call'd Commerce flourishing, and extending every way into all the Corners of the World, the Nations falling generally into Dealing with one another; yet Trade found it self unsufferably streightned and perplext for want of a General *Species* of a compleat intrinsick Worth, *as the Medium* to supply the defect of Exchanging, and to make good *the Balance;* where a Nation, or a

 Market,

Market, or a Merchant, demanded of another a greater quantity of Goods than either the Buyer had Goods *to Answer*, or the Seller had occasion to *take back*.

This nothing could be found in the World of universal and intrinsick Worth enough to Answer, but *Metals*; as being neither consuming in *Quality*, bulky in *Carriage*, or useless in *Nature:* Of these Metals several Nations adhered a long time, to such as their own Country produced; but *Gold* and *Silver*, by their meer intrinsick Worth, prevailed; and they alone retain the universal Character, as it may be called, in all Payments of whatever kind in the World.

The Course of Trade being thus turned, from exchanging of Goods for Goods, or *Delivering* and *Taking*, to *Selling* and *Paying*, all the Bargains in the World are now stated upon the Foot of *a Price* in Money; and tho' it be at any Time an Exchange of *Goods* for *Goods*, yet even those Goods are on either side rated at a *Price* in Money.

Tho' this was a great Assistant to Trade, and gave a liberty to the increase of Commerce more than ever it had before, *yet* such was the great increase of Trade, that it even over-run the Money it self, and all the Specie in the World could not answer the Demand, or be ready just at the Time, Trade called for it. *This occasioned*, That when *A* Bought more Goods of *B* than *A* had Money to pay for; and *B* having no Need of any Goods that *A* had to Sell; it behoved, that *A* should leave his Goods with *B* for a certain Time, in which *A* was to provide the Money for the said Goods: And this was done, both from the Occasion *B* had to sell his Goods, the Occasion *A* had to buy them, and the Opinion *B* had of *A*'s Integrity and Ability for Payment.

And this is the Great Thing call'd CREDIT.

CREDIT is a Consequence, not a Cause; the Effect of a Substance, not a Substance; 'tis the *Sun-shine*, not the Sun;

Sun; the quickning SOMETHING, *Call it what you will,* that gives Life to *Trade,* gives Being to the Branches, and Moisture to the Root; 'tis the *Oil* of the Wheel, the *Marrow* in the Bones, the *Blood* in the Veins, and the *Spirits* in the Heart of all the Negoce, Trade, Cash, and Commerce in the World.

It is produc'd, and grows insensibly, from fair and upright Dealing, punctual Compliance, honourable Performance of Contracts and Covenants, in short, 'tis the Off-spring of universal Probity.

'Tis apparent, even by its Nature, 'tis no way dependent upon Persons, Parliaments, or any particular Men, or Sett of Men, *as such,* in the World; but upon *their Conduct* and *Just* Behaviour. *Credit* never was chain'd to Mens *Names,* but to their *Actions*; not to Families, Clans, or Collections of Men; no, not to Nations; 'Tis the Honour, the Justice, the Fair-Dealing, and the equal Conduct of *Men,* Bodies of Men, Nations, and People, that raise the thing call'd *Credit* among them; wheresoever this is found, CREDIT will live and thrive, grow and encrease; *where this is wanting,* let all the Power and Wit of Man join together, they can neither give her Being, or preserve her Life.

Arts have been try'd, on various Occasions in the World, to raise CREDIT; *Art* has been found able, with more Ease, to destroy *Credit,* than to raise it: The Force of *Art,* assisted by the punctual, fair, and just Dealing *abovesaid*; may have done much to form a *Credit* upon the Face of Things; but we find still the *Honour* would have done it without the *Art,* but never the *Art* without the *Honour.* Nor will Money it self, which *Solomon* says, *answers all things,* purchase this thing call'd *Credit,* or restore it when lost.

It is in vain to talk of *Credit* without this *Probity:* Honesty will raise *Credit* without Money; but all the Money in the World will not raise *Credit* without the Principle.

Principle. *D.* was a Prince of high Birth, a great Character for Wit, Gallantry, and all the Perfections of a Duke and Peer of one of the Politest Nations in *Europe*; he had, *besides*, a noble Fortune, built great Edifices, purchased great Houses, maintain'd a vast Equipage, and did every thing with the Air of an exquisite and most accomplish'd Gentleman; he had a vast Fortune, great Offices at Court, nor did he ever want Money; his Stewards were never without 20000 Pistols in Cash; if *any Summ*, however great, was wanting to support any Point of Honour, for his Play, or to purchase what he had his Eye upon, he knew how to produce it; yet the Barber would not trust him for a Perriwig; the Coachmaker would not let his Chariot go home with a new Sett of Wheels; *What was the matter?* He would pay no Body generously, or honourably; he would be surrounded with Duns as he came out of his Palace, and would go *Incognito* to Court to prevent being insulted: The *Sbirri*, or *Provost's Men* at *Paris*, would stop his Coach in the Street, he has been forc'd to call a Chair, and leave his Coach and Horses in their Possession.

The thing was plain, he had no *Credit*; his great Estate, his high Birth and Quality, his Equipage, his vast Quantity of Gold Plate, his large Cash, they would not add one Inch to the Stature of his *Credit*; but he liv'd as if he was Poor, and was less esteem'd in the Shops of the Marchands than a private Gentleman; nay, than one of the *Burgois*; I had almost said, than a Shoe-maker in the City.

On the other hand, *S* —— is a Gentleman of a moderate Fortune, compar'd to the other, but is also a Man of Quality; he lives Nobly, tho' Frugally; keeps a good Equipage, a handsom Family, does not lay up much, his generous Nature will not permit it; but he pays punctually, no Man comes twice for his Money; if a Tradesman leaves his Bill, he buys no more of him till he comes



for

for his Money; he never Dines till his Wine is paid for; he wears no Cloaths that the Taylor or Mercer can reproach him for, and call THEIRS as he goes along the Street; instead of having his Door crowded with Duns, and his Steward brib'd to pay, he is rather crowded with Shop-keepers to petition for his Custom; his Servants are teiz'd to procure their Lord to buy here or there, and every one studies to leave his Goods for Approbation. The Tradesmen are ready to fight, who shall get in his Goods, and Sell often to Loss, to under-rate one another. What's the Matter? *Credit* stands at his Door; Honour lives there, and *Credit* is her Handmaid. The Count deals justly, pays punctually, every Man's Demands are answer'd, *Credit* courts him, he shall have her Favour, whether he will use her or no.

It is needless to enlarge; Experience tells us the same thing in all Cases, whether private or publick, Personal or National.

*Credit* is the Consequence of just and honourable Dealing; fair Proposals punctually perform'd will bring Credit, let the Person or People be who they will. How do we Trade among the *Turks*, and Trust the *Mahometans*, one of whose Doctrines, in the *Alchoran*, is, not to keep Faith with Christians? They have obtain'd it by a just, punctual, and honourable Practice *in Trade*, and you *Credit them without Scruple*; nay, rather than a Christian.

Upon this Foundation I build what I am in hand with, and bring it down to the present Case: I know no Persons or Parties in my Argument: This Lord Treasurer or another Lord Treasurer, or no Lord Treasurer, it is the same thing to me; a Bank or no Bank, 'tis all one, I'll sell none of my Tallies or Annuities, I'll discount no Exchequer Bills: Dissolve the Parliament or not Dissolve the Parliament, 'tis all one to me; I neither fear, desire, or am anxious about either; nor can I see so much Cause for an Alarm among our People that have Money,



as

as if Credit was pinn'd to the Girdle of a Man, or waited at the Door of the House of Commons; the thing is a Mistake, Credit attends the honourable Management of your *Treasurers*, your *Exchequers*, your *Parliaments*, whether past, present, or to come.

I do not examine what Politic Reasons may induce her Majesty, to change or remove her Great Men in the Ministry; I enquire not whether her Majesty purposes to dissolve the Parliament, or to let them Sit, these things are not concern'd in our Case: The late Lord Treasurer,* I allow, has done Honourably, has manag'd the Finances with great and unusual Dexterity, and has acquir'd thereby the Fame of the Best Officer, that has for many Years acted in that Post; I could be content to spend a whole Page in his Praise; the Nation is infinitely obliged to him; and his Royal Mistress, no doubt, has receiv'd infinite Satisfaction in his Conduct, as appears by rejecting all Attempts against him, and keeping him so long in a Post of so Great Trust.

But after this is said, *Credit*, which has for some Years been the Nations happy Guest, by whose Aid such mighty Things have been done, cannot be said to be the sole Property of my Lord T———r Personally; it is not singly intail'd upon his Family, or his Name; this would be to go a length his Lordship himself has more Modesty than to claim; nor would his Lordship be well pleased with any that could think such coarse kind of Flattery would oblige him.

Our Credit in this Case is a Public Thing; it is rightly call'd by some of our Writers, NATIONAL CREDIT; the Word denominates its Original; 'tis produc'd by *the Nations* Probity, the Honour and exact performing *National Engagements.* In this the Great Officers of the Treasury and Exchequer are, as we may say, perfectly

 Passive;

* Lord Godolphin.

Passive; their Business is indeed Active; so the Wheels of a Clock, their Business is to go round; but they are subject to the Influence of *their Position,* the Operations of the Springs and Wheels that guide *their Motion,* by which they act passively, if that may be said, *that is,* of meer Necessity; and the punctual pointing of the Hand to the Lines shewing the Hour, the Minutes and the Seconds, *are Consequences* of these Motions: These indeed tell us that the Wheels are good, perfectly made, exactly plac'd, and move to a Truth; but the Honour redounds to the *Workman,* who plac'd them in that exact Order, adapted them to their several Uses, and placed such Springs and Wheels about them, which by their like exactness, but all deriv'd from the same Original, oblige every part punctually to perform the End of the whole Movement.

CREDIT is not the Effect of this or that Wheel in the Government, moving regular and just to its proper Work; but of the whole Movement, acting by the Force of its true original Motion, according to the exquisite Design of the Director of the whole Frame.

Thus the *Honour,* the *Probity,* the *exact,* punctual *Management,* which has raised our *Credit* to the pitch it is now arriv'd at, has not been merely the Great Wheel in *the Nations Clockwork,* that turn'd about the Treasure, but the Great Spring that turn'd about that Wheel, and this is the QUEEN and PARLIAMENT. *The one,* the Spring (*still keeping to the Allegory*) that gives Motion or Life to the whole; *the other,* the Balance or Pendulum, that regulates that Motion, keeps it true to, and exact in the performance of the General Work, (*viz.*) the equal and punctual dividing the smallest measures of Time.

*This Nice Case* requires me a little to descend to Particulars, and touch Matter of Fact nearer than was intended; What is it has restored and recovered the Nations *Credit* from the Breaches made in it? The answering

 this

this necessarily requires that I should also ask what made the former Breaches in *our Credit?* I shall do this as Modestly as I can; for it is not the present Work to open Sores, but to heal them, to prevent more from breaking out.

Some of the Reasons which sunk *our Credit,* and made the Breaches in it in the late Reign, were the settling Funds that were in themselves deficient; and making no Provision to supply those Deficiencies. Some would perhaps go farther, and say, It was settling Funds that *were not probable,* and whose Deficiencies Were visible. I shall not go that length; the Error was in the Original; it would be unjust to charge the Deficiency of these Funds upon the Commissioners of the Treasury *for the Time being,* it would be still harder to blame them for the Parliament not supplying those Deficiencies. Some may have said they were to blame in the First Act, because it was their Work to provide Funds, and the Parliament only gave what they ask'd; that they took them and went away satisfied, as sufficient for the supply of the Occasion, and that they were Judges of the probability: *I am not of that mind,* tho' it is not to my purpose here to debate it. But this is Certain, the not supplying the Deficiencies upon the repeated Application of the Persons whose Estates lay in those Deficiencies, seem'd wholly to lye at the Door of the Parliament, and this brought the Tallies on those Funds to intollerable, unheard of Discounts, to the ruin of all that we *called Credit.*

What then has raised *this Credit?* I hope I do not detract from the just Character of him, whom one calls the great Guide of the Nation's Treasure, if I say, It was something else than his Lordship's Management; something Prior to it, *in which* that National Honour and Justice, Resolution of punctual Payment and Concern for the Means of it, *appeared,* which put Life into the Nation, and made those People that had Money think it *as safe,* as well deposited, and the Principal in as *good*

*Hands* as in their own; so that they were perfectly Easie in adventuring their Money, and the longer this went on, the forwarder were the People to bring in their Money: Nay, so forward, that the faster the Government lower'd their Interest, the more eager were the People to bring in their Money.

*Let us see* where this began, and this will tell us *whose doing* it was. After the first Session of Parliament of Her present Majesty, the Queen acquainted the House, That the Funds had more than answered the Sums *they were given for;* there was the capital Wound of Deficiency healed at once. That the Overplus should be apply'd, &c. There was an Assurance, that all Deficiencies, if any happen'd, should be made good. This gave *the Parliament Part* a Brightness that reviv'd the Spirits of the People, help'd open their Purses which had been so long closed, and caused Taxes to be raised without murmuring.

*The Queen* acted the next part; Her Majesty gave constant Assurances, that everything given should be *rightly apply'd*; and to Encourage her People, and shew she was willing *to bear a part* of their Burthen, the Queen generously threw in *an Hundred thousand Pound* of her own Money, *appropriated for the Civil List*, to ease the Nation of so much in that Years Burthen. *These were Steps* no Prince ever was known to take before. *After this* you never heard of a Complaint of the heavy Burthen of the Taxes, tho' greater far than any raised in the former Reign; on the contrary, *the more* you rais'd, *the easier* they were paid; *the more* the Nation ran in Debt, *the higher* their Credit rose every day. *After this* you never had any Commissioners of Accounts ask'd for, or any Question about Misapplication. *No Man* need go far for a Reason for this; *the Credit* centred all in the Queen, whose Concern was so visible for her Peoples good, that she would suffer no Misapplications; that she would Employ none but in



whom

whom she could place entire Confidence; whose Probity and Exactness her Majesty could answer for *to her self,* and was well assured she might be *safe in.*

'Tis no way lessening the Honour of the Servants her Majesty Chose, to say that the Nations Credit depends not on the Reputation of their Conduct; but on her Majesty's Care, in Chosing such Men, whose Conduct would perform all the Nation could expect; and that if they should fail, her Majesty would not fail to remove them, and put in others. This is putting the thing right; the Sum and Substance of the Argument is this, in short.

*Publick Credit* is the Consequence of honourable, just, and punctual Management in the Matter of *Funds* and *Taxes,* or Loans upon them. Where this goes before, Credit always follows.

*This Management* depends not upon the Well-Executing their Offices, by the great Officers of the Treasury, and the Exchequer, but on the *Care, Conduct* and *Vigilance* of her Majesty and the Parliament; *the latter* in Establishing sufficient Funds; and *the former* in Placing able Officers, and obliging them to an honourable Management.

The *Publick Credit* therefore depends upon the Queen and Parliament entirely, and not at all upon the well or ill Management of the Officers, of what kind soever.

Another thing confirms this, (*viz.*) That while the Parliament Concerns it self to prevent the Deficiency of Funds, and the Queen to Place Men of Probity and Honour in the Government of her Treasury; *there is no Question to be made,* but both would concern themselves *upon any Complaints of the Subject,* to enquire into any Mismanagement or Abuse of the People, in the greatest Officers; and not only punish the Offender, but *prevent the Offence,* by removing such Officer, and supplying his Place with others, who should better discharge so weighty a Trust. This resolves the point, That Credit centers



where

where the Government centers; for if the Sovereign displaces those that mis-apply, the Wound to Credit heals of it self; and while the Sovereign carefully prefers Men of Honour and Probity in the Nations Trust, Credit rises by a natural Consequence.

But still it is the NATIONS CREDIT; *that is,* it is built on the Honour of the Queen and Parliament, as above; and this has been the Case of the late Lord Treasurer; the Credit of whose Management must return to the Queen, as to the Center; otherwise this must be call'd *My Lord T . . . 's Credit,* not the *Nations*; and, to our great loss, must dye with his Lordship; which would be very unhappy *for us*; and would imply, that we ought to be more concern'd for his Lordship's long Life than the Queen's; a thing would very ill please even his Lordship to suggest.

Having laid down this as a Foundation, I build this short Fabrick upon it, (*viz.*) *That as* the Publick Credit is *National,* not *Personal,* so it depends upon No *thing* or *Person,* No *Man* or *Body of Men,* but upon the Government, *that is,* The Queen and Parliament; displacing or removing any Minister of State, or great Officer, whose Management under the Sovereign affects our Treasure, can no way influence our *National Credit*; while the Just, Honourable and Punctual Conduct of the Sovereign and Parliament remains the same. Neither does our Credit depend upon the Person of the Queen, *as Queen,* or the individual House of Commons, *Indentically*; as if *no Queen* but her present Majesty, and *no Parliament* but the present Parliament, could support and uphold the Credit of the Nation: *But* it will remain a Truth, that *every Queen,* or *every King,* and *every Parliament,* succeeding the Present, that shall discover the *same Justice* in Government, the *same Care* in giving sufficient Funds, the *same Honesty* in supplying the Deficiencies if they happen, *the same* Concern for the Burthen of the Subject, and *the*

 *same*

*same* Care to put the Treasure into the Hands of Faithful and Experienc'd Officers; shall keep up *the same* Character, have *the same* Credit, and restore all these Declinings to *the same* Vigour and Magnitude as ever.

*From hence it appears,* That our present Loss of *Credit* does not arise from any Doubt, whether the like Conduct can produce this Effect or no; but from a strange Suggestion, That a new Parliament, or a new Ministry, shall either *not Design* or not *Pursue* the same vigorous and wise Resolutions, or mannage with *the same* Integrity, as the last have done. If her Majesty saw room for this Suggestion, I make no doubt, (her Concern for the Publick Good *is such*) that no such Change had been made, or would lodge an Hour longer among her Thoughts; but if her Majesty is of the Opinion, that such a Change will not lessen the Concern *for*, or just Measures *in* the Publick Service, then the Difficulty ends. Her Majesty has now put new Officers into her Treasury: No doubt her Majesty *is satisfied* it shall be in their Power to preserve the *Publick Credit*, and restore it to as great a height as ever it was before, And I will presume to add, That if her Majesty should find it otherwise, it would be an effectual Motive to *farther Changes* till such Hands should be found, in whose Conduct the *National Credit* could not Miscarry.

It seems that the present Discontents are grounded upon *a Supposition*, That a New Ministry shall be less zealous for the Publick Interest, than the present; or, at least, the Objectors argue, that her Majesty has sufficient Experience of the Zeal of the present Ministry, *for her Service*, and for the Publick Good; and therefore it cannot seem rational to run that Risque, and the like, of a New Parliament.

To this may be answer'd; Why should it be suggested, that a New Parliament shall not be equally zealous for

 the

the Liberties of *Britain* with the present? They are to be chosen by the Freeholders, they are to be Englishmen; they are to be Protestants; they are to abjure the Pretender; they are to be join'd with *the same* House of Lords, to be blessed with *the same* Queen; and the Queen, I doubt not, fill'd with *the same* Principles as before; *the same* by which her Majesty, for I must place it there, *restor'd the Nations Credit before,* and raised it to what we have now seen it.

Shall we say, the Parliament will not raise Money to carry on the War? This would be to say, We shall choose such a Parliament as will *declare the Pretender, forsake* the Confederacy, *join* with the Common Enemy, and *Depose* the Queen. These are Fears no thinking Man can suppose to be rational; and are spread about by none *but those* that desire it should be so; and who, crying out loudest of the Fall of *Public Credit,* procure the thing they complain of; and indeed we have no Breach of *our Credit,* but what rises from these Men.

To back their Fears, and make others think them reasonable, they give long Accounts of the Progress of Dr. *Sacheverell,* as if the Folly and Impolitick Vanity of that Gentleman could influence the People of *England,* to send up Men as *mad* and *foolish* as himself: I must profess to think, if Dr. *Sacheverell* thinks he serves the Interest he pretends to appear for, by his mobbing and riotous Progress, he is as much mistaken *as they were,* who made him Popular by a hasty Prosecution, instead of committing his Sermon to the Hang-Man, and kicking him from the Bar for a Lunatic; which if they had done, the Nation had been more in Debt to *their Prudence,* than I think they are now for *their Justice.*

I am against Furies on both sides; nor do I see any such coming in: If her Majesty does let in any such, *I dare presume to say*, it must be for want of having their due Character; and the Term of their Services may probably end when they discover themselves.

But if Men of Moderation, and Men of Integrity come in, I see no room to fear, but *our Credit* shall revive as well under a New Ministry as an Old.

*I know*, that some talk of a Stagnation of the Fountain; that there is a Famine of Funds; that the Nation is exhausted, and we are at a full Stop: This I take to be *an Amusement*, that comes over from *France*, and is calculated very much for the Service of the Enemy. But there are ways to get over the Difficulty, and the best way is Demonstration and Experience; I believe the *French* King does not raise half so much Hopes from our not being able to find any Funds at all, as from our being at a loss for Credit to borrow upon those Funds when they are raised; and he may live to be deceived in both.

But to obviate these things, *I take the liberty to say*, and that not without-book, When the Parliament meets, be it the present Parliament, or a new Parliament; be it the present Ministry, or a new Ministry; as I hope there will not want Zeal in the Members, to supply her Majesty's Occasions for the War; so were this War to hold Seven Years longer, it is easy to propose sufficient Funds for the carrying it on, without that horrid Proposal of mortgaging our *Land-Tax*, or without any *such Taxes*, as shall either be burthensom to the Poor, or scandalous to the Nation.

*As to Credit*, while the Parliament and the Queen continue to preserve those Funds from Deficiencies, to make good such as happen, and to support the Vigour and Honour of the Publick Management; I see no room to doubt, but *Credit* shall revive, and as we have not yet found any Fund the Parliament has rais'd, unsupply'd with Loans and Advances upon it, even faster than could

 be

be desired; so I can see no room to fear the contrary: Yet if such a Thing should happen, a mean Head may find out some Expedient that may not be ineffectual; for a Supply of which, if there should be Occasion, a Proposal shall not be wanting.

---

*FINIS.*

# A LETTER TO A FRIEND.

In which is ſhewn,

The Inviolable Nature OF *Publick Securities.*

*By a Lover of his Country.*

*LONDON:*

Printed for *R. Burleigh,* in *Amen-Corner.*
MDCCXVII.

# A LETTER TO A FRIEND.

## In which is ſhewn, the *Inviolable Nature* of *PUBLICK SECURITIES*.

*SIR*,

YOUR, Project of raising Money for this Years Service, or of paying Debts by *Taxing* or *Lowering the Interest of the Funds*, meets, I think, with too much Approbation amongst some People, who look no farther than *Themselves*, and consider only the *Present* Difficulty, regardless of the Consequences of their Proceedings. The Importance of the Case seems to require that every body should contribute what they can to set this Matter in a true Light, and Examine, without Prejudice, how much the *Interest* of our Country, its *Reputation* and *Honour*, its *future* Good or Evil may be affected by it. This I can assure you, that as I am not concerned in any of the Funds, and *Interest* cannot mislead me in Prejudice to this Project; so the rack-four Shillings in the Pound which I pay to the Land-Tax, is a Motive which would make me *favour* it, if I were not very apprehensive



of

of its fatal Consequences. I cannot but think that *Conscience* is concerned, and *natural Honesty*, and *Publick Justice*, and the *Credit* of the Nation: Every thing that is *sacred* and *inviolable* in *Property*, is nearly affected; All *Obligations* will be in a way of being cancell'd, and in a Word, an indelible Character of *Injustice* cast upon us. I may be mistaken perhaps in my Notions, or misinformed of the nature of your Project; However I will endeavour to state the Case as fairly as I can, and shew the *Unreasonableness* of *Taxing* or *Lowering the Interest of the Funds.* The Case is This.

The Legislative, *i. e.* King, Lords, and Commons in Parliament assembled, has Occasion for, and *borrows* great Sums of Money of the Subject for the Common Service; and *oblige* Themselves to repay the Money borrowed in such a Term of Years, or sooner if they could, and give a *Parliamentary Security* to repay it; and as an *Encouragement* to the Lender, they engage to pay a certain *specified Interest*, and enact that the Sums so lent should *not* be *liable* to any *Taxation.* Your Project is, to *Lower their Interests*, or which is the same thing, *to Tax these Funds*, in order to raise the Money for, or lessen the Debts of the Nation.

Against this Project, however acceptable perhaps it it may be to some, give me leave to propose my Objections, which proceed from neither Interest, nor Favour, nor any other View than the Good of my Country, and a sincere Desire that its *Credit* may remain unsullied to the latest Posterity. And

1*st*, To support and maintain a Mans *Private Credit*, 'tis absolutely necessary that the World have a fixt Opinion of the *Honesty* and *Integrity*, as well as Ability of a Person. If there be good Reason to Object against the One or the Other of These, his *Credit* sinks, no one chooses to *deal* with him, nor does any one care to *trust* him. This is so Universal a Rule, such a First Principle,

 that

that no Man ever call'd it in Question, or disputed its Truth; Nay, so uncontested in Practice, that neither *Art*, nor Superior Genius, has ever been able long to support *Credit*, when *upright open* Dealing, or *Performance* of Promises, of Covenants or Contracts, has been wanting. Indeed *Credit* is the natural Result of being persuaded of the Obligation of that Law of Nature, *Be Faithful to Contracts;* and therefore when once a Person is supposed to have laid aside that Principle, or by any *avowed* Acts declares that He thinks himself free from that Bond, 'tis impossible in the Nature of Things to place any *Confidence* in Him; every body is forced to be on his Guard; nor can they with *Assurance* transact any Business of Moment with him. *Uprightness* and *Honesty* are the Bands of humane Society; and *Credit* is not to be purchas'd, nor acquir'd, till by a continued Series of *fair* and *open* Actions the World is satisfied of our *Sincerity*, and *Integrity*.

As These then are the Basis of *Credit*, every Attempt to blast it, be it upon just or unjust Grounds, has this fatal Effect, that it raises *Jealousies* and *Surmises* in Peoples Minds, and in consequence lessens their Opinions of a Man; so much at least it lessens their Opinions, as Evil Rumors prevail upon them. Scarce ever was there an Evil Report spread abroad, but it gain'd over some credulous Persons, 'twas industriously propagated by a Mans Enemies, it met with Encouragement amongst some; and so far it *impaired* the *Credit* 'twas designed to lessen. And was it ever found an easy matter to *regain* the Reputation of *Honesty* and *Upright Dealing*, when these have been industriously struck at? Was it ever found, but that the Person (whom I suppose even unjustly treated) *lost* a vast deal of his *Credit*, and continued *injured*, notwithstanding all the Care that could be taken to recover his Good Name?

And indeed a *Readiness* and *Willingness* to perform ones Engagements is such a *Fundamental* of *Credit*, that all the

Affluence of Money, and the most immense Riches are of no Consequence, if there be Ground for the *least* Suspicion of Disingenuity. The *Ability* of a Person without *Natural Justice*, rather makes Men *cautious* than *forward* to deal with him. And the Reason of it is plain, because by his *Power* he is able to keep a Creditor out of his Right longer, and to put him to infinite more Trouble and Inconvenience than otherwise 'twould be possible to do. *Honour* therefore and *Uprightness* must attend upon Riches and Ability, or else the meanest Honest Person shall have, a better *Credit* and a more settled good repute, than the Richest *Crassus* with all his Money.

This *true*, This *only* Foundation of *Credit* takes in all Cases, and all Persons, *Publick* as well as Private; National as well as Personal. Just and Honourable Practices, Fair and Open Dealings, a strict Performance of Contracts, a steddy Observance of Engagements will necessarily *gain Credit* every where; and Common Experience teaches us that a *Breach* in These as necessarily *destroys* it.

If therefore the Legislative of Any Country should decline standing to its Contracts, or endeavour to impose other Conditions than what at first were stipulated, I ask, wou'd not such a Conduct as necessarily impair the *Publick Credit*, as it wou'd the *Credit* of a *Private* Person? Has it not the same Tendency to make the Lenders *Jealous* of their *Securities?* Would it not affect the *Honour* of the Nation? Or how is it consistent with *express* Engagements? If not, 'tis very natural to ask again, who will venture to *lend* the Publick a second Time, if once They find themselves not treated *according* to their *Contracts?* May there never be Emergencies, which may again oblige the Publick to borrow Money! And if such Cases should happen; upon what Foundation must They proceed, if an Instance can be produced, an Act of the Legislature, which can never be forgot nor ever can be repaired, to

 shew

shew that *Legal Security* is not a *Security*, and that *Engagements* with such Powers are not to be understood *litterally*. What is the natural Consequence of This, but that no Man will *lend* the Government for the future, but at *such Interest*, and such Advancements, as are full *Equivalents* to the *Hazards* which People may run in Lending? Certain it is that no Man borrows Money for *Pleasure*, but for *Want*: Nor would any Man pay Interest for Money, did not his *Necessities* oblige him to supply his own Deficiencies from the Abundance of Others. So great therefore as a Man's *Necessities* are, so much will he necessarily give to have them supplied. But be his Necessities ever so pressing, yet no Man in his Senses will *lend*, without some Prospect of *Payment*; He will not part with what his Industry and Labour has acquired, or his Ancestors have left him, to one who has forfeited his *Reputation* for *Honesty*, and whom he knows to be *out of his Reach* to compel him to repay, or if he may be *compell'd*, yet the Lender is *assured* there will not be a Competency to satisfy His Demands. If a single Person, therefore, or a Government, (for 'tis much at one) be under such Circumstances as to be forc'd to *borrow* Money, they will endeavour, no doubt, to get it as *Cheap*, i. e. at as *low an Interest* as They can. The first Question then which the *Lender* proposes to himself is, *shall I ever be repaid?* and *what Security shall I have?* If the Borrowers *Credit* be *unspotted*, half the Difficulty is presently removed; and there remains only the Adjustment of Security; a thing neither long in Agitation, nor do any Difficulties occur, which *untainted Credit* doth not instantly remove. But if the stop be at the *Credit* of the Person, who is known to have *broke thro' former* Engagements, and to have *voided Former* Contracts by any *Arts* inconsistent with the *strictest Honour*, what Contests must be strugled with, what Depths must be waded through, to gain the Point? If Money *can* be procured at all, at what Rates must it be? For 'tis allowed on all hands, that common Justice requires a *reasonable* Profit to the Lender, and the Measure of That is in proportion to the *Danger* he ventures. Interest therefore will necessarily run high, where there is a Deficiency of *Security* in the Borrower: If the Deficiency lye on the Part of *Honour,* nothing can be an Equivalent to it: But then if it be on the Part of *Ability,* and the Person is a known *inviolable* Observer of *Honesty* and keeps his *Integrity* clear, This will make amends in some degree for the Other, and procure him what he wants.

But because *Facts* are inflexible Things, and will speak with Authority, I ask, what was the Reason that *Navy Bills* some Years ago were at such prodigious Discount? What was the Reason the *Nations Credit* run so low, that a Man might purchase a Hundred Pounds for Threescore or Threescore and Ten? Why, there was plainly a *Deficiency of the Funds;* and the People not having any *further Security* that those *Deficiencies* shou'd be made *good,* they bought and sold the Government Bills, but at such a Price as they thought the Funds would repay them with some Advantage. They were *sure* of such or such Proportions of their Money, and according to that *Assurance,* the *Credit* of the Government was, higher or lower. Again, What is it then that has *rais'd* the *Credit* of the Government since, and has brought it to such a Pitch, that even Exchequer Bills, which bear so small an Interest, are now not to be bought under such Premiums? This is as plain too. The People have had a *Parliamentary Security* that all *Deficiencies* shall be made *good,* and the Debts contracted shall be paid, and They have *yet* had no Reason in the least to question the *Integrity* of the Parliament, or their *strict Observance* of their Engagements.

If we suppose now your present Project to be receiv'd, and a Parliament should recede from that known and unshaken Resolution to their Pecuniary Engagements, must not our *Credit sink* again in Proportion to the *Fears* and

*Jealousies* of the People? For where is the Difference between a *Defect* in *Ability* to pay, and a *Defect* arising from not *standing to Agreements,* except that the latter in its own Nature more sensibly affects our *Credit?* Must it not *sink* again necessarily, when one of its chief Supports, nay the *very Foundation* of it is so visibly weakned? Credit cannot be maintained without the *strictest Performance* of Covenants: And yet if your Project should be entertained, the most *express* and *plainest Contracts* must be cancelled; and what must be of infinite Concern, a *Spirit of Jealousy* will be rais'd, that 'tis impossible can ever be laid. For no greater *Assurances* can be given to a People to secure their Loans, than what an Act of Parliament can give; and yet if These are broken thro' as 'twill be impossible to obliterate the Fact, so no *Assurance* can be greater than This, *what has been may be.*

Nor must you imagine, Sir, That the Consequences of such a Jealousy, founded upon sufficient Ground, can be confined to the narrow Compass of *Loans,* and to the particular Cases of the Governments *Borrowing.* The Government will be the Sufferer, wherever it deals, or into whatever Engagements it is obliged to enter. Who is there will supply our Fleets with Stores, or furnish our Magazines for our Armies, if, contrary to Contract, their Stipulations may be broke thro'? And what *Assurance* can They have, that They shall not be treated in that manner? Must it be Personal or National? National will be too liable to Exception, if once a *Breach* is made in its *Credit:* And no Personal can be given, because it is supposed to depend on the Ratification of the Publick. So that in short, the Government is reduced to the unhappy pass of Trading all with *Ready Money,* a thing impossible to be practised, or else of paying exorbitantly for what is wanted, because of our *broken Credit.* Is it not the usual method of dealing, and is it not necessary so to deal, that the Seller may not be the Loser by his Com-

 modities?

modities? And how can this be effected, but by proportioning the Price of his Goods, to the Time and Circumstance of his being paid? If therefore he runs a hazard of having his Bargain *alter'd*, *after* he has parted with his Goods; he must rate them accordingly, or run too great a risque of losing by his Trade; which can neither be expected nor desired. *Credit* therefore, i. e. an *Assurance* of having Money in such and such Quantities, and at such and such Times, must be preserv'd *inviolable*, or else the Merchant must be paid in *ready Money*, or lastly we must *pay for* our *want* of *Credit* just as the Vender pleases to rate us.

Judge now, Sir, What must be the Consequence of *breaking* into Parliamentary Securities, and of hurting *National Credit*. You mistake, if you bring into the Account, only the lessening some of our Debts; or the raising some Money for present Emergencies. I grant you, This it will do: But then it doth it just as a Man pays his Debts, by *forcing* another to give him Money, or by *forcing* his Creditors to *abate* of their Contracts. It pays our Debts by bringing such a Mischief upon our selves as never can be remedied. If once our *Credit* suffers the least Diminution, be it by a groundless Suspicion if you please, You must not imagine that it can be *rais'd* again at Pleasure. The very Heart of *National Credit* is stabb'd, when Covenants are *broken* by a *Law*, and it must as necessarily grow faint and languid, till at last it bleeds to Death.

When a Private Person once has forfeited his Credit, He may with Zeal and the utmost Care endeavour to retrieve it; but he must be Master of a great deal of good Conduct, and give a great many Proofs of more than ordinary Integrity, before he can wipe off the Stain, or remove the Ground of Jealousie and Suspicion. *National Credit* is only to be recovered the same Way. But what then must be the *intermediate* State? I put the present

 Case

Case only to shew you, that we shall not ease *Our selves*, as may be imagin'd, by your Project, though 'tis suppos'd that Posterity would be ready to *trust* the Government again, and deal with it fairly without the least Mistrust. What I say must be the *intermediate* State, before the Government can *retrieve* its *Credit*, and the People gain an *entire Confidence* in it? Will the Purses, and the Hearts of the People be open? Will they be ready to bring in their Money upon any Emergencies? Will they subscribe two or three Millions again in two or three Hours, as they used to do? Can it be expected that the present Generation will part as *freely* with their Money as if the *National Credit* had been kept inviolable? No. This would be to expect something contrary to Humane Nature; and consequently if any Difficulties should arise, (as the Enemies of the Government have not shewn themselves unactive hitherto,) We our selves must be infinite Sufferers for want of that *Credit* which your Project must affect. Either therefore we must be *insured* against future straits which may happen in our Times, or the most daring Projector ought to be apprehensive of Danger in striking at the Vitals of That which *never can* be cured *entirely*, and *may immediately* prove Mortal.

The Sum of what hath been said upon this Argument is This; *Publick Credit*, like *Private*, is *entirely* founded upon *Integrity*, and *strict Performance* of Contracts. If once *Covenants* are broke thro' by any Person, it necessarily alarms every body, and makes the parties concern'd *Jealous*, and upon their *Guard*, very *suspicious* of every Motion, and very apt to *misinterpret*, and to put the *worst* Sense upon every Action. They never can think themselves *secure*, and therefore will never *deal* but with Advantages equal to what they think their Hazards are. If a Nation once forfeits its *Credit*, it not only feels the *present* ill Effects, but *latest* Posterity will have a just Sense of such Proceedings; and will never venture with that *Assu-*

*rance* and *Confidence* their Money into the Publick, as if it had literally performed its Engagements: And the Consequence of this is, *ill Will, evil Surmises, Jealousies, Distrust* between the Government and the Subject, *Delays* in raising Money, *losing Opportunities* of Advantage, *encouraging* Enemies; in a Word, *sinking* Publick *Credit*, is big with all the Misfortunes that can attend an unhappy Nation. And does not your Project I am considering immediately affect the *National Credit?* Is it not, that the Legislative should *alter* their Contracts? That the *Stipulations* which have been made for a great many Years past should be *brȯke* thro'; and the *Conditions*, upon which so many Millions have been borrowed *changed?* If *Publick Credit* can withstand such a Shock, it must be founded on something very different from what hitherto has been conceiv'd or known. A

2*d Objection* against your Project is, That it is not calculated to *pay* the Debts, but to *sink* them; 'tis not designed to *discharge* them *fairly* and *honourably*, but in effect to declare that Engagements between the Legislative and the Subject are not inviolable. What a Source of endless Mischiefs is This? and what would be the Difference between the most *Arbitrary* Monarchys and our Constitution, if no regard were to be had to the plainest Statutes? If a Law can be made, and all Assurances possible given to the Subject to *secure* them in what they shall *Lend* the Government, and these over and over repeated, and constant fresh Assurances given to *make good* Deficiencies, and yet at last these Bonds be broke through and the Conditions changed, would not these be Instances of *Arbitrariness?* And must we not at last fall into what we have paid so many Millions to avoid, and shed so much Blood to prevent, if we pursue the Steps which your Project would lead us to? To what end are Laws, if they give a Man no *Security?* and what *Security* are They, if they are made *pliable*, and *bend*

 to

to Purposes directly contrary to their Original meaning? Much *less* are they *Securities,* if *Contracts* are made *Laws* and yet may be *Dispensed* with.

The great end of Government is the *Preservation* of Property; and therefore neither Prince nor Senate can have Authority to *take* to themselves the whole or any Part of it *arbitrarily,* and *at Pleasure.* This is so clear a Truth, and its contrary so full of Miseries, that I do not wonder we struggled so hard against the Power of *France,* and refused no Expences, to ward off *absolute arbitrary* Government. Is it then a *small* Approach to *Arbitrariness,* to annull Laws which were given upon Loans as a *security* to the Lender? Did not the Legislative *engage* to repay the Summs Borrowed, and in the mean while to *pay* them *such* and *such Interest?* Was not *This* the Reason that so much Money was so *readily* advanced? Did not the Lenders *believe* they would, and did not the Borrowers *intend* to act openly and *pay* what was *engaged* for? Could then the most *arbitrary* Government act a stranger Part, than to break thro' all this, as you propose; and when there seems no more Occasion for Borrowing, *refuse* compliance with the Conditions of *their own* Proposals.

The *Credit* of the Nation was *engaged* to pay annually such or such Summs: The Nation reaped the Benefit of the Principal every Year; and Glory, and Honour, and Liberty and Safety, and every thing that was valuable and dear to *Englishmen* flowed in upon us. This was wholly owing to the forwardness of Money'd Men, who were truly sensible of the fatal effects of *Arbitrary* Government. It would look too like forgetting the Benefits we received, if assoon as we are out of Danger from abroad, almost the *First* Step taken to lessen our Debts, should be to *break thro'* the *Engagements* we were under to the very Persons who contributed most to our Safety. If any Man upon a pinch should Borrow upon Bond, and should rate his Interest according to his Necessities, the

 better

better to induce his Neighbour to Lend him what he wanted; should he afterwards find himself *Powerful* enough, ought he in *common Justice* to resolve against paying his Bonds? Ought he in *Honour* to pay no more than what he himself thought fit? Or could he, consistent with *Honesty*, refuse the Conditions which He himself had made? Would it not be looked upon as most *arbitrary* Proceeding in such a Man, to trample upon his Covenants? Or if he ever wanted again, could he expect to Command Money as if he had strictly perform'd his Contracts? No. *Credit* once lost is not to be retrieved again, unless the very *cause* of its sinking be perfectly removed; and *Arbitrariness* is such a mortal Enemy to *Credit*, that 'tis impossible they should Both Thrive in the same Country.

There was, I remember, some Six or Seven Years ago, a very remarkable Coldness in the Nation to *Parliamentary Securities*. Some there were who took all Opportunies to express their Dislike of them; and express'd Apprehensions that One Parliament might vacate what another established. I then pleaded, that nothing but a Subversion of the Government, and an entire Destruction of our Constitution, could ruine the Credit of our Funds; and whenever that should happen, in the common Confusion, *Private* Securities would be no better than *Publick:* I us'd to plead that common Benefits to all would call for common Gratitude from all: That National Justice was as necessary to our Constitution as 'twas to private Persons: That if the Legislature had any Sense of Right and Wrong, they could not but take Care of the Publick Debts, and punctually perform their Obligations: That if they attempted to *Sponge* out the Debts, they must be guilty of such a flagrant piece of Injustice, that they themselves must repent of: That such Proceeding would be a *National Disgrace*, and such a black Reproach that we could never wash off. These Arguments Then weighed with me, and do so much still, that I am not willing to believe it can enter into any Bodies Mind knowingly to Sacrifice our *Publick Credit,* or at all to weaken the National Securities. And yet is not your Project a plain *Sponge* to *wipe* out some of our Debts and not to *pay* them? Doth it not *wipe* away 2 *per Cent.* Interest, which is as much engaged for as the Principal it self? And may not the same Contrivance next time *clear* off 5 *per Cent.* and thus still lessen our Debts? Nay, 'twill more effectually *clear* all our Incumbrances, if the Principal and Interest too be struck away at once. 'Tis but the same *Act of Power* exerted a little farther to make clear Work. For when once it can enter into the Heart of any Man to break through Contracts, and to annull Engagements, I do not see but the same Motives may carry a Man *in infinitum,* and the same Power extend it self as long as it has Objects to work on. When once the plain beaten Track is forsaken, and *resolvedly* deserted, Men may wander uncontrouled till they are lost. The narrow Path of *Right* is uniform and strait, and when once 'tis determined to *quit* That, the same Motives will equally justify any thing. Truth and Honesty, guided by Prudence, never did, nor ever can do any Disservice to Publick or to Private Measures: Arts and Shuffling often have, and ever will. These may keep up the *Shadow* of *Credit* for some Time; but Those are the only *lasting* Foundations of *Credit,* which always did, and always will support it, and can and are ready to stand the Test of Men or Angels.

'Tis not many Years ago since our National *Credit* met with a violent Shock, and sunk very low, because 'twas apprehended that the Measures Then engaged in must necessarily terminate in the *Pretender,* and in *Arbitrary* Power. What was but Guessing then, and arguing from highly Probables, has since been too demonstratively prov'd true. But how did those Measures affect our Credit? And why did it sink at that Rate which it did?

 'Tis

'Tis plain: If the Pretender had succeeded, the *Funds* would have been *Sponged* out: Those *Laws* which have been Enacted to *secure* the Subject, had been *repealed;* and consequently no Man could have laid Claim to his Debt, or had any Title for his Demands. In proportion therefore to the *Jealousies* of People, and their *Suspicions* of the *Integrity* of their future Paymasters, our *Credit* sunk: And so it always will do, if there be Occasion given for ill Surmises. And is there not *just Occasion* given, when we hear of Projects to *alter* or *change* the *Conditions* of those very *Laws* which were to *secure* the Funds? 'Twou'd be a Step, which I cannot but think *too like* what we were apprehensive of from *Arbitrary* Power; and there seems no other material Difference betwixt them, except that This, if it were to succeed according to your Wishes, wou'd be done by the *Gown*, That would have been executed by the Sword. A

3*d Objection* against your Project, or Argument shewing the *Unreasonableness of Lowering the Interest of* or *Taxing the Funds,* is taken from the Consideration of the Nature of our Constitution, and Circumstances, as a *Free People.* We enjoy that *Liberty* which our Neighbours envy, and have this Advantage, that our *Properties* are Sacred, not to be touched but by our own Consent; and one Common Law is made for Sovereign and Subject. The Law is the Standard of all our Actions; nor are we subject to an *arbitrary unlimited* Will, which renders us uncapable of knowing our Duty; nor are we apprehensive of *extempore Decrees,* which always make *Property* very *precarious* and *doubtful.* Great and Glorious Privileges These! such as render us the Wonder of *Europe,* and make all Nations pronounce us Blessed! Oh! that *WE* knew how to *value* these Blessings, and to *BELIEVE* our selves that Happy People which all the World besides *KNOWS* us to be!

From this particular Frame of our Constitution 'tis easy to see in what *Reputation* We must be in all *Europe.*

 The

The Riches of These Parts of the World are no where so *secure* as Here. No Man can *enjoy* his own, or be *known* to have the Possessions which his Industry has acquired, so *safely* as *Here.* In *England* They are *sure* of commanding the Fruits of their Labours; They may Employ them to such Purposes, and in such Measures, and prosecute such Designs as They themselves think fit. Such Privileges as These in necessary Consequence must draw hither the Riches of *Europe,* if we take but the common Care of *preserving our Credit.* Keep but That *unspotted,* and *England* must be the Center of Trade, the Mart of the World, the common Treasury of Merchants, and therefore the Riches of *Europe* must be reposited *Here.* If on the other hand we begin to *violate* our *Engagements,* *i. e.* to remove the Land-mark of *Honesty,* our *Credit* must *sink;* and what before made *Us* the Place of Refuge, being lost, we must find its fatal Effects in Scarcity of Money.

Let our *Credit* therefore be preserved *untouched,* and every thing which tends to its Diminution be rejected, and with how much Ease may this Flood be improved to the Payment of the Debts of the Nation? By a dextrous Management of an *unspotted Credit,* how Easy is it to make it *par* to ready Money? But to put this into a clearer Light.

Money has This in common with all Commodities, that its *Value* is always in Proportion to its *Quantity* or *Scarceness* in a Land. Where there are more Buyers than Sellers, the Markets will always run high: On the other hand where there is a greater Quantity of Commodities than there is of People to purchase, Things are cheap. But Money being usually considered as the Standard of the Value of all other things, and what will readily purchase all other things, and all the World at all times desiring to be Masters of it, the *Quantity* of it alone determines its natural worth, and makes it *cheap* or *dear,*

 *i. e.*

*i. e.* to be borrowed at higher or lower Interest. If there be much *more* Money in a Nation than is imployed in Trade, it necessarily follows that Interest must be *low*, because there will be so many Lenders, who can't tell how to improve their Money by any other Methods. If again the Demands of Trade are such, by reason of an Overballance in other Countries, or on any particular Occasion, as to draw away Money out of a Land, it follows necessarily, that Money must bear a very high Interest, because there will be but *few* Lenders and many Borrowers. I do not concern my self with the nature of Money farther than this, nor with Laws which are or may be made for lowering Interest; nor will I enquire what real Service or Disservice such Laws are to the Publick. 'Tis enough for my Purpose to have shewn that *Plenty* of Money only makes it *cheap*, *i. e.* easy to be borrowed, and at a low Interest, if the *Credit* of the Borrower be untainted.

Consider then the *Situation* of *England*, its *Commerce*, its *Laws* and *Liberties*, its *Credit* hitherto *unspotted*, and what the Consequences of These must be. The Money of all Nations is flowing in upon us, and Those who live under Despotick *Arbitrary* Government, can no where so well *secure* their own as Here. In *England* 'tis safe, and may be commanded as their Occasions require; and besides This, our Commerce is so improved by the Wisdom, Care, and Conduct of his Present MAJESTY, and The Treaties which cramp'd it, altered; and all its Obstacles removed; that in a few Years Time *England* (if it retains its *Credit*) must be the *Richest* Spot in *Europe*, and may command the most Money. As Money will be in consequence *Easy* to be borrowed, and at a *low* Interest, the Funds *redeemable* by Parliament may be with Ease paid off; the litteral Engagements may inviolably be observed, the Laws be litterally kept, every body fully satisfied and contented, and what is of the most Value in the World,

 the

the *Credit* of the Government handed down *unspotted* to Posterity.

I need not observe to You, in Confirmation of what I have here asserted, the *Præmium's* for some Time past given for *Exchequer* Bills, nor the Summs of Money borrowed this Winter in Town at 4 *per Cent.* These and other Instances are sensible Demonstrations of what I have said; and are, let me add, as evident Proofs of the *absolute Necessity* of preserving *Credit* sacred. Nor need I mention the Method which *John de Witt* took in *Holland* to lessen their Publick Debts. The *Lender* must be the Judge, and not the Borrower the *arbitrary Imposer* of his own Terms. If the *Lender* be left at his Liberty to receive his Money, or to let it lye at lower Interest; (in Cases where Funds are *redeemable*;) no Cause can be given of Complaint, No Injury is done, No Hardship is offered, the *Integrity* and *Honesty* of the Borrower is evident, and *Credit* is indisputable. But if the Borrower be his *own Judge*, and his *own Carver*, and flies to an Act of Power because he *can* do it, it as necessarily *sinks* his *Credit*, as it takes away its Foundation. How much your present *Project* affects all this, and takes away the very Foundation of our Abundance, I leave to your impartial Consideration. A

4*th* Consideration is taken from the *Nature* of those Laws which have been made to *secure* the Persons, who so much to their Honour advanced their Money for the *Service* of their *Country*. No Man that knows the nature of our Constitution can doubt of the Power and Right of Parliaments to *make* and to *repeal* Laws. Yet, I think, it cannot be proved that the Legislative of our own or any Country in the World, can extend its Power *absolutely* and *arbitrarily* to the *Lives* and *Fortunes* of their Subjects, without contradicting the *End* and *Design* of Society. *Justice* therefore and *Equity* and *Reason* bounds their Power, and not *Advantage* or *Interest* as has been incul-

19 cated

cated too much by too too many. 'Tis true that the *Interest* of the *Society* is the great End of all Laws: But then That *Interest* is not to be prosecuted by Injustice, by Fraud, or any Evil Arts. He that breaks thro' the Boundary of *Justice* to serve his present Turn, cuts down the Fence of his own Peace and Quiet for ever after.

The Legislature no doubt has a Power to cancel Laws, such as are inconsistent with the Peace and Safety and Good of the Publick: But yet this Power will not, I am apt to believe, authorize them, to cancel *Bonds* and *Covenants* which They Themselves have engaged in. When the *Emperor* some Years ago mortgaged *Silesia* to us for so much Money, 'twou'd have been inconsistent with the Laws of Nations, or with *Common Justice*, afterwards to have *sunk* the *Interest* he *agreed* for, and to have paid but what he thought fit. If it be *Injustice*, when One Nation borrows of Another, to force the *Lender* to accept what Terms the *Borrower* thinks fit to impose after the Loan is received: It seems very like the same Crime, if a Nation borrows of its *own Subjects*, and enters into Articles for their Payment, and yet afterwards *refuses* to comply with *their own* Terms. *To do as one would be done by*, is so evidently a first Principle both of Natural Reason, and of Christianity, that every body who has any Sense of Humanity acknowledges its Obligation, however his Practice may vary from it. If That then be receiv'd as a Standard Rule, *equal* and *just*; I ask, if the Emperor contracted for *Eight per Cent.* Interest, and afterwards would have paid but *Four* or *Three* or any other Summ, or None at all, should We our selves have thought This Proceeding *Just?* Could not His Imperial Majesty have urged in his Defence, the *Debts* he was involved in? The urgent *Necessities* of the *Empire* when he borrowed, which obliged him to offer such large Terms? The Weight of the War, *&c.* And should we have thought these Reasons of sufficient Weight to *justify* the *Breach* of his

 Bargain?

Bargain? But say, that notwithstanding This, We had been *obliged* to have *taken* the *Interest* which He thought fit to *give* us: I ask again, Would we have *trusted* Him again, whatever Occasions he might have had? Would the Promise of *Eight* or *Ten* per *Cent.* or *any* Consideration have invited us to repose our Money in his Hands, who once before had *broke* through all *Engagements* with us? I scarce think that any Inducements would have prevail'd; his *Credit* would have been *lost;* The *Integrity* and *Honesty* upon which we ventured to *Lend,* would have been plainly Sacrificed; and consequently as He would not have been able to ask with any Conscience, We should have been ready to have refus'd him, nay, should have been apt to censure the Discretion of any body else that would Venture their Money upon such *an unsafe Bottom.*

The Reason why I think there is a mighty Difference between Those Laws which have expressly engaged *for* such or such Interests, and have *exempted* the Funds from being chargeable with any *Rates, Taxes,* or *Duties whatsoever,* and Other Laws or Acts of Parliament, is This. The former are plain *Contracts* made between the *Legislature,* and *such of the Subjects* as will accept the Terms specified, and advance the Money wanted. The Legislature here becomes a *Party* to the Covenant, and according to the Fiduciary Power reposed in Them by the Nation, they oblige the Nation in such and such Terms to those particular Persons They Treat with. If the Loan of 200,000 *l.* upon which the Bank was at first established, had been Borrowed by our Legislature, of so many Subjects of *France* or *Spain,* as it was of our *own* Subjects, no Doubt had ever been rais'd about the *Obligation* to *keep* to the Terms *agreed* on. Wherein then is the Difference? None certainly. For the Legislature *lays aside* its Superiority, or at least is *considered* as laying it aside, and makes it self upon a Level with those of whom it Borrows; and makes no Distinction between Natives or

 Foreigners,

Foreigners, or any such meer accident. In other Cases the Legislature makes its Laws extend to every Part or Member of the Society, it prescribes Rules for all their Actions, and is considered justly as *Supreme.* In This Case, 'tis not but by Accident, *Supreme over* the Persons whose Money it Borrows: For when the Emperor Borrowed Money of us, he had no sort of *Supremacy* over us. The *Supremacy* therefore of the Legislature has no Relation to, or concern with these *Laws* or *Contracts,* farther than as They had Power to enter into such *Engagements,* and actually did do it. They become *Debtors* and are to be consider'd as such: And it scarce can be reconciled to any just Conduct of *Debtors,* to make a Law to enable themselves to dissolve their Obligations, and by this means *injure* their respective *Creditors.* Should the Parliament of *Paris,* or the States of *Holland,* or any Legislative Power enact a Law that all the Private Debts which every particular Member of the Legislative owed, should be *void,* and himself free from all Obligations to his Creditors; every body would have a just Abhorrence of such a manifest Breach of Justice. Or should They agree to Sink not All, but a Part of their Just Debts, it would be still a *Breach of Justice,* though not so flagrant, or not so much complain'd against. Now all the Particular Members making up but ONE Legislature, if *That* enters into Covenants and Borrows with other People, the Debt contracted is as much the Debt of that Body, as the Private Debts of any particular Member are his own. And it seems the same *Injustice,* to void the Obligations of the One or the Other without Performance of the Covenants Stipulated.

Upon These Reasons it is that I think it *Unreasonable* to *Tax* the Funds, or to *lower* their Interest by a Law. And here I had concluded, but that I thought it not improper to observe in a few Words, what has been urg'd at Times to my self in behalf of your Project.

*First.* The *Land* has been already *Tax'd* and *Tax'd*, and the Burden of the War has lain upon That so long, that every Landlord has paid above the Price of his Land in Taxes. And

*Secondly.* The *Moneyed* Men have *rais'd* such *immense* Estates from the *Funds*, without contributing any thing to the Burden, that it is highly reasonable they should at length be made *Sharers* in the common Load. And

*Thirdly*, 'Twill be making some *Amends* to the *Landed Men* to *lower* the Interest of Money, and of the *Funds* in particular, because this will *raise* the Value of Land, and by this Means in some Measure *reimburse* those who have paid so much to the War.

The *First* and *Second* of these Objections, I'll consider together. I grant then that the Land has been taxed, and has bore a very heavy Burden during this whole War. But then I add

That the laying the Tax upon *Land* has been *cheaper* to the Landlord, than if it had been laid upon *Commodities*. Let us suppose now the Land free from Taxes, and the Supplies entirely to be laid upon *Commodities*. These are either *Foreign* or *Domestick*. The Merchant that imports the *Foreign* Goods will *never* pay the Tax, but in Course will *raise* their Price so high as to make his Profits, or else he won't import at all. As these therefore *rise* by being Tax'd, *Domestick* ones *fall* as necessarily to the *First Seller*, and consequently make the Tenant if he sits at a Rack-Rent absolutely uncapable of paying his Landlord. The Farmer pays the Malt-Tax, and not the Malster, who makes his Advantage doubly, by beating down the Price of Barley in its *first Sale*, under Pretence of the Tax upon Malt, and pleads the same again to the Buyer to Sell it so much the dearer. The Land-Tax now goes out of the Landlord's Pocket, and he feels its Weight very heavy. He throws it therefore upon the Tenants, for the Taxes must be rais'd. *Domestick* Commodities

 *sink*

*sink* because of the Tax, *Foreign* ones necessarily *rise.* The Tenant therefore that sits at near or full Rent; is utterly incapacitated to pay his Rent, the Landlord therefore must sink his Rents, and consequently pay the very Tax he strives to avoid, by having at the Years end less Money in his Pocket, than if he had paid a Land-Tax. Let me add to this, that if the Day-Labourer and poorer People do but *barely* live now the Tax is upon Land, they must be maintained by the Parish if all *Commodities* were dearer, (as they must be to pay the Taxes, to all but the first Seller,) or else must raise the Price of their Labour. Either of which Inconveniences, or both of them, very much concerning the Tenant, must fall at last upon the Landlord by forcing him to an Abatement of his Rents. Which whether you prefer to a Land-Tax, I leave you to judge.

But however cheap at the long run it may be, yet still 'tis *heavy* upon the Land, and the Monied Men pay nothing, nay, they get Estates, whilst the Landed Men are beggered.

I grant the Landed Men are heavy loaded with the Taxes. But then 1*st,* the Honour of the Nation is at Stake, not to Tax the Monied Men for what they had lent the Nation. *Common Justice* is due to Them as well as to the Land; and if to Tax them you must *break* thro' your *Laws, sacrifice Covenants* and *Contracts*, and *murder* the *Credit* of the Nation, I do not see how it can be done without much greater Detriment, than we can propose Advantage. 2*dly,* The Objection would be allowed, if the Government had *paid* them what they have *lent* to it, *i. e.* if Men made Interest from their Money otherways, and yet contributed nothing towards the common Charge. But upon this Supposition, the Objection would be nothing; it being already lawful to tax Bonds or Securities. 3*dly,* You may complain that the Traders *get Estates,* and that others are impoverish'd; yet, depend

 upon

upon it, the Trader will be the last, do what you will, that will feel Poverty. As long as Commodities must be had, he'll always take Care to *secure* himself, and by such *Prices* as will make others pay his Taxes; and this, tho' somewhat more remotely, comes to the Landlord at last. But I have said so much already to obviate this Objection, that I shall immediately proceed to the

*Last* Objection. 'Twill be making some *Amends* to the Landed Men to *lower the Interest* of Money, and of the *Funds* in particular, because this will *raise* the Value of Land, and in some Measure *reimburse* those who have most contributed to the War.

This I think the common Objection, and it meets with general Reception; and yet I think it full of very great Mistakes, and such as the Landed Gentlemen will find to be so in the Consequence. For 1*st.* The *lowering* the Interest of Money will *not raise* the Value of Land. For this I appeal to plain Experience, Land having Sold for above Twenty Years Purchase all the last Century, when Money has been 10 *per Cent.* and 8 *per Cent.* and 6 *per Cent.* And I ask if they have found that the Price of Land has been *raised* for these last Three Years, that Money has been reduced to Five. 2*dly,* To *lower* the Interest of Money, no more concerns *Land* in its *value,* than it does any *other* Commodity, which any Person shall think fit to deal in. Money of *it self* producing nothing, unless it be by way of *Interest;* if there was no other way of making an Encrease but by laying it out upon *Land,* the Consequence would be good: If they that had Money *must* lay it out that *single* way, it would make a *great many* Purchasers, and in Course the Commodity would be *rais'd.* But let the Legal Interest run as you please, at 5, or 4, or 6 *per Cent.* yet if there be a *Scarcity* of Money, Men will always find ways to *give* and *take* according to that *Scarcity,* and their Occasions: And *That* will be the Standard in the *Market,* whatever the *Legal Stand-*

*ard* may be. When Money is *plentiful*, if the Legal Interest be 5 *per Cent.* yet you may hire for 4; and if it be very *scarce*, notwithstanding all the Provision you can make, you will not be able to procure it under 6 *per Cent.* 3*dly*, The true Reason of Land's selling very *dear*, *i. e.* for Four or Five and Twenty Years Purchase or more, is not very difficult, if we consider *where* it is that it will fetch that Price. 'Tis not the *Goodness* of the Land, nor the *low Interest* of Money, that makes Estates sell so *dear* in *Middlesex*, but what I intimated before, the *Number* of Monied Men who are ready always to buy. And as this is the only Reason, unless by Accident; it may deserve the serious Consideration of those who would *raise* the Value of Land, how much they should *encourage* the Monied Interest. To *raise* the *Value* of Land, *unless* it be designed for *Sale*, is but raising an imaginary Fabrick: And if it be *with* Design to *sell*, then 'tis the *Interest* of the Landlords *not* to *tax* those Funds from which such *Numbers* are enabled to be *Purchasers*. 4*thly*, How must the Gentlemen propose to themselves to be *reimburs'd* by *raising the Value* of Land, unless they propose to *sell* it? The *lowering* Interest will not signify any thing towards *raising* their Rents; and That is the only way of *raising* the Value of Land to him that designs to continue *Possessor* of it. To declare therefore a Design of *reimbursing* themselves by *raising the Value* of Land, is to declare an *open Sale* in Effect, which, whether it will make a *greater Quantity* of Buyers, or a *Scarcity* of them; and in Consequence, whether Land will be *dearer* or *cheaper;* is easy from what has been said to determine.

But still tis asked why the *Funds* should bring in 6 or 7 *per Cent.* and Money as now 'tis settled by Law 5 *per Cent.* and Land will not bring in above 4 or 5 *per Cent.* at most, and yet *this* is Tax'd, and *Those* are thought *unreasonable* to be Taxed.

I answer 1*st*. The Funds are *settled* upon *Terms pro-*

 *pos'd*

*pos'd* by the Legislative, and agreed to by them, as I have more than once observed. *2dly*, Money in *common Justice* ought *always* to be somewhat *higher* than Land, because it can't be imployed in such a *constant* manner as always to produce its Fruits, *viz.* Interest; whereas Land may be cultivated by Landlord as well as by the Tenant, and made to yield such a Profit, as will recompence the Labour. In many Instances, the Produce of Land is without any Labour at all: And 'tis no Detriment to the Proprietor, if he has no Tenant for one part of the Year, because the *whole* Produce of the Land coming at a particular Season, That Season is *all* the Tenant wants and pays for. However, this not being the general Case of Land, it is known that a *good Farm* never wants a Tenant. But Money yields not a *days* Interest more than it is Let for; and is repaid again as often as the Borrower's Turn is served, and lies *dead* till it can be disposed of again, which *may* happen, and actually *does*, much *longer*, and much *oftner*, than any Farms do. Upon which Account 500*l.* worth of Land, *i. e.* 25*l. per Annum*, which *pays* the Tax, at Twenty Years End will put more Money into the Owner's Pocket, than 500*l.* in Money *not Tax'd* will do. But this is not all. For *3dly*, In *Land* the Proprietor can loose but his *Years Profit*, *i. e.* The *Interest* of the Year: The Land cannot be removed, nor can unseasonable Years, breaking of Tenants, or any other Accidents make it contain *fewer* Acres, or be worth much less than when it was Let. But in the Case of *Money*, you run the Chance of *Principal* as well as *Interest*; and therefore there ought to be some *Equivalent* to the *Hazard* you run. No one *Borrows* unless to *supply* his *Wants:* and the Money Lent is always dispers'd into the Hands of others, and in Course the *Lender* suffers in every thing with the *Borrower*, and is involved in all his Misfortunes; and this not only as to the *Interest*, but to the Prime Sum too. This can't be the Case of Landlords, who never can loose *above* the yearly

Rent, and are provided for in numberless Cases prior to all other Creditors, and will be first paid, if the Goods in the House, or the Corn in the Barns, the Stock in the Grounds are sufficient. Hence it is that Money *ought* in *common Equity* to bear a *higher Value, i. e.* to produce a *greater* yearly Increase than Land.

Thus *Sir,* have I given you my Sentiments, upon a Subject I think of the *highest Importance* to the *British* Nation. It appears to me a Question, which ought to be weighed with great Accuracy, and thoroughly examined, before a Proposal be admitted to *alter* the Laws in Being. I do not pretend to have treated this Matter as it ought to be done. If I have given you Occasion to consider this Subject with that Care and Exactness, with that Judgment and Sagacity that you are Master of, 'twill answer the End of,

*SIR,*

*March 7th* *Your most humble Servant.*
1717.

*FINIS.*

AN

# ESSAY

ON THE

# PUBLICK DEBTS

## Of This KINGDOM.

WHEREIN

The Importance of diſcharging them is conſidered; the Proviſions for that Purpoſe by the SINKING FUND, and the Progreſs therein hitherto made, are ſtated and explained; the Sufficiency of thoſe Proviſions are demonſtrated; ſome general Miſtakes about the Nature and Efficacy of this Expedient examined and removed; and the Progreſs of the Sinking Fund deſcribed and computed from *Midſummer*, 1727.

To which is ſubjoined,

An Enquiry into the General Convenience of reducing farther the Intereſt of our Publick Debts below 4 *per Cent per Annum*.

---

*In a* LETTER *to a* MEMBER *of the* HOUSE *of* COMMONS.

---

The THIRD EDITION.

---

*LONDON:*

Printed for J. PEELE, at *Locke's-Head* in *Paternoſter-Row*.

M.DCC.XXVI.

THE

# PREFACE.

*THERE may perhaps appear something too assuming in the Attempts of an Author, to inform the Publick, or to direct their Sentiments about Matters of general Importance, to admit of a better reception or Entertainment from the Town than what Performances of this kind have of late Years generally met with. I have thought therefore, that it may not be improper to mention my Reason for the Publication of the following Sheets, as an Apology for it with the Reader; to whom I can with great Truth and Sincerity represent, that I should never have thought any Knowledge which I had, or any Discoveries in my Power, of our Circumstances with regard to our present Debts, worth the publick Notice, if I had not frequently met with some Mistakes on this Subject, which appeared to me very generally to prevail, and firmly to be insisted on and believed much to the Disadvantage of our Publick Credit, and which at the same Time I have flattered my self, might be confuted and removed, from such Informations only as I should be able, on this Occasion, to collect. I have so often heard it affirmed, that our Publick Debts have increased upon us since the Provisions made for the Discharge of them, that it has sometimes seemed to me to*



*be*

*be the more common Opinion even of those Persons who are most interested to be rightly informed in this Particular; and have almost as often heard it from hence inferred, that those Provisions are therefore insufficient to answer the Expectations we are supposed to have from them. And from the bad Influence that the Belief of this Assertion, and the Inference from it, must have on our Publick Credit, especially when it falls in with any general Apprehensions for the Publick Peace or Welfare on any other Account, I have been induced to think, that as this Fact is not true, nor the Inference from it rightly made, it would be of general Convenience that they were publickly contradicted, and proved to be otherwise; and that this were better done from that less exact and partial Information which I have been able to come at upon this Subject, than not done at all, or perpetually put off in Expectation of its being some time done by such Persons who have the exactest Knowledge of our Circumstances in this Respect, or the best Capacity for improving it for this Purpose.*

*Nor should I have been diverted from communicating the few or partial Discoveries that the following Sheets may be thought to contain, by being told, that such Misrepresentations of our Circumstances were made with Design only, and by Persons who better than my self knew the State of our Affairs in this Respect; because in this Case in particular, it appears to be the Publick Interest, that the Truth should be as generally known as may be, and that every Person who is or may be an Adventurer in our Publick Funds, should, as distinctly as can be, understand the Provisions that have been made for supporting the Credit of them.*

*What I have farther added beyond the General Design, by which I was at first engaged to write upon this Subject, the Reader will judge of on the Perusal of it. I am not insensible that there are several Parts of this Performance open to Exceptions; but I have more hopes of the Reader's*

 *Indulgence*

*Indulgence to these Faults as they shall occur to him, than I have that he will forgive the Recital of them here, or my detaining him by endeavouring in this place to explain away or obviate any Exceptions of this kind. I shall therefore mention but two Particulars, in which I may be thought more than once to have offended. One is, that I have not every where used the utmost Exactness in supposing, stating, or describing the Publick Debts, or the Variations in them. To this Fault, as often as I have been guilty of it from any other Cause than my want of Materials for that purpose, I have been chiefly induced by the Views of being thereby more intelligible: Having presumed that it would be better to omit any such Degrees of Exactness in this respect, as was more than sufficient to answer the General Design of this Essay, which would at the same Time render it more tedious and perplexing. I have also for much the same Reason, been induced to content my self with the Use of some Words in what has seemed to me to have been their more ordinary Acceptation, when applied to this Subject; which in a longer or more elaborate Enquiry, I should have thought my self obliged to define and explain distinctly before I ventur'd upon the Use of them.*

AN

# AN ESSAY ON THE PUBLICK DEBTS.

## *In a Letter to a Member of the* HOUSE of COMMONS.

*SIR,*

UPON recollecting the Conversation that was the Occasion of your desiring my Thoughts in Writing on the Subject of our Publick Debts; I have concluded, that I should best answer your Expectations from me in in this Affair, by confining my Thoughts,

1. To the Consideration of what Advantage to the Publick may be reasonably expected from the Discharge of those Debts, and the Redemption of the Duties provided for the Payment of their Interest.

2. To an Enquiry into the Reasons we have at present to expect or hope that these Debts, or any considerable



Part

Part of them, will within any reasonable Compass of Time be discharged and paid off. And,

3. To such Reflections as have occurred to me upon those Measures that may for the future be enter'd upon, for the more speedy and effectual Discharge of our present Debts, from the Income of the *Sinking Fund* already provided for that purpose; or for still farther increasing the annual Income of that Fund, by such Reductions as may yet be made in the Interest or Annuities payable for the principal Sums of which the present Debt consists.

As to the first of these, or the Advantage arising to the Publick by the Discharge of the present Debts; there seems to be but little room to enlarge, after the Consideration of that great annual Revenue at present levy'd and applied to the Payment of our Debts, which, after the total Discharge of them, will, without any Loss or Injury to private Persons, be redeemed to and become the Property of the Publick. The present yearly Expence to the Government, on Account of our Publick Debts, computing the annual Income of the Sinking Fund and the yearly Interest of those Debts together, will be found to amount to little less than, if not to exceed, the sum of 3,000000*l.* A Revenue exceeding the whole farther annual Expence of our Civil and Military Government in a Time of Peace; and which, together with the ordinary Supplies which our Government requires in a Time of Peace, may perhaps be a Fund sufficient to answer our utmost probable Expences during the most expensive War.

I do not think my self at Liberty to suppose, or promise it as one Advantage arising to the Publick from the Discharge of the present Debts, that the several Duties appropriated to the Payment of them will, as soon as they are redeemed, be immediately removed or determined; for Reasons, which in the following Sheets I shall have a further Occasion to mention: When I



shall

shall recommend it to be considered, whether the Revenues arising from those Duties, or the greatest Part of them, are not raised with more Ease, greater Equality, and more to the common Benefit of the Subjects of *Great Britain*, than some Part of the Supplies that are annually voted for the current Service of the Year; and consequently, how far it may be reasonable to substitute a great Part of the Revenues arising from those Duties, after the Redemption of them, in the Place of our annual Taxes. But it will, I presume, appear no small Convenience to the Publick, arising from the Redemption of the aforesaid Duties, that when they shall be no longer appropriated to the Payment of our Debts, the principal Difficulty will be removed, which has at any Time obstructed the Removal or Lessening any of these Duties, though the Convenience of the Publick may, upon other Accounts, have perswaded to it; either as such Duties may have appeared to give too great Perplexity to Persons employed in Trade, or to prevent or obstruct any profitable Branch of our Commerce with Foreign Countries; as they may have been thought to require too strict an Enquiry, or too great Severity or Expence, in the collecting them; as by being laid on any Commodities universally necessary, they may have seemed too great a Burthen on the poorest of our Inhabitants; or as by bearing too great a Proportion to the Bulk of the Commodities on which they have been laid, they may have made the Gain arising from defrauding the Publick, or the Temptation to attempt it, bear too great a Proportion to the Hazard of being discovered; or, as in any other Respect they may be found to be attended with general Inconvenience, or unreasonable Hardship on particular Persons, Employments or Conditions of Life amongst us.

And however it shall be determined, after the Discharge of our present Debts, as to the Continuance or

Removal of the Whole or any Part of the Duties appropriated for the Payment of them; the Revenues arising from them being redeemed will become the Property of the Publick, and if not from thenceforth removed, will be employed in the room of and take away the Occasion for such other Taxes, as shall then appear a greater Burthen to or to be more unequally levyed upon the Subjects of this Kingdom.

Having mentioned the Quantity of annual Expence to the Government, occasioned by our Publick Debts, it seems unnecessary to proceed further in proving the Importance of discharging them, or to descend to or enumerate any further Inconveniencies, that upon this Account we labour under. An uncomfortable Employment! and which, I hope, I shall be excused from, for this further Reason; That the Inconvenience of our present Debts, and the Importance of discharging them, are so universally believed and felt, and so unanimously agreed to, that I know none of my Fellow-Subjects who want to be convinced of them. I shall proceed therefore to what I proposed in the

2d place, To make out the Probability, and represent the Reasons we have to hope, that the present Publick Debts will, within the Compass of a few Years, be effectually and honourably discharged.

What I have chiefly proposed under this Head, is to describe and explain, as far as my Materials for that purpose will carry me, those Measures which have been already taken for the Discharge of our Publick Debts by the Provision of the Sinking Fund. To which Attempt, though this Provision has already been made as Publick as our Acts of Parliament, and though the Operation and Progress of it, in the Discharge of our Debts, is without any Difficulty to be computed, I find my self induced, from that general Suspicion of the Inefficacy of this Provision to answer the Ends proposed by it; and

 which

which seems to have prevailed amongst some People, who have either not had Leisure for that purpose, or who have declined the Trouble of collecting the Materials for, or making those Computations from them which are requisite, in order to their Satisfaction about the Use and Efficacy of the Sinking Fund.

The first material Provision that was made for discharging the Principal of our present Debts, was enacted in the Third Year of his present Majesty's Reign, by Three several Acts of Parliament at that Time made; the first of which (in the Order that they should have been printed amongst the Statutes published for that Sessions) is intitled, *An Act for redeeming several Funds of the Governour and Company of the Bank of* England, *pursuant to former Provisoes of Redemption; and for securing to them several new Funds and Allowances redeemable by Parliament; and for obliging them to advance further Sums, not exceeding* 2500000l. *at* 5 per Cent. *as shall be found necessary to be employed in lessening the National Debts and Incumbrances; and for continuing certain Provisions formerly made for the Expences of his Majesty's Civil Government, and for the Payment of Annuities formerly purchased at the Rate of* 5 per Cent. *and for other Purposes in this Act mentioned,* Page 331. The Second, intitled, *An Act for Redeeming the yearly Fund of the* South-Sea *Company (being after the Rate of Six Pound* per Cent. per Annum. *and settling on the said Company a yearly Fund after the Rate of* 5 per Cent. per Ann. *and to raise for an Annuity or Annuities, at* 5 per Cent. per An. *any Sum not exceeding* 2,000000*l.* *to be employed in lessening the National Debts and Incumbrances, and for making the said New yearly Fund and Annuities to be hereafter redeemable in the Time and Manner thereby prescribed,* page 375. And the Third, intitled, *An Act for Redeeming the Duties and Revenues which were settled to pay off Principal and Interest on the Orders made forth on Four Lottery Acts, passed in the* 9th *and* 10th *Years of her* *late Majesty's Reign; and for Redeeming certain Annuities payable on Orders, according to a former Act in that Behalf; and for establishing a General Yearly Fund*, &c. pag. 291.

The *Sinking Fund*, of late Years called so from its being understood to be appropriated to the Sinking and Discharging, as far as it will go, the Principal Sums of the present Publick Debt, is made up of Money arising yearly into the *Exchequer*, as the Surplus of the Produce of Three several Funds established by the Three aforesaid Acts of Parliament, by the Names of *the Aggregate Fund, the South-Sea Fund*, and *the General Fund*; the Surplusses of which Three Funds, or what they annually produce more than the yearly Sums to the Payment of which they are first appropriated, are by the last of the aforesaid Acts of Parliament reserved for, and made applicable only to, the Discharge of the Principal and Interest of such Debts as had been before the Year 1716 contracted and provided for by Parliament. The yearly Sums to the Payment of which those Funds are first appropriated, (except the Sum of 700000*l. per Ann.* to his Majesty for the Expence of his Civil Government) are generally the Interest or Annuities payable for several principal Sums, of which our Publick Debts consist. As often therefore as any of those principal Sums are paid off, or the Proprietors of any Part of the Publick Debt are induced to accept of a less Interest or Annuity for the same principal Sums, the Sinking Fund is understood to increase by the yearly Addition of the Interest of such Sums as are paid off, or the Abatement of the Annuity for such Part of the Publick Debt as is agreed to be continued at a lower Rate of Interest. But the Duties, the Surplus of which the Sinking Fund consists of, not bringing in every Year an equal Sum of Money, the Surplus likewise is not every Year alike; and therefore, in order to compute in what Time the present Publick Debt may be discharged by the

Sinking Fund, it is necessary to enquire, from what different annual Sums have of late Years been produced by it, what yearly Sum it is reasonable to suppose may for the future be produced by it at a Medium, or one Year with another. To which yearly Sum we are from Time to Time to add the yearly Interest or Annuity of such principal Sums, part of the present Publick Debt, as may be paid off by it; and all such Abatements of Interest of all or any Part of the Publick Debts, as are already agreed hereafter to take Place, or may for the future be agreed to by any of the Creditors to the Publick.

There are a great many Particulars which you will see, *Sir,* I must want the Knowledge of, in order to make this Supposition with any great Exactness. I could wish here to be able to state the Produce of the several particular Duties, the Excesses of which constitute and supply the Sinking Fund; the different Sums produced by them in different Years, from the Times they were severally granted; to assign the most probable Causes of their Variation, and from thence infer the Probability of their producing more or less for the future. But however unprovided I am with Materials for an Inquiry of this kind, it may be yet worth while to proceed in describing the Proportions in which any determined yearly Sum (though by mistake) supposed to be the present yearly Produce at a Medium of the Sinking Fund, will increase, when apply'd to the Payment of the Publick Debts; as those Proportions will be the same with those in which any other Sum, with more Truth or Probability supposed to be produced one Year with another by the Sinking Fund, will increase when apply'd to the same Purpose.

The best Account I have been able to get of the Produce of the Sinking Fund for some Years last past lies now before me, and states the Produce of the Surplusses of the several Funds, commonly called *the Aggregate Fund,*

13 *the*

*the General Fund* and *the South-Sea Fund* (the Sum of which Surplusses our Acts of Parliament call the *Sinking Fund*) to be from the 31st of *December* 1722, to the same Time in the Year 1723, 619000*l.* and upward; and the Produce of the same Surplusses from thence to the 31st of *December* 1724, to amount to upwards of 653000*l.* This Amount of the Produce of the Sinking Fund for the two Years above-mention'd exceeds the Produce of the same Fund for some Years before, by a greater Sum than can be accounted for by the Discharge or Reduction of the Interest of any Part of the Publick Debt before that Time; and which therefore I am inclined to attribute to several Provisions about that Time made by the Legislature, for preventing Frauds in the Payment, and for the more fully and effectually collecting of several Duties which in part supply the Revenues appropriated to the Payment of our Publick Debts; and of which Provisions I would hope we may long enjoy the Benefit in the Increase of the Sinking Fund. And from hence, I should think, we might venture to expect an annual Produce from the Sinking Fund for the future, equal to the Produce of the same Fund at a Medium for the two Years above-mentioned, ending in *December* 1724; and increasing by the yearly Addition of the Interest of such Principal Sums as may be henceforth paid off, and of the Abatements of the Interest or Annuities of any of the Publick Debts when the same shall take place, that already are or may hereafter be agreed for.

The Abatements of Interest in the Year 1727 are so considerable, and the Time when they are to take place so near, that I believe it will be thought reasonable to step forwards to the Time when the Sinking Fund will be increased by the Addition of those Abatements; and from that Time to consider the Progress that may be made in discharging the present Publick Debt by the Sinking Fund.

From *Midsummer* in the Year 1727, it is already provided, that the Sinking Fund be increased by the Reduction of the Interest from 5 to 4 *per Cent.* or an Abatement of 1 *per Cent. per Annum* on the Principal Sums following.

| | |
|---|---|
| On 13061878*l.* being the Amount of the Publick Debt to the *South-Sea* Company, excluding 3839363*l.* part of it, for which an Annuity at 4 *per Cent.* only is at present payable, | 130618 15 07 |
| On 16901241*l.* 17*s.* of the *South-Sea* Annuities, | 169012 08 04 |
| On 3775027 17 10½ part of the Debt to the Bank of *England*, | 37750 05 06 |
| On 4000000*l.* farther part of the Debt to the Bank of *England*, purchased by them of the *South-Sea* Company, | 40000 00 00 |
| To this, if the annual Income of the Sinking Fund on the 31st of *Decemb.* 1724 be added, supposed to be, | 600000 00 00 |
| And the Increase of it by the Discharge of 600000*l.* *per Annum* of such *Exchequer* Bills as remained uncancelled on the 31st of *Decemb.* 1724, and are made payable out of the Sinking Fund from the said 31st of *December* to the 24th of *June* 1727, *viz.* the Interest and Charge of circulating 1500000*l.* *Exchequer* Bills at 3 *per Cent.* | 45000 00 00 |
| | 1022381 09 05 |

The Amount of the said several annual Sums will be upward of 1022000*l.* the Produce of the Sinking Fund from the 24th of *June* 1727.

 The

The Publick Debts on the 31st of *December* 1724, are stated to amount to 52363471*l.* or thereabouts: From which, if it be allow'd me to deduct 1500000*l.* *Exchequer* Bills above supposed to be paid off by the Sinking Fund on the 24th of *June* 1727, and such further Principal Sums as Provision is made for the Discharge of otherwise than by the Sinking Fund, the Remainder to be paid off on the 24th of *June* 1727 will be considerably less than 50 Millions. Which Sum however, (that I may not be thought to strain Matters in Favour of this Scheme of discharging the Publick Debts by a Sinking Fund) I will suppose to be the Principal Debt to be paid off on the 24th of *June* 1727, and the annual Produce of the Sinking Fund to be from the same Time One Million only. I will likewise suppose, (as is most generally true) that the above-mentioned Principal Sum of 50 Millions will from the same Time carry Interest after the Rate of 4 *per Cent.* And because there are some Persons so sanguine to imagine, that by the Force of our Sinking Fund, or some Schemes formed upon it, the same Debt may be still further reduced to a lower Rate of Interest, and the Sinking Fund increased further by such Reduction; I will likewise suppose such a Scheme to have taken effect, and the above-mention'd Principal Sum to carry 3 *per Cent.* Interest only, and the annual Produce of the Sinking Fund to be increased by an Abatement of 1 *per Cent.* Interest on 50 Millions, to 1500000*l.* Upon both which Suppositions, I shall subjoin a Computation, describing in what Number of Years, from *Midsummer* 1727, the above-mention'd Principal Sum of 50 Millions, or any particular Part of it, may be discharged and paid off; in which, when I had not Time to correct them, I discovered a small Mistake or two; which I hope the Reader will excuse, when I have assured him, that they no where misrepresent the Time in which the aforesaid Debt, or any Part of it, may be paid off by so much as two Days.

## *Computation at* 4*l.* per Cent.

| | *Payments made at* Midsummer *every Year.* | | | *Total of all the Payments from the Beginning in every Year.* | | |
|---|---|---|---|---|---|---|
| 1728 | 1000000 | 00 | 00 | 1000000 | 00 | 00 |
| | 40000 | 00 | 00 | | | |
| 29 | 1040000 | 00 | 00 | 2040000 | 00 | 00 |
| | 41600 | 00 | 00 | | | |
| 30 | 1081600 | 00 | 00 | 3121600 | 00 | 00 |
| | 43264 | 00 | 00 | | | |
| 31 | 1124864 | 00 | 00 | 4246464 | 00 | 00 |
| | 44994 | 11 | 2⅜ | | | |
| 32 | 1169858 | 11 | 2⅜ | 5416322 | 11 | 2⅜ |
| | 46794 | 06 | 10⅛ | | | |
| 33 | 1316652 | 18 | 0½ | 6632975 | 09 | ⅞ |
| | 48666 | 02 | 3¾ | | | |
| 34 | 1265319 | 00 | 4¼ | 7898294 | 09 | 5⅛ |
| | 50612 | 15 | 2½ | | | |
| 35 | 1315931 | 15 | 6¾ | 9214226 | 04 | 11⅞ |
| | 52637 | 05 | 5 | | | |
| 36 | 1368569 | 00 | 11¾ | 10582795 | 05 | 10⅝ |
| | 54742 | 15 | 02⅜ | | | |
| 37 | 1423311 | 16 | 02⅛ | 12006107 | 02 | 0¾ |
| | 56932 | 09 | 05 | | | |
| 38 | 1480244 | 05 | 7½ | 13486351 | 07 | 8¼ |
| | 59209 | 15 | 2½ | | | |
| 39 | 1539454 | 00 | 10 | 15025805 | 08 | 6¼ |
| | 61578 | 03 | 02¾ | | | |
| 40 | 1601032 | 04 | 0¾ | 16626837 | 12 | 07 |
| | 64041 | 05 | 9¼ | | | |
| 41 | 1665073 | 09 | 10 | 18291911 | 02 | 05 |
| | 66602 | 18 | 9½ | | | |
| 42 | 1731676 | 08 | 7½ | 20023587 | 11 | 0½ |
| | 69267 | 01 | 1¾ | | | |

*Computation at* 3*l*. per Cent.

| | *Payments made at* Midsummer *in every Year.* | | | *Total of all the Payments from the beginning in every Year.* | | |
|---|---|---|---|---|---|---|
| 1728 | 1500000<br>45000 | 0<br>0 | 0<br>0 | 1,500000 | 0 | 0 |
| 29 | 1545000<br>46350 | 0<br>0 | 0<br>0 | 3,045000 | 0 | 0 |
| 30 | 1591350<br>47740 | 0<br>10 | 0<br>0 | 4,636350 | 0 | 0 |
| 31 | 1639090<br>49272 | 10<br>14 | 0<br>0 | 6,275440 | 10 | 0 |
| 32 | 1688363<br>50650 | 4<br>17 | 0<br>4½ | 7,963803 | 14 | 0 |
| 33 | 1739014<br>52170 | 1<br>8 | 4½<br>5¼ | 9,702817 | 15 | 4½ |
| 34 | 1791184<br>53735 | 9<br>10 | 9¾<br>8¼ | 11,494002 | 5 | 1¼ |
| 35 | 1844920<br>55347 | 0<br>12 | 6 | 13,338922 | 5 | 7¼ |
| 36 | 1900267<br>57008 | 12<br>0 | 6<br>6¾ | 15,239189 | 18 | 1¼ |
| 37 | 1957275<br>58718 | 13<br>0 | ¾<br>6½ | 17,196465 | 11 | 2 |
| 38 | 2015993<br>60479 | 13<br>16 | 6¼<br>2½ | 19,212459 | 4 | 8¼ |
| 39 | 2076473<br>62544 | 9<br>4 | 8¾<br>1 | 21,289032 | 14 | 5 |
| 40 | 2139017<br>64170 | 13<br>10 | 9¾<br>7¾ | 23,428050 | 8 | 2¾ |
| 41 | 2203188<br>66095 | 4<br>12 | 5½<br>11¼ | 25,631238 | 12 | 7¼ |
| 42 | 2269283<br>68078 | 17<br>10 | 4¾<br>3¾ | 27,900522 | 10 | 0 |

*Computation at 4l.* per Cent.

| | *Payments made at* Midsummer *in every Year.* | | | *Total of all the Payments from the Beginning in every Year.* | | |
|---|---|---|---|---|---|---|
| 1743 | 1800943 | 09 | 09¼ | 21824531 | 00 | 09¾ |
| | 72037 | 14 | 09½ | | | |
| 44 | 1872981 | 04 | 06¾ | 23697512 | 05 | 03½ |
| | 74919 | 04 | 11¾ | | | |
| 45 | 1947900 | 09 | 06½ | 25645412 | 14 | 10 |
| | 77916 | 00 | 04½ | | | |
| 46 | 2025816 | 09 | 11 | 27671229 | 04 | 09 |
| | 81032 | 13 | 02¼ | | | |
| 47 | 2106849 | 03 | 01¼ | 29778078 | 07 | 10¼ |
| | 84273 | 19 | 03¾ | | | |
| 48 | 2191123 | 02 | 05 | 31969201 | 10 | 03¼ |
| | 87644 | 18 | 06 | | | |
| 49 | 2278768 | 00 | 11 | 34247969 | 11 | 02¼ |
| | 91150 | 14 | 01 | | | |
| 50 | 2369918 | 15 | 00 | 36617988 | 06 | 02¼ |
| | 94796 | 15 | 00 | | | |
| 51 | 2464715 | 10 | 00 | 39082703 | 16 | 02¼ |
| | 98588 | 12 | 04¾ | | | |
| 52 | 2563304 | 02 | 04¾ | 41646007 | 18 | 07 |
| | 102532 | 03 | 03½ | | | |
| 53 | 2665836 | 05 | 08¼ | 44311844 | 04 | 03¼ |
| | 106633 | 09 | 00½ | | | |
| 54 | 2772469 | 14 | 08¾ | 47094313 | 19 | 00 |
| | 110898 | 15 | 09½ | | | |
| 55 | 2883368 | 10 | 06¼ | 49977682 | 09 | 06¼ |
| | 115334 | 14 | 09¾ | 22317 | 10 | 05¾ |
| 56 | 2998703 | 05 | 04 | 50000000 | 00 | 00 |
| | 1296 | 14 | 08 | | | |
| | 3000000 | 00 | 00 | | | |

## *Computation at* 3*l.* per Cent.

| | *Payments made at* Midsummer *every Year.* | | | *Total of all the Payments from the beginning in every Year.* | | |
|---|---|---|---|---|---|---|
| 1743 | 2337362<br>70120 | 7<br>17 | 8½<br>5 | 30,237884 | 17 | 8½ |
| 44 | 2407483<br>72224 | 05<br>9 | 1½<br>11½ | 32,645368 | 2 | 10 |
| 45 | 2479707<br>74391 | 15<br>4 | 1<br>7¾ | 35,125075 | 17 | 11 |
| 46 | 2554098<br>76622 | 19<br>19 | 8¾<br>4¼ | 37,679174 | 17 | 7¾ |
| 47 | 2630721<br>78921 | 19<br>13 | 1<br>2 | 40,309896 | 16 | 8¾ |
| 48 | 2709643<br>81289 | 12<br>6 | 3<br>2 | 43,019540 | 8 | 11¾ |
| 49 | 2790932<br>83727 | 18<br>19 | 5<br>9 | 45,810473 | 7 | 4¾ |
| 50 | 2874660<br>86239 | 18<br>16 | 2<br>8½ | 48,685134<br>1,314865 | 5<br>14 | 6¾<br>5¼ |
| 51<br>½ | 2960900<br>39099 | 14<br>5 | 10½<br>1½ | 50,000000 | | |
| | 3000000 | 0 | 0 | | | |

 You

You will be pleased to observe, *Sir,* That the annual Income of the Sinking Fund, in this manner applied to the Discharge of the Principal of the Publick Debts, increases yearly in the same manner and Proportion as a Principal Sum put out and continued at compound Interest, or Interest upon Interest, at such a Rate of Interest as the Principal Sum to be paid off is supposed to carry: That the Increase of it in every Year, is by the Interest of that Principal Sum which was paid off in the Year next before it; and that the whole of the Increase of it in any one Year, from the beginning to apply it in Discharge of the Principal Debt, is the Sum of the Interest of all the Principal Sums that have been in the Year before paid off by it: And that the whole of the Debt proposed to be paid off by a Sinking Fund in this manner applyed, will be compleatly discharged the Year before the Sinking Fund it self is increased by the Addition of the whole Interest of the Debt to be paid off.

From which Observations, it will be easy to compute the Progress of any other annual Sum, greater or less, than what I have supposed to be the Produce of the Sinking Fund in the Year 1727, in the Payment of a Principal Sum of 50 Millions, at 4 *per Cent.* or any other Rate of Interest, or any other Principal Sum which you may think it more reasonable (as our Affairs now stand) to provide for the Payment of, by the common Rules for calculating the Increase of Principal Sums continued at compound Interest.

In the use of which Rules, you will find, *Sir,* if you should think it more reasonable to set the Income of the Sinking Fund, from the Year 1727, at 800000*l.* or (as some Persons have represented it) at 1200000*l.* *per Annum,* that a Debt of 50 Millions, carrying 4 *per Cent.* Interest, would in the first of these Cases be paid off in about 32 Years, and in the other in 25 Years and one Month; or

 if

if in either Case the Sinking Fund should be supposed to be increased by 500000*l*. *per Annum* added to it, from the Interest of the same Debt reduced to 3 *per Cent.* from the same Time, it would appear that it might be fully discharged and paid off, by a Sinking Fund of 1300000*l*. *per Ann.* in about 25 Years, and by a Sinking Fund of 1700000*l*. in 21 Years and 8 Months, or thereabouts.

But whatever may in this manner be observed or proved, relating to the Efficacy or Progress of the Sinking Fund increasing annually by Addition of the Interest of such Debts as are discharged by it, I have heard it objected and strongly insisted on to be true, that our Publick Debts have been far from decreasing or being made less since the Contrivance and Application of this Expedient for that purpose; but, on the contrary, have been growing upon us, and are now considerably greater than they were about the Time when the Surplusses of several Funds were first appropriated to the Discharge of those Debts. And this melancholy Circumstance the same Persons aggravate, with observing, that the Increase of our Debts has been in a Time of almost uninterrupted Peace; and infer, that our Debts must increase still faster upon us, in case of any Publick Troubles.

I have often wondered how so uncomfortable a Mistake could so generally prevail, against the Testimony that the Memory of every Person at all acquainted with Publick Transactions of this kind must bear, that our Publick Loans of late Years (except such as have been made on Funds provided to discharge the Monies advanced upon them within the Year,) have not been equal to the Sums that have within the same Time been paid off; 'till upon further Enquiry upon this Subject, I have had put into my Hands Copies of Accounts, supposed to be made up at the *Exchequer*, stating the Totals of the Publick Debts for different Years, to be greater considerably from the Year 1720, than in that Year, and in that Year to be more than in any Year before it. From which Accounts I cannot but think this Mistake must arise, and prevail with Persons, who satisfy'd themselves with observing the Totals only, and have not attended to the particular Articles of which they were made up; but in examining the particular Articles of which those Totals are made up, they will find that the great Increase of Figures in the Description of our present Incumbrances, is not owing to any real Increase of their true Quantity.

In an Account now before me, of the Amount of the Publick Debts on the 31st *Dec.* in several Years, beginning in 1717, and ending in the Year 1724, the Amount of the Publick Debts in the first of those Years is described to be 47894950*l.* and in the last to be 52363471*l.* Of which great Increase in the Description of our Debts, the chief Reasons are; First, the Subscriptions of several irredeemable Annuities for different Terms of Years into the *South-Sea Company's Stock*, in the Years 1719 and 1720; by which those Annuities were converted into a redeemable Debt from the Government, and purchased back from the Proprietors at higher Rates, or a greater Number of Years Purchase, than were paid by the Proprietors for the same Annuities when they were first purchased from the Government. Before these Subscriptions made, this Part of our Publick Incumbrances is described in the aforesaid Account, by the Principal Sums originally advanced by the Proprietors on the Purchase of them; and afterwards, by the Quantity of redeemable Debt for which by Virtue of the aforesaid Subscriptions they were exchanged; which generally exceeds by four Years and one half's Purchase the Sum originally contributed by the Proprietors of those Annuities, and which upon the whole of the said Annuities at those different times subscribed amounts to about 3,155858*l.* This in the present View must, I think, be admitted to be no real Increase of the Publick Incumbrances, or at

23 least

least not properly brought into the Account of those Years in which the aforesaid Subscriptions were made; those Subscriptions being well enough known and understood to have been of great Advantage to the Publick, and very much to have facilitated the Discharge of the Whole of our present Debts; and it being very obvious, that whatever real Incumbrance has been growing upon us on Account of those Annuities, it is to be attributed only to the increasing Value of those Annuities, and to be computed from the Times of their being valued at higher Prices, and not from the Times of the Subscriptions above-mentioned, by which the further Increase of their Value was most fortunately prevented; and about which, all that we have to wish is, that it had been done sooner.

Another Article increasing in the aforesaid Accounts of the Publick Debts from the Year 1717 to the Year 1724, is of Army-Debentures, or Annuities charged and made payable out of the Fund commonly called the *General Fund,* after the Rate of 4 *per Cent.* for such Principal Sums, as, in pursuance of several Acts of Parliament for appointing Commissioners to state the Debt due to the Army, have been certified to have been due for Services in the late War, and before the Year 1717. This, *Sir,* from 40157*l.* 8*s.* 5*d.* which on the 31st of *Dec.* 1717 is only stated to be due from the Publick under this Article, is on the 31st of *Dec.* 1724, by the aforesaid Accounts described to amount to upwards of 2,140157*l.* But as this Debt was due before the Year 1717, in the present Inquiry whether the Publick Debts are since that Time increased or no, this Sum, now the Quantity of it is determined, is to be reckon'd in the Amount of the Publick Debt, as well in the Year 1717 as in the Year 1724; or, in other Words, to be consider'd as due from the Publick from the Time it was contracted, and not from the Time only when it was certified to be due.

Another Article increasing the Total Amount of the

Publick Debts in the Year 1724 beyond that of the Year 1717, in the aforesaid Accounts, is, that of 1000000*l.* of *Exchequer* Notes made out and lent to the *South-Sea* Company in the Year 1720, and in that Year added to the Amount of the Publick Debts. This Sum, on the Repayment of it by the *South-Sea* Company, would have been deducted from the Amount of the Publick Debts in that Year in which it was repaid, if it had not been provided by a subsequent Act of Parliament, that the aforesaid *Exchequer* Notes should be cancelled and paid out of the Sinking Fund; and that the Sum of 1000000*l.* due from the *South-Sea* Company, should be applied, when paid, to the Discharge of a farther Million of *Exchequer* Notes made forth in the Year 1722, and upon which Money was raised for the Discharge of a like Sum in Arrear to the Navy; which said Sum of 1000000*l.* being in this manner ultimately supplied out of the Sinking Fund, it is necessary to suppose it to have been due from the Publick before the Year 1716, the Sinking Fund being, as I have above observed, about that Time appropriated to the Discharge of such Debts only as were due before that Year; and consequently, this Sum of 1000000*l.* being in the Year 1717 owing, and in Arrear from the Government, should also, in our present Inquiry about the Increase of the Publick Debts, be in that Year added to the Amount of them.

As should also, for much the same kind of Reasons, the following less material Articles, *viz.*

| | |
|---|---|
| Navy-Annuities, a Debt though before due, not brought into the Publick Accounts till the Year 1718. | 110312 00 00 |
| A further Provision for the Sufferers at *Nevis* and *St. Christophers*, about | 41000 00 00 |

| | |
|---|---|
| The Increase of a Deficiency on the *East India* Company's Fund stated in the Publick Accounts, to be from the Year 1717 to the Year 1720, about | 67500 00 00 |
| A Sum in the Year 1723, raised for immediate Service on the Credit of *Exchequer* Notes, the Payment of which was at the same Time provided for by a Tax on the Estates of *Roman Catholicks*, | 100000 00 00 |
| To these Articles are to be added the Three First above-mentioned, *viz.* | |
| The Increase computed on the Subscription of Irredeemables, | 3155858 00 00 |
| Of Army Debentures, | 2100000 00 00 |
| And the Sum raised for discharging Arrears to the Navy, | 1000000 00 00 |
| The Amount of which Sums together is, | 6574670 00 00 |

And this Sum, *Sir*, must be added to the abovemention'd Total of our Publick Debts in the Year 1717, before the comparing it with the Total of the same Debts in the Year 1724 will truly determine how far our Debts are increased or grown less from one Time to the other. Let this then be done.

| | |
|---|---|
| | 47894950 00 00 |
| | 6574670 00 00 |
| And the aforesaid Amount of our | 54469620 00 00 |
| Debts in 1724, deducted from it | 52363471 00 00 |
| | 2106149 00 00 |

And it will appear, that our Debts are not in reality increased from the Year 1717, to the Year 1724; but, on the contrary, are diminished by the Sum of 2106149*l.* or thereabouts.

The same Thing will appear from enumerating the Particulars of the real Increase or Decrease of our Debts from one Time to the other; of which, *Sir*, the following is very nearly a true Account, *viz.*

| | |
|---|---|
| Money at different Times borrowed on the Duty on Coals for Building Churches, more than in the mean Time has been paid off by the particular Provision made for that purpose, | 92778 02 00 |
| Money borrowed for the Service of the Year 1719, more than paid off by the Provision made for that purpose on the 31st of *December* 1724, | 439300 00 00 |
| Money borrowed on the Plate Act for the Service of the Year 1720. | 312000 00 00 |
| Total | 844078 02 00 |

And this Sum of 844078 02 00 is the whole Sum that our Debts can, with any Propriety, be said to be increased by, from the Year 1717. Such other Sums as have been since that Time borrowed having been employ'd in Aid of the Sinking Fund, and applied in Discharge of some other Debts at a higher Interest; of which the following (except what of this kind has been already mentioned) is likewise a true Account, *viz.*

| | |
|---|---|
| Borrowed in the Year 1719 by Lottery, | 500000 00 00 |
| Advanced in the same Year by the *South Sea* Company on the Increase of their Stock and Funds, about | 544142 00 00 |
| Advanced in the Year 1723, towards the Discharge of the Lottery Annuities unsubscribed to the *South Sea* Company, about | 1000000 00 00 |
| Total | 2044142 00 00 |

By which Sum, together with the Sinking Fund, have been paid off from 1717 to 1724, *viz.*

| | |
|---|---|
| Of *Exchequer* Notes | 2924612 00 00 |
| Lottery Annuities unsubscribed | 1204786 00 00 |
| *Bank* Annuities unsubscribed | 235297 00 00 |
| Deficiency of the *East India* Company's Fund | 191028 00 00 |
| Besides, there has been in the same Time paid in part of a Principal Debt contracted by two Lotteries in the Years 1713 and 1714, by Provision for that purpose at the same Time made, about | 429490 00 00 |
| Total | 4985213 00 00 |
| From whence the Total of the last above-mentioned Loans being deducted, *viz.* | 2044142 00 00 |
| The Remainder | 2941071 00 00 |

will be the Sum of what has been paid off from the Year 1717 to the Year 1724 by the Sinking Fund, or otherwise without the Assistance of those Loans.

| | |
|---|---|
| And from thence, | 2941071 00 00 |
| let us farther deduct the Total of the aforesaid Articles by which our Debts have really, in the mean Time, been encreased, *viz.* | 844078 00 00 |
| And that Remainder | 2096993 00 00 |

will be the Sum by which our Debts, within the aforesaid Seven Years, appear by this Computation really to have been diminished; differing indeed from that Sum which I have from the first Computation stated to be the Decrease of the Publick Debts in the same Time by near 10000*l.* but which Difference, if I pretended to the utmost Exactness, might be removed, by either adding to the last Remainder, or reckoning amongst the Particulars by



which

which our Debts have decreased within the Time aforesaid, the Value of such Annuities for Lives as within that Time have reverted to the Crown.

This Sum, perhaps, especially if it be farther reduced by the Deduction of One Million at Two different Times borrowed, to supply the Deficiencies of the Provision for the Expence of His Majesty's Civil Government, consider'd as Part of and an Addition to our Publick Debts, may be thought too inconsiderable a Diminution of our Debts to be boasted of as the Effects of this Expedient for so great a length of Time. But as it is no real Objection to the Truth of those Computations which I have made, of the Progress of the Sinking Fund from the Year 1727, I presume it will likewise be no Discouragement to our Dependance on this Provision for the Payment of our Debts; especially after we have considered the great Addition that will be made to the Sinking Fund in the Year 1727, and have farther observed the much greater Dispatch which a yearly Sum applied to the Payment of any determined Debt at Interest, and increasing annually in the manner above described, will make in the Discharge of such a Debt in a few Years after the first Application of it to that purpose, than it will do when it first begins in that Manner to be applied.

The little Progress however hitherto made in the Diminution of our Debts, leads me to the Examination of another Opinion, which I think I have observed to prevail with the same Persons who affirm our Publick Debts to have increased upon us; which is, that upon the Supposition that such Debts are really increasing upon us by new Loans equal to or exceeding the Discharges made in the same Time by the Sinking Fund, the Sinking Fund is in such Case making no effectual Progress at all in the Diminution of our Debts. It is perhaps the more material to consider here, how far this Opinion is true, for this Reason, that though this Supposition on which it is

 founded

founded has not been true hitherto, it must be however admitted to be not improbable, that some future Exigencies of the Government may make such new Loans necessary as may exceed any Sums in the same Compass of Time produced by or applied to the Discharge of our Debts from the Sinking Fund. And in this Case, upon the Supposition that such new Loans are made upon further Funds found out for Payment of the Interest of the Money so to be advanced upon them, this Opinion, that the Sinking Fund applied as aforesaid would be making no effectual Advance to the compleat Discharge of the Whole of our Publick Debts, would not be true. This will be best explained, if during the Time that the above supposed Sinking Funds are imployed in the Discharge of the aforesaid Debt of 50 Millions, the Whole of our Debts should be supposed, by new Loans upon further Funds borrowed at 4 or 3 *per Cent.* Interest, to be increased by a further Sum of 50 Millions, and that Sum to be discharged in the same Manner, and by the same Sinking Funds, after the Discharge of the first 50 Millions; or if the Account of the Progress of the above supposed Sinking Funds be carried on, till instead of 50 Millions they shall have discharged a principal Debt of 100 Millions.

## *Computation at* 4*l.* per Cent.

| | *Payments made at* Midsummer *every Year.* | | | *Total of Payments from the Beginning in every Year.* | | |
|---|---|---|---|---|---|---|
| 1755 | | | | 49977682 | 09 | 06¼ |
| 56 | 2998703<br>119948 | 05<br>02 | 04<br>07¼ | 52976385 | 14 | 10¼ |
| 57 | 3118651<br>124746 | 07<br>01 | 11¼<br>01¼ | 56095037 | 02 | 09 |
| 58 | 3243397<br>129735 | 09<br>17 | 00½<br>11½ | 59338434 | 11 | 10 |
| 59 | 3373113<br>134924 | 07<br>10 | 00<br>08 | 62711547 | 18 | 10 |
| 60 | 3508037<br>140321 | 17<br>10 | 08½<br>03½ | 66219585 | 16 | 06 |
| 61 | 3648359<br>145934 | 07<br>07 | 11½<br>06 | 69867945 | 04 | 05½ |
| 62 | 3794293<br>151771 | 15<br>15 | 05½<br>00 | 73662238 | 19 | 11 |
| 63 | 3946065<br>157842 | 10<br>12 | 05½<br>05¼ | 77608304 | 09 | 04½ |
| 64 | 4103908<br>164156 | 02<br>06 | 10¾<br>06 | 81712212 | 12 | 03¼ |
| 65 | 4268064<br>170722 | 09<br>11 | 04¾<br>06½ | 85980277 | 01 | 08 |
| 66 | 4438787<br>177551 | 00<br>09 | 11¼<br>06¾ | 90419064 | 02 | 07¾ |
| 67 | 4616338<br>184653 | 10<br>10 | 06<br>09¾ | 95035402 | 13 | 01¾ |
| 68 | 4800992<br>192039 | 01<br>13 | 03¾<br>07¾ | 99836394<br>163605 | 14<br>05 | 05<br>07 |
| 69 | 4993031<br>6968 | 14<br>05 | 11½<br>00½ | 100000000 | 00 | 00 |
| | 5000000 | 00 | 00 | | | |

## *Computation at* 3*l.* per Cent.

| | *Payments made at* Midsummer *in every Year.* | | | *Total of Payments from the Beginning in every Year.* | | |
|---|---|---|---|---|---|---|
| 1750 | | | | 48685134 | 05 | 06¾ |
| 51 | 2960900 | 14 | 10½ | 5164603 | 00 | 05¼ |
| | 88827 | 00 | 05½ | | | |
| 52 | 3049727 | 15 | 04 | 54695761 | 15 | 09¼ |
| | 91491 | 16 | 01¾ | | | |
| 53 | 3141219 | 11 | 05¾ | 57836981 | 07 | 03 |
| | 94236 | 11 | 07¾ | | | |
| 54 | 3235456 | 03 | 01½ | 61072437 | 10 | 04½ |
| | 97063 | 13 | 08¼ | | | |
| 55 | 3332519 | 16 | 09¾ | 64404957 | 07 | 02¼ |
| | 99975 | 11 | 10¾ | | | |
| 56 | 3432495 | 08 | 08½ | 67837452 | 15 | 10¾ |
| | 102974 | 17 | 03 | | | |
| 57 | 3535470 | 05 | 11½ | 71372923 | 01 | 10¼ |
| | 106064 | 02 | 02 | | | |
| 58 | 3641534 | 08 | 01½ | 75014457 | 09 | 11¾ |
| | 109246 | 00 | 07¾ | | | |
| 59 | 3750780 | 08 | 09¼ | 78765237 | 18 | 09 |
| | 112523 | 08 | 03¼ | | | |
| 60 | 3863303 | 17 | 00½ | 82628541 | 15 | 09½ |
| | 115899 | 02 | 03¾ | | | |
| 61 | 3979202 | 19 | 04¼ | 86607744 | 15 | 01¾ |
| | 119376 | 01 | 10 | | | |
| 62 | 4098579 | 01 | 02¼ | 90706323 | 16 | 04 |
| | 122957 | 07 | 04½ | | | |
| 63 | 4221536 | 08 | 06¾ | 94927860 | 04 | 10¾ |
| | 126646 | 01 | 09¼ | | | |
| 64 | 4348182 | 10 | 04 | 99276042 | 15 | 02¾ |
| | 130745 | 09 | 06 | 723957 | 04 | 09¼ |
| 65 | 4478927 | 19 | 10 | 100000000 | 00 | |
| | 21072 | 00 | 02 | | | |
| | 4500000 | 00 | 00 | | | |

From hence, *Sir*, it presently appears, that the above supposed Sinking Funds, in this Manner increasing by the Addition of the Interest of the Principal Sums in every Year paid off, and consequently by Additions in every Year greater than those made to it in the Year before, will be sufficient not only to discharge our present Debts, but any probable Addition in the mean Time to be made to them by further Loans on new-invented Funds, in a few Years after the present Debts shall be discharged; and that the Time required for the Discharge of our Debts increased by any Addition in this Manner made, will by no Means be lengthened out, or the Payment of the Whole of our Debts by the Sinking Fund retarded or delayed, in Proportion to the Addition to or Increase of the Debt itself: The total Payment of our Publick Debts becoming by no Means desperate from any Sinking Fund, however less than those above supposed, upon Account of any determined Increase of or Additions made to them; unless those Additions are supposed to be continued increasing in every Year in the same or a greater Proportion to one another than that in which the Additions yearly made to the Sinking Fund increase. This is so true, that Suppositions about the Increase of the Publick Debt might be carried to the utmost Extravagance, and still appear to be provided for by the above-mentioned Sinking Fund of 1000000*l.* increasing at the Rate of 4 *per Cent.* Compound Interest; which, if it were worth while, might be shewed to be sufficient, in about 105 Years, to pay off a Debt of 1575 Millions, allowing for the Increase of the present Debt of 50 Millions, by an Addition of 15 Millions in every Year in which that Sinking Fund should be so applied. Nor will this at all surprise Persons who have been accustomed to attend to the Increase of Money put out at Compound Interest, or Quantities continued in Geometrical Progression; an Enquiry into which will remove all Doubt about the Truth of what I have here advanced. It would however be true, that if at any Time, on the Discharge of any Part of the Principal of the present Debt, the Interest were not added to and applied in the further Discharge of the remaining Debt, but another equal or greater principal Sum should be borrowed on the same Annuity; the Progress of the Sinking Fund would by such Measures, if the same Sum were borrowed, be stopp'd; and if a greater, be put backwards: But as long as these Measures are not taken, or the Sinking Fund diverted or applied to any other Purpose than the Discharge of our Debts, the full and effectual Payment of all our Debts by this Expedient, is by no Means to be despaired of from the Increase of them by new Loans on further Duties.

And that the Sinking Fund will, from Time to Time, be applied to the Discharge of the Publick Debts, and not be diverted or applied to any other Purpose whatsoever, is what, I think, we may securely promise our selves; from considering that the aforesaid Fund has been appropriated to that Purpose by the Legislature, and our Publick Faith in the same Manner engaged to the Creditors of the Government, that the Surplus of the aforesaid Duties should be applied to the Discharge of the Principal of their Debts, as the Funds themselves to the Payment of the Interest or Annuities contracted for: Which Faith of the Publick in this Manner engaged, I think we have all the Reason in the World to believe will be as inviolably observed in this as in any other Part of their Contract with the Proprietors of the Publick Debts.

This Appropriation of the Sinking Fund to the Purpose aforesaid, you will find, *Sir,* to have been made by the aforesaid Acts of Parliament. In the last of which, taking them in that Order in which I have referred to them, *page* 320, after reciting that by the Two other Acts of Parliaments, the Surplusses of the *Aggregate* and *South-Sea Funds* are provided to be reserved to the Disposition of Parliament only; it is enacted, That the Surplusses of the *General Fund* thereby created, should in like manner be accounted for and reserved for the Disposition of Parliament. And then it is further enacted in the Words following: "That all the Monies to arise from Time to "Time, as well of or for the said Excess or Surplus, by "virtue of the said Act made for redeeming the Funds of "the Governour and Company of the *Bank of England* "[viz. the *Aggregate Fund*] and of or for the said Excess "or Surplus, by virtue of the said Act for redeeming the "Funds of the said Governour and Company of Mer-"chants trading to the *South-Seas, &c.* and of or for the "said Excess or Surplus of the said Duties and Revenues "by this Act appropriated as aforesaid, [viz. *the General* "*Fund*] and the said Overplus Monies of the said General "yearly Fund by this Act established or intended to be "established as aforesaid, shall be appropriated, reserved, "and imploy'd to and for the discharging the Principal "and Interest of such National Debts and Incumbrances "as were incurred before the 25th of *Dec.* 1716, and are "declared to be National Debts, and are provided for by "Act of Parliament in such Manner and Form as shall be "directed and appointed by any future Act or Acts of "Parliament to be discharged therewith or out of the "same, and to and for none other Use, Intent or Purpose "whatsoever."

By these Words, I think, the Surplusses therein mention'd, of which the annual Income of the Sinking Fund is made up, sufficiently appear to have been appropriated by the Legislative Power to the Payment of our Publick Debts, till they shall be intirely discharged and paid off. Nor can this Provision well be understood as made by the Government for what then appeared for publick Convenience only, and consequently to be altered by subsequent Acts whenever it shall appear, or be pretended to be otherwise; but must, I think, be considered as a Contract by the Government with the Publick Creditors, if the Occasion of these Acts of Parliament be attended to. In which Case it will appear, that the several Provisions by these Acts made, were enacted and proposed to the Creditors aforesaid, as Inducements to them to accept of an Interest or Annuity for their Debts by one Sixth Part less than that which till that Time they had received; of which the most obvious Inducement was, that what was thus deducted from the yearly Interest of their Debts, should be applied for the better securing and gradual Discharge of the Principal of the said Debts. To which Security, amongst the other Benefits by the same Acts of Parliament proposed to them, they must I think be considered to have intitled themselves by their Subscriptions afterwards made, subsequent to and in Consideration of such Proposals made to them by the Legislature. And whoever will be at the Trouble of turning over the several subsequent Acts of Parliament relating to the Publick Debts, will find this Provision for the Application of the Sinking Fund frequently repeated and confirmed: And in Cases where by Act of Parliament Application of Monies in the Sinking Fund to the Discharge of Debts that were less obviously or less generally known to have been within the Description of the Debts intended by the Provision above-recited, such Debts have been by the Recitals declared and explained to have been Debts incurred before the 25th of *Dec.* 1716, and provided for by Parliament in a manner that has plainly intimated it to be understood by the Legislature, that the above-recited Provision was an Engagement or Contract of the Government with the Publick Creditors, about the punctual Observation of which from Time to Time they were intitled to have all possible Satisfaction; or at least, that the punctual Application of the above-mentioned Surplusses to the Discharge of our present Debts, was regarded by them as a Matter of the highest Consequence to the

 Publick

Publick Welfare. And as long as the Publick Welfare shall be in the least regarded, and this continues to be the only Expedient for removing such heavy Incumbrances on our Affairs, and redeeming so considerable a Revenue to the Use of the Publick, I think we may confidently expect, that no Persons whatsoever, whose Hands the Administration of our Affairs may at any Time for the future be committed to, can ever be induced to approve of or recommend the Application of the Produce of the Sinking Fund in any possible Exigence of our Affairs, to any other Uses than those to which it stands now appropriated, though there were no other Considerations to inforce it.

For let us inquire a little, what publick Exigencies can be supposed to happen, that can make it at any Time advisable to divert or apply the Produce of the Sinking Fund to any other Purpose till after the intire Payment of our Publick Debts. Let the Expence that the Circumstances of our Affairs may at any Time make necessary, be or be supposed to be ever so much more than what can be conveniently raised within the Year; it must I think always appear more eligible in regard to the Publick Interest, as well as more easy to those Persons in the Administration, to whom the Care of providing the necessary Supplies shall at any Time be allotted, to raise what shall be further wanted by increasing the Publick Debt with further Loans upon Interest provided for by new Duties, than to supply the same Sums in any way from the Produce of the Sinking Fund.

The Computation that I have last made was to shew, That the Time in which the above supposed Sinking Fund of 1000000*l.* will be sufficient to compleat the Discharge of the Publick Debts, will by no means increase equally to the Increase of the Principal Sum of those Debts by further Loans on new Funds: But it may be of further Use to shew, how much less the Increase of the Publick Debts, by borrowing further Sums at Interest

 provided

provided for by new Funds, will retard the Discharge of the Whole of the Publick Debts, than the supplying the same Sums in any way from the Produce of the Sinking Fund would do. Let us suppose, for Instance, that the Government were obliged for 25 Years together to increase the present Debt, by a Million borrowed in every Year at an Interest of 4 *per Cent.* provided for by further Funds, the above-made Computation will shew that that additional Debt of 25 Millions would be paid off by a Sinking Fund of one Million, apply'd as is therein supposed, in little more than 7 Years after the Discharge of the present 50 Millions. But if the same Sum were to be supplied out of the Produce of the Sinking Fund, it is obvious that the Payment of the Publick Debts must stand still for 25 Years, and be by more than Two Thirds of that Time retarded beyond the Time in which they would otherwise be discharged, tho' increased as aforesaid; and the greater the Sum is supposed to be, that in these different Ways is to be supply'd, the greater will be the Proportion in which the Payment of our Debts will be delay'd, by supplying such Expences from the Sinking Fund than by the other way: Or if the Sums in these different Ways supply'd should be supposed less, the difference of the Delay in these two Cases will be indeed less: But on supposition of the smallest Sum to be these two different Ways supplied, the Delay arising to the Discharge of the Publick Debt by this Misapplication of the Sinking Fund, will be at least three times as great as that which will be occasioned by increasing the Publick Debt in the other Method.

The borrowing Money on the Income of the Sinking Fund in any Form, if no more were in any one Year borrow'd than what had been by the Sinking Fund the Year before paid off; and if that Money be supposed to be borrowed at the same Rate of Interest that was payable for the Debt before paid off; will have the same Effect in



delaying

delaying the Payment of the Publick Debts, as the Misapplication of the Revenue of the Sinking Fund the Year before would have had: But if greater Sums be at any Time borrowed on that Fund, the Payment of the Publick Debts will not only be stopped, but put backwards; and that in a manner that obviously leads not only to delay the Payment of the Publick Debts, but the taking away intirely the only Security yet provided, that they shall ever be paid off. For which reason I shall not trouble you, *Sir*, with any Computation of the different Degrees in which different Steps in pursuing these Measures will affect us; but at once suppose it impossible that any Persons can propose to borrow Money, (or much less to succeed in it) on the Credit of Schemes that themselves destroy all probability of the Repayment of it; which, such Measures as these, must evidently appear to do, to those that consider, that we have already had the greatest Advantage from the Reduction of Interest that can with reason be hoped for in the Provision of the present Sinking Fund; which if we once part with in Exchange for an increased Principal Debt at a lower Rate of Interest only, it will be Madness to expect that either such a lower Rate of Interest, or any Alteration in our Circumstances for the better, will admit of the same kind of Provision to be made again for the Payment of our Debts increased by such Measures as these are.

I cannot therefore, *Sir*, amongst the ordinary Vicissitudes of the Affairs of any Nation, not even amongst any long and expensive Wars, that it may be necessary for the Defence and Safety of these Kingdoms to carry on with our Neighbours, find out that Exigence of our Affairs that can make the Misapplication of the Sinking Fund appear necessary, or probable to be put in Practice; while it is so certain, that the Lands, Estates, Expence, or Commerce of *Great-Britain*, will yet easily admit of farther Duties sufficient to furnish new Funds to answer the

 Interest

Interest of such Sums as any publick Occasions that I can represent to my self can call for. Nor can I fear, that such Duties will not be chearfully voted and submitted to, when they shall appear necessary to prevent the Misapplication of an annual Sum imployed in so useful and necessary a Service to the Publick, as the Reduction of our Debts; while that appears to be retarded so much more by discontinuing the Payment of those Debts, than by the Increase of them.

There is another Objection to the Probability of the Payment of our Publick Debts, which if I did not frequently meet with, I should choose not to mention, from my Apprehensions, that in stating of it as I have met with it, I should be obliged to mention my Superiours with less Decency, than that grateful Sense I have of the Happiness we enjoy under the present Reign would on all other Occasions lead me to, or than you, *Sir*, from the same Motives would expect from me. But as you are pleased to admit you have often met with it from others, you will give me leave to mention it, in my way to answer it. The Objection I mean is, That the Continuance of our Publick Debts is, and always must be, the Interest of Persons in the Administration; that the greatest Profit of their Employments arises from hence; and that the necessary Power and Influence to support themselves in those Employments, depend greatly on their having reserved to themselves the Disposition of the various Offices and Employments in collecting and applying the Revenues appropriated to the Payment of the Publick Debts; which, when those Debts shall be discharged, can subsist no longer.

Whatever Truth we should admit to be in this Objection, we have the Pleasure of observing, that it appears to be equally true, from the frequent and earnest Recommendations from his Majesty of the necessary Measures for discharging the Publick Debts to the Care and Endea-



vours

vours of the Legislature; the several Steps that have been taken by them; and the great and effectual Provision that is already made for this Purpose; that nothing can have been or will be more sincerely intended and endeavoured by his Majesty, or the Persons who have had or shall have the Honour to be imployed by him.

But from the Sense I have just now professed to have of the Blessings we enjoy under the present Government, I must confess, I should with no Pleasure look forwards on that Period of Time, when his present Majesty or his Successors should be deprived of the Means of supporting it, or even of rewarding and encouraging the Fidelity and Services of their best Subjects. The chief Use therefore that I have proposed to make of this Objection, is to take an Occasion from it, of considering how far it is probable that such a Reform as is above supposed, of the various Employments in collecting and receiving the present Revenues, will take Place on the Discharge of the Publick Debts; or how far it is reasonable that it should do so. And this Supposition being founded on a Presumption, that the particular Duties now appropriated to the Payment of the Publick Debts will, after the Payment of them, be immediately removed, the Reasonableness of that Presumption will be the Matter in Question.

For the Purpose of this Inquiry, *Sir,* I should propose it to be consider'd, that the Support of our Government necessarily requires a considerable annual Expence, that is at present ordinarily supplyed by other Taxes than those which have been provided to answer the Payment of the Publick Debts; that the present ordinary Provision for that annual Expence has been hitherto determined, rather by the Necessities of the Publick, than by Choice; and that it yet remains to be debated, how far the Duties at present appropriated to the Payment of our Debts, or Part of them, may, after the Discharge of those Debts, be continued and made to answer the ordinary annual

Expence of our Government, more to the Advantage of the Publick, with less Burthen and Expence to the particular Estates of his Majesty's Subjects in this Kingdom, and consistently with a more equal and reasonable Proportion of the Burthen or Expence by every Subject submitted to, to the Benefit he receives from the Support of our Government, than is now done by the present Provision made for the aforesaid ordinary annual Expence.

It is in vain to suppose, that the necessary Expences of a Government are to be supply'd by any Taxes that are no ways burthensome to the Whole or some Part of the Community, and consequently to which some Objections may not be dressed up by Persons interested in avoiding them; which Objections, however, when such Taxes appear necessary, it is unreasonable to propose or aggravate. I shall not therefore point out any Inequality or Hardship that I may apprehend to be in the ordinary annual Provision made amongst us by a Land-Tax; but content my self with making some Observations, tending to recommend the greatest Part of the Duties now appropriated to the Payment of our Debts, as the most convenient and reasonable Taxes to supply the ordinary Expence of our Government, when redeemed by the Payment of those Debts.

Upon enumerating the several Duties which at different Times have been provided to answer the Demands of the publick Creditors, it will appear that the greatest Part of them (whether collected by Custom or Excise) have been laid upon Commodities in general Use and Consumption amongst that Part of the Inhabitants of this Country, whose Circumstances will admit of the Expence.

About these Duties it will appear upon Reflection to be generally true, that they have been added to the Price which those Commodities had before the Imposition of such Duties, and from thenceforth to be ultimately

 paid

paid in the last Price of such Commodities by the Consumer.

Upon which Supposition, if the aforesaid Duties are either, by way of Custom or Excise, generally collected throughout the Country where such Commodities are consumed; it's plain that the said Duties will generally be paid by every Person residing in such a Country, nearly in Proportion to his ordinary annual Expence.

And this, *Sir*, is the Share or Proportion which of all others I think most eligible to be taken from every Person residing in a Country where great Part of the Inhabitants subsist by Commerce, towards the publick Expences of the Government of that Country when it can in this manner be done, without enquiring exactly into the Expence of every particular Inhabitant.

For, first, in this way the publick Expence is least sensibly felt by those who really contribute towards it; every Person being voluntary in his Expence, and gratifying himself while he is contributing from his Estate to the Expence of the Government.

2. Contributions in this manner generally made by the Inhabitants of a Country in Proportion to their Expence, will be likewise made in a near Proportion to the real Value of the Property of the same Inhabitants; perhaps, a nearer than it would be done by a Law made directing the publick Expences to be levyed in that Proportion, from the great Difficulty of finding out and plain Inconvenience of exactly enquiring into the real Value of every Man's Property for a Purpose of this Kind, in a Country so much engaged in Traffick as ours is. Nor will Taxes upon our Expences, vary much from Taxes proportioned to the Value of our Property, (if long continued) from what may at first Sight appear a reason for that Conclusion; I mean, the different Choice of the Thrifty and Extravagant in the Proportion of their Expences; the first of which, by contributing little himself to the publick

 Expence,

Expence, is providing for larger Contributions by his Successors; and the other, by contributing too largely in haste, is incapacitating himself for contributing at all.

I think also, that in those Particulars in which a Tax proportioned to our Expences, either does or may be contrived to vary from one intended to levy the same Sum in proportion to the Value of Property in *Great-Britain*, such a Tax on our Expences appears the more eligible.

1. A Tax proportioned to the Expences of Persons residing in *Great Britain*, will collect a Proportion of the Income of the various profitable Professions and Employments amongst us, and of the annual Gains of Foreign and Inland Commerce; all which being received and enjoyed by Virtue of the Laws, and under the Protection of this Government, should, together with the annual Income of our Property, contribute towards it.

2. It will likewise collect and take in a Proportion of the annual Income of such Estates or Employments, as supply the Expence of Foreigners on different Accounts residing in *Great Britain*, as well as of such of his Majesty's Subjects who chuse to reside here and support their Expences by the Income of Estates in *Ireland*, or any of our Colonies or Plantations in *America* or elsewhere; from whom, in return for the Protection their Estates receive from the Arms or Influence of *Great Britain*, supported at our Expence, no Contributions in common with the Inhabitants of this Kingdom can be thought unreasonable.

Contributions thus made by Persons residing in *Great Britain*, in Proportion to their Expences, will likewise include a Proportion of the annual Income of such Estates as may be brought hither by Foreigners, chusing to settle amongst us, or by any of our own Countrymen returning with their Gains from other Countries.

In short, a Proportion of all Estates whatsoever, whether within or without the Kingdom of *Great Britain*, and whether discovered or not discovered, that any way

 supply

supply the Expences of our Inhabitants in a manner as is above observed, not grievous to or liable to be complain'd of by the Contributors themselves, and with the further good Oeconomy of sparing on ordinary Occasions, and increasing that publick Stock, that unmoveable Part of our Property within this Kingdom, to which in Times of extraordinary Danger and Expence we must necessarily have recourse.

It may likewise be considered, in Recommendation of this manner of supplying the ordinary Expences of our Government by Duties in the manner above supposed, levied in proportion to our Expences, what farther Conveniencies to the Publick may be procured by such Duties, over and above such a Supply to its ordinary Expences; such as discouraging the Consumption of such foreign Commodities as may, in a manner plainly inconvenient to the Publick, interfere with or hinder the Consumption of the Produce or Manufactures of our own Country; abating the extraordinary Price of foreign Commodities, or the exorbitant Gains of Foreigners by the Importation of them; the diminishing a Trade carried on with any of our Neighbours, the Ballance of which is too evidently in their Favour; the encouraging any other more profitable Branch of the *British* Commerce; or the preventing the Increase of any particular Article of Expence, that may too plainly tend to debauch the Manners or abate the Industry of his Majesty's Subjects. Of this kind many are the Conveniencies that may be procured to a Country, by the same Measures that supply the ordinary Expences of its Government. And when it shall be considered to how many publick Uses of this sort several of the Duties appropriated to the Payment of our Debts are subservient, besides the annual Income produced by them; I believe it will appear by no means eligible, and much less necessary, that the Whole of those Duties should, immediately after the Payment of the Publick Debts, be removed and

 determine;

determine; when the same Conveniencies may be still preserved to us by the Continuance of them, and the Income of those Duties be made to supply such of our Expences as are now provided for by less equal or less beneficial Taxes.

Such Considerations as these, I think, are sufficient to remove the above-mentioned Supposition, that the Payment of our Publick Debts is inconsistent with the Interest of a *British* Ministry; in which, however, I could still advance farther, by remarking how remote the Views of any Interest of this kind are placed, by the Length of Time that will be necessarily required for the Discharge of our present Debts from a Sinking Fund; and by observing, that the Removal of any Part of the present Duties, which are any ways inconvenient to the Publick, and are continued now only because appropriated to the Payment of some Part of our Debts, will by no means imply, or even admit of a Reduction of Officers employed in the Collection of those kind of Duties, either by way of Custom or Excise, in the several Ports or Districts in *Great Britain*, in Proportion to the Income of such abolished Duties; and from several other Reflections that have occurred to me on this Subject, if I did not think it unnecessary any farther to follow so groundless and indecent a Jealousy of the Integrity and publick Spirit of such of my Countrymen, who shall for the future deserve and attain to the Favour and Confidence of his Majesty or his Successors.

Thus far I have been endeavouring to make out, that the Provision already made of the present Sinking Fund is an Expedient, from which we may with great Confidence expect the full and effectual Payment of the Principal of our present Debts within a few Years. Upon which, *Sir*, if I have dwelt longer than you may have thought necessary, I hope you will be pleased to consider in Excuse of it, how far I must have been led to do so, by attending to the happy Influence that a general Confidence in the Efficacy of this Expedient would have on the Credit of our Publick Funds, especially in case that the Measures lately taken by some neighbouring Princes should make a Rupture with them necessary to us; and how far such a general Opinion of the Efficacy of this Scheme has a Tendency to forward and increase the Success of it.

I am now brought, *Sir*, to the last Task, that in Obedience to your Commands I have assigned my self; and am to inquire what Measures it may be most for the Interest of the Publick to take in the Application and Use of the Sinking Fund from the Year 1727. About which the only Question that can, as I think, be put is, Whether it shall be from thenceforth adviseable for us to endeavour after a greater Increase of the Sinking Fund, by a farther Reduction of the Interest of the Publick Debts? Or if it may not be then on the whole more for the Publick Interest, to endeavour only after such an Increase of the aforesaid Fund, as will be produced by the Application of it from Time to Time to the Discharge of the Publick Debts, and the Addition of the yearly Interest of such of the said Debts as shall be from Time to Time paid off.

Before I proceed to any other Consideration which it may be thought material to attend to in determining this Question, I shall take leave to state the greater Effect the first of these different Measures would have in accelerating the Payment of the Publick Debts than the other of them. And this I chuse first to do, because in an Affair of this publick Concern, and where we are not to be supposed to give our selves the Trouble of the same Exactness in Computation that we should use in our own private Affairs, I am a little apprehensive that People when they turn their Thoughts to this Subject are apt, upon any Increase of the Sinking Fund, to promise themselves a farther Degree of Dispatch in the Payment of the Publick Debts

 in

in Proportion to such Increase. For an Instance, to explain my Meaning: I fear, that upon stating from the above-mentioned Supposition, that the Sinking Fund of 1000000 *l.* was increased to 1500000 *l. per Annum,* by an Abatement of 1 *per Cent.* Interest on 50 Millions, the Debt supposed to be paid off by it; on stating such a Case, I say, I fear it would be in haste inferred, from the Sinking Fund's being increased to half as much again as it was before, that the Publick Debts would be likewise paid off by the Sinking Fund so increased half as soon again, or that the Publick Debts would be paid off by a Sinking Fund of One Million and a Half *per Ann.* in Two Third Parts of the Time that would be taken up in discharging it by a Sinking Fund of One Million *per Annum* only. But this Inference would not be true, by whatever Means the Sinking Fund were supposed to be so increased; and least true, when the Increase of the Sinking Fund is made by a Reduction of the Interest of the Debt to be paid off by it.

If the aforesaid Fund of 1000000 *l. per Annum* were increased to 1500000 *l.* by an Addition made to it of 500000 *l. per Annum* provided by a new Tax, or any otherwise than by an Abatement of the Interest of the 50 Millions to be paid off, which should continue to carry 4 *per Cent.* Interest; it would be true, that while the said increased Sinking Fund is supposed to be applied to the Discharge of that Debt, it would pay off in every Year half as much again as the Sinking Fund of One Million only beginning at the same Time to be applied to the same purpose would do in the same Year; and at the End of any Number of Years, in which both Funds are supposed to continue so applied, will have paid off a Principal Sum exceeding the Principal Sum paid off by the Sinking Fund of One Million only, by one half Part of the Latter; or in other Words, the Principal Sum paid off by the aforesaid greater Fund will be to that paid off by the Lesser, either

 in

in an equal Number of Years from the Time they begin to be applied, or in any one Year equally distant from that Time, in the Proportion of Three to Two. And in this Sense the aforesaid greater Fund may be said to pay off the Publick Debt half as fast again, as in the same Time it will pay off half as much again. But from hence it is not to be inferred, that the less Fund will be half as long again as the greater in discharging the same Principal Sum; or that the same Principal Sum would be paid off by the greater Fund in Two Thirds of the Time that would be taken up in discharging it by the smaller Fund: And of this the plain Reason will soon appear, on inspecting the above-made Computations; from which it may be observed, That the Sinking Fund applied, as we have all along supposed it, is increasing by an Addition in every Year made to it of the Interest of that Principal Sum which was paid off by it in the Year before; from whence both the Income of the Fund it self, and the Principal Sums annually paid off by it, are in every Year greater than in the Year before, and increasing in every Year by an Addition greater than the Addition made to it in the Year before. From whence it necessarily follows, that in a Series of Payments made by the Sinking Fund for any Number of Years carried on, the Payments towards the latter End of such Series must be considerably greater than those before; and that the Amount of the Payments for any Number of Years separated at the latter End from the rest of the Series, must greatly exceed the Amount of the Payments for any equal Number of Years in any other Part of the same Series. And from hence it must appear, that the Excess of the Payments made by the greater Sinking Fund above those made by the less in the same Number of Years, will not be a Rule for determining the Time in which they must severally be employed in discharging the same Principal Sums.

And it will be further from the Truth, in the case of

 the

the Sinking Fund increased from an Abatement of the Interest of the Debt to be paid off, by an Addition of an annual Income equal to one half Part of its Income before such Increase, to suppose, that from thenceforth the Debt will be discharged in Two Third Parts of the Time which would have been otherwise required; because the Additions from Time to Time made to a Sinking Fund employ'd in the Payment of a Debt carrying 3 *per Cent.* Interest only, do not increase in the same or so great a Proportion, as those made annually to a Sinking Fund in the Discharge of a Debt at 4 *per Cent.* From which Circumstance the less Sinking Fund increasing by this greater Ratio or Proportion, would in a longer Series than I hope we have any Thing to do with in the present Case, have so considerable an Advantage, as to overtake the greater Sinking Fund in its Payments, and from thence to be every Year discharging a greater Debt.

But in the Case we have supposed of a Debt of Fifty Millions, the Time in which we have before computed that that Debt carrying 3 *per Cent.* Interest may be paid off by a Sinking Fund of 1500000 *l.* is 23 Years and one Half nearly, and by the Sinking Fund of 1000000 *l.* the Debt continuing at 4 *per Cent.* Interest in about 28 Years; so that the Time saved in the Discharge of our Debts by the Reduction of them to 3 *per Cent.* Interest, appears, on the aforesaid Suppositions, to be 4 Years and a Half, or thereabouts; which is something less than One Sixth Part of the Time in which the same Debt might be discharged without any further Reduction of the Interest.

Another way of Stating the Advantage to the Publick in this Contraction of the Time which our Debts may take up in the Discharge of them, from 28 to 23 Years and a half, would be to find out and assign that annual Sum, which added to the above supposed Sinking Fund of 1000000 *l.* at the Publick Expence, and without any fur-

 ther

ther Reduction of the Interest of the Debt to be paid off, would answer the same Purpose as the Addition of 500000 *l.* to that Fund taken from the Income of the Publick Creditors, and contract the Time in which the Payment of 50 Millions would be compleated from 28 Years to 23 and a half; and this, *Sir,* will be found almost 322000 *l*: Which yearly Expence to the Government for 23 Years and a half, would answer the same Purpose as the above supposed Deduction of 500000 *l. per Ann.* from the Income of the Publick Debts. And this Advantage I chuse to state distinctly as it is, before I proceed farther; because I think in all the Discourse I have met with on this Publick Affair, I have seldom heard any Distinction made about the Convenience of the several Reductions of Interest from 6 to 5 *per Cent.* and from thence to the Rate of Interest at 4 *per Cent.* which is shortly to take place, or relating to the further Reduction to 3 *per Cent.* which we seem to intend and be providing for: but on the contrary, they seem all to be considered and expected alike as of equal Advantage in dispatching the Discharge of the Publick Debts; though it be at the same Time true, that by the first of these Reductions we came only to have any Sinking Fund at all, and to the second of these Reductions, together with the Provisions at the same Time made about the unredeemable Annuities, we owe it, that the total Payment of our Debts by this Expedient begins to appear practicable. But in those Circumstances in which we now are, and with those Views which we at present have of the Payment of our Debts within no great Length of Time, from the Provisions already made for that Purpose, by the Reduction of Interest hitherto effected or contracted for; I think we are at Liberty, before any further Steps of this kind, to consider of some probable Consequences that may follow upon them; which to have produced as Objections to any former Reductions of Publick Interest, while they ap-

 peared

peared so necessary, might have been thought impertinent or untimely.

It seems to me to have been an Opinion of late Years pretty generally agreed to, (perhaps as long since as the celebrated Mr. *Locke's* Performance on that Subject) That all Attempts to reduce Interest by compulsive Methods, or by Force of any Laws made for that purpose, are not only unlikely to succeed, but on other Accounts inconvenient to the Publick; But I know not if the Interest of the Publick in the Reduction of it by any other Means effected, has been much considered; or if such a Reduction of Interest is not usually expected by us with general Satisfaction, arising from our regarding it as the Effect of the common and natural Causes of a lower Interest in every Country, and such Alterations in our Circumstances as are truly enumerated amongst the Instances of Publick Prosperity.

Mr. *Locke,* in his aforesaid Treatise on this Subject, mentions, as the natural Causes of the Variations of the Rate of Interest in any Country, the Variations of the Proportion that the Quantity of Money bears in such a Country to the Demand for it, arising either from the Quantity of Debts contracted amongst the Inhabitants, or of the Trade carried on by them. To which Occasions of a Demand for Money, I think should be generally added all other Circumstances in the Affairs of such a Country, as may be there supposed ordinarily to contribute to, or be the Occasion of, a greater or less Demand of that kind. And as a further natural and ordinary Cause of a Variation any where in the Rate of Interest, I should chuse to add such Alterations in the Circumstances or Situation of the Affairs of the Country where such a Variation happens, as may make it more or less dangerous or secure to advance Money upon Loans in all or any of the different Scenes of Business, where Negotiations of this kind are usually carried on; by which last Cause I am apt to

 think

think that the more sudden and sensible Variations in the Rate of Interest have been chiefly and most frequently every where occasioned. And when a lower Rate of Interest is supposed to be produced amongst us, by such Causes as these are, it is perhaps most reasonable that it should be regarded with general Satisfaction, as it is a Proof of such a Situation of our Affairs, as is of it self, and independently on this Consequence from it, an Instance and Part of the Description of our general Welfare and Prosperity; and as the monied Man himself has in this Case an Equivalent for what he may be supposed to lose by the Abatement of his Income, in the greater Safety with which, on such an Occasion, he lends his Money, or the less Hazard which he runs of the Repayment of it; as well as in the greater Frequency of Opportunities, which such a Situation in our Affairs produces, of putting out and improving Money with greater Safety. But as far as a lower Rate of Interest may be produced amongst us, either without such compulsive Methods, or the Concurrence of such natural and ordinary Causes for it as are above-mentioned, I apprehend that it yet remains to be inquired into, if it be the Interest of the Publick that it should be so? and, as far as the Success of any Measures entered upon for this Purpose may be uncertain, if it be, with regard to the Publick, adviseable that such a Reduction of our Interest should be attempted or endeavoured after? And in this Case it will be allowed me, that a lower Rate of Interest thus produced, or supposed to be so, is no longer to be considered as a Proof of, or attended with, the above-mention'd Instances of our publick Happiness; such a Rate of Interest having no Tendency in it self to increase our Money, or the Lenders Security for the Repayment of it; nor consequently, being of any effect to produce a real Increase of our Negociations in advancing Money; which while no Provision is made for increasing either, our

Capacity or Disposition to lend Money can by no means become greater, or more frequent, from the greater Application to borrow Money only.

I shall therefore endeavour, *Sir*, to describe such Transactions amongst us with respect to our Publick Debts, as I apprehend may have been supposed to have had a great Share and Influence in producing amongst us lately very great and general Variations in the Rate of Interest, and from which a still further Reduction of the Rate of Interest may be yet expected; I mean, those great Adventures in the Publick Funds, of late Years so apparently undertaken with a View to such Gains as might be quickly made by the different Prices of them, and which have so much contributed to the late great and sudden Variations in the Market-Prices of these Securities. In the Infancy of these Adventures, the chief or only Motives to them probably were those Pieces of Intelligence about the Situation of our Publick Affairs, from the Publication of which the Adventurer might reasonably infer the general Satisfaction or Diffidence of the Proprietors of the Publick Debts in their several Securities. And as far as Intelligence of this kind was true, and the general Sense of the Proprietors upon the Publication of it rightly conjectured or inferred, the Rise or Fall of Stocks produced by these Adventures might be regarded as an Event, which in a longer Time or in a less Proportion would have happened, if these Adventures had not been made; and in this View may not improperly have been called the Growth or Declension of our Publick Credit. But as this Practice grew upon us, it is not to be wondered at, if from the general Industry of great Numbers to be first acquainted with every material Occurrence to the Publick, and to be earliest in the Improvement of their Information in Adventures of this Nature, several Variations in the Prices of our Funds have been produced by Transactions in them, undertaken upon false or uncertain Intel-

 ligence,

ligence, and groundless Inferences and Conjectures from it; which Variations have not been afterwards to be accounted for from any real Alteration in the Posture of our Affairs, or the general Sentiments of the Proprietors of the Publick Debts; and from which, therefore, the real State of Publick Credit at such a Time would be uncertainly, if not falsly, inferred or determined. The latter Variations in the Prices of our Stocks would be still more improperly described to be the Growth or Declension of our publick Credit; which Credit, since the Restoration of our Tranquility, and during the Absence of our Apprehensions for the Publick Safety, can only with Propriety be said not to have been disputed or called in Question; and which cannot, I think, be supposed to have been of late at all attended to by the Purchasers of our publick Securities, at Premiums and advanced Prices far beyond those Sums for the Repayment of which the Credit of the Government is any ways depended on. In short, by whatever Names we have been accustomed, or may chuse to describe the Rise or Fall of our Stocks by, I submit it to such Persons who have made any Observations on the late Transactions in *Exchange-Alley*, if they have not (and especially the Rise of them) been generally occasioned by such Adventures made in them, as Persons have been induced to from the Hopes of Gain from a further speedy Variation in the Price of them, without any regard to the Continuance of it; and if these Variations are not of late come to be expected from any the most inconsiderable Occasions, or perhaps for no Reason at all, but what is to be inquired for in the Market, and amongst the Accounts and Contracts depending there.

While this Disposition continues amongst Numbers to be constantly adventuring in the Publick Funds, and consequently upon Expectations that must be generally supported by the most inconsiderable Reasons, it is hardly to

 be

be doubted but that at any Time in the Absence of our Apprehensions of any general Danger, the Intelligence being spread amongst them that any Scheme or Proposals were to be set on Foot, by which the Rise of Stocks was either intended or supposed, would generally determine these Adventurers to expect and provide for such a Rise of Stocks, and by their Contracts founded on these Expectations in a great Measure to produce it: To effect which Purpose, I hardly think it material, that any further reasonable Provision should be made in the Proposals or Schemes themselves, or that any Thing would be further necessary for this Purpose, than declaring the Rise of Stocks to be intended by them. Such a Rise of Stocks I am almost inclined to believe might be the first Effect of any Intelligence communicated in *Exchange-Alley* at such a Time as I have above supposed, that some Proposals were shortly to be made to all or great Part of the Publick Creditors, to agree to the further Reduction of their Interest or Annuities, as disagreeable as this must at first appear to the greatest Part of the Creditors themselves. But how far such a Rise of Stocks may be in this Case expected, and how far it may proceed in forwarding any Proposals of this Nature, I submit to be conjectured from the following Considerations.

First, Such a Proposal must suppose and lead our Expectations to a Rise of Stocks in general; without which, or at least if the contrary should happen, such a Proposal could by no Means be executed or complied with; it being necessary to the Success of this Proposal, that the Market-Price should, at the Time of making it, offer the Proprietor as much or more, as if he declined to comply with it would be payable to him by the Government. And as the greatest Part of the Proprietors of the Publick Debts have been at different Times incorporated for the Purpose of carrying on certain Trades, from the Profits of which



(as

(as I would willingly hope) 1 *per Cent.* or more has been annually divided over and above the Income of their Interest in the Publick Debts; if their Annuity from the Government when reduced and diminished continues to be valued as before, the Price of that Part which is not liable to any Diminution from these Proposals, may well enough be expected to rise in some Proportion to such a Reduction of their Annuity. Thus, if to the Proprietors of *South-Sea* Stock, for Instance, it were proposed that their Annuities in the Year 1727 should be from thence reduced to 3 *per Cent.* upon the Supposition that their Shares in the Publick Debt should, after such a Reduction, continue to be valued as before at Par, it might be as reasonable to expect that the 1 *per Cent.* continuing to be divided on every Hundred Pound Stock, should be from thenceforth valued in the Price of it at 33 *l.* 6 *s.* 8 *d.* as it was before to expect it should be ever valued at 25 *l.* And from the Rise of that Part of our Publick Securities which fall under this Consideration, some Advance in our other Securities may likewise be expected, as the Money received on the Sale of those Stocks which shall first and in the greatest Proportion rise on this Occasion, is generally observed to be applied to the Purchase of that Part of our Publick Debts which is conceived to be less liable to Variation in the Prices of them.

Secondly, Such Persons as are observed to be constantly adventuring in the Stocks from Expectations of Gain, either from the Rise or Fall of them, must be generally supposed to be determined to these Adventures by the lowest Degree of Probability that they shall succeed in them; and it is hardly therefore to be doubted, but that the ordinary Adventures in our Stocks would be made upon Expectations of the Rise of them, upon the Publication of any Proposals from Authority that supposed the Rise of Stocks, or implied that it was expected by our Superiors.

 Thirdly,

Thirdly, The Rise of Stocks upon this Occasion would be further favoured, by the Disposition of those Proprietors who are not ordinarily engaged in Adventures of this kind to wait for the utmost Advantage to be made of the Rise of Stocks, whatever might be their Sentiments about continuing Proprietors of the Publick Debts when reduced to a lower Interest.

Fourthly, A Rise of Stocks on this, as well as former Occasions, may be still further advanced, by the spreading of false Computations of the Value of our Stocks, and idle Opinions about Credit and Circulation, and by the Force of a general Example, assisted by the Confidence of the Proprietors of our Publick Debts in the Authority by which these Proposals may be recommended.

And when the Stocks shall be sufficiently advanced to colour any Proposals of this Nature, it is perhaps not impossible that the Concurrence of the Proprietors to such Proposals should be obtained; tho' at the same Time they may be generally dissatisfied with the lower Rate of Interest proposed to them, and severally determined on that Account to quit their Interest in the Publick Debts on the next convenient Opportunity. For it is to be considered,

That the Reason for their objecting publickly, or declaring their Sentiments against any Proposals of this kind, is removed by the Price of their Securities at Market, where they are offered for the present as much or more for them, as if they thought proper to decline these Proposals would be payable to them by the Government; and that the general Dissatisfaction of the Proprietors should not determine them to take Advantage of the then Market-Price for the Sale of their Securities, and by that means occasion the Fall of Stocks, and prevent the Success of these Proposals, may in a great measure be accounted for from a general Inclination to have the utmost possible Advantage from the Rise of Stocks, from the Difficulty of



finding

finding on such an Occasion any immediate Improvement for their Money, and their Impatience of its lying by them unemployed, joined with that Dependance which Men generally have on their own Foresight and Skill in the Choice of the fittest Opportunity for this Purpose; from which Motives, while the Bulk of our Publick Securities may be supposed to be kept from Market, that Part of them which shall be brought there, by the more wary or determined of the Proprietors, will be found for a Time provided for by those considerable Sums which the Estates and Credit that Persons engaged in such Adventures in the Stocks as I have above described, will for a Time supply the Market with.

I think, *Sir*, from hence it appears possible, that a Proposal for reducing the Interest of our Publick Debts, though without any reasonable Foundation, may, as our Affairs now stand, succeed even so far as to obtain the Concurrence of the Proprietors. And the Inference which I would from thence make is, that it belongs to them, by whose Influence or Advice such a Proposal shall at any Time be made, first to consider if there be a solid Foundation for it, or if it be likely still farther to succeed; and not to depend on the Consent of the Proprietors in this manner obtained, as a sufficient Proof that such a Proposal was reasonable, or as a Security for the still further Success of it.

Whenever therefore the further Reduction of the Interest of our Publick Debts shall be attempted, it should be first enquired if the real Proportion of our ordinary Necessities for Money to our Capacity and Disposition to supply them, have been so far altered as to admit of it; and if such an Alteration has proceeded from those reasonable and general Causes of it, which are likely long to continue and support it. Nor will such an Alteration be safely inferred from the Market-Prices of our Stocks, any further than those Prices are determined and pro-

 duced

duced by such Purchases only as are made with a View to the Improvement of the Money laid out in these Securities from the Interest or Income of them; by which Purchases of late Years the Prices of our Stocks have so seldom been determined, that perhaps it may be more reasonable in this Case to conclude from an Enquiry into the Rate of Interest ordinarily reserved on private Loans, or into those other Transactions in which we are usually directed by Computations upon the customary Rate of Interest amongst us. These Transactions, however, must, as well as the Prices of Stocks, in this Case be considered and attended to on this Account, that Persons in the Disposition of their Money will, as often as they think themselves equally secure, be determined by the greater Interest they are offered for it; from whence it must be expected, that when the Income of our Publick Securities, compared with the Prices they are sold for, offer a less Improvement for our Money than may with equal Security be made of it by private Loans or otherwise, the general Industry of Mankind to make the best Improvement of their Estates, will quickly reduce either the Price of our Publick Securities, or the Rate of Interest in such private Transactions as aforesaid.

I question therefore, if any Attempts to reduce the Interest of our Publick Debts below 4 *per Cent.* at present will be of any lasting Convenience to the Publick, or ever can be so till such a lower Rate of Interest shall be preceded by its being customarily accepted of upon private Loans on unquestionable Securities. For let it be considered how such a lower Rate of Interest can otherwise appear to be founded on any real Variation in the Proportion of our Necessities for Money to our Capacity or Disposition to supply them; or if the contrary does not appear, from a higher Rate of Interest ordinarily paid at the same Time upon private Loans. And while this continues to be the Case, how reasonable is it to apprehend,



that

that when the Money and Credit of those Adventurers, who first advanced the Price of Stock, shall be withdrawn, the same ordinary Necessities for Money, without any Increase of the Provision for supplying them, will bring the Proprietors of the reduced Securities to expect and look out for the former annual Income for their Money, and thereby occasion a Declension in the Price of these Securities proportioned to the Diminution of their Interest?

How far the Continuance of those Adventures, by which the Price of Stocks is supposed first on such an Occasion to be advanced, may be depended on for the Support of it, may be collected from the Motives by which the Adventurers were first engaged in them; and is from thence to be expected but till the utmost probable Rise of Stocks from such Proposals has been effected: After which that the former Supplies from their Credit and Estates should be withdrawn from Market, is not all that is in this Case to be apprehended; it being further probable that they will be from thence employ'd in depreciating those Securities which were at first advanced by them, with a View to the same kind of Profits from the Fall, as they before expected from the Rise of Stocks. From which, together with the fresh Necessities which the more inconsiderate of these Adventures will naturally produce, it would not be at all strange if the Price of Stocks should be carried lower, beyond the Declension of them in Proportion to the Diminution of their Income, and the Rate of Interest for a Time become higher than it would have been, if such an Attempt for the reducing it had not been made. And this Consequence of a Rise of Stock from Adventures of this kind must some time or other be expected, as far as that Rate of Interest which our real Necessities would produce is varied from or misrepresented by such Adventures. It may not probably immediately succeed a Rise of Stocks by these Means

 effected;

effected; these Adventures in a Time of general Tranquility, may for a considerable Time be protracted by further Views, or the Market supply'd by a Succession of them; and this has often been the Case, till upon the Arrival of some Intelligence about the Situation of our Affairs, which we call bad News, these Views have been given over, and the Declension of our Stocks on that Occasion attributed to and accounted for only from that Intelligence: But if the real Occasion of the great Variation in our Stocks at such a Time were further enquired for, it would be found to be the precipitate Sale of great Quantities of Stock, which, with such Views as aforesaid, had been before bought up; and that this Declension would as certainly, if not so suddenly, have happened from the same Occasion, without the Intervention of such Intelligence, when these Views should have been on any other Account given over; or when (as, I think, I have heard some Persons acquainted with these Transactions express themselves) the Game had been play'd out.

It is true, indeed, that the Government by those Terms on which they borrow, I mean, by engaging only for the Payment of the Interest or Annuities contracted for till the Repayment of the Principal, avoid all Inconvenience from the Interest of Money advancing after their Contract for the Reduction of it, and leave the entire Disappointment upon the Proprietors. But I submit it, how far the Publick can be considered to be unconcerned in a Disappointment of the Publick Creditors, obviously owing to their Concurrence with Proposals recommended to them by Authority; or in that general Mutiny and Discontent, which will be the necessary Consequence of such a Disappointment: Which from a remarkable Instance of this Nature, after the Execution of the late *South-Sea* Scheme in the Year 1720, we must have observed to have been once regarded by the Legislature, as of sufficient Moment to induce them to release the most considerable

 Advantage

Advantage that the Publick had agreed for from that Scheme, though set on Foot upon the Proposals of the Creditors themselves. And if ever the Publick Creditors should be generally disappointed by a considerable Discount upon their Securities, obviously owing to their Concurrence to an Abatement of Interest recommended by Publick Authority, and proposed for the Convenience of the Publick, I doubt if their Expectations of Relief from the Government could be thought less reasonable. I cannot, for my own Part, but think, that the general Submission of the Publick Creditors in their Contracts with the Government, to wait for the Repayment of their Principal till the Publick Convenience will admit of it, and waving any such Agreement about a determined Time for the Repayment of it, as in private Contracts is ordinarily provided, would be far from removing their Expectations of Redress under a Disappointment of this Nature; and rather apprehend, that this Submission would be urged on such an Occasion, as a meritorious Instance of their Confidence in the Care and Protection of our Government, and as a Reason for their expecting in return for it, that what may be then called Publick Credit should be kept up, and their Securities by all possible Means preserved at Par, till the Time when they could be discharged.

The Success attending the Reduction of so great a Part of our Debt from 6 to 5 *per Cent.* and from thence afterwards to 4 *per Cent.* cannot certainly be looked on as a Foundation for expecting the same Event of our Endeavours to reduce Interest still further. As to the first of these Reductions, we shall find it, on looking back, to have been attempted quickly after such an Alteration in the Circumstances of our Affairs, as furnished the best Foundation for our Hopes of succeeding in it: at the End of a long and expensive War, that threatened us with the Loss of every Thing valuable, but more particu-

 larly

larly of that Part of our Property which had been advanced for the Services of the Publick; at a Time when those Necessities of the Government were removed, which had obliged us for several Years before, to be continually increasing the Publick Debts, and at the same Time admitted of no Provisions for the discharging of them; at a Time when the lasting Prosperity of *Great Britain* was lately secured to us by his present Majesty's Accession to the Throne, and soon after the intire Defeat of the last Attempt that was likely to be made to disturb or prevent the present happy Establishment. From such a Foundation as was then laid for the growing Wealth of these Kingdoms from the Increase of our People, our Commerce and Manufacture, and for the particular Security and greater Confidence of the Publick Creditors, it was most reasonable to expect, that the Abatement of Publick Interest then proposed should take place; especially, when these Proposals were attended with the Provisions that were then first made, for securing and rendering practicable the discharging the Principal of the Publick Debts. Nor do I think it unreasonable to have expected, that by Degrees, and from the Fruits and sensible Effects of this happy Alteration in our Circumstances, the further Reduction of Publick Interest to 4 *per Cent.* which has since been agreed for, and which in the year 1727, is generally to take place, might likewise be effected. And though it may be doubted, if the Effect of this last Reduction of Publick Interest has been yet fully try'd, upon recollecting how little the Interest of the Proprietors of the Publick Debts in this Reduction was attended to by themselves, at the Time when it was agreed to; and how possible it is, that a far greater Number of the Proprietors of the present Funds may have proposed to quit their Interest in them, when the Reduction is actually to take place, than will be able to find Customers for it, unless at a considerable Discount: Yet when, on the other hand, it

 shall

shall be considered, how far this Reduction has been precedented by considerable Loans amongst us at the same Rate of Interest, as well before the Exigences of our Government during the late War with *France,* as since his Majesty's Accession to the Throne; I hope we may chearfully conclude, that this Reduction of the Publick Interest may well enough be supported by the regular Application of the annual Income of the Sinking Fund to the discharging of our present Debts. But no Difficulty of finding Employment for Money at 4 *per Cent.* Interest, nor any private Loans at a lower Rate of Interest amongst us, can yet I think lead us to expect that a further Reduction of Publick Interest to 3 *per Cent.* will be for any Length of Time submitted to.

And while this continues to be the Case, and from 4 to 5 *per Cent.* Interest is every Day offered upon unexceptionable Securities, I should think it a more reasonable Use made of recollecting the late Reductions of our Publick Interest, to place them to the Account of our present happy Circumstances; and before we proceed, to expect from the late Alteration in our Affairs a further Reduction of Interest, to consider how far we are indebted to it upon that Account already.

I have indeed sometimes heard it said, that the last Reduction of our Annuities of 4 *per Cent.* still wants to be taken care of; and that the Price of our Publick Securities proportioned to that Rate of Interest, is only to be supported by such Adventures as will be encouraged by keeping in View the Prospect of a still further Reduction of those Annuities to be attempted. From these Persons I very much differ; and cannot but think that this last Reduction (if no new Troubles presently fall out) would be effectually supported by the future regular Application of the Sinking Fund; from which, in a Number of Years, I should rather expect that a further Reduction of Interest may be naturally and reasonably produced, if the

 Effect

Effect of this Provision be not before-hand too far presumed upon and anticipated. But whoever really thinks that the further Reduction of Publick Interest must be kept in View, in order to support the Reductions already made, evidently supposes us to be proceeding in Measures with regard to our Publick Debts, in which we must some where stop, and whenever we do so, repent of every Step we have taken in advancing thither.

For want of Examples amongst our selves, as I suppose, to support our Expectations of the further Reduction of Publick Interest, I have sometimes heard the present low Rate of Interest in some of the Trading Towns of our Neighbours the *Hollanders*, quoted to prove the Probability, that the same or something near the same low Rate of Interest may be made to take place amongst us too. But I see not why the low Rate of Interest in that Country should be more regarded as the Standard for the Rate of Interest amongst us, than the higher Rate of Interest in other neighbouring Countries, unless on account of our greater Commerce and Negotiation with the *Hollanders*. And after I have admitted that the Rate of Interest amongst them is on this Account most likely to have some Influence upon ours; I must expect it should be allowed me, that this lower Rate of Interest than ours having for several Years prevailed amongst the *Hollanders*, has already had its Effect with us in the Reduction of our Interest to that Rate which we now consider it to be brought to; and that the further Effect or Influence of their Example in the Reduction of our Interest, is only to be expected from the further Reduction of the Rate of Interest below what it is at present supposed to be amongst them.

That the Circumstances of our Affairs are the same in all those Particulars that lead to a low Interest in any Country with those of our before-named Neighbours, is by no means in the present Inquiry to be presumed; if

 they

they were so, our Rate of Interest must now be pretty nearly the same with theirs. But if our Rate of Interest considerably exceeds theirs, and has (which as I have been informed is true) for a long Succession of Years constantly done so; it must be inferred, that our Circumstances in some Particulars that influence the Rate of Interest, differ much from theirs. And the Constancy with which our Rate of Interest has been observed for a long Time to have exceeded theirs, is enough to satisfy us that the Occasion of it is to be enquired for in some Difference in our Circumstances which has continued with equal Constancy, and for the same Length of Time; and not amongst any Projects or Contrivances at different Times set on Foot by either of us, to answer any Purpose of this Nature.

The true and general Reason of this Difference between our Rate of Interest and theirs, has perhaps been long since assigned by the abovemention'd Mr. *Locke,* and seems most probably to be the very different Proportion which the Lands or Property of any other Kind producing a certain annual Income amongst the *Hollanders,* taxed as that kind of Property has been with them, bear to the great Stocks and other personal Estates of the Inhabitants of that Country, from that which the Value of Lands and other Property of the same Kind here bear to the personal Estates in this Kingdom. To this Difference it seems owing, that while the *Hollander* can find little other Employment for the Money he can spare from his own Adventures within his own Country, than in supplying the Necessities which their Commerce from Time to Time produces, the monied Inhabitant of this Country, besides the Opportunities offer'd him from the ordinary Necessities of Persons engaged in Trade, is hardly ever without Proposals for the Employment of his Money in supplying the Wants of the Proprietors of our Lands, by either purchasing or advancing Money upon their Estates;

 and

and from hence is in a Condition to demand and obtain a greater Reward for the Use of Money than the *Hollander* can do, where the demand for it in his own Country is so much less. This Difference between us, as far as it will be allowed to have been one Cause why our Interest has hitherto exceeded theirs, will be allowed also as a Reason why it should continue to do so, till the Inhabitants Wealth and Commerce of *Great-Britain* shall have increased in the same Proportion to the Extent and Value of our Lands, as it may be observed they have done in the *Seven Provinces.*

I cannot forbear thinking, that upon this Occasion it deserves most seriously to be considered, how far our late Expectations of continued Attempts to reduce the Rate of Interest, has contributed to promote and increase the aforesaid Traffick in *Exchange-Alley*; a Practice that, in the midst of those Reproaches which it lies under by the Name of Stock-jobbing, and the most serious Complaints of its ill Consequences to the Kingdom upon every Declension of our Stocks, seems to me to be still growing upon us. Whenever it shall be seriously intended to prevent or restrain this Practice, I believe it will appear, that whatever Contrivances may be provided for prohibiting the Contracts in *Exchange-Alley* in the Manner they are now made, or altering the Manner of conveying our Interest in Stocks from one Person to another, while they increase the Difficulty of the most innocent and necessary Transactions in the Publick Funds, will have little further Effect on this Practice, than to force it into some other Channel, and perhaps increase the Profit and Employment of the Banker only, by making his Credit or Assistance further necessary; and that the most reasonable Method of preventing it, will be removing the Encouragement and Temptation to it. And though our Complaints of these Adventures are then only generally made, when they seem to contribute to the Declension of our Stocks, a little Enquiry will convince us, that the Foundation for such a Fall of Stocks, was really laid by those Adventures which seemed to contribute to and attended the Rise of them. If during a Time of general Tranquility, from unlimited Expectations of the perpetual Advance of Publick Credit, countenanced amongst us beyond any sufficient Foundation for it, Persons are induced to spread their Estates upon the utmost Price of our Publick Funds, in such a manner that a Variation of 2 or 3 *per Cent.* in the Price of them threaten them with the Loss of the greatest Part of their Estates; what can be expected but from the earliest Appearance of Publick Troubles, an idle Rumour, tho' improbable to be true, or the Apprehension of any ill Accident, tho' most unlikely to fall out, should determine them in this Situation of their Affairs, to consult their Safety with the utmost Precipitation, and crowd the Market with the Stock of which before they continued Proprietors upon such desperate Terms. A Fall of Stock by this Means occasioned, with Persons less exactly acquainted with the Reason of it, serves as a Confirmation of every false Report at the same Time published to the Prejudice of our Affairs: From hence still further Quantities of Stock are brought to Market, and a further Declension in the Price of them occasioned; from whence, to greater Apprehensions of Publick Danger, and from thence to the further Fall of Stocks, by Turns producing and increasing each other, we may have often been observed to proceed, without any possibility of putting a stop to either of them. Upon such an Occasion as this it has often, and perhaps constantly happened, that several Persons proposing to themselves Gain from the Calamities of the Publick, have on a Presumption of the Fall of Stocks, contracted for the Delivery of Stock which they had not, and could propose to furnish only, by the Purchase of what the growing Apprehensions of others should afterwards bring to Market;

 and

and of these Adventures it has been usual on the Fall of Stocks principally to complain. This is a Practice, which has doubtless often contributed to the Misfortunes of the Publick on an Occasion of this Nature; but which I doubt not would in a great Measure be prevented for the future, if the excessive Adventures in the Purchase of Stocks, in Expectations of Gain from the Rise of them, were first prevented; to which the contrary Practice is chiefly owing. For it will on Enquiry be found, that Stock-jobbing begins from, and People have been usually initiated into this Practice, by general Expectations of the Rise of Stocks; in which when they are once habituated, and the Expectations of Gain from the Variations in the Price of Stock are become the only End of their Transactions, their Despair of Advantage by the Rise of Stock, is quickly changed for Hopes of Profit from the Fall of it.

Besides the unreasonable Prices to which the extravagant Adventures for the Rise of Stock have carried them, must first have taught the more wary and less credulous Adventurers to expect the Fall of them, and have been the Occasion of that Success that has encouraged the Continuance of these Adventures for the Fall of Stocks: Nor would the Performance of their Contracts for the Delivery of Stock, which they had not, at certain Times be generally practicable, but from the Contracts for the same Time ordinarily made for purchasing Stock without providing the Money to be paid for it.

And if it be to these sanguine Expectations of the Rise of Stocks, and the Adventures founded on them, that the frequent and excessive Variations in the Price of them are really and ultimately owing; how dearly do the Publick pay in every Instance of Perplexity in our Affairs, for any Convenience to be reaped from, or Use to be made of, this prevailing Humour in the Absence of our Apprehensions of Publick Danger?

The Rise of our Stocks produced by the Assistance of



such

such inconsiderate Adventures in the Purchase of them as have been above described, is at best of it self, and without attending to any Consequence from it, a Matter of absolute Indifference to the Publick in the Absence of general Danger; but the Consequence of it in the Declension of our Stocks upon the Approach of Publick Troubles is by no means so; then it is that the general Diffidence in our Securities and Wreck of Publick Credit is of the utmost Disservice to us, by rendring difficult, if not impracticable, the raising such Supplies as an Occasion of this kind may necessarily call for; and as the Variation in our Publick Funds at such a Time may be regarded by our Neighbours as the Measure of our Apprehensions from their Attempts upon us, and encourage them in their Presumption on the unsettled Circumstances of our Affairs: All which Difficulties in our Affairs on such an Occasion, attended with false and groundless Reports and Apprehensions of our Danger, general Mutiny and Discontent, seditious Exceptions to the Conduct of our Superiors, and great Distress and Interruption to our Commerce, I cannot but think we in a great measure owe to such inconsiderate Purchases of our Publick Funds during the general Tranquility; and that they might in a great Degree for the future be prevented, if by removing all Encouragement to the extraordinary Rise of Stocks, the Publick Funds were suffered to fall generally into the Hands of such Persons, who, satisfied with their Income, shall purchase them as a Supply for their ordinary Expences, with Money which they are not soon likely to have any other Occasion for.

The Proprietors of our Debts have, as such, not deserved Severity from the Publick; but as Subjects of this Kingdom are intitled to have their Interest regarded by the Government, as far as the Publick Convenience will admit of it. And in this View there may be some

 room

room to consider the unequal Hardship to the Publick Creditors, by the Loss of a fourth Part of the annual Income of their Estates, imply'd in the Success of an Attempt to reduce their Annuities to 3 *per Cent.* And while the Convenience to the Publick, to be obtained by such a Reduction, is supposed to be the earlier Discharge of the Publick Debts; the Hardship appears greater from this Circumstance, that what shall be thus annually deducted and taken from their Income, will not go so far in answering this Purpose, as two Thirds of the same yearly Sum any other way supplied, and for this general Convenience, more equally levy'd upon the Subjects of this Kingdom: 322000*l.* *per Annum,* or thereabouts, raised at the general Expence, and added to the Sinking Fund of 1000000*l.* being, as I have before observed, sufficient on the above-made Suppositions, to effect the total Discharge of the Publick Debts, as soon as the Addition of 500000*l.* *per Annum* deducted from the Interest of those Debts when reduced to 3 *per Cent.* For it should be attended to, that though the Gain or Convenience to the Publick is to be computed upon such of our Debts only as from Time to Time remain unsatisfy'd, and as long as they remain so; yet supposing the Continuance and general Success of this Reduction of our Interest, the Loss to the Publick Creditors is from the Time of such a Reduction to be computed on the Whole of the Annuities that shall be reduced. If this, as a Hardship on the Publick Creditors, should not be proper in this Case to be considered: it may be so, however, for the Purpose of collecting what their Sentiments on this Affair must some time or other be. The Loss and Inconvenience to them by this Reduction, will be so sensibly felt, that no Misrepresentations can possibly long mislead them. The Continuance of their Submission to former Abatements of their Interest has been already accounted for, by the then late Alteration in our Cir-

 cumstances

cumstances for the better, making the Purchaser of our reduced Annuities a large amends in his greater Security, and to the monied Men in general in the Frequency of Opportunities of improving their Estates with Safety. But will the present happy Situation of our Affairs admit of a further equal Alteration in our Circumstances for the better, or that shall in the same Proportion increase our Security in advancing Money upon the Publick Credit? The former Reductions of our Annuities may have been recommended to the Publick Creditors, as the only Means that could render the Discharge of our Debts practicable to the Government; but as far as they are interested in it, is not that End sufficiently obtained? or is the Prospect that the Payment of the Publick Debts may be thereby effected by 4 Years and a half in 28, sooner than it would be otherwise, of Consequence enough to the Proprietor of any Part of them, to induce him for that Purpose only to part with for the future one fourth Part of the annual Income of his Estate? However the Reduction of Publick Interest hitherto effected may have contributed to the Security of the Proprietors, from the next Reduction it is perhaps not unreasonable to apprehend a contrary Effect; and next to the great Difficulty in the discharging of our Debts, the most reasonable Foundation of our Apprehensions may be, it's becoming in the Opinion of some Persons a Matter of too much Indifference to the Publick whether they are ever discharged or no. When the Publick Debts by the further Reduction of their Interest shall sit so easy upon us, as to require but one Moiety of the annual Provision at first made for the Payment of it, and leave the other at the Service of the Publick, the Danger seems to me by no Means inconsiderable, that it may soon after be determined to imploy the annual Income of the Sinking Fund in the room of, and to ease the Publick of some

 other

other Taxes by which our ordinary Expences are supplied; and that it may be thought as reasonable to rest contented with the Recovery of half the annual Income of the Publick Funds without any Expence to us, as to redeem the Whole of them with the Trouble and Expence of really discharging so considerable Debt.

And if this Reduction of Interest be successfully carried on, the Loss and Inconvenience aforesaid cannot be confined to the Proprietors of our Debts only, or to their Property in the Publick Funds; for if it were so, it's plain, the Price of them after such a Reduction must be abated in Proportion to it: It must therefore, if it succeeds, take place in the Interest of all private Loans, in the Profits of all the different Employments of our Money, and by Degrees must affect the Profits of our Commerce, and spread it self throughout the Kingdom: An Effect, which when not produced by, or attended with the Increase of our Wealth, the Revival of Commerce amongst us, the Succession of general Tranquility to a dangerous or unsettled Situation of our Affairs, or other like Instances of general Prosperity, I know not how to regard otherwise, than as an uncomfortable and general Inconvenience in a Country where the personal Estates are so considerable as here they are; which if it should be thought not material to attend to as a Hardship or Inconvenience meerly to particular Persons, should at least put us in mind of the Opposition that must sooner or later be expected amongst us to Measures from which a great Reduction of Interest is apprehended.

Against this great and general Inconvenience to the Proprietors of personal Estates from a lower Interest, I would willingly place any further publick or private Advantage that may arise from it, besides hastening the Payment of our Publick Debts. The chief, if not the only Advantages of this kind that I have met with by any Persons proposed from a lower Interest, have been the

74 Increase

Increase of our Foreign Commerce, and the Advance of the Value of our Lands and irredeemable Annuities of any kind.

As to the first of these, it must be admitted, that Cases may be put about the particular Circumstances of any Country, in which a lower Rate of Interest would have a Tendency to increase their Commerce; as it might be an Inducement to such Persons who could no longer support themselves, or were not contented with the Income of their Estates at such a lower Rate of Interest, to ingage in Trade; and as it might be the Means of furnishing others with Money for the Purpose of undertaking any particular Branch of Trade, at such Interest and upon such Terms as the Profit of such a Trade would only answer. But all the Advantage of this kind that in our Circumstances, and in the present Case we have to expect, is to be collected only by an Inquiry into the present State of our Commerce; from whence, if it cannot be made to appear that there is at present any profitable Branch of foreign Commerce neglected by us, the Profit of which will over and above the Hazard and other Expences of adventuring exactly bear 3 *per Cent.* Interest for the Money employed in it, but will not answer Four; I should think we have more reason to apprehend some ill Consequences from a sudden Reduction of Interest amongst us with relation to our foreign Commerce, which are by no means inconsiderable: Such as

The rashly engaging unexperienced Persons in unprofitable Adventures, to their own and the Nation's Prejudice.

The increasing our Adventures in the several Branches of our present Commerce beyond the Demand for, or the Possibility of vending our Commodities with Advantage at foreign Markets; and thereby rendring the whole of our foreign Commerce for the future less profitable; and by this means,

 The

The furnishing a Temptation to the more skilful and experienced Persons, at present employed in our foreign Commerce, to remove all their Effects, and settle in other Countries, from whence the Commerce they are best acquainted with may be carried on with more Advantage. An Inconvenience which we have the greatest reason to guard against at this particular Juncture, when our Neighbours in the different Parts of *Europe* are so generally attempting to rival us in our foreign Commerce.

And if amongst these Consequences of the sudden Reduction of our Interest, the Money of Foreigners, which either our Government or private Persons amongst us at present have the Use of, (to whom most certainly a higher Rate of Interest than they can have at Home for it, must have been the general Inducement for their trusting it here) should be called from us, and applied to other Uses; a higher Rate of Interest than before may not only be apprehended, but an absolute impossibility of supplying the ordinary Demands of our Commerce for some time at any Rate at all.

As to the Proprietors of our Lands and irredeemable Annuities, I am content to admit that they may reasonably expect a higher Price to be offered for their Estates in some measure proportioned to and regulated by a lower Rate of Interest produced by and in proportion to any solid and reasonable Causes for it. But I think it has been with Truth observed by Mr. *Locke* on this Occasion, that in this higher Price of their Estates, those Proprietors are only interested who have contracted or want to contract Debts upon their Estates; it being of no Consequence to the Person who neither sells nor mortgages his Estate, or intends to do so, what Price he may procure for it; and it being as plain, that the Person who on this Occasion receives a higher Price on the Sale of his Estate, from thenceforth stands in the Place of the monied Man, pos-

 sessed

sessed of a greater Sum of Money indeed than he could have had before, but which will produce no greater annual Income, nor generally speaking go farther in any Provision he has intended for himself or Family, nor in any other Use that he can apply it to (except the Discharge of such Debts as he may have contracted) than a less Sum would have done when the Rate of Interest was higher. The principal if not the only general Advantage of a lower Interest to the Proprietors of Land, is therefore so far as they have contracted Debts; which Advantage to them and to all other Persons who have contracted Debts, is exactly ballanced in the Publick Accounts by an equal Loss and Inconvenience to their Creditors.

I will desire your Attention, *Sir*, but to one Consequence more, which I think will naturally and necessarily follow a further Reduction of our Interest, if it can by any Means be effected, or for any Length of Time prevail amongst us, without the Concurrence of what I have hitherto supposed to be the natural and only reasonable Causes of it, *viz.* a considerable Diminution of our Expences, which the Publick as our Affairs now stand, and the Proprietors of Land in particular, seem to me not a little interested to prevent. A fourth Part of the Income and usual Profits of the personal Estates in this Kingdom, withdrawn and deducted from the Whole of our ordinary annual Expence, must occasion a very considerable Diminution in it, when not supplied by the Increase of those personal Estates, or the growing Wealth of our Inhabitants, and must from thence occasion a considerable Diminution in the Price and Consumption of our Commodities. And this I apprehend will be the sooner and more sensibly felt, as the Interest of Money and the Profits of personal Estates are more generally the Funds for, and supply the Expence of, the Inhabitants of this Metropolis of the Kingdom, than of any other Part of it; and as a Variation in our fashionable Expences here is most likely to

 spread

spread it self by the Force of our Example throughout the other Parts of this Kingdom, where perhaps there may not be the same occasion for it; from hence it deserves well to be consider'd, if the Publick may not lose as much or more in their Revenues arising from different Commodities consumed amongst us, as may be saved by the Reduction of our Interest; or if the Proprietors of Land may not at last find themselves obliged to furnish from their own Revenues those Supplies for the Service of the Government, which have been hitherto furnished by our Expences. And if it be possible that this Diminution of our Expences should proceed further, in reducing the Price of Labour, and from thence of our necessary Provisions and the Produce of our Lands, the Proprietors of those Estates must in their Turn suffer from the Reduction of their annual Revenues.

From such Reflections as these, *Sir*, it has seemed to me not unreasonable, that we should at least for some Time rest contented with such Reductions of Publick Interest as have been hitherto made: From whence I have been further induced to think, that it would be of considerable Convenience to the Publick, if the Application of the present Sinking Fund, which stands now appropriated to the Discharge of the Publick Debts in general, were by Act of Parliament determined as to the Course and Order in which those Debts should be for the future discharged by it. These Measures with regard to the Publick Debts may possibly have not been hitherto proposed, on account of that Advantage which the Publick may have been supposed for the future to be in a Condition to make in the further Reduction of Publick Interest, while they reserved to themselves the Preference of one Creditor to another in the Order of discharging them; but I submit it, how far this Advantage would be prudently exchanged for the following Conveniencies to the Publick, from determining the Order in which the Sinking Fund

 should

should be applied in the Discharge of our present Debts.

First, The annual Income of the Sinking Fund will, by this means, be more fully appropriated to the Payment of the Publick Debts, and the Application of it to that Purpose more effectually secured, by intitling every particular Creditor to expect the Application of it in the Order that shall be so determined.

Secondly, It will be of considerable Use in fixing the Credit of the Publick Funds, and the Confidence of the Proprietors on such Foundations, as will support them in any Time of publick Difficulty, by removing all Grounds for those Apprehensions, which, on such Occasions, are observed greatly to the Disadvantage of the Government to prevail amongst us, that the Income of the Sinking Fund will be applied to some other Purposes than the Discharge of our Debts; and by giving every particular Creditor an Opportunity of computing and satisfying himself in the Value of his Interest in the Publick Funds, from the Knowledge of that Time when his Principal will be punctually paid off.

Thirdly, It will in a great measure prevent Stock-jobbing, by removing the Temptation to it from the great Variations in the Market-Prices of our Debts, from such extravagant Premiums paid for them in a Time of Peace, as if the Income of them was conceived to be an irredeemable Annuity; and such Discounts on the other Hand allowed upon them, in a Time of the least general Apprehension, as if they were regarded as Debts almost desperate.

Fourthly, It will lay a further Foundation for a greater Equality in the Prices of our Publick Debts, by giving an Opportunity to the Proprietors to suit their own Convenience in the Purchase of such Part of those Debts as are determin'd to be payable, as near the Time as possible when they expect any Occasion for their Money; and

 prevent

prevent in a great measure the Necessities of the Proprietors being brought to Market, especially in the Manner in which, when any Declension in the Price of Stocks is apprehended, it may be observed often to be done long before they have any real Occasion for their Money.

Fifthly, It will tend to the Increase of our Credit, and the facilitating both of publick and private Loans at the present, or as far as is reasonable to wish for it, at a lower Rate of Interest, by capacitating such of the Creditors, whose Debts shall be in a less remote Order of Payment, to lend out such Sums as they may have by them reserved for distant Uses, in Expectation of being supplied for such distant Occasions by the Payment of their Share in the Publick Debts in the Order and at the Time appointed for it.

And Lastly, such a Determination of the Order in which the Sinking Fund should be applied in the Discharge of our Publick Debts, and the Notice the Creditors would thereby have when they should be paid off, would give them an Opportunity of looking out for, and providing the most apt and convenient Employment for their Money against the Time of receiving it; a Convenience to the Creditors themselves, which, as the Publick is always interested in the innocent Improvement of our Estates, may I think be esteemed a general Advantage.

I shall conclude, by putting together what I have been endeavouring to represent about the Reduction of our Publick Interest, *viz.* That the general and usual Rate of Interest in every Country is determined by the Proportion that the ordinary Necessities or Demands for Money amongst the Inhabitants, bear to their Capacity and Disposition to supply them; That any other Rate of Interest produced without a Variation in the Proportion aforesaid, or a Foundation laid for it is not likely to continue; That we seem here to have had the Effect of the late



happy

happy Alteration in our Publick Circumstances, in such Reductions of our Interest as have been made already; That the Prospects of a still further Reduction of Publick Interest are a continued Encouragement to Adventures, which though they may be made to contribute to the producing such a Reduction for a Time, are not to be depended on for the Support of it; That these Adventures are themselves at all Times a general Inconvenience, and particularly prejudicial to the Publick on the Approach of Troubles. I have likewise endeavoured to represent, that the further Reduction of Publick Interest is neither equally necessary, nor of equal Advantage to the Publick, as either of those that have been already made; nor does it want to be explained, that the same Addition to the Sinking Fund, to be now made by the next Reduction of the Publick Interest below 4 *per Cent.* will diminish the remaining Income of the Creditors in a greater Proportion than those before made, and be a greater Inconvenience to them. I have recommended it to be considered, how far a Reduction beginning with the Publick Interest must, if it succeeds, necessarily spread it self, and affect the rest of our personal Estates; and from thence the Opposition that Measures for reducing Interest will some time meet with, where some real Alteration in our Circumstances does not perswade to it. I have proposed it to be inquired, if there be any other general Advantage to be obtained by a lower Rate of Interest amongst us, than in regard to our Publick Debts only. And from such Considerations, would submit it, if it might not be convenient, that not only our Measures for further reducing Interest, but our Expectations of it, were at least for some Time suspended; till after the regular Application of the Sinking Fund now provided for a few Years, and the Intermission of such extraordinary Adventures as aforesaid in our Publick Stocks, we might with more Certainty collect what lower

 Rate

Rate of Interest our real Circumstances will admit of.

In what little I have said about the Consequences of a lower Interest on our Commerce and Expences, I have referred my self, *Sir*, to Sentiments in which I have had the Honour to agree with You, and must not pretend to have made out any Thing to general Satisfaction: If I had attempted to do so, I should have been carry'd too far beyond the Design of this Essay; and should have been obliged to examine some prevailing Opinions on this Subject, which seem to me so far from being reasonable or true, that I have sometimes thought, that Part of them which the private Interest of particular Persons have not introduced amongst us, to have been taken up merely on Account of their Resemblance to Paradoxes, and for that Reason affording the greatest Amusement in Conversation.

I would not have it, from any Thing I have said, inferred, that I am in general against any Expedient for the much speedier Discharge of our present Debts; I should be glad if any reasonable Method for this Purpose could be thought of; nor would any new Burthen, or Variation in the present Burthen, on the Subject of this Kingdom, imply'd in any Proposals for this Purpose, be with me an Objection to them, if the Means were but found out of proportioning such a new Burthen, either to the Property or Expences of our Inhabitants in such a manner as would be generally submitted and agreed to: And that such an Expedient were found out, I wish for this general Reason, that whatever in Publick Affairs is thought of great and general Importance to be done at all, should be done, if possible, as soon as it appears to be so; that the most eligible Methods for effecting it are such as may be carried on, and finished under the Direction of the same Persons who were first engaged in them; and that the Success of such Measures should be as little



as

as possible hazarded by the different Sentiments of their Successors. But this Consideration will not go far in recommending the further Increase of the Sinking Fund, by reducing the Interest of the Publick Debts; which upon the Suppositions on which my Calculations have been made, would not, if the Sinking Fund were increased by reducing their Interest to 2 *per Cent.* be paid off in less than 20 Years and a half, or thereabouts; if to 1 *per Cent.* in less than 18 Years and 4 Months; or if the Creditors would be satisfied without any Interest at all till the Payment of their Principal, in less than 16 Years and eight Months.

*I am,* SIR, *&c.*

*FINIS.*

A

# STATE

OF THE

# NATIONAL DEBT,

as it stood

*December* the 24th, 1716.

WITH THE

Payments made towards the Discharge of it out of the *Sinking Fund*, &c.

compared with

The Debt at *Michaelmas*, 1725.

---

*LONDON:*

Printed for R. FRANCKLIN, under *Tom's* Coffee-house, *Covent Garden*. 1727.

# A STATE OF THE *PUBLICK DEBTS*, &c.

THERE have been so many Accounts and States of the National Debts drawn up and published within a few Years past, that I should have thought it very unnecessary to have troubled the Publick upon this Subject, if I had not lately, to my no small Surprize, met with such warm and angry Contentions about it, as have very much disturbed the Peace and Quiet of the Neighbourhood where I live; and it is not unlikely, that they have had the same Effect in other Parts of the Kingdom. This having led me to enquire from whence these unexpected Disputes did arise, I found they were occasioned by a late *Essay* on *the Publick Debts*, which the Author says "he was induced to write, in order to remove some "Mistakes upon this Subject, which he found generally "to prevail, to the Prejudice of the Publick, that our "Debts have *increased* upon us since the Provisions made "for the Discharge of them; and, as he rightly says, it "is the Interest of the Publick that the *Truth* in this "Case should be as generally known as may be."

I was in hopes from hence to have met with a clear and



distinct

distinct Account of what our Debts were at the Beginning of this Reign, or some other fix'd Period of Time; and of the particular Sums which had been discharged in part thereof; and from that plain Proof, to have continued in the Satisfaction which I had for some time enjoyed from the Belief that the *National Debts* were considerably *lessen'd;* which every one might easily imagine them to be, as well from the Provisions made for this Purpose by the *Sinking Fund*, as from the frequent mention made in the Votes, and in the Titles of many Acts of Parliament of the Redeeming of one Fund or other; which I thought was paying off the Debts that had been charged thereupon. This, together with an Absence of some Years from Town and Engagements in Things of another Nature, had induced me not once to question that Fact.

But after reading a very few Pages of this *Writer*, I began to doubt, from his confused Manner of Stating these Accounts, and the little Shifts and Distinctions made use of to disguise them, that I was mistaken; yet being as unwilling to believe it, as this Author seems to be that the Publick should know it, I immediately resolved to procure such Papers and Informations, as I thought necessary to enable me to satisfy my self in this Enquiry, which now much more engaged my Concern than my Curiosity.

And after the strictest and most careful Examination, being convinced of my own Delusion, and seeing the Endeavours used to deceive the Publick, in a Particular, in which it very much concerns them to be truly informed, I have therefore thought it to be of greater Service, than I otherwise should have done, to collect from the Papers, which have been delivered to the House of Commons, as far as they will enable me to do it, a *true State* of our present Debts, and lay the same before them.

As I do not pretend to have any other helps and assistances, but these Papers only, which I think are fully sufficient for this Purpose, as well as authentick, so I do not expect any Credit but what is supported by their Authority. That the Reader's Attention may not be interrupted, nor his Eye disturbed by turning over long Accounts, I have annexed those, which I think necessary, to the End of this Paper, and refer to them as Occasion requires.

The most reasonable and unexceptionable Method of doing what I propose is, I think, to begin with the Account of the *National Debt*, as it is stated from the Exchequer the 14th of *March* 1716, which varies very little, I believe, from what it was the 24th of *December*, 1716, the time that is referr'd to by all our Acts of Parliament.

The several Particulars of this Account have been so often printed already, that I have only made an Abstract of it; but in such a Manner, that it may be very easily examined by any body, who will take the trouble of doing it.

To this Account, as then delivered to the House of Commons, I have added all such Debts as have been stated *since* that time, but were due for Services performed *before*, and consequently do compleat the total Sum of the National Debt, as it stood the said 24th of *December*, 1716.

The Manner of drawing up Accounts, by way of *Debtor* and *Creditor*, being, I believe, most plain and intelligible, I have therefore stated the Accounts this way, placing the Debt before-mentioned on one Side of it, and on the other I have set down all the Payments, which since that time have been made at the Exchequer, out of the Produce of any of the Taxes and Duties appropriated to the Payment of any Part of these Debts; and then such farther Sums as have been applyed towards the Discharge of them out of the Money of the Sinking Fund, from *Michaelmas*, 1715, the Time of its Commencement, to

5 *Michaelmas*,

*Michaelmas*, 1725, to which time only these Accounts are delivered to Parliament.

The Ballance of this Account* thus stated, will, I doubt not, be well understood, and undeniably granted to be the *Total National Debt*, which would have been owing at this Time, in case no Additions had been made to it *since* the 24th of *December*, 1716.

And this Sum appears to be *Forty-five Millions, Five Hundred Fifty-nine Thousand, Seven Hundred Forty-six Pounds.*

The greatest Part of this remaining Debt, with the farther Sums which have been Contracted *since* that Time, having, as it is too well known, changed their Denominations by the Subscriptions into the *South-Sea* Corporation, in the Year 1720; I have therefore thought it for the Reader's ease and conveniency, to form an entire new Account of the Publick Debt, as it now stands, which includes the before-mentioned Ballance, with the Addition of such Debts as have been contracted for Services *since* the 24th of *December*, 1716; and which for that Reason are not in the former Account: and these Sums make the *Debtor* Side of the *second* Account†.

The first Article on the *Credit* Side is the Ballance of the first Account, by which means the Debt to the 24th of *December*, 1716, is deducted out of the Debt, as it now stands. The other Articles are the Payments which have been made of any Part of the Debt *since* the Alterations made by the unhappy *South-Sea* Scheme; and this, either by the Produce of the Funds themselves, or by Money out of the *Sinking Fund*, which could not be brought into the former Account. These two Accounts do therefore contain all the Money which has, at any time, been paid in Part of the National Debt, from the 24th of *December*, 1716, to the 24th of *December*, 1725. And the Ballance

6 of

* *Vide*, the Appendix, No. 1. † No. 2.

of this Account is most certainly the Sum, which has been *contracted* or *added* to the Publick Debt, *since* the Year 1716. And this Addition or Increase amounts to the Sum of *Seven Millions, seven hundred sixty-four Thousand, and thirty-seven Pounds.* And by this means the Debt which would have been reduced, as appears by Account (No. 1.) to *Forty-five Millions, five Hundred fifty-nine Thousand, seven hundred forty-six Pounds*, is now increased to *Fifty-three Millions, three hundred twenty-three Thousand, seven hundred eighty-four Pounds.*

This, I hope, is sufficient to explain to the Reader, That by the *increased Debt* I mean the Sum more than the National Debt would have been at *Michaelmas*, 1725, in case no Additions had been made to it *since* the Year 1716; and will likewise obviate an Evasion, that may probably be made use of, to deceive those who are not conversant in these Things, which is artfully to omit any Notice of the Sums which have actually been *paid* in Part of the Debt due in 1716, and then to compare the State of it at that Time, when it appears to be *Fifty-one Millions, six hundred and forty Thousand, nine hundred thirty-four Pounds*, with the Account of it at *Michaelmas* 1725, which is *Fifty-three Millions, three-hundred twenty-three Thousand, seven hundred eighty-four Pounds;* and from thence argue that there has been little *Addition* made to the Publick Debts.

In Answer to this, it must be considered that some Part of the Debt in 1716, has been constantly *paying off* out of the Produce of the Funds originally appropriated to the Payment of the Money borrowed upon them; and other Sums have from Time to Time been *paying off*, out of the Produce of the *Sinking Fund*, which begins from *Michaelmas*, 1715.

And if this *Author* should be living at the End of 28 Years, and the whole *old Debt* of *fifty Millions* should then be paid off, as he supposes, and yet the National Debt

 should

should, notwithstanding, be still *fifty Millions*, would he have the Confidence to affirm that there had, in this Time, been no *Addition* to, or *Increase* of the Publick Debts?

This is just the present Case, tho' in a smaller Sum.

I believe this Account will, in some Measure, remove the Author's "Wonder how the *uncomfortable* Mistake, "as he is pleas'd to call it, that our Debts have *encreased* "upon us *since* the Provisions made for the Discharge of "them, has so generally prevailed." And that it has not arose from any designed Misrepresentation of our Circumstances, but is a most certain, and unhappy Truth, which must surprize every body who reads his positive* Assertions, That our Debts have in this Time been really *diminished* the Sum of *two Millions, ninety-six Thousand, nine hundred ninety-three Pounds.* For allowing him to deduct out of the Ballance of the *increased* Debt the *three Millions, one hundred fifty-five Thousand, eight hundred fifty-eight Pounds,* increased by the Subscription of the *Irredeemables,* which, for the Reasons I shall afterwards mention, there is no Ground for; yet notwithstanding this, the Difference between his Assertions and the true State of the Debt will be *four Millions, six hundred eight Thousand, one hundred seventy-nine Pounds;* To which adding the Sum of *two Millions, ninety-six Thousand, nine Hundred ninety-three Pounds,* which he affirms the Debt is *diminished,* the total Difference is no less than *six Millions, seven hundred, five Thousand, one hundred seventy-two Pounds.*

If to the *increased* Debt of *seven Millions, seven hundred sixty-four Thousand and thirty-seven Pounds,* as it stands in this State, there is added the *five hundred Thousand Pounds borrowed upon* the Victuallers Tax, the Deficiency of *one hundred and one Thousand, three Hundred Pounds,* still unprovided of the Supply for the Year 1724, the



---

* P. 72. and 74.

Deficiencies of the *Land-Tax* and *Malt* for the Years 1724 and 1725 (not to mention 1726,) which have not been yet made good, with the extraordinary Expences of the *Fleets* abroad, and the unusual Supply of an unlimited Sum for *Services unknown* or *unnamed*, a like Instance whereof I have not before met with in the Journals of Parliament; I am afraid that the *increased Debt* of this Kingdom, at *Christmas* next, will not be much less than *ten Millions;* and this in about *ten* Years; and, as the Author truly says, in a Time of almost *uninterrupted* Peace.

One would think the Writer of the *Essay* had from hence made his Calculation of the Sum he supposes we may be obliged to run in Debt annually for 25 Years to come: nay,* he thinks it not only probable that the Exigencies of the Government may make *new Debts* necessary, but afterwards seems to intimate that the Increase may be *fifty Millions* more than the present Debt. Or else to what Purpose does he wast his own Time, or trouble his Reader with that laborious and comfortable Computation of the Time, in which the *Sinking Fund,* is to pay this *one hundred Millions.* He further tells us,† "That the Lands, Estates, Expences or Commerce of "*Great Britain* will yet easily admit of farther Duties, to "answer even any Expence."

As they may very likely be soon wanted, he would have done well to have pointed out some of these *easy* Taxes. To assist him in this Work, I have at the End of these Papers annexed a View of all the several *Taxes, Duties,* &c. which have been laid upon the Subject, since the *5th* of *November* 1688, over and above all *Taxes* payable at that Time, and have, from Time to Time, been continued, till they were most of them very lately made *perpetual,* and are not to cease till the National Debt is paid off.



* P. 75, 76. † P. 85.

I believe very few of my Country-men have seen or considered this in the manner it is now laid before them; and I confess it was so unpleasing a Task, that nothing could have extorted it from me, but the Mis-representations and extravagant Assertions of this Author, *that we are still able to bear a great many more;* for whose Information I have been prevailed on to draw up this Abstract, which I think well deserves the serious Consideration of the Publick. And for his farther Information, I think it may not be unnecessary to acquaint him, that the *doubling* or *encreasing* any of these Duties, will be of very little use to his Purposes. For though the *Customs* may now be reckoned at least four times greater than they were before the *Revolution;* yet whoever examines these Revenues, will find that they do not produce above one half more than they did before the Additions to them. So that altho' *Trade* is burthened and oppressed, yet the Publick has not the Benefit expected from these *multiplied, encreased* Duties.

It is impossible to read many Pages in this Writer, without being put in mind of the *Empsons* and *Dudleys,* those great Oppressors of Old, who, in their most cruel Treatment of the People, never discovered a more merciless Disposition than this Author, in his Assertion of the *Easiness* of laying *more Taxes* upon them. And since it is Pity he should lose his Reward, I wish he may be made the *Collector,* as well as the *Inventor* of them.

I must confess, I did not think it possible to have found any *Briton* so void of Compassion to his Country, and all Sense of Duty to his Majesty, who has so often and so earnestly recommended the *Payment of our Debts,* as to allarm his Dutiful and Loyal Subjects with these terrifying *Suppositions,* and instead of giving them hopes of being eased of some of the numerous *Taxes* they now pay, to insult the People with telling them that they may not only *easily* bear more, but that they may be continued *for ever* upon them; which is the plain and certain Consequence of his Doctrine, and seems to be the whole Tenour and Design of his Book.

It is an Observation of the *Naturalists*, that every *venomous* Creature, by the Goodness of Providence, carries with it the Antidote of its own Poison; and nothing being more plain, than that the Intention of this Author is to encourage us to run into *new Debts*, upon the pretence of shewing us the *Easiness* of paying off our *Old* ones, by the help of the *Sinking Fund*, and thus turning to our certain Destruction the only Means left for our Preservation; it is to be hoped, that since, by this Instance, we are warned that the Kingdom may produce those, who think like this Author, the Nation will therefore be upon its Guard, to prevent such Doctrines being put in Practice. We are, I believe, in no danger at present, that they should receive the least Encouragement or Countenance; since, as I am informed, the Gentlemen in the Administration very justly place no small Part of their Glory and Merits in encreasing and supporting the Publick Credit, which, they must be sensible, cannot be more effectually destroyed, than by publishing such dangerous and pernicious Insinuations.

When therefore it was impossible that this Writer could ever think to make his Compliment to them, it justly encreases our Wonder, what Motives could induce him to this Attempt, and what vain Presumption could persuade him to imagine, that by a confused Jumble of Figures, he should be able to pass such a gross Imposition as this upon his fellow Subjects, that our debts are really *decreased* above *two Millions*.

I think we may venture to draw a farther Confirmation from it, of what I just now mentioned, that this Performance owes its Birth to the ill judged Officiousness of the Author, and not to any Encouragement from his Superiours, who, I believe, will give him little Thanks for

 this

this Instance of the Respect which he pretends to have for them. For if it was possible to believe, that any of them could have a Desire that the *National Debts* should be thought of in the Light which this Author would put them; was not the only Way of doing this, to leave them, as before, to be talked of in general words? By which Means, with the Help of a little Authority, and some Assurance, modest Knowledge would be often born down, not only in Conversation, but even in Places where it is of much greater Importance that the Truth should be known. But *Facts* and *Figures* are the most stubborn Evidences; they neither yield to the most persuasive *Eloquence* nor bend to the most imperious *Authority.*

I have therefore thought it much more for the Reader's Satisfaction, to lay a plain Account of the Debt before him, than to waste his Time in taking any Notice of this Author's laboured Piece of Confusion; but think it necessary to acquaint him, that the Sums I have inserted in the Account, as paid at the *Exchequer* upon the several *Lotteries* of the Years 1713, 1714, and 1719, and likewise Part of the Sum towards the Discharge of *Exchequer Bills,* is rather Guess, than Certainty, by reason of the Ignorance or Negligence of the Person, whom my Friend sent to make the Enquiry; for I do not suppose, for many Reasons, that the Answer which he sent me was true. The only Difference will be, that in case the Sums which I have set down on these Heads, as paid off, are not so, the Debt is the greater.

I do not apprehend that there is any other Objection or Pretence for the least Cavil, except placing the *one hundred ten Thousand, three hundred twelve Pounds Navy Annuities,* as a Debt *since* the Year 1716; for though it is true, as the Author says, that this was an Arrear due to the *South-Sea Company before* the Year 1718, when it was provided for, yet whoever reads the Act 4° *Geo.** or the

12 Act

* P. 262.

Act 5° *Geo.** will see no Reason to believe that it was grown due before the Year 1716, but the contrary. And were it otherwise, there is ample amends for it made, by placing the whole Arrear of *one hundred ninety-one Thousand, twenty-eight Pounds* to the *East-India* Company, as a Debt *before* the Year 1716, when above *one hundred twenty-seven Thousand, five hundred Pounds* of it was contracted *since* that Time; but I was not willing to break the Sum, lest it might give trouble to any Body who is pleased to examine the Accounts.

As for the other Sums, which the Author excepts out of the *present* Debt, because the Money was borrowed in Aid of the *Sinking Fund;* which are the *Lottery* 1719, the *Money* advanced by the *South-Sea* Company, for taking in the *Lottery* 1710, and the *Exchequer Bills* applyed to the Payment of the *Lottery Annuities,* due Credit is given for them by the Payments in the Account towards the Discharge of the Publick Debt.

But I must ask leave to set the Author right in one Thing, which is, That the whole *five hundred forty-four Thousand, one hundred forty-two Pounds,* advanced by the *South-Sea* Company, was not employed in Aid of the *Sinking Fund;* for *one hundred eighty-eight thousand, two hundred and twenty-six Pounds* was allowed to the Company to make good an Arrear of Interest incurred in the Years 1719 and 1720, and when Interest is turned into Principal, I suppose it may be called a *Debt;* and the farther Sum of *thirty-three Thousand, two hundred forty-two Pounds,* though it does not appear in any of the Accounts to be accounted for to the Publick, yet it is the Sum which, I suppose, was allowed the Company for their Benefit by this Subscription, pursuant to the Act, and is Part of the *thirty-seven Thousand, five hundred Pounds,* which they were to have had, in case the whole Sum

13 remaining

---

* P. 287.

remaining unpaid of the *Lottery* 1710, had been subscribed; but as it was not, if their Proportion was to go hand in hand with the Sum of *seven hundred seventy-eight Thousand, seven hundred and fifty Pounds,* the Publick was in that case to have had, and the Sum of *five hundred forty-four Thousand, one hundred forty-two Pounds;* which they did receive, it will be found that the *South Sea* Company received *seven thousand and forty Pounds* above their Proportion. It is very probable that I may be laught at, for taking notice of such a Trifle, who have the Simplicity to think, that nothing is so, which will be the least Help towards lessening the Debt of the Kingdom.

As I cannot see any Reason, why the Author has deducted out of the Debt since the Year 1716, the *three Millions, one hundred twenty-three Thousand, one hundred eighty-seven Pounds* (and not *three Millions, one hundred fifty-five Thousand, eight hundred fifty-eight Pounds,* as he makes it) which was allowed the *Annuitants,* upon Subscribing their Annuities to the *South-Sea* Corporation, in the Year 1720: So I do not know in what other Period of Time to place it; for it would appear very unreasonable to place it to the Account *before* 1716, when there are so many living Instances of Publick Justice upon those, who have been punished, in a very exemplary Manner, for bringing this Debt upon us. For it is well-known the chief Reason for giving this advanced Price, was because the Publick was to be reimbursed it with a greater Sum, towards the Discharge of the National Debt, by the *seven Millions* which were to have been paid for this Bargain; and no Body doubts but the Loss and Injury the Publick suffered upon this Occasion, as well as the private Calamities of the Subject, were considered in the Punishment. And this Writer is sure very unlucky in the choice of this unhappy Article, which is so very fresh in all our Memories, and is, of all others, the most afflicting and grievous to the remembrance of every honest

*Briton*, and is too strongly fixed upon the Nation, to be removed by his Exception to it.

But was it otherwise, neither the Author, I believe, nor myself have any Authority to enquire by what *Means* or *Methods* our Debts have been *contracted* or *increased:* for if we had, I might possibly with as good Reason except very large Sums out of the Debts *before* 1716, and others might enter into Enquiries of this kind, that I believe would not be very agreeable.

But I think such Examinations of no use in the present Case; nor that it is very becoming either of us to be pointing at any Debts that may be thought to have been *contracted* by the *Weakness* or *Wickedness* of any *Ministry*, to give handles to make Comparisons of one Reign or one Administration with another.

I shall therefore content my self with stating the Debt as it is; and have carefully chosen Periods of Time to avoid the least Suspicion of any such Reflections; Truth and nothing more being the End of the present Enquiry, which I hope will appear plain and satisfactory by this State of the National Debt.

And, to obviate every Objection I can think of, it is necessary to acquaint the Reader that he will find charged *one Million* in *Exchequer Bills* made out for the *Navy Debt*, and *five hundred thousand Pounds* raised by the *Lottery* 1719, for paying off *Exchequer Bills*, is given Credit for in the Account; neither of which Sums are inserted in the Accounts of the *Sinking Fund*.

The *State* of the *Debt*, being settled, naturally leads me to the Consideration of the *Provisions* made for the *Payment* of it, as stated by the Author of the *Essay;* who, for Reasons which he does not explain, is pleased to quarrel with the Order of printing the Statutes, because the Act for *Redeeming several Funds of the Governours and Company of the* Bank *of* England, *&c.* is not put *before* the two others, which he recites. But I think he had much

 better

better Grounds to have found fault that a *certain Act* of the *first* of the King is printed *before those Acts* of the *third* of the King, because it very unluckily flatly contradicts his Assertion, *That the* first *material Provision that was made for discharging the Publick Debts, was by the* Acts *he mentions,* which were all passed 3° *Geo*ij. And every body, who has made the least Enquiry into these Things, or has turned over the *Statute Book* knows very well that the Act 1° *Geo*ij. *for Enlarging the Fund of the Governour and Company of the* Bank *of* England, *&c.* establishes the *aggregate Fund,* which is the first great Branch and Foundation of the *Sinking Fund.* I am sorry the Author has no better Notions of *Truth* and *Candour,* than to think this sly Compliment, made at the Expence of the Honour and Memory of the *Dead,* could be acceptable to *those,* whose Merits do not stand in need of such low Artifices to gild them.

I suppose the *Estimate* which he has made of the Produce of the *Sinking Fund,* is taken from the Accounts delivered to the *House of Lords;* for they not only differ in the Times they are made up for, from those delivered to the *House of Commons,* and directed by the Acts of Parliament, but likewise in the annual Sums; but as the Differences are not very considerable, I shall not trouble the Reader with them; but only take Notice that it would have been some Advantage to his Argument, if he had made his Calculation from the Accounts of the *Sinking Fund* laid before the *House of Commons* for the two Years ending at *Michaelmas* 1725; for in the last of them the Produce is *seven hundred seventy-five Thousand, seven hundred twenty-six Pounds;* and this, notwithstanding a Sum of *one hundred, one thousand, eight hundred, thirty-five Pounds* is taken (as it is said) to make good so much owing to the *Civil List,* which I suppose is not to be an annual Deduction: but I must confess I don't understand what is the meaning of it, which I could wish had been a

16 little

little explained; since, after no small Pains in examining the Accounts of the *Sinking Fund,* I find that the full *seven hundred thousand Pounds* per Ann. established by Parliament for the *Civil List,* has been constantly deducted; and therefore I am not able to find the Reasons for the Deduction of this farther Sum of *one hundred thousand Pounds.*

I am also at a loss for the Reason that, in the Account of the *Sinking Fund* to *Michaelmas* 1725, there is said to be then remaining in the *Exchequer,* the Sum of *five hundred forty-seven thousand, six hundred fifty-four Pounds;* and this Account is dated the 25th of *February,* 1725. For by Act 9° *Geo*ij. it is expressly ordered that *this Money* should be applied, from Time to Time, as it arises, to the Discharge of *Exchequer Bills;* and a Paymaster is directed to be, and I suppose has been appointed for this Purpose, to whom by this Act of Parliament it seems, this Money should have been paid long before; except there has been any other express Directions since that Time, as I am told there has not; but must confess I have not seen the Acts since. And the Author, who is a very Great Man at Compound Interest, will, I believe, find that this is a Loss to the Publick of near *eight thousand nine hundred Pounds.* But, what is worse, it hurts his Computation of the certain Payment of the Debt in about 28 Years: since every Interruption or Delay, in applying the *Sinking Fund,* puts it back. And is he sure that nothing more of this kind will happen in such a Number of Years, since this may be said to be stumbling at the Threshold?

I hope the Reader will excuse me for giving one Instance of the Author's great Care and Exactness in the Use of his Papers, upon this Occasion, as well as of his great Sagacity in the Observation he is pleased to make, that the Produce of the *Sinking Fund* in the Years 1723 and 1724, " exceeds the same Fund for some Years

 " before,

" before, by a greater Sum than can be accounted for by " the Discharge or Reduction of the Interest of any Part " of the Publick Debts; and he is therefore inclined to " attribute it to the Provisions made about that Time for " preventing *Frauds* in the *Revenue*, &c."

I hope, and do not doubt, that the Publick will in time find the Benefit of this Act: but whoever considers that it takes place from the 25th of *March*, 1722, only, and is never so little acquainted with these Things, and knows the many Branches of Trade, which are concerned in the *Sinking Fund*, with the numberless Accidents that may occasion little Variations one Year more than another, will, I believe, think the Author a little too hasty in his Conclusion, that the Difference, which appears in these two Years Produce of this Fund, is owing to the immediate Effect of this Act; and at the same time overlook a much more probable, and, I may say, certain Cause, which is (contrary to his Affirmation) the most remarkable Reduction of Interest since the Year 1720, viz. *sixty thousand, two hundred thirty-nine Pounds* per Ann. upon the Annuities of *one Million, two hundred and four Thousand, seven hundred eighty-six Pounds* from *Lady-Day*, 1723, and *twelve Thousand, four hundred fourteen Pounds* per Ann. upon *two hundred thirty-five Thousand, two hundred ninety-seven Pounds*, from *Lady-Day* 1724, and if he will add these Savings of Interest to *five hundred ninety-seven Thousand, one hundred twenty-four Pounds*, the Produce of the *Sinking Fund* for the Year 1720, he will find it exceeds either of the Years 1723 or 1724.

Or if the Author will examine the Produce of the great Branches of the *Customs* for the Years 1719 and 1720, he will find them *more* than in his favourite Periods of 1723 and 1724.

As I have hitherto looked upon the Establishment and Appropriation of the *Sinking Fund* to the Payment of the National Debts, as the wisest and most beneficial

 Provision,

Provision, which, in our Circumstances, could have been thought of; I cannot but be pleased to see any Advocate for the Improvement and strict Application of it to this great and good Use; and I am not a little glad to see an Opinion, I have always entertained, confirmed by this Author* *viz.* "That the *Sinking Fund* is grounded upon "a Contract between the *Government* and the Publick "*Creditors*, they on the one hand accepting one sixth Part "less of their Annuity or Interest, upon the Assurance "and Security given them by the Legislature, that this "Saving should be inviolably applyed to the Payment of "their Principal; to which Purpose it is in such a "Manner appropriated by the Legislature, that it is not "*alterable* by any *subsequent Acts* of Parliament, upon "Pretence of any publick Conveniency whatsoever. And "that we may confidently expect that no Person whatso-"ever, to whose Hands the Administration of our Affairs "may at any Time be committed, can ever approve or "recommend the Application of the Produce of the "*Sinking Fund*, in any possible Exigency, to any other "Uses than those to which it stands now appropriated." A Declaration thus clear and full, from one whose Maxims do not much favour the only good End proposed by this Fund, viz. *the Payment of our Debts,* would be very satisfactory, if, in my looking over Papers upon this Occasion, I did not meet with a Difficulty which I cannot solve; and that is, that without any great Exigency, as I think, in our Affairs, this *Fund* has been a Security for *Payment of Money* raised for the *Current Service* of the Year, which certainly has nothing to do with our Debts *before* 1716, and must have been provided for, if no such *Fund* were in being. I know there is a Proviso, that in case the Funds do not prove sufficient for the Purposes for which they were granted, they are then to be made good out of

 the

* P. 81, 82.

the first Aids of the next Year; but in case that fails, the *Sinking Fund* stands engaged, and is no doubt looked upon as the *Security*, or otherwise it would be to no purpose to name it. Whether this is not a Practice that may be dangerous, I shall leave to others to consider: for if there should be a necessity, upon any Occasion, to raise large Sums for the Service of any one Year, and the Deficiency of the Funds should be too great to be provided for out of the Supplies of the next Year, the *Sinking Fund* will be then probably obliged to make good that Deficiency, and diverted from the Uses to which it is most strictly appropriated; and this without any Benefit that I can learn to the Publick; for is it not equal in Point of Advantage to the Kingdom, whether we save a higher Interest by paying off our old Debts, or take the Money that ought, preferable at least to all other Considerations, to be applyed to the Payment of them, only to make a Merit of Raising the Supplies for the Current Services at a *Lower Interest*, in prejudice to the *Publick Credit*, and to the insensible *Increase* of our Debts?

And in the Times of Peace and Prosperity which we have enjoyed, I believe no body, who is acquainted with Trade and Business and the regular Payments upon the *Land-Tax* and *Malt*, and knows any thing of providing Necessaries for the *Navy*, &c. as I have done, would find any great Difficulty to supply the Money for the Year's Service, from time to time, as it is wanted, without putting the Kingdom to the Expence of *Two per Cent.* Interest. I have been informed that the late Earl of *Godolphin* did not, for the Services at home, pay above *Four per Cent.* or 4½ in the Heat of the War; but indeed, I believe he was not of Opinion, that the Wealth, Trade, and Riches of these Kingdoms were *too considerable* to stand in need of any *frugal Management:* and after many Years presiding at the Head of the *Treasury*, he left no Acquisitions by his Employment, but, without the

 accidental

accidental Falling in of the paternal Estate, he would have dyed in *Want;* a glorious Example for all his Successors to follow! And who is there, that has any Sense of publick Merit, who does not sincerely wish that his Honour and Memory may be perpetuated for ever, and his Family distinguished with the most lasting and uninterrupted Happiness?

I must confess, that Arguments for the Preservation of the *Sinking Fund* have a very odd Appearance in *one*, the whole Intent of whose Writing seems to be, to pervert the great and good Ends proposed by it, to the most pernicious Purposes that the Wit or Wickedness of Man could have thought of, *viz. An Encouragement and Foundation of a Succession of endless Debts and Taxes;* and his extraordinary Zeal for it puts one in mind of the *common Jugglers*, who amuse you with bidding you hold fast the Money, which they are then dexterously taking from you.

For would it not have been much better, that there never had been any such Thing as a *Sinking Fund*, than that it should be made the Instrument and Means of *encreasing*, instead of *lessening* our Debts, as this Author is pleased to argue, and tell us in very plain words*, "That it will always appear more eligible, in regard to "the Publick Interest, *as well as more* easy *to those Persons in the Administration*, to raise what shall be farther "wanted, by *increasing* the Publick Debts with *farther* "*Loans* upon Interest provided for by *New Duties*, than "to supply the same Sums from the *Sinking Fund*."

The Writer must have a very mean Opinion of his Readers, if he thinks the putting this by way of *Supposition* will be a sufficient Security from the just Reproach of such *Insinuations*, which are followed with very express *Declarations* of his Meaning.

21 For

* P. 83.

For* where he argues against the *Reduction* of the Interest of the Funds to *three per Cent.* he tells us, that in case this should be done, "The danger seems to him by "no means *inconsiderable,* that it may soon after be deter-"mined to employ the *Sinking Fund* in the room of our "*other Taxes,* and leave the Debt upon the Kingdom for "ever." How is this to be reconciled with his strong Assurances and firm Belief before-mentioned, That the *Publick Faith* and *Justice* was so strongly engaged for the Security of *this Fund,* that there was no Danger of any Violation of it? To what purpose then does he frighten the *Publick Creditors* with the Apprehensions of *Exigencies* happening, in which it might come into a Competition, which was most eligible. To seize upon the Produce of the *Sinking Fund,* or to *contract New Debts* upon *New Loans,* on the Prospect of paying them off by this Security; and is not this the most certain Consequence of his Reasoning?

For if it is reasonable that the *Present Ministry* should, for *their Ease,* be allowed to *encrease* the National Debt; will not the same Plea hold for the *next,* and so on? Nay, will not any *succeeding Ministry* have much stronger Reasons for *adding* to the Debt, not only from the *Precedent* of their *Predecessors,* but by their having *anticipated all Taxes* which the Wit of the sharpest Projectors could invent, and consequently left no Room to raise *any Sum* for the Necessities of the Government?

I must confess, the Author's Reasoning, upon this Occasion, seems but a very odd Complement to *any Ministry;* for I always thought their great *Honour* consisted in their *Skill* and *Ability* to *extricate* their Prince and Country out of the *Difficulties* in which they were involved; and not in pursuing Measures that must end in the *Destruction* of both, however *easy* and *beneficial* they

 may

* P. 119, 120.

may be to *themselves:* But this Author having very wisely, as he supposed, secured his *own Interest* by taking the *Present Ministry* under his Protection, leaves the *next* Reign and Ministry to shift for themselves; and if his Doctrine is pursued, they will find it no *easy* Task, unless the *Riches* of the Kingdom, and the *Patience* of the People are equally inexhaustible: For he has not been so kind to his Country, as to fix the happy *Æra,* when an End is to be put to *multiplying* of *Taxes* and *Debts;* and till then, he might have spared himself the trouble of making any Computation of Time, when it is probable *the* Debt *of the Kingdom will be* paid.

In the mean time, it may not be improper to consider, that the Kingdom of *Great Britain* only already pays, for the *Current Services* of the Government, and *Interest* of our *present Debts,* between *six* and *seven Millions* a Year; besides the *vast* and *unlimited Charge* of *Managing, Collecting,* and *Bringing in the same.*

I must leave it to those, who are best acquainted with the State of the Nation, to judge what *farther Sum* they think may be annually raised upon the Kingdom; this being near as much as was granted in the most expensive Years of the late *great War.* And to encourage us in the ſarther Prosecution of it, I doubt not that many remember we were flattered. "That the Revenues of the "Crown, at the *Revolution,* being about *two Millions, two-* "*hundred Thousand Pounds per Annum,* exclusive of the "Charges of *Collecting,* the *Expences* of the Government, "both *Civil* and *Military* at the End of the War, would "be under *one Million, one hundred* and *twenty Thousand* "*Pounds, per Annum;* and the Kingdom would certainly "gain a Saving, to all Futurity, of above a *Million per* "*Annum.*" From what Causes then these *annual Expences* have in so short a time been *encreased* to above *three Millions* a Year, and what is like to be the *Consequences* of it, I must leave to the Consideration of those,

 who

who have a *Right* to make this *Enquiry*, and who cannot forget, That the Crown at King *James's* Accession, when his own Revenue, as *Duke of York*, was consolidated with it, did little exceed *one Million, seven hundred thousand Pounds*, exclusive of all Charges of *Collection*, for all *Expences Civil* and *Military;* which, upon Occasion of *Monmouth's* Rebellion, and other Exigencies, was afterwards encreased *four hundred thousand Pounds*, and Part of this Sum was given for *five*, and some for *eight* Years only.

With this Revenue it is well known, that King *James* paid *Debts* of the *former* Reign, of near *eight hundred thousand Pounds*, and left no *inconsiderable Sum* in the *Exchequer;* and all this, in as little Time almost, as we have seen *one Million* of Debt contracted upon *one Branch* only of our annual Expence. And we may believe, that the *wicked Designs*, which this King was at the same time carrying on, to introduce *Popery*, and *Arbitrary Power*, and over-turn the *Constitution* of these Kingdoms, might require, at least, as great a Sum for *secret Service Money*, as may have at any time since been necessary to support them.

It is certain from the Assistance we at present receive by our *Paper Credit*, that we are less sensible, than we otherwise should be, of the constant great and unusual *Expences* of the Publick; And this *Credit*, managed with *Prudence*, and kept within *due Bounds*, may be of great Use and Service to us in our present Circumstances; yet, if it should be extended *too far*, will be its own Destruction; and it is necessary for us not to suffer our selves to be deluded by it, into a vain Confidence and Dependance upon *greater Riches* than we really possess; for this will have very fatal Effects; and, by hiding from us our Poverty, and hindering us from taking *proper Measures* in time to prevent its growing upon us, we shall be exposed to the greatest Extremities, and shall find ourselves, when

24 Distress

Distress comes upon us, plunged into *Necessities* and *Debts* without Remedy.

And since it is possible, that the Author of the *Essay* may not have fully considered the *Consequences* of *running in Debt;* I shall beg Leave to tell him a little History, that is very well known in a certain County of *Great Britain;* and I wish there was this single Instance only in the Kingdom.

A certain Family was possessed of an Estate of *two Thousand Pounds* a Year, upon which the Grand-Father left a Debt of *two Thousand Pounds* only, the National Interest being then eight *per Cent.* The Son, soon after he came to the Estate, had the Misfortune to engage in a Competition for the County with his Neighbour, who was a Gentleman of a much better Estate. The fashionable Hospitality of that Time, encreased by this Contention, (that Source of *Corruption and Ruin*) engaged this unhappy Gentleman to make a great *Addition* to the *first Debt:* but *Interest* being some time after reduced to *six per Cent.* he very prudently took the Advantage of it, to change the Mortgage; at which time several little Debts being uneasy to him, he took up Money enough upon this Occasion, to pay them off, and *added* the Sum to the *Old Mortgage;* but resolved to keep the *two per Cent.* saved sacred towards discharging his Debt; not reflecting that by the *last Addition* to it, there was little more than *one and a half* left for this Purpose: But what was worse, The Fancy which from hence he entertained of *clearing his Debt,* made him not so careful as he was before, to *regulate his Expences,* to the *yearly Income* now remaining, which was *farther lessened* by the *Publick Taxes,* and his Debts multiplyed upon him faster than his *saving by Interest* paid them off; and it becoming generally known that the Estate was mortgaged near its Value, no Body would lend any more, which reduced him and his Family to *Poverty* and *Misery.*

However melancholly this Story may be thought, yet it will not be surprizing to a Gentleman, who has been *accustomed to attend to the* Increase *of Money put out at* Compound *Interest,* and consequently knows, that an annual Payment of *seven Thousand Pounds* only will, at *five per Cent.* amount to the *whole* Value of an Estate of *forty-nine Thousand Pounds per Annum,* in less than *forty-three* Years.

This is so true, that I believe it may be affirmed, that near *nine* in *ten* of the Families in this Kingdom have been undone, by paying *Interest* for the Incumbrances upon their Estates: For in this case, there are but *two* possible ways for a Man to avoid his Ruin; either by consenting to give up the Vanity of owning a Title to a *greater Estate* than he possesses, and selling Part of it at once, to discharge the *Debt;* which is generally the wisest Way; or, what perhaps is still more difficult, resolutely and obstinately keeping his *Expences* within his *real Income.*

Are not *Kingdoms* a Collection of *Families?* And if any one doubts, whether *devouring Interest* is not as certain Destruction, as a *consuming Land War,* he will need no other Proof of it than this Author's Arguments, upon the *Easiness* of paying the *National Debt,* by the Benefits arising from *Compound Interest,* which I hope he will give me leave to make a little use of, to shew from thence the *Mischief of running into Debt.*

In order to this, I must desire the Reader to remember, that this Author tells us*, that the *Sinking Fund* encreases every Year, *by the* Addition *of the* Interest *of the principal Sums in every Year paid off;* and it is therefore very obvious to every Body, that it will in a much shorter time pay off a *greater Debt* at the end of *twenty-eight Years,* than it did at the *Beginning* of this Time; therefore,

26 though

* P. 79.

though the Debt of *twenty-five Millions* more, which this Writer supposes may be *added* to the *present fifty odd Millions,* may be paid off in little more than *seven Years,* after the *twenty-eight,* in which he proposes the *present Debt* may be paid off from *Midsummer* next, provided that the *fifty Millions* are then entirely discharged. Yet is there not something more to be considered in this case than the *Time?* Is the *Money,* that is to be raised upon the People, not worth thinking of? For, upon the Author's own Supposition of contracting this *New Debt* of *twenty-five Millions,* by *one Million* a Year only, there must be *raised* upon the Subject, by some *New Tax,* the Sum of above *eighteen Millions, three hundred thousand Pounds,* for the *Interest* of the *Principal Money,* at the end of *five and twenty Years,* at *four per Cent.* and then for the *Interest* of the *whole Capital of twenty-five Millions,* for *eight Years* more, it will require above *nine Millions, two hundred thousand Pounds;* which *two Sums* added to the *Principal,* make above *fifty-two Millions,* over and above the *Old Debt* of *fifty odd Millions,* which the Publick must pay for this *New Debt,* in case it should be contracted; which God forbid!

But to do the Author Justice, his Reasonings are of a Piece; and he seems to think himself such a Master of *Figures,* that he can impose upon his Readers at pleasure. Therefore* where he talks of reducing the *Present Debt* from *four* to *three per Cent.* which he does not approve, he tells us that the *Benefit* by this *Reduction* would only be to discharge the *Debt* about *four Years and a half sooner;* and if you will raise a *New Tax* of *three hundred twenty-two thousand Pounds per Annum* more than the Nation now pays, to add to the *present Sinking Fund,* it will pay the Debt in the same time, though it is continued at *four per Cent.* I must here again put this Writer in mind, that if

 he

* P. 96.

he will make use of his *Arithmetick*, he will find that this *New Tax* will, in *twenty-three* Years, cost the People above *eleven Millions, seven hundred* and *ninety thousand Pounds.* And *one per Cent. Interest,* reduced upon *fifty Millions* Debt, will be a *real Saving* to the Kingdom, in this time, of *eighteen Millions, three hundred thousand Pounds:* So that the Difference in Advantage to the Publick, by the *Reduction* of *Interest,* and this Proposal of an *Additional New-raised Fund,* is a Saving of above *thirty Millions,* with this farther Benefit, that in *one case* there is *less* Money sent out of the Kingdom, for the *Interest* due to *Foreigners;* and in the *other, more Money* is raised at Home to be *sent Abroad.* Can a Nation fail to thrive under *such Politicians* as this Author? Who, out of his great Zeal and Concern for the Happiness of his Country, has thought it worth his time and trouble, to compute *how many Years* are required to pay a Debt of *fifteen hundred and seventy-five Millions Sterling!*

When the Author, to whom every Thing of this kind is, I doubt not, very easy, has found out the *Taxes* for *sixty-nine Millions* a Year, to pay the *Interest* of this *Debt,* with the Provision for the *current Services* of the Year, and *Sinking Fund* for it; as much an Enemy as I am to the *Contracting* of any Debts, he shall have my Consent even for this *Debt;* and I don't know, but that may be as significant as the *Intimation* which he has been pleased to give us*, that the Author is one of that *Importance,* that his *Promise* would be sufficient to make us hope for an *End* of the *present Taxes,* after the Payment of the *publick Debt:* A *Grace,* however, which he does not think fit to *grant,* though he might very safely have *promised* it, in case he has the *Power* to put his *own Doctrine* into Practice, if he had the Certainty of living to the Age of old *PAR.*



* P. 54.

It is to be hoped, that this *uncommon Genius* will, in the mean time, give the Publick a Demonstration of that *New* and *Curious Proposition*, "* That an *Increase of Figures* is "not any *real Increase* of the *true Quantity of the Debt.*" For when they are convinced of this Truth, it will remove all Uneasiness about *Multiplying of Debts,* even to the *fifteen hundred Millions Sterling.*

What a Loss is it to the Kingdom, that such an *excellent Head* should not be *better employed?* For I am afraid, these fine Speculations will neither divert the Publick from *thinking*, nor the People from *feeling* the Weight of their *Debts.*

I believe the Author need not have given himself the trouble which he has done, upon the Subject of *Reducing* the *Interest* of the National Debt from *Four* to *Three per Cent.;* which I am so far from *fearing*, as he seems to do, that I think it very desirable, as soon as it is practicable: but I am afraid that we are not yet ready for that Consideration; since it will, very probably, be thought adviseable to see a little what Influence the *Reduction* of above *fifty Millions* to *Four per Cent.* may have upon our Affairs, before we proceed *farther;* and I am confirmed in this Opinion, by the late Caution of our *Superiours* upon this Occasion; for whom I have as great Respect as this Gentleman; and They thought it more prudent, to give the *Bank* about *seventy-five thousand Pounds* for their Consent to a certain Reduction of *three Millions, seven hundred seventy-five Thousand, and twenty-seven Pounds,* from *Five* to *Four per Cent.* at *Midsummer*, 1727, than run the hazard of offering to pay them off *that Sum,* in case of their Refusal; although this Sum would, in *thirty Years,* have paid off a Debt of above *two hundred and forty-four thousand Pounds;* And this at a Time, when the least Apprehensions of Danger seemed to be at a great Distance; which



* P. 69.

which have since, in a very *sudden* and *surprizing* Manner, laid hold on us.

The Gentlemen in the Administration are, no doubt, fully informed of the *Sum* we owe to *Foreigners;* and have the most exact Knowledge of the particular Circumstances of the Kingdom, in regard to our *Coin,* and the *Ballance* of our *Trade;* and therefore are able to judge, whether, if, upon a *farther Reduction* of Interest, *Foreigners* should draw their Money in large Sums, it is likely to be any Inconveniency or not to us: Considerations, that will be allowed to be very necessary; and this shows us one more Mischief of *continuing in Debt,* by cramping our *Ministers* in any Designs they may have for the Publick Good, in which I wish them to enjoy as great Liberty as they themselves can desire: but this is not to be expected in our present Condition; which, to the no small Mortification of every *Briton,* renders us, in some Measure, *Slaves* to the *Nations we despise;* for the *wisest* and *richest* Prince, who ever sat on a Throne, tells us, *that the* Borrower *is a* Slave *to the* Lender.

I shall not trouble the Reader with the several Arguments which have been used in relation to fixing the *Rate of Interest,* in which two very great Men, *one* for his *practical Knowledge,* and *Experience in Trade and Business;* and the *other* for his *Extent of Thought, and Justness of Reasoning,* did formerly a little differ; but I believe, were they now to debate the Case, they would agree.

For, when the great *Increase* of the *personal Estates* of this Kingdom, since the *Restoration,* is considered, plain and Obvious Reasons will lead us to think, That it will be most agreeable to Justice and Policy, to keep even the *Interest* of the *Funds,* near what Mr. *Locke* calls the *Natural Interest of Money.*

As to the Author of the *Essay's* Arguments against the *Reduction* of the *Interest* of the *Publick Debt* from *Four* to *Three per Cent.* upon the Principles and Practices of *Stock-Jobbing*, in which he seems, to me at least, to be a very *great Master;* I am in Truth so great a Stranger to them, that it would be very ridiculous in me to pretend to judge of them.

But I think they offer the strongest Reasons against *increasing the National Debt,* from the great Inconveniences and Mischiefs arising to the Publick by this most pernicious and destructive Traffick, which diverts the Thoughts, Industry, and Money, that would otherwise be usefully employed in carrying on and promoting our *Trade;* the only true and lasting Support of these Kingdoms. But every Body must know, that as long as there is so much greater a Quantity of the *Funds* at Market, than can be purchased by the *Money* there is to place out upon *Interest;* great Part of the *running Cash* of the Nation will be laid out in them; and from hence the frequent and unavoidable Occasions and Necessities there will be of the *Stocks* shifting from one hand to another, will as certainly cause a *Rise* and *Fall* in their Value, as there will be an *Ebbing* and *Flowing* in the *Thames:* and one may as well think to stop the one, as pretend to prevent the other, by any other means, but *lessening the Publick Debt;* and whoever gives his Consent to the *Increase* of it, is a greater Promoter of *Stock-Jobbing,* than the busiest *Broker* upon the *Exchange,* let his Clamours be never so great against it.

I believe there is no Man, who wishes well to his Country, but is grieved to see the Property of above *fifty Millions* of his Fellow-Subjects, in a Coin that is in the Power of such *wicked Craft,* to be raised and lowered at the Pleasure of the *vile Dealers* in it; and this without the Stamp of Royal Authority, or the least Benefit to the King or Kingdom; and by dextrous Management of pretended *new Projects and Designs* at home, or Alarms from abroad, may, great Part of it, in the Compass of a few Years, be brought into as few *private Coffers,* to the no small Impoverishing of the Nation, for want of that necessary *Circulation of Money*, without which, it will be impossible to manage our *Trade* at home, much less to carry it on abroad.

If Mr. *Locke's Calculation* is near the Truth, *That a* thriving Trade *cannot be carried on in any Country* (for the Reasons he gives) *with a less Proportion of Money than* a fiftieth Part *of the* Labourers *Yearly Wages*, one Twentieth *Part of the* Brokers *or* Retailers *Yearly Returns in* Money, *and* one Quarter *of the* Landholders *annual Revenue;* and *that every Kingdom wants more or less* Money *in Proportion to the* Slowness *or* Quickness *of the* Circulation *of it in that Country;* it deserves our Consideration, what are likely to be the Consequences of enlarging a *Traffick*, that has so great a Tendency to cause a *Stagnation* in the *Current Cash* of the Kingdom, by confining the Circulation of it to *Exchange Alley*. And they who live in the *Cloathing Parts*, and Places where the *chief Manufactures* are carried on, are best able to judge if they feel no *Effects* of it already.

These, with numerous other Considerations which will occur to every Body will, it is to be hoped, excite our Zeal, encourage our Endeavours, and determine our Resolutions to put a stop to the *Increase* of the *National Debts;* that we may in time make use of the Advantages of the *Trade* we now enjoy, to the *effectual Paying them off*. For, we are not secure of always possessing it in the same Degree; and this not only from the frequent Changes, that from many unforeseen Accidents happen in the *Trade* of all Countries, which the common Interruptions of *War*, which, though temporary only, yet, in our Circumstances, are not wantonly to be engaged in, but if possible to be avoided, where the immediate Preservation of the King and Kingdom do not require it.

But we must also have in our View, what seems more immediately to threaten us: the *new Trades* and

*Manufactures* that are daily growing up, and increasing in most Parts of *Europe*, where they were unknown before. All our neighbouring Princes, who have long neglected the Care of this great Good, seeming to begin to be now sensible of their Errors, are turning their Thoughts and Endeavours to settle it in their Countries, and making their utmost Efforts to cherish and improve it. The Effects of these Measures we have for some time past felt; though we have willingly *deceived ourselves,* by imputing them to *other Accidents,* rather than to the *true Causes.*

For, I believe, every Body who heard the Arguments relating to the Prohibition of *East-India* Silks, *&c.*, was fully convinced that the great Reason of the Decay of our coarse Woollen Manufactures (the great Article in the Consumption of our Wooll) is owing to the making of this Sort of Goods in *Prussia,* and those Parts of *Germany,* which, though not so good as ours, yet, by the Wisdom of their Governments, are wholly made use of in Cloathing their Troops, and the Generality of their People; and they do, in great Measure, supply with these Commodities the Northern Crowns, and even *Russia,* which formerly received these Goods from Us.

The Loss we have suffered, by the Prohibition of our Stuffs in *Flanders,* is fresh in every Man's Memory. And what we are likely to suffer by the late great Misfortune of the Prohibition of our Manufactures in *Sicily,* and the Designs of Erecting them in the *Imperial* Dominions to supply those Parts, is not yet known nor felt. But what seems most surprizing is, that it does not appear that we have made any Stipulations with the Emperor for the Security of our *Trade* in a Kingdom we conquer'd at our own Expence, and generously gave him; for if we had, those Engagements would, no doubt, have been made the Foundation of our *Complaint* of their Infraction, and not the *Declaration* of the $\frac{25\ Febr.\ 1712.}{8\ Mar.\ 1713.}$ made at *Utrecht* with the King of *Sardinia*, then Possessor of that Kingdom; but this is the *only* Treaty printed and appealed to in the *Courant* of the 6th of *August* last, in which I shall be very glad to be mistaken; but if true, it is a very melancholy Consideration, that the fatal Oversight, in relation to *Ostend*, has not been a sufficient Warning to us, to take Care of our own Country, when we are giving Kingdoms to others. And in case of a *War*, who knows what we may farther suffer by Prohibitions in other Nations?

For I am afraid, let our Forces and Expences at Sea and Land be never so great, they will not be able to recover the *Trade* we have lost, nor hinder any Princes or States from erecting such Companies and Manufactures as they think fit in their own Dominions, whatever the Mischief may be to ours. And, whatever Success we may flatter ourselves with, in the uncertain Events of War, by Reason of our great Superiority at Sea; yet we may believe it must be some very great Injury and Provocation that will engage us in it, since it may be very dangerous to a Nation, that wholly subsists upon *Trade*, to hazard the diverting the most profitable Branches of it into other Channels; for that may be a much more lasting Evil than the Quarrels which occasioned it.

And I wish we don't find all Endeavours to force a *Trade* to have just the same Consequence in publick, which it is known to have in private Affairs.

The only true and certain Means will be to *lessen*, as soon as possible, the *Publick Debts*, which will put us in a Condition, as we see Occasion, to ease those Branches of Trade that require it; which *Paying* Debts with one hand, and *Contracting* with another, and so making the continuance of the *same* Duties and Taxes still necessary, can never enable us to do.

But these extraordinary Burthens upon our Trade will in time get the better even of those great Advantages we



naturally

naturally have for the Improvement of it, beyond any of our Neighbours; and deprive us of those Benefits, which a judicious Writer thought and said, many Years since, were, by the Bounty of Providence, inseparably annexed to these Kingdoms.

That we may therefore neglect no Endeavours to prevent so great an Evil, it is necessary that we should not be discouraged, nor artfully diverted from the steady Pursuit of those Measures which will enable us to struggle with any Difficulties, from the Causes before-mentioned, and put us into a Condition of Opening new Branches of Trade, in case of the Failure of any of the old ones.

I hope that we now are, and, by the prudent Management of the Administration, always shall be able to pay off, (in the gradual Manner it must be done) the utmost Sum which the greatest Improvement of the *Sinking Fund* can produce, towards the Discharge of the Publick Debts, without being sensible of the least Inconveniency by the Money owing to *Foreigners;* and shall not therefore be amused with the vain Apprehensions, that the Payment of our Debts would carry away our Money, which I have lately with great surprize heard mentioned by Men of no mean Rank, nor Understanding; and I am now convinced from whence such Insinuations arise, and wish others would take Notice from what Quarter they come, and the Designs they are meant to serve. For if it is once come to be generally believed, that the Payment of the *National Debt* is either *desperate* or *dangerous,* it will soon be thought that *Adding* to it is no harm; but the doing it may be looked upon as an Act of *Address* and *Skill;* and he may be esteemed the *ablest* Minister who can *increase* it the fastest.

If any Thing could make me merry upon so serious a Subject, it is the great Concern and Tenderness which this Author expresses for our *Ministers,* in the Objection which he gravely tells us, Himself and his Friend have frequently met with ('tis pity he did not say in *what Company*) against the Payment of the *National Debts*, "Because the Continuance of them is necessary for the "*Profit* that arises from them to our *Ministers*, who without the *Influence* and *Power* this gives them, to reward "their *Creatures* and *Dependants* by their Grants to them "of the several Offices and Employments which they "have *reserved to themselves* for this Purpose, would not "be able to support themselves in their Authority and "Grandeur." So that if we have *no Debts*, the King will have no *Ministers;* which puts me in mind of a Saying of one, "That no Government was *worth serving* without "*some Jobbs.*" And it must be allowed that our *Debts* have been no bad one to *some*.

However, great as this Evil is, I cannot help wishing it was put to the Trial. And it is possible that some generous *Briton* may arise, who will undertake this Burthen, even with this great Disadvantage. But I hope there is not so degenerate a One now living, who can have any Comfort in the *Profit* that may arise to him by the *Continuance* of the *Miseries* of his Country. And if there should be such a *Wretch*, yet I doubt not that, as long as a *British Parliament* has a Being, there is no Danger that the Interest of these Kingdoms should be sacrificed to the *Avarice, Ambition*, or *Power* of the most *meritorious Minister*. And in this Assurance we are happily confirmed by His Majesty, who, in almost all his *Speeches*, has, with the most compassionate Earnestness, recommended the Paying of the *National Debt;* well knowing that the antient Splendour and Dignity of the Crown, which suffers by publick Necessity, is to be recovered by this Means only; and that the *Glory* of the Prince consists in the *Riches* and *Ease* of his People.

Upon what Principles therefore this Author founds his Reasoning, I shall leave others to judge: but it is the first



time,

time, I believe, that it was so publickly intimated, *That the* Poverty *of Prince and People were* necessary *to* reward *and* enrich *the MINISTERS;* and it will scarce be denied, that they must be the *wickedest of Servants* who think so.

But to remove this Gentleman's Fears and Apprehensions, "Of looking forward with *no pleasure* to that Period "of Time (*which every honest* Briton *longs and wishes for*) "least the *Payment* of the *publick Debt* should deprive his "Majesty or his Successors, of the Means to *reward* his "faithful Servants:" I would ask him, whether he does not think, that a *Minister* would rather choose to ask the Excesses of a *Civil List Expence*, from a People *Rich* and *Easy*, than in *Necessity* and *Distress?*

And who is there that has the least Regard to the Honour of the *Revolution*, and the *Protestant Succession*, who does not heartily wish that the Circumstances of our Affairs had permitted us to discharge *one Debt* at least, the common Invective of the inveterate Enemies of both, instead of *adding ten thousand Pounds* more to it this Year, that Sum being, by an Account delivered to the House of Commons, acknowledged to have been paid in part of the *Million*, out of the *Six-pences*. It is indeed a small Sum; but as I do not remember to have seen in the Votes any *Message* from the *Crown* for it, If it should have been given without this, or taking any of the *usual Steps* observed in granting Money, (that great and essential Part of our Constitution) and this should be the least weakened by such a Precedent, may it not make the *Civil List* Debt to be remembred much longer than every good Subject wishes it may be?

The Author, as a farther instance of his Zeal and Concern for our *Ministers*, and to give us some Hopes that the *Debt* of the Kingdom will not be absolutely *necessary* to be continued at their Pleasure, and for their *Profit only*, has luckily found out other Reasons to recommend the securing the *same* Benefits to them by *Continuing* the *Duties* and *Taxes* we now pay for the annual Supplies of the Government, *after the Payment of our Debts.*

As this is a Case not very likely to happen in the Time of many Men now living; few, I believe, need trouble themselves with this Consideration, but leave it to the next Age, to judge for themselves, with our hearty Wishes that they may not act *as we have done.*

I shall however venture to say, that tho' there may be some of the Conveniences which the Author mentions in raising Money by *Excises* and *Customs;* yet the Benefits are not so great as he imagines. And this Nation has always expressed the greatest Aversion to them, as *Badges of Slavery,* and *Encroachments* upon the *Liberties* of a Free People. And whoever reads Mr. *Locke* upon this Subject (which well deserves the Perusal of every Gentleman) will, I believe, be fully convinced, that there is in Truth no Benefit to the *Landed Interest by it;* though Gentlemen are apt to fancy the contrary, because it does indeed fall in with our present Way of Thinking, both in publick and private Affairs; for it only removes from our Sight, a present Uneasiness, at the Expence of a much greater and more lasting Evil; and I believe no Gentleman will doubt the Truth of it, who will order his Steward to look back and compare his yearly Expences in any Commodity (*Candles* and *Soap, Coffee,* &c. for Instance) *before* and *since* the Tax was laid upon them. And the Contests, as Mr. *Locke* justly observes, which are set on foot, and sometimes encouraged between the *Landed* and *Moneyed* or *Trading* Interests, only shew the Decay of the *Wealth,* and *Riches* of any Kingdom, or the Uneasiness of their *Taxes.*

For where the Bulk of the Property of any Country is *Land* (which is not the Case of *Holland*) the greatest Part of the publick Expences will terminate there, and Gentlemen have no other way of relieving themselves,

 but

but by keeping them within due Bounds; for shifting the *Names* of the *Taxes* will only deceive them for a Time, but will at last fall the heavier upon them; it being with Kingdoms as it is with Families, neither of which can be happy nor easy who spend more than their Income.

And by this Author's Proposal, we are to lose one of the *greatest Benefits*, which I believe most People hope for, by the *Payment* of our Debts; That is, the being freed from a vexatious Army of *Officers*, who, under the Names of *Commissioners, Secretaries, Clerks, Inspectors, Collectors, Surveyors, &c.* are scarce Inferiour to the usual Establishment of *Guards* and *Garrisons* in Time of Peace, either in *Number* or *Charge*, and have always been looked upon as not much less *dangerous* to our *Liberties*; and are *Troops*, whose Number and Pay *is augmented* and *reduced* at the pleasure of their Superiours, without Application to *Parliament*.

If any Thing can equal the Author's Reasoning for keeping up this *Standing Army*, it is his Arguments against the *farther Reduction* of the Interest of the Funds, lest it should put a Check to our *present Luxury*, and we should be the terrible Example of a Kingdom, undone by *Frugality*: such Reasons as these, he may be very secure, will for ever remain unanswered.

I did not intend to have troubled the Reader any farther, but that I find I have forgot to take Notice of the great Advantages this Writer says the Publick received by the *Increase* of our Debts in one Instance; which was the *Subscription of the Annuities for Terms of Years*, in order to make them *Redeemable*.

I hope I shall be indulged, upon this Occasion, in a few Observations upon this *destructive Project*; from which we may at least reap this Advantage, to be *warned* by *Errors*, that had almost proved *fatal* to us, to avoid the like Dangers.

I believe there is no better Way of doing this, than to

 resolve,

resolve, upon all Occasions, to make some use of our own *Understandings,* and not blindly to give into any *Proposal* from an Opinion, that Men, who are at the *Head* of *Societies* or *Employments,* are always the *best,* or *only Judges* of the Affairs under their Direction: We ought no doubt to pay a just and due Deference to them, by willingly and readily receiving any *Proposals* from them; but it is our Duty to consider, and examine them with the same Care and Caution, as if they came from Persons of less Note and Eminence; for a little Observation upon Ancient or Modern Times will tell us, that the great *Distinction* of one Man above another is sometimes owing to the *Corruption of the Heart,* and not always to the *Clearness of the Head.*

But nothing is more necessary, than for us to be upon our Guard, against pretended *Confidences,* and *secret Motives,* to influence us to Actions which our Reason does not approve; in which the Experience of most Men, who have lived any time in the World, will satisfie them, that they have commonly been deceived and misled: and if this Hint prevents them from falling into the like *Weaknesses,* it will abundantly make them amends for the *little Shame* such Reflections may give them.

There are few Things so intricate in Business, but a little Attention will enable us to judge of them; and they, who are often thought to understand them best, are sometimes most Mistaken.

There cannot, I believe, be a plainer Instance of this, than in the prevailing Opinion, which I heard was the great Temptation to the *South-Sea* Scheme; *That it was in vain to think of any* Reduction, *unless the* Annuities *could be made* Redeemable. But has not Experience shewn us, that the Publick had no more Reason to be afraid of their advanced Price at Market, than at the Rise of the Value of Land, in which no Body is concerned but the Buyer and Seller? for the Publick could pay no more than the *certain Annuities.* As to the Point of *Credit,* That would and, it is plain, hath an Influence upon them, in *raising* and *falling* their Value in Proportion to other Things: but the *Annuities* would have had little or no Effect upon the *Credit* in general, and in all probability much less than they have now, by their being changed from the *settled Estates* they generally were; and this I believe would be found true, if they were now all *unsubscribed.* This Mistake would however have been of less Consequence, if it had not drawn on another more mischievous, which was, that all *Arts* were set on foot, and encouraged to engage the *Proprietors* of these *Annuities* to *subscribe* them, by magnifying imaginary Benefits, instead of providing such as had a real and solid Foundation; by which only Justice could have been done to the *Subscribers,* and the *Publick,* who were to receive no less than a Sum of *seven Millions,* for a *Liberty* to the *Proprietors* of the publick Debts, to unite themselves into one Body.

But may we not now ask, out of what was this great Sum to be raised, unless the *Subscribers Properties?* For bateing the *Assiento* Contract, and the *Fishery,* I never heard of any Advantages they were to have but the Profits of a *Colony* abroad, which may be truly called an Estate in *Terra incognita;* and this afterwards refused them: and these Grants were to enable them to pay *seven Millions,* and an Interest to the Proprietors *equivalent* to the advanced Price of the Stock.

This shews us that the Case would have been very little altered, if the *Bank* had succeeded in this great Struggle. For can any Man think that a little extending of their Credit in *Loans,* and *Discounting Bills of Exchange,* &c. would have enabled them to have paid *five Millions,* and an *Interest* to their Proprietors in Proportion to the advanced Price of their *increased Capital?* By this we may likewise learn, that the Opposition to the *South-Sea,*

41 in

in favour of the *Bank,* was not quite so *meritorious* as it has been thought; for the encouraging the Contentions between the *two Companies,* for Reasons that are no Secrets, was no small Cause of the Madness, which followed from an Opinion of the unerring Wisdom and Prudence of *one* of these Bodies.

And the Proposers and Encouragers of these *Chimerical Schemes* were thought to be Men of great *Knowledge* and *Understanding* in these Things.

I am not so uncharitable, as to distrust that the great Motive to this Design was the Hopes of gaining a considerable Sum, towards the Discharge of the *National Debt;* for surely there is no *Minister,* but must wish and have a Pleasure to see it *decreased* under his Administration; and I hope it will be no Reflection to say, that there was some Prospect of Advantage to the *Contrivers,* and *Managers* of it; for no Man is so foolish and unreasonable, as to grudge *any Ministry* a just Share in the Benefit of Things, that are proposed and conducted by them for the Good of the Publick.

And something of this Kind might have been made very beneficial to the Kingdom, if too much Regard had not been shewn to a *cunning, designing Money-Jobber* (who I, have been assured, stole the *Project* from *another,* and then spoiled it by his Alterations) from a common mistaken Opinion, that because such Men are conversant and acquainted with the Tricks of *Stock-jobbing,* and the low Arts of *Usury,* and have possibly been found useful in that Way, that they are therefore proper Judges of all *Affairs* relating to *Money:* But these Mens notions of Things seldom reach beyond their own narrow Experience and Practice, without the necessary Principles of general Knowledge to direct their Reasonings, which are usually biassed with little Views of their own Gain. It is not therefore to be wondered at, that they should mislead all those who listen to them, or trust them in Points of a

*National Concern;* in which they are generally miserably ignorant, as the *unfortunate Event* in this Case has sufficiently shewn.

For it is not natural to suppose, that the *Directors* themselves foresaw that Deluge of Misery and Mischief, which they were bringing upon the Kingdom; and, in Consequence of it, their own Ruin, (as it might have been very reasonably expected:) but it was *boundless Avarice,* with *Ignorance* and *Inability* to conduct an Affair so much above their *Capacity,* that led them into the *monstrous Measures* they pursued; and for which the *Managers* could not be too much punished, because of the numberless variety of Villanies which they committed in the Execution of this *Project:* and this was followed with a Proceeding, the sad Effects whereof my self, with many other *unhappy Families,* have long felt; though I have but very lately met with the Particulars in Print; which whoever reads will find as *extraordinary* as any Part of the *Proceedings* upon this *delusive Scheme:* I mean the *TREATY* between the *two Companies,* for the mutual Support of each other; which appears to have been carried on with the greatest *Deliberation,* and concluded in the most *Solemn Manner,* before Witnesses of *great Rank* and *Figure;* and the *AGREEMENT* then *Authentically published.* The many unhappy Families, who had hitherto escaped the general Madness, and were by this means involved in the *common Ruin,* is too well known, and too melancholy a Consideration to be enlarged upon; especially by those, who owe their *Misfortunes* to this *unexampled Transaction,* and cannot therefore speak of it with the *Decency* due to *some Persons,* who appear to have been concerned in it. I shall therefore leave it to the Reflections of every Man who will take the trouble to read it, in a late printed *Case of the Directors,* who, whatever their Inclinations might be, yet, one may believe, would scarce dare to publish a *Falsehood* in this particular.

I shall only add, that as *Faith* and *Justice* are the only Bonds of human Society, and the Foundation of all Government, and I have never yet met with any Reasons for the *Violations* of them, for any publick Good, or Conveniency, I should be glad to be informed, in what Cases our *Modern Politicks* make this allowable and necessary; that we may be upon our Guard when to expect them.

After this short View of this *unhappy Project*, and the *Calamities* attending it; I believe it will not be unacceptable to the Reader, to see what the Condition of the Publick would have been at this Time, in regard to the *National Debt*, in case no other Measures had been pursued, but a strict Application of the *Funds* appropriated by Parliament for the Paying these Debts, with the *Additions* which have been made to them by the *Reduction* of the *Interest* to *five per Cent.* which, no Body will deny, would have been very easily effected *without* this Project.

To make this as clear as I can, I have distinguished the *Debt* under the two Heads, by which they are usually called; The *Redeemable*, and *Irredeemable;* the case of the *one* being so very different from the *other*, that it will not otherwise be easy to make any *Estimate* or *Comparison* of the *Advantages* or *Disadvantages*, which have arisen to the Publick by this *Scheme*, which was once so much applauded by all Parties; for they who, since the unhappy Success of it, condemn it most, yet, as I am informed, made *no Objection* to the *Project* it self, when it was *proposed*, but only contended *who* should have the Honour of executing it.

In the *Account* No. 3. is a *View of the whole Debt*, under the *two Heads* before mentioned, as it stood at the Year 1715, when the *Sinking Fund* commences, with the *Addition* of the *Debts* for Services *before* that Time, but adjusted *since*. The only Difference between this and the former *State* is, that, in this Account I have set down the whole Sum allowed to the *Adventurers* by the Acts of

 Parliament

Parliament upon the *four Lotteries*, to prevent the Confusion that would have arisen by breaking into the Produce of these *Funds* from their first Establishment, the *Credit* whereof is taken into the *Account*.

By this *State* it appears, that in case the respective *Funds* appropriated by Parliament to the Payment of the *Redeemable Debt*, with the *saving* by the *Reduction* of the *Interest* to *five per Cent.* had been applied to the Payment of it, the *Debt* remaining at *Michaelmas* last would have been no more than *thirty Millions, nine hundred sixty-five thousand, eight hundred seventy-two Pounds.*

And, without any other *Addition* to the *Funds*, upon the Credit whereof this Money was first borrowed, or any *Improvement* of them, but the *Falling in* of the *Funds* for the *nine per Cent. Annuities*, and the *Lottery* 1710, after the Payment of the *Debt* upon them, at the End of *sixteen Years* from *this Time*, this remaining Debt of *thirty Millions, nine hundred sixty-five thousand, eight hundred seventy-two Pounds*, would be paid off in less than *twenty Years.* But if we take in the *Additions* made to the *Sinking Fund* by *unappropriated Money*, and some *accidental Improvements*, without any Regard to the *South-Sea Project*, and consider that in this Case the Principal Money would have been paid off weekly at the *Exchequer*; I believe it may be truly affirmed, that this Debt would have been paid off in *eighteen Years*, and there would have been above *three and thirty Millions* less raised upon the People at *five per Cent.* by the Ceasing of all those *Duties* and *Taxes* for the *Redeemable Debt*, that, according to the *Author of the Essay's* Calculation, must be continued *ten Years* longer to Discharge the *National Debt*; and comparing this with our present Circumstances, it increases our melancholy Reflections, to think that in case any Part of these Debts had been *Reduced* to *Four per Cent.* (and what Reasons are there to believe they might not?) they would then have been paid off in a shorter time.

 But

But we may, even from these unhappy Mistakes, receive this Comfort, That the *Payment* of the National Debt is by no means *desperate*, as I have heard some are pleased to suggest; for it is evident from these Accounts, that many now living will have the Satisfaction to see their Country discharged from this Burthen, with *Justice* and *Honour*, in case the Produce of the *Sinking Fund* is constantly and inviolably applied, as it arises towards the Payment of it; and this will not only give new Life to our *Credit*, by the daily *Decrease* of our Debt, but put these Kingdoms into such a State of Prosperity at home, and give us that Consideration and Influence abroad, as was never known in any former Age; and we may hope will be a sufficient Encouragement to us, to struggle with any Difficulties, rather than make the least *Addition* to it.

But supposing the Interest to continue at *Five per Cent.* the present legal Interest, we should in the Year 1744, or there-abouts, have no other Debt subsisting, but the *Long Annuities*, and the greatest Part of them, as I mentioned before, would have continued in the Nature of *settled Estates*, and few of them been brought to Market: but the *Alteration* of them, by the *South-Sea Subscription*, has thrown *twelve Millions, seven hundred thousand Pounds* into it, to increase the detestable Trade of *Stock-Jobbing*.

And one *fourth* Part of the Time of these *Annuities*, one with another, being elapsed, the Nation was sure to be discharged of this Debt at the End of a Term, not much above the common Age of Man: and, as we have no Way to judge of the *future*, but by the *past*, if Things go on as they have done, there is no great Certainty of their being now redeemed *sooner*; and Posterity must determine, whether they would not have had greater Obligations to us, if by this Debt, being left in the State it was first contracted, some Part at least of the *Revenues* of the Kingdom had not been in the Power of their Fathers to have mortgaged even beyond that time; and if some

Stop is not put to the *increasing* our Debts, they will soon so much affect every Gentleman's Estate in *Great-Britain*, as to deserve a Consideration in their *Settlements*, as well as any *other Incumbrance*: for, I believe, it will not be denied that, under the present *Land-Tax* of *two Shillings*, and considering the great Variety of *Duties* upon almost all the Necessaries used in a Family, there is scarce a Gentleman, who spends a *thousand Pounds* a Year, who does not pay near *three hundred Pounds in* Taxes.

And till the National Debt is paid off, this is a *real Mortgage* upon the Estates of the Kingdom: for I will, for once, suppose, what idle unthinking People may have sometimes said, (but no sober Man, I am confident, ever did or will think) that when the Bulk of our *increasing Debt* is become too burthensome, there is a *short Way* to get rid of it. Well, admit this to be done: no Man, in his Wits, can imagine that it is to be attempted without a *total Subversion of the Constitution*; and can he be so silly as to think that the Power, which is sufficient to do this, will not be able to seize these *Revenues*? nay, that there will not be an absolute necessity of doing it, to support this Act of *Injustice* and *Violence*?

And, what will be the Condition of the Kingdom then, but that all these numerous *Duties* and *Taxes*, will, in the *literal* and most *extensive* Sense, become *perpetual* and without Hopes of *Redemption for ever*? Let us therefore turn our Thoughts which way we please, we shall find that there is neither *Probability* nor *Possibility* for us to transmit our Estates to our Children without these Incumbrances, nor to secure to them the Possession of them, but by *Paying off the National Debt*; which, if we had not hearkened to the vain and chimerical Pretences of *Ministers, to pay off Debts without Money*; or, which is the same Thing, to pay a *great Sum* with a *little Money*, it is plain most of the *present Age* might have had the happiness to have seen almost discharged: and it might then

 have

have been hoped, that the Smart they had felt, and the Danger they had escaped, would have produced *one Law more*, which, I have heard, was once proposed, and seems necessary to make the rest worth preserving: *That, unless in case of an* Invasion, *it should be* Capital *for any* Minister *to create* a greater Expence *in any one Year, than what the* Money *actually raised by the* Provisions *made for the Service of that Year would pay*. This would not only restrain them from running into *wanton* and *unnecessary* Profusions, but oblige them to preserve some *Decency* at least, in proposing *Funds* to the Parliament, and not to name the first Thing which any *idle Projector* puts into their Heads, without any Regard or Concern whether it will be *deficient* or not, because they think the *publick Faith* in general is always at hand, to be a *Security* for their *Follies* and *Extravagancies*. There have indeed been *Profligates* in all *Ages*, who spend their Estates without any Regard for their Posterity; but the *Body* of the Gentlemen of a Nation must certainly be perswaded, that to leave a *secure* and *flourishing Inheritance* to their Families, is infinitely preferable to any *uncertain temporary* Advantages from *Places, Employments*, &c. by which they themselves become *dependant* in their Life-time, and their *Children* may be made *Beggars* and *Slaves* after them; who, not being secure that they shall be *equally fortunate* in the Smiles of the *Ministers* of their Times, may, with the most sensible Grief and Regret, feel the Weight of their *Fathers Compliances*.

It is well known, that That once Great and August Body the *Senate of Rome*, to whose Empire the greatest Part of the then known World was either subject or dependant, fell from this high State, and became the most abject *Slaves* to their *Emperours*, humoured and gratified them in all the mad *Caprices*, and *wild Extravagances*, which unbridled Lust, and licentious Power could think of. Yet, in their utmost Degeneracy, they kept firm to



one

one Point, to preserve *inviolable their own Properties*, and those of the *Roman People;* of which there cannot be a more remarkable Instance, than in the Reign of the *best of Men and Princes, Marcus Antoninus:* for notwithstanding the *Revenues* of the Empire, as it is well known, had been considerably diminished by the unavoidable Wars carried on by himself and his Predecessors, (Emperours likewise of great *Frugality* and *Virtue*) and the People of *Rome* were terrified with a fresh Breaking out of the *Germanick War;* a War which of all others they dreaded most; yet They would not supply him with on *Obolus* towards this *Expedition*, though they had Money to spare to buy all the *rich Furniture, Jewels,* and *Rarities* of the *Imperial Cabinet, Pictures,* and *Statues,* even to the *Habits* of the *Emperour* and *Empress,* which this Emperour was forced to *sell,* to enable him to carry on this War; and, after the Conclusion of it, This good Prince, by a *Frugal Management* of his Treasury, saved Money to *re-purchase* every Thing which he had sold in this Necessity; that he might have the Satisfaction to leave the Succession of the Empire in the *same Splendour* he received it.

To the *different Condition,* which it appears, by the *State* before-mentioned, that we might have been in, to what we now are, with regard to our *Debts,* I must add, that, in case the *Funds* had continued as they were first appropriated, we should have avoided the great *Inconveniences* and *Hazards* we are liable to, by the *Alteration* of the antient established Manner of Paying off the *Loans Weekly* at the *Exchequer;* by which Method, as is before observed there would not only have been a *considerable Saving of Interest,* but every *Lender* would have been a very good *Inspector,* for the Publick as well as himself, into the *Produce* of each particular *Fund,* by reason his *Interest* ceased the Moment there was Money in the *Exchequer* to pay him off. And when any of the *Duties* had discharged the Money lent upon them, the *Surplus*

 plainly

plainly appeared at the Foot of the *Register*, without going to another Place to state an Account what it was.

But it is well known that it is otherwise now; for the *Companies* trouble themselves no farther than to receive their *Annual Interest* without any Enquiry after a *Surplus* towards the *Discharge* of their *Principal*, which is not their Business to look into.

And, as far as I can guess, by the Papers delivered to the *House of Commons*, and some other Informations, the stating the Accounts of the *Surplusses* which make the *Sinking Fund*, is looked upon as no small *Mystery*, nor a very *easy Task;* since four or five Months are taken to collect the *necessary Papers* from the *several Offices*, as it is said, to enable them to adjust the *Ballance* of it: and neither the *Original Papers* from which it is made, nor any *authentick Certificate* from the respective Offices, do appear to the *House* to *support* and *justify* Accounts of this very great Consequence which I believe every Body now wishes there had been; since it would have prevented *Mistakes* that have been committed in them; for it is plain that there is an Omission of no less than *one Million, five hundred thousand Pounds*, in the Account of the *Sinking Fund*, there being no Notice taken of the *five hundred thousand Pounds*, raised of the *Lottery* 1719, for paying off *Exchequer Bills*, nor of the *Million Exchequer Bills* made out for the *Navy Debt*, and without Supplying these Defects, every Body who tries, will find (as I did) that neither the Account of the *Publick Debt*, nor the *Produce* of the *Sinking Fund* can be *truly stated.*

I believe there is no Wrong yet done to the Publick, because these Sums as I suppose are omitted on both Sides of the Account; for I take it for granted, that the *Total Sum* taken Credit for *Exchequer Bills*, cancelled out of the Money of the *Sinking Fund*, is over and above the *five hundred thousand Pounds*, cancelled by the Money of the *Lottery*. But allowing this (which is only to be

 guessed

guessed at) no Body can say that the *Account* is right; and whoever understands any thing of Accounts, must be sensible that in a little Time, when *Facts* are out of Memory, *other Mistakes* and *Injuries,* from thence may arise to the Publick; for *Errors in Accounts* are of all others most fruitful, and become the more intricate and difficult to be discovered by multiplying one another.

But what is more surprizing, it is now owned, that these are not the *only Mistakes* in these *Accounts;* for since writing this, I have been acquainted with the Reasons given for taking the *one hundred* and *one thousand, eight hundred thirty-five Pounds* before-mentioned, from the last Years produce of the *Sinking Fund,* upon which Occasion I am assured it was publickly acknowledged, in the House of Commons, that they have never yet had any true Account of this *Fund* laid before them; for this Sum of Money, it is said, was taken to make good so much short of the *seven hundred thousand Pounds per Annum,* for his Majesty's *Civil List,* that has arose by a Train of Errors and Mistakes committed every Year, in all the Accounts which have hitherto been made for the *Sinking Fund,* from their very Beginning in the Year 1715, to the last of them in the Year 1725.

I confess this seemed to be very improbable, not to say impossible, considering the great *Penalties* attending the *least misapplication* in this Case; that I could not give any Credit to it, till it was confirmed to me in such a manner, as left me no Room to doubt the Truth of it: when it is considered that the Property of above *fifty Millions* depends upon the Truth and Justice of these Accounts, as well as the only Hopes and Security we have to be freed from this great Load of Debt, we cannot have the least Doubt, that the Guardians of the Properties of the Publick and the People, will omit no Industry nor Endeavours, to examine thoroughly into a Fact of this extraordinary Nature, and vast Importance to the Nation.

 And

And whatever other Consequences it may have, we may be assured that it will not fail to produce such *farther* Laws, as shall be found necessary effectually to prevent the Possibility of such Mistakes in the Accounts of this sacred Treasure, with Directions for making them up in such a plain and clear Method, and to carry such authentick Proof of their Certainty in every Particular along with them, as may remove the least Doubt or Jealousy of the Justice done to the Publick, in a Point in which they are so nearly concerned.

And this will appear to be highly reasonable, when it is considered, that the meanest *Retailer* in the Kingdom, though he can neither write nor read, is yet obliged by a late Act of Parliament, to keep such Books and Accounts, as will satisfie the Officers of the Revenue, to a *Pound of* Coffee *or* Tea *every Day bought or sold by him;* and if through Ignorance, Negligence, or Design, he commits any Mistake, he will incur, and is sure to suffer the Penalty for so doing. And when the Legislature has been thus careful to prevent the Publick's being injured, either by *Mistake* or *Fraud*, in so *small* a Matter as the Duty of a *Pound of* Tea *or* Coffee, it is not to be imagined, they will be *less* circumspect in securing the just and due Application of the *whole Revenues* of the Kingdom; of which the Nation has no other Satisfaction or Assurance, than from the Accounts of the *Sinking Fund.*

*Corruptions* in other Offices, which have been formerly thought to deserve publick Examination, are yet Trifles in comparison of Abuses here, which strike at the very Being of the Constitution; and we have been at a very vain Expence of Blood and Treasure, if these Funds, which have hitherto been looked upon as no small Bulwark of our Safety, should by our fatal Neglect to guard them from the rapacious Hands of any *future Ministers*, become the Means of the Destruction of those Liberties,

 whilst

whilst they are a glorious, though expensive, Monument of our Zeal to preserve them.

But I hope all Apprehensions of this Kind will soon be removed, and the Kingdom will receive the most sensible and convincing Proofs, that we are in earnest in our Resolutions to pay off the *National Debt*, by constantly applying the Produce of the *Sinking Fund*, towards the Discharge of that Part of the Debt, which is more generally known than the *Exchequer Bills*, to the Cancelling whereof it hath been hitherto applied; but as I presume they are now all paid off, I may conclude for the very strong Reasons given by the Author of the *Essay*, that this Money will not be employed to any *other* Use, and whatever now remains in the *Exchequer*, can no way be of greater Service; for it will scarce be denied that even *five hundred thousand Pounds* applied in this manner, will do more towards the Support of the *publick Credit* under any Difficulties, than any Thing that has been done for this Purpose since the Time of contracting the Debt; and this may be no unseasonable Prop to that *lofty Edifice* of *Merit* and *Fame*, which has been built upon it, and which every Well-wisher to his Country heartily desires may prove to be on a *solid* and *lasting* Foundation.

I shall now put an End to what I proposed to say upon this Subject, which will afford many other Reflections, neither proper nor necessary for me to insist upon. I know it would be a very vain Addition to the Trouble I have already given the Reader, to imagine any Professions I can make will obtain the least Indulgence from him farther than he thinks these Papers deserve, I do however assure him that I have taken the best Care I can to prevent any Mistakes; yet as the most careful may err in a Multitude of Figures, I hope he will have the Candor to believe that I have not willingly committed any; for I have no other Expectation of Favour or Credit, but from a strict Observation of *Truth,* and I shall be very glad, if in the pursuit of it, I may have avoided giving any *Offence.*

But as I have been very plain in expressing my Opinion in some Things, which are not agreeable to the Way of thinking that I understand is at present countenanced and encouraged, I have not the folly to think to escape the usual Treatment of *mercenary Malice* upon these Occasions; and I assure them, that they may exert their utmost Talent of Railing, without any Contradiction. I shall however have the Charity to give them one Caution, *viz.* That they do not, out of their great Zeal to abuse these Papers, forget their Duty to his Majesty; for the *Royal Declaration* and *Authority* will fully justify the warmest Concern I have shewn for the *Payment of the National Debt.* But if this should not be a sufficient Protection, as I write neither for *Praise* nor *Reward,* but to satisfy one of the strongest and most laudable Inclinations as well as one of the highest Obligations of human Nature, *Love* and *Duty* to my Country, which I am not in Circumstances to serve any other Way, I shall be contented.

*Æquissimo animo ad honestum consilium per* mediam infamiam *tendere. Nemo mihi videtur pluris æstimare* virtutem, *nemo illi esse magis* devotus, *quam qui* boni viri famam *perdidit, ne* conscientiam *perderet.* Sen.

AS I am thus strongly determined my self, so I hope no Reproaches on the same Account, will ever discourage any of my fellow Subjects, from making use of that *Liberty,* which they are born to as *English-men,* whenever they think it necessary for the Good of their Country; for we can neither expect nor deserve that this Blessing should long continue amongst ourselves, or descend as an

Inheritance to our Children, if we are either *afraid* or *ashamed* to appear in the Defence of it; it is this, and this only, which gives any Man a Title to be ranked amongst *Those*, who are, or desire to be, thought *Lovers* of it; and not the adhering to *vain* and *empty Names*, when the Pretenders of them have manifestly departed from *those* Principles, which first gave them their *Esteem* and *Respect* amongst their fellow Labourers in this *glorious Cause;* and nothing but the extreamest Vanity can make them hope for the *Continuance* of the *same Regard* from them, when they appear to be influenced by *those Principles*, and pursue *those Practices*, which have in all Ages been constantly *opposed* by the *Assertors of Liberty*, and *Lovers of their Country;* who cannot fail to look upon such Men, as *more dangerous*, than the *avowed Patrons* of *Tyranny* and *Arbitrary Power;* which will not change its Nature, nor become less grievous, if it should be brought upon us by *those*, who once joined with us in *Opposing* it.

But it is our own Fault if we are deceived by them, or misled by those, who, for their *Interest*, have blindly given up their *Understanding* and *Consciences* to their Directions; for we have seen such *different Behaviour* of Persons in *different Circumstances* of their Lives, and the most zealous Followers of all *Parties* have so frequently been sacrificed to the least *personal Pique*, or *private View* of their *LEADERS*, that I hope my Country-men will no longer be amused with these *Idle* and *Mischievous Contentions*, set on foot, and encouraged with no other Design, but to *divert* them from attending to Things of *real Concern* to the Publick, and have been hitherto the only Pretence for continuing upon us the great *Expences* and *Dangers* of maintaining so *numerous* and *unusual* a *Standing Army* in time of *Peace*. It is therefore high Time for us to be convinced of our *past Errors*, and put an End to

 these

these *destructive Animosities*, and, without *distinction*, unite in pursuing the *true Interest* of our Country, and in supporting, upon all Occasions, *such Measures* as plainly tend to promote the *Trade* and *Wealth*, and to preserve the *Liberties* of these Kingdoms, in Opposition to all *Endeavours* to entail upon us a Succession of endless Debts, attended with their natural and necessary Consequences, *Poverty*, and *Slavery*.

---

# APPENDIX.

An ACCOUNT of the NATIONAL DEBTS, as which have been made towards the Discharge of 1725. *viz.*

No. I. Debtor.

| | | |
|---|---|---|
| To the Principal Money advanced to the Publick, for the Purchase of Annuities, Granted by several Acts of Parliament, in the Reigns of King *William* and Queen *Anne* for 99 Years | | 9,859,617 07 01 |
| To Ditto, for Annuities for Lives, with the Advantage of Survivorship | | 108,100 00 00 |
| To Ditto, for Annuities on 2 and 3 Lives | | 192,152 06 03 |
| To Ditto, for Annuities at the Rate of 9 *per Cent.* for 32 Years, from *September* 29. 1710. | | 900,000 00 00 |
| To the Principal Sum advanced upon the Lottery, payable in 32 Years from the said *September* 29. 1710. | | 1,500,000 00 00 |
| To satisfy the full sum of 1,328,526 *l* lent by several Bankers to K. *Charles* II. | 664,263 00 00 | |
| To Principal Money remaining unpaid of the Class and 10 *l.* Lotteries payable in 32 Years from *September* 29. 1711. | 4,192,040 00 00 | |
| To Ditto remaining of 2 like Lotteries payable in 32 Years from *Sept.* 29. 1712 | 4,570,585 00 00 | |
| | | 9,426,888 00 00 |
| To Ditto of the Civil List Lottery, payable in 32 Years from *September* 29. 1713. | | 599,190 00 00 |
| To Ditto of the Lottery, payable in 32 Years from *September* 29. 1714. | | 1,812,100 00 00 |
| To the principal Money advanced 1mo. *Geo.* for Annuities at 5 *per Cent.* payable at the Bank of *England*, which by Mistake is put down short 10000*l*, in the first *Exchequer* Accounts, but is rectify'd in all the succeeding Accounts | | 1,079,000 00 00 |
| To the Bank of *England*, for Money advanced on their Original Fund | 1,600,000 00 00 | |
| To Ditto, for Cancelling *Exch.* Bills | 3,775,027 17 10½ | |
| | | 5,375,027 17 10½ |
| Carried forward | | 30,852,075 11 02½ |

they stood, *December* 24. 1716. with all Payments the said Debts, to the Twenty-fourth of *December*,

## No. I. Creditor.

| | | | |
|---|---|---|---|
| By Principal Money paid in Part of the Lottery 1714. by Produce of the said Fund before the Subscription into the *South-Sea* Company | 104,090 00 00 | | |
| By Ditto upon Lottery 1713— | 35,890 00 00 | | |
| | 139,980 00 00 | | |
| By Principal Money paid out of the Produce of the Fund of Lot. 1714. in part of the Sum not subscribed to the *S. S.* Com. | 208,400 00 00 | | |
| By Ditto paid in full of Ditto out of the sinking Fund | 95,640 00 00 | | |
| | | 304,040 00 00 | |
| By Principal Money paid out of the Produce of the Fund for Lottery 1713. in full of the Sum remaining unsubscribed to the *South-Sea* Company | | 98,310 00 00 | |
| Lotteries 1713, and 1714. paid off | | | 542,330 00 00 |
| By Lottery Annuities Unsubscribed to the *South-Sea* Company, paid out of the sinking Fund | | | 1,204,786 03 04½ |
| By Bank Annuities at 5 *per Cent.* Unsubscribed, paid out of Ditto | | | 235,297 18 04 |
| Carried forward | | | 1,982,414 01 08½ |

An ACCOUNT of the NATIONAL DEBTS, as which have been made towards the Discharge of 1725, *viz.*

No. I. Debtor.

| | | | |
|---|---|---|---|
| Brought forward | | | 30,852,075 11 02½ |
| To the *East-India* Com. for the Money advanced by them | | | 3,200,000 00 00 |
| To the *South-Sea* Company for Money advanced at several times by them | | | 10,000,000 00 00 |
| To *Exchequer* Bills remaining Uncancelled | | | 2,561,025 00 00 |
| Total Sum | | | 46,613,100 11 02½ |
| To the foregoing Total must be added the following sums, which, though adjusted since, were for Services performed before *December* 24. 1716. *viz.* | | | |
| Deficiency of Grants, 1716. | | 509,127 05 06 | |
| To pay Bills of Exchange on Account of the Expedition to *Canada* | | 24,195 18 01 | |
| Deficiency on the Duty on Candles | | 346,793 07 10 | |
| Ditto, on low Wines | | 66,812 09 02 | |
| *Ed. Clent* Esq; for an Army Debent. lost | | 585 07 01 | |
| | | 947,514 07 08 | |
| To Army Debentures | | 2,152,927 00 07¾ | |
| To Debentures for Sufferers at *Nevis* and *St. Christophers* | | 141,093 15 01¼ | |
| To the Equivalent due to the Kingdom of *North-Britain* | | 248,550 00 09 | |
| To a Deficiency of the Duty on Hops, Anno 1711. | | 12,480 09 01 | |
| To Ditto on the *East-India* Company's Fund for several Years, computed to *Michaelmas* 1719 | | 191,028 16 06½ | |
| | | 3,693,594 09 09½ | |
| To the Navy Debt to 31 *Dec.* 1716 | 1,043,336 19 09¾ | | |
| To an Encrease of the said Debt since this Ac. as appears by the 2 Sums on the other side, which have been paid in discharge thereof | 290,902 16 03½ | | |
| | | 1,334,239 16 01¼ | |
| | | | 5,027,834 05 10¾ |
| | | | 51,640,934 17 01¼ |

they stood *December* 24. 1716. with all Payments the said Debts, to the Twenty-fourth of *December*

## No. I. Creditor.

| | | |
|---|---|---|
| Brought forward | | 1,982,414 01 08½ |
| By *Exchequer* Bills paid out of the sinking Fund | | 2,561,025 00 00 |
| By a Deficiency in the Duty on Hops, *An.* 1711. paid out of Ditto | | 12,480 09 01 |
| Dy Do. of the *East-India* Fund, Ditto | | 191,028 16 06½ |
| By Navy Debt in Part of said Debt to *Dec.* 31. 1716. by Annuities at 4 *per Cent. per Act* 3° *Georgii*, for Redeeming 4 Lotteries. | 334,239 16 01¼ | |
| By Ditto in further Part of said Debt by *Excheq.* Bills out of the sinking Fund | 1,000,000 00 00 | |
| | | 1,334,239 16 01¼ |
| | | 6,081,188 03 05¼ |
| Balance is the Debt provided for or incurred before *Decemb.* 31. 1716. which remains unsatisfied | | 45,559,746 13 08 |
| | | 51,640,934 17 01¼ |

## A State of the National Debt, as it stood *Decemb.*

since *Dec.* 24. 1716. with the Sums which have been Paid in Part scriptions to the *South-Sea* Company, *&c.*

### No. II. Debtor.

| | | | |
|---|---|---|---|
| To the Bank of *England* — | | 5,375,027 17 10½ | |
| To Ditto for Part of the *S. Sea* Capital transferr'd to them | | 4,000,000 00 00 | |
| | | | 9,375,027 17 10½ |
| To the *East India* Company | | | 3,200,000 00 00 |
| To the *S. S.* Comp. for their Cap. Stock as now augmented by Subscriptions pursuant to Acts of Parl. of 5 & 6 *Georgii* | | 16,901,241 17 00 | |
| To *South-Sea* Annuities —— | | 16,901,241 17 00 | |
| | | | 33,802,483 14 00 |
| To the following Capital Sums payable at the *Excheq.* which were not subscrib'd to the *S. Sea* Comp. *viz.* | | | |
| Annuities for 99 Years —— | | 1,837,533 00 09 | |
| Annuities with Benefit of Survivorship —— | | 108,100 00 00 | |
| Annuities on 2 and 3 Lives — | | 192,152 06 03 | |
| | | | 2,137,785 07 00 |
| Annuities at 9 *per Cent.* for 32 Years | | 161,108 06 08 | |
| Annuities on Lottery 1710. Ditto | | 111,512 04 05¼ | |
| | | | 272,620 11 01¼ |
| Part of 110,312 17 04 for Navy Annuities —— | | 2,510 00 00 | |
| Part of 947,514 07 08 Tallies of Sol. 3 *Geo.* —— | | 198,958 08 03 | |
| P. of 1,603,987 08 01½ Army Debent. certified to 21 *March* 1719 as by 6 *Geo.* | 393,194 14 05½ | | |
| More since —— | 548,939 12 06¼ | | |
| | | 942,134 06 11¾ | |
| Annuities on the Plate Act. 6. *Geo.* | | 312,000 00 00 | |
| *Nevis* Debentures —— | | 141,093 15 01¼ | |
| New Churches —— | | 380,787 00 00 | |
| Part of 500,000 *l.* for 1st. Lot 1719. | | 58,300 00 00 | |
| Part of 500,000 *l.* for 2d. Lot. 1719 | | 65,395 00 00 | |
| | | | 2,101,178 10 04 |
| To *Exc.* Bills lent the *S. Sea* Comp. | | 1,000,000 00 00 | |
| To Ditto pursuant to Act 8. *Geo.* towards the Navy Debt | | 1,000,000 00 00 | |
| To Ditto pursuant to Act 9. *Geo.* to redeem Annuities | | 1,000,000 00 00 | |
| | | | 3,000,000 00 00 |
| To the Civil List Debt —— | | | 1,000,000 00 00 |
| Equivalent due to the Kingdom of *North-Britain* | | | 248,550 00 09 |
| The Debt of the Navy at *Decemb.* 1725 —— | | | 1,255,491 09 04¾ |
| | | | 56,393,137 10 05½ |

## 24 1725. in which is included the Debt contracted thereof, and the Alterations made in the National Debts by the Sub-

### No. II. Creditor.

| | | |
|---|---|---|
| By the Principal Sum remaining unpaid of the Debt due *Decemb.* 24. 1716. as appears by the foregoing Account | | 45,559,746 13 08 |
| By the following Sums paid off at the *Exchequer* viz. | | |
| Navy Annuities | 2,510 00 00 | |
| 1st Lottery, 1719. | 58,300 00 00 | |
| 2d Lottery, 1719. | 65,395 00 00 | |
| Loans on Coals for New Churches about | 285,152 00 00 | |
| | | 411,357 00 00 |
| By *Excheq.* Bills supposed to be Cancell'd out of the Money rais'd for this Purpose, in the Year 1719. by a Lottery on the Sinking Fund, tho' it does not appear in any Account | 500,000 00 00 | |
| By D° out of Money repaid by the *S. S.* C. | 1,000,000 00 00 | |
| By Ditto out of the Sinking Fund | 610,341 17 09¾ | |
| | | 2,110,341 17 09¾ |
| By Balance remaining upon the Account of the Sinking Fund at *Michaelmas* 1725. applicable to this Service | | 547,654 03 10 |
| | | 48,629,099 15 03¾ |
| Balance is the Debt *increased* since *December* 1716. over and above all Payments out of the Sinking Fund, *&c.* | | 7,764,037 15 01¾ |
| | | 56,393,137 10 05½ |

A View of that Part of the NATIONAL DEBT have been applyed towards the Payment of it, out of the ment for this Service, and the Savings by the Reduction *Michaelmas* 1726, in Case no Alteration had been made in

## No. III. Debtor.

| | | |
|---|---|---|
| To the Bank of *England* | | 5,375,027 17 10½ |
| To the *East-India* Company | | 3,200,000 00 00 |
| To the *South-Sea* Company | | 10,000,000 00 00 |
| To *Exchequer* Bills Uncancell'd, 1715 | | 2,561,025 00 00 |
| To 4 Lotteries of the 9th and 10th of the Queen and Bankers Debt. *viz.* | | |
| 10*l*. Lottery, 1711. | 1,928,570 00 00 | |
| Class Lottery, 1711. | 2,602,200 00 00 | |
| 10*l*. Lottery, 1712. | 2,341,740 00 00 | |
| Class Lottery, 1712. | 2,341,990 00 00 | |
| Bankers Debt | 664,263 00 00 | |
| | | 9,878,763 00 00 |
| To Civil List Lottery, 1713. | | 633,010 00 00 |
| To Lottery, 1714. *viz.* | | |
| Blanks | 1,157,360 00 00 | |
| Prizes | 719,040 00 00 | |
| | | 1,876,400 00 00 |
| To 5 *per Cent.* Annuities 1mo *Georgii* | | 1,079,000 00 00 |
| Carried forward | | 34,603,225 17 10½ |

called Redeemable, with the Sums which might
Produce of the respective Funds, appropriated by Parlia-
of Interest, with the State of it as it would have stood at
it by the *South-Sea* Scheme.

## No. III. Creditor.

| | |
|---|---|
| By the Produce of 270,999*l.* 7*s.* *per Annum*, appropriated to the paying off, and cancelling principal *Exchequer* Bills from *Michaelmas* 1715, to *Michaelmas* 1726. 11 Years. | 2,980,992 17 00 |
| By Interest saved upon Two Millions of *Exchequer* Bills, cancelled by the Bank at *Christmas* 1717, for which they received an Annuity of 5*l.* *per Cent.* the Expence before being 7*l.* 4*s.* *per Cent.* but reckoning only a saving of 40,000 *per Annum*, for 8¾ Years, to *Michaelmas* 1726, is | 350,000 00 00 |
| By a Saving on the Remainder of the principal *Exchequer* Bills, being 2,561,025, the Charge whereof was reduced from 7*l.* 4*s.* to about 4*l.* 10*s.* *per Cent.* which at least makes a Saving of 2*l.* 10*s.* *per Cent.* or 64,025*l.* 12*s.* 6*d.* *per Annum*, which for the same time is | 560,224 04 04½ |
| By 100,000 *per Annum*, on reducing the Interest on the *South-Sea* Company's Original Stock of Ten Millions from 6 to 5 *per Cent.* at *Midsummer* 1718, for 8¼ Years to said *Michaelmas* 1726. | 825,000 00 00 |
| By 17,750*l.* 9*s.* 7*d.* ½ *per Annum*, on reducing the Interest of 1,775,027*l.* 17*s.* 10*d.* ½ from 6*l.* to 5*l.* *per Cent.* for the same time, being an Allowance to the Bank of *England* for *Exchequer* Bills, which they formerly cancelled. | 140,441 09 05 |
| Carried forward | 4,862,658 10 09½ |

A View of that part of the NATIONAL DEBT, have been applied towards the Payment of it, out of the ment for this Service, and the Savings by the Reduction *Michaelmas* 1726, in Case no Alteration had been made in

No. III. Debtor.

| | |
|---|---|
| Brought forward | 34,603,225 17 10½ |
| To several Sums incurred for Services performed before the 24 of *Dec.* 1716, altho' adjusted and provided for since that time as by Particulars in the foregoing Account | 3,693,594 09 09½ |
| To the Navy Debt as it stood in *Dec.* 1716 | 1,334,239 16 01¼ |
| | 39,631,060 03 09¼ |

The Debt called Irredeemable.

| *Per Annum.* | | | |
|---|---|---|---|
| 667,278 06 06¼ | Annuities for long Terms | 9,859,617 07 01 | |
| 7,567 00 00 | Annuities on Survivorship | 108,100 00 00 | |
| 20,833 10 03 | Annuities for 2 & 3 Lives | 192,152 06 03 | |
| 695,678 16 09½ | —¼ part of this time is elapsed— | | 10,159,869 13 04 |
| 81,000 00 00 | Annuities at 9*l. per Cent.* for 32 Years from *Michaelmas* 1710. | 900,000 00 00 | |
| 135,000 00 00 | Lottery 1710, for the same time | 1,500,000 00 00 | |
| 216,000 00 00 | ½ of this time is elapsed at *Michaelmas* 1726. | ———— | 2,400,000 00 00 |
| 911,678 16 09½ | *Per Annum.*--Total—Principal— | | 12,559,869 13 04 |

called Redeemable, with the Sums which might
Produce of the respective Funds, appropriated by Parlia-
of Interest, with the State of it as it would have stood at
it by the *South-Sea* Scheme.

## No. III. Creditor.

| | |
|---|---|
| Brought forward | 4,862,658 10 09 |
| By the following Sums which would have been paid off at *Michaelmas* 1726, in part of the Principal Money advanced on the Lotteries under-mentioned out of the respective Funds, appropriated to each Lottery, *viz.* | |
| Two Lotteries 1711. | 1,588,117 08 00 |
| Two Lotteries 1712. | 1,603,537 13 00 |
| Lottery 1713. | 160,941 03 00 |
| Lottery 1714. | 449,932 14 00 |
| | 8,665,187 08 09 |
| Redeemable Debt which would have remained unsatisfied at *Michaelmas* 1726. | 30,965,872 15 00¼ |
| | 39,631,060 03 09¼ |

An ACCOUNT of the Yearly Sum, which at *Michaelmas* 1726, would have been applicable to the Discharge of the redeemable Debts, in Case no Alteration had been made in them by the *South-Sea* Subscription, *viz.*

No. IV.

| | | *Per Annum.* |
|---|---|---|
| The Sum appropriated to the paying off and cancelling principal *Exchequer* Bills by Acts of the 7*th* and 12th of Queen *Anne.* | | 270,999 07 00 |
| Interest saved upon Two Millions of *Exchequer* Bills cancelled by the Bank at *Christmas* 1717, for which they received an Annuity of five *per Cent.* the Expence provided for before, being Seven Pounds Four Shillings *per Cent.* but reckoning the Saving only at two *per Cent.* is | | 40,000 00 00 |
| Interest saved on the Remainder of *Excheq.* Bills being 2,561,025*l.* the Charge whereof was reduced from Seven Pounds Four Shillings *per Cent.* to about Four Pounds Ten Shillings *per Cent.* or | | 64,025 12 06 |
| Interest saved on reducing the *South-Sea* Original Capital of Ten Millions from Six to Five *per Cent.* at *Midsummer* 1718 | | 100,000 00 00 |
| Interest saved on reducing the Interest from Six to Five *per Cent.* at the same time on 1,775,027*l.* 17*s.* 10*d.* ½ *Exchequer* Bills, formerly cancelled by the Bank. | | 17,750 09 07 |
| Lotteries 1711, at *Michaelmas* 1717, when they were reduced from 6*l.* to 5*l. per Cent.* had for their sinking Fund the Sum of | 112,508 07 00 | |
| Which at *Michaelmas* 1726, would have been encreased by the Interest of 1,240,580 10 00 which that Fund had cancelled | 62,029 00 06 | |
| | | 174,537 07 06 |
| Carried forward | | 667,312 16 07 |

## No. IV.

| | | |
|---|---|---|
| Brought forward | | 667,312 16 07 |
| Lotteries 1712, at *Michaelmas* 1717. | 117,316 10 00 | |
| Increased by the Interest of 1,293,597 18 00 which would have been paid off at *Michaelmas* 1726 | 64,679 18 00 | |
| | | 181,996 08 00 |
| Lottery 1713. Sinking Fund | 9,679 12 00 | |
| Interest on 160,945 03 00 which would have been paid off at *Michaelmas* 1726 | 6,437 13 00 | |
| | | 16,117 05 00 |
| Lottery 1714——*Per Annum* | 116,573 12 00 | |
| Now in the *South-Sea* | | |
| At 5 *l. per Cent.* 43,262 10 00 | | |
| At 4 *l. per Cent.* 21,548 16 00 | | |
| | 64,811 06 00 | |
| | | 51,762 06 00 |
| Total | | 917,188 15 07 |

*FINIS.*

A

# DEFENCE

OF AN

# ESSAY

ON THE

# PUBLICK DEBTS

## of this Kingdom, &c.

In Anſwer to a Pamphlet, entitled,

*A State of the National Debt*, &c.

---

By the Author of the ESSAY.

---

*Et Patriæ muros & Te ſervabimus* Hanno.
Sil. Ital.

---

*LONDON:*

Printed for J. PEELE, at *Locke's Head* in *Pater-Noster-Row.* 1727.

# *A* DEFENCE *of an* ESSAY *on the* Publick Debts, *&c.*

IT is now almost Ten Months since I published a Pamphlet, entitled, *An Essay on the Publick Debts of this Kingdom;* a Subject, that notwithstanding the Importance of it, seemed to me to be generally but little understood; and a Subject which farther recommended itself to me upon this Account, That whatever I had to advance about it, as Matter of Fact, might be stated, or corrected, with as much Exactness as I pretended to, from our Acts of Parliament, and with the Evidence of those publick Records; or whatever Inferences I had to make from Facts of this Nature, were generally to be supported by the Certainty of Demonstration. From the same Confinement, on Account of my Health, that was the Occasion of my writing that Essay, I was for some time hindred from knowing the Sense of the Town about it, farther than I could collect it from observing that the Letter-Writer in the *London Journal* had taken me into his Protection, and by his Civilities, as I supposed, exposed me to the Resentments of a Correspondent of Mr. *Mist*, who in great Heat tells his Reader, *that he had not, and would not read me; and that what the* London Journal

Journal *had represented me to say, was false, if that was true which an honest Gentleman, a Neighbour of his in the Country, told him.* I did not from this contemptible Attack upon me, conjecture at any general Sense about my Performance, or yet in the least suspect that my Book was to become the Subject of a Party Dispute amongst us. What I had any where asserted in it, I knew to be true, and, as I thought, had made appear to be so; and whatever I have any where persuaded to, I was induced to it from no Motive in Nature, but that I thought it reasonable. As far therefore as I could presume that any thing which I had advanced was new, or Matter of Information to any Reader, I concluded it would be agreeable to him, whatever Party he was of; with an Exception only to such Persons amongst us, as are too apt, on some Occasions, to betray real Impatience at the Welfare and Prosperity of their own Country; and from whose Dislike of me, as far as I may at any time be known to them, I find no Inclination to withdraw myself.

My Subject, where it led me to speak of our Ministry, furnished me with no just Occasion for complaining of them. But from hence I could not imagine it would be inferred that I wrote to flatter them, or to recommend what might be thought to be their Sentiments in particular, only because they were theirs; and this too against the Evidence of those Proofs to the contrary that might be produced from the Book itself, nay, that in Fact have been produced by the Writers against me themselves, tho' not, as far as I can judge, admitted by them to clear me from this groundless Imputation.

I have carefully reviewed every thing in my Treatise that I have heard objected to, and can't find the least Foundation for that ridiculous Charge upon me, of proposing or recommending the Increase of our Publick Debts. I can defy my Adversaries to produce one single

 Sentence

Sentence truly quoted from me, where I have mentioned it as upon any account eligible, but as the Means of effecting the speedier Reduction of them, and consequently as the least expensive Method to the Publick of supplying their own Necessities.

Let me ask the warmest Patriot, what more could be said about the Inconvenience of misapplying the Sinking Fund, upon the Supposition that it was probable that it would be misapplied, than what might be produced for the same Purpose, in proving that the Misapplication of it was improbable, under the Direction of the present Ministry?

Was it possible for me so long to survey the Burthen of our present Debts without Emotion? Is it true, that I have not frequently expressed my Concern upon this Subject? But yet I must profess myself to believe, and would have the Enemies of *Great-Britain* hear it, "that "her Lands, Estates, Expence and Commerce will yet "easily admit of farther Duties, sufficient to furnish new "Funds to answer the Interest of whatever Sums may "be for the future necessary for her Defence and Safety." And it is with Pleasure that I reflect upon it, that they must soon hear that her Quarrels will be supported without suspending the Provisions made for the Payment of her Debts, or even, as I hope, without any Addition made to them.

Is it to be doubted for the future if the Lands, Estates, Expence and Commerce of *Great-Britain* could yet furnish the Interest of a new Debt upon Emergencies, after the Resolution of her Parliament lately taken to supply the principal Sum that is this Year wanted, beyond our ordinary Supplies, by a further Tax upon Land only, and from one only of those Funds to which I have referred myself?

This is, I think, as much as need to be said in answer to any Exceptions that I have yet seen in print to my

Performance, till the Publication of a late Pamphlet, entitled, *A State of the National Debt,* &c. containing, besides the same general Reflections upon me, which I have hitherto proposed to obviate, a laboured Representation of the State of our Debts at present; by which he would have it understood, at least by his Readers, That in my Essay upon this Subject, I have greatly misrepresented it. As this Author agrees with me, that it very much concerns the Publick to be truly informed in this Particular, he must excuse me, if I take all the Freedom upon this Occasion, that I think is any ways necessary for determining the Question, Whether he or I have deceived, or endeavoured to deceive, the Publick in what either of us have printed upon this Subject.

The most important Debate between the Author and myself, is, Whether our Debts have increased or decreased since the Provisions made for the Reduction of them from the Sinking Fund? Those Provisions I have represented to have been made after the 25th of *December,* 1716. and to have been the Appropriation of what should from thenceforth arise as the Surplusses of several Funds to that Purpose; and I have proceeded to state the Amount of the Publick Debts at *Christmas,* 1717. (before which Time, no Payment of any Part of them was in Fact, or perhaps could be made in Consequence of these Provisions) and then to state (what was then only in my Power) the Amount of our publick Debts at *Christmas,* 1724. and proposed that these different Amounts should be compared together, and their Difference be determined to be the Increase or Decrease of the Publick Debts between those two Periods of Time.

The Author of the *State of our Debts* begins first to differ with me about the Time of the Sinking Fund's Commencement, for a Reason which I could not discover till I read on to the Place* where he charges me with

6 *want*

* *Page* 146.

*want of Truth and Candor, in attempting a sly Compliment, made at the Expence of the Honour and Memory of the Dead, to those whose Merits do not stand in Need of such low Artifices to gild them.* And to support this Charge, he takes Notice, That I have said, that *the first material Provision that was made for discharging the Publick Debts, was by several Acts passed* 3° Georgii; whereas he says, That *the Aggregate Fund* (one of those Funds whose Surplusses are appropriated to the Payment of the Publick Debts) *was established by an Act passed* 1^mo^ Georgii. And *this Aggregate Fund,* he says, *is the first great Branch and Foundation of the Sinking Fund.* From whence it is, as I suppose, that he states the Commencement of the Sinking Fund from *Michaelmas* 1715, the Commencement of the Aggregate Fund, as established by that Act of Parliament, 1^mo^ *Georgii.*

I profess sincerely, that I did not know, nor do yet know, that the Act of Parliament 1^mo^ *Georgii,* and those which I have referred to as passed 3° *Georgii,* were passed under the Direction of different Persons at those different Times in the Management of our Finances. But what Temptation does my Subject offer me to enquire into this Particular? For though the aforesaid Act, 1^mo^ *Georgii,* establishes the Aggregate Fund for the Purposes therein mentioned, it does not establish it for the Purpose of reducing the Publick Debts, nor contain the least Provision, that I know of, for appropriating the Surplus of it to this Purpose in particular. This Appropriation was first made in the Act which I have cited 3° *Georgii,* and was therefore the first Provision for Discharging the Publick Debts, and the first Foundation of what has been since called the Sinking Fund; and from thence therefore, and not from *Michaelmas* 1715, (as this Gentleman would have it) is the Progress or Effect of the Sinking Fund to be computed.

To the Method which I have above-mention'd, for

determining whether our Debts are indeed diminish'd from *Christmas* 1717 (the true Time from whence the Progress of the Sinking Fund is to be computed) to *Christmas* 1724, *viz.* of comparing the Amount of our Publick Debts as they really were at those Two different Times together, and stating the Difference to be the real Decrease of our Publick Debts, I have yet added another, *viz.* of comparing the Amount of the several Articles of Addition to our Publick Debts from one Time to the other, with the Amount of all such Payments, as have within the same Time been made, in Discharge of any Principal Sums of which those Debts consisted; and have stated the Difference of those Amounts to be the real Decrease of our Publick Debts from *Christmas* 1717, to the same Time in the Year 1724. I then thought, and yet think, that these Methods in the proposed Enquiry, were each of them separately the plainest and most intelligible that could be for this Purpose thought of, and true with all the Evidence of a Demonstration. But I have for the Reader's farther Satisfaction, if it could be possibly wanted, by the Use of both these Methods, added a farther Proof of them from their Agreement with each other.

I must leave it therefore to the Reader to judge why this Writer, after professing the same Enquiry with mine, and contradicting me so materially, in his Report about the Matter, upon the Credit of another Method of stating this Account, is pleased to take no other Notice of my Methods of accounting, than to call them* *confused, and disguised with little Shifts and Distinctions made use of for such a Purpose;* or has satisfied himself in declaring me to be so widely and grossly mistaken, as the Ballance of his Accounts have represented me, without attempting to point out the Falshood of any Facts advanced by me in

8 my

* Page 134.

my Accounts, or any of the Shifts he mentions to disguise them, that will any way account for the prodigious Difference between us. After he had found out the Truth, he might have found out too, where I had been mistaken, or, as he charges me, had endeavoured to mislead my Readers; and by these Means, to the Reader's Satisfaction and my Ease, put an End to this Dispute at once, or brought it at least to its proper Issue, upon the Foot of those Accounts which I had proposed for the Purpose of this Enquiry. I had, perhaps, reason to expect that my Accounts or Facts should be examined before they were contradicted; but that he should leave the Reader to chuse his Opinion in a Controversy of this Importance, by suffering the Evidence of my Accounts to remain in full Force against the Truth of his, will, I hope, be a Presumption in Favour of my Accounts, and lead the Reader to infer, that he could not discover the Shifts which he has accused me of, and that he expresses his own Conviction, and not mine, when he says, *That Facts and Figures are the most stubborn Evidences.*

But when I regard the Importance of this Subject, I think myself obliged, however unreasonable it may be in him to expect it of me, to attend this Author through his own Accounts; and endeavour to explain to the Reader the various Mistakes committed in them, as far as such a Task is practicable, in examining Accounts made up of Assertions and States, which are neither true nor false, and where, I begin to perceive, my greatest Difficulty will be to find his Meaning.

The Reader will, I believe, most easily judge of the Plainness, Truth or Evidence of the manner in which these Accounts are carried on, after he has attended to the Design of them, or the Enquiry which he proposes to satisfy from stating of them; and this I believe he would have us understand to be, if our Debts have been increased from *Christmas* 1716 to *Michaelmas* in 1725, and what has been within that Time the real Increase of them; and he explains himself in one Place* by the increased Debt within that Time, to mean *the Sum more than the National Debt would have been at* Michaelmas 1725, *in case no Additions had been made to it since the Year* 1716.

The Sum more than the National Debt would have been at *Michaelmas* 1725, in case no Additions had been made to it since the Year 1716, is plainly the same and no other than the Sum or Amount of the Additions that have been made to it from the Year 1716, to *Michaelmas* 1725; and I could wish that this had been indeed his Meaning, or that he would have confined himself to it. If this had been what he proposed to represent or state to us, he must, I think, have seen immediately that the shortest and plainest Way to do so, was to give us an Account of those particular Sums that, within this Interval of Time, have been added to the Publick Debts, and a Computation of the total Amount of those Additions; nor had any thing that I had advanced been contradicted by his producing 7,764,037*l.* or any greater Sum to be the Amount of those Additions. I have sufficiently described and explained my Enquiry to be after the neat Decrease of the Publick Debts, or the Sum by which the Payments within the Interval of Time which my Accounts refer to, exceed the Additions within the said Time made to them; which might well enough be what I stated it to be, though the Additions were as great as, or greater than he has here described them; nay, the Truth of what I have advanced, if this was all his Meaning, would be, in a great measure, confirmed by his own Accounts; in the first of which he reckons up 6,081,188*l.* as the Amount of several Discharges of the Publick Debt from 1716 to *Michaelmas* 1725; to which in his second Account he adds, as further, within the same Period of Time, discharged of the

10 Publick

* Page 137.

Publick Debt, the Sum of 3,069,353*l.* 2*s.* The Amount of which together to 9,150,541*l.* compared with 7,764,037*l.* will give a considerable Sum for the neat Decrease of the Publick Debts, within the Time which his Accounts refer to, and a greater than I should ask for, if 3,155,158*l.* the Increase of our Debts in the publick Accounts, from the Subscription of the Irredeemables, were allowed me to be no real Increase of the true Quantity of our Incumbrances.

But this Testimony of his about his own Meaning, is too much in my Favour to be depended on from this Author, who has taken so much Pains to prove the Falsehood of what I have advanced about the Publick Debts; and who, referring himself to what he calls the increased Debts, as he has stated it from his own Accounts, tells his Reader,* *That we should differ by upwards of the Sum of six Millions, tho' he should allow me what I have asked from the Subscription of the Irredeemables.*

From hence therefore I have been driven from the Body of his Treatise to the Accounts that he refers to in his *Appendix,* to find what other Meaning he might possibly have in what he calls the *Increase of our Publick Debts.* And here I find the aforesaid Sum of 7,764,037*l.* the Ballance of his second Account, and there described to be *the Debt increased since December,* 1716. *over and above all Payments out of the Sinking Fund,* &c.

Here I must confess myself more at a Loss than ever for the Author's Meaning. The Words in which he has chosen to express himself about the aforesaid Ballance, *that it was the Increase of our Debts, over and above all Payments from the Sinking Fund,* led me to suppose he meant, that all Payments out of the Sinking Fund were a still farther Increase of our Publick Debts, beyond that Ballance. But this Conjecture about his Meaning the Absurdity of it soon removed, and put me upon supposing

 that

* Page 138.

that he would have said, That this Ballance was the neat Increase of our Publick Debts, or the Difference or Excess of the Additions made to them, within the Time that those Accounts refer to, above the Payments in the same Time from the Sinking Fund, &c. But that this should be his Meaning, it was as difficult for me to believe, from the surprising Falshood of it.

In this Perplexity about what this Writer understands himself, or would have us understand by this Ballance of his Accounts, I must propose it to the Reader to look into the Accounts themselves; from which, if we do not find out what he means himself, I am in hopes however we may make out the only Inference that can be truly made from them, and consequently what he only should have meant and recommended to the Belief of his Readers upon the Evidence of these Accounts. And that we may make all the use that can be of this necessary Labour of attending to the various Confusion of what he has here put together for the Purpose of confuting me, I shall endeavour to prove, from the Authority of his own Papers, the Truth of that Particular which I have advanced relating to the Decrease of our Publick Debts, and about which he has taken so much seasonable Pains to contradict me. I shall beg Leave to repeat what I have stated to be the Fact, which he proposes to prove the Falsehood of.

I have said, that from *Christmas* 1716, to the same Time in 1724, (beyond which Time I had no Materials to carry forward this Account) our Publick Debts were diminished by about the Sum of 2,100,000*l.* about which I have both in stating the Design of my Enquiry, and in the manner of proving what I have reported from it, fully explained myself to mean the neat Decrease of our Publick Debts, or the Excess of those Payments by which our Debts had been diminished, beyond those Additions by which they had been within the same Time encreased; and I can

 hardly

hardly believe that my Meaning can have been mistaken, but by Persons, who, like this Gentleman, seem not to understand their own. To bring this State of the Decrease of our Debts within the Reach of all the Evidence that can possibly arise from my Answerer's Computation, I shall carry it forward to *Christmas* 1725, to be nearer the Time that his Accounts refer to: And here I have the Pleasure of informing the Reader, that from *Christmas* 1724. to *Christmas* 1725, by several Payments made, consisting principally of Exchequer Notes from the Income of the Sinking Fund, the neat Decrease of our Debts, clear of a trifling Addition in the same Time made to them upon the Fund for building Churches, was 1,247,152*l.* and which, in order to state the neat Decrease of our Debts from *Christmas* 1717 to *Christmas* 1725, must be added to the same Decrease of 2,100,000*l.* at *Christmas* 1724, and will make it about 3,347,152*l.*

I shall proceed to find how this State of the neat Decrease of our Publick Debts is contradicted by the Accounts before us.

In the first Account referred to in his *Appendix*, (stated by way of *Debtor and Creditor*, as he expresses himself, * *and calls it the most plain and intelligible manner of drawing up Accounts*) in that Column which he entitles *Debtor*, he gives us his State of the Publick Debts, as they stood in *December* 1716. and makes the Amount of them to be 51,640,934*l.* 17*s.* The Author, by mistaking almost equally on both sides of the Question in Debate between us in the particular Articles of the Publick Debt, has produced a Total, to which I have little or no other Exception, but his refusing to allow my Addition to it of the Increase of our Debts in the Exchequer Accounts from the Subscription of the Irredeemables; but this, together

13 with

* Page 135.

with my Exceptions to particular Articles in this Account, I shall reserve for future Notice.

In the Column which he entitles *Creditor,* he has placed several Payments of our Publick Debts, from 1716 to *Michaelmas* 1725, and which, * he says, *are all the Payments, which since that Time have been made at the Exchequer, out of the Produce of any of the Taxes and Duties appropriated to the Payment of any Part of these Debts, and then such farther Sums as have been applied towards the Discharge of them out of the Money of the Sinking Fund, from* Michaelmas 1715, *the Time of its Commencement, to* Michaelmas 1725.

The Ballance of this Account, *thus stated,* he says, (and I must here particularly desire the Reader's Attention) *will be well understood, and undeniably granted to be the Total National Debt which would have been owing at this Time,* viz. *at* Michaelmas 1725, *in case no Addition had been made to it since the 24th of* December, 1716. *And this Sum,* he says, *appears to be* 45,559,746*l.*

The Ballance of this Account, thus stated, the Reader will observe to be the Remainder of 51,640,934*l.* 17*s.* stated by him to be the Amount of our Publick Debts at *Christmas* 1717, after a Deduction of the Amount of such Payments made from that Time to *Michaelmas* 1725, in Discharge thereof, as he has specified on the Credit-side of his Account, and computes to amount to about 6,081,188*l.*

But what he expects here should be undeniably granted him, *viz.* That this Ballance or Remainder is the Total National Debt, which would have been owing at this Time, in case no Additions had been made to it since *December,* 1716, it is most unreasonable to ask, for a plain Reason that could not but lay before him; I mean, that

14 those

* Page 135, 136.

those Payments by the Amount of which he reduces the Publick Debt in 1716. to 45,559,467*l.* were in a great Part made by Money raised, from equal Additions to our Debt made at the same Time, and for the Purpose of making those Payments, and which could not have been made, if those Additions had not been made likewise. Most certainly the Debt reduced by Payments made from equal Additions to it at the same Time, Payments which could not have been made but by those Additions, must never be called what that Debt would have been if those Additions had not been made to it; nor could it, I believe, have been called so, even by this Author, till he had confounded himself with those Formalities, which he depends upon as the plainest Method of drawing up Accounts.

But I have it in view to help this Writer to a Meaning, if I can possibly, and would not have it my Fault, if after all the Reader should not understand him. I shall therefore admit, that if he had confined himself to the Deduction of such Payments only as were made without the Assistance of Additions, from the Amount of the Publick Debt, as it stood in 1716. the Remainder would have been, I was going to say, the Remainder; (for I can make nothing more of it,) but to oblige the Author, I am content to call it *the Total National Debt, which would have been owing, in case no Additions had been made to it since* 1716. And I heartily congratulate him upon his Success in the Use of this plain and easy Method of discovering it.

But the most notable Use of this Discovery is made in his Account, N°. II. Here the Author seems to me almost to have found out (for I can't admit him to be fully satisfied about the Matter) That if our Debts, as they stood in 1716, would have been by Payments since made reduced to about 45 Millions; the difference between that Sum and the Amount of them at *Michaelmas* 1725, must consist of Additions made to them within that Interval of Time.

 If

If I allow him to make this Inference from a true State of the Amount of our Publick Debts in the Years 1716 and 1725, it must be upon these express Conditions, 1. That he confines himself in reducing the Debt as it stood in 1716. by such Payments only as have been made without the help of any Additions made to it: And 2. That he contents himself with calling what he finds to be the Difference, on a Computation of this Nature, the Sum of the Additions made to our publick Debts from 1716. to 1725: For I can be upon no Terms with him, if he persists in calling any Ballance, he may draw from an Account of this kind, *the Debt increas'd since* 1716, *over and above all Payments made from the Sinking Fund*, &c. or pretends that the Increase of our Debt, this way stated, is in the least a Contradiction to what I have advanced about it.

Nor can I by any Means allow him, that this is either a plain or easy Way of stating the Additions to the Publick Debt, by inferring and computing it from the Payments in Discharge of it. The Additions of the Publick Debt, whatever they are, must necessarily have been made publickly, and the Quantity of those Additions determined by such Acts of Parliament as those additional Debts have been contracted by; from whence the Particulars of those Additions might have been at once stated with the greatest Evidence and Propriety, and would have required no further Computation, than that of the Amount of them, for his Reader's Satisfaction; and if he really intended to state the Additions to the Publick Debt only from 1716 to 1725, I should be concerned to find him, for want of thinking of this easier and more obvious Method of doing so, obliged to infer and compute them from Payments at the *Exchequer* in discharge of them; his Account of which, he says, * *is rather Guess than Certainty; nay*



* Page 142.

*which for many Reasons he supposes to be not true. But for which, after condemning his Friend's Friend as guilty of Ignorance or Negligence, in making the necessary Enquiry on this Occasion,* he makes this Apology for himself, *That the only Difference will be,* viz. from his Mistakes about it, *that in Case the Sums which he has set down on these Heads as paid off, are not so, the Debt is the greater.*

I have hitherto been induced to account for most of this Author's Mistakes from his Ignorance of the Subject only, and his want of all Conception of the Matters which he has engaged himself in a Dispute about: But I wish here he don't design to impose upon us. The only Mistake which he would have us suppose the Ignorance and Negligence of the Person employed could lead him into here is, of setting down *a greater Sum as paid off, than really was so*; and if this should be the Case, he tells us, *the Debt will be the greater:* About which I would desire the Reader to determine, if he does not mean *that our present Debt will be the greater, and the Increase of our Debts greater than he has represented it.* But can it be allowed the Author to be so ignorant of his own Accounts, as not to know that the Increase of our Debts from 1716 to 1725, as he has inferred and stated it from the Payments made in discharge of them within the same Time, will be greater in proportion as those Payments are stated to be greater, and greater than it really is, as those Payments are stated to be greater than they really are; and that that Ballance which he calls the *Increased Debt,* &c. as it is form'd from his Accounts, increases by all the Sums that he sets down as paid in discharge of the Publick Debts.

I must confess myself to have been for this Reason greatly at a Loss to account for it, why this Author has not placed all the Sums which he states to have been paid off from 1716 to 1725, on the Credit Side of his first Account. He produces us in his two Accounts together, several Particulars of Money paid in discharge of our

Debts from 1716 to 1725, amounting to 9,150,541*l.* the whole of which the Reader will, I believe, perceive should be placed on the Credit Side of his first Account, and deducted from the Amount of our Debts in 1716, for the same Reason that any Part of it is so. But instead of this the Author has chose to pick out of it 6,081,188*l.* to place on the Credit Side of his first Account, where it serves to aggravate the Increase of our Publick Debts; and has reserved 3,069,353*l.* 2*s.* to place on the Credit Side of his second Account, where it serves a quite contrary Purpose, and is a Deduction from what would otherwise come out as the Ballance of his second Account for the Debt increased, &c. And for this Distinction between the same kind of Payments, and within the same Time made, I do not find that he any where assigns the true Reason. But having, as I believe, at last found out what really induced him to it, I think myself obliged to let the Reader into it. I take it, that the Author having set down as many particular Payments as amounted to upwards of six Millions, began to consider that he had sufficiently, and fully to his Satisfaction, provided for the Increase of the National Debt to 1725; and wisely recollected, that, if he went on to place the whole there, he should have nothing left to place on the Credit Side of his second Account, but that single Article which he calls the Ballance of his first Account. This, the Reader will observe, would have looked but awkwardly, to be placed by it self in a whole Column provided for it, and that too under the Title *Creditor*, when it was necessary to describe it not to be Credit, in any Sense that is familiar amongst Accountants, but the Reverse of it, a Debt, and a Debt unpaid too.

But I can't but observe, that this Motive, trifling as it may appear, has been of no little Service to the Publick; for had the Author went on as he had begun to the End of his first Account, and placed the Whole 9,150,541*l.* on

 the

the Credit Side of it, and the Ballance of it by this Means, the only Article of Credit in the next Account, had been reduced to 42,490,393*l.* the fatal Consequences of it are too obvious to want explaining. Our Debt had been increased by those Means by almost fourteen Millions, instead of 7,764,037*l.* to which in his great Moderation he has thought proper to confine it.

I have pointed out in general the Absurdity of this Attempt, to infer and compute a Ballance at the Foot of these Accounts, as an Addition and Increase of the Debt from 1716 to 1725, from Payments within that Time made, without distinguishing between such Payments as have been without Additions to it, and such Payments as have been made by and from Additions to it, and could not have been made otherwise. But from the Idea I have collected of this Author's Capacity as an Accountant, I believe it will be further necessary for his Conviction, to explain my self upon some one particular Instance of this kind in his own Accounts.

For this Purpose I would desire him to observe, That amongst the Articles on the Credit Side of his first Account, by the Amount of which he reduces the Publick Debts as they stood in 1716 to 45,559,746*l.* he mentions by the Name of Lottery-Annuities unsubscribed to the *South-Sea* Company, paid out of the Sinking Fund, an Article of 1,204,786*l.* 3*s.* 4*d.* He knows very well, that the Money for making this Payment was raised partly by a new Loan upon *Exchequer* Bills, and partly by Money then remaining in the Sinking Fund, *viz.* by 1,000,000*l.* borrowed upon *Exchequer* Bills, and 204,786*l.* remaining in the Sinking Fund; and accordingly in his State of the Debt at *Michaelmas* 1725, on the Debtor Side of his second Account, he mentions this Million of *Exchequer* Bills as a Debt created 9° *Georgii* to redeem Annuities. I do not enough understand his Accounts, to determine for him, whether he supposes this Million to be or not to

 be

be Part of our Debts at *Christmas* 1725; but let him suppose which he pleases, this Sum amongst others is manifestly to be deducted from that 7,764,037*l.* the Ballance of his second Account, which he calls the Debt increased since 1716. If this Sum was paid on the 24th of *December* 1725, he ought not to have stated it as part of our Debts at that Time, and then it is to be deducted from that 56,393,137*l.* which he represents on the Debtor Side of his second Account to be at that Time the Total of them. If it was not paid, it ought not to have been deducted by him from the 51,640,934*l.* which he describes to be the Amount of our Debts in 1716. And either his Total of our Debts in 1725 should be made by one Million less, or the Ballance of his first Account placed in his second, as the first Article on the Credit Side of it, should be one Million more; in either of which Cases, the Ballance of his second Account, whatever he means by it, would be by one Million less.

But, upon a Presumption that he may still persist in his good Opinion of that plain Method which he has fallen into of drawing up Accounts, I can't forbear the Vanity of showing him how far I could exceed him in the Use of it, for this useful Purpose of increasing our Publick Debts.

After I had stated with him in his first Account the Amount of our Debts in 1716 to be 51,640,934*l.* I could for the same Reason that he deducts from it any Part of those Payments amounting to 6,081,188*l.* which were made with Money raised upon new created Debts, proceed further to deduct in his Manner,

| | |
|---|---|
| By *Exchequer* Bills paid off and cancelled by the *Bank of England* since *Dec.* 1716, in Consideration of a redeemable Debt added to their Stock and Funds. | 2,000,000 |

 By

By several Debts at 6 *per Cent.* Interest since the same Time discharged by Annuities at 5 *per Cent.* commonly called *Lottery Annuities* and redeemable by Parliament, } 9,534,357

From hence I might, with as much Reason, advance to the Discharge of various Incumbrances by their Subscription into the *South-Sea* Company, to the Payment of 4,000,000*l.* to that Company, by the Addition of an equal Debt to the *Bank of England;* from whence, together with several other Items formed from Variations in the Form of our present Debts, without any Variation in their real Quantity, I should not doubt my Abilities to prove, in the Author's Manner, that the Whole of our Debt in 1716, has been since paid off; and with the same Evidence that he produces, proceed to infer from it, that the whole, or even more than the Amount of our Debt at present, is the Debt increased, or an Addition made to it from 1716 to 1725.

I have, I fear, trespassed upon the Reader's Patience, in remarking upon Accounts formed, as it seems to me, by the Author, upon no one intelligible Design, unless it be that of making them unintelligible, and securing himself from any Reply to his Pretences of having contradicted me by drawing Conclusions from them without any distinct, and as I think, without any kind of Meaning in them, which he has not himself somewhere or other in the Body of his Book, or in some Part or other of his Accounts, expressly contradicted. If there is indeed any Inference to be truly made from those Accounts, or either of them, that is any way inconsistent with what I have advanced about the Decrease of our Publick Debts, I must desire he would explain himself upon it; and in the mean time I must submit it to the Reader how far the Account that I have given of the neat Decrease of our Debts from 1717 to 1724, by the

Sum of 2,100,000*l.* or thereabouts, and from the same time to 1725, by about the Sum of 3,347,152*l.* is contradicted by the States this Author has produced of the Amount of our Debt in 1716, and in 1725.

In 1716, he says, our Debts amounted to 51,640,934*l.* to which, if he will allow me, for the present only, to add the Increase of our Debts in the *Exchequer* Accounts from the Subscription of the Irredeemables, as I have computed it to be, 3,155,858*l.* the total Amount of our Debts will be in 1716, 54,796,792*l.* and by about 327,172*l.* more than 54,469,620*l.* which I have stated it to be in 1717. The general Reasonsof this Difference between us are, that he has reckoned amongst our Publick Debts, as well in 1716 as in 1725, 248,550*l.* the Equivalent due to *Scotland*, which not being in my Account, was left out by me both in 1717 and 1724. He has likewise reckoned as Part of the Debt in 1716, a Debt to the Navy of 334,139*l.* which if he will look again into that Act 3° *Georgii*, which he quotes as a Proof of this Arrear, and of the Satisfaction of it by Annuities at 4 *per Cent.* he will find to be included in what he has charged in another Article of the same Account, and calls Deficiency of Grants, 1716. These two Sums together should make his State of the Debts in 1716, exceed mine in 1717, by the Sum of 582,789*l.* or thereabouts; but he has omitted in his Account of the Debt in 1716, to charge, as any Part of it, 110,312*l.* Navy Annuities, and represents the Amount of the Debt on the Four Class Lotteries and Bankers Annuities together, to be 9,426,888*l.* only; which, however it may be charged in the Papers he made use of, was then, and is frequently recited in several Acts of Parliament to have been 9,534,357*l.* and by 107,469*l.* more than he has stated it to be. He has therefore charged as due in 1716 582,789*l.* which I have omitted, and omitted what I have charged to have been due about the same Time 217,781*l.* The difference of which two

22 Sums

Sums is so nearly equal to the Sum, by which his State of the Debt in 1716, with the Addition of what I have asked with regard to the Irredeemables, exceeds my State of the Debt in 1717; that if, with regard to these Observations, the Reader will correct his State of the Debts and mine, he will find them, though computed for different Times, agree nearly enough for our proceeding together in our Enquiry after the Decrease of them to *Christmas* 1725. The Difference of what he has overcharged in 1716, *viz.* 334,239*l.* and what he has omitted to charge 217,781*l.* is 116,458*l.* which I propose should be deducted from 54,796,792*l.* and the Remainder will be 54,680,334*l.*

To my State for *Christmas* 1717, of 54,469,620*l.* I must add, to bring my Accounts as near to his as may be, the Equivalent Debt of 248,550*l.* and then my State will be 54,718,170*l.* and the Difference between us will be little more than 38,000*l.* which, whether it be from my Mistake or his, the Reader will I believe excuse me from contending with him, when he considers our Accounts are taken from different Papers, and refer to different Points of Time.

The Equivalent Debt was not in my Accounts, either of the Debt in 1717 or 1724, about which likewise no Dispute that is material to the present Question can be started; since if it be considered and accounted for as a Publick Debt both in 1717 and 1725, it can occasion no Variation in the Sum that shall be from thence computed to be within that Time the Decrease of our Publick Debts.

The Author, in his Second Account, which he calls a State of the National Debt, as it stood in *December* 1725, has not, as I think, stated any Sum at all to be then, or at any other Time, the Amount of our Publick Debt. He does indeed cast up the several Articles on the Debtor Side of his Account, and makes them amount to

 56,393,137*l.*

56,393,137*l.* but this I think he does not give us for the Amount of our Debts at *Christmas* 1725; for the Creditor Side of his Account admits that several Articles on the Debtor Side were not due at *Christmas* 1725, but before that Time paid off and satisfy'd. The Amount of these Articles taken from the Creditor Side of this Account is 3,069,353*l.* which I should presume upon his Leave to deduct from 56,393,137*l.* and to take the Remainder 53,323,784*l.* for what he would give us for the Debt in 1725, if it was not for the contrary Use which he makes of Payments in the same manner, and under the same Title enter'd in his first Account of Increasing the Publick Debt by them: However, since he admits himself to be uncertain about his Payments, he will give me leave to settle them from my Papers.

The whole Remainder of what was due at *Christmas* 1725 for the *Exchequer* Bills, or any other *Exchequer* Bills (exclusively of what had been then lately made out to supply his Majesty's Civil List Expences, and which have been since discharged from the Contributions on the last Lottery) was 560,312*l.* 10*s.* The Author therefore in charging 3,000,000*l.* under this Head, charges 2,439,687*l.* 10*s.* more than was really due.

The whole Remainder of what was unpaid at *Christmas* 1725 of Money at any Time advanced for building Churches, was 68,665*l.* This Debt the Author in charging at 380,787*l.* charges it at too much by 312,122*l.*

Of the Debt on the second Lottery 1719, all that was not subscribed to the *South-Sea* Company was paid off before *December* 1725. The Author therefore wrongly charges, under this Article, 65,395*l.*

He should not have reckoned amongst our Debts in 1725, 2,510*l.* Navy Annuities, for that Sum was before paid off.

And from the Sum of 192,152*l.* 6*s.* 3*d.* placed against the *Item* of Annuities for two and three Lives, the Sum of

24 4,102*l.*

4,102*l.* is to be deducted on account of such Annuities as before *Christmas* 1725 were reverted to the Crown.

If the Amount of these Sums with which he has overcharged the Publick, and which as I compute it, is 2,823,816*l.* 10*s.* be deducted from 56,393,137*l.* 10*s.* the Remainder is 53,569,321*l.* to which is to be added, what he has omitted, a Debt on the Lottery 1713, at *Christmas* 1725, of 32,260*l.* This added to the last Remainder of 53,569,321*l.* will make it 53,601,581*l.* and will be his State of the Publick Debt at *Christmas* 1725, if he will admit of my Assistance in correcting those Particulars in his Accounts where he supposes himself mistaken.

But to bring his Accounts and mine together, I must further deduct from his, which were not charged as Publick Debts in the Papers which I made use of, 1,000,000*l.* charged by him for the Civil List Debt, and 1,255,491*l.* 9*s.* which he calls the Debt of the Navy; and then his State of the Debts at *Christmas* 1725 will be reduced to 51,346,089*l.* 11*s.* And this Sum I would propose should be compared with the above mentioned Sum of 54,718,170*l.* the Amount of the Debt in 1717, and the Amount in 1725 thus reduced to 51,346,089*l.* deducted from it, in which Case the Remainder 3,372,081*l.* thus produced as the Neat Decrease of our Debts at *Christmas* 1725, and compared with 3,347,152*l.* which I have from my Papers described to be the Decrease of them in the same Time, will show what Shifts or Disguises I have any where made use of, to impose upon my Readers a false Account of the Decrease of our Publick Debts.

I followed indeed the Accounts as made up at the *Exchequer*, in not charging the Sum of One Million borrowed to supply the Deficiencies of the Civil List, and charged in a particular Manner upon the Payments from that Revenue, amongst our Publick Debts. But I was so far from attempting to conceal it, that I have, in my *Essay upon the Publick Debts*, produced and mentioned it, and

 by

by no means opposed the Deduction of it from what I then just before stated to be the Decrease of our Debts, within the Time referred to.

No Body, I believe, will wonder that I did not, in a State of our Debts at *Christmas* 1724, mention a Debt to the Navy, stated, as he says, to *Christmas* 1725. The Truth is, I had no Account of any Debt upon the Navy at the Time of publishing that Essay; but if I had, I should, perhaps, have thought it improper to call it a Publick Debt, or stated it amongst Debts provided for by Parliament, till the Legislature had made it so. And if I could take this Gentleman's Word for the Quantity of it at *Christmas* 1725, I should be at a Loss in what manner to state it for the Purpose of my Enquiry, unless he had informed me what Part of it was incurred before 1717, and what Part of it since that Time. But what I have a little Reason to be surprised at, is, that this Gentleman, who informs us he has been employed *in providing Necessaries for the Navy,* should seem to be no more apprized of the necessary Uncertainty of the precise State of the Debt upon this Score, to the very Time of making-up any Account of it that may be enquired for. I know not from what Papers he may have taken the Sum, which he says is the State of this Debt to *Christmas* 1725; but I could almost venture to refer my self to his own Papers for the Proof of it, that he has taken this Sum not from a State, but from an Estimate of the Navy Debt.

The Author* has refused me a Place for 110,312*l.* Navy Annuities, in the Account of our Debts before 1716; for he says, *whoever reads the Act* 4° Georgii, *or* 5° Georgii, referred to in his Margin, *will see no Reason to believe that the Arrear of Interest, which this Debt was created to satisfy, was grown due before the Year* 1716; *but for this,* he says, *he has made amends in allowing a like*

26 *Arrear*

* Page 142.

*Arrear to the* East-India *Company, to be due before that Time, though above* 127,500*l. of it has been contracted since.* Here this Gentleman seems to me determined to proceed in his own Way; he will not allow me one Debt to be due before 1716, for he does not know whether it was so or no; but another greater Debt he will allow me to be so, though he pretends to know the contrary. In the next Page he asks Leave to set me right in one Thing, and tells me, *that* 544,142*l. advanced by the* South-Sea *Company, was not employed in Aid of the Sinking Fund, because* 188,296*l. was allowed out of it to the Company, to make good an Arrear of Interest incurred in* 1719, *and* 1720, about which he adds, *that when Interest is turned into Principal, he supposes it may be called a Debt.* I can't see that what he supposes done in the Case before us, *viz. the discharging an Arrear of Interest in making up an Account between the Government and this Company,* is turning Interest into Principal, and therefore I do not know what he aims at here; but if this was the Case, I agree with him, that when Interest is turned into Principal, that Principal may be called a Debt; and in return for this Concession, I hope, he will allow me, that the Interest was a Debt likewise before the turning it into Principal: And then with regard to this Arrear, the Arrear discharged by Navy Annuities, and the Deficiency in the Payment of the *East-India* Company's Annuity, if the Time when these Debts were contracted becomes the Question; the Answer, I think, must be the Time when the Contract was made to pay them, which was then only, when the Government contracted with these Companies to pay them Interest, and which I suppose is well enough known to have been before 1716. And if the Author will not take my Sense about this Matter, I must refer him to that of the Legislature, as it is expressed upon the Subject of the *East-India* Company's Deficiency, now in Question before us, in the Act 7° *Georgii*, Pag. 498. But what

 can

can be the Meaning of any Dispute about this Particular; or who ever expected more from the Surplusses called the Sinking Fund, to the Discharge of our principal Debts, than what was more than sufficient to pay their Interest?

As to the Author's Objections, or rather unmeaning Opposition, to what I have advanced relating to the Subscription of the Redeemables, I must leave the Difference between us to the Reader's Judgment, upon the Evidence of what I have already represented upon this Subject. I have said, that the Sums originally contributed for the Purchase of these Annuities, and by which they were described in the *Exchequer* Accounts, before their Subscription into the *South-Sea* Company, did not truly describe the Quantity of these Incumbrances upon the Government; that they were before that Subscription an Incumbrance at least, to the full Value or Price of them at Market, which was, before that Subscription, greater than the redeemable Debt for which they were exchang'd; and consequently that our Debts, when the Quantity of our Incumbrances is to be attended to in the Description of them, were not increased by that Subscription. Is there any-body, but this Author, who does not assent to this, as soon as it is proposed to him? Or is this less true, because the *South-Sea* Scheme was an ill-contrived, or an ill-executed one upon any other Accounts?

This Author asks a great many Questions foreign to the Subject I have treated of, and which, weary of the Difficulty of finding out his Meaning, I must excuse myself at once from answering, as by no Means contradicting me, or as stated from Papers that I know nothing of; but there is one of them, which though not objected to me, relates to the Account of our Debts in Dispute between us, and as it seems, has been one great Occasion of this Gentleman's Perplexity in stating of it.

He has proposed it in different Places in his Performance,

28 but

but has at last placed it at the Head of a long Complaint, and formal Reasoning about the Inconvenience of Mistakes in our National Accounts: * *It is plain,* he says, *that there is an Omission of* 1,500,000*l. in the Account of the Sinking Fund, there being no Notice taken of the* 500,000*l. raised of the Lottery* 1719, *for paying off* Exchequer *Bills, nor of* 1,000,000*l.* Exchequer *Bills made out for the* Navy *Debt; and without supplying these Defects, every-body who tries, will find (as I did) that neither the Account of the Publick Debt, nor the Produce of the Sinking Fund, can be truly stated.*

I should sooner have understood the Grievance he here complains of, if instead of saying, *that every-body who tries, will find (as I did)*, he had express'd it by saying, *every one who tries (as I did) will find,* &c. and I could almost leave him in his Perplexity upon this Account, but that I find he thinks he has got over it, and throws the Blame of it upon other People. He does not find this 1,500,000*l.* in the Account of the Sinking Fund: Why does he want to find it there? Was it the Produce of the Sinking Fund; or was it, as he says, raised upon the Lottery 1719, and in 1722, upon the Credit of *Exchequer* Bills? I who know his Accounts, know it would answer his Purpose, to have it (though falsly) represented, to be the Produce of the Sinking Fund; and he has in his first Account accordingly supposed it to be so, and from that very Circumstance inferred these, amongst other Articles, to be an Increase of our Publick Debts.

† Another Thing which he complains of as a Trespass upon *the great and essential Part of our Constitution,* is, that last Year a Million was raised to pay off the Civil List Debt, contracted the Year before upon the Credit of *Exchequer* Bills, of which 990,000*l.* he says, was all that then remained unpaid; and from hence he infers, that a new Debt of 10,000*l.* for the Service of the Civil List, was at

 this

* Page 180. † Page 167.

this Time contracted, *without any Message from the Crown*, &c. This is likewise a Complaint that I am not concerned in, and should not therefore answer, but that it is in my Power to do so, by appealing to the Act of Parliament by which he supposes this Debt to be contracted.

I must propose it to him, to turn over the Act of Parliament, for raising this Million upon the last Lottery; he will find there, that the Commissioners of the Treasury are empowered to reward the Managers, and to make Allowances for prompt Payment, out of the Monies contributed upon that Act. One Million of Money was all that was to be raised in Pursuance of it, and 990,000*l.* to be paid out of it, and the Remainder, 10,000*l.* all that would be left, for the Charges of the Lottery, and Allowances for prompt Payment. Let him adjust by himself, what he pleases to allow for these Purposes, and then consider what Part of this 10,000*l.* he is so much in haste for an Account of.

It may be expected from me possibly, that I should take some Notice of this Author's third Account, after he has been at so much Pains about it; but he must excuse me in making what haste I can from it, when he reflects on the Pains I have been at already, to make any Thing of his two first Accounts. He calls it *a View of that Part of the Debt called Redeemable, with the Sums which might have been applied towards the Payment of it*, &c. *by* Michaelmas, 1726, *in Case no Alteration had been made in it by the* South-Sea *Scheme.*

I expected from this Title, to find *the Sums that might have been applied towards the Payment of it* accounted for as the Produce of the Sinking Fund, in which the Amount of the Surplusses of almost every particular Fund was brought together; but instead of this, the Author gives an Account of several Surplusses and Savings variously mistaken in the Particulars, both previously to, and as the consequence of that Provision, and produces an

 Account

Account of them greatly exceeding the Produce of the Sinking Fund within the Time that he refers to. This Circumstance, I think, sufficiently proves the Falshood of his Account in general, unless he would represent to us, that the aggregating particular Surplusses in the Provisions of the Sinking Fund has diminished the Total Quantity of them; which, it is impossible, I should think he can suppose, after declaring, with such an Appearance of being in earnest, *That he has * hitherto looked upon the Establishment and Appropriation of the Sinking Fund to the Payment of our National Debts, as the wisest and most beneficial Provision, which in our Circumstances could have been thought of.*

This Author † has charged me with presuming upon my Skill in Figures, to impose upon my Readers at Pleasure, and proceeds to say, *That I have told them that the Benefit of reducing the Interest of the present Debt from* 4 *to* 3 per Cent. *would only be to discharge the Debt in about four Years and a half sooner:* And this I am represented to say would be the *only* Benefit of this Reduction, for no other Reason that I can think of, but because it just then occurred to the Author, that I had likewise stated the Benefit of this Reduction with regard to the Publick Expence of coming at it in another Manner; which, as he immediately reports himself, I have said, would be 322,000*l.* *per Annum* for about 23 Years. I can't enter into his Reasons for rebuking me ‡ for not having used my Arithmetick for ascertaining the Total of this Expence in 23 Years. But from his strange Report about this Matter, that it would amount to upwards of 30 Millions, I have been induced to multiply this annual Sum by 23, and find the Produce to be 7,406,000*l.* the Amount of this Annuity, and 4,765,600*l.* to be about the present Value of it at 4 *per Cent.* Compound Interest. What this Gentleman

31 means,

* Pages, 148, 149. † Page 157. ‡ Pages, 157, 158.

means therefore, by his 30 Millions, I can't imagine, unless he has computed the Amount of this Annuity at Compound Interest, and wisely supposed, that if the Government raised this Sum annually, the Consequence would be (what can't possibly be supposed, but as the Consequence of their not raising it,) I mean, that they must pay Interest upon Interest, to be computed upon this Annuity. From whence he must, as I conceive, have proceeded to this further Mistake of supposing, that because the Benefit of 500,000*l. per Ann.* gained to the Publick, by reducing Interest, was equal to the Benefit of 322,000*l. per Ann.* without reducing it, it was therefore equal to the Amount of both together, and has upon this Foundation added to the Amount of the first Annuity, the Amount of this last too, computed in the same manner. What a misfortune is it, to understand Arithmetick with no better luck in the Application of it!

But what Reason has this Gentleman (unless from the Authority of another Pamphlet published against me) for supposing, that I propose this Addition precisely to be really made to the Annual Expence of the Publick for the Reduction of our Debts? I have mentioned it only as a different Method of stating the Advantage to the Publick, from the Reduction of Interest from 4 to 3 *per Cent.* upon Fifty Millions, supposed to be the Amount of our present Debts, and which I had just before stated in another manner.

It can't, I think, be expected that I should take particular Notice of several other Instances, where this Author has seemed to me to misrepresent purposely my Meaning, for his own or his Readers Diversion or Amusement only. I hope they have entertained his Readers, but I can't apprehend they have imposed upon them.

I can't but be serious upon this Subject of our Publick Debts, and therefore wish this Author had gravely endeavoured to show me where I have my self objected to the Payment of them; or if I any where appear to admit or foresee an Objection to it, which I have not endeavoured to remove and answer. I never thought, nor have I any where supposed, that the Money due to Foreigners from the Publick was an Objection to it; or that we should suffer from hence any Inconvenience from discharging it. This is a Circumstance attending our present Debts, which in my Opinion makes the Payment of them, as soon as it can be reasonably effected, more eligible, if possible, than it would be otherwise. I have indeed met with this Objection, and often accounted for it from a prevailing Habit amongst us, of refining too much upon Subjects of this Nature, and paying too little regard to the plainer Truths that offer themselves in the usual Scenes of Business. What other *Quarter* Insinuations of this kind arise from, I am at a Loss to know, unless I could see any Designs going forward, that these Opinions would have any Tendency to promote amongst us.

Nor have I used this, or indeed any other Argument against the Reduction of Interest, as far as it is reasonable to expect it may be supported amongst us afterwards; but should, on the contrary, for this Reason amongst others, while we remain indebted to Foreigners, wish for it as much as this Author can do. I have no where opposed the Reduction of Interest, but where I have explained my self to mean the sudden Appearance only of reduced Interest amongst us, produced by such Views and Adventures as I have described to be not long likely to be continued, or to support any Reduction of Interest that may seem for a Time to be effected by them: From which the only Inconvenience that I have hinted at, with regard to our Debt to Foreigners, I have supposed to arise from our being, upon such an Occasion, induced to purchase of Foreigners their Interest in our Funds, upon

 such

such Terms as may soon afterwards oblige us to offer it to them again at much lower Prices.

This Author, who, I suppose, thinks it below him to receive any Information *from the Principles and Practices of Stock-jobbing,* however material it may be, in judging of the Reasonableness of reducing Interest for the Publick Service, has found out another way of determining, that *it will be most agreeable to Justice and Policy, to keep even the Interest of the Funds near what Mr.* Locke *calls the Natural Interest of Money.*

Justice and Policy, I think, join in directing us to keep the Interest of the Funds, at that Rate which the Government has contracted to pay the Publick Creditors, till a reasonable Method or Occasion shall be found out or offer it self, of obtaining their deliberate Consent to the Reduction of it. Such a Reduction would certainly be a Convenience to the Publick: And for this Reason, Policy directs us to every reasonable Expedient for reducing the Natural Rate of Interest. And if I do not think this likely to be effected by Schemes formed from a confined Attention to our Funds and Money only; we may, however, in my Opinion, most reasonably expect it from such Policies, as shall preserve our Tranquility, secure our Commerce, assure our Properties inviolably, support the Credit of our Government, and enforce the Punctuality of private Persons in their Contracts with one another. From such Causes as these, the Author very much mistakes me, if he thinks I fear a Reduction of the Rate of Interest. But when he gives us his Advice upon this Subject, does he conceive that the Common Rate of Interest is to be determined absolutely by the Choice of our Superiours? I always took it for granted, that when we considered the Provision of the Sinking Fund, and the Reduction of Interest from 6 to 5 *per Cent.* together, we regarded that Provision as the Effect of Interest reduced amongst us, and not the Cause of it: Whoever thinks

34 otherwise

otherwise, differs from what appears to have been at that Time, the Sense of the Legislature, which the Reader will find by turning to those Acts of Parliament, which I have referred to as the first Provision of the Sinking Fund: There he will observe, *the Common Interest of Money being very much lessen'd under his Majesty's most auspicious Government,* recited as the Foundation of the Provisions made by those Acts of Parliament. And of this Reduction of Interest, as far as our Debts were then redeemable, the proper Advantage for the Publick Service was then reasonably and wisely taken, and will, I hope, be always for the future taken, of every farther Reduction of the Common Rate of Interest.

This Author has, I think, unjustly charged me, in several Places, with Intimations and Insinuations which I never thought of. All that I have meant any where, I have endeavoured to explain as expressly as I could. But in return for it, I think, I meet with several intire Pages in this Author, which are only Intimations. I can't suppose, that they relate to me; but, if they should do so, till I am let into the Drift of them, they must remain unanswered.

As to what I have advanced, that it is more eligible *to raise what Money may be farther wanted, by increasing the Publick Debts with farther Loans upon Interest, provided for by New Duties, than to supply the same Sums from the Sinking Fund:* It is true, it is a Truth of Publick Consequence to be attended to, and what I have therefore explained and proved to be a Truth; and it must therefore out-live all the Pleasantries that have been excited by it. Nor can I think that there can be any great Difficulty in understanding it, by any Person who will attend to the Difference of the Increase of the same Sum at the same Rate of Simple and Compound Interest. If the Government, by the Addition of a new Debt for the Publick Service, pay Simple Interest for it only, and by supplying it from the Sinking Fund, lose the Benefit of Compound Interest for the same Sum, can it be long doubted, which of these Methods of supplying our Necessities are least expensive to the Publick, or will longest delay the Total Payment of our Debts? I have not in any Part of my *Essay* recommended an Addition to our Debts, but upon an Occasion when it would be absolutely necessary, to prevent the Misapplication of the Sinking Fund: And if the Interest of this Kingdom in these different Measures, upon any such Occasion, was not before generally attended to, or understood, I have so much the greater Reason to be satisfied in having recommended it to the Publick Notice.

I can hardly believe, that any of my Countrymen are more sensible than I am of the Burthen of our present Debts, or wish more sincerely for the Reduction of them. Such thoughts as these were in reality my greatest Inducements to the Publication of my *Essay;* in which, if I have (as this Author says) discovered an extraordinary Zeal for the Preservation of the Sinking Fund, I have given, in my Opinion, a sufficient Proof of my Aversion to the Increase of our Debts, whenever it can by any reasonable Expedient be avoided.

If it is indeed for me (as this Author is pleased to say it is) that he has given us his fourth View, or Abstract of the present Taxes, I can assure him he never more misapplied his Time. I have often attended to them with as much Concern as he can have upon this Account, and almost as often, in the most comprehensive Views I have been capable of, considered the Manner and Degree, in which the Estates of Gentlemen, and the Rewards of Industry amongst us, are affected by them. But I know no Foundation for an Outcry upon this Subject, or any Measures going forwards, but what are consistent with the same Sentiments in the Gentlemen in the Administration, and their really desiring the Reduction of our

 Debts

Debts as soon as possible. If this was otherwise, or ever should be so; should I ever see any Measures remarkably neglected, that would contribute to this Purpose, or any Measures enter'd upon that had a Tendency to obstruct or delay the Payment of our Publick Debts, this Author could not, I believe, be readier than I should be to advertise the Publick of it.

I account for it from this Author's Mistake about me, that he chuses for his Diversion to represent me, as objecting the Interest of the Ministry to the Payment of the Publick Debts. I have mention'd it as an Objection I had heard made to the Probability of their being paid; an Objection that I have not made; that I have stated only with a Design to answer it: And in this I would willingly be thought to have succeeded. But this Author, I hope, reasons in a Manner peculiar to himself, when from hence he infers, that I have a Share in any Advantage that may arise from those Necessities of the Publick, or supposes that, if I had so, I should chuse unnecessarily to excite a general Attention to it.

I have taken Notice of as much of this Author's Performance, as I have hitherto thought material, or, at least as much, as amidst the necessary Avocations of a particular Employment, my Leisure would by any Means admit of, consistently with that dispatch with which I judged it reasonable, that so great a Misrepresentation of the Increase of our Debts under the present Reign ought at this Time to be publickly contradicted. This I thought it my Duty in particular to attempt, as my Treatise had been the Occasion of it. And if I should, from the Diversion given me from my ordinary Business, and in a Matter which requires so much distinct and deliberate Attention, have any where committed a Mistake in it, I hope the Reader will regard it with all reasonable Indulgence.

I could not possibly find out the Means of accommodating to an Enquiry after the Diminution of our Debts

 from

from any one Time to another, the Method which this Gentleman calls *the plainest Manner of drawing up Accounts by way of Debtor and Creditor.* Nor do I know any Use of Forms in the drawing up Accounts, which the Design of our Enquiries from them does not point out to us. In the Computations I have made of the Progress of the Sinking Fund, I must appear, to Persons versed in Affairs of this Nature, to have taken more Pains, for the Purpose of being generally understood, than was necessary for my own Satisfaction, as to the Truth of what I have advanced about it; and this too, at the Expence of appearing less skilful in Numbers than I should do otherwise. Nor would I have avoided the Pains or at least the Pomp of a long Account, if I thought it could be of the least Use to explain, that the Difference of the Amount of our Debts in 1716, and the Amount of them in 1724, rightly computed, was a true State of the real or neat Increase or Decrease of them, within those two Periods of Time.

I find, by the Conclusion of this Author's Treatise, he expects to be rail'd at for it, and calls this Usage *the usual Treatment of* Mercenary Malice *upon these Occasions.* If this Description is intended as a Compliment to me, I am pleased to think that he will find himself disappointed. I have met, throughout the whole Book, with so much Reason for believing, that this Gentleman was in reality himself mistaken, or imposed upon, before this Attempt to mislead his Readers, that I can't prevail upon myself, to dispute with him the Account he gives of his Views in the Publication of it. If he *indeed* thought I had so grossly abused the Publick, in my Account of their Debts, as he says I have done, let it be *Love* and *Duty* to his Country (if he pleases) that prompted him in this manner to oppose me in it; but let me assure him, the same laudable Inclination, the same Sense of Duty to my Country, led me to the Publication of the Treatise which he is so angry with. I know what little Credit is to be given to an Author upon his own Word as to this Particular; nor can I expect to be sooner believed than other People in these Pretensions, after so much Pains taken to represent me differently to the Publick: But true it is, that a real and sincere Regard to the Publick Interest was my Inducement to the writing the *Essay upon our Debts;* and from the same Motive I would, as far as possible, support the Credit of it against this prevailing Method of interpreting a Book wrote upon any Publick Subject, not from the plainest Expressions in it, but an idle Conjecture about the Author's Design in the Publication of it. I must declare therefore, that as I intended only the Publick Service in writing it, without any regard to the Sentiments or Convenience of any particular Persons or Party whatsoever, so I never produced myself as the Author of it, with a View to any Advantage of my own from any Person, or on any one Account soever. I had, I have no Engagements or Dependance that should prejudice me on any Side of a Question of general Importance in this Country. A disinterested Regard to our common Safety and Happiness has indeed long since attached me to the Protestant Succession, as established amongst us in his Majesty and his Royal Family, and made me a determined Enemy, as far as my Condition of Life would to any purpose admit of it, to those who would disturb us in it: Whatever Partiality therefore against the Interest of my Country, any Party Engagements might render me suspected of, I have no other but this, and from this I have no Apprehensions that it can mislead me.

I some Years since published a Pamphlet, recommending to the Proprietors of the *South Sea* Company the Proposals made them for an Engraftment; and though I have since observed some Mistakes in it, owing to my then wanting sufficient Information upon those Subjects, I have had however an Opportunity of observing, that

 my

my Sentiments were agreeable to the Sentiments of the Legislature, as appears by two Acts of Parliament made afterwards, which proved to be of the greatest Service to the General Credit of the Publick; one of them for transferring four Millions of the *South-Sea* Company's Funds to the Bank of *England*, to raise Money for the Discharge of the *South-Sea* Company's Incumbrances; and the other of them for separating from their Stock one Moiety of their Annuities.

The Success of my *Essay upon our Publick Debts*, with the more reasonable and unprejudiced Part of my Fellow-Subjects; the Satisfaction of hearing from the Throne, that what this Author calls my extraordinary Zeal for the Preservation of the Sinking Fund, cannot have been disagreeable to his Majesty, give me a Pleasure that certainly those Gentlemen never knew, who will not allow me that this alone is a sufficient Inducement to it, an ample Reward for an Attempt to serve their Country.

I know nothing of what this Author means * by *Secret Motives*, or *pretended Confidences*. *Standing Armies*, and *Badges of Slavery*, have been so often repeated lately without a Meaning to them, that I have almost forgot to receive the least Impression from them. But let this Author explain himself, from whence he thinks the Liberties, the Ease, the Honour of his Country, to be indeed in Danger. I cannot be *afraid*, I hope I should not be *ashamed, to appear* early *in the Defence of them*, in this way at least, in this, in which *only I am in Circumstances* to serve the Publick.

This Author and I have differed about a Representation of our Circumstances, in which I thought the Honour of our Country concerned. But had I at any Time the same Occasion, I see no reason for his inferring from hence, that I should appear more indifferent about her

 Liberties

* Pag. 170.

Liberties, her Ease or Safety. To preserve these, I entirely agree with him, That it requires our utmost Care to prevent the unnecessary Increase of our Debts, and to promote, as much as possible, the Reduction of them; a Matter of that Consequence to this Kingdom, that if I should ever see it neglected, no Considerations in Nature, could restrain me from exposing it; upon such an Occasion I should think

*Fas mihi Graiorum sacrata resolvere jura,*
*Fas odisse viros, atque omnia ferre sub auras.*

I have added, to relieve the Reader from the Perplexity which the Dispute between this Author and my self may have given him upon the Face of his Accounts, a new, and, I think, an exact State of our Debts in 1717, with the Increase from the Subscription of the Irredeemables added to it; and on the other Side, a State likewise of our Debts at *Christmas* 1725: And the Difference of their Amounts, I have added to the Debt in 1725, as the Ballance of an Account, and stated to be the neat Decrease of our Publick Debts, within that Time. This Ballance, the Reader will undeniably grant me to be the real Decrease of them, with a Reserve to his own Opinion about the Navy Debt at that Time, or the Million borrowed for the Service of the Civil List; and excuse me for the Future from Taking Notice of any Objections to me, but what shall be made upon the Face of this Account, and by Exceptions either to such Articles in particlar, as are contained or omitted in it, or to the Computation made by me of the Amount of them. As I have taken all possible care about the Truth of what I have now stated to be the Quantity of the Debts mentioned in it, at the two different Times referred to, I hope the Reader will be able from it to correct such Mistakes, as either my Adversary or I may have before committed, and render it unnecessary for me to point out the less material Particulars, in which my former Account of the Debt in 1717 may differ from this, either from any Mistake made in it, or such Variations in the Account of our Debts from *Christmas* 1724, to 1725, as make this Difference at present necessary. I shall therefore mention the chief Occasion only of the Difference of what I have before stated, and what I now state to be the Debt in 1717.

I have before stated the Debt in 1717 to be 54,469,620*l.* and by the Addition of the Equivalent Debt to be 54,718,170*l.* I now state it to have been only 54,636,912*l.* 17*s.* 4*d.*¼ and from this different Amount of our Debts in 1717, a different Sum comes out for the neat Decrease of them at *Christmas* 1725.

This Difference arises principally from my having stated 100,000*l.* raised for immediate Service upon the Credit of *Exchequer* Bills, tho' at the same Time the early Discharge of it was provided for by a Tax on *Roman Catholicks*, to be a Debt at *Christmas* 1717. I found it in the Account of our Publick Debts; but as it was no real Increase of them, or at least was to remain so only till that Tax could be collected in, or the Deficiency of it, when ascertain'd, be made good by Parliament, I therefore carry'd it to the Account of our Debts in 1717, by which the same Purpose, only in the Enquiry I proposed, was answered, as if I had (which I must have done otherwise) deducted it from the Amount of our Debts, amongst which it then stood in 1724.

This indeed was a *Shift*, as the Author of the *State* calls it; but I hope he will see it was necessary to me, in order to avoid what I find him full as angry with, *distinguishing* about this Article. This for the Reader's Ease only, and to prevent Perplexity, in the Way to what I had more generally in View to represent to him, I chose to avoid in this Place, by a Method that could occasion no Difference in the Sum which I was to produce, as the Decrease of our Debts to *Christmas* 1724. but in carrying this

Account forwards, to *Christmas* 1725, I think it necessary for the Reader's Satisfaction to state this particular Article by it self distinctly.

I found this Sum in the Account of our Publick Debts, but could upon the Whole have wished that this, any more than the Loans upon any other of the Annual Grants, had not been there. It was a Sum voted for the Service of the Year 1723, and a Provision was made for raising it by a Tax for that Year upon the Estates of *Roman Catholicks*, and the further usual Provision made about it, that the Deficiency of that Tax should be supplied out of such Aids as should be granted by Parliament next after that Deficiency should be ascertained. But it was further provided, for the immediate Service of the Government, that it might be raised upon the Credit of *Exchequer* Bills, payable from the Sinking Fund. And in Consequence of this, what should be collected from this Tax, or granted afterwards by Parliament to supply the Deficiency of it, would belong to the Sinking Fund, to replace the Sum that should be in this Manner taken from it. With regard to this Provision for it, the same in reality as is annually made for the Loans on the Land or Malt Tax, I could not consider this Sum amongst the Amount of our Publick Debts at *Christmas* 1724, when it was not probable that any Part of it was discharged from the particular Tax provided for it. But at *Christmas* 1725, it is to be presumed that the greatest Part of what could be collected from the Tax on *Catholicks* was brought to the *Exchequer*, placed in the Sinking Fund, and from thence reissued in Discharge of such *Exchequer* Notes as were uncancelled at *Christmas* 1724, and of which this Article in particular was then a Part.

It appears from the Act for laying a Duty on Victuallers, *Page* 318. that the Sum of 44,621*l.* 2*s.* 4*d.* was supplied out of the Aids for the Year 1726, to make good the Deficiency of this Tax on *Papists:* from whence it is

43 to

to be inferred, that 55,378*l.* 17*s.* 8*d.* was collected from that Tax, and, together with the Produce of the Sinking Fund, applied to the cancelling of *Exchequer* Notes before *Christmas* 1725. As much therefore of this Sum as at *Christmas* 1725, is stated to have been discharged from the general Provision for the Reduction of our Publick Debts, must be allowed to have been before a Part of them. But the Remainder 44,621*l.* 2*s.* 4*d.* part of 560,312*l.* *Exchequer* Bills, stated in the Schedule annexed to be unsatisfied at *Christmas* 1725, is still to be objected to as no part of those Debts which our Enquiry here relates to, and may be added to the Ballance there produced, to form the exact State of the Decrease of our Publick Debts at *Christmas* 1725.

I endeavour to be as intelligible as I can upon this Subject, and hope the Reader will make all reasonable Allowances for the real Difficulty of settling so long and various an Account of our Incumbrances, in one View, with great Exactness, for the Purpose of an Enquiry that appears hitherto to have been so much neglected by us.

*A State of our Publick Debts at* Christmas 1717, *with the Increase of them from the Subscription of the Irredeemables.*

| | l. | s. | d. |
|---|---|---|---|
| ORIGINALLY contributed for sundry Annuities for long Terms of Years | 9,859,617 | 7 | 1 |
| Ditto for Annuities of Survivorship | 108,100 | 0 | 0 |
| Ditto on Annuities on 2 and 3 Lives | 192,152 | 6 | 3 |
| Ditto for the 9 *per Cent.* Annuities | 900,000 | 0 | 0 |
| Ditto for the commonly call'd Lottery 1710 Annuities | 1,500,000 | 0 | 0 |
| Annuities at 5 *per Cent.* commonly call'd Lottery Annuities | 9,534,357 | 13 | 11¾ |
| The same commonly called Bank Annuities | 1,079,000 | 0 | 0 |
| The same commonly called Navy Annuities | 110,312 | 17 | 4¾ |
| Annuities at 4 *per Cent.* on Tallies of Sol. | 947,514 | 7 | 8 |
| The same for Army Debentures | 2,152,927 | 0 | 7¾ |
| Debentures to the Sufferers at *Nevis* and *St. Christopher's* | 141,093 | 15 | 1¼ |
| The Equivalent Debt | 248,550 | 0 | 9 |
| A Deficiency on the Duty of Hops | 12,480 | 9 | 1 |
| The same on the *East India* Company's Fund | 191,028 | 16 | 6½ |
| Debt on the Lottery 1713 | 588,120 | 0 | 0 |
| The same on the Lottery 1714 | 1,779,020 | 0 | 0 |
| *Exchequer* Bills | 2,561,025 | 0 | 0 |
| Debt to the Bank of *England* | 5,375,027 | 17 | 10¼ |
| The same to the *South-Sea* Company | 10,000,000 | 0 | 0 |
| The same to the *East-India* Company | 3,200,000 | 0 | 0 |
| An Arrear to the Navy since paid from the Sinking Fund | 1,000,000 | 0 | 0 |
| Increase of the Debt in the Publick Accounts, from the Subscription of the Irredeemables which I have since with more Exactness computed to amount to | 3,156,585 | 5 | 0 |
| Total | 54,636,912 | 17 | 4¼ |

*A State of our Publick Debts at* Christmas 1725.

| | *l.* | *s.* | *d.* |
|---|---|---|---|
| DUE to the *South-Sea* Company and their Annuitants | 33,802,483 | 14 | 0 |
| The same to the Bank of *England* | 9,375,027 | 17 | 10½ |
| The same to the *East India* Company | 3,200,000 | 0 | 0 |
| *Debts remaining unsubscrib'd into the* South-Sea *Company in* 1720, *and unsatisfy'd at* Christmas 1725, *viz.* | | | |
| Annuities on Tallies of Sol. | 198,958 | 8 | 3 |
| Army Debentures | 942,134 | 6 | 11¾ |
| Debt remaining on the Lottery 1713 | 32,260 | 0 | 0 |
| The same on the first Lottery 1719 | 58,300 | 0 | 0 |
| *Exchequer* Bills | 560,312 | 10 | 0 |
| Annuities on the Duties on wrought Plate | 312,000 | 0 | 0 |
| *Nevis* and *St. Christopher's* Debentures | 141,093 | 15 | 1¼ |
| Loans on Coals for Building Churches | 68,665 | 0 | 0 |
| Originally contributed for the Purchase of 131,458*l.* 12*s.* 8*d.* *per Ann.* Annuities, for long Terms remaining unsubscrib'd into the *South-Sea* Company. | 1,837,533 | 0 | 9 |
| The same for 29,925*l.* 1*s.* 1*d.* Annuities for short Terms | 272,620 | 11 | 1¼ |
| The same for Annuities on Survivorship | 108,100 | 0 | 0 |
| The same for Annuities for Lives subsisting at *Christmas* 1725 | 188,050 | 6 | 3 |
| Equivalent Debt | 248,550 | 0 | 9 |
| Total | 51,346,089 | 11 | 0¾ |
| Ballance the neat Decrease of our Publick Debts from *Christmas* 1717 to *Christmas* 1725 | 3,290,823 | 6 | 3½ |
| | 54,636,912 | 17 | 4¼ |



*P. S.*

*P. S.* Amongst the various Exceptions taken to my *Essay upon the Publick Debts,* there is but one, and that repeated by two Writers against me, that have induced me to propose an Amendment to it. This is in *Page* 119 where I do not know how it happen'd, that I have, *Line* 33, said, That the Danger *seems to me,* by no means inconsiderable. Whoever consults the general Intention of that Paragraph, will find I should have said, the Danger *may seem to them* by no means inconsiderable. In this manner, I hope the Reader will be so good as to correct my Copy, without insisting that I should charge that as a Mistake upon the Printer, which I indeed suspect I was guilty of my self. There are so many other Instances, in which my Sense has been misrepresented, by Methods that I believe yet want a Description in the Art of Criticism, that it would be an endless Labour, (at least, it is what my Employment will not admit of) to attempt to explain upon them. My Sense is open to every reasonable and unprejudiced Reader, and as far as it is of any Consequence either to him or me to know, whether I have been fairly quoted or not, I doubt not but he will attend to it; but I am sorry that I have Reason to advertise him, that I have seen my self quoted even with Words foisted in upon me, and which I have not used in the Passages quoted from my *Essay,* and this very Forgery afterwards used as the only Cause of railing at me.

*FINIS.*

# REPRESENTATION

OF THE

# HOUSE OF COMMONS

TO

# HIS MAJESTY GEORGE II.

SHEWING THE STATE OF THE

# NATIONAL DEBTS

IN 1716 AND 1726.

---

*Commons Journals*, 8 *April*, 1728.

*** We have referred in the Preface to this volume to the discussions which took place in the House of Commons upon the question agitated in the last three tracts, that is, whether the National Debt had been increased or diminished in the interval between 1716 and 1726. It may seem surprising that there should have been any room for doubt or controversy about such a matter. But owing to the extremely confused manner in which the public accounts were then kept, it was one in regard to which it was by no means easy to arrive at a satisfactory conclusion; and the speakers, whether on the one side or the other, were able, with little difficulty, to deduce apparently well-founded results in favour of their views. In the end, however, it was established, beyond all doubt, that in the interval referred to the principal of the debt had been diminished by above £2,500,000; and that the income of the Sinking Fund amounted, in 1726, to about £1,200,000 a year. To show the results which had been effected, and what was the true state of the public incumbrances in 1716 and 1726, the minister, Sir Robert Walpole, submitted, on the 8th of March, 1728, certain Resolutions to the House of Commons: and these having been carried, formed the groundwork of the following Representation or Report, which the House adopted and ordered to be laid before his Majesty. It was written by Walpole, and is at once elaborate and satisfactory.

# REPRESENTATION.

---

Most gracious Sovereign,

Your Majesty's most dutiful and faithful Subjects, the Commons of *Great Britain*, in Parliament assembled, having, in Duty to your Majesty, for the Sake of Truth, and for the better Information and Satisfaction of all your good People, taken into their Consideration the State of the national Debt, in regard to what Debts have been discharged and paid off, since the Establishment of the Sinking Fund for that Purpose, and what new Debts have, within the said Time, been contracted and incurred, beg Leave, with all Duty and Submission, to lay the same before your Majesty in this our most humble Representation.

The national Debt of this Kingdom contracted in carrying on Two long and expensive Wars, before the happy Accession of your Majesty's late royal Father to the Crown of these Realms, as it was a Matter of the last Consequence to the Nation, was become the Care and Concern of all, who wished well to our present and future Prosperity. This produced several Considerations in Parliament, to find out, and settle, some Means of putting this great Debt into a Method of being gradually reduced and diminished; and the Sinking Fund was at last happily established to general Satisfaction. This Fund became immediately the favorite Article in all parliamentary Considerations, relating to the publick Revenues, and was considered as a national Interest, worthy of the highest Regard and Attention; which was, by all possible Means, to be cherished and improved, and the Produce of it set apart, and kept distinct, from all other Services and Pur-



poses,

poses, and was appropriated by Parliament, to pay off and discharge national Debts, incurred before the Twenty-fifth Day of *December*, 1716.

Hence arose that Distinction in the publick Revenues, which has ever since been so far continued and kept up, that the Nation has seemed to have Two different Interests; one, in the Produce of the Sinking Fund, for the Discharge of the national Debt, another, in the annual Supplies, granted to the Crown, for carrying on the current Service of the Year.

But several Controversies having of late Years been started, concerning what real Benefit had accrued to the Nation from the Produce and Application of the Sinking Fund, if considered and compared with new Debts, supposed to have been incurred within the same Time; the Commons of *Great Britain,* truly sensible of the Weight of this national Debt, a Burthen of itself sufficient to create some Uneasiness in the minds of the People, without the Help of any Aggravations, or Misrepresentations, thought it a Duty incumbent upon them, so far to enter into the Consideration of this important Affair, as to examine, and state, how much of the national Debt, incurred before the Twenty-fifth of *December*, 1716, had been actually paid off, or discharged, and what new Debts had been really contracted and incurred in Support of the Publick, and in carrying on the current Service of the several Years, since that time.

It is well known, with what Content and Chearfulness your Majesty's Subjects have all along paid and contributed towards the annual Interest of this national Debt contracted and incurred in securing to them the inestimable Blessings of your Majesty's most auspicious Reign, and the Protestant Succession in your illustrious Family, and in Defence of their Religion, Liberties, and Properties which they always thought, could not be purchased and preserved, at too dear a Rate; and, from the Time they had the Comfort of having a Sinking Fund settled and established, that gave them the Prospect and Hopes of seeing this great Debt gradually reduced, and discharged, it was a Satisfaction, that rendered the Burthen easy and light; and your People seemed even to forget the great Expence they had been at, happy in the free and full Enjoyment of all that was dear and valuable to them, the Fruit and Return of so much Treasure, necessarily and usefully employed.

Notwithstanding this flourishing State of the publick Credit, and the good Effects of this happy Situation, there were not wanting those, who attempted to disturb the Quiet and Satisfaction, that almost universally prevailed in the Minds of your People, by publishing and promoting, with the greatest Industry, most notorious Misrepresentations of the true State of our Debts, and of the Provisions made for the Discharge of them; and by infusing groundless Jealousies and Insinuations, as if the Produce of the Sinking Fund had been but little and inconsiderable, or that by wrong and imprudent Measures, bad Economy, Neglect, or Mismanagement, unnecessary Expences had been made, and new Debts contracted, that not only equalled, but exceeded by several Millions the Amount of the old Debts, that had been discharged.

These artful Insinuations and Misrepresentations served to a double Purpose, to make our Fellow-subjects restless and uneasy under their present Difficulties, by persuading them, they were endless, and inextricable; and, at the same time, so apprehensive of new Engagements, that they might be prepared rather to suffer all Sorts of Insults and Injuries, than by endeavouring to do themselves Justice, to enter into new Expences, everywhere represented as destructive and intolerable.

This prevailing Mischief called for an immediate Remedy and made it necessary to enter into a strict Disquisition of the Truth and Certainty of these Affairs, that your

 Majesty

Majesty might be truly informed, and your faithful and well-affected Subjects have the Satisfaction to see, how grossly the World had been imposed upon by these groundless Misrepresentations; and that your Enemies might be convinced, that the Wealth and Power of *Great Britain* is not so exhausted, as to render this Nation, under your Majesty's happy Government, less considerable and formidable, than in the Time of any of your royal Predecessors.

We observed, that what gave any Foundation for the Belief of these notorious Falshoods, was the Liberty which some misinformed, or ill-designing, Persons had taken from the several Alterations, which had been made of late Years in the Shape or Denomination of our publick Debts, to make and publish imaginary States of the Whole of those Debts, by putting fictitious Values upon them, at their own Will and Pleasure, and from thence making Balances that might serve their Purpose, but were not really true.

But the Difficulties of making up this Account in that Manner, with any Certainty, made us carefully avoid going into a Method, which might be afterwards liable to Cavil and Disputes, according to the Humour, Caprice, or private Opinion, of every Man.

That we might therefore avoid, as much as possible, any Doubt or Perplexity, we proceeded to state the Truth of this Fact in a Method, that was plain, obvious, and intelligible to the meanest Capacity; and took an Account of the several national Debts, incurred before the Twenty-fifth Day of *December*, 1716, which, since that time, had been actually paid off, or discharged, and also an Account of the several national Debts, that, since that time, had been contracted or incurred, and were still subsisting; upon comparing of which together, it will appear, whether the national Debt is, since the Establishment of the Sinking Fund, increased, or decreased, and to what Amount.

Having now gone through this Enquiry with as much Care and Exactness, as was possible, we beg leave, in the most dutiful Manner, to lay before your Majesty Two Accounts; the First containing the several particular Articles of national Debts, incurred before the Twenty-fifth Day of *December*, 1716, and since discharged; which is as followeth:

An ACCOUNT of such national Debts, incurred before the 25th of *December*, 1716, as have been since discharged; *viz.*

| | | | | Debts discharged. | | |
|---|---|---|---|---|---|---|
| | £ | s. | d. | £ | s. | d. |
| The capital Sum of the Lottery Annuities, established by the Act 3° *Geo.* Imi, which creates the General Fund, and also the Sinking Fund, was . . . . | 9,534,357 | 13 | 11¾ | | | |
| Of which there was subscribed into *South Sea* Stock . . . | 8,329,571 | 10 | 7 | | | |
| The Remainder, paid off, is . | | | | 1,204,786 | 3 | 4¾ |
| Annuities at £ 5 *per Cent.* redeemable by Parliament, and transferrable at the Bank of *England*, were granted by an Act 1° *Geo.* Imi, for . . | 910,000 | — | — | | | |
| Of which there was subscribed into *South Sea* Stock . . | 706,175 | 15 | — | | | |
| The Remainder, paid off, is . | | | | 203,824 | 5 | — |
| Other Annuities, of the same Kind, were granted same Year for . . . . | 169,000 | — | — | | | |
| Of which there was subscribed into *South Sea* Stock . . . | 137,526 | 6 | 8 | | | |
| The Remainder, paid off, is . | | | | 31,473 | 13 | 4 |
| Annuities at £ 4 *per Cent.* redeemable by Parliament, and transferrable at the Bank of *England*, were created for Tallies of Sol, Act 3° *Geo.* Imi, for . | 947,514 | 7 | 8 | | | |
| Of which there was subscribed into *South Sea* Stock . . . | 748,555 | 19 | 5 | | | |
| The Remainder, paid off, is . | | | | 198,958 | 8 | 3 |
| The like Annuities were granted by sundry Acts, for Army Debentures, certified before the 21st of *March*, 1719, for | 1,603,987 | 8 | 1½ | | | |
| Of which there was subscribed into *South Sea* Stock . . | 1,210,792 | 13 | 8 | | | |
| The Remainder, paid off, is . | | | | 393,194 | 14 | 5 |
| The principal Sum remaining due at *Christmas*, 1716, on Lottery, 1713, was | 599,210 | — | — | | | |
| Of which there was subscribed into *South Sea* Stock . . . | 464,990 | — | — | | | |
| The Remainder, paid off, is . | | | | 134,220 | — | — |

| | | | Debts discharged. |
|---|---|---|---|
| | | £ s. d. | £ s. d. |
| The like on Lottery, *Anno* 1714 . . | | 1,812,100 — — | |
| Of which there was subscribed into *South Sea* Stock . . . | | 1,403,970 — — | |
| The Remainder, paid off, is . | | | 408,130 — — |
| The Exchequer Orders, for Army Debentures, certified since the 21st *Mar.* 1719, are all paid off, being . . | | . . . | 548,939 12 6¼ |
| The Deficiency of the Duty on Hops, *Anno* 1711, which was directed by Act of Parliament to be paid off, was . | | . . . | 12,480 9 1 |
| The like of the *East India* Company's Fund stated to *Christmas,* 1716, and paid out of Sinking Fund, was . | | . . . | 79,339 17 5 |
| The 3 *per Cent.* Annuities in the Million Lottery, which were returned as Cash into the Exchequer, and which were, by an Act 13° *Geo.* I^mi^, applied to discharge *Nevis* Debentures, were . | | . . . | 103,272 10 — |
| The principal Sum standing out in Exchequer Bills on 25th *December,* 1716, was . . . . . . | | 4,561,025 — — | |
| Interest and Premium due thereon . | | 35,159 15 7½ | |
| Total Debt in Exchequer Bills . . | | 4,596,184 15 7½ | |
| Of which Two Millions were converted into a Bank Annuity, at £5 *per Cent.* by the Act 3° *Geo.* I^mi^; so deduct that . . . | £ s. d.<br>2,000,000 — — | | |
| And, towards discharging the rest of these Bills, £500,000 was raised by a Lottery. *Anno* 1719, and charged on the Aggregate Fund, of which £441,700 was afterwards subscribed into, and still remains Part of, the *South Sea* Stock, and the remaining £58,300 has been since paid off; so deduct only. . | 441,700 — — | | |
| Total of these Deductions . . | | 2,441,700 — — | |
| The Remainder is the net Debt on this Head, that is paid off | | | 2,154,484 15 7¼ |

| | | Debts discharged. |
|---|---|---|
| | £ s. d. | £ s. d. |
| The Duty on Coals, for building of Churches, *&c.* was granted before 1716, for several Terms of Years, to expire at *Michaelmas*, 1725, and the whole Produce of that Duty was appropriated for those Services, which may be estimated as a Debt at 1716, of . . . | 540,000 — — | |
| *Anno* 1719, £360,000 was granted for these Services, to be raised on a Fund of £21,000 *per Annum*, for 32 Years, in lieu of the Provision by the former Terms, and of that £360,000 there remains undischarged but . . . | 193,140 — — | |
| The Remainder may be estimated so much Debt discharged . . | | 346,860 — — |
| The Debt of the Navy, as it stood on the 31st *December*, 1716, deducting the Effects in the Treasurers Hands, was . | 1,043,336 15 9¾ | |
| Deduct thereout the Sum then unissued on this Head of the Supplies *Anno* 1716, afterwards provided for by £4 *per Cent.* Annuities, Part of the Tallies of Sol, subscribed into, and still remaining in, *South Sea* Stock . . . | 334,239 16 1¼ | |
| The Remainder is the net Debt of the Navy at 1716 . . . . . | | 709,096 19 8½ |
| £29,925 4*s.* 1*d.* *per Annum* of the short Annuities remaining unsubscribed into *South Sea* Stock, which being valued at 14 Years Purchase, the Rate at which they were subscribed into *South Sea* Stock, *Anno* 1720, makes a Debt at 1716, of . . . . . . . | 418,952 17 2 | |
| Deduct the present Value of these Annuities, in which there were but 14 Years 3 Quarters to come at *Christmas*, 1727, at 10 Years Purchase . . . | 299,252 — 10 | |
| The Remainder is so much discharged | | 119,700 16 4 |
| Total Debts discharged . . . . £ | | 6,648,762 5 1½ |

In the stating of which Account, we beg Leave humbly to represent to your Majesty, that the Articles, stated therein by way of Estimate, are the Interest and Pre-

 mium,

mium, said to be due on the Exchequer Bills, the Debt for the building of Churches, and the Value of the Difference in the Terms for the short Annuities; which Articles are so small in respect of the Whole, that any Alteration in those estimated Values would make no material Difference in the real Increase, or Decrease, of the whole Debt.

We beg Leave further humbly to represent to your Majesty, that all the Articles in this Account are stated as the Debts stood on the Twenty-fifth of *December*, 1716, except the First Article of the Lottery Annuities, which is stated at the Sum, that was made Principal at *Michaelmas*, 1717, by the Act, that established the General Fund, and also the Sinking Fund, from which Time only the Sinking Fund commenced; for which Reason, no Credit is taken in this Account for any principal Money, paid off in Part of the Four Lotteries, comprehended in that Sum, between *Christmas*, 1716, and *Michaelmas*, 1717; nor is any thing charged therein for the Deficiencies of Funds standing out at *Christmas*, 1716, and unprovided for, although the Deficiencies of Three of those Lottery Funds, only amounted at *Lady-day*, 1717, to above Two hundred and seventy thousand Pounds; so that, notwithstanding, upon the Subscription of those Lotteries into redeemable Annuities, one Quarter's Interest, due thereon between *Midsummer* and *Michaelmas*, 1717, was made Principal, amounting to £140,884. 6*s.* 3¼*d.* or thereabouts, yet the same was much short of the Deficiencies then incurred on those Funds, and therefore properly charged amongst the Debts incurred before the Twenty-fifth of *December*, 1716.

And we think it proper further to observe upon the Article of the short Annuities remaining unsubscribed, which are stated at £29,925 4*s.* 1*d.* *per Annum*, that it appears, the real Sum did amount to but

 £24,335 17*s.*

£24,335 17*s. per Annum;* which Mistake did arise by a Mis-recital in the Act, of the Sixth Year of your Majesty's late royal Father; which Difference, being valued at the same Rate, that the whole Annuities are herein valued at, makes a Difference of £22,357 8*s.* 4*d.* to be deducted out of the total Sum of the Debts discharged.

The next Account, which is most humbly submitted to your Majesty's Consideration, contains, the several particular Articles of Debts, contracted and incurred since the Twenty-fifth of *December,* 1716, and now subsisting; which is as followeth:

AN ACCOUNT of national Debts, contracted and incurred since the 25th of *December,* 1716, and now subsisting.

| | £ s. d. | |
|---|---|---|
| By *South Sea* Stock, for so much of the Money, agreed to be advanced by the *South Sea* Company on the Subscription of the Lottery, 1710, as was recounted or deducted by them, pursuant to the Act 5° *Geo.* Imi, for making good the Deficiency of their original and additional Funds; *viz.* | | |
| For the Deficiency of their original Fund for Two Quarters, ending at *Midsummer,* 1719 . . . . . . | 141,547 19 1½ | |
| For *ditto* for one Quarter at *Christmas,* 1719 . . . . . . . | 14,846 18 8 | |
| For the Deficiency of their additional Fund for Two Quarters, ending at *Midsummer,* 1719 . . . . . | 25,831 4 10 | |
| | 182,226 2 7½ | |
| By so much of the £5 *per Cent.* Annuities (created by virtue of a Clause in the Land Tax Act 5° *Geo.* Imi, for replacing to the Treasurer of the Navy the Sum he had issued to the *South Sea* Company, for making good the Deficiency of their original Fund at *Midsummer,* 1718) as was subscribed into *South Sea* Stock, the Remainder being paid off . | 107,802 17 4½ | |
| Total Debts contracted, for making good the Deficiencies of the *South Sea* Company's Funds . . | | 290,029 — — |

| | £ | s. | d. | £ | s. | d. |
|---|---|---|---|---|---|---|
| By *South Sea* Stock, for so much of the Money, agreed to be advanced by the *South Sea* Company on the Subscription of Lottery 1710, pursuant to the Act 5° *Geo.* I$^{mi}$, as was paid by them into the Exchequer, and applied to the Sinking Fund . . . . | . | . | . | 328,673 | 4 | 10½ |
| By Annuities at £4 *per Cent.* redeemable by Parliament, charged on the Duty on wrought Plate by the Act 6° *Geo.* I$^{mi}$ . . . . . . | . | . | . | 312,000 | — | — |
| By the Benefit Tickets in Lottery 1719, charged on the Duty on Coals 5° *Geo.* I$^{mi}$, for . . . . . . | 500,000 | — | — | | | |
| Of which there has been paid off | 65,395 | — | — | | | |
| The Remainder was subscribed into *South Sea* Stock . . . | | | | 434,605 | — | — |
| By Exchequer Bills, standing out, and charged on the Duty on Victuallers by the Act 12° *Geo.* I$^{mi}$. . . . | . | . | . | 486,600 | — | — |
| By the like Exchequer Bills, charged on Surplus of Coals 13° *Geo.* I$^{mi}$ . | . | . | . | 338,800 | — | — |
| By the Debt of the Navy, as it stood on the 31st *December*, 1727, deducting the Effects then stated to be in the Hands of the Treasurers . . . . . | 1,937,023 | 4 | 9¼ | | | |
| Deduct the Sum, then unissued to the Treasurer of the Navy, of the Supplies *Anno* 1727, which has been since issued to him . . . . . . . | 199,742 | 2 | 6 | | | |
| The Remainder is the net Debt on this Head . . . . | | | | 1,737,281 | 2 | 3¼ |
| Total of these Debts . . . . . £. | | | | 3,927,988 | 7 | 1¾ |

From these Two Accounts, we presume most humbly to represent to your Majesty, that the several national Debts, incurred before the Twenty-fifth Day of *December*, 1716, which have been since discharged, after deducting the before-mentioned Sum of £22,357. 8*s*. 4*d*. do amount in the whole to the Sum of Six millions Six hundred and Twenty-six thousand four hundred and Four Pounds Sixteen Shillings, and Nine Pence Half-peny; and that the several national Debts, incurred since the said twenty-fifth day of *December* 1716, and now subsisting, amount

10 together

together to the Sum of Three millions Nine hundred Twenty-seven thousand Nine hundred Eighty-eight Pounds, Seven shillings, and One Peny Three Farthings.

Which being deducted out of the Amount of the Debts discharged, the difference is so much real Decrease of the national Debt since the Twenty-fifth Day of *December*, 1716, being Two millions Six hundred Ninety-eight thousand Four hundred and Sixteen pounds, Nine Shillings, and Seven pence Three Farthings. And, that the State of the new-contracted Debts may appear in a true Light, we think it necessary, for the better Information of your Majesty, to distinguish them under the proper Heads of Services, for which they were contracted, and, by way of Explanation, to observe, that a considerable Part of the new contracted Debt, amounting to the Sum of £703,740 6*s.* 2½*d.* was occasioned by the annual Provisions, made by Parliament for making good the yearly Deficiencies of the General Fund to and for the year ending at *Michaelmas* 1726, pursuant to the Directions of the Act establishing the General Fund, the Surplus whereof composes Part of the Sinking Fund; and by these Means the Sinking Fund has received annually some Proportion out of the Supplies of the Year:

And, that the further Sum of £290,029 has been raised by new-contracted Debts, and is included therein, for making good at several Times the Deficiencies of the original and additional Funds of the *South Sea* Company; which Two Sums, amounting together to the Sum of £993,769 6*s.* 2½*d.* having been applied towards making good Deficiencies of the General Fund, and other Funds, established before the 25th Day of *December*, 1716, ought to be distinguished from the national Debt incurred since that *Time:*

As likewise the sum of 328,673*l.* 4*s.* 10½*d.* another Part of the said new-contracted Debts, which was occasioned by Stock created for so much of the Money to be advanced by the *South Sea* Company, upon the Enlargement of their Capital Stock by the Subscription of the Tickets in the Lottery, *Anno* 1710, pursuant to an Act, of the Fifth Year of the Reign of your Majesty's late royal Father, as was paid into the Exchequer; and, as the same was applied to the Uses of the Sinking Fund, and no Part of it to any other publick Services, this Sum ought also to be distinguished from the rest of the Debts, contracted since the Establishment of the Sinking Fund: Which Three Sums making together the Sum of £1,322,442. 11*s.* 1*d.* and being deducted out of the said Sum of £3,927,988. 7*s.* 1¾*d.* the remaining Sum of £2,605,545. 16*s.* —¾*d.* is the whole national Debt, that has been contracted or incurred, for answering or defraying the annual Charges and Expences of the Publick for the current Service of the several Years since the 25th Day of *December*, 1716, including therein the whole Debt of the Navy, as it stood on the 31st Day of *December*, 1727.

And further, to obviate any Objections that may be made to the stating of the Account of national Debts, contracted and incurred since the Twenty-fifth of *December*, 1716, and still subsisting, it is proper to observe, that no Notice is taken therein of the Debts by Loans, or Exchequer Bills, on the annual Land Taxes, or Malt Duties; because, as those Loans, or Bills, are weekly discharged out of the Produce of those Taxes, and as often as any Deficiencies happen thereon, they, as well as the Deficiencies of Grants, are not suffered to remain as Debts, but are constantly from Year to Year, discharged by being made Part of the Supplies, granted for the current Service of the subsequent Years; and accordingly Provision has been already made for such of them as can be anyways ascertained, out of the Supplies for the Service of the Year 1728; therefore, they were not proper to be brought into this Account.

Having thus humbly represented to your Majesty the



true

true State of the Decrease of the national Debts since the 25th day of *December*, 1716, and the Establishment of the Sinking Fund, with the Occasions and Services for which the several new Debts have been incurred, we beg Leave, by this our humble Representation, to lay before your Majesty the Circumstances this Nation was in, with regard to the national Debt, before the Establishment of the Sinking Fund, and what happy Consequences have arisen from the Establishment thereof.

At the Accession of your Majesty's late royal Father to the Throne of these Realms, a great part of the publick Debts, consisted of absolute Annuities, granted for very long Terms of Years, which were only to be discharged by the wearing out of those Terms; other great Parts thereof were the capital Stocks of the Bank, the *South Sea* and *India* Companies, at very high Interest; other Debts were charged upon particular Funds, appropriated to pay off and discharge the principal Moneys, with Interest at very high Rates, in course, to Multitudes of People, both at home and abroad; other great Parts thereof were in Exchequer Bills, circulated and exchanged at very high Rates for Interest, Premium, and Charges; and the Debts of the Army, which were very considerable, were not then liquidated, nor had any provision at all then been made for the Discharge of them: Besides this, the Funds themselves appropriated for these Debts, were most of them deficient; so that, if these Debts had been suffered to continue in this State, so far would they have been from being lessened to any degree, that new Burthens must have been laid on the Nation, for securing the Debts unprovided for.

Soon after his late Majesty's Accession, an unnatural Rebellion broke out, during which, not only all Thoughts for any Method for the more speedy Payment of our Debts were of Necessity suspended, but new and heavy Debts were contracted; and in the Year 1715, Annuities, at Five Pounds *per Cent.* redeemable by Parliament, were sold for £1,079,000 besides a considerable Addition to the capital Stock of the *South Sea* Company.

But no sooner was that Rebellion defeated, and the Fears of the People removed, but the Parliament immediately began to set about the great Work of putting the national Debt in a Method of being sooner discharged with Honour and Justice; and, in the Year 1717, the Foundation was laid, by establishing the Sinking Fund; the Consequences and Advantages whereof will best appear, by considering, what it is, and by what Means it was perfected.

The only Methods, that could be thought of, for paying off the national Debts, must be, either by improving and augmenting the Produce of the Funds, already settled for the Payment of the Principal and Interest, or by granting new Taxes and Impositions upon the People, or by a Reduction of the Interest, made payable on the several Debts; and, as the first Method would have been found not sufficient to answer this desirable End, and the Second would have been very grievous and burthensome to the People, the principal Method, that was then thought expedient, and most free from Objections, was to reduce the high Interest, and other Charges, payable on all the publick Debts; But, as great Part of those Debts were not subject to any Power of Redemption, and as none of them were redeemable, but on Payment of the principal Money, it manifestly appeared, that such a Reduction could never be made, without the voluntary Consent of the Proprietors of such, as were irredeemable, or a legal Tender to the others of their principal Money; both which seemed at that time almost impracticable; but, by an extraordinary Zeal and Application to the publick Service, this Difficulty was surmounted, with respect to the whole of the Debts, that were then redeemable, by procuring, not only the voluntary Consent of the *South*

*Sea* Company to the Reduction of the Interest on their whole capital Stock, then consisting of Ten Millions, from £6 to £5 *per Cent.* and of the Bank to a like Reduction on an Annuity, then payable to them in respect of a Sum of upwards of £1,775,000, and to a great Abatement in their Allowances for circulating Exchequer Bills, then amounting to more than £4,500,000, at an annual Charge of above £7 *per Cent.* but also by engaging those Corporations to furnish sufficient Sums for paying the principal Money to such of the Proprietors of other redeemable Debts, amounting to more than Nine Millions, as would not voluntarily choose to accept an Interest at £5 *per Cent.* for the future.

This Provision being made, the Act passed in the Third Year of his late Majesty's Reign, for establishing the General Fund; whereby the Proprietors of certain Debts therein mentioned, all carrying an Interest at £6 *per Cent.* had their free Election, either to accept an Interest at £5 *per Cent.* per Annum, or to receive their principal Money: and so general was the Satisfaction of all the Proprietors, that few and very inconsiderable Sums were demanded to be paid off; but the principal Sums, that were voluntarily reduced to £5 *per Cent.* amounted to £9,392,311 4*s.* 2½*d.* or thereabouts; and by this Method more than £25,800,000 was at once voluntarily reduced from £6 *per Cent.* or upwards, to £5 *per Cent.* which was an annual Saving of above £320,000.

By the same Act, not only the Surplus of this General Fund, but the Surplusses of several other Funds, were appropriated to the Discharge of national Debts, contracted before the Twenty-fifth of *December*, 1716: And this was the Beginning and Establishment of the Sinking Fund.

From this happy Event arose such general Satisfaction in all Degrees of People, that though the Interest of the publick Debts was reduced, and the Proprietors received a less Income from them, than before, yet their Security for their Capital being so much mended, the Rate or Price for the Purchase of these Debts soon advanced to a much higher Value, than they were at before the Reduction; and it was easy to foresee, that, in Process of Time, a further Reduction might have been made by the same just and honourable Methods, without any extraordinary Advantages to be granted for the effecting it.

Had this Method (begun and executed so successfully and with such Satisfaction), been further pursued and without Interruption, the dangerous and mischievous Part of the late *South Sea* Scheme might have been avoided; and yet the further Reduction of Interest might have been obtained, and taken place, much sooner than it has done by the execution of that Scheme.

But now, at length, not only the Reduction from £5 to £4 *per Cent.* settled by the *South Sea* Act, has taken place, but a voluntary Reduction hath also been made, by the Bank of *England*, from £5 to £4 *per Cent.* Interest or Annuities, for Two principal Sums belonging to them, amounting together to upwards of £3,775,000, and by these several Reductions a further Addition is made to the Sinking Fund of more than £377,000 *per Annum*, from *Midsummer* last: By all these Means, and by the Savings of Interest of the Debts, that have been already discharged, and by several wise Provisions for the Improvement of the Funds themselves, this Sinking Fund is risen to, and may be reasonably estimated at £1,200,000 *per Annum*, or thereabouts; and will be every Year increasing from the further Savings of the Interest of the remaining Debts, from time to time, as they shall be paid off.

But, if anything were further necessary to demonstrate the immediate and certain Advantages, that have accrued to the Publick from the Methods used and established to discharge the national Debts, it is sufficient only to reflect, that the Interest of the greatest Part of the Debt, being now actually reduced from £6 to £4 *per Cent.* makes a Saving of One-third of the Interest of such Debt; which, being in the Hands and Possession of the Government, and applicable, from time to time, to the Discharge of the Principal, makes a Gain and Profit to the Publick, equal to the Discharge of One-third of such Principal.

And, if the Amount of the Produce of the Sinking Fund did appear originally to be about £400,000 *per Annum* only, the Produce of the said Fund being now raised to about £1,200,000 *per Annum,* the Addition of £800,000 *per Annum* to the Sinking Fund, which is just so much gained by the Publick, if valued at Twenty-five Years Purchase, at which Rate all Annuities are now currently sold, makes a real Profit to the Publick, amounting to Twenty Millions.

This is the happy State of the Sinking Fund, taken separately, and by itself; but, if we cast our Eyes upon the State of our publick Credit in general, it must be an additional Satisfaction to us, that by preserving the publick Faith inviolable, by the Discharge of the old Exchequer Bills, and the Reduction of the high Interest on all our standing Debts, the whole Credit, that is taken on the annual Funds, for carrying on the current Service of the Year, is and may be supplied for the future at £3 *per Cent.* or less, for Interest, Premium, and Charges, by Exchequer Bills, created, just as the Occasions of the Publick require, without any Loans, or being obliged to any Persons for Money to be advanced or lent, on the Credit of them; and so far is the Publick from being under the former Necessities of allowing extravagant Interest, Premiums, or Discounts, for any Money they want, that the only Contest now among the Creditors of the Publick is, that every one of them desires to be the last in course of Payment.

Permit us then, Most gracious Sovereign, to congratulate your Majesty on the comfortable Prospect we have

 now

now before us, if, notwithstanding the many Difficulties this Nation has laboured under since the happy Accession of your Majesty's late royal Father to the Throne, notwithstanding the unnatural Rebellion, which soon after broke out, and the many heinous Plots and Conspiracies, which have since been formed and carried on for overturning the Religion and Liberties of our Country, and the Protestant Succession in your most illustrious Family, the many Disturbances, which have arisen, and the uncertain and embroiled Condition of the Affairs of *Europe,* not a little fomented and encouraged by the false Intelligence, and malicious Insinuations, which have been industriously spread abroad by your Majesty's and our Enemies, of the uneasy and perplexed State of our Affairs at home, as if that had rendered it almost impossible for this Nation effectually to exert themselves in Defence of their own just Rights and Possessions, and for establishing, and securing, the publick Peace and Tranquillity; if, notwithstanding these and many other Difficulties, which we laboured under, and while the Sinking Fund was yet in its Infancy, and so much less than it now is, we have been able to diminish the national Debts so much already, what may we not hope for in regard to a more speedy and sensible Discharge of them for the future, now the Sinking Fund is so greatly increased, and our publick Credit in so flourishing a Condition?

The finishing and perfecting this great Work seems to be a peculiar Glory reserved for your Majesty's Reign. From your known Goodness and Wisdom, the present Age may promise themselves the certain and immediate Benefit of your Majesty's particular Regard to the public Credit, and your universal care and Concern for the Ease and Happiness of your People, which our latest Posterity must remember, and acknowledge with Duty and Gratitude.

*** The subsequent history of Sir Robert Walpole's Sinking Fund is given at considerable length in the tract by Dr. Price in a subsequent part of this volume. Here it may be sufficient to observe that some disguised inroads were made on it in the period between 1727 and 1733. But, in the latter year, it was directly charged with £500,000 required for the public Service; and in the following year £1,200,000 was taken from it. In 1735 and 1736 it was in great part anticipated and mortgaged.

These invasions of the fund occasioned lengthened debates both in the Lords and Commons, which, however, present few features of interest. The question really at issue was not clearly stated. But, however disguised, it plainly regarded the policy or impolicy of an increase of taxation; for if the Sinking Fund were to be kept up it could only be by imposing taxes to make good those deficiencies of revenue which the Minister proposed to supply by diverting the fund from what was supposed to be its proper object.

The following protest against the alienation of the fund in 1733 was signed by a great number of peers:

Dissentient,

"BECAUSE the Sinking Fund, being composed
" of the surplusses of funds originally granted as a
" security to the creditors of the public; and these sur-
" plusses arising principally from a reduction to 4 *per cent.*
" of the interest granted them for the most part at 6 *per*
" *cent.* we cannot but think that this saving ought to be
" applied, according to the most inviolable rules of equity,
" and according to the known design, and the repeated
" and solemn engagements of parliament, to a gradual
" payment of the principal to these creditors of the public,

" who have parted with a third of their revenue in this " view, and upon this confidence."

" BECAUSE we apprehend, that the method of apply-" ing large portions of the Sinking Fund to the service of " the current year, must, in effect, perpetuate the debts " and taxes which lie on the nation, and is, therefore, " injurious to the public. Had this whole fund been " strictly applied from the beginning to its proper use, we " think it may be demonstrated, not only that much more " of the national debt might have been discharged, but " that those taxes, which are most oppressive to the poor, " and most prejudicial to trade, might have been already " taken off, since upwards of 480,000*l. per ann.* belonging, " as we conceive, to this fund, has been applied to other " uses."

" BECAUSE we conceive, that if the whole produce " of the Sinking Fund were not to be applied to the dis-" charge of the public debts, it would be much more for " the ease of trade and advantage for the nation, that some " of those grievous taxes out of which it arises should " cease, than that they should be continued to supply the " current service at 4 *per cent.* which might certainly be " supplied by other ways at a cheaper rate. Most of " these taxes were laid during the necessity of two long " and expensive wars, and were granted only for terms of " years, that so the principal and interest of the loans " made on them might be paid off in a certain limited " time. Thus, the nation consented to pay in some man-" ner a double tax, in order to avoid the long and uncer-" tain continuance of such grievous impositions; and " according to the first design, many of them would have " been very near the expiration of their term at this hour. " The wisdom of parliament, indeed, thought fit after-" wards to throw these taxes, and the method of discharg-" ing these public debts, into another form, which now

 " subsists.

" subsists. But we cannot conceive that this was done
" with a view to continue our taxes and debts the longer.
" On the contrary, we are sure it was done in the view of
" discharging both the sooner; and it is this very view
" which, we apprehend, must be fatally disappointed, if
" the present method of diverting any part of the Sinking
" Fund from the payment of the public debts be suffered
" to continue."

" BECAUSE we apprehend, that this method may
" create the utmost uneasiness in the minds of his
" Majesty's subjects; and may tend, if not timely pre-
" vented by the wisdom and authority of this house, to
" diminish their affection for his person and government.
" Hitherto, whilst they have laboured under the weight
" of taxes, and groaned under the oppression of excise
" laws, the hope of seeing speedily an end put to both has
" been their sole consolation. But nothing can maintain
" this hope, except a due application of the entire Sinking
" Fund to the discharge of those debts, for the discharge
" of which these taxes were given. If some parts of this
" fund, therefore, continue to be mortgaged off, and other
" parts to be applied to the current service, even in the
" midst of profound peace, this hope must sink, and despair
" arise in its stead, &c. &c."

*Bedford, Craven, Gainsborough, Winchelsea* and *Nottingham, Gower, Bridgwater, Bruce, Carteret, Bathurst, Shaftsbury, Sunderland, Coventry, Thanet,* &c. &c.

OF

# PUBLIC CREDIT,

BY

DAVID HUME, Esq.

FROM

## ESSAYS,

MORAL, POLITICAL, AND LITERARY,

PUBLISHED IN

1752.

## Of Public Credit.

IT appears to have been the common practice of antiquity, to make provision, during peace, for the necessities of war, and to hoard up treasures before-hand, as the instruments either of conquest or defence; without trusting to extraordinary impositions, much less to borrowing in times of disorder and confusion. Besides the immense sums above mentioned*, which were amassed by Athens, and by the Ptolemies, and other successors of Alexander; we learn from Plato†, that the frugal Lacedemonians had also collected a great treasure; and Arrian ‡ and Plutarch || take notice of the riches which Alexander got possession of on the conquest of Susa and Ecbatana, and which were reserved, some of them, from the time of Cyrus. If I remember right, the scripture also mentions the treasure of Hezekiah and the Jewish princes; as profane history does that of Philip and Perseus, kings of Macedon. The antient republics of Gaul had commonly large sums in reserve §. Every one knows the treasure seized in Rome by Julius Cæsar, during the civil wars: and we find afterwards, that the wiser emperors, Augustus, Tiberius, Vespasian, Severus, &c. always discovered the prudent foresight, of saving great sums against any public exigency.

On the contrary, our modern expedient, which has become very general, is to mortgage the public revenues,



and

* Essay V. † Alcib. I. ‡ Lib. iii.

|| Plut. *in vita* Alex. He makes these treasures amount to 80,000 talents, or about 15 millions sterl. Quintus Curtius (lib. v. cap. 2.) says, that Alexander found in Susa above 50,000 talents.

§ Strabo, lib. iv.

and to trust that posterity will pay off the incumbrances contracted by their ancestors: And they, having before their eyes, so good an example of their wise fathers, have the same prudent reliance on *their* posterity; who, at last, from necessity more than choice, are obliged to place the same confidence in a new posterity. But not to waste time in declaiming against a practice which appears ruinous, beyond all controversy; it seems pretty apparent, that the ancient maxims are, in this respect, more prudent than the modern; even though the latter had been confined within some reasonable bounds, and had ever, in any instance, been attended with such frugality, in time of peace, as to discharge the debts incurred by an expensive war. For why should the case be so different between the public and an individual, as to make us establish different maxims of conduct for each? If the funds of the former be greater, its necessary expences are proportionably larger; if its resources be more numerous, they are not infinite; and as its frame should be calculated for a much longer duration than the date of a single life, or even of a family, it should embrace maxims, large, durable, and generous, agreeably to the supposed extent of its existence. To trust to chances and temporary expedients, is, indeed, what the necessity of human affairs frequently renders unavoidable; but whoever voluntarily depend on such resources, have not necessity, but their own folly, to accuse for their misfortunes, when any such befal them.

If the abuses of treasures be dangerous, either by engaging the state in rash enterprizes, or making it neglect military discipline, in confidence of its riches; the abuses of mortgaging are more certain and inevitable; poverty, impotence, and subjection to foreign powers.

According to modern policy war is attended with every destructive circumstance; loss of men, encrease of taxes,



decay

decay of commerce, dissipation of money, devastation by sea and land. According to ancient maxims, the opening of the public treasure, as it produced an uncommon affluence of gold and silver, served as a temporary encouragement to industry, and atoned, in some degree, for the inevitable calamities of war.

It is very tempting to a minister to employ such an expedient, as enables him to make a great figure during his administration, without overburthening the people with taxes, or exciting any immediate clamours against himself. The practice, therefore, of contracting debt will almost infallibly be abused, in every government. It would scarcely be more imprudent to give a prodigal son a credit in every banker's shop in London, than to impower a statesman to draw bills, in this manner, upon posterity.

What then shall we say to the new paradox, that public incumbrances, are, of themselves, advantageous, independent of the necessity of contracting them; and that any state, even though it were not pressed by a foreign enemy, could not possibly have embraced a wiser expedient for promoting commerce and riches, than to create funds, and debts, and taxes, without limitation? Reasonings, such as these, might naturally have passed for trials of wit among rhetoricians, like the panegyrics on folly and a fever, on BUSIRIS and NERO, had we not seen such absurd maxims patronized by great ministers, and by a whole party among us.

Let us examine the consequences of public debts, both in our domestic management, by their influence on commerce and industry; and in our foreign transactions, by their effect on wars and negociations.

Public securities are with us become a kind of money, and pass as readily at the current price as gold or silver. Wherever any profitable undertaking offers itself, how expensive soever, there are never wanting hands enow to embrace it; nor need a trader, who has sums in the public stocks, fear to launch out into the most extensive trade; since he is possessed of funds, which will answer the most sudden demand that can be made upon him. No merchant thinks it necessary to keep by him any considerable cash. Bank-stock, or India-bonds, especially the latter, serve all the same purposes; because he can dispose of them, or pledge them to a banker, in a quarter of an hour; and at the same time they are not idle, even when in his scritoire, but bring him in a constant revenue. In short, our national debts furnish merchants with a species of money, that is continually multiplying in their hands, and produces sure gain, besides the profits of their commerce. This must enable them to trade upon less profit. The small profit of the merchant renders the commodity cheaper, causes a greater consumption, quickens the labour of the common people, and helps to spread arts and industry throughout the whole society.

There are also, we may observe, in ENGLAND and in all states, which have both commerce and public debts, a set of men, who are half merchants, half stock-holders, and may be supposed willing to trade for small profits; because commerce is not their principal or sole support, and their revenues in the funds are a sure resource for themselves and their families. Were there no funds, great merchants would have no expedient for realizing or securing any part of their profit, but by making purchases of land; and land has many disadvantages in comparison of funds. Requiring more care and inspection, it divides the time and attention of the merchant; upon any tempting offer or extraordinary accident in trade, it is not so easily converted into money; and as it attracts too much, both by the many natural pleasures it affords, and the authority it gives, it soon converts the citizen into the country gentleman. More men, therefore, with large stocks and incomes, may naturally be supposed to continue in trade, where there are public debts; and this, it must be owned, is of some advantage to commerce, by diminishing its profits, promoting circulation, and encouraging industry.

But, in opposition to these two favourable circumstances, perhaps of no very great importance, weigh the many disadvantages which attend our public debts, in the whole *interior* œconomy of the state: You will find no comparison between the ill and the good which result from them.

*First*, It is certain, that national debts cause a mighty confluence of people and riches to the capital, by the great sums, levied in the provinces to pay the interest; and perhaps, too, by the advantages in trade above mentioned, which they give the merchants in the capital above the rest of the kingdom. The question is, whether, in our case, it be for the public interest, that so many privileges should be conferred on LONDON, which has already arrived at such an enormous size, and seems still encreasing? Some men are apprehensive of the consequences. For my own part, I cannot forbear thinking, that, though the head is undoubtedly too large for the body, yet that great city is so happily situated, that its excessive bulk causes less inconvenience than even a smaller capital to a greater kingdom. There is more difference between the prices of all provisions in PARIS and LANGUEDOC, than between those in LONDON and YORKSHIRE. The immense greatness, indeed, of LONDON, under a government which admits not of discretionary power, renders the people factious, mutinous, seditious, and even perhaps rebellious. But to this evil the national debts themselves tend to provide a remedy. The first visible eruption, or even immediate danger of public disorders, must alarm all the stock-holders, whose property is the most precarious of any; and will make them fly to the support of government, whether menaced by Jacobitish violence or democratical frenzy.

*Secondly,* Public stocks, being a kind of paper-credit have all the disadvantages attending that species of money. They banish gold and silver from the most considerable commerce of the state, reduce them to common circulation, and by that means render all provisions and labour dearer than otherwise they would be.

*Thirdly,* The taxes, which are levied to pay the interests of these debts, are apt either to heighten the price of labour, or be an oppression on the poorer sort.

*Fourthly,* As foreigners possess a great share of our national funds, they render the public, in a manner, tributary to them, and may in time occasion the transport of our people and our industry.

*Fifthly,* The greater part of the public stock being always in the hands of idle people, who live on their revenue, our funds, in that view, give great encouragement to an useless and unactive life.

But though the injury, that arises to commerce and industry from our public funds, will appear, upon balancing the whole, not inconsiderable, it is trivial, in comparison of the prejudice that results to the state considered as a body politic, which must support itself in the society of nations, and have various transactions with other states in wars and negociations. The ill, there, is pure and unmixed, without any favourable circumstance to atone for it; and it is an ill too of a nature the highest and most important.

We have, indeed, been told, that the public is no weaker upon account of its debts; since they are mostly due among ourselves, and bring as much property to one as they take from another. It is like transferring money from the right hand to the left; which leaves the person neither richer nor poorer than before. Such loose reasonings and specious comparisons will always pass, where we judge not upon principles. I ask, Is it possible, in the nature of things, to overburthen a nation with taxes, even



where

where the sovereign resides among them? The very doubt seems extravagant; since it is requisite, in every community, that there be a certain proportion observed between the laborious and the idle part of it. But if all our present taxes be mortgaged, must we not invent new ones? And may not this matter be carried to a length that is ruinous and destructive?

In every nation, there are always some methods of levying money more easy than others, agreeably to the way of living of the people, and the commodities they make use of. In GREAT BRITAIN, the excises upon malt and beer afford a large revenue; because the operations of malting and brewing are tedious, and are impossible to be concealed; and at the same time, these commodities are not so absolutely necessary to life, as that the raising of their price would very much affect the poorer sort. These taxes being all mortgaged, what difficulty to find new ones! what vexation and ruin of the poor!

Duties upon consumptions are more equal and easy than those upon possessions. What a loss to the public, that the former are all exhausted, and that we must have recourse to the more grievous method of levying taxes!

Were all the proprietors of land only stewards to the public, must not necessity force them to practise all the arts of oppression used by stewards; where the absence or negligence of the proprietor render them secure against enquiry?

It will scarcely be asserted, that no bounds ought ever to be set to national debts; and that the public would be no weaker, were twelve or fifteen shillings in the pound, land-tax, mortgaged, with all the present customs and excises. There is something, therefore, in the case, beside the mere transferring of property from the one hand to another. In 500 years, the posterity of those now in the coaches, and of those upon the boxes, will probably have

 changed

changed places, without affecting the public by these revolutions.

Suppose the public once fairly brought to that condition, to which it is hastening with such amazing rapidity; suppose the land to be taxed eighteen or nineteen shillings in the pound; for it can never bear the whole twenty; suppose all the excises and customs to be screwed up to the utmost which the nation can bear, without entirely losing its commerce and industry; and suppose that all those funds are mortgaged to perpetuity, and that the invention and wit of all our projectors can find no new imposition, which may serve as the foundation of a new loan; and let us consider the necessary consequences of this situation. Though the imperfect state of our political knowledge, and the narrow capacities of men, make it difficult to foretel the effects which will result from any untried measure, the seeds of ruin are here scattered with such profusion as not to escape the eye of the most careless observer.

In this unnatural state of society, the only persons, who possess any revenue beyond the immediate effects of their industry, are the stock-holders, who draw almost all the rent of the land and houses, besides the produce of all the customs and excises. These are men, who have no connexions with the state, who can enjoy their revenue in any part of the globe in which they chuse to reside, who will naturally bury themselves in the capital or in great cities, and who will sink into the lethargy of a stupid and pampered luxury, without spirit, ambition, or enjoyment. Adieu to all ideas of nobility, gentry, and family. The stocks can be transferred in an instant, and being in such a fluctuating state, will seldom be transmitted during three generations from father to son. Or were they to remain ever so long in one family, they convey no hereditary authority or credit to the possessor; and by this means, the several ranks of men, which form a kind of independent

 magistracy

magistracy in a state, instituted by the hand of nature, are entirely lost; and every man in authority derives his influence from the commission alone of the sovereign. No expedient remains for preventing or suppressing insurrections, but mercenary armies: No expedient at all remains for resisting tyranny: Elections are swayed by bribery and corruption alone: And the middle power between king and people being totally removed, a grievous despotism must infallibly prevail. The landholders, despised for their poverty, and hated for their oppressions, will be utterly unable to make any opposition to it.

Though a resolution should be formed by the legislature never to impose any tax which hurts commerce and discourages industry, it will be impossible for men, in subjects of such extreme delicacy, to reason so justly as never to be mistaken, or amidst difficulties so urgent, never to be seduced from their resolution. The continual fluctuations in commerce require continual alterations in the nature of the taxes; which exposes the legislature every moment to the danger both of wilful and involuntary error. And any great blow given to trade, whether by injudicious taxes or by other accidents, throws the whole system of government into confusion.

But what expedient can the public now employ, even supposing trade to continue in the most flourishing condition, in order to support its foreign wars and enterprizes, and to defend its own honour and interest, or those of its allies? I do not ask how the public is to exert such a prodigious power as it has maintained during our late wars; where we have so much exceeded, not only our own natural strength, but even that of the greatest empires. This extravagance is the abuse complained of, as the source of all the dangers, to which we are at present exposed. But since we must still suppose great commerce and opulence to remain, even after every fund is mortgaged; these riches must be defended by proportional

 power;

power; and whence is the public to derive the revenue which supports it? It must plainly be from a continual taxation of the annuitants; or, which is the same thing, from mortgaging anew, on every exigency, a certain part of their annuities; and thus making them contribute to their own defence, and to that of the nation. But the difficulties, attending this system of policy, will easily appear, whether we suppose the king to have become absolute master, or to be still controuled by national councils, in which the annuitants themselves must necessarily bear the principal sway.

If the prince has become absolute, as may naturally be expected from this situation of affairs, it is so easy for him to encrease his exactions upon the annuitants, which amount only to the retaining money in his own hands, that this species of property would soon lose all its credit, and the whole income of every individual in the state must lie entirely at the mercy of the sovereign: A degree of despotism, which no oriental monarchy has ever yet attained. If, on the contrary, the consent of the annuitants be requisite for every taxation, they will never be persuaded to contribute sufficiently even to the support of government; as the diminution of their revenue must in that case be very sensible, would not be disguised under the appearance of a branch of excise or customs, and would not be shared by any other order of the state, who are already supposed to be taxed to the utmost. There are instances, in some republics, of a hundredth penny, and sometimes of the fiftieth, being given to the support of the state; but this is always an extraordinary exertion of power, and can never become the foundation of a constant national defence. We have always found, where a government has mortgaged all its revenus, that it necessarily sinks into a state of languor, inactivity, and impotence.

Such are the inconveniencies, which may reasonably be foreseen, of this situation, to which GREAT BRITAIN is



visibly

visibly tending. Not to mention, the numberless inconveniencies which cannot be foreseen, and which must result from so monstrous a situation as that of making the public the chief or sole proprietor of land, besides investing it with every branch of customs and excise, which the fertile imagination of ministers and projectors have been able to invent.

I must confess, that there is a strange supineness, from long custom, creeped into all ranks of men, with regard to public debts, not unlike what divines so vehemently complain of with regard to their religious doctrines. We all own, that the most sanguine imagination cannot hope, either that this or any future ministry will be possessed of such rigid and steady frugality, as to make a considerable progress in the payment of our debts; or that the situation of foreign affairs will, for any long time, allow them leisure and tranquillity for such an undertaking. *What then is to become of us?* Were we ever so good Christians, and ever so resigned to Providence; this, methinks, were a curious question, even considered as a speculative one, and what it might not be altogether impossible to form some conjectural solution of. The events here will depend little upon the contingencies of battles, negociations, intrigues, and factions. There seems to be a natural progress of things, which may guide our reasoning. As it would have required but a moderate share of prudence, when we first began this practice of mortgaging, to have foretold, from the nature of men and of ministers, that things would necessarily be carried to the length we see; so now, that they have at last happily reached it, it may not be difficult to guess at the consequences. It must, indeed, be one of these two events; either the nation must destroy public credit, or public credit will destroy the nation. It is impossible that they can both subsist, after the manner they have been hitherto managed, in this, as well as in some other countries.

There was, indeed, a scheme for the payment of our debts, which was proposed by an excellent citizen, Mr. HUTCHINSON, above thirty years ago, and which was much approved of by some men of sense, but never was likely to take effect. He asserted, that there was a fallacy in imagining that the public owed this debt; for that really every individual owed a proportional share of it, and paid, in his taxes, a proportional share of the interest, beside the expence of levying these taxes. Had we not better, then, says he, make a distribution of the debt among ourselves, and each of us contribute a sum suitable to his property, and by that means discharge at once all our funds and public mortgages? He seems not to have considered, that the laborious poor pay a considerable part of the taxes by their annual consumptions, though they could not advance, at once, a proportional part of the sum required. Not to mention, that property in money and stock in trade might easily be concealed or disguised; and that visible property in lands and houses would really at last answer for the whole: An inequality and oppression, which never would be submitted to. But though this project is not likely to take place; it is not altogether improbable, that, when the nation becomes heartily sick of their debts, and is cruelly oppressed by them, some daring projector may arise with visionary schemes for their discharge. And as public credit will begin, by that time, to be a little frail, the least touch will destroy it, as happened in France during the regency; and in this manner it will *die of the doctor*.

But it is more probable, that the breach of national faith will be the necessary effect of wars, defeats, misfortunes, and public calamities, or even perhaps of victories and conquests. I must confess, when I see princes and states fighting and quarrelling, amidst their debts, fund, and public mortgages, it always brings to my mind a match of cudgel-playing fought in a *China* shop. How can it be expected, that sovereigns will spare a species of property, which is pernicious to themselves and to the public, when they have so little compassion on lives and properties, that are useful to both? Let the time come (and surely it will come) when the new funds, created for the exigencies of the year, are not subscribed to, and raise not the money projected. Suppose, either that the cash of the nation is exhausted; or that our faith, which has hitherto been so ample, begins to fail us. Suppose, that, in this distress, the nation is threatened with an invasion; a rebellion is suspected or broken out at home; a squadron cannot be equipped for want of pay, victuals, or repairs; or even a foreign subsidy cannot be advanced. What must a prince or minister do in such an emergence? The right of self-preservation is unalienable in every individual, much more in every community. And the folly of our statesmen must then be greater than the folly of those who first contracted debt, or, what is more, than that of those who trusted, or continue to trust this security, if these statesmen have the means of safety in their hands, and do not employ them. The funds, created and mortgaged, will, by that time, bring in a large yearly revenue, sufficient for the defence and security of the nation: Money is perhaps lying in the exchequer, ready for the discharge of the quarterly interest: Necessity calls, fear urges, reason exhorts, compassion alone exclaims: The money will immediately be seized for the current service, under the most solemn protestations, perhaps, of being immediately replaced. But no more is requisite. The whole fabric, already tottering, falls to the ground, and buries thousands in its ruins. And this, I think, may be called the *natural death* of public credit: For to this period it tends as naturally as an animal body to its dissolution and destruction.

So great dupes are the generality of mankind, that, notwithstanding such a violent shock to public credit, as a voluntary bankruptcy in ENGLAND would occasion, it would not probably be long ere credit would again revive in as flourishing a condition as before. The present king of FRANCE, during the late war, borrowed money at a lower interest than ever his grandfather did; and as low as the BRITISH parliament, comparing the natural rate of interest in both kingdoms. And though men are commonly more governed by what they have seen, than by what they foresee, with whatever certainty; yet promises, protestations, fair appearances, with the allurements of present interest, have such powerful influence as few are able to resist. Mankind, are, in all ages, caught by the same baits: The same tricks, played over and over again, still trepan them. The heights of popularity and patriotism are still the beaten road to power and tyranny; flattery, to treachery; standing armies to arbitrary government; and the glory of God to the temporal interest of the clergy. The fear of an everlasting destruction of credit, allowing it to be an evil, is a needless bugbear. A prudent man, in reality, would rather lend to the public immediately after we had taken a spunge to our debts, than at present; as much as an opulent knave, even though one could not force him to pay, is a preferable debtor to an honest bankrupt: For the former, in order to carry on business, may find it his interest to discharge his debts, where they are not exorbitant: The latter has it not in his power. The reasoning of TACITUS *, as it is eternally true, is very applicable to our present case. *Sed vulgus ad magnitudinem beneficiorum aderat: Stultissimus quisque pecuniis mercabatur: Apud sapientes cassa habebantur, quæ neque dari neque accipi, salva republica, poterant.* The public is a debtor, whom no man can oblige to pay. The only check which the creditors have upon her, is the interest of preserving credit; an interest, which may easily be overbalanced by a great debt, and by a difficult



* *Hist. lib.* iii.

and extraordinary emergence, even supposing that credit irrecoverable. Not to mention, that a present necessity often forces states into measures, which are, strictly speaking, against their interest.

These two events, supposed above, are calamitous, but not the most calamitous. Thousands are thereby sacrificed to the safety of millions. But we are not without danger, that the contrary event may take place, and that millions may be sacrificed for ever to the temporary safety of thousands*. Our popular government, perhaps, will render it difficult or dangerous for a minister to venture on so desperate an expedient, as that of a voluntary bankruptcy. And though the house of Lords be altogether composed of proprietors of land, and the house of Commons chiefly; and consequently neither of them can be supposed to have great property in the funds. Yet the connections of the members may be so great with the proprietors, as to render them more tenacious of public faith, than prudence, policy, or even justice, strictly speaking, requires. And perhaps too, our foreign enemies may be so politic as to discover, that our safety lies in despair, and may not, therefore, show the danger, open and barefaced, till it be

17 inevitable

---

* I have heard it has been computed, that all the creditors of the public, natives and foreigners, amount only to 17,000. These make a figure at present on their income; but in case of a public bankruptcy, would, in an instant, become the lowest, as well as the most wretched of the people. The dignity and authority of the landed gentry and nobility is much better rooted; and would render the contention very unequal, if ever we come to that extremity. One would incline to assign to this event a very near period, such as half a century, had not our fathers' prophecies of this kind been already found fallacious, by the duration of our public credit so much beyond all reasonable expectation. When the astrologers in FRANCE were every year foretelling the death of HENRY IV. *These fellows*, says he, *must be right at last*. We shall, therefore, be more cautious than to assign any precise date; and shall content ourselves with pointing out the event in general.

inevitable. The balance of power in EUROPE, our grandfathers, our fathers, and we, have all deemed too unequal to be preserved, without our attention and assistance. But our children, weary of the struggle, and fettered with incumbrances, may sit down secure, and see their neighbours oppressed and conquered; till, at last, they themselves and their creditors lie both at the mercy of the conqueror. And this may properly enough be denominated the *violent death* of our public credit.

These seem to be events, which are not very remote, and which reason forsees as clearly almost as she can do any thing that lies in the womb of time. And though the ancients maintained, that, in order to reach the gift of prophecy, a certain divine fury or madness was requisite, one may safely affirm, that, in order to deliver such prophecies as these, no more is necessary than merely to be in one's senses, free from the influence of popular madness and delusion.

*FINIS.*

# ACCOUNT

OF THE

# NATIONAL DEBT,

FROM

BLACKSTONE'S COMMENTARIES,

BOOK I. CAP. 8.

## Account of the National Debt.

IN order to take a clear and comprehensive view of the nature of this national debt, it must first be premised, that after the revolution, when our new connections with Europe introduced a new system of foreign politics, the expenses of the nation, not only in settling the new establishment, but in maintaining long wars, as principals, on the continent, for the security of the Dutch barrier, reducing the French monarchy, settling the Spanish succession, supporting the house of Austria, maintaining the liberties of the Germanic body, and other purposes, increased to an unusual degree: insomuch that it was not thought advisable to raise all the expenses of any one year by taxes to be levied within that year, lest the unaccustomed weight of them should create murmurs among the people. It was therefore the policy of the times to anticipate the revenues of their posterity, by borrowing immense sums for the current service of the state, and to lay no more taxes upon the subject than would suffice to pay the annual interest of the sums so borrowed: by this means converting the principal debt into a new species of property, transferable from one man to another at any time and in any quantity. A system which seems to have had it's original in the state of Florence, *A.D.* 1344: which government then owed about 60000*l.* sterling: and, being unable to pay it, formed the principal into an aggregate sum, called metaphorically a *mount* or *bank*, the shares whereof were transferable like our stocks, with interest at 5 *per cent.* the prices



varying

varying according to the exigencies of the state.[1] This policy of the English Parliament laid the foundation of what is called the national debt: for a few long annuities created in the reign of Charles II. will hardly deserve that name. And the example then set has been so closely followed during the long wars in the reign of queen Anne, and since, that the capital of the national debt, (funded and unfunded) amounted in January 1771* to above 140,000,000*l.* to pay the interest of which, and the charges for management, amounting annually to upwards of four millions and a half, the extraordinary revenues just now enumerated (excepting only the land tax and annual malt tax) are in the first place mortgaged, and made perpetual by parliament. Perpetual, I say; but still redeemable by the same authority that imposed them: which, if it at any time can pay off the capital, will abolish those taxes which are raised to discharge the interest.

By this means the quantity of property in the kingdom is greatly increased in idea, compared with former times; yet, if we coolly consider it, not at all increased in reality. We may boast of large fortunes, and quantities of money in the funds. But where does this money exist? It exists only in name, in paper, in public faith, in parliamentary security: and that is undoubtedly sufficient for the creditors of the public to rely on. But then what is the pledge, which the public faith has pawned for the security of these debts? The land, the trade, and the personal industry of the subject; from which the money must arise that supplies the several taxes. In these therefore, and these only the property of the public creditors does really



[1] *Pro tempore, pro spe, pro commodo, minuitur eorum pretium atque augescit.* Aretin. See Mod. Un. Hist. xxxvi. 116.

* We quote the edition published in 1773: the "Commentaries" were originally published in 1765.

and intrinsically exist: and of course the land, the trade, and the personal industry of individuals, are diminished in their true value just so much as they are pledged to answer. If A's income amounts to 100*l. per annum*; and he is so far indebted to B, that he pays him 50*l. per annum* for his interest; one half of the value of A's property is transferred to B the creditor. The creditor's property exists in the demand which he has upon the debtor, and no where else; and the debtor is only a trustee to his creditor for one half of the value of his income. In short, the property of a creditor of the public consists in a certain portion of the national taxes: by how much therefore he is the richer, by so much the nation, which pays these taxes, is the poorer.

The only advantage, that can result to a nation from public debts, is the increase of circulation by multiplying the cash of the kingdom, and creating a new species of currency, assignable at any time and in any quantity; always therefore ready to be employed in any beneficial undertaking, by means of this it's transferable quality; and yet producing some profit even when it lies idle and unemployed. A certain proportion of debt seems therefore to be highly useful to a trading people; but what that proportion is, it is not for me to determine. Thus much is indisputably certain, that the present magnitude of our national incumbrances very far exceeds all calculations of commercial benefit, and is productive of the greatest inconveniences. For, first, the enormous taxes, that are raised upon the necessaries of life for the payment of the interest of this debt, are a hurt both to trade and manufactures, by raising the price as well of the artificer's subsistence, as of the raw material, and of course, in a much greater proportion, the price of the commodity itself. Nay, the very increase of paper-circulation itself, when extended beyond what is requisite for commerce or foreign exchange, has a natural tendency to increase the price of provisions as well as of all other merchandize. For, as it's effect is to multiply the cash of the kingdom, and this to such an extent that much must remain unemployed, that cash (which is the universal measure of the respective values of all other commodities) must necessarily sink in it's own value, and every thing grow comparatively dearer. Secondly, if part of this debt be owing to foreigners, either they draw out of the kingdom annually a considerable quantity of specie for the interest; or else it is made an argument to grant them unreasonable privileges in order to induce them to reside here. Thirdly, if the whole be owing to subjects only, it is then charging the active and industrious subject, who pays his share of the taxes, to maintain the indolent and idle creditor who receives them. Lastly, and principally, it weakens the internal strength of a state, by anticipating those resources which should be reserved to defend it in case of necessity. The interest we now pay for our debts would be nearly sufficient to maintain any war, that any national motives could require. And if our ancestors in king William's time had annually paid, so long as their exigencies lasted, even a less sum than we now annually raise upon their account, they would in the time of war have borne no greater burdens, than they have bequeathed to and settled upon their posterity in time of peace; and might have been eased the instant the exigence was over.

The respective produces of the several taxes beforementioned were originally separate and distinct funds; being securities for the sums advanced on each several tax, and for them only. But at last it became necessary, in order to avoid confusion, as they multiplied yearly, to reduce the number of these separate funds, by uniting and blending them together; superadding the faith of parliament for the general security of the whole. So that there are now only three capital funds of any account, the *aggregate* fund, and the *general* fund, so called from such union and addition; and the *south sea* fund, being the produce of the taxes appropriated to pay the interest of such part of the national debt as was advanced by that company and it's annuitants. Whereby the separate funds, which were thus united, are become mutual securities for each other; and the whole produce of them, thus aggregated, liable to pay such interest or annuities as were formerly charged upon each distinct fund; the faith of the legislature being moreover engaged to supply any casual deficiencies.

The customs, excises, and other taxes, which are to support these funds, depending on contingencies, upon exports, imports, and consumptions, must necessarily be of a very uncertain amount; but they have always been considerably more than was sufficient to answer the charge upon them. The surplusses therefore of the three great national funds, the aggregate, general, and south sea funds, over and above the interest and annuities charged upon them, are directed by statute 3 Geo. I. c. 7. to be carried together, and to attend the disposition of parliament; and are usually denominated the *sinking* fund, because originally destined to sink and lower the national debt. To this have been since added many other intire duties, granted in subsequent years; and the annual interest of the sums borrowed on their respective credits is charged on and payable out of the produce of the sinking fund. However the neat surplusses and savings, after all deductions paid, amount annually to a very considerable sum; particularly in the year ending at Christmas 1768, to almost two millions of money. For as the interest on the national debt has been at several times reduced, (by the consent of the proprietors, who had their option either to lower their interest or be paid their principal) the savings from the appropriated revenues must needs be extremely large. This sinking fund is the last resort of the nation; it's only domestic resource, on which must chiefly depend all the hopes we can entertain of ever discharging or moderating our incumbrances. And therefore the prudent application of the large sums, now arising from this fund, is a point of the utmost importance, and well worthy the serious attention of parliament; which was thereby enabled, in the year 1765, to reduce above two millions sterling of the public debt; and about three millions in the three succeeding years.

*FINIS.*

AN

# A P P E A L

TO

# THE PUBLIC,

On the SUBJECT of the

# NATIONAL DEBT.

---

A NEW EDITION.

WITH

An APPENDIX.

---

By RICHARD PRICE, D.D. F.R.S.

---

LONDON:

Printed for T. CADELL, in the STRAND.

M.DCC.LXXIV.

# PREFACE

## TO THE

# SECOND EDITION. (a)

IN perusing this Appeal to the Public, it will be found, that one of my chief purposes in it has been to prove the following proposition: "That to alienate a fund, "appropriated to the payment of public debts, while it "can be avoided, by borrowing money at simple interest "on new taxes or savings, is a most pernicious measure." And it may be depended upon, that, if there is any certainty in numbers, this has been proved beyond the possibility of reasonable doubt.

Dr. DAVENANT, in the reign of King *William*, warned the kingdom of the danger which would attend breaking into appropriated funds. He was disregarded; and the public debts increased so much as to be generally thought, in the year 1716, *insupportable*. This gave occasion to the establishment, in that year, of a general saving under the name of the SINKING FUND; which repeated laws declared should be applied to the payment of the public debts, and *to no other purpose whatever*. This fund soon became the only hope of the kingdom; and, could it have been defended against alienation, it would, in a few years, have accomplished all that was expected from it. Notice was given of this, in the year 1726, by a writer of great abilities



(a) The first edition was published in 1771.

abilities (*a*); and the public was a *second* time warned of the fatal consequences which would follow alienations. But this warning was also neglected; and, in consequence of this, our debts, instead of being annihilated, as they might have been, have increased from 17 millions, their amount in 1699, and from 52 millions, their amount in 1726, to 140 millions, their amount nearly in the present year.—There is now one farther attempt made to bring back the State to the path of rectitude and safety by a writer indeed of much less weight, but possessed of the same good intentions. He knows that he cannot expect to be regarded. The same measures will be pursued; and it is easy to foresee in what they will terminate.

"In FRANCE the custom of borrowing on Funds, in-
"stead of levying money for the necessary supplies within
"the year, was begun in 1678. M. COLBERT perceived
"the tendency of it; and after remonstrating against it
"in vain, he told the ministers who advised it, that they
"should answer to God for the mischief they would do to
"the king and the state, by introducing so pernicious a
"practice(*b*)."—The managers of our affairs will have more to answer for. They have not only introduced this pernicious practice; but they have defeated the effect of an establishment, which would have preserved us from all the dangers attending it.—The greatest sufferers by this practice will in the end be the moneyed people themselves; or those creditors of the public, who are now maintained by the contributions of the poor, and the labour of the industrious.—It is impossible that debts always increasing, should not in time sink the kingdom. They have already done us unspeakable mischief. A considerable part of our people is lost. By extending the influence of the

4 crown

(*a*) Tract No. III. in this volume.

(*b*) I have related this fact from the most respectable authority.

crown, they have undermined the foundation of our liberties. It is doubtful also, whether they have not turned the balance of trade against us, by raising the price of our manufactures, and carrying out of the kingdom about a million and a half every year, in payments of dividends to foreigners. The late augmentation of the navy, though probably a right measure, has, by taking a large annual sum from the SINKING FUND, removed us to a greater distance than ever from the possibility of discharging them. An unfavourable turn of events in the *East Indies*, or any considerable deficiencies in the revenue, might destroy our ability of paying even the interest of them. At least, it is to be feared, that another war would exhaust our resources, and bring our affairs to a *crisis*.

In these circumstances; some vigorous measures for our own preservation, ought to be entered into immediately. More especially, it seems to be time for the public creditors to think of securing their capital. The law once gave them the Sinking Fund as a sacred and unalienable security. Would it be wrong to require a *restitution* of it; and to make this a condition of future loans?

Upon the whole. It is my sincere conviction, that a policy, too narrow and selfish, has brought us into threatning circumstances. I have written under this conviction; and, if my feelings have drawn from me any language improperly severe, I hope I shall be excused.

I will only add, that I think myself much obliged to the civility of *some* who have addressed remarks to me. But their objections have not yet led me to any change of sentiments.—Whenever I am made sensible of having fallen into any material mistakes, I shall think myself bound to acknowledge and retract them. In the mean time, I must beg leave to avoid disputes; and to refer in silence all I have written to the decision of the public.

# ADDITIONAL

# PREFACE.

THE foregoing Preface was written near two years ago.—In a new edition of my Treatise on *Reversionary Payments*, published since that time, I have given an account of a plan for discharging in forty years, a hundred millions of the national debt, with a *surplus* of a million *per annum*. This plan is an improvement of a scheme proposed in the former editions of the same *Treatise*, and referred to in this pamphlet.—It contains a method of reducing public debts which, with respect to expedition and efficiency, cannot be far from the utmost limits of possibility; and I have shewn, that, were it established, it would at all times lessen the public burdens, and operate as a preservative of the kingdom from calamities that are otherwise unavoidable.—I am in hopes that every competent judge who will examine that plan must find this to be true. At the time it was published, the kingdom was possessed of the very surplus it required; but I am obliged to take the present opportunity to mention, with regret and pain, that this is now no longer true.

In consequence of the decline of trade, and the loss of an annual payment of 400,000*l.* from the *East-India Company*, the surplus of the revenue has suffered a diminution that leaves us little to expect from it: And last year, had it not been for the money raised for paying the debts of this Company, the whole revenue of the nation would have been scarcely sufficient to bear its current and



necessary

necessary expences (*a*)—This, I think, never before happened in a time of peace, since the first establishment of the Sinking Fund.

Two years ago trade had been carried much beyond its natural limits; and, aided by luxury and false credit, had occasioned an unusual flow of money into the Sinking Fund, and produced all the appearances of increasing wealth and prosperity.—But it might have been seen that these appearances were deceitful and transient.— False credit cannot be permanent; and every thing, when it has got beyond a certain point, must sink.—Accordingly, in the summer of 1772 fictitious credit broke; and the ease with which money had been procured by issuing paper, being lost, the appearance of a general scarcity of money followed; many were involved in ruin; and trade, before overdone, stagnated and declined.—In this condition we now find ourselves; our merchants, fearful of the hazards of commerce and the competitions of adventurers, calling in their capitals (*b*): all sorts of provisions at an exorbitant

7 price;

(*a*) In 1772, a million and a half of the 3 *per cents* was paid off. At opening the budget that year, this was declared by Lord *North* in the House of Commons to be *the commencement of a plan for paying off in ten years* 17 *millions of the national debt*, and thus increasing in that time the Sinking Fund half a million *per ann.* and preparing the nation for bearing another war.—But in the very next year, only 800,000*l.* was paid; and this was done, not with real surplus money, but with part of 1,400,000*l.* borrowed on *Exchequer Bills*, and lent to the *East-India* Company to enable them to pay arrears of customs and other debts due to government.—Should, therefore, as some expect, this loan (or the greatest part of it) never be re-paid; more will have been added last year to the public debts than was taken from them.—It must be soon known how much will be paid this year.

(*b*) To this chiefly has been owing the late alteration of foreign exchanges in our favour; and not, as has been strangely asserted, to the Coin-Act.—An Act, which, by oppressing the poor, distressing traffic at a very critical time, and increasing *Paper-money*, has, I am afraid, done more harm than good.

price; our manufacturers starving; the poor an intolerable burden; and multitudes leaving the kingdom.

These evils are perhaps *temporary;* and a revival of trade may succeed the glut which speculation and extravagance have occasioned. But should the contrary happen; should trade, opprest by the permanent incumbrances upon it, go on to languish; the time must soon arrive when, instead of enjoying any SURPLUS in the revenue, DEFICIENCIES will arise; and when, consequently, it will be necessary, in order to bear the expences of the peace-establishment, either to impose new taxes, or to make reductions in the Funds (*c*). Every one must be sensible of the alarm this would give, and the danger into which it would bring us.

What renders our prospect in these circumstances more



(*c*) Our circumstances and those of the *French*, are in this respect extremely different. Among us, through misconduct, which the nation will rue and execrate, the expence of every war remains till another war comes. Among them, the expences of wâr are soon cleared away. They have more than once, by acts of power to which no resistance has been made, but which would *here* unhinge all government, reduced their funds one half; and I am informed, that since the last war their finances have been improved several millions *per annum*, and are at this time in a very good state.

The state of public credit, among us, for the last twenty years, may be learnt from the following account of the average prices of the 3 *per cent.* funds.

From 1751 to 1755, they kept between 104 and 106.—In 1755, the war which begun in that year reduced them to 92; and, in 1756, to 89.—In 1757 and 1758 they fluctuated between 89 and 93—In 1759, between 89 and 82—In 1760, between 84 and 75—In 1761, between 80 and 71.—In 1762, they fell to 62.—In 1763, the peace raised them to 94: But from that year to the present, though there has been no interruption of peace, they have been sinking; and are now at 86¼; that is, lower than they were at any time during the first four years of the last war; and near 20 *per cent.* lower than in the peace that preceded it.

threatning is, the tender and precarious nature of *Paper-credit.* This is now our chief support.—BANK NOTES, in particular, make the principal part of our cash; and were they to lose their credit, all the money in the kingdom would not much exceed the annual amount of the taxes; the revenue would fall to nothing, and general devastation would take place. For this reason, it may be said with truth, that more depends at present on the wisdom and good conduct of the BANK DIRECTORS than on the whole Legislature—One wrong step in them; an improvement in the art of forgery; or any event that should produce a general disposition to prefer *coin* to their *paper*, would undo us.—Paper-money, having only a local and imaginary value, can bear no alarm. It shrinks at every approach of danger. *Suspicion* subverts it: and when it falls, it gives no warning, but falls at once. The condition, therefore, of every state in which this prevails must be always critical in proportion to the quantity of it, and the degree of dependence upon it.

The History of *France*, in the year 1720, furnishes us with a striking proof of the truth of these observations. The *Royal Bank* in that kingdom had issued paper to the amount of above a hundred millions sterling. While this paper maintained its currency, it produced all the effects of a sudden importation of so much real money into the kingdom. The price of every thing was raised excessively. Estates were sold at 80 years purchase. The interest of money was reduced to 2 *per cent.* New buildings arose in town and country. Industry revived; luxury prevailed; and wealth and plenty reigned every where.—— But this state of seeming prosperity was of short duration. An *arret of council*, intended to reduce the price of provisions, and also to give permanency to the circulating paper, produced in one day its ruin (*d*). General poverty

9 and

(*d*) This arret was published on the 21st of May 1720; and "the

and misery followed; and Paper-credit in that kingdom has never since recovered itself.

It is well known that the frenzy of this memorable year was not confined to *France*. At the breaking of the *South-sea Bubble*, our own bank was in some danger; and had paper circulation failed then *here* as well as in *France*, we might *now* have been only the happier. The public debts then existing would have been annihilated, and could not easily have been afterwards renewed; and we should at this moment have had only the *recollection* to trouble us of distresses still in our view; and which, every year that has since passed, has been rendering more and more terrible when they come.

Before the *Revolution* the supplies of every year were raised within the year by *temporary* taxes.—After the *Revolution* this became too difficult; and money was raised by perpetuating and anticipating the taxes, and forming them into funds for discharging the principal and interest of sums borrowed upon them. But even in this way, sufficient supplies for carrying on King *William's* and Queen *Anne's* wars could not have been procured, had it not been for the establishment of the BANK. This provided a substitute for money which answered all its purposes, and enabled the nation to make payments that it could not otherwise have made.

From that period, *Paper-credit* and *taxes* have been increasing together.—When *moderate*, these *promote* trade, by quickening industry, supplying with a medium of traffic, and producing improvements. But, when *excessive*, they *ruin* trade, by rendering the means of subsistence too

10 dear,

following day a person might have starved with "a hundred millions in his pocket." See Sir *James Steuart's* Enquiry into the Principles of Political Œconomy, vol. II. book IV. chap. 26, &c. where a particular account is given of the events to which I have here referred.

dear, distressing the poor, and raising the price of labour and (*e*) manufactures.—They are now among us in this state of excess: And, in conjunction with some other causes, have brought us into a situation which is, I think, unparalleled in the history of mankind.—Hanging on paper, and yet weighed down by heavy burdens.—Trade necessary to enable us to support an enormous debt; and yet that debt, together with an excess of Paper-money, working continually towards the destruction of trade.—Public spirit, independence and virtue undermined by luxury; and yet luxury necessary to our existence.—Other kingdoms have enacted sumptuary laws for suppressing luxury. Were we to do this with any considerable effect the consequence might prove fatal.—In short: were our people to avoid destroying themselves by intemperance, or only to leave off the use of one or two foreign weeds, the revenue would become deficient, and a public bankruptcy might ensue.—On such ground it is impossible that any kingdom should stand long.—A dreadful convulsion cannot be very distant. The next war will scarcely leave a chance for escaping it. But we are threatened with it sooner.—An open rupture with our colonies may bring it on immediately.

*Newington-Green,*
*Feb.* 16*th*, 1774.



(*e*) The poor-rate alone is now equal to all the ordinary taxes formerly; and the expences of *peace* DOUBLE to those of *war* in King *William's* time.

# APPEAL

## TO

# THE PUBLIC, &c.

---

## PART I.

IN a late Treatise on *Reversionary Payments, Annuity-Schemes*, and *Population*, I have offered to the public several observations on a subject, now highly interesting to this kingdom: I mean, the NATIONAL DEBT. These observations appeared to me important; and in this opinion of them I have been since confirmed, by the concurring opinions of some of the best judges. But they have not yet, as far as I know, been favoured with the attention of the managers of our affairs; and this is one of the reasons of the present Appeal to the Public. Could our Governors be engaged to take them into consideration, they would perhaps see them to be worth their regard. Be this, however, as it will, I cannot make myself easy, without begging from the Public one further hearing on this subject.

I have observed in page 163 of the Treatise I have mentioned, that in order to justify the Alienation of the SINKING FUND, it has been usual to plead, that when money is wanted, it makes no difference, whether it is taken from hence, or procured by making a new loan charged on new funds.



funds.

funds. I have called this a SOPHISM: and asserted in opposition to it, that the difference between these two ways of procuring money is no less than *infinite*. Those who have entered into my ideas, cannot possibly want any other proof of this assertion than I have given. But, as it is a point of particular consequence, and some have objected to it, I shall here give as distinct and clear an explanation of it as I can.

A SINKING FUND, according to the most *general* idea of it, signifies " any SAVING or SURPLUS, set apart from the rest of an annual income, and appropriated to the purpose of paying off or sinking debts."

There are *three ways* in which a kingdom may apply such a saving.

1*st*. The *interests* disengaged from time to time by the payments made with it, may be themselves applied to the payment of the public debts.

Or, 2*dly*, They may be spent on current services.

Or, 3*dly*, They may be immediately annihilated by abolishing the taxes charged with them.

In the first way of employing a *Sinking Fund*, it becomes a fund always increasing itself. Every new *interest* disengaged by it, containing the same powers with it, and joining its operation to it; and the same being true of every interest disengaged by every interest, it must act, not merely with an *increasing* force, but with a force the *increase* of which is continually accelerated; and which, therefore, however small at first, must in time, become equal to *any* effect. In the *second* way of applying a *Sinking Fund*, it admits of no increase, and must act for ever with the same force.—In other words, A *Sinking Fund*, according to the first method of applying it, is, if I may be allowed the comparison, like a grain of corn sown, which, by having its produce sown and the produce of that produce and so on, is capable of an increase that will

 soon

soon stock a province or support a kingdom.—On the contrary. A *Sinking Fund*, according to the second way of applying it, is like a seed the produce of which is consumed; and which, therefore, can be of no farther use, and has all its powers destroyed.

The *former*, be its income at first ever so much exceeded by the new debts incurred annually, will soon become superior to them and cancel them.—The *latter*, if at first inferior to the new debts incurred annually, will for ever remain so; and a state that has no other provision for the payment of its debts, will be always accumulating them till it sinks.

What has been now said of the *second* mode of applying a fund is true in a higher degree of the *third*. For in this case, the disengaged interests, instead of being either added to the fund, or spent from year to year on useful services, are immediately given up.

In short, a fund of the *first* sort is money bearing *compound* interest—A fund of the *second* sort is money bearing *simple* interest—And a fund of the *third* sort is money bearing *no* interest—The difference between them is, therefore, properly infinite. And this is so evident, that I cannot go on with this explanation without some reluctance. I will, however, rely on the candour of those who must be already abundantly convinced, while I endeavour to illustrate these observations by the following example.

Let us suppose a nation to be capable of setting apart the annual sum of 200,000*l.* as a fund for keeping the debts it is continually incurring in a course of redemption; and let us consider what its operation will be, in the THREE ways of applying it which I have described, supposing the public debts to bear an interest of 5 *per cent.* and the period of operation 86 years.

A debt of 200,000*l.* discharged the first year, will

 disengage

disengage for the public an annuity of 10,000*l.* If this annuity, instead of being spent on current services, is added to the fund, and both employed in paying debts, an annuity of 10,500*l.* will be disengaged the *second* year, or of 20,500*l.* in both years. And this again, added to the fund the *third* year, will increase it to 220,500*l.*; with which an annuity will be then disengaged of 11,025*l.*; and the *sum* of the disengaged annuities will be 31,525*l.*: which added to the fund the *fourth* year, will increase it to 231,525*l.*, and enable it then to disengage an annuity of 11,576*l.* 5*s* and render the *sum* of the disengaged annuities in *four* years, 43,101*l.* 5*s.*—Let any one proceed in this way, and he may satisfy himself, that the *original Fund*, together with the *sum of the annuities disengaged*, will increase faster and faster every year, till, in 86 years, the *fund* becomes 13,283,414*l.* and the *sum* of the disengaged annuities 13,083,414*l.*(*a*)—The full value, therefore, at 5 *per cent.* of an annuity of 13,083,414*l.* will have been paid in 86 years, that is, very nearly, 262 millions of debt; And, consequently, it appears, that tho' the state had been all along adding every year to its debts three millions; that is tho' in the time supposed it had contracted a debt of 258 millions, it would have been more than discharged, at no greater expence than an annual saving of 200,000*l.*—But if the same fund had been employed in the *second* of the three ways I have described, the annuity disengaged by it would have been every year 10,000*l.*; and the sum of the annuities disengaged would have been 86 times 10,000*l.* or 860,000*l.*;—The *discharged* debt, therefore, would have been no more than the value of such an annuity, or 17,200,000*l.* But besides this, it must be considered, that there will be an expense *saved*, in consequence of applying every year the disengaged annuities to current services,

 for

(*a*) See Appendix, note A, Table I.

for which otherwise equivalent sums must have been provided by new taxes, or assessments 10,000*l.* will be saved at the beginning of the *second* year; 20,000*l.* at the beginning of the *third;* 30,000*l.* at the beginning of the *fourth;* and 850,000*l.* at the beginning of the 86th year (*a*); and the sum of all these savings is 36,550,000*l.* which, added to 17,200,000*l.* the debt *discharged,* makes 53,750,000*l.* Substract the last last sum from 262 millions, and 208,250,000*l.* will be the complete loss of the public arising, in 86 years, from employing an annual sum of 200,000*l.* in the second way rather than the first.

Little need be said of the effect of the same fund applied in the *third* way. It is obvious that the whole advantage derived from it, would be the discharge of a debt of 200,000*l.* *annually;* or of 17,200,000*l.* in all.

Similar deductions might be made on the supposition of lower rates of interest and shorter periods.—Thus; let a state be supposed to run in debt two millions annually, for which it pays 4 *per cent.* interest. In 70 years, a debt of 140 millions would be incurred. But an appropriation of 400,000*l.* *per ann.*, if employed in the *first* way, would, at the end of this term, leave the nation *beforehand,* six millions; whereas, if applied in the *second* way, the nation would be left in debt, 73 millions; and in the *third* way, 112 millions.

It is an observation of particular importance here, that there can be no reason for employing a *fund* in the *second* of the ways I have mentioned, rather than the *first.* In both cases, the taxes are continued during the operation

17 of

(*a*) This is an Arithmetical Progression; and the sum of every such progression is found by multiplying the *sum* of the first and last terms by *half* the number of terms; or, in the present case, by multiplying 860,000 by 42½.

of the fund. In the former, a disengaged tax or annuity is employed to *pay* debts; and in the latter, it is employed to *save* debts which must have been otherwise incurred. If employed to *pay* debts it will obtain for the public other annuities, and those others *in infinitum.* But if it is employed to *save* debts; or, which in the present case is the same, the *interests* of debts, as those interests would not themselves have borne interest, no farther profit could arise—In short, in the one case the disengaged annuity is PROLIFIC, and contains in itself a number continually growing of other annuities—In the other case, it is a BARREN annuity.—To employ a fund, therefore, in the latter way rather than the former, is preferring an exemption from the burden of ONE annuity, to an exemption from MANY; and subjecting a kingdom to the loss of 208 millions in the *first* example, and 79 millions in the second, only for the sake of avoiding one expence by continuing another equal expence.

In the third or last way of employing a Fund, the Public will obtain some advantage by the abolition of taxes. But it is an advantage unspeakably overbalanced by disadvantages.—In the first example, we have seen, that it is gaining 36 millions and a half at the expence of 262 millions; or, in other words, procuring an ease from taxes which, in 86 years, would have been increased to 850,000*l.* *per annum,* at the expence of a Fund that, in the same time, would have eased the Public of above THIRTEEN MILLIONS *per annum* in taxes.—But I need not insist on the folly of this, the abolition of taxes being what we have hitherto known little of in this country.

It must have been observed, that a *Fund* of the *second* sort is a greater check on the increase of public debts, than a Fund of the *third* sort. But the difference is not considerable, and there is one circumstance which, I think, reduces it almost to nothing.—It supposes a strict and inviolable application of the perpetuated annuities to the purpose of saving equivalent debts. But such an application of them is scarcely practicable. When small, they would be neglected; and, when large, they would, like the savings of persons in private life, only occasion an abatement of frugality: and, for this reason, if a *Fund* is not applied in the first way, it might, for ought I know, be best that it should be employed in the last way; for a kingdom would then be sure of receiving *some* relief, whereas otherwise it might receive *none*.

Perhaps, indeed, one might observe, in general, that if a *Sinking Fund* is not employed in the first way, and rendered absolutely inaccessible and unalienable, it would be most for the benefit of a State to be without any such provision. For, in these circumstances, tho' incapable of doing much good, it might do much harm by encouraging extravagance, and supplying Ministers of State with more money to be spent in maintaining undue influence and corruption.

But it is time to enter into a more explicit confutation of the plea commonly used to justify the alienation of the *Sinking Fund*, and which has been mentioned at the beginning of this Essay.

This alienation, it is well known, is become a fixed measure of Government among us. We owe to it our present heavy debt, and if continued much longer, there will, I am afraid, be no possibility of escaping some of the worst calamities. It is, therefore, necessary that the reason on which it has been grounded, should be particularly examined and refuted. And in order to do this, I must beg leave to bring again to view some of the preceding observations.

There is, let us suppose, a million wanted for the necessary supplies of the year. It lies ready in the *Sinking Fund*, and a minister, in order to obtain leave to seize it, pleads, "That, since such a sum must be had, it is indif-

" ferent whether it is taken from hence, or procured by
" making a new loan. If the former is done, an *old* debt
" will be continued. If the latter is done, an *equal new*
" *debt* will be incurred, which would have been otherwise
" saved; and the public interest can be no more affected
" by one of these than the other. But the former is
" easiest. And it will save the disagreeable necessity of
" laying on a new tax."—This argument appears plausible: and it has never yet failed of success.—But what must prove the consequence?—If such reasoning is good one year, it is good every year; and warrants a total alienation of the *Sinking Fund*, if the annual expences of Government are such as always to require a sum equal to its income. And thus, it will lose its whole efficacy; and a Fund that, if not alienated, would have been OMNIPOTENT, will be converted into just such a *feeble* and *barren* one, as the *second* or *third* in the former account.

The fallaciousness of this argument consists in the supposition, that no loss can arise to the Public from continuing an *old debt*, when it cannot be discharged without incurring an *equal new debt.*—I have demonstrated this to be a mistake; and that by practising upon it, or *alienating* rather than *borrowing*, an INFINITE loss may be sustained. —Agreeably to this, I have in the Treatise on Annuities shewn, that had but 400,000*l.* *per annum* of the *Sinking Fund* been applied, from the year 1716 *inviolably*, THREE MILLIONS *per annum* of our taxes might now have been annihilated.

I will here add, that had the whole produce of it been thus employed (*a*), we might now have been in possession of a very considerable SURPLUS, instead of being *in debt*, A HUNDRED AND FORTY MILLIONS.—But I will go



farther.

(*a*) An explanation and proof of this may be found in the Appendix, Note B.

farther.—Had even the money that, at different times, has been employed in paying off our debts, been applied but in a different manner (*a*); that is, had it been made the produce of a *Sinking Fund*, which, from 1716 to the present year, had never been alienated; above HALF our present debts would have been cancelled.—Such is the importance of merely the MANNER of applying money.—Such is the prodigious difference, in the present case, between *borrowing* and *alienating*.—Nor is there anything in this mysterious. The reason has been sufficiently explained.—When a state borrows, it pays, I have said, only *simple* interest for money. When it alienates a Fund appropriated to the payment of its debts, it loses the advantage of money, that would have been otherwise improved necessarily at *compound* interest (*b*). And can there be any circumstances of a State which can render the latter of these preferable to the former? Or can the inconveniences, which may attend the imposition of a new tax, deserve in this case to be mentioned? What a barbarous policy is that which runs a Kingdom in debt, MILLIONS, in order to save THOUSANDS; which robs the Public of the power of annihilating ALL taxes, in order to avoid a small present increase of taxes?—This, in truth,

 has

(*a*) I reckon that about 20 millions of the income of the *Sinking Fund* have, at different times and in different ways, been employed in paying public debts. Fifty-six yearly payments of 357,000*l.* make nearly this sum; and, had it been divided into such payments and inviolably applied in the manner I have explained, from the year 1716; SEVENTY-ONE MILLIONS of debt, bearing 4 *per cent.* interest, would now have been discharged.—I hope it will be remembered, that in mentioning the results of calculations of this kind, I generally give the nearest round numbers, my design not requiring greater exactness.

(*b*) I must beg the reader, if he has here any doubt, to consult Note C, in the Appendix.

has been our policy; and it would be affronting common sense to attempt a vindication of it.

I confess myself incapable of speaking on this subject with calmness.—Let the Reader think of the facts I have mentioned: let him consider the difference in our favour, which an inviolable application of the *Sinking Fund* would have made: Let him compare what, in that case, we *should* have been, with what we *are;* and let him, if he can, be unmoved.

I have, hitherto, argued on the supposition of a *total* or *constant* alienation of the Sinking Fund. It may be proper just to mention the effect of a *partial* alienation of it.

Let us then suppose, that its produce is taken from it only every other year. Most persons will, perhaps, be ready to pronounce, that this could only take from it, in any given time, *half* its effect. But the truth is, that such an interruption might destroy almost its whole effect. —An annual Fund of 200,000*l.* would (it has been shewn) in eighty-six years, pay off 262 millions, bearing interest at 5 *per cent.* But if its produce is taken from it every other year, it would, in the same time, pay off no more than twenty-eight millions.

In like manner; a Fund of a million *per annum*, which commenced at the time of the establishment of our *Sinking Fund* would by this time, (that is, in fifty-six years) have paid off TWO HUNDRED MILLIONS bearing interest at 4 *per cent.* But if alienated every other year, it could not have paid off above FIFTY MILLIONS. *(a)* And, if alienated two years in every three, it could not have paid off TWENTY-SEVEN MILLIONS.

I mean this on the supposition of a faithful application of its whole growing produce, in the years when it is not

 alienated.

(*a*) See the Appendix, Note D.

alienated. But this is a supposition which, when applied to the management of our Sinking Fund, is much too favourable. It has seldom happened that, in any one year, its whole produce has been applied to its proper use. In most years, it has been wholly alienated; and in some years, anticipated and mortgaged.—Can we then wonder, that it has done us so little service?

From these observations the truth of the following assertion will be very evident.

"A State may, without difficulty, redeem all its debts "by borrowing money for that purpose, at an equal or "even any higher interest than the debts bear; and with- "out providing any other Funds than such small ones, as "shall from year to year become necessary to pay the "interest of the sums borrowed."

For Example. Suppose our Parliament, 56 years ago, had resolved to borrow half a million annually for the purpose of redeeming the debts of the kingdom. The *National Gain*, supposing the money applied, without interruption, to the redemption of debts bearing 4 *per cent.* interest, would have been a HUNDRED MILLIONS, being *debt redeemed*, or the sum nearly to which an annuity of half a million will accumulate in 56 years.—On the other hand. The *National Loss* would have been, TWENTY-EIGHT MILLIONS; being *debt incurred*, or the sum of all the loans.—The balance, therefore, in favour of the nation, would have been (*a*) SEVENTY-TWO

 MILLIONS.

(*a*) It seems to me scarcely proper to take into this account, the produce of the taxes laid to pay the interest of the debts contracted from year to year. Let this, however, be charged.—The produce of the taxes laid to pay the interest of the first half million, will be 55 times 20,000*l.* or 1,100,000*l.* For the second, third, fourth, &c. half-millions, the payment of taxes will be 54, 53, 52, &c. times 20,000*l.* And the sum of all these payments will be 30,800,000*l.* Add this

MILLIONS. — During this whole period, the revenue account would have been the same that it has been, except that it would have been charged, towards paying the interest of the money borrowed, with an annuity increasing at the rate of 20,000*l.* every year. In the present year, therefore, this annuity would have been 55 times 20,000*l,* or 1,100,000*l.* But it should be remembered, that 100 millions having been redeemed, the kingdom might have been now eased of the annual expence of *four millions.*

Again, Suppose only half a million annually to be now capable of being spared from the *Sinking Fund.* This, if applied to the redemption of the 3 *per cents.* at *par,* would pay off no more than 61 *millions* in 52 years. But let half a million be borrowed annually, for only 23 years to come; and 99 *millions* will be redeemed in the same time. (*a*) That is; 38 millions more than could have been otherwise redeemed, at the extraordinary expence of only *eleven millions and a half.*

WAR, while such a scheme was going on, would increase its efficiency; and any suspension of it then, would be the *madness* of giving it a mortal stab, at the very time it was making the quickest progress towards the accomplishment of its end. — Suppose, for instance, that, within the period I have mentioned, two wars should happen; one

24 to

---

sum to 28 millions; and 58,800,000*l.* will be the whole *national loss:* which deducted from 99,902,770 (the *exact national gain*) leaves 41,102,770*l.* the balance in favour of the public. See the Appendix, Note C.

(*a*) Such a scheme as is here proposed might be more helped than can well be imagined by various kinds of management; and, particularly, when the *stocks* are under *par,* by purchasing them for the public at the prices in the *Alley.*—There are no sums so trifling, as not to be capable in this way, of being applied to the payment of the public debts.—The *smallest gleanings* of a fund might be thus improved, in a better manner than any other parts of it.

to begin five years hence, and to last 10 years; the other to begin 35 years hence, and to last also 10 years, and both raising the interest of money in the *Funds* (*a*) to 4½ *per cent.* It may be easily calculated, that on these suppositions 145 *millions,* instead of 99 millions, would be paid off by such a scheme. But, should it be suspended during the continuance of the two wars, it would in the same time (that is, in 52 years) pay off no more than 40 *millions.*

I know these Observations will look more like *visions* than *realities,* to those who have never turned their thoughts to these subjects; or who have not duly attended to the amazing increase of money, bearing compound interest. — The duration of the lives of *individuals* is confined within limits so narrow, as not to admit, in any great degree, of the advantages that may be derived from this increase. But a period of 50, or 60 or 100 years being little in the duration of *kingdoms,* they are capable of securing them in almost any degree: And if no kingdoms should ever do this; if, in particular, a nation in such circumstances as ours, should continue to neglect availing itself of them: one fact will be added to the many in the political world, which tho' they cannot *surprize* a philosophical person, he must consider with concern and regret.

Money bearing compound interest increases at first slowly. But, the rate of increase being continually accelerated, it becomes in some time so rapid, as to mock all the powers of the imagination. — ONE PENNY, put out at our Saviour's birth to 5 *per cent. compound* interest, would, before this time, have increased to a greater sum,

25 than

(*a*) That is; so high as that it shall be an advantage to the Proprietors of the 3 *per cents.* to dispose of them at about 67.

than would be contained in A HUNDRED AND FIFTY MILLIONS OF EARTHS, all solid gold (*a*).—But if put out to *simple* interest, it would, in the same time, have amounted to no more than *seven shillings and four pence half-penny*.—Our government has hitherto chosen to improve money in the *last*, rather than the *first* of these ways.

Many schemes have at different times been proposed for paying off the National Debt. But the inventors of them might have spared their labour. Their schemes could not deserve the least notice. The best scheme has been long *known*. It has been *established*; but, unhappily for this kingdom, it was crushed in its infancy. Still, however, if our deliverance is possible, it must be derived from hence. The strictest mathematical evidence proves, that the natures of things don't admit of any method of redeeming public debts so expeditious and effectual.—RESTORE, THEN, THE SINKING FUND. And if the WHOLE of it cannot be unalienably applied to its original use, let SOME PART of it be so applied; that the nation may, at least, enjoy a *chance* of being saved.—"The *Sinking Fund* "(says a great writer) is the last resort of the nation; its "only domestic resource, on which must chiefly depend "all the hopes we can entertain of ever discharging or "moderating our incumbrances. And, therefore, the "*prudent* application of the large sums now arising from "this fund, is a point of the utmost importance, and well "worthy the serious attention of Parliament."(*b*)—I should offer an injury to truth, were I to say no more, than that I have pointed out the most PRUDENT application of this *fund*. I am persuaded that I have pointed out the



(*a*) See Treatise on Reversionary Payments, &c. Introduction page 13.

(*b*) See Mr. Justice BLACKSTONE'S Commentaries on the Laws of England, Vol. I. page 329 (and *ante*, p. 300).

ONLY application of it, that can do us any essential service. Time must discover whether the PARLIAMENT will think it worthy of any attention.

## PART II.

I HAVE frequently spoken on the supposition that the *Sinking Fund,* as it was originally established by the Legislature, was such a fund as I have explained in the preceding pages. The following brief account of the origin of this *fund,* and of the measures of Government with respect to it, will, I think, prove this; and at the same time, perhaps, convince every person, that this is a subject on which the nation has indeed no small reason for complaint.

Before the establishment of this *fund,* there had existed many smaller *funds* of the same nature. That is; such duties or taxes had been provided, for paying the interests of particular loans, as afforded surplusses by which the principal itself was to be gradually redeemed. This seems to have been the common practice in the reigns of King WILLIAM and Queen ANNE. Most of the public duties were given for terms of years; and at the end of those terms they ceased of course, unless continued for farther terms by new acts of *Parliament.* And, in general, it was provided, when any money was raised, that the principal should be cancelled either by *time,* as in the case of the sale of long and short annuities, or by the *surplusses* of the duties charged with the payment of the interest. This was certainly an excellent plan. But it was by no means carried steadily into execution.—In the year 1720, most of the long and short annuities were converted into redeemable *perpetuities,* at the expence of above *three millions:* and the surplusses of the

 duties

duties, charged with particular loans, were often so broke into by being either charged with new loans before they had cancelled the old, or spent on current services, as to be rendered incapable of answering the end intended by them (*a.*)—In consequence partly of this bad management, our debts at the *accession* of the present Royal Family were so much increased, as to be generally reckoned *insupportable;* and their reduction was made one of the first objects of parliamentary attention. This gave rise, in the year 1716, to the institution of the *fund* of which I am giving an account; the *father* of which, as is well known, was Sir ROBERT WALPOLE.—All the taxes charged with the National Debt were now made perpetual, and digested into *three* funds called the *Aggregate*, the *South-sea* and the *general* funds.—At the same time a considerable saving was obtained, by the reduction of interest from 6 to 5 *per cent.;* and this saving, together with former savings, and all that should afterwards arise, were to be collected into



(*a*) Dr. DAVENANT, in his Essay on the *probable Method of making People Gainers in the Balance of Trade*, published in 1699, complains of this in very strong language, and represents it as full of danger to the trade and liberties of the kingdom.—" A sufficient provision " (says he) is not made against diverting the public treasure, and " against breaking into appropriated *funds.*—The laws have not " made this criminal enough.—The Exchequer should be fenced about " with all possible skill.—Stopping the principal, tho' the payments " of interest are continued, may prove *fatal.*—More danger may arise " to our liberties from breaking into old funds appropriated, than " from making new and forced levies on the subject."—The reason he gives for these assertions is " that in consequence of such diver- " sions of the public *funds* the public debts (then estimated by him " at 17 millions) would increase, and ministers come in time to be " supplied with a revenue so large as would enable them, with the " help of a standing army, to make Parliaments useless and to over- " throw the constitution."—What would this excellent writer say were he now living? See Davenant's works lately published by Sir CHARLES WHITWORTH, vol. 2d. page 286, &c.

a *fourth* fund, distinguished under the name of the SINKING FUND the account of which was to be kept separate, and the whole produce of which was to be appropriated inviolably to the payment of the National Debt.

A considerate person might have suspected, that the same causes that had rendered former partial appropriations ineffectual, would destroy the efficacy of this. There seemed, however, to be reason for hoping the contrary. For,

In the first place, The future happiness and glory of the Kingdom were considered as depending on this appropriation; and the law which established it was declared to be a fundamental law of the realm.

In conformity to this, secondly, The words of the law were made as strong as they could well be (*a*). For, concerning all the Surplusses to arise from time to time in the three Funds I have mentioned, it declares, that they *shall be appropriated, reserved and employed to and for the discharge of the principal and interest of such national debts and incumbrances as were incurred before the* 25*th of December* 1716, *and to and for no other use, intent or purpose whatever.*—It was, therefore, impossible, that any alienation of these Surplusses should take place, without a direct breach of this law.

Again. One of the considerations, that induced the public creditors to accept of an interest of 5 instead of 6 *per cent.* was the security given to their principal by this appropriation. It was a sacred Deposit or Pledge made over to them; and at that time it was, I believe, universally reckoned, that no alienation of it could take place, without injustice to the public creditors, and a violation of the faith and honour of Parliament.



(*a*) This law was afterwards repealed in an act of the 5th of George I. chap. 3.

Particular notice should be taken of the words of the *Act of Parliament*, as they have been just recited. It is evident, that they make this *Fund* such a *Fund* as that upon which I have all along argued. The public taxes were made perpetual; and all the surplusses were to be applied to the discharge of the public debts, and to no other purpose whatever. When, therefore, a debt had been paid off, the addition arising from that payment to the surplusses, or the annuity disengaged by it, became a part of the Fund, and, together with it, was to be employed in discharging farther debts. And, the same being true of every successive annuity disengaged *by every* payment, the Fund was rendered such an increasing Fund as the first I have described; or a *Fund*, which, if never misapplied, must have operated in sinking the public debt, in the same way that money *accumulates*, when put out to bear compound interest. And in this way this Fund did in fact operate for a few years.—While in its infancy, it was watched over with great care. The improvement and the inviolable application of it were recommended in most of the Speeches from the Throne, and echoed back in the Addresses of the *House of Commons* (*a*).—In

30 consequence

(*a*) King's Speech at opening the Parliament, February 20, 1717. —" You are all sensible of the *insupportable* weight of the National " Debt, &c."—Answer of the *Commons* :—" We are all but too sensible " of the *insupportable* weight of the National Debt; and, therefore, " will not neglect to apply ourselves, with all possible diligence and " attention, to the *great and necessary work* of reducing and lessening " by degrees this heavy burthen, which may prove the most effectual " means of preserving to the Public Funds a real and certain secu- " rity, &c."—King's Answer.—" Your resolution of applying your- " selves to ease my people, by gradually reducing the heavy load of " the Public Debts, deserves my hearty thanks, &c."—King's Speech, May 6, 1717.—" I must recommend to you, as I did at the beginning " of the Session, to take all proper methods of reducing the Public

RXTSA

P.O. DATE: 9-13-72

AUTHOR

TITLE

A SELECT COLLECTION OF SCARCE AND VALUABLE TRACTS ON THE NATIONAL DEBT AND SINKING FUND (1857), KELLEY REPRINTS

SLC 10-25-72

mw

| PUBLISHER | PUB. DATE |
|---|---|
| NEW YORK | 1966 |

| EDITION | VOLS. | COPIES | | |
|---|---|---|---|---|
| | | 1 | | 450872 |

| RICHARD ABEL & CO., INC. | LIST PRICE | NET PRICE | SALES TAX | SELLING PRICE |
|---|---|---|---|---|
| | 26.00/01 | | | |

F.

consequence of the increase of public credit occasioned by it, a *second* reduction of interest from 5 to 4 *per cent.* took

 place

" Debts."—Answer of the *Commons.*—" We are truly sensible, how " much the ease and prosperity of your subjects, depends on the " accomplishing that great and necessary work of reducing the Pubic " Debts, and are resolved to carry it on in the most effectual manner." —King's Speech, 1718.—" I have the pleasure to observe to you, " that the *Funds*, appropriated for sinking the Public Debts, have " answered above expectation."—Address of the *Commons* on presenting a Money Bill, 1722.—" They have omitted no opportunity of " easing the Public incumbrances, and of putting the National Debt " into a method of payment. For no sooner had your Majesty, by " the vigilance of your Councils, and the success of your arms, " restored and secured the public peace, but your Commons " immediately found means to reduce the interest of the National " Debt, and thereby set a-part a Fund, which, by a farther reduction " of interest since made by your Commons, will, in a few years, be " considerably increased, and the payment of the Principal become " practicable."—King's Speech, January 9, 1724.—" I must, *in a* " *particular manner*, recommended to your care the Public Debts of " this Kingdom, as the MOST NATIONAL CONCERN YOU CAN POSSIBLY " TAKE INTO YOUR CONSIDERATION. I am persuaded it must be a " great satisfaction to all my faithful Subjects, to see the *Sinking* " *Fund* improved and augmented, and the Debt of the Nation " thereby put into a method of being so much the sooner reduced " and paid off."—Reply of the Commons.—" We are highly sensible " of your Majesty's goodness to all your people, in recommending, " particularly, at this time, to our consideration the Public Debts of " the Kingdom, which are so heavy a load and so much *a national* " *concern*, that we should be wanting to ourselves, if we did not " assure your Majesty, that we will use our utmost endeavours to " improve and augment the *Sinking Fund*, and thereby put the " National Debt into a method of being gradually reduced and paid. " And as your Majesty is pleased to encourage our undertaking so " great and noble a design, so we are fully persuaded, that the wis- " dom and *steadiness* of your Majesty's Government will enable us to " perfect this great undertaking."—The King's Answer to the Representation on the Subject of the National Debt (ante p. 249) was as follows :—" The provision made for gradually discharg- " ing the National Debt is now become so certain and con- " siderable, that nothing but some unforeseen event can alter or

place in the year 1727, and near 400,000*l.* *per ann.* was added to its income.—So far were our ministers from being then deceived by the sophism which has since done so much mischief, that, whenever money was wanted for defraying the necessary expences of Government, it was always (*a*) borrowed, and never taken from hence.

32 It

" diminish it; which gives us the fairest prospect of seeing the old " debts discharged; and you may be assured, that it shall be my " particular care and study to maintain public credit, to *improve the* " *Sinking Fund*, &c."—Who, at this time, could have thought, that the very administration which declared all this anxiety about *improving* and *cherishing by all possible means* the *Sinking Fund*, would introduce the practice of constantly *plundering* it?

| | | £ |
|---|---|---|
| (*a*) In 1718 was borrowed towards the Supplies | | 505,905 |
| 1719 | — — — | 312,737 |
| 1720 | — — — | 500,000 |
| 1721 | — — — | 1,000,000 |
| 1725 | — — — | 500,000 |
| 1726 | — — — | 370,000 |
| 1727 | — — — | 1,750,000 |
| 1728 | — — — | 1,230,000 |
| 1729 | — — — | 550,000 |
| 1730 | — — — | 1,200,000 |
| 1731 | — — — | 500,000 |

The *Sinking Fund* might have supplied all this money; but rather than take any sums from it, the Land-tax was in the year 1726 raised from 2*s.* to 4*s.* in the pound; the nation being then under the apprehensions of a war.—In 1727, these apprehensions continuing, the King in his speech at the opening of the PARLIAMENT, after congratulating them on the great addition that would be made that year to the *Sinking Fund*, warns them against being led by the NECESSITIES OF THE NATION to a diversion of it.—" Let all that wish well to " the peace and quiet of my Government, have the satisfaction to " see, that our PRESENT NECESSITIES shall make no interruption in " the progress of that desirable work of gradually discharging the " National Debt. I hope, therefore, you will make a provision for " the immediate application of the produce of the *Sinking Fund* to " the uses for which it was so wisely contrived, and to which it stands

It deserves to be particularly mentioned here, that in 1726, an opinion had been propagated, that, notwithstanding the establishment of this *Fund*, the public debts had been for some years increasing rather than decreasing. This occasioned the publication of a very curious and important pamphlet, in defence of the *Sinking Fund* and the Ministry, entitled, *An Essay on the Public Debts of this Kingdom.* (No. III. in this volume.) I have now by me the fourth edition of this pamphlet, and I wish I could put it into every hand in the kingdom (*a*). It contains an

33 excellent

now appropriated."—Reply of the *Commons.*—" And that all that " wish well to the peace and quiet of your Majesty's government, may " have the satisfaction to see, that our PRESENT NECESSITIES shall make " no interruption in the progress of that desirable work of gradually " reducing the National Debt, we will consider of the most proper " method for immediately applying the produce of the *Sinking Fund* " to the uses for which it was so wisely contrived, and to which it " stands now appropriated."

In the following year the *House of Commons* voted, that the monies issued towards discharging the National Debt, from 1716 to Lady-day 1728, were 6,648,000*l*.

In 1729, the nation being still threatened with a war, extraordinary supplies were wanted; and the Sinking Fund would have afforded all that was necessary. But the King in his speech, at the opening of the Sessions, " recommended it to the care of the *House* " *of Commons* to apply it to its proper use." And the *Commons*, in their reply, assured him that it should be so applied.—Accordingly a million of the South-sea Annuities was ordered to be paid off.—At this time, however, the zeal of the ministry for the preservation of the *Sinking Fund* was much abated, and indeed meant no more, than that it should not be robbed of any gross sums. In the preceding year, the surplusses belonging to it had been charged with the interest of the money then borrowed; and the same was done this year.

(*a*) This pamphlet cannot, I suppose, be now easily procured.—It was answered in a pamphlet, entitled, *A State of the National Debt* (No. IV. in this vol.); and this produced a second pamphlet by the Author of the ESSAY, entitled, *A Defence of an Essay on the Public Debts of this Kingdom, in Answer to a Pamphlet, entitled, A State of*

excellent account of the importance of discharging the public debts, and of the provision made for that purpose by the institution of the *Sinking Fund.* It proves particularly, in opposition to the opinion I have mentioned, that the public debts had decreased; and that of the 52 millions then due, 50 millions would, in 28 years, (*a*) be extinguished by the *Sinking Fund.* The same explanation is given of the nature of this Fund with that which I have given. The same representation is made of its powers: and the same arguments used to demonstrate the evil of alienating it, in order to avoid making new loans charged on new *Funds.* In answer to a suspicion which was then entertained, that the practice of alienating it would be introduced by our ministers, the author observes, that this would be to pursue a measure which would destroy all probability of the payment of our debts; and, therefore, he pronounces that, "as long as the public welfare was in the least "regarded, the nation might confidently expect, that no "person into whose hands the administration of its affairs "might fall, would ever approve of or recommend any "such measure, *in any possible exigence of our affairs.*"

34 After

*the National Debt.*—(No. V. in this vol.) From the following words in this *Defence,* I conclude, that some reference had been made to the ESSAY, in one of the King's Speeches.—"The success of my *Essay* "*on the Public Debts,* and the satisfaction of hearing from the throne, "that my zeal for the preservation of the *Sinking Fund* cannot "have been disagreeable to his Majesty, gives me a pleasure that "alone is an ample reward for my attempts to serve my country."—

It is a reflection which in my enquiries into the History of the Sinking Fund, has occurred to me with pain; that, while a ministerial measure, it was no object of the zeal of the *Patriotic Party.* But as soon as it came to be deserted by the ministry, they took it up warmly.

(*a*) Mr. SMART also published, at this time, calculations of the same kind. See his TABLES OF INTEREST, dedicated to the GOVERNOR and DIRECTORS of the Bank of England, page 98, 99.

—After this he goes on in the following words.— "There is another objection to the probability of the "payment of our public debts, which, if I did not "frequently meet with it, I should chuse not to mention, "from my apprehension that in stating it, as I have met "with it, I should be obliged to mention my superiors "with less decency, than that grateful sense of the happi- "ness we enjoy under the present reign, would, on all "other occasions, lead me to. The objection I mean is, "that the continuance of our public debts is and always "must be the interest of the persons in the administra- "tion (*a*); that the great profits of their employments "arises from hence; and that the necessary power and "influence to support themselves in their employments "depend greatly on their having reserved to themselves "the disposition of the various offices and employments "in collecting and applying the Revenue appropriated "to the payment of the public debts."—In answering this objection, this writer acquaints the public, that whatever truth there might be in it, nothing can have been or will be more sincerely endeavoured by the servants of the crown, than the discharge of the public debts. He takes notice of the remoteness of those views of interest which might render our ministers unwilling to give up the public debts; and then concludes with this general inference from all his observations—"That the provision which had "been made of the *Sinking Fund*, was an expedient, from "which the full and effectual payment of the principal "of the national debt, in a few years, might, with great "assurance, be expected."

35 Such

(*a*) Apprehensions of this kind were entertained likewise in Dr. Davenant's time.—"Some modern politicians (says he) have run "upon another notion, and several persons have thought, that the "more funds are erected, the more the people are engaged to preserve "the present Government:" Davenant's Works, Vol. II. 297.

Such was the language, and such were the sentiments of the ministry and its friends, in the year 1726.—Would to God they had continued in these sentiments. But they soon changed; and it appeared that the suspicions which this writer had taken pains to remove, and which he had called *indecent jealousies*, were but too well grounded.

Charging the income of the *Sinking Fund* with the payment of the interest of new loans, is an encroachment upon it, no less subversive of its efficacy, than depriving it of *gross* sums; there being evidently no difference between taking from it the *annual interest* of a sum, and that sum itself.—This writer saw this, and therefore declared, "that, in his opinion, it was IMPOSSIBLE it "should ever be done."—But how miserably was he deceived by the confidence he placed in his friends in power?—In a little time after this, that alienation which he thought could never be *proposed*, much less *succeeded in*, was begun in the very manner that he had declared to be IMPOSSIBLE. Between the year 1727, and 1732 several new loans were made; and surplusses, that of right belonged to the *Sinking Fund*, were charged with them. This reduced its income considerably below what it should have been. But, being an encroachment of a less open nature, it did not, as far as I can find, produce any particular opposition.—From this period, however, we must date the ruin of the *Sinking Fund*. The finishing blow was given it on the following occasion.

In the year 1732, the land tax had been reduced to 1*s*. in the pound; and, in order to supply the deficiency arising from hence, half a million had been procured for the current service, by the revival of the salt duties, which, but two years before, had been repealed, because reckoned too burthensome on the poor.—In the year 1733, in order to keep the land-tax as low as it had been the year before, it was necessary either to borrow another half million, or to take it from the *Sinking Fund*. The last

 method

method was chosen and proposed by Sir ROBERT WALPOLE to the *House of Commons.*—Long and warm debates ensued.(*a*) A proposal to alienate, in a time of profound peace, a *fund* which the law had made sacred, and the alienation of which no possible exigence of public affairs could justify, only for the sake of keeping the land-tax for one year at 1*s.* in the pound, justly kindled the indignation of the Patriotic Party. They urged the prohibition of the law, the faith of Parliament, and the security of the kingdom. The proposer of the alienation was reminded of his inconsistency and treachery, in endeavouring to beat down that very monument of Glory which he had boasted of having erected for himself; and Sir JOHN BARNARD warned him, that he was drawing upon himself the curses of posterity.* — But all arguments were vain. — The



(*a*) See Vol. viii. of the History and Proceedings of the *House of Commons.* Or, the *Historical Register*, Vol. xviii. page 218.—In the account of this debate I don't find the argument, on which alienations have been since grounded, once intimated. After the publication I have mentioned, it could scarcely deceive any person: Nor, indeed, in the present case, could it have been urged with any tolerable decency; for there was no public exigence which rendered an extraordinary supply necessary.

* In the House of Lords also this alienation was warmly opposed. Lord CARTERET, Lord BATHURST, and others, insisted, that the application of the Sinking Fund to any other use than the payment of the public debts, was robbing the public creditors, because it was depriving them of their security for their principal; and doing injustice to the whole people of England, because it was taking from them the only means, by which they could expect to be freed from the taxes under which they groaned. See The *History and Proceedings of the House of Lords*, Vol. 4th, pag. 155, &c. "It is true, that "after a certain provision had been made for paying off the principal, in a term within every man's view, it began to be a contest "among the public creditors, who should be *last* paid off. But if "two or three more misapplications should be made, the only contest "will be, who shall be *first* paid off; because every man will begin

ministry pleaded that the landed interest wanted ease; that there was no occasion for being in a hurry to pay the National Debt; and that the circumstances of the kingdom had altered so much since the establishment of the *Sinking Fund*, that the competition then among the public creditors was, not who should be *first*, but who should be *last* paid. Thus argued among others Sir ROBERT WALPOLE. His reasons prevailed; and the *House of Commons*, not used to refuse him any thing, consented.

The practice of alienating the *Sinking Fund* having been thus begun, it went on of course. In the next year, or 1734, 1,200,000*l.* was taken from it. In 1735, it was even anticipated and mortgaged.

Thus then expired, after an existence of about eleven years, the SINKING FUND—that sacred Blessing—Once the Nation's only hope—prematúrely and cruelly destroyed by its own parent.—Could it have escaped the hands of violence, it would have made us the envy and the terror of the world, by leaving us at this time, not only TAX-

38 FREE,

---

" to be afraid, that an entire stop will be put to the annuity, as well " as the payment of the principal, before the last creditors could be " paid off." *Ibid.* p. 511.—" When any additional tax is imposed, the " public feel the weight of the annual public expence. This puts them " upon enquiring into the necessity of that expence; and when they " can see no necessity for it, they murmur, and those murmurs be- " come dangerous to the ministers. Whereas no man feels what is " taken from the Sinking Fund; therefore no man enquires into the " necessity of that expence, which occasions its being plundered; " and for this reason it will be always looked upon by ministers as a " fund which they may squander with safety. But this may, and will " probably at last, fall heavy on some prince of his majesty's family. " At the same time that he will see almost all the revenues in the " kingdom mortgaged for old debts, he may find himself engaged in " a war as expensive as was that war which occasioned these debts. " And this is so melancholy a prospect, that the mere possibility of " its existing must give the most affecting sorrow to every man who " has the security and honour of the present Royal Family at heart." *Ibid.* p. 511.

FREE, but in possession of a treasure, greater perhaps than was ever enjoyed by any kingdom.—But, let me not dwell on a recollection so grievous.

It is unavoidable here to enquire, how the conduct of our *Parliaments* or *Ministers,* in this instance, can be accounted for—Were they indeed ignorant of the powers of the *Sinking Fund?*—I doubt not but this has been true of most of our late ministers. But that recital of facts which I have given proves, that, in the period of which I am speaking, it could not have been true.—I am afraid therefore, that the most candid will, on this occasion, find themselves under a necessity of giving way to the suspicion, which the excellent author I have so often quoted, has called an *indecent jealousy.* The powers of the *Sinking Fund* were, perhaps, but too well known. It had been demonstrated, as we have seen, in a performance generally read and even referred to from the throne, that, in a few years, it would have annihilated the whole National Debt. In consequence of having been carefully nursed and cherished for eleven years, it had acquired a vigour, that promised much more than was ever expected from it. The loss, therefore, of the *dependence* created by the National Debt, and of the security it gave to the *Hanoverian* succession and the administration, was brought in too near view. And in these circumstances, it is not strange, that the policy of our Governors should take a new turn, and that the *ruin* of the *Sinking Fund* should become no less a measure of state, than its improvement had been.—My conscience obliges me to take this opportunity to add, that similar measures were, at this time, pursued in another instance of no less importance. For like reasons, and with like views, a PERNICIOUS INFLUENCE was maintained and promoted in the *House of Commons,* which has sapped the constitution; and which may in time establish among us a tyranny of the most intolerable kind; a tyranny attended with the mockery of all the forms of liberty; a tyranny created, supported and sanctified by a PARLIAMENT.—This is, in truth, the *fundamental* grievance of the kingdom; and that Patriotism, the first object of which, is not the removal of it, can be nothing but an imposture. To this grievance we owe, among other evils, the loss of the *Sinking Fund.* Had the guardians of the State been under no undue influence, they would have been more faithful; and could not have given up this great security of the kingdom.—Unhappy BRITAIN!—How long art thou to lie thus bleeding?—How long are thy dearest rights to be sacrificed to *temporary expedients,* and a narrow and selfish policy?—When shall thy PARLIAMENTS recover independence and dignity, and become once more awful to Ministers of State?

But I am in danger of digressing too far.

I have been frequently obliged to refer to the Observations on the National Debt in my Treatise on *Annuities.* Indeed, one of my designs in this Appeal, is to engage attention to those Observations; and, therefore, I will here beg leave to recapitulate some of the chief of them, that all who will look into this Pamphlet may be able to judge how far they deserve notice.

First, Such a *Fund* as I have proposed in that Treatise, and here more fully explained, would discharge the *largest* debts that a State could have occasion to contract, at a *small* expence, and in as little time as its interest could possibly require.—For example. An annual saving of 200,000*l.* applied, without interruption, from the year 1700, would, long before this time, have discharged above eighty millions of our debts (*a*), gradually and insensibly,



and

(*a*) In this year it would have paid off 96 millions and a half, and

and without interfering with any of the other measures or resources of Government.—A tax on celibacy alone might, in this way, have been made the means of bearing most of the Public Expences; and at the same time that, by promoting population, it increased the number of our people.—A Fund yielding 1*l.* *per cent.* surplus annexed to a loan at 6 *per cent.* would, besides paying the interest, discharge the principal in thirty-three years. A Fund producing the same surplus annexed to a loan at 5 *per cent.* would discharge the principal, in thirty-seven years; at 4 *per cent.* in forty-one years.—A saving of a million and a half *per annum* continued for twenty years, (or only for eighteen years, supposing management used, (sic in orig.) or a war to come) might, (with the help of a saving of 200,000*l.* which will arise in 1781, from the reduction of the 4 *per cents*) be so improved as to ease the Nation, at the end of that term, of a MILLION AND A HALF *per annum* of the most oppressive taxes; and, at the end of forty-one years, of THREE MILLIONS *per annum* more in taxes (*a*); And the

41 nation

---

disengaged 3,555,000*l.* of the public taxes. And (in pag. 307.) it is shewn, that in eighty-six years, supposing it all along applied to the redemption of debts bearing 5 *per cent.* interest, it would pay off 262 millions.—In short; there is not a PENNY wasted in the management of the Revenue, or *worse* than wasted, by being given to hungry dependents, which might not be made a *mine* of inexhaustible wealth to the Kingdom.

(*a*) See Treatise on Annuities, p. 156.—Were the managers of our affairs to enter with zeal into such a proposal as this, they might probably find means of improving the *Sinking Fund* so far, as to make it capable of yielding the whole annual sum here mentioned, over and above all the sums necessary for supplying the deficiencies of the peace establishment.—Let this, however, be granted to be impossible; and let the sums it wants of such a surplus be borrowed every year. From what has been already stated it may be inferred, that this (supposing the sums borrowed not to exceed half a million annually) would make no great difference in the efficiency of the

nation, if capable of bearing its increasing burdens for some time longer, would be then completely extricated.

2ndly, Such a Fund would render it of little or no consequence what interest a State paid for any loans.—Concerning reductions of interest it has been proved, that they are not attended with the advantages commonly imagined; and that, has hitherto managed among us, they have been indeed only *expedients* which have *postponed* a



---

scheme: And, at the same time, by providing for the public creditors a way of returning part of the money annually paid them, it would be attended with some advantages.—Every such measure is, I have shewn, only a course of borrowing sums at *simple* interest, in order to improve them at *compound* interest: And, as the benefits hence arising become in time infinite, THERE IS NOTHING THAT A STATE MAY NOT DO BY IT.—With the effect of such a scheme, compare the effect of paying off a *million*, or a *million and a half*, now and then, in a time of peace only.—This is the paltry plan we are pursuing.—With a *Sinking Fund* which, at an average, has for several of the last years yielded *two millions and a quarter*; and with the land tax also at 4*s.* and 3*s.* in the pound; we have, during a peace of near ten years, paid off about *eight millions*; and, in this way of going on, we shall, if the peace lasts NINETY YEARS, reduce our debts to the state they were in eighteen years ago.—Have such measures any *tendency* to save us? Is there any probability, that the payment of even *two millions* annually, from this time to the commencement of another war, would do us any great service?—Miserable reflection! —That it should be possible for our ministers, in defiance of a law which has established the most efficacious of all plans, and the kingdom sinking; to go on in such a way.—Had the scheme here proposed been begun as soon as the last war ended, we should now have seen ourselves, within a few years of the extinction of a *third* of all the taxes that pay the interest of the National Debt. The 3 *per cents* also would now have been near *par*: and when a war came (supposing the kingdom convinced that no more alienations would take place) all the money necessary to carry it on might have been procured on easy terms.

public bankruptcy, by *lessening the possibility* of avoiding it. (*a*)

3dly, A war would either have *no* effect on the public Funds; or, if it had, would *accelerate* the payment of the public debts, in proportion to that effect (*b*).

4thly. That fluctuation in the Stocks would be prevented, which now lays the foundation of so much evil; and which (with the help of *annual Lotteries*) is likely in time to destroy all honest industry among us, and to convert us into a nation of gamblers.

5thly, Public credit would be always kept firm and flourishing by such a Fund; and all those dangers which attend our present exorbitant debt would be removed.

6thly, It is not possible, there should be any method of discharging public debts so cheap and effectual. All methods of paying debts or raising money by Life-Annuities are, in particular, shewn to be wasteful, the same ends being equally attainable with less trouble, and at near half the expence. Should, therefore, the managers of our affairs ever determine to enter into vigorous measures for reducing our debts, they will be eased of all trouble in examining schemes. They have nothing to do, but to carry into execution a scheme which lies before them, and which the law has long since established.

Among the evils produced by the National Debt, there is *one* of which the Public has not been yet sufficiently apprized; and which, therefore, I must here beg leave particularly to mention. I mean; that DEPOPULATION which has been going on among us, ever since it began. A Depopulation so great, as to have reduced the number of inhabitants in ENGLAND and WALES, near a QUARTER

 in

---

(*a*) Treatise on Annuities, pag. 140, &c.

(*b*) *Ibid.* p. 157, &c. (See also, *ante* p. 324.)

in eighty years; or from about SIX MILLIONS, to about FOUR MILLONS AND A HALF. In the *Supplement* to the Treatise on Annuities, I have given an account of the facts which prove this; and there is nothing that ought to alarm more, or to engage more the immediate attention of Government.(*a*) Among the causes of it, I have mentioned the engrossing of farms; the emigrations to our settlements in the *East and West Indies;* and the great increase, since the REVOLUTION, of our continental connexions, of our navy and army, and of commerce and luxury.—But the National Debt is likewise to be reckoned

44 one

(*a*) Perhaps it is hardly necessary to observe that these statements in regard to the decrease of the population are entirely erroneous. They were first put forward by Price in his Treatise on Annuities; and were afterwards repeated, and the evidence on which they rested more fully explained in an "Essay on the Population of England and Wales," which he published in a separate form in 1780. In it he states, as the result of his investigations, that the population, which had amounted at the Revolution to about 6,500,000, had fallen off in 1777 to 4,760,000, or at most 5 millions. (P. 14, &c.) But the fallacy of the evidence on which Price built his conclusions, and of the conclusions themselves, was speedily established in two very able pamphlets published in the course of the following year (1781)—"An Examination of Dr. Price's Essay," by the Revd. John Howlett, A.B., and "An Inquiry into the Present State of the Population of England and Wales," by William Wales, F.R.S. The elaborate researches which have since been made into the progress of the population during last century show that it must have been nearly as follows, viz.

| | | | | | | |
|---|---|---|---|---|---|---|
| 1700 | — | 5,134,516 | — | 1760 | — | 6,479,730 |
| 1720 | — | 5,345,351 | — | 1780 | — | 7,814,827 |
| 1740 | — | 5,829,705 | — | 1800 | — | 9,172,980 |

During the present century the progress has been

| | | |
|---|---|---|
| 1820* | — — — — — — | 11,902,463 |
| 1840* | — — — — — — | 15,739,994 |
| 1850* | — — — — — — | 17,735,871 |

* 1st of March in each year.—Note by ED.

one of its principal causes. Its necessary tendency is to produce this effect.—It is a common observation, and probably not very far from the truth, that *half* the price of all the articles of consumption is caused by our taxes. They *double*, therefore, the price of every thing; and, by increasing the difficulties of supporting a family, they discourage marriage and promote licentiousness.—There is no political maxim more certain, than that population thrives in a country, in proportion to the ease with which the means of subsistence can be procured. In a country, therefore, where they are all loaded with taxes, population must decline.—It has, I know, been asserted in answer to this, that though taxes increase the price of the means of subsistence, they increase also in an equal proportion the price of labour; and, consequently, cannot render the support of a family less easy. But no observation can be more groundless than this. It is true only of an increase in the price of the means of subsistence, produced by the importation of money into a country. As far as it is produced by taxes, it has exactly the same effect with a *scarcity*.—When there is an increase of money in a country, it will by degrees get into the hands of all, and therefore, all will be as well able to pay *more* for every necessary of life, as they were before able to pay *less*. But this cannot be the case if *more* must be paid, and yet the quantity of money remains the same. In this case, poverty and difficulties must be introduced: And these will be increased, if *luxury* co-operates with *taxes*, by producing a greater number of wants, and rendering more of the articles of consumption necessary.—*Moderate* taxes may, by quickening industry, be so far an advantage: But they always check population. And there is a limit which, when they exceed, they must produce ruin. In a word; not only the preservation of our TRADE (*a*) and LIBERTIES; but the

 very

(*a*) Nothing, in my opinion, can be more replete with mischief to

very BEING OF THE STATE depends at present on the reduction of our debts.

There is one objection which, probably, has been often offering itself to every reader; and which, tho' I cannot answer it, I must mention.—"Suppose," it will be said, "such a *fund* established, as has been here described;" or, which is the same, "suppose the SINKING FUND "restored. What security can be obtained for the faith-"ful and inviolable application of it?"—Were I to propose, in answer to this enquiry, guarding the *Sinking Fund*, by pains and penalties; and making all encroachments upon it, no less TREASON than an attempt to kill the King; I should be conscious of making a very vain proposal. For such a security would be only the security of law; and this has been already given without effect. *Parliaments* can give no defence against themselves. Nor is there any thing that one Parliament can *do*, which a succeeding Parliament, or even the same Parliament, may not *undo*.—This, however, is an objection which our Statesmen cannot make with any decency; because it implies a confession, that they must not be expected to continue faithful to the public interest.—And if this be indeed true; if a succession of such wise and honest administrations is impossible, as is necessary to execute a

46 plan

a free people, than such a debt as ours is.—I have mentioned (in the Treatise on Annuities, pag. 161.) the danger to which it exposes us from *foreign enemies*, by making us fearful of war; and from *domestic enemies*, by making us fearful of the consequences of opposition to arbitrary measures. Indeed, I look upon the public creditors as little better than a band of pensioners to the Government; and it is more than probable, that had the nation been encumbered with our present debts in the reigns of King CHARLES the Ist. or JAMES the IId. the former would never have lost his *life*, nor the latter his *crown*.

plan that requires steadiness of counsel for a course of years; and if, on this account, the kingdom must despair of ever seeing the SINKING FUND permanently and efficaciously restored—then, in the name of justice and humanity, LET IT BE EXPUNGED FROM OUR PUBLIC ACCOUNTS; and let us not be any longer mocked with the SHADOW of an invaluable blessing, once solemnly promised us; but which, it seems, for want of public virtue, we can *never* enjoy.

But it is time to dismisss this subject.

I have written freely the sentiments of my heart; and the public is now left to judge.—With the *desire*, but not with much *hope* of success, I have stepped forth to convey to my country an information, which all who will consider it must see to be of great importance. Should it be entirely neglected, the pain I shall feel will not be on my own account. I know I have *meant* to act the part of a good citizen; and I shall return to obscurity and silence, satisfied with this reflexion; and happy in the consciousness of wanting nothing this world can give me.

# APPENDIX.

## Note (A).

### TABLE I.

Shewing the Progress of a Fund of 200,000*l.* *per Annum*, applied *unalienably* to the Payment of public Debts, bearing 5 *per cent.* Interest.

| Yrs. | Produce of the Fund at the beginning of every year. | Total of debts paid at the beginning of every year. | Yrs. | Produce of the Fund at the beginning of every year. | Total of debts paid at the beginning of every year. |
|---|---|---|---|---|---|
| | £. | £. | | | £. |
| 1 | 200,000<br>Add 10,000 | 0.200,000 | 12 | 342,068<br>17,103 | 3.183,425 |
| 2 | 210,000<br>Add 10,500 | 0.410,000 | 13 | 359,171<br>17,959 | 3.542,596 |
| 3 | 220,500<br>Add 11,025 | 0.630,500 | 14 | 377,130<br>18,856 | 3.919,726 |
| 4 | 231,525<br>Add 11,576 | 0.862,025 | 15<br>&c. | 0.395,986<br>&c. | 4.315,712<br>&c. |
| 5 | 243,101<br>12,155 | 1.105,126 | 30<br>&c. | 0.823,227 | 13.287,769 |
| 6 | 2.55,256<br>12,763 | 1.360,382 | 50<br>&c. | 2.184,266 | 41.869,600 |
| 7 | 268,019<br>13,401 | 1.628,401 | 70<br>&c. | 5.795,509 | 117.705,702 |
| 8 | 281,420<br>14,071 | 1.909,821 | 86 | 12.650,870<br>Add 632,543 | 261.668,284 |
| 9 | 295,491<br>14,775 | 2.205,312 | 87<br>&c. | 13.283,414 | 274.951,698 |
| 10 | 310,266<br>15,513 | 2.515,578 | 100 | 25.047,858 | 522.005,020 |
| 11 | 325,779<br>16,289 | 2.841,357 | | | |

 *N.B.* The

*N.B.* The whole profit, in 100 years, by this fund, supposing it alienated every year, to avoid borrowing at 5 *per cent.* simple interest sums equal to its produce, would be 69.500,000*l*, including the principal sums borrowed, together with all their interests.

The WHOLE PROFIT by it, if *never* alienated, would, it appears, be, in the same time, 522 millions. The COMPLETE LOSS, therefore, by alienation, would be 452 millions and a half. (*ante* p. 317) It is shewn, that, in 86 years, the loss would be 208.250,000*l*. And this forms the strictest demonstration, that, while there is a possibility of avoiding alienation, by borrowing money at simple interest, it must be, in the highest degree, pernicious to a state not to do it. But this will be farther explained in the following notes.

Note (B).

I HERE suppose the operation of the fund to begin at Midsummer, 1717, and to be applied from that time to Midsummer, 1727, to the payment of debts bearing 5 *per cent.* interest. From 1727 to 1756, I suppose it applied to the payment of debts bearing 4 *per cent.* interest; and from 1756 to Midsummer 1772, to the payment of debts bearing 3 *per cent.* interest. I further suppose the produce of the fund to have been, from the first, 1.200,000 *per ann.*—In the first of these periods, such a fund, unalienably applied, would have paid off 17 millions. In the second period, or the next 29 years, it would have paid off 126 millions. And in the last 16 years, it would have paid off 129 millions. In all then, 255 millions might have been paid; or 115 millions more than our present debt.

In this calculation no account is taken of the benefit derived from the alienations of the *Sinking Fund.* Let these be supposed to have been equivalent to a million *per Ann.* which the public must have otherwise borrowed, and paid interest for, at 4 *per cent.* from Midsummer, 1733, to Midsummer, 1771.—By the alienation in 1733, the public would have been saved a million, together with 38 annual payments of interest money. In 1734, 1735, 1736, &c. it would have been saved the same sum, together with 27, 26, 25, &c. annual payments of interest money. It may be easily found, that all these savings added together, will amount nearly to 68 millions. And this sum I reckon much more than equivalent to the profits we have made by alienations. But it has appeared that, had there been no alienations, 255 millions would have been paid off. Subtract then, from this sum, 68 millions, and also the present debt, estimated at 140 millions; and the remainder, or 47 millions, will be the SURPLUS, which the public must have been now possessed of, after discharging, not only all the present debts, but likewise *all the extraordinary expences, including*



interest

*interest monies*, which must have been incurred by avoiding alienations.

Somo will probably think, that this surplus ought to be further diminished by the amount of the debts that have been actually paid off. I have supposed these about 20 millions, but let them be 27 millions; and still there will be left a surplus of 20 millions.

In short. Let any one calculate on any suppositions that he may think nearest to the truth; and he will find the losses, occasioned by the diversions which have been made of the *Sinking Fund*, to be at least equal to the whole of our present debts; losses, I must add, which there could be no occasion for incurring: which have had no advantages to balance them; and which I have shewn, in the last part of this pamphlet, to have been brought upon us, in opposition to the authority of an express law.

I have supposed the income of the sinking fund to have been equivalent to 1,200,000*l.* *per ann.* from the year when it was first established. It is of no particular consequence, whether this supposition is exactly right or not. The probability seems to be, that it falls short of the truth; for it should be remembered, that the *Sinking Fund* has been plundered in more ways than by taking from it gross sums—1st. Many savings have been kept from it, which should have been brought into it. And 2dly, The income of it has, in many instances, been charged with the payment of the interest of new loans. Had no alienations of any kind been practised, and the intention of the law sacredly observed, its income would have been considerably greater than it has been, and the surplus we should have been now possessed of, after paying all our debts, would have been greater than can well be estimated. What its actual income has been, will appear from the following account.

Medium of the annual produce of the *Sinking Fund*, from its commencement,

| | | £. |
|---|---|---|
| to 1726 | — — | 0.577,614 |
| From 1727 to 1736, | both inclusive | 1.132,251 |
| 1737 to 1746 | — — | 1.062,170 |
| 1747 to 1756 | — — | 1.356,578 |
| 1757 to 1766 | — — | 2.059,406 |

The chief reason of the increase after the years 1726 and 1756, was the reductions of interest which then took place.

 Note (C).

Note (C.)

EVERY one who has attended to my reasonings, must see, that when a state borrows to avoid alienating, I always suppose the interests of the sums borrowed to be paid either by a new tax, or by creating some new saving. If the interests of the sums borrowed are taken from the *Sinking Fund*, its efficacy will be as effectually destroyed, as if those sums themselves had been taken from it ; the powers of the fund depending entirely on the interests disengaged from time to time being suffered to remain there, in order to carry interest by being employed in paying debts, and consequently in disengaging *farther* interests.

The two following tables, will, I hope, explain this sufficiently.

TABLE II.

Shewing the Progress of *two* Funds ; *one* alienated every Year, by taking from it GROSS SUMS equal to its Produce : And the other unalienable.

| I. Yrs. | II. Annual produce of the fund. | III. Debts paid off bearing 4 *per cent*. interest. | IV. GAIN by ALIENATION, being the totals, to the beginning of every year, of the sums alienated, together with the totals of the interests at 4 *per cent.* which must have been paid for those sums, had they been borrowed. | V. GAIN by NON-ALIENATION, being the totals of the debts paid off at the beginning of every year, in consequence of avoiding alienation. | VI. BALANCE, at the beginning of every year, in favour of non-alienation, being the excess of the numbers in column V. above those in column IV. |
|---|---|---|---|---|---|
| | £. | | £. | £. | £. |
| 1 | 1.000,000 | . . . . | 1.000,000 | 1.000,000 | 0.000,000 |
| 2 | 1.000,000 | . . . . | 2.040,000 | 2.040,000 | 0.000,000 |
| 3 | 1.000,000 | . . . . | 3.120,000 | 3.121,600 | 0.001,600 |
| 4 | 1.000,000 | . . . . | 4.424,000 | 4.246,464 | 0.006,464 |
| 5 | 1.000,000 | . . . . | 5.400,000 | 5.416,323 | 0.016,323 |
| 6 | 1.000,000 | . . . . | 6.600,000 | 6.632,975 | 0.032,975 |
| 7 | 1.000,000 | . . . . | 7.840,000 | 7.898,294 | 0.058,294 |
| 8 | 1.000,000 | . . . . | 9.120,000 | 9.214,226 | 0.094,226 |
| 9 | 1.000,000 | . . . . | 10.440,000 | 10.582,795 | 0.142,795 |
| 10 | 1.000,000 | . . . . | 11.800,000 | 12.006,107 | 0.206,107 |
| &c. | | . . . . | | | |
| 56 | 1.000,000 | . . . . | 117.600.000 | 199.805,540 | 82,205,540 |
| 70 | 1.000,000 | . . . . | 166.600,000 | 364,290,459 | 197.690,459 |
| 100 | 1.000,000 | . . . . | 298.000,000 | 1237.623,700 | 939.623,700 |

 TABLE III.

## TABLE III.

Shewing the Progress of *two* Funds; *one* alienated every Year, by taking from it the Interests at 4 *per cent.* of gross Sums, equal to its Produce: And the other unalienable.

| I. Yrs. | II. Annual produce of the fund. | III. DEBTS paid off bearing 4 *per cent.* interest. | IV. GAIN by the *fund* to the beginning of every year being the totals of the sums paid off, together with the totals of the interest taken from the fund to avoid creating new taxes. | V. GAIN, to the beginning of every year, by non-alienation. | VI. BALANCE at the beginning of every year in favour of non-alienation, being the difference between the numbers in column IV. and V. |
|---|---|---|---|---|---|
| | £. | £ | £. | £. | £. |
| 1 | 1.000,000 | 1.000,000 | 1.000,000 | 1.000,000 | 0.000,000 |
| 2 | 1.000,000 | 1.000,000 | 2.040,000 | 2.040,000 | 0.000,000 |
| 3 | 1.000,000 | 1.000,000 | 3.120,000 | 3,121,600 | 0.001,600 |
| 4 | 1 000,000 | 1.000,000 | 4.240,000 | 4.246,464 | 0.006,464 |
| 5 | 1.000,000 | 1.000,000 | 5.400.000 | 5.416,323 | 0.016,323 |
| 6 | 1.000,000 | 1.000,000 | 6.600,000 | 6.632,975 | 0.032,975 |
| 7 | 1.000,000 | 1.000,000 | 7.840,000 | 7.898,294 | 0.058,294 |
| 8 | 1.000,000 | 1.000 000 | 9.120,000 | 9.214,226 | 0.094,226 |
| 9 | 1.000,000 | 1.000,000 | 10.440,000 | 10.582,795 | 0.142,795 |
| 10 | 1.000,000 | 1.000,000 | 11.800,000 | 12.006,107 | 0.206,107 |
| &c. | &c. | &c. | &c. | &c. | &c. |
| 56 | 1.000,000 | 1.000,000 | 117.600,000 | 199,805,540 | 82.205,540 |
| &c. | &c. | &c. | &c. | &c. | &c. |
| 70 | 1.000,000 | 1.000,000 | 166,600,000 | 364,290,459 | 197,690,459 |

The numbers in the 5th columns of these Tables, are calculated in the same manner with the numbers in the third columns of Table I. page 348: and the numbers in the *fourth* columns, in the manner explained in page 315. The former numbers exhibit the amount of a million *per ann.* bearing 4 *per cent.* COMPOUND interest; and the latter numbers exhibit the amount of the same annual sum bearing 4 *per cent.* SIMPLE interest. It appears, therefore, undeniably, from these Tables, that the superior efficacy of an *unalienable fund*, depends on the improvement of money in it at compound interest; and that to



divert

divert the produce of a fund, appropriated to the payment of debts, in order to avoid making new loans, and providing new savings for paying the interest of those loans, is the very same with taking money from *compound* interest, in order to put it out to *simple* interest.—It appears, likewise, that the losses arising from hence, though at first small, soon become very great; and that, consequently, the reason which has been used to justify this practice, is, indeed, what I have represented it, a DANGEROUS SOPHISM. In no long time, it will probably, if no vigorous measures are soon entered into, cost this nation all the troubles of a public bankruptcy.

It may deserve to be mentioned, that the sums supposed to be borrowed every year in consequence of non-alienation, being balanced by equal sums paid every year; the total of these sums, to the beginning of every year, may be deducted from the sums in the 4th and 5th columns; and there will remain in the 4th column, the produce of all the taxes imposed to pay off the debts in the 5th column.—Thus from 117.600,000*l.* in the 4th column, and also from 199.805,540*l.* in the 5th column, deduct 56 millions, and the remainders will shew, that at the expence of taxes or assessments, all the payments of which would, in 56 years, make 61.600,000*l.* the public would pay off 143.805,540*l.* Or, (which comes to the same) that at the expence of taxes, beginning with 40,000*l.* *per ann.* and increasing gradually till the last annual payment become 2.200,000*l.* the public might ease itself, at the end of 56 years, not only of all these extraordinary taxes, but also of *other* taxes to the amount of 5.752,000*l.*—The *Sinking Fund* then, had its income from the first been only a million *per ann.* might, by this time, besides paying off a sum equal to the whole present amount of the national debt, have paid off 56 millions principal money borrowed to avoid alienation; and also, a part of 61.600,000*l.* contributed by the public from time to time to pay the interest of the money borrowed. Has not then alienation been a pernicious measure? Can it be possible, that an enlightened kingdom, with ruin before it as the consequence, should go on with such a measure?

These Tables exhibit only the effects of *constant* alienations. If these are pernicious, *partial* alienations must be also pernicious. In what degree they are so, will appear in the next note.

It is necessary I should observe farther, with respect to these Tables, that the 4th column in Table II. shews exactly the *whole loss* the public would sustain, by borrowing a million annually at 4 *per cent. including the whole produce of every tax for paying the interest of every loan* ; and column the 5th shews the gain arising from employing that annual sum in the payment of debts bearing the same interest. These Tables, therefore, explain and demonstrate the observations in pages 324 and 325.

Were it indifferent, when any sums are wanted, whether they are procured by new loans charged on new taxes, or by alienating an appropriated fund, the gain by a fund *always* alienated for current services, would be the same, in every period of its progress, with the gain by an equal fund *never* alienated ; and consequently the gain by a million spent annually on current services, would (by column 5, Table II.) be equivalent, in a hundred years, to 1237 millions : And the gain by a *penny* spent at our Saviour's birth, equivalent to 150 millions of earths, all solid gold ; for to this sum would a penny, bearing 5 *per cent.* interest, in an unalienable fund, have by this time amounted.

Upon the whole. It is not in my power to imagine more than the following cases, in which alienations can be excusable. 1st. After a fund has operated its full time, it may be right to employ it in defraying the expences of any services that may happen *then* to be necessary. For example. Our *Sinking Fund*, had it been preserved from alienation, would, in the present year, have extinguished all our debts, and given the public the command of an income of at least seven or eight millions *per ann.* And, had a war become now unavoidable, no inconveniences could have arisen from employing this income in bearing the expences of the war. This would have enabled the kingdom to carry it on without making any addition to its incumbrances ; and when a peace came, all the perpetual taxes might be abolished : and the establishment of a small new fund, at the commencement of any subsequent war, would be sufficient for ever to keep the public debts within the bounds of safety.

Secondly. The alienation of a fund is excusable, when a state cannot borrow money at any rate of simple interest ; or, which comes to the same, when no taxes or savings can be procured for paying the interest of new loans, but such as either necessarily *must*, or certainly *would* have been brought into the fund, and improved there at compound interest, whether there had been any new loans or not. Every one must see, that this is a case which cannot happen while a state has the power of creating taxes or savings, that neither *must*, nor probably *would* have been created, had it not been for the emergency that occasions them.—It may, indeed, be said concerning every tax or saving, created to avoid alienating a fund, that it *might* at that time have been created, and likewise brought into the fund, though the reason for creating it had

 not

not existed. But if, though it *might*, it either certainly or probably *would* not, the losses by alienation remain the same.—It is very absurd to assert concerning any measure, that it would have been taken, though the reason for it had not existed. The contrary may be always depended upon. With respect to our own government in particular, we know, that it has never yet, with any permanency, improved money at compound interest. Nor has there been ever a time, when it could have been said with truth, that, had it avoided alienation, the very tax necessary in that case to pay the interest of the sum which must have been borrowed, would have been provided, and made a part of an unalienable fund. But this leads me to mention.

Thirdly, That the alienation of a fund would be excusable, were a new tax or saving, producing the interest of the sum alienated, *always* created, and *immediately* brought into the fund, to be improved there in the same manner with the rest of its produce.—This is, likewise, a case that has never happened in this kingdom, alienations having been practised among us, *on purpose* to avoid new taxes.

It deserves to be here mentioned, that a wise state will, if possible, put even such alienations as these out of the power of the managers of its affairs: for, the facility of obtaining money in this way, might tempt to alienation, when services absolutely necessary did not call for money; and the new taxes necessary to replace the interest of the sums alienated, might often be postponed, or prove deficient; in all which cases, losses would be incurred, and the efficiency of a fund might be so much lessened, as to be rendered useless.

Lastly. Alienations might be justified, were a kingdom got to its utmost limit in taxation, and so far exhausted as to be incapable of making any new savings for paying interest of new loans. In these circumstances, necessity having no law, it might be right to take from a fund, any sums which the salvation of the kingdom required. But this, likewise, is a case that cannot be our own, till all the reductions possible have been made in the number of places and pensions, in the pay of the great officers of state, and in the collection and expenditure of the revenue.—Perhaps, indeed, we cannot go much further in *taxation*. An addition to an *old* tax, might destroy its own effect by diminishing consumption. The imposition of a *new* tax might also destroy its own effect by clashing with some *old* tax. And the effect of a general *productive* increase of taxes, could it be accomplished, would most probably destroy its own source by accelerating depopulation.—Some think this not to be a very wrong account of our present state with respect to taxation. But I hope they are mistaken.

 It

It gives me much concern to be obliged to be so minute and tedious as I have been in this note. But the common and strong prejudices in favour of alienations, and the objections of some very respectable persons, have convinced me, that there is more occasion for this minuteness than I once imagined ; and that, though supported by demonstration, I ought not to omit even the argument taken from the authority of those who have writ before me on this subject. (The Dr. then goes on to say, that for the reason now stated, he had subjoined some farther extracts from the Tract of Sir Nathaniel Gould, *ante* No. IV., but these we have of course suppressed.)

## Note (D). See *Ante* Page 322.

## TABLE IV.

Shewing the whole Effect, in 56 Years, of a Fund yielding a Million *per Ann.* appropriated to the payment of Debts bearing 4 *per cent.* Interest, but alienated every other Year.

| Mid-summer. | Produce of the fund at Midsummer every year. | Total of the debts paid from Mid-summer, 1717, to the beginning of every year. | Sums alienated every other year. | Expence saved by alienation, being the sum alienated, together with all its interests from the year of alienation, to Midsummer, 1771. |
|---|---|---|---|---|
| | £. | £. | £. | £. |
| 1717 | 1.000,000 | 1.000,000 | . . . . | . . . . . |
| 18 | 1.040,000 | 1.000,000 | 1.040,000 | 3.244,800 |
| 19 | 1.040,000 | 2.040,000 | . . . . | . . . . . |
| 20 | 1.081,600 | 2.040,000 | 1.081,600 | 3.288,064 |
| 21 | 1.081,600 | 3.121,600 | . . . . | . . . . . |
| 22 | 1.124,864 | 3.121,600 | 1.124,864 | 3.329,470 |
| 23 | 1.124,864 | 4.246,464 | . . . . | . . . . . |
| 24 | 1.169,858 | 4.246,464 | 1.169,858 | 3.369,176 |
| 25 | 1.169,858 | 5.416,322 | . . . . | . . . . . |
| 26 | 1.216,652 | 5.416,322 | 1.216,652 | 3.406,622 |
| 27 | 1.216,652 | 6.632,975 | . . . . | . . . . . |
| 28 | 1.265,319 | 6.632,975 | 1.265,319 | 3.441,635 |
| 29 | 1.265,319 | 7.898,294 | . . . . | . . . . . |
| 30 | 1.315,931 | 7.898,294 | 1.315,931 | 3.474,048 |
| 31 | 1.315,931 | 9.214,226 | . . . . | . . . . . |
| 32 | 1.368,569 | 9.214,226 | 1.368,569 | 3.503,507 |

TABLE IV. Continued.

| Midsummer. | Produce of the fund at Midsummer every year. | Total of the debts paid from Midsummer, 1717, to the beginning of every year. | Sums alienated every other year. | Expence saved by alienation, being the sum alienated, together with all its interests, from the year of alienation, to Midsummer, 1771. |
|---|---|---|---|---|
| | £. | £. | £. | £. |
| 1733 | 1.368,569 | 10.582,795 | . . . . | . . . . |
| 34 | 1.423,311 | 10,582,795 | 1.423,311 | 3.529,795 |
| 35 | 1.423,311 | 12.006,107 | . . . . | . . . . |
| 36 | 1.480,244 | 12.006,107 | 1.480,244 | 3.552,559 |
| 37 | 1.480,244 | 13.486,351 | . . . . | . . . . |
| 38 | 1.539 454 | 13.486,351 | 1.539,454 | 3.571,528 |
| 39 | 1.539,454 | 15.025,805 | . . . . | . . . . |
| 40 | 1.601,032 | 15.025,805 | 1.601,032 | 3.586,303 |
| 41 | 1.601,032 | 16.626,837 | . . . . | . . . . |
| 42 | 1.665,073 | 16.626,837 | 1.665,073 | 3.596,531 |
| 43 | 1.665,073 | 18.291,911 | . . . . | . . . . |
| 44 | 1.731,676 | 18.291,911 | 1.731,676 | 3.601,885 |
| 45 | 1.731,676 | 20.023,587 | . . . . | . . . . |
| 46 | 1.800,943 | 20.023,587 | 1 800,943 | 3.601,808 |
| 47 | 1.800,943 | 21.824,531 | . . . . | . . . . |
| 48 | 1.872,981 | 21.824,531 | 1.872,981 | 3.596,118 |
| 49 | 1.872,981 | 23.697,512 | . . . . | . . . . |
| 50 | 1.947,900 | 23.697,512 | 1.947,900 | 3.584,136 |
| 51 | 1.947,900 | 25.645,412 | . . . . | . . . . |
| 52 | 2.025,816 | 25.645,412 | 2.025,816 | 3.565,424 |
| 53 | 2.025,816 | 27.671,229 | . . . . | . . . . |
| 54 | 2.106 849 | 27.671,229 | 2.106,849 | 3.539,490 |
| 55 | 2.106,849 | 29.778,078 | . . . . | . . . . |
| 56 | 2.191,123 | 29.778,078 | 2.191,123 | 3.505,783 |
| 57 | 2.191,123 | 31.969,201 | . . . . | . . . . |
| 58 | 2.278,768 | 31.969,201 | 2.278,768 | 3,463,718 |
| 59 | 2.278,768 | 34.247,969 | . . . . | . . . . |
| 60 | 2.369,918 | 34.247,969 | 2.369,918 | 3.412,674 |
| 61 | 2.369,918 | 36.617,988 | . . . . | . . . . |
| 62 | 2.464,715 | 36.617,988 | 2.464,715 | 3.352,007 |
| 63 | 2.464,715 | 39.082,703 | . . . . | . . . . |
| 64 | 2.563,304 | 39.082,703 | 2.563,304 | 3.281,028 |
| 65 | 2.563,304 | 41.646,007 | . . . . | . . . . |
| 66 | 2.665,836 | 41.646,007 | 2.665,836 | 3.199,001 |
| 67 | 2.665 836 | 44.311,844 | . . . . | . . . . |
| 68 | 2.772,469 | 44.311,844 | 2.772,469 | 3.105,163 |
| 69 | 2.772,469 | 47.094,313 | . . . . | . . . . |
| 70 | 2.883,368 | 47.094,313 | 2.883,368 | 2.998,702 |
| 71 | 2.883,368 | 49.977,682 | . . . . | . . . . |

| | |
|---|---|
| Total of the expences saved by alienation — | £92.701,035 |
| Add the total of debts paid — — — | 49.977,682 |
| Whole gain by the fund — — — | 142.678,717 |
| Gain by the same fund, supposed *unalienable*, being the total of the debts which it would have paid off — — — — — | 199.805,540 |
| Deduct the gain with alienation — — | 142.678,717 |
| Remains, the uncompensated loss in 56 years, by a fund yielding a million *per ann.* alienated every other year — — — — | 57.126,823 |

It should not be forgotten, that in this and the preceding Tables, the expences saved by alienation are greatly over-rated for the following reasons.

First. They suppose that not only the principal sums alienated, but all the annual interests of these sums, are so much money saved, which would have been otherwise certainly paid by the public: whereas, there is all the reason possible for believing, that the liberty to alienate encourages profusion; and that, had there been always a necessity for borrowing on new taxes to avoid alienation, more care would have been used in the management of the public finances.

Secondly. They suppose the present value of every annuity to be equal to the number of payments which will be made of it. For instance, An annuity of 41,600*l.* payable for 53 years, as interest at 4 *per cent.* for 1.040,000*l.* is reckoned worth 53 years purchase; or 2.204,800*l.*; which sum added to 1.040,000*l.* makes 3,244,800*l.* the whole expence saved by alienation in the year 1718, according to this Table.

*FINIS.*

# EXTRACTS

FROM A TRACT ENTITLED

# THE CHALLENGE;

OR,

PATRIOTISM PUT TO THE TEST,

*In a Letter to the Rev. Dr. Price.*

---

By JOS. WIMPEY.

---

LONDON:
MDCCLXXII.

# EXTRACTS.

THAT the SINKING FUND, at the time of its institution, was a proper measure, and would have effectually answered the intended purpose of discharging the national debt is clearly demonstrable; provided Government had taken care to have raised Supplies sufficient to discharge current expences as they arose. But every one must surely see the mighty difference there is between providing for the payment of the interest, and discharging a debt of fifty-five millions, (the amount of the debt at that time) and a debt of one hundred and forty millions, the amount of the present debt. If the interest of the first is two millions, the interest of the last is five millions six hundred thousand pounds. The nation at that time might be very able to bear the payment of two millions standing interest, and the current supplies of the year; it may now be able to pay the interest of twice that sum, and the current expences of the year, and yet be utterly incapable of paying the interest of the present debt, and the necessary incidental expences. But as in the course of your treating this subject, in your Appeal to the Public, there are several things that are either above my comprehension, or contrary to my reason; I will beg leave to refer to the Appeal, and take them in course as they offer.

In p. 313.* you say, " That in order to justify the Aliena-
" tion of the SINKING FUND, it has been usual to plead,
" that when money is wanted, it makes no difference
" whether it is taken from hence, or procured by making



" a

* These references are all to this volume.

"a new loan charged on new funds. I have called this a
"SOPHISM, and asserted, in opposition to it, that the dif-
"ference between these two ways of procuring money, is
"no less than *infinite*."

You then proceed to define the *general* idea of a SINKING FUND, which I think you have done very truly.

You then point out three ways, in which a kingdom may apply such a saving.

"1st, The *interests* disengaged from time to time by the
"payments made with it, may be themselves applied to
"the payment of the public debts."

"Or, 2dly, They may be spent in current services."

Now, Sir, you make the difference between these two ways of appropriating the fund no less than *infinite*.

The first proposition, I think, is evidently true; for a fund that produces annually more than will pay the interest of the debt, being constantly applied towards the discharge of the interest and debt, *must* annually diminish, and finally will discharge the same. But when the sense of both propositions are considered as they relate to the good and ill, or rather profit and loss of the public, I cannot make out the infinite difference you so clearly see, or, indeed, any difference at all.

I am not in love with the statesman's SOPHISM, I am desirous of avoiding all SOPHISMS, be they from whence they may. Let us suppose then, that a NATION is indebted to the amount of 140 millions, that the interest on the same is 5,600,000, and that its ability will extend no farther than to furnish 6,600,000, by any possible means

 whatever.

whatever. However, in conformity to Dr. Price's opinion and advice, it is resolved to apply the whole 6,600,000 to pay the interest due at the end of the year, and towards discharging the debt. This being repeated year after year, it would operate exactly in the manner the doctor has said. At the end of the first year one million; at the end of the second, a second million, together with the interest of the first; at the end of the third year, a third million, together with the interest of the two former millions, and the interest of the interest of the first. And thus would it go on till the whole debt and its interest were paid.

The next consideration is, how to provide money to defray the current expences of the year. A resolution is taken to act in this also conformably to the doctor's opinion; which is to borrow money for the purpose. Indeed it has no choice left; for six millions being the utmost its ability will by any means extend to, and that being applied as above, borrowing is the last and only resource. Let us suppose a million is found necessary for this purpose, and the interest to be four per cent. the same as the interest of the million discharged at the end of the first year. At that time the account will stand thus.

| | |
|---|---|
| To the amount of the national debt — | £140,000,000 |
| To one year's interest — — — — | 5,600,000 |
| | 145,600,000 |
| By amount of all the resources of the state — | 6,600,000 |
| Total of the old debt at the end of the first year — | 139,000,000 |
| To second year's interest — — — | 5,560,000 |
| | 144,560,000 |
| By amount of resources, as before — — | 6,600,000 |

| | |
|---|---|
| Total amount at the end of the second year — | £137,960,000 |
| To third year's interest — — — | 5,518,400 |
| | 143,478,400 |
| By amount of resources, as before — — | 6,600,000 |
| Total amount at the end of the third year — | 136,878,400 |
| To fourth year's interest — — — | 5,475,136 |
| | 142,353,536 |
| By resources, as before — — — | 6,600,000 |
| Total Amount at the end of the fourth year — | 135,753,536 |

And thus we might proceed till the whole debt should be discharged. By the above calculation it appears, that £4,246,464 would be discharged from the old debt in four years; that is, four millions from the resources, and the remainder of the sum by means of the operation of the interest.

Now let us see how we stand in respect to the New Debt, which we are contracting for the annual service of the year.

| | |
|---|---|
| Borrowed at £4 per cent. for the current service of the first year — — — — — — | £1,000,000 |
| To one year's interest at the end of the second year — | 40,000 |
| Amount of the new debt at the end of the second year | 1,040,000 |

*N.B.* As the nation annually disposes of the whole amount of its resources, and therefore cannot discharge the interest of the money it borrows, that at the end of every year becomes Principal; or, which is the same thing, it must borrow as much more at the end of each year, as may be necessary to pay the interest of the preceding years, and so on from year to year.

Brought

| | |
|---|---|
| Brought over the amount of the new debt at the end of the second year — — — — | £1,040,000 |
| Borrowed for the service of the second year — | 1,000,000 |
| | 2,040,000 |
| To third year's interest — — — | 81,600 |
| Total amount of the debt at the end of the third year | 2,121,600 |
| Borrowed for the service of the third year — — | 1,000,000 |
| | 3,121,600 |
| To fourth year's interest — — — | 124,864 |
| | 3,246,464 |
| Borrowed for the service of the fourth year — | 1,000,000 |
| Total amount of the new debt at the end of the fourth year — — — — — | 4,246,464 |

Which being exactly the sum the old debt decreased in the same time, being added to the remainder, makes the sum total precisely the same, and puts the NATION *in statu quo.*

## PROOF.

| | |
|---|---|
| Amount of the old debt at the end of the 4th year — — — — | 135,753,536 |
| Amount of the new debt at the end of the same year — — — | 4,246,464 |
| Total amount of the national debt — | £140,000,000 |

at the end of the fourth year, without the least diminution whatever. And should such a measure be pursued 40 or even 400 years, the debt would remain exactly the same.

The doctor's comparison of a "*Sinking Fund* to a corn "of grain sown, which, by having its produce sown, and

" the produce of that produce, and so on, is capable of an " increase that will soon stock a province or support a " kingdom," is very pretty; but I am afraid not just. I should rather compare it to a parson's barn, which is always open to receive whatever is brought to it; but never increases the quantity till the next tithing brings a fresh recruit of stock. The doctor seems to speak of a *Sinking Fund* as a spring or fountain, whereas at best it is no more than a reservoir, which depends entirely upon other springs or sources, as we shall see by and by; when they are stopt or cease to flow, the reservoir of course is speedily drained and continues empty and useless. But you go on page 315.

" The *former*, be its income at first ever so much " exceeded by the new debts incurred annually, will soon " become superior to them, and cancel them.—The *latter*, " if at first inferior to the new debts incurred annually, " will for ever remain so; and a state that has no other " provision for the payment of its debts, will be always " accumulating them till it sinks."

I humbly conceive, doctor, the calculations now made fully disprove the first part of this observation. For without supposing the income of the former way to be *ever so much* exceeded by the new debts incurred annually, it appears from thence, that the new debts must ever increase as the old ones diminish, and that the state gains no advantage by the mode recommended.

As to the latter part of the observation, if the provision at first, or indeed at any time after, is inferior to the new debts incurred annually, the debts must continue to increase, so long as the provision for discharging them may fall short of their amount; which in time would accumulate to a height that would infallibly sink the state. But

 pray,

pray, doctor, give me leave to ask, if there is no medium? Should the state find it has ability to discharge the interest of the present debt annually, and provide for the current services of the year, and should take their measures accordingly, the present debt might stand as it does now an hundred years, without the least tendency to sink the state below what it is at this moment. For so long as the people can furnish money to discharge the whole current expences of the year, with an overplus; such overplus being applied as it ought, will certainly diminish the debt. But when these expences exceed their utmost ability, the debt, in spite of all management, will increase; and I conceive it can make no difference how any former surplus's may be applied, if towards the discharge of the old debts new ones must be contracted, with an interest daily accumulating.

But it is time to enter thoroughly into this business. I have said above, the *Sinking Fund* has nothing in it of the nature of a spring; it must be supplied from time to time, or it will necessarily cease to act, and to be anything more than a name. The only *Source* is the *Purse* of the people; when that is drained, good bye to all FUNDS, call them by what name you please. Their infinite difference and omnipotent powers immediately vanish.

A *Fund* of £200,000 per ann. or a million per ann. continued for 500 years, would avail nothing, unless the people could besides, and over and above those sums, discharge the interest of the present debt, and defray the current expences. Without such abilities, *a Sinking Fund* is a mere chimera, and a new debt might accumulate with twice the rapidity that the old one could be cancelled. 'Twould be like holding a double chalk in one hand, and a sponge in the other, and making two strokes with the right, while one was rubbed out with the left; the longer you chalk and rub, the larger and longer would be the account.

That money, at compound interest, would accumulate in the surprizing manner you have said, is demonstrably certain; and it is just as certain, that the interest of money borrowed, if not punctually discharged, would accumulate in the very same manner, and with equal celerity. That it has not been discharged without incurring new debts, is abundantly manifest from the present frightful extent of the *National Debt*. Nor is it always right, or does it signify to inveigh against *Administration*. *Ministers* are but men, and are too frequently necessitated to pursue measures by a majority of the people, for which they are reviled and condemned by the rest.

What can the Ministry do against the general bent and inclination of the people? In a full House, a very few days since, was there a single *Member* who opposed the reduction of the *Land-Tax*, from four to three shillings? Ask the first hundred freeholders you meet, if they are for reducing the Land-Tax to three shillings, or keeping it up to four, in order to reduce the *National Debt*; if you meet with one out of the hundred who would vote for the latter, I shall be much surprized. There was a time when the *Sinking Fund* might have answered so desirable a purpose; but even then not with so much ease as is generally imagined; for how far soever the doctor's honest zeal for the permanent prosperity of his country may carry him, ninety-nine in an hundred are for the enjoyment of the present hour; and Administration *dare* not tax the people for a long series of years in *peace*, as they may in *war*.—The burden is heavy and grievous, they have borne it long, and are very apt to think it is made more oppressive than is necessary. In times of imminent danger, when their fears are alarmed, they are generous

 and

and free, and will strain every power; but in times of peace, he that may dare to insist upon such a degree of painful exertion, will be considered as a *traitor* and a *robber*, and would be treated accordingly.

You think, Sir, the operation of the *Sinking Fund* is so clear and certain, that all further explanation is unnecessary. But all this is upon certain conditions that lurk *in petto*. The reader not perceiving those *latent* conditions, attends to the argument as it stands, and assents to the conclusion, as demonstrably certain.

"A nation capable of setting apart the annual sum of £200,000, interest at 5 per cent. might in 86 years accumulate above 260 millions; which would discharge the present *National Debt*, and leave 120 millions as a capital to answer any future expence that might accrue." Now this is a fact which is clearly demonstrable; and therefore 'tis concluded that to continue the nation groaning under its oppressive weight, argues folly, madness, or some cause of a more malignant nature, arising from the depravity and corruption of ministers. But this amazingly great, good work, is to be performed only upon certain conditions, which conditions do not appear. The *Conditions* are, That during the time the sum of £200,000 is annually set apart to accumulate, the nation shall pay and discharge the whole interest of the present debt, together with all and every incidental charge and expence that may accrue in time of war or peace, for and during the said term of 86 years. A *Condition*, which if any regard is to be paid to past events, absolutely vacates and annuls the benefit and advantage of the whole measure. For admitting that certain branches of the *Revenue* do produce a surplus of £200,000 per ann. which is sacredly applied towards the discharge of the national debt, according to the true intention and meaning of the *Sinking Fund*. If the

 circumstances

circumstances of the times, from the intolerable burden the people groan under during the same, should render it necessary for Government to borrow £400,000 annually, together with the interest from year to year on the accumulating debt; the state of the *National Debt*, then, instead of having paid off its present debt, and raising a *capital* of 120 millions, would be this: At the end of the term it would be 260 millions in debt, which is greater than the present debt by 120 millions. This would then be our true and most deplorable situation; and this, the history of past times fully declare and confirm.

In 1716 the *Sinking Fund* was instituted, the national debt at that time was about 55 millions, this was 56 years ago, and the debt is now about 140 millions; so that it is increased in that time the surprizing sum of 85 millions. To this you remark, this increase of debt is owing entirely to the Sinking Fund's being misapplied to the payment of current annual expences, instead of being applied towards the discharging the old debt. This I beg leave to say, Sir, I conceive to be a great mistake; for had the Sinking Fund been applied as you desire, and new debts contracted to the same amount, these, with their interest, would have accumulated to the very same sum as the old ones discharged with its interest, and in the same time. But if you will set apart a sum of money, and calculate its effects from the operation of compound interest on the one hand, and borrow the same sum of money, leaving out its operation of compound interest on the other, by that means you may discharge any debt, or raise any fortune, let the extent of the sum be what you please. Was it as easy, doctor, to discharge the national debt, as it is to make figures and raise schemes of calculation, you and I could jointly or separately exonerate the whole, and set the *Nation*, in a few minutes, as clear as it was at the REVOLUTION. But I must beg leave to insist, that there

12 is

is no doing it by means of a *Sinking Fund*, unless such *Fund* be supplied from time to time by levies raised on the people. This is a task they have not been equal to, since the commencement of the debt, which is abundantly evident from its continual increase to the present amount. The longer it lasts, the heavier the burden grows, and of course in length of time will become so heavy as no longer to be borne.

These observations being duly attended to, will, I apprehend, satisfactorily answer all you have advanced in favour of the superiority of a sinking fund; and therefore I need not apply them to every particular case you mention, though they are equally applicable to each. But there are some peculiar matters, which I must not pass over in silence. You say,

"It is an observation of particular importance here, "that there is no benefit to be derived from employing a "*fund* in the *second* of the ways I have mentioned, rather "than the *first*. In both cases the taxes are continued "during the operation of the fund, and the national "burdens are the same. In the former, a disengaged tax "is employed to *pay* a debt, and in the latter, to *save* a "debt, which must have been otherwise incurred; and "*thus far*, the two funds are perfectly equal in their "influence on the public." There is a wide difference then, Sir, between your opinion and mine, and I am apt to think, between your's and the public; or I cannot see what should induce them to divert the sinking fund from its intended course. The ultimate influence, in respect to the amount of the debt, would be equal; but certainly the difference of the present influence is very great. Suppose the nation has a million more to raise than it can conveniently find ways to do, and that sum lies ready in the sinking fund, 'tis resolved therefore to use that million for the purpose. By that means Administration is relieved from the difficulties that would attend the raising it, and the people are relieved by paying a million less than otherwise they must have done. Therefore 'tis plain, what would have been a present burden, and probably a very grievous one, is entirely avoided by such an application of a million from the sinking fund, and the old debt remains the same to be paid hereafter instead of the present time. But you say,

" The difference which will appear on tracing them " farther," (speaking of the two ways of applying the fund) " is a difference entirely in favour of the former fund; " and a difference too, which is not balanced by any kind " of loss or expence.—A disengaged annuity, if employed " to *pay* a debt, will obtain for the public another annuity, " and that another *in infinitum.* Whereas if employed to " *save* a debt; or, which is the same, the *interest* of a debt, " as that interest would not itself have borne interest, no " farther advantage could arise.—In short; in the one " case the disengaged annuity is PROLIFIC, and contains " in itself a number continually growing of other annuities. " —In the other case, it is a BARREN annuity."

I will not call this reasoning *fallacious,* because I am thoroughly convinced Dr. Price does by no means intend to mislead the Public; but I must beg leave to say, I think he is much mistaken. The Propositions are, that the applying the fund towards the discharge of the debt, is entirely in favour of that way, which is not balanced by any kind of loss or expence.—That in the first way it bears a compound interest; in the second, its interest bears no interest; in the first case it is *prolific,* in the second, it is *barren.* But why does it bear no interest in the second way of applying it? Suppose I borrow £1000 of Dr. Price, at 5 per cent. At six months end

 he

he calls for his interest, I then pay him £25. On the morrow he calls again, and says, I find I shall not want this money, give me your note for it with interest, and you may have it for six months if you please, which is done accordingly. At the end of six months more, he calls again for £25. due for interest on the £1000 at that time, which I pay him. He then pulls out his note for £25, which I gave him before, saying, You may as well take this note, pay me 12*s.* 6*d.* the interest due on the same, and give me your note for £50, to carry interest from this time, and there is your former note, and the £25 you paid me. Thus we might go on from time to time till the interest equalled the principal, or any time you please. Now the question between the doctor and me is, whether I have paid, and he has received interest upon interest or not? In the eye of the *law* I have not; that is, not in such a way as will render him culpable and subject to punishment; but in reality and fact I have to all intents and purposes.

In this manner it operates exactly between the public and its creditors. A gentleman has money in the funds, for which he receives a dividend of £1000; it is at his option either to invest that interest again in the funds, or dispose of it otherwise; but which way soever he chuses, it makes no difference to the public, if their necessities oblige them to borrow; it does not signify, whether it is the money they paid for interest, or whether it is a fresh sum from a different hand, it subjects them to the payment of a fresh interest, and operates exactly in the same way, and to equal disadvantage as if they should pay interest upon interest, and is equally PROLIFIC in every respect to the *first* method.—As to what the doctor says of "preferring an exemption from the burden of ONE "annuity, to an exemption from MANY, and subjecting "a kingdom to the loss of 208 millions, only for the sake "of saving a debt, rather than paying an equal debt, that "is, from a regard to a circumstance in itself absolutely "frivolous," I conceive to arise from his partial manner of stating the case. The loss to the kingdom would not be 208 millions, nor so many pence, in one way more than the other, but exactly the same. The reason of the apparent difference is, that he reckons compound interest on the money paid by the sinking fund in discharge of the debt; but reckons no interest on the same money when applied in discharge of current services; or, which is the same thing, the people must pay in the *first* way as much more money than they do in the *second*, as is equal to the sum paid by the sinking fund; and a compound interest reckoned upon that surplus, be the sum what it will, will render the disbursements exactly equal to the public, and consequently is a matter of no signification.

This method of reasoning runs through the whole of the doctor's writings on this subject. Whereas had he considered, that money in the hands of individuals is equally valuable as it is in the hands of Government, and that its interest will accumulate by their use of it equally fast at least, often much faster, he never could have thought that any sum employed in one way of paying debts, could have been so far exceeded by another. The different ways or MANNER of application is nothing, the difference arises solely from the public's paying (according to his plan of a sinking fund) a large sum of money annually in that way more than they do in any other, and that with its interest constantly accumulating produces the mighty sums he ascribes to the mere MANNER of applying the money. Whereas, was the national debt continued, and these sums which compose the savings or surplusses of the sinking fund suffered to remain with the individuals that furnish them, the same sums would produce the mighty ones the doctor quotes, besides many further advantages the extra use of it would produce in their hands, over and above the common rate of interest.

I do not mean to insinuate, that the paying off or lessening the national debt is not a desirable object; I should heartily rejoice to see any measure adopted for that purpose, which would in any degree answer consistently with the peace, safety and tolerable subsistence or well-being of the people; but to augment taxes already much too burthensome and grievous, to exonerate posterity from like burdens, would, I fear, be introducing a scene of wretchedness and misery we might very soon repent, and prove exceedingly dangerous for Administration to attempt. But you say,

"From these observations the truth of the following "assertion will be very evident."

"A state may, without difficulty, redeem all its debts by "borrowing money for that purpose, at an equal or even "any higher interest than the debts bear; and, without "providing any other Funds than such small ones, as "shall from year to year become necessary to pay the "interest of the sums borrowed."

If you can reconcile this *assertion* to practice, doctor, according to the obvious, literal meaning of the same, you will be the greatest *Benefactor* to individuals as well as the public, the world ever knew. I will venture to say, this is a secret no man is master of but yourself; and it is therefore well worth the study and labour of every one to make himself fully acquainted with.

But I will beg leave to make an observation or two, which will furnish an infallible rule to try the truth of

 this,

this, and all other assertions of the same kind by.—Whenever the public or individuals are once in debt, they *must* ever remain so as long as their expences or outgoings equal their income. Suppose A. is indebted in the sum of £100, and spends the whole of his income as fast or faster than he receives it, he may get further into debt, but should he live a hundred years he could never get out, nor in the least diminish his debt.—Should he, upon your plan, borrow money of others, at an equal rate of interest, by that means he might shift the debt from his present creditors to others, but he would be the same debtor still, without the least relief from borrowing. But should he borrow at a higher rate of interest, (as you say he may, and notwithstanding that diminish his debt) 'tis very evident to me, his debt would increase in proportion to the advance of interest.—But I am not a stranger to the salvo you here call in to your aid, I mean the *provisoe*, formerly mentioned. I should be sorry to offend, doctor; but I must beg leave to say, this appears to me to be downright begging the question, as may appear by what follows.

You say, Sir, "Suppose our Parliament, in the year "1706 had resolved to borrow half a million annually for "the purpose of redeeming the debts of the kingdom. "In *private life*, such a measure would be justly deemed "absurd: But in a *State* it would be the effect of the "soundest policy. For in the present year the *National* "*Gain*, supposing the money applied without interruption, "to the redemption of debts bearing 4 per cent. interest, "would have been an HUNDRED MILLIONS, being *debt* "*redeemed*, or the sum nearly to which an annuity of half "a million will accumulate in 56 years.—On the other "hand, the *National Loss* would have been TWENTY-"EIGHT MILLIONS, being *debt incurred*, or the sum of all "the loans.——The clear balance, therefore, in favour of "the nation, would have been SEVENTY-TWO MILLIONS."

18 Now

Now let us examine this with candour and impartiality. 'Tis asserted that half a million borrowed annually for 56 years, and applied to the discharge of our debts at 4 per cent. interest, the nation would have gained — — — £100,000,000
The national loss in the same time would be 28,000,000

The clear balance in favour of the nation £ 72,000,000

This great national gain of seventy-two millions is ascribed to the plan of borrowing. Now, I am of opinion that the nation would not receive the least gain or advantage by such a measure. But at the end of 56 years, without borrowing a shilling, *ceteris paribus*, (consider this matter in whatever way you please) the event would have been precisely the same.

Let me endeavour to explain this by a clear state of the question. Suppose in the year 1716 the national debt was 72 millions, that it paid 4 per cent. interest for the same, that its whole taxes and resources could by no means be extended farther than to pay the interest of the debt of 72 millions, and the current expences of the year, its ability could not extend a shilling farther; so that its debt must continue the same. However, it is resolved to try, by way of expedient, if the borrowing half a million annually at the same rate of interest, would not afford relief, and in time lessen the debt by a constant application of it for that purpose.

| | | |
|---|---|---|
| In the year 1716, the national debt suppose | | £72,000,000 |
| One year's interest at 4 per cent. is — | | 2,880,000 |
| | | 74,880,000 |
| The amount of the fund is — — | 2,880,000 | |
| Borrowed — — — — | 500,000 | |
| | | 3,380,000 |

| | |
|---|---:|
| The amount of the debt in 1717 — — | £71,500,000 |
| One year's interest on this sum is — | 2,860,000 |
| | 74,360,000 |
| Deduct the fund, and money borrowed as before — — — — | 3,380,000 |
| The debt in 1718 — — — | 70,980,000 |
| One year's interest on this sum — — | 2,839,200 |
| | 73,819,200 |
| Deduct the fund, &c. as above — — | 3,380,000 |
| The debt in 1719 — — — | 70,439,200 |
| One year's interest on this sum — — | 2,817,568 |
| | 73,256,768 |
| Deduct the fund, &c. — — | 3,380,000 |
| The debt in 1720 — — — | 69,876,768 |
| One year's interest on this sum — — | 2,795,070 |
| | 72,671,838 |
| Deduct the fund, &c. — — — | 3,380,000 |
| The debt in 1721, which deducted from the original debt, shews how much the debt | £69,291,838 |
| is reduced in 5 years — — | 2,708,162 |
| The state of the new debt for the same time. | |
| Borrowed at the end of the year 1716 — | 500,000 |
| One year's interest on the same, at 4 per cent. | 20,000 |
| | 520,000 |
| Borrowed in 1717 — — — | 500,000 |
| Debt in ditto — — — — | 1,020,000 |
| One year's interest on this sum — — | 40,800 |
| Borrowed in 1718 — — — | 500,000 |
| Debt in ditto — — — — | 1,560,800 |
| One year's interest on this sum — — | 62,432 |

| | |
|---|---|
| | £1,623,232 |
| Borrowed in 1719 — — — — | 500,000 |
| Debt in ditto — — — — — | 2,123,232 |
| One year's interest on this sum — — — | 84,929 |
| Borrowed in 1720 — — — — | 500,000 |
| | 2,708,161 |
| Fractions — — — — — | 1 |
| Amount of the new debt in 1721 — — | 2,708,162 |
| being the exact sum paid off on account of old debt, to which add the sum now due on the same — | 69,291,838 |
| Due jointly on the old and new debt — — | £72,000,000 |

at the end of five years; the precise sum that the nation was in debt when this measure was commenced; and thus would it operate was it to be carried on for 56 or 560 years. This state of the question shews, I think, in the clearest and strongest manner, that money *borrowed* of one to *pay* another, effects nothing towards paying off a debt, indeed it is impossible it should.—The thing is exactly the same, whether the debt be owing by the public or an individual, it makes not the least difference. You allow such a measure in *private life* would be justly deemed absurd: Indeed, every one perceives it to be so; and in a *State* it is equally so, but from its extent and magnitude it is more difficult to comprehend. But money borrowed to pay debts in either case, operates exactly the same: They only differ as more and less, but their relations, proportions, and effects, are immutably the same.

It may be objected, that the doctor did not intend the interest should be calculated on the money borrowed. If so, to that I answer, then his scheme would be too partial to be just: For the interest is as much a debt as the principal, and must be paid even with more punctuality.

 But

But it may be said, that compound interest should not be allowed. I answer, there is no foundation for such an assertion: For if money is to be borrowed to discharge the interest, it then becomes principal, and is subject to interest, and that interest again to interest, and so on, *ad infinitum.*—But it may be said, it is plain the doctor intended the interest of the sums borrowed should be discharged by taxes laid on the people; otherwise what does he mean, by saying, "Without providing any "other Funds than such small ones as shall from year "to year become necessary to pay the interests of the "sums borrowed." I answer, I admit that to be his meaning, and must beg leave to think 'tis plainly begging the question. For, the *Nation* either has it in its power to discharge its debts, or it has not; if it has, then borrowing money for *that* purpose is an unnecessary measure, and should by all means be avoided. But if it has it not in its power, then to say it shall provide Funds to discharge the interest of the sum borrowed, is to subject it to a burden it is confessed it is not able to bear, which inability suggested the necessity of the measure of borrowing. And though the Funds, for that purpose, are called SUCH SMALL ONES, yet if they are considered as accumulating for the term mentioned, they will be found to equal the *large* debt discharged.

But, if we should admit (though I by no means think it admissible) that the Nation could provide Funds for any length of time for the payment of the interest of the sums that is proposed to be borrowed, over and above the interest of the present debt, and all current and incidental expences. I then insist, that borrowing money for the payment of the debt is an unprofitable measure, and altogether unnecessary. For if the Nation can pay the interest of the money borrowed, that is, if they can pay an annuity increasing at the rate of £20,000 every year,

22 that

that sum applied annually for 56 years towards the discharge of the *National Debt*, will as effectually answer the purpose, and discharge as much of the *Debt* as the borrowing half a million annually for that purpose. And I appeal to the doctor, as a Gentleman of *veracity* and *honour*, if this be not precisely the case? If so, why then should we deceive ourselves with schemes of borrowing, and give a seeming utility and important advantage to a measure which is a mere matter of amusement?

This brings me back to the sense of my former universal *maxim*, viz. If the *income* of a *State* exceeds its *outgoings*, the *surplus* being inviolably applied towards discharging its debts, they would be continually diminishing, and in time it would totally discharge them. But, on the other hand, if its outgoings exceed its income, its debts would constantly increase, and finally terminate in inevitable ruin. To borrow money, or to depend upon the powers of a sinking fund, would be only to deceive ourselves; our fate in such a deplorable situation would be absolutely fixed, and without all remedy, unless we should grow wise in time, and bring our expences within our ability to bear them. Indeed, where the outgoings of a State exceeds its income, there can be no such thing, properly speaking, as a *Sinking Fund;* there may be *surplus's* of particular funds, which may be called by that name, and they may be applied towards the discharge of the *National Debt* in the way you recommend, and as was originally designed; but what relief would such an application afford, if while you discharge or redeem half a million of debt by the sinking fund, you contract or incur a new debt annually to twice that amount; that is, while you pay off one million, you contract a new debt of two; so that by the time you have redeemed SEVENTY-TWO MILLIONS of debt, you will find yourselves ONE HUNDRED and FORTY-FOUR further in debt. In short, I have no idea of a

 sinking

sinking fund, or its efficacy under such circumstances; we may fancy its effects as omnipotent as we please; but a superior rising debt would be more omnipotent than it, if I may so speak, and would render null and void its whole efficacy and power.—We may call it paying simple interest for the money we borrow; but all who know the use of money, know, that every one who pays the interest punctually when it becomes due, pays compound interest, or what in every sense is equal to it. For should he borrow money on interest, or discount bills to pay it, that would be paying compound interest in express terms. But should he have cash to pay it without, that cash would at least have made an interest which still amounts to the same thing. * * *

As to the *Sinking Fund*, though you have treated of its nature and operations so fully, I find, by the conversation of several, they have quite mistaken your meaning; and, instead of being informed, have been mislead. You every where compare it, in its operations and effects, when applied in discharge of the National Debt, to money bearing compound interest; and that it accumulates in the same beneficial manner. This, as a comparison, very well serves to illustrate and explain your meaning; but many, it seems, have mistaken the *thing* it is compared to, for the *thing* itself; between which I observed there is an infinite difference. They replied, if so, there must be a strange fallacy in the doctor's argument which they had not discovered. I told them that was for want of attending to the whole of it. I will therefore endeavour to explain this matter in the easiest and clearest manner I can.

The general idea of *A Sinking Fund* (as the doctor has well defined) signifies "any SAVING or SURPLUS, set "apart from the rest of an annual income, and appro-

 "priated

"priated to the purpose of paying off, or sinking debts."—The original intention of instituting such a *Fund*, was, that it should be inviolably applied towards the discharge of such debts as had or might be contracted during times of extraordinary expence, when they might happen to be so great, as to render it imprudent or inconvenient to tax the people so high as such outgoings made necessary. Therefore it was thought a more eligible way to borrow money for the present, and to apply the sinking fund towards the discharge as it should arise hereafter.

But, in process of time, it has so happened, that our expences or outgoings have been so exceedingly multiplied, that the *National Debt* is grown to an enormous size, far beyond what it was thought possible, even by the ablest statesmen, for the nation to bear. So that to discharge the interest of the present debt, and pay current expences, requires the raising annually much heavier taxes *now*, than the state required *then*, even in the times of the greatest *Exigence*, when it was thought more prudent to borrow than to distress the people by taxing them higher.

This has put Administration under great difficulties. The people groan under a load of taxes, which are become intolerable; therefore, let the exigences of the state be as great as may be, to increase a load already much too great, is universally opposed. The general voice then, is, borrow more money, or apply what you have in the *Sinking Fund*, rather than multiply or augment the taxes, which the people *cannot*, which it is feared they *will* not bear.—As the least evil, that of applying the money in the *Sinking Fund* to the discharge of current expences, is adopted, and the payment of the former debts thereby procrastinated. This is the alienation the doctor complains of; and maintains, that it would be infinitely better to borrow money for the purpose; for, by means of such alienation, you run the kingdom in debt MILLIONS, in order to save THOUSANDS; meaning, that if the money in the sinking fund was applied to the payment of the former debts, it would bear *compound interest*, and if money was borrowed in its stead, for it, the kingdom would only pay *simple interest*. This it is that has imprinted a false idea of this matter on the minds of many.

In order to set this in a clear, and at the same time, a true light: Let us suppose the interest of the *National Debt*, and the current services, require taxes to be raised annually to the amount of six millions; that however eight millions is the amount of the present taxes, beyond which they cannot be extended, without distressing the people beyond all measure. Here is a clear *Surplus* or *Saving* of two millions per ann. which passes into the Sinking Fund, and by it is applied towards the discharge of the National Debt. From hence it is clear, two millions of debt would be discharged annually, so long as the Fund and its application should be continued; besides the interest of each two millions at the end of each succeeding year, and also the interest of such interest. Let us suppose this measure to continue three years only. At the end of the first year two millions of debt is discharged; at the end of the second, two more, together with the interest of the first two millions; at the end of the third, two more, together with the interest of four millions, and the interest of the interest of the first two millions. At this time a war happens to break out, and the current service of the state requires eight millions in the room of six; therefore Administration must either increase the burden of taxes a fourth, that is, from eight to ten millions: or else they must apply the two millions in the Sinking Fund to current service, and let the National Debt continue till better times. Should we go on in this way for twenty or an hundred years, the *debt* would continue the same exactly, without the least increase or diminution Whereas had the six millions paid in the three former years, together with the interest upon it, been money at, or operated like money at compound interest, this could not have been the case; for then those sums would have daily accumulated as money at compound interest doth, and in time would have totally discharged the National Debt, was its magnitude ten times as great as it is. Here then it is the doctor's comparison totally fails.

The truth is, the money arising from the Sinking Fund, as suppose the six millions abovementioned, or any other sum, applied as above, neither is money at compound interest, nor are its effects analagous thereto. Two millions applied by the sinking fund, or any other way towards the discharge of the debt, would reduce the sum so much, and consequently the interest of the same. But there its whole efficacy or power determines and ceases for ever. The question then is, supposing this to be true, what is the interest, and the interest upon interest above talked of, and how is it produced? I answer, that it owes its existence to quite another *Source*, which is the *people's pocket.* The money paid, as suppose the six millions abovementioned have wrought their whole effect, the interest of two millions paid the first year, the interest of the four millions paid the first and second year, and the interest of the interest paid the first year, let the amount be what it will, not a shilling of it was produced by the said six millions, but was so much money paid by the people for the interest of four millions of debt they had before discharged. And it would have operated exactly in the same manner, had the same sums the interest amounted to been paid towards the discharge of the debt, so far as they extend, whether the six millions had been

 paid

paid or not. So that the whole interest, which is said to accumulate from such payments, *do not at all arise from the payments, but from the money paid by the people from time to time, over and above the interest of the present debt.*

*FINIS.*

# NOTE

ON

# THE SINKING FUND

ESTABLISHED

BY MR. PITT,

IN

1786.

## *SINKING FUND of* 1786.

THE National Debt, which had appeared to Hume of appalling magnitude in 1752, was largely increased by the war terminated in 1763, when it amounted to about 139 millions. Rather more than 10 millions were paid off in the subsequent peace, so that it stood at between 128 and 129 millions at the beginning of the American war. But that unfortunate contest nearly doubled its amount, which in 1784 was about 250 millions. This rapid increase of the public debt, coupled with the disordered state of the finances, which exhibited a large deficit, and the supposed injurious influence of the independence of the American States, excited the greatest apprehensions in the public mind. And though the last-mentioned ground of alarm was entirely visionary, the crisis was such as could be averted only by the adoption of an improved system of financial policy. And happily the vigour and perseverance of Mr. Pitt succeeded in great measure in effecting this object. The complexity in the public accounts was mostly got rid of by bringing the various funds which had hitherto been distributed under different heads into a single or consolidated fund. Various retrenchments were at the same time effected, and some new taxes having been imposed, the deficit of revenue was made good and a surplus realised.

Meanwhile, the cry for the adoption of vigorous measures for the diminution of the public debt had become very general. The tract published by Dr. Price in 1772, in which the imaginary virtues of a sinking fund operating at compound interest were so highly extolled, might



have

have been forgotten. But similar statements and calculations were brought before the public over and over again, in the popular and widely circulated tracts written by the Doctor against the American war, and in those which he published in 1783 and 1784 on the public debts and finances. And the clearness of his style, the earnestness with which his theories were enforced, and their consolatory character, procured for them a very general support. Not being subjected to any very searching examination, and the conclusive answer which Wimpey had made to them, having either attracted no attention or been forgotten, they were generally believed to be as sound as they were striking and encouraging. The extinction of that debt which had so long excited the alarms of philosophers, of financiers, and of the public, was now supposed to be not only a possible but an easy task. A few hundreds of thousands of pounds set apart as a peculiar fund to increase through the magical influence of compound interest, were all that was said to be necessary to ensure so very desirable and so unlooked for a result.

Ministers, it might have been expected, would have known better. But they were carried away by the general delusion. Having succeeded in getting a surplus revenue, Mr. Pitt lost no time in consulting Price upon the establishment of a sinking fund. And the latter, after having maturely considered the subject, drew up the following schemes for the formation of such fund which he accompanied with the subjoined memorandum.

## PLAN I.

Million *per ann.* Surplus, aided by the falling in of the Temporary Annuities, Life Annuities, Expenses of Management, and converting sixty millions of the *three per cents.* into *four per cents.*, by providing in the first five years £600,000 *per ann.* for paying the difference of interest.

| FUND. | 3 per cents redeemed. £ | STOCK REDEEMED. £ |
|---|---|---|
| Surplus - - | 1000,000 at 75 - | 1,333,333 |
| Received in exchange for six millions of *three per cents.* converted into 4 *per cents.*, at 18⅓ *per cent.* - | 1,100,000 at 75 - | 1,466,666 |
| Interest of £1,333,333 and £1,466,666 - | 84,000 | |
| Expence of management, at 562½ *per* million - | 1,575 | |
| Short Annuity for ten years lapsed - - | 25,000 | |
| Life Annuities lapsed, at £2000 *per ann.* - | 2,000 | |
| Management on the Short Annuity - - | 351 | |
| Received for 18 millions of *three per cents.* converted into *four per cents.* at 20 *per cent.* - - | (3,600,000) at 78 - | 4,615,384 |
| One year from the first payment - - | 1,112,926 at 78 - | 1,426,828 |
| Interest of £4,615,384 and £1,426,828 - - | 181,266 | |
| Expence of management | 3,611 | |
| Life Annuities lapsed - | 2,000 | |
| Received for 12 millions of *three per cents.* converted into *four per cents.* at 20 *per cent.* - - | (2,400,000) at 81 - | 2,962,962 |
| Two years from the first payment - - - | 1,299,803 at 81 - | 1,604,695 |
| Interest of £2,962,962 and £1,604,695 - - | 137,029 | |
| Expence of management | 2,568 | |
| Life Annuities lapsed - | 2,000 | |
| Received for 12 millions of *three per cents.* converted into *four per cents.* at 20 *per cent.* - - | 4 per cents. redeemed. (2,400,000) at par - | 2,400,000 |
| Three years - - | 1,441,400 - | 1,441,400 |
| Interest of £2,400,000 and £1,441,400 - - | 153,656 | |
| Expence of management - | 2,160 | |
| Life Annuities lapsed - | 2,000 | |

| Fund. | | | Stock redeemed. |
|---|---|---|---|
| | 4 per cents. redeemed. | | |
| Received for 12 millions of *three per cents.* converted into *four per cents.* at 20 *per cent.* - - | £ (2,400,000) | - | £ 2,400,000 |
| Four years - - | 1,599,216 | - | 1,599,216 |
| Interest of £2,400,000 and £1,599,216 - - | 159,968 | | |
| Expence of management | 2,250 | | |
| Life Annuities lapsed - | 2,000 | | |
| Exchequer Annuities lapsed | 56,250 | | |
| Five years - - | 1,819,684 | - | 1,819,684 |
| Interest of £1,819,684 - | 72,787 | | |
| Expence of management | 1,023 | | |
| Life annuities lapsed - | 2,000 | | |
| Six years - - | 1,895,494 | - | 1,895,494 |
| Interest of £1,895,494 - | 75,820 | | |
| Expence of management | 1,066 | | |
| Life Annuities lapsed - | 2,000 | | |
| | 5 per cents. redeemed at par. | | |
| Seven years - - &c. | 1,974,380 &c. | - | 1,974,380 |

| | Free Revenue. | | Stocks Reemeded | |
|---|---|---|---|---|
| In 25 years after the first payment | £ 5,190,980 | - | £ 13,409,869 | three per cents. |
| | | | 52,959,990 | four per cents. |
| | | | *19,953,649 | five per cents. |
| | | Total | £86,323,508 | |
| In 30 years after the first payment | 6,345,566 | - | 13,409,869 | three per cents. |
| | | | 81,128,473 | four per cents. |
| | | | 19,953,649 | five per cents. |
| | | Total | £114,491,991 | |



* In this plan 25 millions of stock are paid off in seven years. The *five per cents.* therefore become redeemable at par, and the whole debt in that stock is discharged at the end of 15 years. From that period the payment of the *four per cents.* again commences, and the whole of them is paid off in the 32d year, from which time the *three per cents..* continue to be redeemed at par during the remainder of the term.

| | Free Revenue. | | Stocks redeemed. | |
|---|---|---|---|---|
| | £ | | £ | |
| In 35 years after the first payment | 7,511,358 | - | 35,633,625 | three per cents. |
| | | | 93,074,916 | four per cents. |
| | | | 19,953,649 | five per cents. |
| | | Total | £148,662,190 | |
| In 40 years after the first payment | 8,731,523 | - | 75,557,308 | three per cents. |
| | | | 93,074,916 | four per cents. |
| | | | 19,953,649 | five per cents. |
| | | Total | £188,585,873 | |

## PLAN II.

Million *per annum* Surplus, aided by the falling in of the Temporary Annuities, Life Annuities, Expence of Management, and £600,000 *per ann.* added to the Million Surplus by new Taxes, or Savings, in the first five Years without Conversions.

| Fund. | | | Stock Redeemed. |
|---|---|---|---|
| | | 3 per Cents redeemed. | |
| | £ | | £ |
| Surplus - - | 1,000,000 | at 75 - | 1,333,333 |
| Interest - - | 40,000 | | |
| Management - | 750 | | |
| Annuities lapsed - | 25,000 | | |
| Management on those Annuities - - | 351 | | |
| Life Annuities lapsed | 2,000 | | |
| One year - - | 1,068,101 | at 78 - | 1,369,360 |
| Interest - - | 41,081 | | |
| Management - - | 770 | | |
| Life Annuities lapsed - | 2,000 | | |
| Additional Tax* - | 60,000 | | |
| Two years - - | 1,171,952 | at 81 - | 1,446,854 |
| Interest - - | 43,405 | | |
| Management - | 814 | | |
| Life Annuities lapsed | 2,000 | | |
| Additional tax - | 180,000 | | |

 Fund.

* The additional taxes have been introduced into this Table a year too late, by which the Fund loses the interest of £600,000 for a year, that is £24,000, which would have made the free revenue, after 40 years, about £4,000 more than it is by this Table, and the total of Stock redeemed in the same time about £100,000 greater.

| Fund. | 4 per cents. redeemed. £ | | Stock redeemed. £ |
|---|---|---|---|
| Three years - - | 1,398,171 | at par - | 1,398,171 |
| Interest - - | 55,927 | | |
| Management - | 786 | | |
| Life Annuities lapsed - | 2,000 | | |
| Additional tax - | 120,000 | | |
| Four years - - | 1,567,884 | - | 1,576,884 |
| Interest - - | 63,075 | | |
| Management - | 887 | | |
| Life Annuities lapsed - | 2,000 | | |
| Exchequer Annuities lapsed | 56,250 | | |
| Additional tax - | 120,000 | | |
| Five years - - | 1,819,096 | - | 1,819,096 |
| Interest - - | 72,763 | | |
| Management - - | 1,023 | | |
| Life Annuities lapsed | 2,000 | | |
| Additional tax - | 120,000 | | |
| Six years - - | 2,014,882 | - | 2,014,882 |
| Interest - - | 80,595 | | |
| Management - | 1,123 | | |
| Life Annuities lapsed | 2,000 | | |
| Seven years - - | 2,098,600 | - | 2,098,600 |
| &c. | &c. | | &c. |

| Free Revenue. | £ | Stocks redeemed. £ | |
|---|---|---|---|
| In 25 years - | 5,212,370 | 21,258,225 | three per cents. |
| | | 32,769,418 | four per cents. |
| | | *19,968,691 | five per cents. |
| | | Total £73,996,334 | |
| In 30 years - | 6,069,709 | 48,983,157 | three per cents. |
| | | 32,769,418 | four per cents. |
| | | 19,968,691 | five per cents. |
| | | Total £101,721,266 | |



* At the expiration of 13 years £20,780,355 in the *four per cents.* and 4,974,151 Stock in the *three per cents.* are paid off. From this period, therefore, the *five per cents.* become redeemable. These are all discharged the beginning of the 20th year, and in two years more the remainder of the *four per cents.* is redeemed. From the 22d year the *three per cents.* are paid off at par, to the end of the term.

| Free Revenue. | | | Stocks redeemed. | |
|---|---|---|---|---|
| | | £ | £ | |
| In 35 years | - | 7,060,130 | 81,258,874 | three per cents. |
| | | | 32,769,418 | four per cents. |
| | | | 19,968,691 | five per cents. |
| | | Total | £133,996,983 | |
| In 40 years | - | 8,206,994 | 118,784,226 | three per cents. |
| | | | 32,769,418 | four per cents. |
| | | | 19,968,691 | five per cents. |
| | | Total | £171,522,335 | |

# PLAN III.

Million *per annum* Surplus, aided only by the falling in of the Temporary Annuities, Life Annuities, and Expences of Management.

| Fund. | | | | | Stock redeemed. |
|---|---|---|---|---|---|
| | | | 3 per cents. redeemed. | | |
| | | £ | | | £ |
| Surplus | - - | 1,000,000 | at 75 | - | 1,333,333 |
| Interest | - | 40,000 | | | |
| Management* | - | 750 | | | |
| Ten years Annuity lapsed | | 25,000 | | | |
| Life Annuities lapsed | - | 2,000 | | | |
| One year | - - | 1,067,750 | at 78 | - | 1,368,910 |
| Interest | - - | 41,067 | | | |
| Management | - - | 770 | | | |
| Life Annuities lapsed | - | 2,000 | | | |
| Two years | - - | 1,111,587 | at 81 | - | 1,372,329 |
| Interest | - - | 41,170 | | | |
| Management | - - | 772 | | | |
| Life Annuities lapsed | - | 2,000 | | | |
| | | | 4 per cents. redeemed. | | |
| Three years | - - | 1,155,529 | at par | - | 1,155,529 |
| Interest | - - | 46,221 | | | |
| Management | - - | 650 | | | |
| Life Annuities lapsed | - | 2,000 | | | |



* Since these Tables were computed, the expences of management have been reduced to £450 per million *per ann.*; but the difference this makes in the results is too inconsiderable to deserve notice.

| Fund. | | | Stock redeemed. |
|---|---|---|---|
| | 4 per cents. redeemed. | | |
| | £ | | £ |
| Four years* - - | 1,204,400 | - | 1204,400 |
| Interest - ' - | 48,176 | | |
| Management - - | 677 | | |
| Life Annuities lapsed - | 2,000 | | |
| Exchequer Annuities lapsed | 56,250 | | |
| Five years - - | 1,311,503 | - | 1,311,503 |
| Interest - - | 52,460 | | |
| Management - - | 738 | | |
| Life Annuities lapsed - | 2,000 | | |
| Six years - - | 1,366,701 | - | 1,366,701 |
| Interest - - | 54,668 | | |
| Management - - | 769 | | |
| Life Annuities lapsed - | 2,000 | | |
| Seven years - - | 1,424,138 | - | 1,424,138 |
| &c. | &c. | | &c. |

| | Free Revenue. | Stocks redeemed. | |
|---|---|---|---|
| | £ | £ | |
| In 25 years - | 3,892,831 | 4,074,572 | three per cents. |
| | | 30,390,243 | four per cents. |
| | | 18,039,875 | five per cents. |
| | Total | £52,504,690 | |
| In 30 years - | 4,579,731 | 21,056,177 | three per cents. |
| | | 34,283,074 | four per cents. |
| | | 18,039,875 | five per cents. |
| | Total | £73,379,126 | |
| In 35 years - | 5,330,252 | 45,416,595 | three per cents. |
| | | 34,283,074 | four per cents. |
| | | 18,039,875 | five per cents. |
| | Total | £97,739,544 | |
| In 40 years - | 6,196,104 | 73,747,452 | three per cents. |
| | | 34,283,074 | four per cents. |
| | | 18,039,875 | five per cents. |
| | Total | £126,070,401 | |

10 MEMORANDUM.

* All the redemptions in these plans, after the first three years, are supposed to be made at par. Exchequer Annuities, amounting to £80,000, fall to the fund in the 20th year, and £404,332 *per ann* (being the 30 years annuity) in the 22d year.

## MEMORANDUM.

"In the first of these plans, the *three per cents.* are supposed at 75, and the difference of price between them and new *four per cents.* supposed to be made *first* redeemable when under par, but *ir*redeemable when above *par* till 60 millions of other stocks were redeemed, is reckoned at $18\frac{1}{3}$.—The market difference of price between the *present* four per cents. redeemable at pleasure, and the South Sea three per cents. when this plan was formed (the latter being then at 68,) was above 20. Was it not reasonable, therefore, to expect that the holders of these annuities would eagerly have taken at $18\frac{1}{3}$ *per cent.* an exchange of them for such new four per cents. as those just described, and therefore much more valuable?"

"£18 6*s.* 8*d.* for every £100 three per cent. stock converted into a four per cent. stock would have produced just £1,100,000 for the conversion of six millions. £20 for the conversion of every £100 stock would have produced £1,200,000, for the conversion of six millions."

"This conversion was taken in the first place at $18\frac{1}{3}$ *per cent.* the first year, and only six millions were supposed to be converted, and £1,100,000 then gained for the fund, because the first year was supposed to be a year of experiment only, and therefore more liberal terms were supposed to be offered.—Should the experiment have succeeded, and the difference of price between the three per cents. and the new four per cents. have risen above £20, the former being above 75, a conversion might have been offered the second year at 20 *per cent.* of 18 millions into four per cents. not redeemable till a larger amount of stocks should have been previously redeemed; and afterwards, in the three following years, a third, a fourth, and a fifth conversion, at the same price of twelve millions each year. as specified in this plan, the amount of stocks to be previously redeemed to be increased every successive year; in consequence of which the last 12 millions would, without any effect on the efficiency of the plan, have come to be declared the last redeemable of 108 millions."

"Should the Stocks have risen, as is supposed in these plans, greater sums than these specified would probably have been gained by the proposed conversions, and therefore the results in the first plan increased.—There were advantages, not immediately apparent, which would have been gained by these conversions.—First, the public would have availed itself by them of the want of confidence in a plan of redemption which more or less have taken place at first.

first. For the less the public confidence had happened to have been, the greater would have been the effect of the regulation proposed in raising the value of the new four per cents., and consequently in gaining money for the fund."

"Secondly, it is particularly worth attention that it would have diminished the loss that might have accrued from an interruption of the scheme, should an interruption have happened after £600,000 *per ann.* had been added to a million surplus for carrying on the scheme. Should, for instance, the scheme have been interrupted in the seventh year of its operation, and after the fund had increased, according to the first Table to £1,974,380, and redeemed 25 millions, and, by the 2nd Table to £2,098,600 but redeemed only eleven millions; the public would have gained, by the measure of conversion, the excess of the interest of 27 millions above 13 millions; and, therefore, the addition of £600,000 *per ann.* to the fund in the first five years (which both the first and second Table suppose) would have been nearly replaced, if the plan in the first Table had been adopted. Two advantages, therefore, would in this way have been obtained.—1st The advantage of a redemption of fourteen millions more than could have been redeemed by the plan in the 2d Table. And, 2dly, the advantage (should the scheme have ever been resumed) of having had 60 millions of four per cents. to be redeemed by a Sinking Fund, instead of 60 millions of three per cents., and consequently a much more easy and rapid course of redemption."

"At the end of the 40 years it is to be observed that the plan in the first Table would have redeemed 188½ millions, and the plan in the second Table 171½ millions; but that even in the first *four* years the first plan would have redeemed 19½ millions, whereas the second would have redeemed in the same time only 5½ millions, and but little more than the plan in the third table. This pointed out a farther and very considerable recommendation of the first plan, and that was, the particular vigour with which it would have operated at its outset, when vigour was most wanted, and would consequently have brought the five per cents into a course of redemption in six years, which would not have been done by the 2d plan in less than 13 years; nor will it be done by the third (which is now carrying into execution) in less than 16 years."

---

Mr. Pitt, influenced no doubt by the very reasonable desire to avoid the imposition of new taxes, adopted the last and least efficient of the schemes suggested by Price. It was carried into effect by stat. 26 Geo. III, c. 31, which provides that £250,000 a-quarter, or £1,000,000 a-year, shall be paid over to Commissioners, who "shall apply the same to the reduction of the National Debt, and to no other intent or purpose whatever." The Commissioners were to receive the dividends on the stock purchased by them; and these, with the annual million, and certain annuities specified in the act, were to be continuously employed to purchase up additional stock. A clause is also inserted authorising the Commissioners to subscribe the funds at their disposal towards any loan that might be negociated for the public service.

In 1792 it was further enacted, (stat. 32 Geo. III, c. 55) that besides providing for the interest of loans that might afterwards be contracted, additional taxes should be imposed to form a sinking fund of one per cent. on the subscribed capital of such loans.

The sum annually appropriated to the Sinking Fund was also raised in 1792 from £1,000,000 to £1,400,000; and it amounted in 1793 and subsequent years to £1,200,000 a-year.

Such was Mr. Pitt's famous sinking fund. But though it was established with the full concurrence of parliament, and of the vast majority of the public, there were some who were clear-sighted enough to perceive the entire hollowness of the principles on which it was founded, and who did not scruple to communicate their views to the public. Of these, the unknown author of the following tract, which was either published when the bill for the establishment of the fund was before parliament, or immediately after, was perhaps one of the ablest. But though nothing can be more convincing than his reasoning in opposition to the bill, it had no effect. The belief in the efficacy of Price's panacea was too unreasoning and too intense to be in any degree affected by any statements, however conclusive, of an anonymous writer. It is indeed most probable that they attracted no notice.

*FINIS.*

# CONSIDERATIONS

ON THE

# ANNUAL MILLION BILL,

AND ON THE

# REAL AND IMAGINARY PROPERTIES

OF A

# SINKING FUND.

---

LONDON:
PRINTED FOR T. PAYNE AND SON, AT THE
MEWS-GATE.

---

M.DCC.LXXXVII.

## Considerations on the Annual Million Bill.

I SHALL not trouble the reader with any apology for writing on a subject that has lately undergone such variety of discussion: so long as the funds shall exist, the subject will not cease to be interesting; and what is here said will at least have brevity to recommend it; an encouragement which modern book-makers do not always hold out to a reader.

The nation has long been accustomed to hearing complaints and apprehensions of our enormous debts and taxes, even at times when they were trifling compared to what they now are: nevertheless, contrary to all reasonable expectation, the public credit has kept up: whence people are led to imagine all former fears were groundless, and, trusting that our resources are inexhaustible, to discard all apprehensions for the future; not considering that the increase of property and money in the nation has not been equally rapid with the increase of debt.

It is not in the power of speculation, or within the reach of human wisdom, to determine how long, and to what magnitude, the debts of a nation may be extended, where the interest due to the creditors, with the expence of a peace establishment, exceeds the amount of the revenue, and recourse is perpetually had to the faith of the public for fresh loans to make up deficiencies. Certainly such a system cannot be expected to endure for a long time, without either taxing the funds, or, which is the same thing, lowering the interest in a certain proportion; or some compounding measure between the creditors and government.

That such is our situation at present, I will not insist



upon

upon; such, however, since the close of the late war, has been our situation; and I sincerely wish it were in the power of any of the most strenuous assertors of the public prosperity to make appear we are not still very near it.

The plan held out in the late bill for reducing the national debt, proposes a million annually to be appropriated to the purchasing of stock. If such a surplus is realized, the method of disposal is advantageous; but, unfortunately, the surplus is calculated to arise, not from what the revenue exceeds the present expenditure, but from what it is said the excess will be some years hence. This, I am afraid, is supposing more than any experience has warranted; it is taking for granted, that whatever may now be the case, the time is to arrive when the expenditure shall be confined within its proper limits, and when there shall be no more extravagance or mismanagement.

If seven or eight years are to pass by, after a war, before the expences of a nation can be reduced to the regular peace establishment, and before the proposed surplus of revenue is to commence, it can be no discredit to the wisdom of any man, that he distrusts the benefit of such distant œconomy.

Of our ability to establish a surplus of much more than a million per annum, in time of peace, there can be little doubt: and if the ministry heartily set about it, by œconomy as well as by taxes, it is to be hoped no impediment will be thrown in their way; and that the leisure afforded by peace will not be lost to the public: for, should no progress be made in lessening our debt during the peace, who will be found hardy enough, when another war breaks out, to risk their money on government credit?

If the surplus should fall short, to apply a million annually in purchasing stock, money must be borrowed. The benefit or loss attending such a measure, will almost wholly depend upon the fluctuation in the price of stocks.

4 Dr.

Dr. Price and others, in describing the nature of a sinking fund, have asserted, and endeavoured to prove, that it is practicable to borrow money at simple interest, whilst, by means of a sinking fund, they can pay at compound interest: and so far has this doctrine obtained credit, that it has been advanced the nation might safely continue to run in debt for ever, provided there was a regular application of only a few hundred thousand pounds per annum as a sinking fund.

The Doctor, in his Appeal to the Public, puts the following case, " Let a state be supposed to run in debt " two millions annually, for which it pays 4 per cent. " interest: in 70 years a debt of 140 millions would be " incurred: but an appropriation of £.400,000 per annum, " employed in manner of a sinking fund, at compound " interest, would, at the end of this term, leave the nation " beforehand 6 millions."

If this were true, it follows that two millions might be annually borrowed at 4 per cent. of which £.1,600,000 might be yearly expended without incurring any more debt than would be paid by a regular appropriation of the remaining £.400,000. But if the interest of such an annual loan is paid by new annual taxes, those taxes would, in a small number of years, exceed the loan itself; and the tax for the last year only, on account of such a loan would amount to £.5,600,000, that is, £.3,600,000 more than the two millions borrowed: so that in this instance the debt, which is said to be redeemed by the appropriation of the annual £.400,000 sinking fund, is redeemed wholly by the taxes. For, supposing only £1.600,000 borrowed annually and expended, and the £.400,000 remaining to be entirely out of the question; the taxes necessary in the former instance would equally the same have discharged the debt.

All money lent or borrowed may be reckoned at simple interest from the time of the loan till the day the first

 payment

payment of interest becomes due. If then, and at future stipulated times, the payment of the interest cannot be delayed or evaded, the debt acts with all the effect of compound interest; as either the money that pays the interest is prevented from decreasing the capital, or perhaps, to pay the interest, a fresh debt must be incurred, which likewise bears interest.

Suppose government could borrow a million at 5 per cent. per annum, and not be called upon for the interest for a number of years, say 10; if the creditors, at the end of ten years, will be satisfied with ten times £.50,000 as the interest of their money, this may be called a loan at simple interest.

From arguments not founded on true arithmetical principles, Dr. Price lays down, as evident, the following maxim—that " a state may, without difficulty, redeem all " its debts by borrowing money for that purpose, at an " equal or even any higher interest than the debts bear; " and without providing any other funds than such *small* " ones as shall from year to year be necessary to pay the " interest of the sums borrowed*."

In this position the Doctor has not attributed the effect to the real cause: the loan is supposed to do that which is done only by the *small* annual funds provided to pay the interest of the sums borrowed. Many instances are given to prove what is said to be evident; but in every one it will, on examination, appear, that borrowing answers no other purpose than to entangle and perplex; and that the redemptions could have been effected only by the taxes supposed necessary for the loan. Of several examples, I have taken the following: " Suppose our parliament, 56 " years ago, had resolved to borrow half a million annually, " for the purpose of redeeming the debts of the kingdom. " The *National Gain*, supposing the money applied, with-

 " out

* Appeal to the Public.

" out interruption, to the redemption of debts bearing
" 4 per cent. interest, would have been a hundred millions,
" being debt redeemed, or the sum nearly to which an
" annuity of half a million will accumulate in 56 years.
" —On the other hand. The *National Loss* would have
" been twenty-eight millions, being debt incurred, or the
" sum of all the loans.—The balance, therefore, in favour
" of the nation, would have been 72 millions." In a note
at the bottom, the Doctor adds, " It seems to me scarcely
" proper to take into this account, the produce of the
" taxes laid to pay the interest of the debts contracted
" from year to year. Let, this, however, be charged.—
" The produce of the taxes laid to pay the interest of the
" the first half million, will be* 55 times £.20,000, or
" £.1,100,000. For the 2d, 3d, 4th, &c. half millions,
" the payment of taxes will be 54, 53, 52, &c. times
" £.20,000. And the sum of all these payments will be
" £.30,800,000. Add this sum to 28 millions; and
" £.58,800,000 will be the whole national loss; which,
" deducted from £.99,902,770 (the exact national gain)
" leaves £.41,102,770, the balance in favour of the public."

By the foregoing calculation Dr. Price makes the nation, in consequence of the loan, a clear gainer of 41 millions, and that 72 millions of debt would be cleared.

The redeemed annuities he reckons (and rightly) at compound interest; but the taxes paid annually on account of the loan, he values only at 31 millions, which is the sum total of the taxes, without any allowance of interest. The benefit of borrowing is asserted in consequence of this omission; and herein consists the mistake: for it will be found, that the same taxes, applied as a sinking fund, would, without the help of a loan, have produced exactly the effect described above; that is, of clearing 72 millions



* It should have been 56 times, and for the 2d half million 55 times £.20,000, &c.

of debt. For, the taxes necessary for the 1st year's interest would have been £.20,000, and for the last £.1,120,000, being the interest of 56 half millions at 4 per cent. Now £.20,000 of the national debt, at 4 per cent. paid 55 years ago, would have made the debt at present £.172,926 less, by a proper application of the interests saved. The tax necessary for the 2d year's interest would have been £.40,000, which, paid 54 years ago, would have made a reduction, by the same management, of £.332,550 at this time; and by continuing the calculation, it will appear that the annual loan of half a million may be entirely left out of the plan, without altering the effect. The evident inference is, that if the payments made by the nation have the effect of compound interest, the sums borrowed will likewise act in the same manner; and, that borrowing to pay is, in the instance just recited, only creating unnecessary perplexities, and incurring useless charges of management.

Nor can borrowing money and paying money on the same terms, by any just mode of arithmetical reasoning, be found to have any other consequence: for the simple fact is, that the whole of the national debt acts at compound interest—whatever is employed to pay any part off, acts at compound interest—and likewise, whatever is borrowed, whether for the purposes of a sinking fund, or any other purpose, acts at compound interest: in short, every increase and decrease, alike act at compound interest.

I have been at this pains chiefly to prove, that to create new debts, merely for the purpose of paying old debts, where no reduction of interest is obtained, is inefficacious, and of no use. So mistaken an idea, as that of money borrowed acting at simple interest, whilst a sinking fund acts at compound interest, might be no small encouragement to extravagance; as it supposes a sinking fund capable of redeeming any new debt at much less expence than it was contracted.

To pay old debts by contracting new, can only be done with advantage, where the money borrowed bears a lower rate of interest, than the debt it is to pay.

In other instances Dr. Price appears to have bewildered himself in his calculations. By what he says respecting reduction of interest, I do not well comprehend whether he means to prove it of no advantage. Certainly his arguments have been so understood by many. On a plan of an annual saving or surplus properly applied, he says, it deserves particular attention, that it will be of *less importance* to a state what interest it is obliged to give for money: for the higher the interest, the sooner will such a fund pay off the principal.

"Thus, 100 millions, borrowed at 8 per cent. and bear-
" ing an annual interest of 8 millions, would be paid off,
" by a fund producing annually £.100,000, in 56 years;
" that is, in 38 years less time than if the same money
" had been borrowed at 4 per cent*."

By this it can scarcely be meant, that it is of little importance, whether 8 per cent. or 4 per cent. is given for 100 millions, the contrary being so very evident: for, if such a sum was borrowed at 8 per cent. an annual fund of £.8,100,000 would, besides paying the interest, only afford a surplus of £.100,000; but if at 4 per cent. the same fund would pay the interest, and give £.4,100,000 surplus. Again: If a fund of 7 per cent. is raised, for the purpose of paying the interest and reducing the capital of a debt bearing 6 per cent. interest, it would discharge the principal in 33½ years: lower the interest to 5 per cent. the same fund will discharge the principal in 26 years: and if the interest is lowered to 4 per cent. the principal will be paid off in less than 22 years.

But supposing, when the interest is lowered, that the

9 fund

* Price on Reversionary Payments, chap. 3.

fund allotted for its payment is lowered likewise, a consequence by no means of necessity, still there would be gained the advantage of the public burthens being lessened; which, surely, may be reckoned a matter of some importance.

The Doctor, however, adds, that reduction of interest may prove hurtful, by furnishing funds for further debts, and supplying deficiencies occasioned by profusion, &c. The same may be said of every surplus, and, if allowed, would make an argument against every increase of revenue. Let us suppose the interest of our present debt could be lowered one per cent. it is possible we should, in consequence, grow more remiss in our exertions; yet it cannot be denied that such a reduction would at least put it in our power to make a rapid progress in the discharge of the principal. On the other hand, if the interests of all the sums now owing were raised up to the terms of the original bargains, it would be utterly out of our ability to lessen a penny of the principal, or to prevent its increase. Certainly, not to reduce the interest of our debts, when proper opportunities offer, is neglecting the means of good when in our reach.

As to the management described by Dr. Price, as so contrived that war would accelerate the redemption of the public debts, and the more, the longer it lasted*; I confess not clearly to understand his arguments; neither have I much faith in such management.

Finance is so connected with numbers, that it might have been expected to afford no hook whereon to hang doubtful positions: it has, however, not escaped being entangled and obscured by strange paradoxes and mistaken hypotheses; the common fate of almost every topic on which more than one book has been written. Among

 other

* Price on Reversionary Payments, p. 204, 4th edition.

other new and extraordinary opinions, it has been argued, that the national debt is a great benefit to the kingdom; and some calculators, in reckoning the amount of national property, add to the value of the land, houses, specie, goods, &c. the whole of our debt, as so much gain. Another author on finance asserts, that, before public credit is carried to too great a height, war, maintained by national loans and taxes, may be accounted an advantage to the state. "It is of service to the poor," he says, "because the price of their labour increases with the "demand for labourers. It is of use to the rich, for the "greater occasion there is for money, the greater is the "profit of those who have money to lay out." Thus a modern author attempts to prove, that war, independent of the cause or end proposed, may be beneficial and desirable. Of the poor who are thus said to be benefited, a great part are forced into the service of the navy, or inveigled into the army; where, for one that becomes richer, twenty perish or are crippled; and for one that becomes honester, twenty, at least, are rendered more dissolute. As to the labourers who share no part of the danger, many of them, in common with those who surmount the dangers, are, at the close of a war, left destitute of employment. Nor can it be reckoned an advantage to the state, that the rich shall have opportunities of making themselves still richer, by extortionate loans.

To return to the surplus bill.—Parliament has engaged to apply a million annually to redemption of debts. If there is no surplus, either the plan must drop to the ground, or the million must be raised by new taxes, or by a new loan. If the latter should ever be intended, what I have already said, may be sufficient to prove, that such a measure would not be attended with advantage. However, let us examine it more closely.

When the 3 per cents. were at 78, the 4 per cents. were at 99; suppose them, for the sake of even numbers, to rise till the 4 per cents. should be a fraction above par, and the 3 per cents. 79, and that they should continue at that price. Government could then get money at 4 per cent. A million so raised, applied in redeeming 4 per cents. is doing nothing; if applied in purchasing 3 per cents. the account will stand as follows:

| | GAIN. | | LOSS. | |
|---|---|---|---|---|
| | Redeemed Capital 3 per cents. | Redeemed Annuity. | Capital increased 4 per cents. | New Annuity incurred. |
| By 1 million borrowed at 4 per cent. to purchase 3 per cents. at 79. | 1,265,823 | 37,975 | 1,000,000 | 40,000 |
| Second Year. | | | | |
| Loan — 1,000,000 | | | | |
| Add — 37,975 { Annuity redeemed. | | | | |
| Deduct 40,000 { New Annuity incurred. | | | | |
| Remains 997, 975 { To purchase 3 per cents | 1,263,260 | 37,898 | 1,000,000 | 40,000 |
| Effect of the first 2 years — | 2,529,083 | 75,873 | 2,000,000 | 80,000 |

In this calculation the most favourable terms have been supposed for government, and nothing charged for brokerage or management. The balance gives an advantage of £.529,083 nominal capital redeemed; for which the public burthens are increased with an additional perpetual annuity of £.4,127. It is to be noticed, that the 2d year's million is not so productive as the first; and likewise, that every future year the redemptions would decrease, whilst the new loan and annuity incurred, would advance with unaltered pace.

But if taxes were raised to pay the interests of the new loan, and the redeemed 3 per cents. given to the sinking fund, still the advantage would not be equal to what

 might

might be gained by the application of the same taxes without any money borrowed, and especially if the taxes were applied to the payment of 4 per cents.

This may be seen by the following comparison of the effect which might be produced by each method in 10 years.

1st. By an annual million loan, the interests being paid by new taxes.

| | £. | | £. |
|---|---|---|---|
| Annual Million sinking fund would redeem, in 10 years, of 3 per cents. at 79— | 15,627,400* | Annuity redeemed — | 468,822 |
| Against which set off the new loan —— | 10,000,000 | New annuity incurred | 400,000 |
| Gross capital lessened | 5,627,400 | Annuity lessened — | 68,822 |

2d. By the same taxes, without any loan, applied to the payment of 4 per cents. there would be redeemed,

Capital 2,486,330, and annuity 99,453.

Here the loan, applied to the purchase of 3 per cents. reduces £.3,141,070 of the gross amount of the capital more than is reduced by the simple application of the taxes; but the redeemed annuities are not so much by £.30,631.

A sinking fund, supported by an annual loan, can have no effect, unless the interests of the loan are provided for by taxes; but, besides that the debt might be better lessened by a proper application of the same taxes, without any loan (as has been already shewn); such a plan

13 requires

* As by a loan, the stock may be purchased at the beginning of each year, whilst the taxes for paying the interests of the loan are not applied before the end of a year; to bring the result of each method to the end of the 10th year, I have increased the sum of the 3 per cents. purchased at the beginning of each year, by the quantity of the same stock which the total of the annuities saved at the end of the 10th year (£.451,670) would have purchased.

requires taxes continually increasing, and fresh burthens annually added to the old: which is beginning at the wrong end.

To say, "Be of good cheer, for the worst is to come; pay "only £.40,000 this year, and you shall pay twice as much "the next, and three times as much the year after, &c." this is not much encouragement. If a debt is to be reduced by taxes, subject to annual variation, it would have a more promising appearance to begin with the greatest payment, and gradually lessen, till you end with the least. This mode requires most vigour in the outset, but, in return, gives an immediate prospect of better days, and with the same sums would redeem a larger portion of our debt.

The different effects this method would have, is obvious; for, suppose the taxes necessary to pay the interest of an annual loan of a million, for 10 years, at 4 per cent. were applied as a sinking fund, the first year's tax would be £.40,000, the second year's £.80,000; and, thus increasing £.40,000 every year, the last year's tax would be £.400,000. Invert the order of these taxes, beginning with the £.400,000 and ending with the £.40,000; here the greatest sums would have the longest time to act, and consequently be more productive.

Money borrowed at 4 per cent. to buy up 3 per cents. at any price above 75, must be attended with a loss of interest, and will increase the real burthens of the public, for the sake of decreasing a nominal capital. Converting 100 millions of 3 per cents. into 79 millions of 4 per cents. would increase the annuities paid to the public creditors £.160,000. To load the public with such an additional perpetual annuity, for no other purpose than lessening the nominal capital 21 millions, would be disposing for ever of a fund, which, by a different application, might, in no great number of years, redeem the 21 millions capital, with its real interest.

To lessen the capital is doubtless an object of consequence: but too high an idea of the advantages attending such a reduction may lead into improvident measures.

The plan proposed in the House of Lords, by Earl Stanhope, to decrease the capital by inviting the 3 per cent. stockholders to subscribe their consent to accept of 90 pounds for every hundred of their present capital, whenever the public shall be desirous of redeeming the said capital at such price, and, in return, to give their stock the preference of redemption, would, I apprehend, be subjecting the public to great inconvenience, for a very remote and almost hopeless chance of benefit. For,

First, if the 3 per cents. should never rise to above 90, government would be fettered, and never reap any advantage in return.

Secondly, the money to be employed in reducing the debt, by being confined to the redemption of the new subscribed 3 per cents. might enable those stockholders to raise their stock to an unreasonable price.

Thirdly, should the 3 per cents. get up to more than 90, still it would be a loss to the public to be obliged to pay off the 3 per cents. at that pricc, whilst any debt, bearing above $3\frac{1}{3}$ per cent. interest, remained.

By this plan the restraint on the public would be immediate and constant, and probably the time might never arrive when the stockholder should be called upon to perform his engagement. There is little doubt that the proprietors of 3 per cents. when they comprehended the plan, would readily subscribe; but that is far from being a proof that the plan is in favour of the public.

I agree with Dr. Price, and believe almost every considerate man will think the same, as to the ill policy of borrowing, by creating an addition to the capital more than the sum received, when it might have been avoided by giving, nominally, but not in reality, higher interest; and would have been less disadvantageous though such good bargains as Dr. Price supposes might not have been obtained. In funding the last debts at 5 per cent. much of this disadvantage was avoided; but a new one incurred, by making the debt irredeemable and irreducible till 25 millions of the old debt should be paid. Instead of which, it were to be wished, that the limitation had been for a specified number of years, and the liberty of redemption made less dependent upon accident.

This restriction on the 5 per cents. is one reason in favour of redeeming the 3 per cents. in preference to the 4 per cents. as 25 millions of 3 per cents. may be sooner paid than the same quantity of any other stock; and the 5 per cents. thereby sooner rendered redeemable. But were it not for the prospect of being entitled to lower the 5 per cents. more solid advantages would be realized by paying the 4 per cents. though at par, than by redeeming 3 per cents. at 78; for greater annuities would fall in every year, and the sinking fund would increase faster.

This difference, in favour of paying or redeeming 4 per cents., arises from the 4 per cents. being proportionably cheaper than the 3 per cents. and yielding to the purchaser higher interest for his money*; which is occasioned by the apprehension that at some future period, when money can be procured on lower terms, the interest of the 4 per cents. may be reduced: and this consideration will probably prevent the 4 per cents. or indeed any redeemable annuities, from ever rising much above par; for, suppose the market price of any redeemable stock were 105, it would be in the power of government to raise money by issuing out new stock of the same kind at 104, and paying off the old stock at par. The standard rate of

16 interest,

* The prices of stocks have lately been considerably more in favour of redeeming 4 per cents. than what I have stated; partly perhaps in consequence of the purchases on account of government.

interest, therefore, will, in general, be more justly estimated from the price of the 3 per cents. than of any other stock; they being the most stable and unchangeable, and the only stock which has not hitherto experienced reduction of interest.

In redeeming the public debts, no great allowances ought to be made for probabilities of future rise or fall in the price of stocks. The best judgment is as likely to be deceived as any other, except where advantage may be taken (not a fair one) of receiving earlier intelligence than the public of such events as may affect the funds. The price of the day is that which is most generally imagined will be the price hereafter; for, if there was a strong and general belief that the price of stocks would next year, or any future year, be 10 per cent. higher than now, such a persuasion would immediately raise the present price to nearly, if not quite, what they were expected to rise at hereafter. Should there happen any considerable rise in the stocks, perhaps most gain would accrue in consequence of having previously bought up 3 per cents: but, merely on this supposition, to purchase 3 per cents. in preference to 4 per cents. would be giving up a certain benefit on speculation, which, if the stocks should fall, would turn out the contrary way. The terms of the 5 per cents. however, is a sufficient consideration for employing money at present in redeeming that stock which bears the lowest price.

I will beg the reader's attention to a few words more on the subject of a sinking fund unalienable, at the same time that the expences of the state are partly supported by new loans.

The progress made in the redemption of our debts, by a sinking fund, depends on the revenue being raised so high as to answer, 1st. the common exigencies of the state; 2d. the interest of all the debts; and, 3d. the sum a sinking fund is supposed to apply annually towards diminishing the principal. Thus, suppose the current service of the nation to be $5\frac{1}{2}$ millions—the interest due to the public creditors $9\frac{1}{2}$ millions—and the revenue 16 millions, affording 1 million annual surplus, which is to be applied as an unalienable sinking fund—in 40 years, if interest was at 4 per cent. 95 millions would be paid, and £.3,800,000 annuities redeemed; the payment to be made by the sinking fund for the next year would be £.4,800,000. But if, in this 40 years, unforeseen events should have made new loans necessary, to the amount of 95 millions, and, as this money is borrowed, new funds are provided for paying the interests, which, f at 4 per cent. is £.3,800,000 per annum; the debt, at the end of 40 years, will be the same as at the beginning: and the efficacy of the sinking fund will rest upon what is called an *improved revenue*; that is, upon the public being burthened with supplying a revenue to government increased £.3,800,000 more than at the beginning: for the revenue, at the end of 40 years, must be £.19,800,000; that is,

| | £. |
|---|---|
| To answer the current service —— —— | 5,500,000 |
| For paying the interests of unredeemed debts | 5,700,000 |
| For annual surplus for the sinking fund —— | 1,000,000 |
| For redeemed annuities to be given to the sinking fund —— —— —— | 3,800,000 |
| For paying the interest of new debts —— | 3,800,000 |
| Total | £.19,800,000 |

This statement will prove that a sinking fund, without œconomy, is no ease to a nation; and that the most rigid unalienation cannot at all keep off the weight of new loans: for, in the foregoing instance, however much the annual produce of the sinking fund has increased at the end of 40 years, yet, balancing the new loans with the sinking fund, the whole gain is taxes additional, to the amount of £.3,800,000 per annum. Take away those taxes, and the debt would be in the same state as at the outset.

 That

That every new loan should have new funds to pay the interest, is universally agreed; and those funds ought to be sufficient, not only to pay the interest of the sums borrowed, but to afford a small surplus; by which the new debts would be immediately put on terms of redemption.

Should new loans increase faster than taxes can be provided to satisfy the interests, no sinking fund could be of service; but the debt must increase as long as any one could be found to trust.

Almost all writers on the funds, who have proposed schemes for reducing the national debt, are the declared advocates for increase of taxes. True it is, that without heavy ones nothing can be done in the way of redemption. But, seeing how greatly our burthens may be increased by new loans, notwithstanding the most faithful appropriation of a sinking fund, it is most of all important to avoid, if possible, creating any necessity for borrowing. If we must borrow, it is no bad proviso, in the annual million bill, which empowers the commissioners of the sinking fund to subscribe to new loans; as it secures to the sinking fund the interest of the money taken from it: and, by lessening the sum to be raised, may enable government to procure money on more reasonable terms than otherwise. But let us hope that public credit will be allowed time to recover breath. Every new loan* may be considered as a step towards insolvency: if we borrow without necessity, it argues waste or mismanagement; and if with necessity, it is a certain sign that our expences exceed our income.

A minister who is a real œconomist, is the truest friend to his country; and though, in an age so dissipated, a rigid œconomist might not on all hands meet with applause

 and

* Such loans excepted as are procured at a low interest, for the sole purpose of redeeming debts that bear higher interest.

and gratitude, yet, what to a good man is better, he would be conscious of having deserved it.

To reduce our debts, a clear surplus or excess of the revenue above the expenditure, must be provided. Such a surplus can only be created two ways—by taxes, or by savings; methods which merit very different degrees of praise, yet both almost equally necessary, as the produce of either singly can have but little effect.

Taxes, however, there is not much occasion to recommend, as little reason has been given lately to complain of want of attention on that score: yet, with a certainty of a frugal application, more heavy taxes than those we at present labour under, might be borne with cheerfulness.

*FINIS.*

AN

# INQUIRY

CONCERNING

THE RISE, PROGRESS,

*REDEMPTION, PRESENT STATE,*

AND

MANAGEMENT,

OF THE

# NATIONAL DEBT

OF

Great Britain and Ireland.

THE THIRD EDITION, ENLARGED.


BY *ROBERT HAMILTON, LL.D.F.R.S.E.*

PROFESSOR OF MATHEMATICS IN THE MARISCHAL COLLEGE
ABERDEEN.



Edinburgh:

PRINTED FOR OLIPHANT, WAUGH, AND INNES.

1818.

# PREFACE
TO THE
## *SECOND EDITION*

THE author of the following Inquiry has attended for a course of years to the progress of the national debt, from the interest which he felt as a member of the community in a subject of so much importance, and which has now assumed so alarming an aspect. As he has observed that many persons, in general well informed, were imperfectly acquainted with the facts, and entertained crude views of the principles of finance, he trusts that what he now submits to the public may not be altogether useless.

In the first part, he lays down and enforces some general principles of finance. A person unacquainted with the management of our national debt, may blame him for bestowing labour to prove *truisms,* or principles which cannot be controverted; but to those who know that our financial measures have been conducted for a course of years upon opposite principles, the arguments adduced will not appear unnecessary.

In the second part, a particular detail is given of the origin, progress, management, redemption, and present state of the national debt. A part of these facts is generally known; but as few are possessed of full information on the subject, a publication of this kind seemed wanted. The author could not well have fixed upon a certain degree of information as what his readers already possessed, and supplied the remainder. Had he attempted to do so, his work would have presented a mutilated appearance, without being a great deal shorter. He has therefore drawn up such a narrative as may communicate all necessary information to a young person or a foreigner, who has no previous knowledge of the subject.

The materials for the statements previous to the year 1786, are drawn from the best authorities that could be procured; and, if not altogether correct, at least, cor near to the facts.—Those since 1786, are taken from the official papers presented to the House of Commons, and the acts of Parliament relative to finance. The author cannot expect that, in so great a variety of figures and statements, no error has been committed: but he trusts that the errors are neither numerous nor important.

In the third part, the propriety of the measures adopted in the management of our finance, is examined. It cannot give any reasonable ground of offence, that the plans of respectable authors, and the measures of eminent statesmen, are discussed with freedom. The author is not conscious of having censured any person with asperity: But wherever he thought their opinions erroneous, or their measures improper, he was under the necessity of assigning his reasons for doing so.

In this edition, the statements are continued to the present time, and have been carefully revised. and some errors corrected. An account and examination of Mr. Vansittart's plan of finance, adopted in the operations of the year 1813, is added;—also some general observations on sinking funds. An Appendix is subjoined, containing an account of the several stocks,—of the East India Company,—and of the manner of transacting loans, and transferring stock;—and several additional Tables are inserted in the concluding Appendix.

---

## POSTSCRIPT.

In this third edition, a fuller detail is given of the progress of the national debt before the French revolution. Some account of this part of the work will be found in Note XII.

The Tables and calculations are brought up to 1st February, 1817, and a sketch of the transactions since, added in a Postscript. An additional Table is inserted, exhibiting the operations on the present plan of finance, since its commencement in 1813; and various articles, containing information on points connected with the subject, are introduced.

To accomplish all this, and accommodate the whole to a time of peace, many alterations have been necessary. We are aware, that such alterations, in subsequent editions, are not in general allowable; but, in a work of this kind, they must be admitted.

We consider it as an imperious duty, if, on reviewing a subject, there appear cause to alter an opinion formerly given, in whole or in part, to acknowledge it, and assign the reasons. Accordingly, we have modified, though not entirely altered, the opinion given in our former editions, Part III. Chap. VI., in regard to the system of funding by an increase of capital.

# CONTENTS.

APPENDIX I.



APPENDIX II. TABLES.



---

AN

# INQUIRY

CONCERNING THE

# NATIONAL DEBT.

## INTRODUCTION.

THE decision of national contests, in ancient times, depended upon the numbers, courage, and military talents of the contending nations. The invasions of barbarous hordes, destitute of wealth, and impelled to undertake these invasions by poverty, have often accomplished the subversion of large and wealthy nations, amply provided with all the means of warfare that wealth can furnish, and long renowned for military prowess; but fallen from their former pitch of valour, in consequence of the luxury which wealth gives rise to. In this manner were the Roman empires, western and eastern, subverted; and in this manner have the opulent and luxurious nations of the East been repeatedly subdued by indigent and hardy barbarians.

The great alteration in the state of mankind in modern times, and the changes introduced into the art of war, have, in some measure at least, transferred the decision of national contests to a different principle. Money is said to supply the sinews of war; and gold, rather than steel, is accounted the instrument which leads to victory. It cannot be doubted that this is true in a certain degree, although not to the extent that some maintain.

In the middle ages, when the ferocious spirit which had formerly animated the northern nations, had in some degree subsided; while commerce was still in its infancy, and little national wealth accumulated; wars were carried on languidly, and were generally of short duration. Their operations were frequently interrupted by truces, and sometimes discontinued through mere feebleness. A victorious army, conducted by a warlike leader, was obliged to stop short in a successful career, from want of resources.

It is not our object at present to inquire into the sources of weakness, and incapacity for foreign expeditions, inherent in the feudal system, then more or less established in every nation in Europe. Under any system of government, the general wealth was insufficient to supply the expense of those extensive and long continued wars, which have been waged in later times. The revenue of the sovereign was derived partly from lands reserved as a royal demense, and partly from feudal casualties, and afforded a slender provision for maintaining the royal state, and defraying the ordinary expenses of government; but was altogether inadequate to the support of numerous and permanent armies. Supplies from the people were obtained to a certain extent; but the people neither possessed the means, nor had acquired the habit of granting liberal supplies. Princes, under any emergency, real or supposed, or actuated by any scheme of ambition, had recourse to the measure of borrowing. The loans which they raised were partly compulsory; and as the repayment was ill secured, the rate of interest was high. Sometimes the jewels of the crown were pledged, and sometimes the crown lands were mortgaged. In this manner, the revenues of most of the powers of Europe were anticipated and encumbered.

This irregular mode of borrowing gradually gave way to one more systematic; which has now been carried by this nation to an extent far beyond what was ever known in any other age or nation; far beyond what any person at its commencement, or even after its considerable

 advancement,

advancement, believed to be practicable. This system is still expanding. The public debt, which was inconsiderable at the Revolution, has increased, in little more than a century, to its present magnitude. The increase during every reign, except the pacific reign of George I. has been greater than during the preceding. The increase during every war has been greater than during the preceding. The increase during the latter period of every war, except the late one, has been greater than in the earlier period. The increase, by every national exertion, has been greater than administration held forth when the measure was undertaken. The part of the national debt paid off, in intervals of peace, has borne a small proportion to that contracted by the preceding war. No man can foresee how far this system may be carried, or in what manner it will terminate.

It, however, presents an aspect sufficiently important and alarming to command our most serious attention. In various periods of its progress it has obtained the attention, perhaps of statesmen, who were unwilling to publish all they thought; certainly of men who were skilled in the principles of political economy, and well acquainted with the state of our finances; and none of these, it is believed, have considered it in a trivial point of view. Perhaps the unexpected magnitude to which the public debt is carried, and the ease with which the funds for its annual augmentations are procured, have contributed of late to blunt the public feelings on this important subject.

Various schemes have been proposed, by means of sinking funds, for diminishing, and, in course of time, discharging our national incumbrances; and some of these have been carried into execution to a certain extent. The confidence placed in the efficacy of these schemes has contributed further to ease the alarm which the magnitude of the public debt would otherwise have produced. Their principles and probable result ought to be scrutinized in

 the

the strictest manner. If they be adapted to the relief and ultimate discharge of our national burthens, contracted under the system of expensive warfare in which we have been engaged, let us enjoy the comfort, which such a prospect affords, upon rational grounds. If they be, in whole or in part, deceptious, it is proper that the deception should be pointed out, and that we should know the hazards and the limits of our financial system. If we shut our eyes to national dangers of whatever kind, we are most likely to be overwhelmed by them. If we see them in their true colours, we stand the fairest chance of encountering them with success. If a candid enquiry into this subject should lead to results less favourable than those which have been held forth by high authority, and are readily adopted by the sanguine disposition of the public, the enquirer performs the part of a true friend to his country, and ought not to be charged as acting from factious motives.

In the following Inquiry we propose,

First, To lay down some general principles, which, if established, would lead to general conclusions, concerning our financial system, and in a great measure, supersede the necessity of examining particular plans which have been proposed or adopted.

Secondly, To give a narration of the manner in which we have proceeded in conducting and accumulating our public debt, and a statement of its present amount and annual charge, and an account of the plans which have been proposed or adopted for its discharge, and their operation. The necessary tables in illustration of these particulars will be subjoined in an Appendix.

Thirdly, By means of the general principles, to scrutinize the efficacy of the schemes to which we trust for the relief of our national burthens; and examine the propriety of the methods we have adopted in conducting our financial operations.

# PART I.

## GENERAL PRINCIPLES OF FINANCE.

I. THE annual income of a nation consists of the united produce of its agriculture, manufactures, and commerce. This income is the source from which the inhabitants derive the necessaries and comforts of life; distributed, according to their stations, in various proportions; and from which the public revenue, necessary for internal administration, or for war, is raised.

II. The portion of national income which can be appropriated to public purposes, and the possible amount of taxation, is limited; and we are already far advanced to the utmost limit.

III. The amount of the revenue raised in time of peace, ought to be greater than the expense of a peace establishment, and the overplus applied to the discharge of debts contracted in former wars, or reserved as a resource for the expense of future wars.

IV. In time of war, taxes may be raised to a greater height than they can in peaceable times; and the amount of the additional taxes, together with the surplus of the peace establishment, should be applied for defraying the expense of the war.

V. The expense of modern wars has been generally so great, that the revenue raised within the year is insufficient to defray it. Hence the necessity of having recourse to the system of funding, or anticipation. The sum required to complete the public expenditure is borrowed on such terms as it can be procured for; and taxes are imposed for the payment of the interest; or perhaps to a greater extent, with a view to the gradual extinction of the principal.

VI. In every year of war, where this system is adopted, the amount of the public debt is increased; and the total increase of debt during a war depends upon its duration, and the annual excess of the expenditure above the revenue.

VII. In every year of peace, where the excess of the revenue above the expenditure is properly applied, the national debt is diminished; and the amount discharged during any period of peace, depends upon the length of its continuance, and the amount of the annual surplus.

VIII. If the periods of war, compared with those of peace, and the annual excess of the war expenditure, compared with the annual savings during the peace establishment, be so related, that more debt is contracted in every war than is discharged in the succeeding peace, the consequence is a perpetual increase of debt; and the ultimate consequence of a perseverance in this system must be, its amount to a magnitude which the nation is unable to bear.

IX. The only effectual remedies to this danger, are the extension of the relative length of the periods of peace; frugality in peace establishment; lessening the war expenses; and increase of taxes, whether permanent, or levied during war.

X. If the three former of these remedies be impracticable, the last affords our only resource. By increasing the war taxes, the sum required to be raised by loan is lessened. By increasing the taxes in time of peace, the sum applicable to the discharge of debt is increased. These measures may be followed to such an extent, that the savings in time of peace may be brought to an equality with the surplus expenditure in time of war, even on the supposition that the periods of their relative duration shall be the same for centuries to come, that they have been for a century past.

XI. When taxation is carried to the extent just

 mentioned,

mentioned, the affairs of the nation will go on, under the pressure of existing burthens; but without a continual accumulation in debt, which would terminate in bankruptcy. So long as taxation is below that standard, accumulation of debt advances; and it becomes more difficult to raise taxation to the proper height. If it should ever be carried beyond that standard, a gradual discharge of the existing burthens will be obtained; and these consequences will take place in the exact degree in which taxation falls short of, or exceeds the standard of average expenditure.

XII. The excess of revenue above expenditure is the *only real sinking fund* by which public debt can be discharged. The increase of the revenue, and the diminution of expense, are the only means by which this sinking fund can be enlarged, and its operations rendered more effectual: And all schemes for discharging the national debt, by sinking funds, operating by compound interest, or in any other manner, unless so far as they are founded upon this principle, are *illusory*.

THE greater part of these propositions are so incontrovertible, that it may appear superfluous to adduce any arguments in support of them, and the others may be inferred from these, by a very obvious train of reasoning. Yet measures inconsistent with them have not only been advanced by men of acknowledged abilities, and expert in calculation, but have been acted on by successive administrations, annually supported in parliament, and ostentatiously held forth in every ministerial publication. These seemed to have gained possession of the public mind, and we hear them daily extolled and confided in by persons, in other respects candid and intelligent. This not only supplies an apology for examining the principles minutely, but renders such an examination necessary.

I. *The annual income of a nation consists of the united produce of its agriculture, manufactures, and commerce. This income is the source from which the inhabitants derive the necessaries and comforts of life; distributed, according to their stations, in various proportions; and from which the public revenue, necessary for internal administration, or for war, is raised.*

In every nation, a part of the public income must be withdrawn from the use of the inhabitants, and applied to public purposes. This constitutes the national revenue, and is levied from the people by taxes. The amount required for this purpose, even in peaceable times, and when all practical economy is observed, is considerable. The administration of justice and police, the support of such an army and navy as the present state of surrounding nations renders necessary, and various other objects, require a large expenditure. In time of war, the public expenditure is greatly increased.

This expenditure, however reasonable and necessary, is defrayed by subtracting from the funds which supply the wants of the people, and tends to lessen their enjoyments. Taxation, therefore, although necessary, is not desirable. It may arise to a magnitude which will press severely on the comforts, and even encroach on the necessaries, of the middling and lower ranks. Unnecessary public expenditure, whether occasioned by engaging in wars which might be avoided, or conducting necessary ones with improper prodigality, or by extravagance in internal administration, is a serious evil to the public.

The proposition here laid down concerning taxation, will not be universally admitted. Taxes are affirmed to be harmless, and even useful, upon two principles. They are said to be a spur to industry; and the money collected is said to be no loss to the community, as it is returned,

 by

by various channels, to the people from whom it was raised.

It is foreign to the object of our present inquiry to enter into a full examination of the arguments adduced in support of these opinions; and it could not be done without a full discussion of the principles of political economy.

In regard to the first, we may briefly observe, that the desire inherent in every man to improve his circumstances, is a sufficient and effectual incitement to exertion. The farmer raises all the produce he can from his land. If he be deficient, it arises from want of capital, or of agricultural knowledge. The manufacturer extends his operations as far as his capital, the extent of the market, and the number of hands he can employ, permit him. In time of war, the sums exacted in taxes lessen the abilities, and consequently the exertions of both. In regard to commerce, the effects of war are various. Many branches are circumscribed, or altogether destroyed. Others go on with increasing alacrity: but taxation is never the cause of their enlargement. The merchant generally advances the tax, and, as this employs part of his capital, he is obliged to circumscribe his speculations. He is afterwards reimbursed, perhaps with profit, by raising the price of his commodities, and thereby devolving the tax on the consumer; but the enhancement of price can never increase the quantity of merchandize sold. The only classes of men upon whom taxation can be reasonably supposed to operate as a spur to industry, are those of the lower order, who earn their subsistence, from day to day, by the labours of agriculture or manufactures. If a man can maintain himself and family by four days work in the week, he will not, it is said, work for six. In regard to those employed in agriculture, this seldom takes place. The unremitted labours of the

 peasant

peasant are obvious to every one. In regard to manufacturers and tradesmen, there is more foundation for the observation. A few intemperate tradesmen, unless compelled by necessity, may spend a day or two weekly in the ale-house. But it is notorious, that the greater number continue regularly at their work, except upon rare occasions; and not a few wear out their constitutions by excessive and too long continued exertions. It is a comparatively small part of the taxes which falls upon persons in these stations of life.

The other argument (that taxes are only an imaginary evil, because the money is returned, by various channels, to those from whom it was collected,) *is founded upon the principle of the mercantile system, that money constitutes wealth*—a principle which has been ably refuted by writers on political economy, and is now generally abandoned. The farmer pays part of his produce, or its value, in taxes, and has so much the less for other purposes; that is, he is so much poorer. The money may be brought back to him to purchase another part of his produce for the consumption of the army or navy; but the same men who constitute the army and navy must have been maintained, and his produce would have found a market. Even if money were admitted to constitute wealth, it is not true that all the money raised by taxes returns to those who pay them. A large part is sent abroad for subsidies to foreign powers, and for the support of armies employed in foreign service.

II. *The portion of national income which can be appropriated to public purposes, and the possible amount of taxation, are limited; and we are already far advanced to the utmost limit.*

THE truth of the first part of this proposition is so



obvious,

obvious, that it may seem unnecessary to enlarge on it. Yet the unexpected increase of the public revenue has drawn off the attention of many from its ultimate limit. They will not affirm that it may be extended to an indefinite magnitude; but, as it has been carried so much farther than our fathers, or we ourselves in early life, believed to be practicable, they maintain, that its future extension may be greater than any one now conjectures; and that its reaching a maximum is so distant an event, that the prospect of it ought not at present to have any influence on our public measures.

It may, however, be evinced, that a large proportion of our resources is already exhausted; and that the continued increase of revenue, at a rate equal to what has taken place these last twenty years, cannot be carried on for a long term of future years.

The whole annual income cannot, under any exigency, be appropriated for public revenue. A sufficiency must be reserved for supplying the necessaries of life. The surplus only can be applied to public purposes, and the proportion which can be actually applied to them for any length of time falls much below this limit.

Taxes upon articles of luxury, if raised beyond a certain pitch, lessen their consumption, and become unproductive. The same holds in some degree with regard to taxes on every article not indispensably necessary; and our government has hitherto wisely been sparing of taxes on the necessaries of life. Taxes upon commerce, for the same reason, have their limit; and it seems to be believed, that the system of indirect taxation, in some respects the most eligible, is now carried nearly as far as it can be done: For, instead of raising all the revenue wanted by taxes of this kind for some years past, recourse has been had to the system, little used before, of direct taxation.

Our direct taxes are of two kinds. The first is a tax upon legacies and successions in case of intestacy, being a certain proportion of the moveable property left by every person at his death, varying according to the propinquity of the successor to the deceased, and amounting to ten per cent. on property left to remote relations or strangers. Of the same nature is another tax, a stamp duty on the probates or inventories of personal estates, wherein no abatement is allowed, in whatever relation the successor may stand to the deceased.

The second and more considerable branch of direct taxation is that of a certain proportion of every man's income, from whatever source it arises. This has been considered as a war tax, and was first imposed in 1799, under the name of the income-tax, at the rate of ten per cent. After a short intermission during the peace which succeeded the treaty of Amiens, it was revived in 1804, under the name of the property-tax, at the rate of five per cent.; raised in 1806, to six and one-fourth per cent.; and in 1807 to ten per cent., at which rate it continued until the conclusion of the war. Incomes under L.50, arising from annuities or professional gains, were exempted; and incomes of that sort under L.150, were entitled to certain deductions according to an established scale; but every income, however small, arising from capital of any kind, was subject to the full tax of ten per cent. The assessed taxes raised upon houses and windows may also be referred to the head of direct taxation.

The amount of property-tax levied, at an average of three years preceding 5th January, 1813, was L.13,281,509; and the whole average amount of taxes, permanent and annual, raised during these years, after deducting drawbacks, &c. was L.64,860,192. If the property-tax be ten per cent. upon the general amount of income, the whole taxation is nearly fifty per cent., or one-half. The lower classes indeed were exempted, or relieved in a certain proportion from the property-tax; and it is probable, that among the higher classes who ought to have paid ten per



cent.

cent. considerable evasions took place: But as the higher and middling ranks pay almost the whole of the assessed taxes, and a larger proportion of the taxes on consumption, their taxation cannot fall much below one-half of their income; and therefore we are already far advanced to the utmost limit which taxation can ever reach. The lower classes indeed pay a smaller proportion; but it will hardly be thought prudent or practicable to raise the taxes upon them in a higher proportion than is done upon their superiors.

If we be nearly right in this view, it is impracticable, in the present state of public wealth, to double our present revenue by increased taxation; and it would be a measure of great difficulty and danger to enlarge it by one-half.

We do not, however, affirm, that the nominal, or even the real amount of our revenue, can never, at any future period, amount to double of its present magnitude. A nominal increase may arise from the depreciation of the value of money, which has taken place rapidly for a century past, and is probably still advancing. This depreciation is necessarily accompanied by a nominal increase of public expenditure; as every article which government has occasion to purchase, and the pay of every person in civil or military employment under government, must be increased in the same proportion. The increase, therefore, of nominal revenue, while its effective power remains the same, affords no advantage to the public.

The increase of the money price of commodities arises from two distinct sources, of which, although the effects be blended, the principles, when analyzed, are of a very different nature. The first is the relative increase of the circulating medium, compared with the mass of commodities in circulation. This, so far as it arises from addition to the quantity of gold and silver in circulation, although it first takes place in the nations that are proprietors of the mines of these precious metals, has a tendency, in no long time, to diffuse itself, nearly equally, among all nations connected by a regular commercial intercourse. The effect of it is to subject every creditor, public or private, to a loss in proportion to the extent of the deterioration of the value of money. It consequently discharges part of the public debt; but it produces little effect upon the actual revenue, or the state of commerce. An increase of circulating medium, by the artificial means of paper credit, has the same effect upon the price of commodities, and upon the property of creditors, as an increase of circulating coin: But this, although adopted under one form or other by most mercantile nations, has not the same tendency to equalization, and may occasion considerable changes in the state of commerce; always to the disadvantage of the nation where fictitious circulating medium most prevails.*

The second cause of the increase of the price of commodities, is the taxes imposed upon manufactures, of which we have now a great variety, and upon merchandize imported. The amount of the tax is incorporated with the natural price of the commodity, and paid along with it by the consumer. It is nearly the same as if the consumer paid the natural price of the commodity to the manufacturer or importer, and paid at the same time a tax to government, in proportion to the extent of his consumption. Something of this sort actually took place in what was called the Commutation Tax. When government found it expedient to repeal a part of the duties upon tea, it imposed a tax upon every person for the quantity of tea he was conjectured to consume, as ascertained by the number of windows in the house he possessed. This part of the price of commodities, unless drawn back upon exportation, operates as an obstruction to commerce; and

22 even

* See Note I.

even when drawn back, the relief is only partial. For it is not merely the amount of the tax which the manufacturer must lay upon his commodities: He must have an allowance for the advance of money, and for the additional wages paid to his workmen to enable them to pay the taxes on what they consume. Creditors, public or private, do not sustain any special injury by this part of the increase on the price of commodities. They only contribute their share, along with others, to the increased exigencies of the public.

A real increase of revenue may arise from an increase of national wealth; and this increase of revenue will be obtained by the existing taxes becoming more productive, without the imposition of new ones. Our wealth has increased to an amazing magnitude, and we do not affirm it has reached its utmost limit. But, considering the extent to which our commerce, a chief source of our wealth, is already carried, it is not reasonable to depend upon its further increase, under growing burdens, as an inexhaustible source for supplying all our exigencies in a state of continued warfare.

III. *The amount of the revenue raised in time of peace, ought to be greater than the expense of a peace establishment, and the overplus applied for the discharge of debts contracted in former wars, or reserved as a resource for the expense of future wars.*

THE propriety of this conduct is obvious, and it has been adopted to a certain extent, but has not been followed out with important efficacy.

In the earlier part of our history, the ordinary revenue was hardly sufficient for the ordinary expenditure; and parliamentary supplies in time of peace, were rarely granted. Henry VII. was the last, and we believe, the only English king, in modern times, who amassed a considerable treasure by a parsimonious and oppressive administration, during a reign the greater part of which was passed in peace. This treasure was dissipated in a short time by his successor. It is unnecessary to enter into a detail of the financial measures of each reign, from that time to the Revolution. Although the period, compared with that which followed, was on the whole pacific, it never afforded any surplus of revenue.

The nature and efficacy of the different kinds of sinking funds established since the Revolution, will be considered in the third part of this inquiry.

The amount of the payments of the public debt, in time of peace, subsequent to the Revolution, has been as follows:

During the peace which followed the treaty of Ryswick, being a period of four years, from 1697 to 1701, there was discharged L.5,121,040 of funded debt, being L.1,280,260 annually at an average;* and at the rate of L.5.95 per cent. on the public debt existing at the termination of the preceding war.

During the peace which followed the treaty of Utrecht, being a period of twenty-six years, from 1713 to 1739, there was discharged L.4,190,734, of funded debt, being L.161,182 annually, at an average; and at the rate of L.0.31 per cent. of the debt existing at the termination of the preceding war.

During the peace which followed the treaty of Aix-la-Chapelle, being a period of eight years, from 1748 to 1756, there was discharged L.4,961,560, being L.620,195 annually, at an average, and at the rate of L.0.78 per cent. of the debt existing at the termination of the preceding war.

During the peace which followed the treaty of Paris, being a period of twelve years, from 1763 to 1775, there was discharged L.10,281,795, being L.856,816 annually,

 at

* See Part II. Chap. I.

at an average, and at the rate of L.0.62 per cent. of the funded debt existing at the termination of the preceding war.

During the peace which followed the American war, being a period of ten years, from 1783 to 1793, there was redeemed by the commissioners for the reduction of the national debt, L.10,242,100, being L.1,024,210 annually, at an average, and at the rate of L.0.43 per cent. of the funded debt existing at the termination of the preceding war. But as the unfunded debt was increased during the peace, the discharge of debt was only L.5,732,993, being L.573,299, at an average, and at the rate of L.0.23 per cent. of the whole debt existing at the termination of the preceding war.

No debt was paid off in the short space which followed the treaty of Amiens in 1802.

IV. *In time of war, taxes may be raised to a greater height than in peaceable times; and the amount of the additional taxes, together with the surplus of the peace establishment, should be applied for defraying the expenses of the war.*

It is not intended to affirm that the power of a nation to bear taxes is increased in consequence of its being engaged in war. The contrary is always the case. Commerce, manufactures, and agriculture, are the sources from which all revenue is derived. The two former may be ameliorated in certain branches by war, but they are depressed on the whole; and agriculture also suffers in some degree. But the necessity of the case, real or supposed, has a powerful influence on the public mind, and reconciles the community to submit to privations, which in peaceable times would be accounted insupportable.

Before the introduction of the funding system national exertion was limited by the revenue which could be raised

 within

within the year: but so soon as that system was established, the selfish practice of devolving the burthens, arising from the exigencies or passions of the present age, upon posterity, was adopted in its full extent. The first attempt to defray any considerable part of the war expenses by taxes raised within the year was under Mr. Pitt's administration, in 1798, when the aid and contribution tax was imposed, being a large addition to the former assessed taxes on houses, windows, servants, horses, carriages, &c. regulated by an increasing scale according to the amount of the former assessment.

This tax, not succeeding to expectation, only subsisted one year, and was succeeded by the income and property taxes, already mentioned. Another war tax, first imposed in 1798, was an additional duty on all goods exported and imported, partly according to a table, and partly at so much per cent. on their real value, as ascertained by the oath of the merchant, together with a tax upon the tonnage of shipping. This tax is sometimes called the convoy tax, being considered as a compensation for the security which our trade receives in time of war by sailing with convoy. These, together with additional excise duties, were imposed during the continuance of the war, and amounted in 1812 to L.21,838,166, and in 1815 to L.24,213,930, being about one-third of our whole taxation.

The property-tax, and some other of the war taxes, have been discontinued since the peace. Some of them have been continued for a limited time, and others rendered perpetual. How far the promised relief will extend, and prove permanent, is still among the secrets of futurity. Past experience shows, that taxes have been often imposed at first for limited terms, and afterwards rendered perpetual; and the incroachments that have been already made upon the war taxes, do not promise fair for their speedy removal. In the years 1798, 1799, 1800, a sum of no less than L.56,445,000 was charged upon the war taxes,



and

and distinguished from what was then called the *permanent* funded debt, being intended to be discharged by continuing the war taxes after the restoration of peace. This system, however, was abandoned under Mr. Addington's administration, and the above sum consolidated with the rest of the funded debt. The war taxes were discontinued during the short peace. The system adopted by Lord Henry Petty, in 1807, would have entirely absorbed the war taxes for an indefinite period, if it had been continued; and during the only year it subsisted, the war taxes were mortgaged for the interest and sinking fund of the loan of that year, for a term of at least fourteen years,

| | |
|---|---|
| to the extent of - - - | L.1,200,000 |
| and in 1809 the charges of the loan were again laid upon the war taxes, amount, - - - - | 1,040,000 |
| Sum for which the war taxes are pledged, - - - - | L.2,240,000 |

The war taxes are also charged with the interest, &c. of the loan 1811, but certain additional duties imposed that year are added to the war taxes, which are expected not only to defray that charge, but to afford a surplus. The measure, however, of blending the war taxes in this manner, with the general revenue, is not favourable to the prospect of their speedy removal.*

V. *The expense of modern wars has been generally so great, that the revenue raised within the year is insufficient to defray it. Hence the necessity of having recourse to the system of funding, or anticipation. The sum required to compleat the public expenditure is borrowed on such terms as it can be procured for; and taxes are imposed for the*

27 *payment*

* See Note II.

*payment of the interest; or perhaps to a greater extent, with a view to the gradual extinction of the principal.*

VARIOUS causes may be assigned for the increased expense of war in modern times; the nature of our military weapons; the entire separation of the character of the soldier from that of the citizen; the extensive system of colonization and foreign settlements, in consequence of which, a national contest, which a few centuries ago would have been decided by a battle on the frontiers of the contending nations, now extends the ravages of war to every corner of the globe: And since the system of the balance of power has prevailed, large sums have been granted by more opulent states, as subsidies to others supposed to be interested in the same common cause. While these and other causes have led to great expense, the increase of national wealth has supplied the means; and the rulers of this nation in particular, by a strict adherence to public faith, and by a well regulated system of transfer, have been able to draw forth a large proportion of the wealth of their subjects, and a share of that of foreigners, for the exigencies of the public. The progress of our public debt, and manner of conducting it, will be detailed in the second part of this inquiry.

VI. *In every year of war, where this system is adopted, the amount of the public debt is increased, and the total increase of debt during a war depends upon its duration, and the annual excess of the expenditure above the revenue.*

VII. *In every year of peace, where the excess of the revenue above the expenditure is properly applied, the national debt is diminished; and the amount discharged during any period of peace depends upon the length of its continuance and the amount of the annual surplus.*

VIII. *If the periods of war compared with those of peace, and the annual excess of the war expenditure compared with the annual savings during the peace establishment, be so related, that more debt is contracted in every war than is discharged in the succeeding peace, the consequence is a perpetual increase of the debt; and the ultimate consequence of a perseverance in this system must be its amount to a magnitude which the nation is unable to bear.*

THE two former of these propositions appear incontrovertible, and the first part of the other follows from them as a necessary consequence.

The doctrine of our national debt amounting to a magnitude which the nation is unable to bear, will not be easily relished. We are accustomed to hear of our inexhaustible resources, and we have experienced the amount of our debt to an amazing magnitude with less pressure than might have been expected.

The observations already made in illustration of the second proposition show how far our resources are already exhausted.

In Part II. Chapter 1. there is given a statement of the amount of the funded debt at the commencement of each war, and of each peace, from the Revolution to the year 1816, inclusive, being a period of 128 years, and the amount of debt, contracted in each period of war, and discharged in each period of peace. The number of years of war in that period is 66, and those of peace 62. But the duration of war expenditure compared with that of peace establishment will be found considerably greater than that proportion; for,

1st. A long time is required at the termination of a war, before affairs can be brought to the situation of a peace establishment, and a large expense is incurred during that period. If we add a year of war expenditure to the duration of each war on this account, we shall not go beyond the fact.

2d. Besides the wars enumerated in the statement, the nation has been put to expense by several armaments, when national disputes assumed the appearance of war, although they were adjusted with slight or no hostilities. Something of this kind occurred in regard to Spain oftener than once in the early part of the 18th century, and again with the same power, in 1770, from a dispute concerning the Falkland islands in the south extremity of South America; and in 1790, from a dispute concerning Nootka Sound in the northern extremity of North America. When these circumstances are attended to, the period of war expenditure will be found considerably greater than that of peace establishment.

The whole debt contracted during 66 years of war is L.802,819,790, being L.12,163,936 annually, at an average.

The whole debt discharged during 62 years of peace is L.44,837,399, being L.723,814 annually, at an average.

But the average sums are not those which chiefly claim our attention. It appears by inspection of the table how rapidly the debt contracted in the latter part of the period has increased; and future events will more probably assimilate to that than to an earlier period.

The whole debt contracted during the period of war is to the whole debt discharged during the period of peace, as 17.9 to 1.

The average debt contracted annually in war is to the average debt paid annually in peace, as 16.8 to 1.

It is maintained by many that there is no cause to be alarmed at the magnitude of the national debt, because the greater part of the national creditors are our fellow citizens, and a debt owing by one part of the community to another is in effect no debt at all. Some go as far as to maintain that the national debt is a part of our national

 wealth

wealth, and ought to be reckoned, along with the value of our commerce, manufactures, and agriculture, in estimating the amount of the national capital.

With these last we shall not undertake to argue. Towards the others we shall partly concede the point. But when every reasonable concession is made, enough still remains to place the magnitude of the national debt in an alarming point of view.

The large amount which the public have been able to borrow is a proof of a large capital existing among the community, and affording a surplus after the demands of commerce, manufactures, and agriculture, in their actual state, are supplied. But we are not warranted to affirm that the existence of a large public debt is necessary for employing this capital, or that it could not have been invested in various ways to the further increase of our public wealth in its genuine sources. This would have diffused an additional share of the comforts of life through every rank of society. The taxes, which the public debt requires, lessen these comforts. The wars in which money has been expended, if not unnecessary, are certainly unprofitable. The interest of the public debt, at least of a large part, is drawn from the profits of the industrious part of society, and paid to the idle and luxurious. It is drawn from the merchant, the manufacturer, the farmer, and paid to the stockholder. The amount so drawn may be augmented till it occasion the ruin of those who pay it, and ultimately the ruin of the stockholder, involving the whole community in distress and confusion.

Perhaps some think, though they seldom venture to say, that matters may be restored, by means of a public bankruptcy: and that this nation, after such a measure, will retain the same degree of internal wealth, and support the same strength and importance in its relations to foreign states, as if no national debt had ever existed.—It will not be necessary to enter into a long refutation of this opinion.

 The

The extent of distress attending a public bankruptcy, whether brought on systematically, or overtaking us as the necessary consequence of our being overwhelmed with the magnitude of our debt, would be so great; the present overthrow of every thing valuable so complete; and their future extrication so uncertain, that we can hardly conceive a greater public evil. Among its probable consequences we may reckon internal insurrections, and foreign invasions by rival or hostile nations, taking advantage of the time of our distress and weakness.

Every friend to Britain, every friend to humanity, must deprecate such an event. And a proper sense of the calamities in which it would involve us, should keep us at a cautious distance from the verge of so dreadful a precipice.

" Does the circumstance of our creditors being our " fellow citizens afford no relief to the magnitude and " burthen of our national debt, and are we in the same " situation, as if we were indebted to foreigners?" We do not affirm so. So long as public faith is maintained, there are two ways in which the burthen of our debts is alleviated by having our countrymen for our creditors.

1st. A part of the taxes raised for the payment of interest, and also for other purposes, falls upon the stockholder, and this part is more considerable as the national debt increases, and bears a greater proportion to the whole of the national revenue.

2nd. The expenditure of the stockholder increases the profit of the industrious citizen.

But allowing for these advantages, still, the greater part of the burthen falls upon the industrious, and it receives only a partial relief from any advantage resulting from the expenditure of the idle.

It is argued by those who still retain the generally exploded opinions concerning money, that all the money raised in taxes, at least all that comes to the stockholder, is

 spent

spent among those who pay it, and that therefore it is no loss to them. This is no less absurd than the defence of a house-breaker, who being convicted of carrying off a merchant's money, should plead that he did him no injury, for the money or part of it would be returned to him in purchasing the commodities he dealt in.

Were a national bankruptcy ever to take place, perhaps less evil might attend it if our creditors were foreigners. It would not in that case occasion internal distraction and convulsion. The evil to be dreaded would be war with the injured nations. And as we would retain our full national strength, and our resources would then be unincumbered with debt, they might not find it prudent to attack us. However, as we hold a breach of national faith in detestation, we recollect with pleasure, that the far greater part of our creditors are our fellow citizens.*

In part of the foregoing argument we have spoken of the industrious citizen and the stockholder as being separate persons, and, in some respects, of opposite interests. In many individuals these characters are blended: But, in most cases, the one or the other character predominates, and if, in a few, they be nearly equally balanced, it does not affect the general argument.

IX. *The only effectual remedies to this danger are the extension of the relative length of the periods of peace; frugality in the peace establishment; lessening of the war expenses; and increase of taxes, whether permanent, or levied during war.*

As the object of the present inquiry relates to our national revenue, debt, and resources, we shall avoid, as far as possible, the collateral subject of an examination of

 the

* See Note III.

the necessity or rashness, the expediency or inexpediency, the justice or injustice, of the wars in which we have been engaged. A wise nation will at all times engage in wars with much circumspection, and terminate them as soon as can be done with safety. If the result of our inquiry should be, that we are not able for another century to carry on our warlike system in a manner similar to that which we have done in the period now reviewed, this furnishes additional reasons for such wise and moderate conduct.

If nations could derive wisdom from past experience, and from the judgment which is formed of many former wars, now that the passions which excited them are subsided, much might be urged in favour of a pacific system. It will be admitted that we have frequently engaged in war for trivial or unattainable objects—that the objects have generally not been attained—that, under pretence of guarding against distant and improbable dangers, we have incurred present and imminent ones—that passion and national pride, rather than rational views of national interest, have been often the ruling principles of our public conduct—that, as we have engaged in war rashly, we have persevered in it with obstinacy, and rejected offers of pacification more favourable than those which we were afterwards under the necessity of accepting.

The view we entertain of any present war is seen through a different medium. Every thing valuable to us as men, and as a nation is supposed to be at stake—our national prosperity, our national honour, our national existence—our liberties and lives. No exertion can be too great —The power of our enemy is so formidable, and his ambition so insatiable, that we have no alternative but to prosecute the war with the utmost vigour, till we lay him prostrate at our feet. No pressure of increasing burthens is to be regarded; no dread of exhausting our resources entertained. If he make repeated overtures of



pacification,

pacification, they are to be considered as insidious, and rejected with scorn.

While these passions prevail, any arguments against our belligerent conduct, whether drawn from past experience, or from a cool view of present circumstances, will be urged in vain. As the judgment we now form of the measures of our ancestors is different from theirs, it may happen that the judgment formed of the measures of the present day by posterity, or by the younger part of our fellow citizens, when in advanced life, may be different from ours.

Admitting that our situation in the scale of nations, at the termination of the late war, is nearly the same as it has been for some centuries past, can it be reasonably expected that the succeeding period will be more pacific than the past? We can hardly expect it would. If reason and past experience were listened to, they have much to urge: but the world is not now in its infancy, and experience has long furnished the same lessons of the inefficacy and destructive tendency of war, in vain. It is likely the same passions will involve rival nations again in the calamities of war, upon slight or no grounds. If there be any circumstance likely to assuage the passion for war, it arises from the pressure of public debt, a system peculiar to modern times, the effects of which, when carried to its utmost extent, have not yet been submitted to the test of experience.

In regard to the public expense during peace, it was generally believed during the late war that the state of Europe, under any terms by which it could be concluded, would be such as to render it necessary to keep up a higher peace establishment than had been formerly done. And experience since has verified this opinion in its full extent.

In regard to the expense of future wars, it is not in general wise, admitting their necessity or propriety, to be sparing in exertion in those points where the contest is likely to be effectually decided. Our operations ought to be as prompt and vigorous as we can make them. Neither ought we to be sparing in any expense that contributes to the health and comfort of the soldier, the care of the sick and wounded, the comfortable provision for the worn-out and disabled. But there are other points in which, without enfeebling national exertion, or without encroaching on the demands of humanity, economy may be properly practised. The following questions in regard to the expenses of past wars may be proposed. Have there been no unnecessary and ineffectual expeditions undertaken? Have not considerable armies been kept in places where they could be of little or no use? Has there been no lavish expenditure in fortifications and barracks? Has not the system of increasing the number of our foreign colonies, and consequently the expense of establishments and garrisons, been followed to the utmost extent, and in quarters where it did not weaken our enemy; and where, by employing a part of our disposable force, it weakened our exertions in points of more importance? Have the national expenses been conducted with all prudent frugality? or have not enormous fortunes been amassed by public contractors? Have not large sums been retained for long periods of time in the hands of public accountants? and have not large sums been ultimately lost by the insolvency of some of these accountants, from whom sufficient security had not been taken? Have not large subsidies been granted to foreign powers whose fidelity we had just cause from experience to distrust, and who actually proved unfaithful?

Most of these questions will be generally answered in the affirmative of misconduct: and yet we find the estimates of the expense of each succeeding year are formed on a larger scale; that the execution generally exceeds the estimate; and that motions for inquiry into the public expenditure and correction of abuses, are generally discouraged;

couraged; and that even where abuses in public offices are admitted, speedy and effectual measures are not taken for their correction.

X. *If the three former of these remedies be impracticable, the last affords our only resource. By increasing the war taxes, the sum required to be raised by loan is lessened. By increasing the taxes in time of peace, the sum applicable to the discharge of debt is increased. These measures may be followed to such an extent, that the savings in time of peace may be brought to an equality with the surplus expenditure in time of war, even on the supposition that the periods of their relative duration shall be the same for centuries to come that they have been for a century past.*

THE difficulty and danger of a further increase of our taxes have been already considered. Every new imposition, as we approach the limit of taxation, becomes more oppressive and more unproductive. But if we cannot or will not adopt more frugal or more pacific measures, there is no alternative but an increase of our taxes to the extent above mentioned. And, if we cannot bear this increase, it is impossible to escape national bankruptcy.

We are far advanced to the utmost extent to which taxation can be carried. But we have also gone far towards defraying our annual expenses by money raised within the year. During the last ten years, and upwards, though we have been engaged in a war of unprecedented expense, the amount of our taxes has been greater than the expense of the war, but insufficient to answer, along with that expense, the interest of the debt formerly contracted. Taxation is now carried, perhaps, as far as is necessary upon the supposition that the intervals of peace in future will be equal to the time of war. We have been engaged in war for twenty years, with scarcely any

 interval

interval, and have not yet fully attained the state of a peace establishment; and some have maintained, that since the former system of Europe was dissolved, there was no *safety* for us but in *perpetual war*. These, if they were consistent, would perceive the necessity of raising our taxes to the amount of our full expenditure. We reprobate the idea of eternal war, as barbarous and impracticable: But if we have still the prospect of frequent war, prudence requires us to raise our taxes to the measure of our expenditure; which, however severe a pressure it may occasion at present, must, if deferred, occasion a still heavier pressure at a future period, when our public debt is further accumulated.

So long as the practice was followed of defraying almost all the war expenses by loans, and imposing taxes only for the payment of interest, the burthens of the war were so lightly felt, that the national promptness to engage in war was scarcely under any restraint. Now, when a great part of the expense is raised within the year, and much of it by direct taxation, the burthen is far more heavy, and this pressure would go far to indispose the nation for war, except in a situation where the necessity for prosecuting it was considered as great, or where hostile passions were excited to a more than usual height. Still, however, our burthens were not raised to the measure of our expenditure, and therefore the restraint did not operate so far as it ought. We ought to have felt the full extent of our burthens, and then it would have been tried how far our relish for war would continue. Justice to posterity required this.—Every generation has its own struggles and contests. Of these, and of these only, it ought to bear the burthen. We at present labour under a heavy debt contracted by our ancestors, in wars, perhaps unnecessary, certainly arising from causes now past and gone, with which we have no concern; and, under a still heavier one, arising from wars waged in our own

 days

days, the burthens of which, at the time, we were unwilling to bear. Had the debt accumulated in these wars not existed, our present taxes would have been more than sufficient to defray all the expenses of the late war, widely as it was extended, and lavishly as it was conducted.

XI.—*When taxation is carried to the extent mentioned above, the affairs of the nation will go on, under the pressure of existing burthens, but without a continual accumulation of debt, which would terminate in bankruptcy. So long as taxation is below that standard, accumulation of debt advances, and it becomes more difficult to raise taxation to the proper height. If it should ever be carried beyond that standard, a gradual discharge of the existing burthens will be obtained, and these consequences will take place in the exact degree in which taxation falls short of, or exceeds the standard of average expenditure.*

XII. *The excess of revenue above expenditure is the only real sinking fund by which the public debt can be discharged. The increase of the revenue, or the diminution of expense, are the only means by which this sinking fund can be enlarged, and its operations rendered more effectual; and all schemes for discharging the national debt, by sinking funds operating by compound interest, or in any other manner, unless so far as they are founded upon this principle, are illusory.*

THE progress and discharge of the debt of a nation are regulated by the same principles as those of an individual; and experience shews, that measures of public finance are often conducted with a degree of imprudence seldom exhibited in the management of private affairs. We may, however, extend our views to a greater length of time, in regard to the former.

It is true that, upon abstract principles, the smallest sum lent out for compound interest will, in length of time, increase to an indefinite magnitude:* But it is obvious, that the improvement of money in that way would be limited, at a certain amount, by the want of demand from borrowers, and the impossibility of investing it in productive capital of any kind. It is restricted within a much narrower limit by the mutability of human measures, and the actual impossibility of adherence to the same system, conducted by successive trustees through many generations. It is true that if the system were invariably adhered to, the sum would increase at the rate which calculation points out, until it was limited by the impossibility of finding borrowers, or employing it in any profitable manner.

The system of accumulating a national treasure has been long laid aside, and is not likely to be revived. We may therefore dispense with any further consideration of nations storing up wealth, and bestow our attention on the actual case of nations labouring under debt; sometimes endeavouring to discharge it; often obliged to increase it.

Suppose an individual has contracted a certain extent of debt, and afterwards attains to circumstances which enable him to discharge it. If no oppressive and usurious measures be practised against him by his creditors, and if he pay the interest regularly, the sum which he must pay altogether, before he be clear of debt, is the amount of the money he borrowed, and the simple interest of each portion of the same, from the time of its being borrowed to the time of its repayment. Suppose he borrows

 L.10,000

* See Note IV.

L.10,000, and that for ten years he pays the interest, but no part of the principal. If the rate of interest be 5 per cent. he pays during that time L.500 annually for interest, or L.5000 altogether: and if, by a sudden acquisition of wealth, he is able to discharge the debt at the end of ten years, he pays exactly L.15,000 altogether. But suppose, by an amelioration of his circumstances, he is enabled to pay L.1000 annually to his creditors, for principal and interest. The first year he pays L.500 for interest, and L.500 towards the discharge of the principal. The remaining debt is L.9500, and the interest of this being L.475, if he can pay L.1000 next year, he discharges L.525 of the principal, leaving a debt of L.8975. The interest of this is L.448 15s. and next year, by paying L.1000, he discharges L.551 5s. of the principal, and reduces the debt to L.8423 15s. If he continue to act in this manner, the whole debt will be discharged in about 14¼ years; and the whole sum which he pays including the L.5000 paid during the first ten years, is L.19,250 nearly, being the amount of the principal, of 10 years interest on L.10,000, of 11 years interest on L.9500, of 12 years interest on L.8975, of 13 years interest on L.8423 15s. and so on; altogether, the principal, together with the simple interest of each portion of the same, from the time that the debt was contracted, till the time that portion was repaid. If he can only spare L.750, and therefore discharge L.250 of the principal the first year, it will require somewhat above 22 years to discharge the whole; and if he can only spare L.600 and therefore discharge L.100 of the principal the first year, it will require 37 years. In all these cases, it is the surplus of L.500, of L.250, or of L.100, which the debtor can spare above the interest, that enables him to discharge the principal.

Instead of conducting the business in this manner, he may pay only the L.500 of interest to his creditors, and

 lend

lend out the other L.500 at interest, and lend again L.500 more at the end of the next year, and so on, accumulating the sums lent by compound interest, till it amount to L.10,000, and then discharge his whole debt at once. It will require exactly the same time of 14¼ years to accomplish this. If he transact the business himself, the second way will be attended with more trouble, but the result will be the same. If he employ an agent to transact the loans, he will be a loser by following the last mentioned method, to the extent of the fees paid for agency.

If the debtor be able to pay no interest during the first ten years, the creditors will either insist on accumulating, the interest with the principal, in the manner of compound interest, or the debtor must borrow annually from other hands, to pay the interest annually to his original creditors, and must also borrow more each succeeding year, to pay the interest of the debts thus contracted. In either way, his debt at the end of ten years will amount to L.16,289, the interest of which being L.814 9s. an annual payment of L.1000 would discharge only L.185 11s. of the principal debt the first year, and would require about 35 years to discharge the whole, whether he pay the L.1000 annually to his creditors to lessen the principal, after payment of the interest, or whether he accumulate the overplus by compound interest till he be able to pay the whole debt at once.

Substitute millions, or tens of millions, or hundreds of millions, for thousands, and the above reasoning is equally applicable to the public debt of a nation.

If the debt be ever discharged, which can only be done by a surplus revenue, and if the business be transacted as private affairs are, where the creditor is entitled to no more than the sum lent, together with the interest, the time required for the discharge of a public debt will be the same as that for a private one, when the proportion of surplus revenue is the same; and this holds whether the surplus be paid annually to the creditors, in discharge of part of the debt, so far as it will go, or accumulated in a sinking fund, in the hands of Commissioners appointed for that purpose.

The whole sum paid to the public creditor, before the debt be discharged, is equal to the sum advanced by him together with the simple interest of each portion of the same, from the time it was advanced to the time it is repaid, providing the interest be paid regularly from the time the debt is contracted. But if the payment of the interest be suspended for a certain time after the debt is contracted, then the whole sum paid is equal to the principal debt, together with the compound interest of the same, during the period of suspension, and the simple interest of each portion of this accumulated sum, from the time it is put in a train of payment, till that portion be paid.

But the manner in which our public debt is conducted is greatly more unfavourable to its repayment than in the case of private business. A certain capital in the 3 per cents. or other fund, is assigned to the public creditor for every L.100 advanced, according to the price of the funds at the time, and allowing always a profit to the lender. He is repaid according to the price of the funds at the time of repayment; and as the repayment is in time of peace, when the funds are generally much higher than in time of war, the sum repaid is, in such case, much greater than the sum advanced, together with the interest.

There is generally a collateral circumstance in favour alike of the public and private debtor, which was already mentioned in the illustration of the second general proposition, arising from the alteration of the value of money. In regard to either, if the interval between the time of borrowing and repaying be considerable, the nominal sum paid is likely to be of less real value than a like nominal sum at the time the debt was contracted.

Neither this advantage which the public debt possesses in common with the private one, nor the disadvantage which the public debt labours under from the above mentioned imprudent manner in which it is conducted, has any relation to the argument concerning the inefficacy of the sinking fund.

Let us next consider the case of a nation engaged in war, the expense of which it is unable or unwilling to bear during the year. Suppose the annual expenditure of the war, added to the peace establishment and interest of former debts, exceed the present revenue by 11 millions. That sum must be raised by loan, or additional taxes, and should be raised by the latter as far as the nation can bear them.

If no additional taxes be imposed, the annual loans of 11 millions will accumulate against the nation with all the disadvantages of compound interest.

If a sum less than the interest be raised by additional taxes, the loans will accumulate in some degree with the disadvantage of compound interest.

If a sum equal to the interest be raised by additional taxes, the nation will be burdened at the conclusion of the war, or at any period of its continuance, with a capital debt equal to the amount of the loans, and with additional perpetual taxes equal to the amount of the simple interest of the same.

Suppose the war to continue ten years, and the loans to be raised in the 5 per cents. at par. The whole sum borrowed will be 110 millions, and the interest of each loan being L.550,000, the whole additional interest will be L.5,500,000.

The surplus of the revenue, now burthened with this additional sum, above a peace establishment, is the only fund from which this debt can be discharged during a subsequent peace.

If a sum greater than the interest of the loan be raised

 by

by additional taxes, there will be less accumulation of capital; and the further taxation is carried, the more accumulation is restricted; but, until taxation is carried so far as to defray the expenses within the year, there will be a certain accumulation; and till it be carried so far as to confine the accumulation within the limit that may be reasonably expected to be discharged in a subsequent peace, the system will prove ultimately ruinous.

The restraint given to the accumulation of debt in any period, short or long, depends altogether upon the excess of the additional taxes above the interest of the loans; and it makes no difference whether they be considered simply as war taxes, or permanent taxes, according to future exigencies; or whether they be connected with a sinking fund of any kind.

Suppose that additional taxes amounting to L.610,000 are imposed every year; as this does more than cover the interest of the loan, and part of it may be applied to the expense of the war, a less loan than L.11,000,000 will be sufficient, and the loan will be less in each succeeding year, so long as L.11,000,000 is the sum wanted.

The progress of the funded debt will be as follows,

The first year L.550,000 * from the additional taxes being applied in payment of the interest of the loan, there will be a surplus of L.60,000 applicable to the service of the second year.

The loan required the second year will therefore be L.10,940,000, and the amount of the loans, in the two first years, L.21,940,000, the interest of which is L.1,097,000, and as L.610,000 more of additional taxes are imposed the second year, or L.1,220,000 in these two

45 years,

* All the calculations in this inquiry, unless when otherwise mentioned, are made at 5 per cent. interest; the 3 per cent. funds are valued at 60, the 4 per cents. at 80, and the 5 per cents. at par.

years, there will be a surplus, after paying the interest, of L.123,000 applicable to the service of the third year, and the loan required for that year will be L.10,877,000.

The amount of loans during these three years is therefore L.32,817,000, the interest thereof, L.1,640,850, the additional taxes imposed during these three years, L.1,830,000, affording a surplus of L.189,150, applicable to the service of the fourth year.

The progress during ten years is exhibited in the following table.

| Years. | Loan each year. | Amount of Loans. | Amount interest. | Amount add. taxes. | Surplus. |
|---|---|---|---|---|---|
| 1st | 11,000,000 | 11,000,000 | 550,000 | 610,000 | 60,000 |
| 2d | 10,940,000 | 21,940,000 | 1,097,000 | 1,220,000 | 123,000 |
| 3d | 10,877,000 | 32,817,000 | 1,640,850 | 1,830,000 | 189,150 |
| 4th | 10,810,150 | 43,627,850 | 2,181,393 | 2,440,000 | 258,607 |
| 5th | 10,741,393 | 54,369,243 | 2,718,462 | 3,050,000 | 331,538 |
| 6th | 10,668,462 | 65,037,705 | 3,251,885 | 3,660,000 | 408,115 |
| 7th | 10,591,885 | 75,629,590 | 3,781,480 | 4,270,000 | 488,520 |
| 8th | 10,511,480 | 86,141,070 | 4,307,043 | 4,880,000 | 572,947 |
| 9th | 10,427,053 | 96,568,123 | 4,828,406 | 5,490,000 | 661,594 |
| 10th | 10,338,406 | 106,906,529 | 5,345,326 | 6,100,000 | 754,674 |

Thus, at the end of ten years, when additional taxes are imposed annually to the extent of L.610,000, the amount of funded debt is L.106,906,529, instead of L.110,000,000, which it would have been, if the additional annual taxes had been only L.550,000.

If, instead of conducting the business in this manner, we trace the effects of the system, actually followed, of transferring L.1,200,000 annually from the public revenue to Commissioners appointed for the reduction of the national debt, by whom also the interest of the sums redeemed are applied each succeeding year, in addition to the above mentioned sum, for its further redemption, the result will be found exactly the same.

As L.11,000,000 is annually wanted to complete the war expenses, and L.1,200,000 to be transferred to the

 Commissioners,

Commissioners, the annual loan must be L.12,200,000 and the amount of the loans in ten years, L.122,000,000.

The first year, L.1,200,000 of the debt is redeemed, leaving L.11,000,000 unredeemed.

The second year, L.60,000, the interest of this redeemed debt being added to the L.1,200,000, the sum applied by the Commissioners for the redemption of the public debt is L.1,260,000, and this redeeming an equal sum in the 5 per cents. the whole sum redeemed the two first years is L.2,460,000, and the loans of these years being L24,400,000, the unredeemed debt at the end of the second year is L.21,940,000.

The interest of the redeemed debt now amounts to L.123,000, which being added to L.1,200,000 gives L.1,323,000, applicable to the redemption of debt. The whole sum borrowed the first three years is L.36,600,000: the whole sum redeemed, L.3,783,000; and the unredeemed debt L.32,817,000.

The progress during ten years is as follows:

| Years. | Loan each year. | Amount of Loans. | Debt redeemed each year | Amount of debt redeemed. | Interest on debt red. | Debt remaining unredeemed. |
|---|---|---|---|---|---|---|
| 1st | 12,200,000 | 12,200,000 | 1,200,000 | 1,200,000 | 60,000 | 11,000,000 |
| 2d | 12,200,000 | 24,400,000 | 1,260,000 | 2,460,000 | 123,000 | 21,940,000 |
| 3d | 12,200,000 | 36,600,000 | 1,323,000 | 3,783,000 | 189,150 | 32,817,000 |
| 4th | 12,200,000 | 48,800,000 | 1,389,150 | 5,172,150 | 258,607 | 43,627,850 |
| 5th | 12,200,000 | 61,000,000 | 1,458,607 | 6,630,757 | 331,538 | 54,369,243 |
| 6th | 12,200,000 | 73,200,000 | 1,531,538 | 8,162,295 | 408,115 | 65,037,705 |
| 7th | 12,200,000 | 85,400,000 | 1,608,115 | 9,770,410 | 488,520 | 75,629,590 |
| 8th | 12,200,000 | 97,600,000 | 1,688,520 | 11,458,930 | 572,947 | 86,141,070 |
| 9th | 12,200,000 | 109,800,000 | 1,772,947 | 13,231,877 | 661,594 | 96,568,123 |
| 10th | 12,200,000 | 122,000,000 | 1,861,594 | 15,093,471 | 754,674 | 106,906,529 |

Thus it appears that the amount of unredeemed debt at the end of ten years, when the system of the sinking fund is strictly followed, is L.106,906,529, the same as the amount of the debt under equal expenditure and taxation when no sinking fund is established. It is the



same

same every year of that period, and will remain the same for any length of time. The surplus of taxes applicable to the expense of the war on the one system answers to the interest of debt redeemed, applicable to its further redemption, on the other.

If, instead of funding in the 5 per cents. at par, the transactions be made in the 3 per cents. at L.166 13s. 4d. capital, for L.100 borrowed (and this is nearly what has been done), the nominal sums funded and redeemed are increased in the proportion of 5 to 3, but no alteration is made in the interest, or the real value of the debt.

If the L.11,000,000 required yearly be funded in the 3 per cents. the capital funded is L.18,333,333, and if a sinking fund of 1 per cent. on this nominal sum be established for its redemption, the sum required to be raised by additional taxes yearly for that purpose is L.183,333. This will have a greater effect in preventing accumulation or increasing the sum redeemed than a surplus of L.60,000 in proportion to the sums: But the reasoning adduced in regard to the one is equally applicable to the other.

We have now examined the supposed effects of sinking funds, in the cases of diminishing debt during peace, and of increasing debt during war, with a degree of prolixity which so clear a subject little required, had not the efficacy of a sinking fund, and omnipotence of compound interest been strongly urged by respectable authority, and taken possession of the public mind, and influenced the public measures of finance for a course of years. We trust we have demonstrated their futility. No person ever doubted that increase of taxation, and saving of expenditure, are means of retarding the accumulation of debt. We ought to embrace the former as far as we are able, and the latter, as far as safety permits. But the point at issue is whether, taxation and expenditure being the same, a sinking fund produces any beneficial effect.

If a period of peace were protracted till the public

debt were discharged, the taxes might and would be diminished to the limit of a peace expenditure, for nobody now thinks of accumulating national treasure for future purposes. If the periods of war and peace be so related, that the debt contracted in the former be discharged in the latter, the amount of the debt vibrates, and this system may go on for an unlimited length of time. But, if more debt be contracted every war, than is discharged in the subsequent peace, (and this has hitherto been the real case) and if the accumulation be in a greater proportion than the increase of national wealth, there is a limit beyond which the system cannot be supported.

# PART II.

## HISTORY OF THE PUBLIC DEBT OF GREAT BRITAIN.

---

## CHAPTER I.

*Progress of the Funded Debt.*

---

### SECTION I.

### PERIOD BEFORE THE FRENCH REVOLUTION.

THE funded system commenced at the Revolution. The public debt before that time was inconsiderable, and not reduced to any regular form. During the war waged by King William against the abdicated monarch, and the king of France, who supported his claims, it was found impracticable to raise the requisite sums within the year, and recourse was had to loans; for discharging which taxes were imposed, to continue for a limited number of years; it being expected that the produce of these taxes would discharge the debts in the periods for which they

 were

were granted. These expectations were seldom realized, and as the public exigencies required the taxes to be mortgaged again, for new loans, often before their former term was expired, they were prolonged from time to time, and at last, almost in every instance, rendered perpetual. Loans were also raised during that war on annuities for lives, on very high terms.

The legal rate of interest at the commencement of the funding system was 6 per cent, and it was reduced in the year 1714 to 5 per cent.* The rate of interest granted for the public debt has been often higher than the legal rate: But instead of assigning capital to the public creditor equal to the sum borrowed, and a rate of interest which it could be procured for, according to the circumstances of the times, the practice in the later period of that system has been to fix upon a low rate of interest, and grant the lender other advantages, generally by assigning to him a capital larger than the sum borrowed. The greater part of the loans has been made in funds bearing 3 per cent. interest on the nominal capital, some in a fund at 4 per cent. and some in one at 5 per cent.

Some loans have been contracted altogether on annuities for lives or years: But most of these annuities, which at present amount to a large sum, have been granted as a collateral advantage to the public creditor, who received the greater part of his recompence in a capital bearing interest at three, four, or five per cent.

Annuities for lives have sometimes been granted upon schemes called *Tontines*, in which the benefit of survivorship is allowed. The subscribers to these schemes appoint nominees, who are divided into classes, according to their ages, and a proportionate annuity is assigned to each; and when some of the lives fail, the amount of the annuities

 appertaining

* See Note V.

appertaining to each class is divided among the survivors, so long as any remain, or at least till the annuity amount to a large sum, according to the terms of the scheme.

Tontines seem adapted to the passions of human nature, from the hope every man entertains of longevity, and the desire of ease and affluence in old age; and they are beneficial to the public, as affording a discharge of the debt, although a distant one, without any payment. They have been extensively adopted in some foreign countries, but seldom in Britain. The first, which was proposed in the beginning of king William's reign, only succeeded to a small extent; the second, attempted in the year 1766, almost totally failed; and, in the third and last, undertaken in 1789, although the sum proposed to be raised in this way was only L.1,002,500, the persons who contracted with Government for the whole were unable to complete it without loss; and an alternative was afterwards allowed them of a long annuity.* Some schemes of this kind, undertaken in Ireland in the years 1773, 1775, and 1776, were more successful.

The annuities for fixed terms now existing (called Long Annuities) all terminate at the same time, in 1860. The first of these was granted in the year 1761, being an annuity of L.1 for 99 years, upon every L.100 subscribed to the loan of L.11,400,000 contracted that year, in addition to the permanent annuity of L.3 on a capital equal to the sum advanced. Many other annuities of this kind have been since granted, and all of them for such periods as to terminate at the same time. The amount of these annuities for Britain, on the 1st February, 1817, was L.1,225,431, and, except what was granted in place of the tontine of 1789, they are all in addition to the perpetual annuities on the capitals of the loans.

 The

* See Note VI.

The part of the public debt to which a perpetual annuity is annexed is called the *redeemable debt,* because it may be redeemed by Parliament, on repayment of the capital. The part invested in annuities for lives or years is called the *irredeemable debt,* as these cannot be redeemed during the term agreed on, without the consent of the holder.

Another collateral advantage has sometimes been granted to the public creditors from lotteries. Tickets have been granted to the subscribers to the loans, on terms considered as beneficial, and instead of paying money to the holders of the fortunate tickets, the prizes were assigned them in capital stock of that kind in which the loan of the year was funded. This method was introduced in king William's reign, and continued in many of the loans of the three following reigns. During the peace which followed the seven years war, the lotteries were several times connected with the schemes adopted for discharging a part of the public debt. In the lottery of 1769, the prizes were paid in money; in 1776, the system of funding the prizes was revived. The lotteries, from 1777 to 1784 inclusive, were connected with the loans, but the prizes paid in money. In 1785, the tickets were sold at a profit to the public, and the prizes paid in money; and this method has been adhered to in all the lotteries since.

The profit which the public draws from lotteries has been considered as a tax on the spirit of gaming, and in this view may be added to the amount of the other taxes. In order to secure all that can be raised this way to the public, private lotteries are prohibited under heavy penalties. But a lottery was granted in 1720 to the York Building Company, to assist them in the purchase of the estates forfeited by the rebellion, 1715; and another in 1758, for the benefit of the British Museum, and a few others have been granted since for private purposes.

It will appear from the following detail, that part of the loan has been frequently raised by lottery on easier terms than the remainder. The profits which the lottery would have yielded were, in effect, assigned as a *bonus* to the lenders.

The system of lotteries, however, has been much and justly reprobated, as tending to corrupt the morals of the lower ranks, and lead on many to idleness and ruin; and these consequences become more extensive from their being combined with fraudulent schemes of insurance, which, though prohibited by law, have never been effectually suppressed.

Although the public creditor cannot demand payment of the capital debt,* the mode of transferring it, even in small sums, is so conveniently arranged, and the dividends so regularly paid, that it is considered as an eligible property. The value of the funds is liable to considerable fluctuation. It depends chiefly upon the proportion between the interest they bear, and the profit which may be obtained by applying capital to other purposes. It is influenced by the plenty or scarcity of capital, and by the amount of the loan required at the time; and it is impaired by any event which threatens the safety, or weakens the credit of government. It is generally much higher in time of peace than in time of war; and is affected by every event and even by every report, in time of war, favourable or unfavourable. False reports are frequently raised by designing people for that purpose.

The public debt is distinguished into funded and unfunded. The funded debt consists of the capital or annuities assigned for loans, and generally transferable at the Bank of England. The unfunded debt may arise

 from

* The Loyalty Loan is an exception from this.

from any transaction which constitutes a claim against the public; but the greater part from the issue of Exchequer and Navy Bills, the nature of which will be explained afterwards. These are convertible into funded debt, and have been funded to a great extent: that is, capital in one or more funds has been assigned to the holders of these bills, instead of payment, on such terms as they were willing to accept of.

---

## REIGN OF WILLIAM III.

---

THE only debt subsisting before the Revolution, which is now blended with the mass of our national incumbrances, took rise from the measure of shutting the Exchequer in the year 1672. On that occasion, L.1,328,526, which had been advanced on the credit of supplies voted by the House of Commons, was retained. Interest was paid to the creditors for some years, at 6 per cent., but was discontinued before the death of Charles II.; and no provision was made by Parliament for this debt till the last year of king William's reign, when the hereditary excise was charged with the interest of the above mentioned sum, at 3 per cent. redeemable upon payment of L.664,263, or half the principal. This has been called the Bankers' debt, and was incorporated with other public debts in the general fund established in 1716.

There was also due for arrears to the army and other demands at the Revolution, about L.580,000, and L.60,000 to the late king's servants; but the money in the Exchequer and in the hands of the receivers was sufficient to discharge these demands.

More difficulty was found in raising the comparatively moderate sums required in king William's reign, than in obtaining much larger loans in later times. This may be partly attributed to the inferiority of the national wealth, and greater value of money; and partly to the novelty of the system, and want of public confidence. Measures of various kinds were had recourse to.

1. The most general measure was that already mentioned, of imposing taxes for a limited, generally a small, number of years, and mortgaging their produce to the lenders for payment of their

 principal

principal and interest. Upon this system the following loans were authorized by Parliament,* though some of them were not completed.

|  |  |  |
|---|---|---|
| 1690.— | Loan, charged on certain excise duties, for four years, interest 8 per cent. for what was advanced before 10th June, and 7 per cent. afterwards, - - - - - | L.250,000 |
| | Loan, charged on duties of tonnage and poundage, for four years, interest as above, | 500,000 |
| 1691.— | Loan, charged on duties on East India goods, &c. for 5 years, interest 8 per cent. - | 300,550 |
| | Loan, charged on duties on wines, &c. continued from 1693 to 1696, interest 8 per cent. - - - - - - | 700,100 |
| | Loan, charged on additional excise duties, for 4 years, interest 7 per cent. payable quarterly, - - - - - - | 1,000,000 |
| 1693.— | Loan, charged on additional duties on importation, for years, at 8 per cent. - - | 510,000 |
| | Loan, charged on duties on wines, &c. continued from 1696 to 1698, at 8 per cent. - | 500,000 |
| 1694.— | Loan, charged on stamp duties, now first introduced, for 4 years, at 8 per cent. - - | 330,000 |
| 1695.— | Loan, charged on tonnage and poundage duties, for 4 years, at 8 per cent. - - | 1,250,000 |
| | Loan, charged on duties on bachelors, widows, marriages, births, and burials, for 5 years, at 8 per cent. - - - - - | 650,000 |
| | Loan, charged on glasswares, for years, at 7 per cent. - - - - - | 564,700 |
| 1696.— | Loans, charged on continued duties on wines, &c. for 3 years, at various rates of interest, | 1,500,000 |
| | Loan, charged on house and window duties, for 7 years—the first L.000,000, at 7 per cent., and the remainder at 8 per cent.† - | 1,200,000 |
| | Loan, charged on duties on low wines, &c. for years, at 7 and 8 per cent. - - | 515,000 |

At the peace of Ryswick, in 1697, it appeared that many of the funds on which the loans had been granted, would prove defective, and the Exchequer tallies in the hands of the public creditors sold at great discount. The amount of these, including advances on a scheme of a land Bank, which did not take effect, was L.5,160,495;



* We have not included the sums borrowed in anticipation of the land tax, or other taxes, which were repaid, or intended to be repaid, within the year.

† See Note VII.

to provide for which the Bank of England was authorized to receive them on subscription, and enlarge their capital; and funds were provided, by the prolongation of various duties to 1706, which were expected to yield L.800,000 per annum, to discharge these debts, with interest, at 8 per cent. within that period. This has been called the *first general mortgage*, several similar measures having been adopted afterwards.

The system of borrowing on duties for short terms was continued after the peace, to discharge arrears, or answer other exigencies, as follows:

| | |
|---|---|
| 1697.—Loan, charged on additional duties on malt, &c. for two years, by lottery, (which proved deficient,) - - - - - - | L.1,400 000 |
| 1698.—Loan, charged on additional duty on coals, for 5 years, at 7 and 8 per cent. - - | 500,000 |
| 1701.—Loan, charged on continuation of various duties, for years, at 6 and 7 per cent. - | 300,000 |
| Loan, charged on weekly payments of L.3,700 from the excise, for 5 years, at 6 and 7 per cent. | 820,000 |

II. During this reign, the Bank of England, and a new East India Company, were incorporated, and advanced the following sums to the public.

| | |
|---|---|
| 1694—Loan from the Bank of England, at 8 per cent. besides L.4000 for management, - - | L.1,200,000 |
| 1698.—Loan from the East India Company, at 8 per cent. - - - - - - | 2,000,000 |

III. Besides the above mentioned debts, which can only be discharged by the repayment of the principal, others were contracted this reign on annuities for lives, or terms of years; which therefore became extinct by the failure of the lives, or the lapse of time.

The first operation of this kind was in the year 1692, when it was proposed to raise a million, for which the contributors were to receive 10 per cent. for seven years, and afterwards 7 per cent. on the lives of their nominees, with the benefit of survivorship, till the number was reduced to seven. Advantageous as these terms were, the sum raised on it was only L.108,100, and the annuity after seven years, L.7,567.

An alternative was allowed of an annuity on a single life, at 14 per cent.; the sum raised on which was L.773,393, amounting, with the former, to L.881,493; and by an act of the following year, the million was completed on the same terms. The payment of these

 annuities

annuities was charged on an additional duty on ale, &c. for 99 years, which was afterwards rendered perpetual.

In the year 1694, annuities were granted for one, two, or three lives, in the option of the purchasers, on which the following sums were raised.

| | *Principal.* | *Annuity.* |
|---|---|---|
| On single lives, at 14 per cent. - - - | L.107,847 | L.15,098 |
| On two lives at 12 per cent. - - - | 170,917 | 20,510 |
| On three lives, at 10 per cent. - - | 21,335 | 2,123 |
| | L.300,000 | L.37,712 |

By several acts passed this reign, the holders of annuities on single lives were empowered, upon advancing additional sums, to convert them into long annuities, of 96 years certain duration. By an act of 1695, the additional sum required was 4½ years purchase, or L.63; and if the annuitant declined this, strangers were entitled to purchase the long term, subject to the former life annuity, for L.70, or five years purchase. A like offer was repeated several times in the succeeding year, sometimes at four, and sometimes at five years purchase; aud at last, the whole subsisting annuities, amounting originally to L.139,964, but reduced by death to L.134,122, were converted into long annuities. The sum of L.139,964, annuities, was again completed in the first year of queen Anne's reign, by selling L.5,842, long annuities, on 15 years purchase, by which L.87,630 was raised.

In 1694, a million was raised on annuities for sixteen years, at 14 per cent. by way of lottery.

The amount of annuities subsisting at the end of this reign, including the above mentioned transaction at the commencement of the following one, were

| | *Principal.* | *Annuity.* |
|---|---|---|
| Long annuities, which expired in 1792, | L.1,584,265 | L.139,964 |
| Annuities for 16 years, which expired in 1710, - - - - | 1,000.000 | 140,000 |
| Annuities for two lives, - - | 170,917 | 20,510 |
| Annuities for three lives, - - | 21,235 | 2,123 |
| Tontine annuities, - - - | 108,100 | 7,567 |
| | L.3,884,518 | L.310,166 |

IV. The measure of raising money by issuing Exchequer bills was introduced in this reign, in the year 1696; and has been annually continued, and much extended since.

## REIGN OF QUEEN ANNE.

I. The measure of raising money by loans on particular branches of the revenue mortgaged for a limited number of years was continued in the early part of this reign. The whole sum raised by eight loans of this kind, almost all at 6 per cent. interest, payable quarterly, was L.4,713,405, exclusive of the loan of L.1,296,552, raised in 1710, charged at first on the continuation of the impost on wines, tobacco, &c. from 1716 to 1720; but transferred next year to the South Sea Company.—On these loans no additional capital was granted.

II. L.1,200,000 was advanced in 1708 by the East India Company, without interest, and L.400,000 by the Bank of England, in 1709, without interest after the two first years, on the prolongation of their respective charters.

III. The South Sea Company was established in 1711. At this time great arrears had been incurred upon the navy, victualling, transport, and ordnance departments, and other branches of the war expenditure; to liquidate which the holders of these debts, and also of the loan of 1710, were incorporated and invested with the exclusive privilege of trading to the South and West coast of America; and they advanced L.500,000 to Government for current services.

| | |
|---|---|
| The amount of arrears and deficiencies above mentioned, with interest, was reckoned at - - - - - - | L.7,213,572 |
| Loan of 1710, - - - - - - | 1,296,552 |
| Interest on the same, to 25th March, 1711 - - | 74,876 |
| | L.8,585,000 |
| Interest on above, to 25th December, 1711, - - | 386,325 |
| Sum advanced for public services, - - - | 500,000 |
| Amount capital, by act 9 Anne, chap. 21. - - | L.9,471,325 |
| However, on making up their accompts, it was found only to amount to - - - - - - | 9,177,967 |

On this, their original capital, they received 6 per cent. interest, and L.8000 per annum for management.

IV. Large sums were raised on annuities for 99 years, at different rates; money was also raised in 1705, on annuities for one, two, or

58 three

three lives, which were afterwards converted, upon advancing additional sums, into long annuities. The amount raised in this manner was L.8,191,942, and the amount of the annuities was L.527,174.

The payment of these annuities was charged on certain branches of the revenue; and as these were already mortgaged for a certain term at the time when the money was wanted, a farther sum was raised, in addition to that applied to the public service, for payment of the annuity, till the branch of revenue in which it was charged should become free. Thus, in 1704, the sum raised by annuities was L.1,018,867, charged on weekly payments from the excise; but L.900,000 only of this was applied to the public service, and L.118,867 was reserved for payment of the annuities until the 25th December, 1705, when that fund should be disengaged. A like arrangement, obviously very disadvantageous to the public, was made in several following financial operations.

V. In the year 1710, the sum of L.2,400,000 was raised by two acts, on annuities for 32 years, at 9 per cent.

VI. In the latter part of this reign, when, from the continuance of the war, the difficulty of obtaining money became greater, recourse was had to a method which increased the capital of the public debt to a much greater extent than the money raised. The loans were raised by lotteries, in which every ticket was intitled to a capital equal to the sum advanced; and the fortunate tickets or prizes to a large additional capital—both bearing interest at 6 per cent., and proposed to be repaid, with interest, in 32 years, funds being allocated for that purpose, which were reckoned sufficient for their discharge in that time. The sums raised in this manner, by six lotteries, including one which was appropriated to discharge the debt on the civil list, and one which was granted after the peace of Utrecht, to discharge arrears, amounted to - - - L.9,000,000
and the benefits to fortunate tickets, - - - 2,723,910

Sum added to the public debt, - - - L.11,723,910

 The

The terms of the loans, and amount of money borrowed and capital funded, and interest and annuities incurred, during queen Anne's reign, were nearly as follows.

| | *Sum borrow ed.* | *Capital funded.* | *Interest.* | *Annuit.* |
|---|---|---|---|---|
| 1703. | | | | |
| Loan, charged on continuation of coal duty, the first L.200,000 at 5 per cent. and the remainder at 6 per cent. - - | 500,000 | 500,000 | 28,000 | |
| 1704. | | | | |
| By annuities for 99 years, from 25th March, 1704, at 15 years purchase, charged on weekly payments of L.3700, from the hereditary excise, after 25th Dec. 1705. - - - | 1,018,867 | – | – | 67,924 |
| By annuities for one, two, or three lives, charged as above,* | 364,384 | – | – | 36,821 |
| 1705. | | | | |
| By annuities for 99 years, from 15th December, 1705, at 15 years purchase, charged as above, - - - - | 690,000 | – | – | 46,000 |
| By prolongation of life annuities for 99 years, from 25th March, 1704, - - - | 187,930 | | | |
| Loan, charged on prolongation of duties on low wines, &c. from 1706 to 1710, at 6 per cent. - - - - | 700,000 | 700,000 | 42,000 | |
| Loan, charged on the duties called the two-thirds subsidy, for 4 years, at 6 per cent. - | 636,957 | 636,957 | 38,217 | |
| 1706. | | | | |
| By annuities for 99 years, charged on sundry continued duties, at 15½ years purchase, | 2,855,761 | – | – | 184,242 |
| 1707. | | | | |
| By annuities for 99 years, charged on sundry continued duties, at 16 years purchase, | 1,155,000 | – | – | 72,187 |
| Loan, charged on continuation of various duties to 1712, at 6 per cent. - - | 822,381 | 822,381 | 49,343 | |
| 1708. | | | | |
| By annuities for 99 years, charged on continuation of duties and surplus monies, at 16 years purchase, by two acts, | 1,920,000 | – | – | 120,000 |
| | 10,851,280 | 2,659,338 | 157,560 | 527,174 |

* See Note VIII.

| | Sum borrowed. | Capital. | Interest. | Annuit. |
|---|---|---|---|---|
| Brought forward, - | 10,851,280 | 2,659,338 | 157,560 | 527,174 |
| 1708. | | | | |
| From the East India Company, without interest, on the prolongation of their charter, | 1,200,000 | 1,200,000 | | |
| Loan, charged on continuation of various duties to 1714, at 6 per cent. - - - | 729,067 | 729,067 | 43,744 | |
| 1709. | | | | |
| From Bank of England, without interest, - - - | 400,000 | 400,000 | | |
| Loan, charged on continuation of various duties to 1716, at 6 per cent. - - - | 645,000 | 645,000 | 38,700 | |
| 1710. | | | | |
| By annuities for 32 years, at 9 per cent. charged on continuation of wine duty, and additional duty on houses, raised by lottery, - - - | 1,500,000 | - | - | 135,000 |
| By annuities for 32 years, charged on additional excise duties, &c. at 9 per cent. - | 900,000 | - | - | 81,000 |
| Loan, charged on additional candle duty, at 6 per cent. | 500,000 | 500,000 | 30,000 | |
| Loan of L.1,296,552, charged on mortgaged duties, but added next year to the other advances by the South Sea Company. | | | | |
| 1711. | | | | |
| By lottery of 150,000 tickets of L.10, to be repaid, with 6 per cent. interest in 32 years, charged on various duties, continued for that term, - | 1,500,000 | 1,500,000 | 90,000 | |
| with an additional bonus to fortunate tickets of - | | 428,570 | 25,714 | |
| By lottery of 20,000 tickets of L.100, to be repaid, with 6 per cent. interest, in 32 years, charged on additional stamp duties, &c. - - - | 2,000,000 | 2,000,000 | 120,000 | |
| with a bonus to fortunate tickets of - - - | | 602,200 | 36,132 | |
| Loan, charged on duty on hops, at 6 per cent. - | 180,000 | 180,000 | 10,800 | |
| Stock of South Sea Company, at 6 per cent. - | 9,177,967 | 9,177,967 | 550,678 | |
| Carried forward - - | 29,583,314 | 20,022,122 | 1,103,328 | 788,174 |

| | *Sum borrowed.* | *Capital.* | *Interest.* | *Annuit.* |
|---|---|---|---|---|
| Brought over, - - - | 29,583,314 | 20,022,122 | 1,103,328 | 788,174 |
| 1712. | | | | |
| By lottery, to be repaid with 6 per cent interest, in 32 years, charged on duties on soap, &c. | 1,800,000 | 1,800,000 | 108,000 | |
| with a bonus to fortunate tickets of - - - | | 541,740 | 32,504 | |
| By lottery, to be repaid with 6 per cent. interest, in 32 years, charged on duties on hides, &c. | 1,800,000 | 1,800,000 | 108,000 | |
| with a bonus to fortunate tickets of - - - | | 541,990 | 32,520 | |
| 1713. | | | | |
| By lottery, to discharge the debt of the civil list, to be repaid, with 4 per cent. interest, in 32 years, charged on annual sum of L.35,000, taken from the civil list, - - | 500,000 | 500,000 | 20,000 | |
| with a bonus to fortunate tickets of - - - | | 133,010 | 5,320 | |
| And to discharge arrears, | 33,683,314 | 25,338,862 | 1,409,672 | 788,174 |
| 1714. | | | | |
| By lottery, to be repaid, with 4 per cent. interest, in 32 years, charged on additional duties on soap, &c. - - | 1,400,000 | 1,400,000 | 56,000 | |
| with a bonus to fortunate tickets of - - - | | 476,400 | 19,056 | |
| | 35,083,314 | 27,215,262 | 1,484,728 | 788,174 |

| | |
|---|---|
| The amount of money raised by loans, charged on funds mortgaged for short terms, was- - - | L.4,713,405 |
| From Bank of England and East India Company, - | 1,600,000 |
| From South Sea Company, - - - - | 9,177,967 |
| On annuities for 99 years - - - - | 8,191,942 |
| On annuities for 32 years, - - - - | 2,400,000 |
| By lotteries, - - - - - - | 9,000,000 |
| | L.35,083,314 |
| Bonus to fortunate lottery tickets, - - | 2,723,910 |
| | L.37,807,224 |

The amount of debt contracted during this or the former reign is not exhibited by adding the loans. For, as some of them were con-

 tracted

tracted on the mortgage of certain branches of the revenue for short terms, and were discharged, or, at least, much reduced, within these periods, the existing debt at any time consisted of the undischarged balances, added to the amount of the debts of a more permanent kind. The same system of paying former debts and contracting new ones then prevailed, which, under a different form, has been so extensively followed in later times.

---

## REIGN OF GEORGE I.

This reign was a period of uninterrupted peace. Notwithstanding this, the capital of the public debt was very little diminished; but important alterations took place in our financial system, and the interest of the debt was much reduced. The most important measures were the following:

I. Instead of mortgaging certain branches of the revenue for a limited time, the loan of 1715 was raised on perpetual annuities, redeemable by Parliament, on repayment of the principal, but funds assigned for payment of the interest only. This method has been generally followed since. But several loans were raised this and the following reign, on the former system, by the renewal, and several prolongations of the salt duties.

II. A separate account had been hitherto kept of each loan, and of the funds on which it was charged. This method was found inconvenient, as the produce of some of the taxes fell short of the expected amount, while that of others exceeded it, and the multiplicity of funds occasioned confusion. For these reasons, the various branches of the revenue, soon after the peace of Utrecht, were united into a few funds. The *aggregate fund* was established in 1714, and the *general fund* in 1716. The *South Sea fund*, which had been established some years before, underwent some new regulations. To each of these funds a variety of duties was appropriated, comprehending altogether the whole revenue, except the land and malt tax granted annually, and the branches then appropriated to the support of the civil government;* and each of them was charged with the payment of certain annuities. The management of the debt and receipt of future loans was transferred from the Exchequer to the Bank,



* See Note IX.

Bank, and that convenient mode of transference established, which is still in use.

III. The united surplus of these three funds formed the basis of the first sinking fund, established in 1716, and proposed to be inviolably applied to the discharge of the national debt. A particular account of this fund will be given in the following chapter.

IV. The more beneficial measures embraced this reign were those for the reduction of the interest on the national debt. We have mentioned that most of the loans in king William's reign were made at 8 per cent. interest, and those in queen Anne's reign at 6 per cent. In 1714, the legal rate of interest was reduced to 5 per cent.; but upwards of two years passed before Government took advantage of this reduction. To accomplish this with more facility, Government treated with the Bank and the South Sea Company, who not only agreed to abate the interest on the debts due them, (except that on the original stock of the Bank) from 6 to 5 per cent.; but to advance, the former L.2,500,000, and the latter L.2,000,000, for the payment of such creditors as should refuse to accede to a like agreement: but no demand from these companies was necessary, as almost all the public creditors agreed to the proposed reduction. This took place in 1717.

Although there has been no farther reduction of the legal rate of interest, yet, the actual rate having fallen, Government was enabled to obtain a reduction of the interest on the debts due to the Bank and South Sea Company, from 5 to 4 per cent. in 1727. The interest on the debt due to the East India Company underwent a like reduction in 1732. At this time, almost all the redeemable debt was due to these three companies.

V. The transactions with the South Sea Company during this reign were extensive and important. We have already noticed, that the original capital of this company, at its establishment in the former reign, was L.9,177,967. In 1715, this capital was increased to L.10,000,000, chiefly by adding arrears of interest unpaid to their former capital. In 1719, part of the annuities granted in 1710, for thirty-two years, at 9 per cent., or $11\frac{1}{9}$ years purchase, were subscribed into the company's stock, notwithstanding the part of the term elapsed at $11\frac{1}{2}$ years purchase, and the company advanced L.544,142 to Government; by which operations, their capital was raised to L.11,746,844.

In 1720, a scheme was formed for uniting all the public debts into one fund; and for that purpose, this company was authorised to purchase the debts and annuities due by Government, on the most advantageous terms they could. The amount of these debts and

 annuities

annuities (besides those due to the Bank and East India Company, not comprehended in the scheme) was—

| | |
|---|---|
| Redeemable debts, bearing interest at 5 per cent. - | L.11,779,660 |
| Ditto, bearing interest at 4 per cent. - . - | 4,776,822 |
| | L.16,556,482 |
| Long annuities, granted for 99 years, - - | 666,821 |
| Short annuities, granted for 32 years, not formerly subscribed, - - - - - - | 127,260 |
| | L.794,081 |

And they were to have an addition to their capital of twenty years purchase for the long annuities, and fourteen years purchase for the short annuities, at 5 per cent. interest, and an equal stock for the perpetual annuities, at the respective rates of interest which they bore: but the interest of the 5 per cents. to be reduced to 4 per cent. in 1727. The company farther agreed to pay into the Exchequer, for the liberty of purchasing the perpetual annuities, L.4,156,306 towards the discharge of the national debt; and to pay L.450 for every L.100 of terminable annuities which they should purchase.

This gave rise to an extraordinary scene of national infatuation, generally called the *South Sea Bubble.* The expectations entertained of advantage from this agreement with Government, and from the extension of their trade to the South Sea, were so extravagant, that the price of their stock rose in a short time to 1000 per cent., and soon after fell as rapidly, to the ruin of many. The folly of this national credulity was the more surprising, as a similar delusion of the Mississippi Company had taken place in France about a year before, attended with consequences still more fatal.

The greater part, however, of the public debt was subscribed into the South Sea Company, and their capital was raised to L.37,802,483; of which, four millions were purchased by the Bank in 1722. Upon the disasters which befell this company, they were exempted from the stipulated payments to Government.

These operations, so far as they related to the redeemable debt, were merely a change of arrangement, and made no alteration either in the capital or interest of the public debt. To understand the alteration produced upon the irredeemable debt, we must observe that the long annuities, in consequence of the reduction of interest, now sold at a higher price than the sum originally advanced, notwithstanding the part of the term elapsed. These annuities had been granted at different rates, as already mentioned, most of them about 16 years purchase. The company, by purchasing L.100 annuity, for which L.1600 had been originally paid, became entitled to a capital of L.2000. Thus, the public, instead of an annuity which terminated by the course of time without repayment, became burthened at present with an equal one, which could only be extinguished by the payment of a sum greater by one-fourth than what had been advanced. But, in return for this, the debt was rendered redeemable, and a reduction of interest to 4 per cent. in 1727, agreed on; and, in consequence of the option of redemption, Government was enabled afterwards to reduce the interest to 3 per cent. along with that of the other public debts.

These measures have been much commended; but their advantage to the public seems equivocal. An interest or perpetual annuity, susceptible of reductions, and actually reduced, was substituted for a temporary annuity, which admitted of no reduction: But the sure and complete relief which the course of time would have given many years ago, without repayment, was abandoned; and the public was burthened with a permanent debt, exceeding the sum originally advanced by L.3,034,769.

Although the amount of the public debt was nearly stationary this reign, considerable loans were made for discharging the unfunded debt, and for compensating the sums paid by the sinking fund, or otherwise. These were nearly as follows:

| | *Principal.* | *Interest.* |
|---|---|---|
| 1715.—Loan, at 5 per cent. transferable at the Bank, - | L.910,000 | L.45,500 |
| Additional loan, at the same rate, | 169,000 | 8,450 |
| 1717.—Loan on the general fund, for supplying sundry deficiencies, at five per cent. - | 952,042 | 47,602 |
| And for discharging Canada bills, at 4 per cent. - | 24,195 | 968 |
| 1719.—Loan, by lottery, at 4 per cent. including expense of drawing, | 505,995 | 20,240 |
| By another lottery, at 4 per cent. | 500,000 | 20,000 |
| Loan at 5 per cent. - | 520,000 | 26,000 |
| 1720.—Loan, charged on plate duty, at 4 per cent. - | 312,000 | 12,486 |
| 1726.—Loan, by lottery, for the civil list, charged on pension duty, at 3 per cent. - | 1,000,000 | 30,000 |
| 1727.—Loan, charged on duty on coals, at 4 per cent. - | 370,000 | 14,800 |

All the redeemable annuities not subscribed into the South Sea Company, were paid off from the sinking fund during this reign. The irredeemable subsisting annuities were nearly as follows:



Long

| | *Principal.* | *Annuity.* |
|---|---|---|
| Long annuities, not subscribed into the South Sea Company, - - | L.1,836,275 | L.131,203 |
| Short annuities, which expired in 1742, not subscribed, - - - | 270,398 | 24,322 |
| Tontine of 1692, - - - | 108,100 | 7,567 |
| | L.2,214,773 | L.163,092 |
| Annuities for two or three lives, granted in 1694, original sum, - - | 192,152 | 22,633 |

The three first of these articles remained permanent for many years; but the last article was diminished gradually by the failure of lives.

The whole debt, funded and unfunded, at the end of this reign, has been estimated at L.52,092,235, and the interest, L.1,217,551.

## REIGN OF GEORGE II.

During the first and pacific part of the reign of George II. financial business was conducted nearly in the same manner as in the former reign. The system of contracting new debts, and applying the sinking fund to the discharge of former debts, was for some time continued, but the debt was, on the whole, diminished. The loans were nearly as follows:

| | *Principal.* | *Interest.* |
|---|---|---|
| 1728.—Loan, from Bank, at 4 per cent. | L.1,750,000 | L.70,000 |
| 1728.—Loan, from Bank, at 4 per cent. | 1,250,000 | 50,000 |
| 1731.—Loan at 3½ per cent. - | 400,000 | 14,000 |
| and by lottery, at 3 per cent. | 800,000 | 24,000 |
| 1732.—Loan, charged on salt duties, revived for three years from Lady-day, 1732,* at 3 per cent. | 500,000 | 15,000 |
| | L.4,700,000 | L.173,000 |
| 1734.—Loan, charged on salt duties, continued for 7 years from 1735, at 4 per cent. - - | 1,000,000 | 40,000 |
| 1735.—Loan, charged on salt duties, continued for 5 years from 1742, at 4 per cent. - - | 500,000 | 20,000 |
| 1736.—Loan, charged on the sinking fund, at 3 per cent. - | 600,000 | 18,000 |
| Carried forward, - | L6,800,000 | L,251,000 |

67

* When the loan was raised on the mortgage of duties for a limited time, we have mentioned the duties on which it was charged, but not when the interest only was provided for.

| | *Principal.* | *Interest.* |
|---|---|---|
| Brought over, | L.6,800,000 | L.251,000 |
| 1737.—Loan, at 3 per cent. - - | 500,000 | 15,000 |
| 1738.—Loan, charged on the sinking fund, at 3 per cent. - - | 300,000 | 9,000 |
| | L.7,600,000 | L.275,000 |

We have not mentioned several loans charged on the growing produce of the sinking fund, from which they were repaid soon after.

" Britain and Spain were in a state of equivocal hostility from the beginning of the year 1739, or earlier, and war was declared between them in October of that year : But there do not seem to have been any loans for that war, except what were charged on the growing produce of the sinking fund, till 1741. War was not declared against France till March, 1744, though hostilities were carried on between the countries long before."

The terms of the loans, and amount of money borrowed, capital funded, and interest and annuities contracted, during the war of 1740, were nearly as follows.

| | *Sum borrowed.* | *Capital.* | *Interest.* | *Annuit.* |
|---|---|---|---|---|
| 1741. | | | | |
| Loan, at 4 per cent. charged on prolongation of salt duties, from 1746 to 1753 - | 1,200,000 | 1,200,000 | 48,000 | |
| 1742. | | | | |
| Advanced by the Bank, without interest, in consideration of the renewal of their charter, - - | 1,600,000 | 1,600,000 | | |
| Loan, at 3 per cent. charged on sinking fund, | 800,000 | 800,000 | 24,000 | |
| 1743. | | | | |
| Loan, at 3 per cent. - | 1,000,000 | 1,000,000 | 30,000 | |
| and by lottery at the same rate, - - | 800,000 | 800,000 | 24,000 | |
| 1744. | | | | |
| From the East India Company, on the prolongation of their charter, at 3 per cent. | 1,000,000 | 1,000,000 | 30,000 | |
| Loan, at 3 per cent, but L.3 deducted from each L.100 at payment, - | 1,164,000 | 1,200,000 | 36,000 | |
| and by lottery, at 3 per cent. | 600,000 | 600,000 | 18,000 | |
| 1745. | | | | |
| Loan, at $3\frac{1}{2}$ per cent. charged on prolongation of salt duties, from 1753 to 1759, - | 1,000,000 | 1,000,000 | 35,000 | |
| Carried forward, - | 9,164,000 | 9,200,000 | 245,000 | |

| | Sum borrowed. | Capital. | Interest. | Annuit. |
|---|---|---|---|---|
| Brought forward, - | 9,164,000 | 9,200,000 | 245,000 | |
| Loan at 3 per cent. - | 1,500,000 | 1,500,000 | 245,000 | |
| and by lottery, each subscriber of L.300 to the loan to have ten tickets, at L.10, | 500,000 | 500,000 | 15,000 | |
| and a life annuity of L.4 10s. | – | – | – | 22,500 |
| 1746. | | | | |
| Loan, at 4 per cent. - | 2,500,000 | 2,500,000 | 100,000 | |
| and by lottery, each subscriber of L.500 to the loan to have 10 tickets, at L.10, | 500,000 | 500,000 | 20,000 | |
| and a life annuity of L.9, | – | – | – | 45,000 |
| Advanced by the Bank, for cancelling Exchequer bills, at 4 per cent.* | 986,800 | 986,800 | 39,472 | |
| 1747. | | | | |
| Loan at 4 per cent. with an additional capital of 10 per cent. - - | 4,000,000 | 4,400,000 | 176,000 | |
| and by lottery, at 4 per cent. | 1,000,000 | 1,000,000 | 40,000 | |
| 1748. | | | | |
| Loan, at 4 per cent. each subscriber of L.100 to have a gratuitous lottery ticket, value L.10 - - | 6,300,000 | 6,930,000 | 277,200 | |
| 1749. | 26,450,800 | 27,516,800 | 957,672 | 67,500 |
| Navy bills, &c. charged on sinking fund, at 4 per cent. | 3,072,472 | 3,072,472 | 122,898 | |
| 1750. | | | | |
| Loan at 3 per cent. to discharge part of the debt of the navy, charged on the sinking fund, - - | 1,000,000 | 1,000,000 | 30,000 | |
| | 30,523,272 | 31,589,272 | 1,110,570 | 67,500 |

It appears from this account, that the loans were raised on easy terms till 1745, when the alarm excited by the rebellion rendered it necessary to grant a life annuity, in addition to the interest of the loan,—and the same was done to a greater extent the following year; and in the two last years of the war, an additional capital of 10 per cent. was granted. A small additional capital had been granted in 1744.

The most important financial measure in the succeeding peace was the reduction of the interest on the greater part of the public debt to 3 per cent. For this purpose, it was enacted, in 1749, that all



* See Note X.

all the public creditors at 4 per cent. who should signify their consent to accept of 3 per cent. after 25th December, 1757, should have their present interest continued till 25th December, 1750, and 3½ per cent. interest, till December, 1757. The amount of these debts was L.57,703,475. The greater part of the creditors accepted of this offer: but, as some had declined it, a like offer was repeated next year, in which the interest at 3½ per cent. was only continued till 25th December, 1755. Most of the remaining creditors accepted, and those who declined it were paid off. These debts were united into a fund, since called the *three per cent. reduced annuities*; and the debts, which then bore only 3 per cent. interest, were united into another fund, called the *three per cent. consolidated annuities.* The interest on the South Sea stock of L.3,662,784 was continued at 4 per cent. till December, 1757; but that on the South Sea annuities underwent the same reduction as the other debts: and L.2,100,000 was borrowed in 1751, transferable at the South Sea House, to pay off those who declined the reduction.

The funded debt discharged during the peace was,

| | |
|---|---|
| Navy debt, charged on sinking fund, in 1749, - - | L.3,072,472 |
| To holders of South Sea annuities, who did not agree to the reduction of interest, in 1751, - - - | 2,276,843 |
| To other public creditors, for the same reason, - | 830,989 |
| | L.6,180,354 |

The funded debt at the commencement of the seven years war was nearly the same as at the conclusion of the former war; but the greater part of the unfunded debt was paid off during the peace.

The terms of the loans, and amount of money borrowed and capital funded, and interest and annuities contracted, during the seven years war, were as follows.

| | *Sum borrowed.* | *Capital.* | *Interest.* | *Annuit.* |
|---|---|---|---|---|
| 1755. | | | | |
| Loan, at 3 per cent. by lottery, - - | 900,000 | 900,000 | 27,000 | |
| 1756. | | | | |
| Loan, at 3½ per cent. redeemable after 15 years, and redeemed in 1771, - | 1,500,000 | 1,500,000 | 52,500 | |
| Also, by lottery, at 3 per cent. - - | 500,000 | 500,000 | 15,000 | |
| 1757. | | | | |
| Loan at 3 per cent. with an additional life annuity of 22s. 6d. per L.100, - | 3,000,000 | 3,000,000 | 90,000 | 33,750 |
| Carried forward, - | 5,900,000 | 5,900,000 | 184,500 | 33,750 |

| | *Sum borrowed.* | *Capital.* | *Interest.* | *Annuit.* |
|---|---|---|---|---|
| Brought forward, - | 5,900,000 | 5,900,000 | 184,500 | 33,750 |
| 1758. | | | | |
| Loan, at 3½ per cent. reduced in 1782 to 3 per cent. - | 4,500,000 | 4,500,000 | 157,500 | |
| and by lottery at 3 per cent. | 500,000 | 500,000 | 15,000 | |
| 1759. | | | | |
| Loan, at 3 per cent. allowing L.115 capital for every L.100 borrowed, - - | 6,600,000 | 7,590,000 | 227,700 | |
| 1760. | | | | |
| Loan, at 4 per cent. for 21 years, and then reduced to 3 per cent. allowing L.103 capital for L.100 borrowed, | 8,000,000 | 8,240,000 | 329,600 | |
| 1761. | | | | |
| Loan, at 3 per cent. with an additional annuity of L.1 2s. 6d. for 99 years, | 11,400,000 | 11,400,000 | 342,000 | 128,250 |
| and by lottery, at 3 per cent. | 600,000 | 600,000 | 18,000 | |
| 1762. | | | | |
| Loan, at 4 per cent. for 19 years, and then reduced to 3 per cent. with an annuity of L.1 for 98 years, - | 12,000,000 | 12,000,000 | 480,000 | 120,000 |
| 1763. | | | | |
| Loan, at 4 per cent. - | 2,800,000 | 2,800,000 | 112,000 | |
| and by lottery at the same rate, - - | 700,000 | 700,000 | 28,000 | |
| Transactions after the peace, to discharge arrears. | 53,000,000 | 54,230,000 | 1,894,300 | 282,000 |
| 1763. | | | | |
| Navy bills, charged on the sinking fund, at 4 per cent. and paid off in 1765, 1766, and 1767, - - | 3,483,553 | 3,483,553 | 139,342 | |
| 1765. | | | | |
| Navy bills, funded in the 3 per cent. reduced, - | 1,482,000 | 1,482,000 | 44,460 | |
| | 57,965,553 | 59,195,553 | 2,078,102 | 282,000 |

The loans of 1758, 1761, 1763, 1767, and 1768 were aided by the profits of lotteries.

A considerable sum of navy and other debts, contracted this war was never funded, but paid off in the subsequent peace.

## REIGN OF GEORGE III.

We have already, for the sake of connection, mentioned the financial operations to the conclusion of the seven years war.

During the succeeding peace, the following loans were contracted, chiefly to discharge other debts which bore a higher rate of interest:

| | |
|---|---|
| Loan of 1766, at 3 per cent. - - - | L.1,500,000 |
| Loan of 1767, at 3 per cent. - - - | 1,500,000 |
| Loan of 1768, at 3 per cent. - - - | 1,900,000 |
| | L.4,900,000 |

And the following debts were paid off:

| | | *Sum paid.* | *Capital.* |
|---|---|---|---|
| 1765 1766 1767 | Navy debt, charged on sinking fund, in 1763, by four equal payments of L.870,888, | L.3,483,553 | L.3,483,553 |
| 1768 1769 | Loan of 1763, at 4 per cent. discharged by 4 equal payments of L.875,000, at par. | 3,500,000 | 3,500,000 |
| 1771. | —Loan of 1756, at 3½ per cent. at par. - - - | 1,500,000 | 1,500,000 |
| 1772 | —Various 3 per cent. funds, paid off at 90 per cent. each holder of L.100 being allowed four lottery tickets, at L. 12. 10*s*. - - | 1,350,000 | 1,500,000 |
| 1774. | —Various 3 per cent. funds, paid off at 88 per cent., each holder of L.100 being allowed six lottery tickets, at L.12 10*s*. - - - | 880,000 | 1,000,000 |
| 1775. | —Various 3 per cent. funds on the same terms, - | 880,000 | 1,000,000 |
| | | L.11,593,553 | L.11,983,553 |

In 1773, L.1,253,700 bearing interest at 4 per cent. till 1781, being part of the loans of 1760 and 1762, was subscribed into the 3 per cent. cons., allowing the proprietors the profits of the lottery of that year. The remainder of these loans was added to the 3 per cent. reduced in 1781.

The terms of the loans, and amount of money borrowed, capital funded, and interest and annuities contracted, during the American war, and to discharge arrears, were as follows.*

| | *Sums borrowed.* | *Capital funded.* | *Interest.* | *Annuit.* |
|---|---|---|---|---|
| 1776. At L.107 10s. funded, for L.100 borrowed in the 3 per cents. - - - - | 2,000,000 | 2,150,000 | 64,500 | |
| 1777. At par, in the 4 per cents. with an annuity of 10s. for 10 years - - - - | 5,000,000 | 5,000,000 | 200,000 | 25,000 |
| 1778. At par, in the 3 per cents. with an annuity of L.2 10s. for 30 years, or for life, in the option of the subscribers | 6,000,000 | 6,000,000 | 180,000 | 150,000 |
| 1779. At par, in the 3 per cents. with an annuity of L.3 15s. for 29 years, or for life, - | 7,000,000 | 7,000,000 | 210,000 | 262,500 |
| 1780. At par, in the 4 per cents. with an annuity of L.1 16s. 3d. for 80 years, - - - - | 12,000,000 | 12,000,000 | 480,000 | 217,500 |
| | 32,000,000 | 32,150,000 | | |
| 1781. At L.150 in the 3 per cents. and L.25 in the 4 per cents. | 12,000,000 | 21,000,000 | 660,000 | |
| 1782. At L.100 in the 3 per cents. and L.50 in the 4 per cents. with an annuity of 17s. 6d. for 78 years, - - - | 13,500,000 | 20,250,000 | 675,000 | 118,125 |
| 1783. At L.100 in the 3 per cents. and L.25 in the 4 per cents. with an annuity of 13s. 4d. for 77 years, - - - - | 12,000,000 | 15,000,000 | 480,000 | 80,000 |
| 1784. At L.100 in the 3 per cents. and L.50 in the 4 per cents. with an annuity of 5s. 6d. for 75½ years, - - - L.2000 being forfeited by the failure of a subscriber. - | 6,000,000 | 8,998,000 | 299,940 | 16,500 |
| Carried forward - | 75,500,000 | 97,398,000 | 3,249,440 | 869,625 |



* See Note XI.

| | *Sums borrowed.* | *Capital funded.* | *Interest.* | *Annuit.* |
|---|---|---|---|---|
| Brought over. | 75,500,000 | 97,398,000 | 3,249,440 | 869,625 |
| 1785. | | | | |
| Navy and victualling bills, funded in the 5 per cents. at L.107 10s. 6d. - - - | 6,397,900 | 6,879,342 | 343,967 | |
| 1786. | | | | |
| Navy victualling and transport bills, and ordnance debentures, funded in the 5 per cents. at L.111 8s. - - | 9,865,942 | 10,990,651 | 549,532 | |
| | 91,763,842 | 115,267,993 | 4,142,939 | 869,625 |

---

The amount of the national debt, and interest and annuities thereon, at the commencement and termination of each war, were as follows.*

| | | *Principal.* | *Interest and Annuities.* |
|---|---|---|---|
| Debt at Revolution, - | 1689 | L.664,263 | L.39,855 |
| Debt at Peace of Ryswick, | 1697† | L.21,515,742 | L.1,721,259 |
| Debt at the commencement of queen Anne's war, - | 1701, | | |
| Bank of England, - | | L.1,200,000 | L.96,000 |
| East India Company - | | 2,000,000 | 160,000 |
| Banker's debt - - | | 664,263 | 39,855 |
| Other permanent debts, - - | | 6,976,529 | 542,958 |
| Annuities for terms of years or lives, being the original sums raised, deducting what had fallen in by death, - - - - - | | 2,884,518 | 310,165 |
| Unfunded debt, interest 6 per cent. | | 2,669,392 | 161,964 |
| | | L16,394,702 | L.1,310,942 |



Debt

---

* See Note XII.

† We have not met with a detailed account of the national debt at this period. The interest is here charged at 8 per cent.

| | *Principal* | *Interest and Annuities.* |
|---|---|---|
| Debt at peace of Utrecht, 1713 | | |
| Bank of England, - - | L.1,600,000 | L.96,000 |
| Exchequer bills, circulated or cancelled by the Bank, - - | 6,451,840 | 442,070 |
| East India Company, - - | 3,200,000 | 160,000 |
| South Sea Company, - - | 9,177,967 | 550,678 |
| Bankers' debt, - - - | 664,263 | 39,855 |
| Other permanent debts - - | 13,471,687 | 949,357 |
| | L.34,565,757 | L.2,237,961 |
| Annuities for terms of years or lives. | 12,545,356 | 912,027 |
| | L.47,111,113 | L.3,149,988 |
| Unfunded debt, at various rates of interest, - - - - | 5,034,250 | 201,370 |
| | L.52,145,363 | L.3,351,358 |
| Debt at the commencement of the war, - - - 1739. | | |
| Bank of England, - - - | L.8,600,000 | L.376,000 |
| and for cancelling Exchequer bills, | 500,000 | 20,000 |
| East India Company, - - | 3,200,000 | 128,000 |
| South Sea Company, - - | 27,302,203 | 1,092,088 |
| Civil list debt,* - - | 1,000,000 | 30,000 |
| Other permanent debts - - | 4,203,521 | 138,864 |
| | L.44,805,724 | L.1,784,952 |
| Annuities for terms of years or lives, | 2,324,220 | 194,835 |
| Unfunded debt, interest 4 per cent. | 824,685 | 32,987 |
| | L.47,954,629 | L.2,012,774 |
| Debt at peace of Aix-la-Chapelle, 1748. | | |
| Bank of England, - - - | L.11,686,800 | L.430,450 |
| and for cancelling Exchequer bills, | 500,000 | 20,000 |
| East India Company, - - | 4,200,000 | 158,000 |
| South Sea Company, - - | 27,302,203 | 1,092,088 |
| Civil list debt, - - - | 1,000,000 | 30,000 |
| Carried forward - - | L.44,689,003 | L.1,730,538 |

75 Other

* This debt was funded in 1726, and is therefore stated here though it was not introduced into the official accounts till a later period.

| | *Principal* | *Interest and Annuities.* |
|---|---|---|
| Brought forward - | L.44,689,003 | L.1,730,538 |
| Other permanent debts - - | 25,609,071 | 933,761 |
| | L.70,298,074 | L.2,664,299 |
| Annuities for terms of years or lives, | 2,042,723 | 155,260 |
| Ditto, for which no money was raised, - - - | - - | 62,857 |
| Unfunded debt, interest 3 per cent. | 6,952,916 | 208,587 |
| | L.79,293,713 | L.3,091,003 |
| Debt at the commencement of the seven years war, - - 1755.* | | |
| Bank of England, - - - | L.11,686,800 | L.393,038 |
| East India Company, - - | 4,200,000 | 126,000 |
| South Sea Company, - - | 25,025,309 | 864,107 |
| Ditto, for loan of 1751, - - | 2,100,000 | 63,000 |
| Civil list debt, - - - | 1,000,000 | 30,000 |
| Other permanent debts, - - | 26,839,146 | 880,096 |
| | L.70,851,255 | L.2,356,241 |
| Annuities for terms of years or lives, | 2,029,131 | 149,022 |
| Ditto, for which no money was raised, - - - | - - | 61,759 |
| Unfunded debt, interest 3 per cent. | 1,451,767 | 43,553 |
| | L.74,332,153 | L.2,610,575 |
| Debt at the peace of Paris, 1763. | | |
| Bank of England, - - - | L.11,686,800 | L.350,604 |
| East India Company, - - | 4,200,000 | 126,000 |
| South Sea Company, including loan of 1751, - - - - | 27,125,309 | 813,759 |
| Civil list debt, - - - | 1,000,000 | 30,000 |
| Other permanent debts, - - | 81,069,145 | 2,652,239 |
| Annuities for terms of years or lives, | 2,020,380 | 147,961 |
| Ditto for which no money was raised, | - - | 343,739 |
| Debt charged on sinking fund, at 4 per cent. - - - | 3,483,553 | 139,342 |
| Unfunded debt, interest 3 per cent. | 8,280,243 | 248,407 |
| | L.138,865,430 | L.4,852,051 |

 Debt

* Hostilities commenced in America and at sea in 1755, though war was not declared till 1756. The debt is stated as it was in the beginning of 1755.

| | *Principal.* | *Interest and Annuities.* |
|---|---|---|
| Debt at the commencement of the American war, - - 1775. | | |
| Bank of England, - - - | L.11,686,800 | L.350,604 |
| East India Company, - - | 4,200,000 | 126,000 |
| South Sea Company, including loan of 1751. - - - | 25,984,685 | 779,541 |
| Civil list debt, - - - | 1,000,000 | 30,000 |
| | L.42,871,485 | L.1,286,145 |
| Permanent debts, at 4 per cent.* - | 18,986,300 | 759,452 |
| Ditto. at 3½ per cent.† - - | 4,500,000 | 157,500 |
| 3 per cent. cons. - - - | 38,251,696 | 1,147,551 |
| 3 per cent. reduced, - - | 18,353,774 | 550,613 |
| | L.122,963,255 | L.3,901,261 |
| Annuities for terms of years or lives, | 2,020,380 | 147,961 |
| Ditto, for which no money was raised | - - | 314,549 |
| Unfunded debt, interest 3 per cent.‡ | 3,600,000 | 108,000 |
| | L.128,583,635 | L.4,471,771 |
| Debt at peace of Versailles, 1783. | | |
| Bank, East India, and South Sea Companies, and civil list debt, as above, | L.42,871,485 | L.1,286,145 |
| 3 per cent. cons. - - - | 107,399,696 | 3,221,990 |
| 3 per cent. reduced, - - - | 37,340,074 | 1,120,202 |
| 4 per cent. cons. - - - | 32,750,000 | 1,310,000 |
| 5 per cent. navy, - - - | 17,869,993 | 893,500 |
| | L.238,231,248 | L.7,831,837 |
| Annuities for years or lives, - - | 2,020,380 | 147,961 |
| Do., for which no money was raised, | - | 1,183,974 |
| Unfunded debt, interest 3 per cent.§ | 9,600,000 | 288,000 |
| | L.249,851,628 | L.9,451,772 |



* These were reduced to 3 per cent. in 1781, and added to the 3 per cent. reduced.

† These were reduced to 3 per cent. in 1782, and added to the 3 per cent. cons.

‡ Viz. Exchequer bills, L.1,250,000 ; navy debt, L.1,850,000 ; civil list debt, L.500,000.

§ This sum is probably too small.

| | *Principal.* | *Interest and Annuities.* |
|---|---|---|
| Debt at the commencement of the French Revolution war, 1793. | | |
| Funded debt as above, - - | L.238,231,248 | L.7,831,837 |
| Of which, purchased by the Commissioners for the Redemption of the National Debt, in the 3 per cents. - | 10,242,100 | 307,263 |
| | L.227,989,148 | L.7,524,574 |
| Annuities for years or lives,* - - | - - | 1,293,870 |
| | | L.8,818,444 |
| Unfunded debt, interest 3 per cent. | 16,129,487 | 483,884 |
| | L.244,118,635 | L.9,302,328 |
| Debt at peace of Amiens, 1802.* | | |
| Funded debt. See appendix, II. tables II. and III. - - - | L.567,008,978 | L.18,466,040 |
| Of which redeemed,† - - - | 67,255,915 | 2,043,851 |
| | L.499,753,063 | L.16,422,189 |
| Annuities for years or lives, - - | - - | 1,604,915 |
| Unfunded debt, interest 3 per cent. - | 20,554,038 | 616,621 |
| | L.520,207,101 | L.18,643,725 |
| Debt after first expulsion of Bonaparte, - - - 1814.‡ | | |
| Funded debt, - - - - | L.932,201,881 | L.31,006,776 |
| Of which redeemed, L.253,354,220 | | |
| Loyalty loan paid, - L.2,017,773 | | |
| Converted into life annuities, - - 2,795,340 | | |
| | 258,167,333 | 7,866,178 |
| | L.674,034,548 | L.33,140,598 |
| Annuities for years or lives, - - | - - | 1,303.585 |
| Life annuities for stock converted, - | - - | 185,878 |
| Unfunded debt, - - - | 68,580,524 | 2,017,415 |
| | L.742,615,072 | L.26,647,476 |



* This debt is stated as it was 1st February, 1803.

† The sums transferred for the purchase of land-tax are not deducted in this or the following similar articles.

‡ This debt is stated as it was 1st February, 1815.

| | | *Principal.* | *Interest and Annuities.* |
|---|---|---|---|
| Debt after second expulsion of Bonaparte, and peace of - - 1815.* | | | |
| Funded debt, - - - | | L.1,003,090,283 | L.33,584,595 |
| Of which redeemed, | L.273,418,402 | | |
| Loyalty loan paid, - | 2,103,758 | | |
| Converted into life annuities, - - | 3,097,551 | | |
| | | 278,619,711 | 8,421,469 |
| | | L.724,470,572 | L.25,163,126 |
| Annuities for years or lives, - - | | - - | 1,303,375 |
| Life annuities for stock converted, - | | - - | 199,845 |
| Unfunded debt, interest 3 per cent. - | | 48,725,359 | 1,461,761 |
| | | L.773,195,931 | L.28,128,107 |
| Debt after a year of peace, 1st February, - - - 1817. | | | |
| Funded debt, - - - - | | 1,006,090,283 | 33,674,595 |
| Of which redeemed, - | L.291,719,172 | | |
| Loyalty loan paid, - | 2,321,590 | | |
| Converted into life annuities, - - | 3,449,955 | | |
| | | 297,490,717 | 9,052,028 |
| | | L.708,599,566 | L.24,622,567 |
| Annuities for years or lives, - - | | - - | 1,302,779 |
| Life annuities for stock converted, - | | - - | 225,254 |
| Unfunded debt, interest 3 per cent. - | | 50,047,088 | 1,501,412 |
| | | L.758,646,654 | L.27,652,012 |

PROGRESS OF THE NATIONAL DEBT.

| | | | |
|---|---|---|---|
| Debt at the Revolution, | 1689. | L.664,263 | L.39,855 |
| Debt contracted during king William's war, - - - - | | 20,851,479 | 1,681,404 |
| Debt at peace of Ryswick, | 1689. | L.21,515,742 | L.1,721,259 |
| Debt paid during peace, - | - | 5,121,040 | 410,317 |
| Debt at commencement of queen Anne's war, - - - | 1702. | L.16,394,702 | L.1,310,942 |
| Debt contracted during war, | - | 35,750,661 | 2,040,416 |
| Carried forward - | - | L.52,145,363 | L.3,351,358 |

79 Debt

* This debt is stated as it was 1st February, 1816.

| | | *Principal.* | *Interest and Annuities.* |
|---|---|---|---|
| Debt at peace of Utretcht, - | 1713. | L.52,145,363 | L.3,351,358 |
| Debt paid during peace,* - - | | 4,190,734 | 1,338,584 |
| Debt at commencement of war, | 1739. | L.47,954,629 | L.2,012,774 |
| Debt contracted during war, - - | | 31,339,084 | 1,078,229 |
| Debt at peace of Aix-la-Chapelle, | 1748. | L.79,293,713 | L.3,091,003 |
| Debt paid during peace, - - | | 4,961,560 | 480,428 |
| Debt at commencement of 7 years war, | 1756. | L.74,332,153 | L.2,610,575 |
| Debt contracted during war, - - | | 64,533,277 | 2,241,476 |
| Debt at peace of Paris, - | 1763. | L.138,865,430 | L.4,852,051 |
| Debt paid during peace, - - | | 10,281,795 | 380,480 |
| Debt at commencement of American war, - - - | 1775. | L.128,583,635 | L.4,471,571 |
| Debt contracted during war, - - | | 121,267,993 | 4,980,201 |
| Debt at peace of Versailles, | 1783. | L.249,851,628 | L.9,451,772 |
| Debt paid during peace, - - | | 5,732,993 | 149,444 |
| Debt at the commencement of the French Revolution war, - | 1793. | L.244,118,635 | L.9,302,328 |
| Debt contracted during war, - - | | 276,088,466 | 9,341,397 |
| Debt at peace of Amiens, | 1802. | L.520,207,101 | L.18,643,725 |
| Debt contracted during renewal of war, before Bonaparte's first expulsion, | 1803. | 222,407,966 | 8,003,951 |
| Debt at Bonaparte's first expulsion, | 1814. | L.742,615,067 | L.26,647,676 |
| Debt contracted during second renewal of war, - - - - | | 30,580,864 | 1,480,431 |
| Debt at Bonaparte's second expulsion, | 1815. | L.773,195,931 | L.28,128,107 |
| Debt paid during year of peace, | 1816.† | 14,549,277 | 476,095 |
| | | L.758,646,654 | L.27,652,012 |



RECAPITULATION

* This sum might have been stated at L.5,190,734; but L.1,000,000 of debt was contracted for the civil list, charged on the pension duty, in 1726.

† This great reduction of the debt was occasioned by part of the loans of the former year being applied to the services of the present.

## RECAPITULATION.

| | | | |
|---|---|---|---|
| Debt at the Revolution, - - - - | | L.664,263 | Annual average. |
| Contracted in war commencing 1689, of 8 years, | | 20,851,479 | 2,606,435 |
| — in war commencing 1701, of 12 years, | | 35,750,661 | 2,979,222 |
| — in war commencing 1739, of 9 years, | | 31,339,084 | 3,482,120 |
| — in war commencing 1756, of 7 years, | | 64,533,277 | 9,219,039 |
| — in war commencing 1775, of 8 years, | | 121,267,993 | 15,158,499 |
| — in French Revolution wars of 22 yrs. | | 529,077,296 | 24,061,614 |
| Viz. war of 1793, - 9 years, | L.276,088,466 | 802,819,790 | 12,163,936 |
| — of 1803, - 12 years, | 222,407,966 | | |
| — of 1815, - 1 year, | 30,580,864 | | |
| 22 years, | L.529,077,296 | | |
| Years of war, | 66 | | |
| Debt paid in peace of - 1697, of 4 years, | | 5,121,040 | 1,280,260 |
| — in peace of - 1713, of 26 years, | | 4,190,734 | 161,182 |
| — in peace of - 1748, of 8 years, | | 4,961,560 | 620,195 |
| — in peace of - 1763, of 12 years, | | 10,281,795 | 856,816 |
| — in peace of - 1783, of 10 years, | | 5,732,993 | 573,299 |
| — in peace of - 1802, of 1 year, | | - - | |
| — in peace of - 1815, of 1 year, | | 14,549,277 | |
| Years of peace, - | 62 | 44,837,399 | 723,814 |
| Debt at Revolution, - - - - | | 664,263 | |
| Debt contracted in six (or eight) wars, - | | 802,819,790 | |
| | | 803,484,053 | |
| Debts paid in periods of peace, - - | | 44,837,399 | |
| | | 758,646,654 | |
| Amount funded debt, by official account, 1st February, 1817, - - - - - | | 682,769,314 | |
| To which add, deductions for land-tax redeemed, | | 25,290,994 | |
| and for unclaimed dividends, - - | | 539,258 | |
| | | 708,599,566 | |
| Unfunded debt, - - - - | | 50,047,088 | |
| Amount debt, 1st February, 1817, - - | | 758,646,654 | |

The progress of the funded debt was as follows:

| | |
|---|---|
| Funded debt, 31st December, 1739. - - - | L.44,805,724 |
| Debt funded during war of 1739, - - - | 27,516,800 |
| Carried forward - - - - | L.72,322,524 |

| | |
|---|---|
| Brought forward - - - | L.72,322,524 |
| Funded debt discharged during war, including L.584,500 charged on salt duties, L.481,400 charged on victuallers' act, &c. - - - - | 2,024,450 |
| Funded debt at peace of Aix-la-Chapelle, - - | L.70,298,074 |
| Funded after peace, to discharge arrears, - - | 4,072,472 |
| Funded in 1751, to pay off South Sea annuities, - | 2,100,000 |
| Other additional funded debt during peace, - - | 561,063 |
| | L.77,031,609 |
| Funded debt paid during peace, - - - | 6,180,354 |
| Funded debt at the commencement of the seven years war, - - - - - | L.70,851,255 |
| Debt funded during seven years war, - - - | 54,230,000 |
| | L.125,081,255 |
| Debt funded after the war, to discharge arrears, - | 4,965,553 |
| | L.130,046,808 |
| Debt funded during peace of 1763, - - - | 4,900,000 |
| | L.134,946,808 |
| Debt paid during peace, - - - - - | 11,983,553 |
| Debt funded during American war, - - - | L.122,963,255 |
| and to discharge arrears, - - - - | 115,267,993 |
| | L.238,231,248 |

Which underwent no alteration till the establishment of Mr. Pitt's sinking fund, in 1788.

The annuities for terms of years or lives then existing was, L.1,193,674.

---

## SECTON II.

### PERIOD SINCE THE FRENCH REVOLUTION.

SINCE the establishment of the present sinking fund, in 1786, part of the funded has been annually redeemed. In order to exhibit a distinct view of this subject, we shall first state the progress and present amount of the funded debt, and charges on the same, without regard to the redemption; and then the extent of the redemption and the amount now unredeemed.

 At

At the commencement of the war in 1793, the capital funded debt, stated as in 1786, consisted of

| | | |
|---|---|---|
| 3 per cents. - - - - - - | | L.187,611,255 |
| 4 per cents. - - - - - - | | 32,750,000 |
| 5 per cents. - - - - - - | | 17,869,993 |
| Amount funded debt,* - - - - - | | L.238,231,248 |
| But there had been redeemed by the sinking fund, in 3 per cents. - - - - - | | 10,242,100 |
| Unredeemed debt, - - - - - | | L.227,989,148 |
| Interest of 3 per cents. - - - - - | | L.5,628,338 |
| of 4 per cents. - - - - - | | 1,310,000 |
| of 5 per cents. - - - - - | | 893,499 |
| Amount Interest, - - - - - | | L.7,831,837 |

And the annuities to which some additions were made since 1786, were

| | | | |
|---|---|---|---|
| Annuities which expired in 1805, | | L.53,655 | |
| — — in 1806, | | 7,776 | |
| — — in 1807, | | 14,892 | |
| — — in 1808, | | 418,333 | |
| | | L.494,656 | |
| Long annuities which expire in 1860, - - - - | | 704,740 | |
| | | L.1,199,396 | |
| Tontine 6 Geo. III. - | L.540 | | |
| 29 Geo. III.† | 18,442 | | |
| | L.18,982 | | |
| Annuities for lives, | 75,492 | | |
| | | 94,474 | |
| | | | L .1,293,870 |
| Management of capital debt, - | | L.98,869 | |
| of annuities, - | | 17,258 | |
| | | | 116,127 |
| Interest, annuities, and management, - - | | | L.9,241,834 |
| Deduct interest redeemed, - - - | | | 307,263 |
| Remainder unredeemed, - - - | | | L.8,934,571 |

Since the commencement of the war, loans have been contracted every year, and Exchequer and navy bills have been frequently funded

83

* See a statement of the several funds in which this capital was invested, in Table I.

† This is afterwards stated at L.18,847. See Note XIV.

funded. A part of most of the loans since 1797 has been for the use of Ireland, and in 1809 a part was for Portugal. Some loans have been transacted in Britain for Ireland, which, though not connected with any British loan, are guaranteed by Britain, and the interest payable there. The particulars of these operations are as follows:

1793.

| | | |
|---|---|---|
| A. Loan, sum raised, - - - - | | L.4,500,000 |
| Capital funded, at the rate of L.100 in 3 per cent. cons. for L.72 raised, - - - - | | L.6,250,000 |
| Interest, - - - - - - | | L.187,500 |
| Management, L.450 per million, - - | | 2,812 |
| Total charge, - - - - | | L.190,312 |

1794

| | | |
|---|---|---|
| B. Loan, sum raised, - - - - | | L.11,000,000 |
| Capital funded at L.100, in 3 per cent. cons. - | | L.11,000,000 |
| and L.25 in 4 per cents., - - - | | 2,750,000 |
| Total funded, - - - - | | L.13,750,000 |
| Interests of 3 per cents., - - - | | L.330,000 |
| of 4 per cents., - - - | | 110,000 |
| | | L.440,000 |
| And an annuity of 11s. 5d. for $66\frac{1}{4}$ years, - | | 62,792 |
| Management of capital, at L.450, - | L.6,187 | |
| and for long annuities, - - | 706 | |
| | | 6,894 |
| Total charge, - - - - - - | | L.509,687 |
| C. Navy and victualling bills funded, amount - | | L.1,907,451 |
| Capital funded at L.101 in 5 per cent. navy, - | | L.1,926,526 |
| Interest, - - - - - | | L.96,326 |
| Management at L.450, - - - | | 867 |
| Total charge, - - - - - | | L.97,193 |

1795.

| | | |
|---|---|---|
| D. Loan, sum raised, - - - - - | | L.18,000,000 |
| Capital funded at L.100 in 3 per cent. cons., - | | L.18,000,000 |
| and L.33 6s. 8d. in 4 per cent., - - | | 6,000,000 |
| Total funded, - - - - | | L.24,000,000 |

| | | |
|---|---|---|
| Interest of 3 per cents., - - - | | L.540,000 |
| of 4 per cents., - - - | | 240,000 |
| and an annuity of 9s. 6d. for 65¼ years, - | | 85,500 |
| Management of capital, at L.450, | L.10,800 | |
| and for long annuities, | 962 | |
| | | 11,762 |
| Total charge, - - - - - | | L.877,262 |

| | |
|---|---|
| E. Navy and victualling bills funded, amount - | L.1,490,647 |
| Capital funded at L.108, in 5 per cent. navy, - | L1,609,898 |
| Interest, - - - - - - | L.80,495 |
| Management at L.450, - - - - | 724 |
| Total charge, - - - - - | L.81,219 |

| | | |
|---|---|---|
| F. Loan, (Dec.) raised, - - - - | | L.18,000,000 |
| Capital funded at L.120, in 3 per cent. cons. - | | L.21,600,000 |
| and L.25 in 3 per cent. reduced, - - | | 4,500,000 |
| | | L.26,100,000 |
| Deduct a deficiency by non-payment of - - | | 4,200 |
| | | L.26,095,800 |
| Interest. - : - - - - | | L.782,874 |
| And an annuity of 6s. 6d. for 61¼ years, - | | 58,500 |
| Management of capital, at L.450, - | L.11,743 | |
| and for long annuity, - - | 658 | |
| | | 12,401 |
| Total charge, - - - - | | L.853,775 |

The imperial loan of this year is stated afterwards.

1796.

| | | |
|---|---|---|
| G. Loan. Sum raised, - - - - | | L.7,500,000 |
| Capital funded at L.120, in 3 per cent. cons. - | | L.9,000,000 |
| and L.25 in 3 per cent. reduced, - - | | 1,875,000 |
| | | L.10,875,000 |
| Deduct a deficiency by non-payment of - | | 81,175 |
| | | L.10,793,825 |
| Interest, - - - - - | | L.323,815 |
| And an annuity of 5s. 6d. for 63¾ years, - | | 20,582 |
| Management of capital, at L.450, | L.4,857 | |
| and for long annuities, - | 231 | |
| | | 5,089 |
| Total charge, - - - - | | L.349,486 |

H. Navy and victualling bills funded, amount, - L.4,226,727

| | | |
|---|---|---|
| Of which L.2,398,927 | funded at L.104 in 5 per cent. cons. | L.2,494,884 |
| and 1,827,800 | funded at L.105 in ditto according to their dates, | 1,919,190 |
| L.4,226,727 | | L.4,414,074 |

| | |
|---|---|
| Interest, - - - - - | L.220,703 |
| Management at L.450. - - - | 1,986 |
| Total charge, - - - - | L.222,689 |

1796. (Nov.)

I. Navy and Exchequer Bills funded.*

| | Navy Bills. | Exch. Bills. | Total. |
|---|---|---|---|
| Amount bills, - - - | 11,595,529 | 1,433,870 | 13,029,399 |
| Funded in 3 per cent. cons. - | 16,438,175 | 1,999,699 | 18,437,874 |
| in 4 per cents. - - | 765,428 | 104,432 | 869,860 |
| in 5 per cent. navy, - | 2,034,890 | 270,202 | 2,305,092 |
| Total funded, - - - | 19,238,493 | 2,374,333 | 21,612,826 |
| Interest of 3 per cents. . - | 493,145 | 59,991 | 553,136 |
| of 4 per cents. - - | 30,617 | 4,177 | 34,794 |
| of 5 per cents. - - | 101,744 | 13,510 | 115,254 |
| Amount interest, - - - | 625,507 | 77,678 | 703,185 |
| Management at L.450, - - | 8,657 | 1,069 | 9,726 |
| Total charge, - - - - | 634,164 | 78,747 | 712,911 |

K. Loyalty Loan.† (Dec.) Sum raised, - L.18,000,000

| | |
|---|---|
| Funded at 5 per cent. in a separate fund, at L.112 10s. - - - . - | L.20,250,000 |
| Deduct a deficiency by non-payment of - - | 125,157 |
| | L.20,124,843 |
| Interest, - - - - - | L.1,006,243 |
| Management at L.450, - - - - | 9,056 |
| Total charge, - - - - - | L.1,015,299 |

86

L. Joint

* See Note XV. † See Note XVI.

1797.

L. Joint loan for Britain and Ireland, funded at L125 in 3 per cent. cons. L.50 in three per cent. reduced, L.20 in 4 per cents, and an annuity of 6s. for 62¾ years.

| | Britain. | Ireland. | Total. |
|---|---|---|---|
| Sums raised, - - - - | 13,000,000 | 1,500,000 | 14,500,000 |
| Cap. fund. in 3 p. cent. cons. - | 16,250,000 | 1,875,000 | 18,125,000 |
| in 3 per cent. red. - | 6,500,000 | 750,000 | 7,250,000 |
| Capital funded in 3 per cents. - | 22,750,000 | 2,625,000 | 25,375,000 |
| in 4 per cents. - | 2,600,000 | 300,000 | 2,900,000 |
| Total funded, - - - - | 25,350,000 | 2,925,000 | 28,275,000 |
| Interest of 3 per cents. - - | 682,500 | 78,750 | 761,250 |
| of 4 per cents. - - | 104,000 | 12,000 | 116,000 |
| Amount interest, - - - | 786,500 | 90,750 | 877,250 |
| Long annuities, - - - | 39,000 | 4,500 | 43,500 |
| Management of capital at L.450, | 11,418 | 1,305 | 12,723 |
| And for long annuities, - - | 446 | 44 | 490 |
| Total charge, - - - - | 837,364 | 96,599 | 933,963 |

The Imperial Loan of this year is stated afterwards.

1798.

M. Joint loan for Britain and Ireland, funded at L.150 in 3 per cent. cons. L.50 in 3 per cent. reduced, and an annuity of 4s. 11d. for 61¾ years.

| | Britain. | Ireland. | Total. |
|---|---|---|---|
| Sum raised, - - - - - | 15,000,000 | 2,000,000 | 17,000,000 |
| Cap. fund. in 3 p. cent. cons. - | 22,500,000 | 3,000,000 | 25,500,000 |
| in 3 per cent. red. - | 7,500,000 | 1,000,000 | 8,500,000 |
| Capital funded in 3 per cents. - | 30,000,000 | 4,000,000 | 34,000,000 |
| Interest, - - - - - - | 900,000 | 120,000 | 1,020,000 |
| Long annuities, - - - | 36,875 | 4,916 | 41,791 |
| Management of capital, at L.450, | 13,500 | 1,800 | 15,300 |
| And for long annuities, - - | 415 | 55 | 470 |
| Total charge, - - - - | 950,790 | 126,771 | 1,077,561 |

| N. Loan. (December.) Sum raised, | L.3,000,000 |
|---|---|
| Capital funded at L.100 in 3 per cent. cons. | L.3,000,000 |
| and L.87 9s. 6d. in 3 per cent. reduced, | 2,624,250 |
| | L.5,624,250 |
| Interest, | L.168,727 |
| Management at L.450, | 2,530 |
| Total charge, | L.171,257 |

1799.

O. Joint loan for Britain and Ireland, funded at L.125 in 3 per cent. cons. and L.50 in 3 per cent. reduced.

| | Britain. | Ireland. | Total. |
|---|---|---|---|
| Sums raised | 12,500,000 | 3,000,000 | 15,500,000 |
| Cap. fund. in 3 p. cent. cons. | 15,625,000 | 3,750,000 | 19,375,000 |
| in 3 per cent. red. | 6,250,000 | ·1,500,000 | 7,750,000 |
| Capital funded in 3 per cents. | 21,875,000 | 5,250,000 | 27,125,000 |
| Interest, | 656,250 | 157,500 | 813,750 |
| Management at L.450, | 9,843 | 2,362 | 12,205 |
| Total charge, | 666,093 | 159,862 | 825,955 |

1800

P. Joint loan for Britain and Ireland, funded at L.110 in 3 per cent. cons. and L.47 in 3 per cent. reduced.

| | Britain. | Ireland. | Total. |
|---|---|---|---|
| Sums raised, | 18,500,000 | 2,000,000 | 20,500,000 |
| Capital fund. in 3 p. cent. cons. | 20,350,000 | 2,200,000 | 22,550,000 |
| in 3 per cent. red. | 8,695,000 | 940,000 | 9,635,000 |
| Capital funded in 3 per cents. | 29,045,000 | 3,140,000 | 32,185,000 |
| Interest, | 871,350 | 94,200 | 965,550 |
| Management at L.450. | 13,070 | 1,413 | 14,483 |
| Total charge. | 884,420 | 95,613 | 980,033 |



Q. Joint

1801.

Q. Joint loan for Britain and Ireland, funded at L.125 in 3 per cent. cons. and L.50 15s. in 3 per cent. reduced.

| | Britain. | Ireland. | Total. |
|---|---|---|---|
| Sums raised, - - - - - | 25,500,000 | 2,500,000 | 28,000,000 |
| Capital fund. in 3 p. ct. cons. - | 31,875,000 | 3,125,000 | 35,000,000 |
| in 3 per cent. red. - | 12,941,250 | 1,268,750 | 14,210,000 |
| Capital funded in 3 per cents. - | 44,816,250 | 4,393,750 | 49,210,000 |
| Interest, - - - - | 1,344,488 | 131,812 | 1,476,300 |
| Management at L.450, - - | 20,167 | 1,977 | 22,144 |
| Total charge, - - - - | 1,364,655 | 133,789 | 1,498,444 |

1802.

R. Exchequer bills funded at L.25 in 3 per cent. cons. L.25 in 3 per cent. reduced, L.50 in 4 per cent. cons. L.25 in 5 per cents. joined to Loyalty Loan, and an annuity of 10s. 9d. for 58¾ years.

| | | |
|---|---|---|
| Amount bills funded, - - - - | | L.8,910,450 |
| Capital funded in 3 per cent. cons. - - | | L.2,227,612 |
| in 3 per cent. reduced, - - | | 2,227,612 |
| Capital funded in 3 per cents. - - - | | L.4,455,225 |
| in 4 per cents. - - - | | 4,455,225 |
| in 5 per cents. Loyalty Loan, - | | 2,227,612 |
| | | L.11,138,063 |
| Interest of 3 per cents. - - - - | | L.133,657 |
| of 4 per cents. - - - - | | 178,209 |
| of 5 per cents. - - - - | | 111,381 |
| Long annuities, - - - - - | | 7,796 |
| Management of capital at L.450, - | L.5,012 | |
| And for long annuities, - | 87 | |
| | | 5,099 |
| Total charge, - - - - - | | L.436,142 |

S. Joint loan for Britain and Ireland, funded at L.65 in 3 per cent. cons. L.60 in 3 per cent. reduced, and L.6 19s. 3d. in 3 per cent. cons. the interest of which is deferred till the year 1808.*

| | Britain. | Ireland. | Total. |
|---|---|---|---|
| Sums raised, - - - - - | 23,000,000 | 2,000,000 | 25,000,000 |
| Capital fund. in 3 p. ct. cons. - | 14,950,000 | 1,300,000 | 16,250,000 |
| in 3 per cent. red. - | 13,800,000 | 1,200,000 | 15,000,000 |
| Capital funded in 3 per cents. - | 28,750,000 | 2,500,000 | 31,250,000 |
| in 3 p. ct. cons. deferred, - | 1,601,375 | 139,250 | 1,740,625 |
| Total funded, - - - - - | 30,351,375 | 2,639,250 | 32,990,625 |
| Present interest, - - - | 862,500 | 75,000 | 937,500 |
| Deferred interest, - - - | 48,041 | 4,178 | 52,219 |
| Total interest, - - - | 910,541 | 79,178 | 989,719 |
| Management at L.450, - - | 12,937 | 1,125 | 14,062 |
| Amount present interest and management, - - | 875,437 | 76,125 | 951,562 |

1803.

T. Joint loan for Britain and Ireland, funded at L.80 in 3 per cent. cons. L.80 in 3 per cent. reduced, and an annuity of 6s. 5d. for $56\frac{3}{4}$ years.

| | Britain. | Ireland. | Total. |
|---|---|---|---|
| Sums raised, - - - - - | 10,000,000 | 2,000,000 | 12,000,000 |
| Capital fund. in 3 p. ct. cons. - | 8,000,000 | 1,600,000 | 9,600,000 |
| in 3 per cent. red. - | 8,000,000 | 1,600,000 | 9,600,000 |
| Capital funded in 3 per cents. - | 16,000,000 | 3,200,000 | 19,200,000 |
| Interest, - - - - - - | 480,000 | 96,000 | 576,000 |
| Long annuities, - - - - - | 32,083 | 6,417 | 38,500 |
| Management of capital at L.340 | 5,440 | 1,088 | 6,528 |
| And for long annuities, - - | 273 | 54 | 327 |
| Total charge - - - - - | 517,796 | 103,559 | 621,355 |



* See Note XVII.

1804.

U. Joint loan for Britain and Ireland, funded at L.100 in 3 per cent. reduced, and L.82 in 3 per cent. cons.

| | Britain. | Ireland. | Total. |
|---|---|---|---|
| Sums raised, - - - - - | 10,000,000 | 4,500,000 | 14,500,000 |
| Capital fund. in 3 p. ct. cons. - | 8,200,000 | 3,690,000 | 11,890,000 |
| in 3 per cent. red. - | 10,000,000 | 4,500,000 | 14,500,000 |
| Capital funded in 3 per cents. - | 18,200,000 | 8,190,000 | 26,390,000 |
| Interest, - - - - - - | 546,000 | 245,700 | 791,700 |
| Management at L.340, - - - | 6,188 | 2,785 | 8,973 |
| Total charge, - - - - - | 552,188 | 248,485 | 800,673 |

1805.

V. Joint loan for Britain and Ireland, funded at L.150 in 3 per cent. cons. and L.22 in 3 per cent. reduced.

| | Britain. | Ireland. | Total. |
|---|---|---|---|
| Sums raised, - - - - - | 20,000,000 | 2,500,000 | 22,500,000 |
| Capital fund. in 3 p. ct. cons. - | 30,000,000 | 3,750,000 | 33,750,000 |
| in 3 per cent. red. - | 4,400,000 | 550,000 | 4,950,000 |
| Capital funded in 3 per cents. - | 34,400,000 | 4,300,000 | 38,700,000 |
| Interest, - - - - - - | 1,032,000 | 129,000 | 1,161,000 |
| Management at L.340, - - - | 11,696 | 1,462 | 13,158 |
| Total charge, - - - . - | 1,043,696 | 130,462 | 1,174,158 |

W. A separate loan for Ireland, in Britain, funded at L.24 in 5 per cent. navy, and an annuity of L.5 for $54\frac{3}{4}$ years.

| | | |
|---|---|---|
| Sum raised, - - - - - | | L.1,500,000 |
| Sum funded in 5 per cent. navy, - - - | | L.360,000 |
| Interest, - - - - - - - | | L.18,000 |
| Long annuities, - - - - - - | | 75,000 |
| Management of capital at L. 340, | L.122 | |
| and for long annuities, | 638 | 760 |
| Total charge, - - - - - | | L.93,760 |



X. Joint

1806.

X. Joint loan for Britain and Ireland, funded at L.100 in 3 per cent. cons. and L.66 in 3 per cent. reduced.

| | Britain. | Ireland. | Total. |
|---|---|---|---|
| Sums raised, - - - - - | 18,000,000 | 2,000,000 | 20,000,000 |
| Capital funded in 3 p. cent. cons. - | 18,000,000 | 2,000,000 | 20,000,000 |
| in 3 per cent. red. - | 11,880,000 | 1,320,000 | 13,200,000 |
| Capital funded in 3 per cents. - | 29,880,000 | 3,320,000 | 33,200,000 |
| Interest, - - - - - - | 896,400 | 99,600 | 996,000 |
| Management at L.340, - - - | 10,159 | 1,129 | 11,288 |
| Total charge, - - - - - | 906,559 | 100,729 | 1,007,288 |

1807.

Y. Joint loan for Britain and Ireland, funded at L.70 in 3 per cent. cons. L.70 in 3 per cent. reduced, and L.10 12s. in 5 per cent. navy.*

| | Britain. | Ireland. | Total. |
|---|---|---|---|
| Sums raised, - - - - - | { 12,000,000 }<br>{ 200,000 } | 2,000,000 | 14,200,000 |
| Capital funded in 3 per cent. cons. - - - - - - | { 8,400,000 }<br>{ 140,000 } | 1,400,000 | 9,940,000 |
| in 3 per cent. red. | { 8,400,000 }<br>{ 140,000 } | 1,400,000 | 9,940,000 |
| in 5 per cent. navy, | { 1,272,000 }<br>{ 21,200 } | 212,000 | 1,505,200 |
| Total funded, - - - | 18,373,200 | 3,012,000 | 21,385,200 |
| Interest of 3 per cents. - - | { 504,000 }<br>{ 8,400 } | 84,000 | 596,400 |
| of 5 per cents. - - | { 63,600 }<br>{ 1,060 } | 10,600 | 75,260 |
| Total interest, - - - | 577,060 | 94,600 | 671,660 |
| Management at L.340, - - | { 6,145 }<br>{ 102 } | 1,024 | 7,271 |
| Total charge, - - - | 583,307 | 95,624 | 678,931 |

92 Z. A.

* See Note XVIII.

Z. A separate loan for Ireland, in Britain.

| | |
|---|---|
| Sum raised, - - - - - | L.1,500,000 |
| Capital funded at L.160 12s. 10d. in 3 per cent. cons. - - - - - - | L.2,409,625 |
| Interest, - - - - - - | L.72,289 |
| Management at L.340, - - - - | 819 |
| Total charge, - - - - - | L.73,108 |

1808.

*A*. Joint loan for Britain and Ireland, funded at L.118 3s. 6d. in 4 per cent. cons.

| | Britain. | Ireland. | Total. |
|---|---|---|---|
| Sums raised, - - - - - | 8,000,000 | 2,500,000 | 10,500,000 |
| Capital funded in 4 per cents. - | 9,454,000 | 2,954,375 | 12,408,375 |
| Interest, | 378,160 | 118,175 | 496,335 |
| Management at L.340, - - - - | 3,214 | 1,004 | 4,218 |
| Total charge, - - - - | 381,374 | 119,179 | 500,553 |

*B*. Exchequer Bills funded.

| | |
|---|---|
| Bills funded at L.105 in 5 per cents. - - - | L.3,524,200 |
| Bills funded at L.63 in 5 per cents. and L.50 in 4 per cents. - - | 475,800 |
| Amount Bills, - - - - - - | L.4,000,000 |
| Capital funded in 5 per cent. navy, - | L.3,700,410 |
| and, - - | 300,944 |
| | L.4,001,354 |
| Capital funded in 4 per cents. - - - | 237,900 |
| Total funded, - - - - - - | L.4,239,254 |
| Interest of 5 per cents. - - - - - | L.200,068 |
| of 4 per cents. - - - - - | 9,516 |
| Total Interest, - - - - - - | L.209,584 |
| Management at L.340, - - - - - | 1,441 |
| Total charge, - - - - - - | L.211,025 |
| Interest of part of the loan of 1802, for Great Britain, deferred till this year,* - - | L.48,041 |

93 *C*. Joint

* See Note XVII.

1809.

*C.* Joint loan for Britain, Ireland, and Portugal, funded at L.60 in 3 per cent. reduced, L.60 in 4 per cent. cons. and an annuity of 8s. 10d. for $50\frac{3}{4}$ years.*

| | Britain. | Ireland. | Portugal. | Total. |
|---|---|---|---|---|
| Sum raised, - - - | 11,000,000 | 3,000,000 | 600,000 | 14,600,000 |
| Capital funded in 3 per cent. reduced, - - | 6,064,478 | 1,800,000 | 895,522 | 8.760,000 |
| in 4 per cents. | 6,960,000 | 1,800,000 | | 8,760,000 |
| Total funded, - - - | 13,024,478 | 3,600,000 | 895,522 | 17,520,000 |
| Interest of 3 p. cents. - | 181,934 | 54,000 | 26,866 | 262,800 |
| of 4 per cents. - | 278,400 | 72,000 | | 350,400 |
| Total interest, - - | 460,334 | 126,000 | 26,866 | 613,200 |
| Long annuities, - - | 51,233 | 13,250 | | 64,483 |
| Management, - - - | 4,864 | 1,337 | 304 | 6,505 |
| Total charge, - - - | 516,431 | 140,587 | 27,170 | 684,188 |

*D.* Exchequer Bills funded.†

| | |
|---|---|
| Bills funded at L.103. 5s. in 5 per cents. | L.6,483,200 |
| Bills funded at L.81. 8s. in 5 per cents. and L.26 5s. in 4 per cents. | 1,448,900 |
| Amount bills funded, - - - - | L.7,932,100 |
| Capital funded in 5 per cent. navy, - - | L.6,693,904 |
| and, - - | 1,179,404 |
| | L.7,873,308 |
| Capital funded in 4 per cent. cons. - - | 380,336 |
| Total funded, - - - - | L.8,253,644 |
| Interest of 5 per cents. - - - - | L.393,665 |
| of 4 per cents. - - - - | 15,214 |
| Total interest, - - - - - | L.408,879 |
| Management at L.340, - - - - | 2,806 |
| Total charge, - - - - - | L.411,685 |



*E.* Exchequer

* See Note XIX. † See Note XX.

1810.

*E.* Exchequer Bills funded.

| | |
|---|---|
| Amount bills funded at L.103. 5s. in 5 per cent. navy, - - - - - - | L.8,311,000 |
| Capital funded, - - - - - | L.8,581,108 |
| Interest at 5 per cent. - - - - | L.429,055 |
| Management at L.340 and L.300, - - | 2,917 |
| Total charge, - - - - - | L.431,972 |

*F.* Joint loan for Britain and Ireland, funded at L.130 in 3 per cent. reduced, and L.10 7s. 6d. in 3 per cent. cons.

| | Britain. | Ireland. | Total. |
|---|---|---|---|
| Sums raised, - - - - - | 8,000,000 | 4,000,000 | 12,000,000 |
| Capital funded in 3 p. ct. red. - | 10,400,000 | 5,200,000 | 15,600,000 |
| in 3 per cent. cons. - | 830,000 | 415,000 | 1,245,000 |
| Capital funded in 3 per cents. - | 11,230,000 | 5,615,000 | 16,845,000 |
| Interest, - - - - - | 336,900 | 168,450 | 505,350 |
| Management, - - - - - | 3,818 | 1,909 | 5,727 |
| Total charge, - - - - | 340,718 | 170,359 | 511,077 |

*G.* A separate loan for Ireland in Britain, funded at L.130 in 3 per cents. reduced, and L.10. 7s. 6d. in 5 per cent. cons.

| | |
|---|---|
| Sum raised, - - - - - | L.1,400,000 |
| Capital funded in 3 per cent. cons. - - | L.1,820,000 |
| and in 3 per cent. reduced, - - - | 145,250 |
| Total funded, - - - - - | L.1,965,250 |
| Interest, - - - - - | L.58,957 |
| Management, - - - - - | 667 |
| Total charge, - - - - - | L.59,624 |

1811.

*H.* Exchequer Bills funded.

| | |
|---|---|
| Amount bills funded at L.103. 14s in 5 per cent. navy - - - - - | L.7,018,700 |
| Capital funded, - - - - - | L.7,278,392 |
| Interest at 5 per cent. - - - - | L.363,919 |
| Management, - - - - - | 2,385 |
| Total charge, - - - - - | L.366,304 |

*I.* Loan to complete L.12,000,000.

| | |
|---|---|
| Sum raised, - - - - - | L.4,981,300 |
| Capital funded in 5 per cent. navy, at L.72 for L.70 raised, - - - - - | L.5,166,319 |
| Interest, - - - - - - | L.258,316 |
| Management, - - - - - | 1,550 |
| Total charge, - - - - - | L.259,866 |

*K.* Loan of L.12,000,000, of which L.4,500,000 is for the service of Ireland. But as Britain undertook to pay the interest, the whole is charged to the account of Britain.

| | |
|---|---|
| Sum raised, - - - - - | L.12,000,000 |
| Capital funded at L.100 in 3 per cent. reduced, - | L.12,000,000 |
| and L.20 in 3 per cent. cons. - - | 2,400,000 |
| | L.14,400,000 |
| And L.20 in 4 per cent. cons. | 2,400,000 |
| Total funded, - - - - - | L.16,800,000 |
| Interest of 3 per cents. - - - - | L.432,000 |
| of 4 per cents. - - - - | 96,000 |
| Total Interest, - - - - - | L.528,000 |
| Annuity for 48¾ years, at 6s. 11d. - - - | 41,500 |
| Management, - - - - - | 5,392 |
| Total charge. - . - - - | L.574,892 |

 *L.* Exchequer

1812.

*L.* Exchequer Bills funded, amount - - - L.5,431,700

Capital funded at L.108 in 5 per cent. navy, - L.5,866,236

Interest at 5 per cent. - - - - L.293,312
Management, - - - - - 1,760

Total charge, - - - - - L.295,072

*M.* Exchequer Bills funded, and loan in supplement amount - - - - - L.6,789,625

Capital funded at L.108 in 5 per cent. navy, - - L.7,332,795

Interest at 5 per cent. - - - - L.366,639
Management, - - - - - 2,200

Total charge, - - - - - L.368,839

*N.* Joint loan for Britain and Ireland, and the East India Company, funded at L.120 in 3 per cent. reduced, and L.56 in 3 per cent. cons.

| | Britain. | Ireland. | East India Company. | Total. |
|---|---|---|---|---|
| Sums raised, - | 15,650,000 | 4,350,000 | 2,500,000 | 22,500,000 |
| Capital funded in | | | | |
| 3 per cent. red. | 18,780,000 | 5,220,000 | 3,000,000 | 27,000,000 |
| in 3 p. ct. cons. | 8,764,000 | 2,436,000 | 1,400,000 | 12,600,000 |
| Total funded, - | 27,544,000 | 7,656,000 | 4,400,000 | 39,600,000 |
| Interest at 3 p. ct. | 826,320 | 229,680 | 132,000 | 1,188,000 |
| Management, - | 8,263 | 2,414 | 1,320 | 11,997 |
| Total charge, - | 834,583 | 232,094 | 133,320 | 1,199,997 |

1813.

*O.* Excheqeur Bills funded, amount - - L.12,000,000

Capital funded at L.115. 10s. in 5 per cent. navy - L.13,860,000

Interest at 5 per cent. - - - - L.693,000
Management at L.300, - - - - 4,158

Total charge, - - - - - L.697,158

 *P.* Exchequer

| | |
|---|---|
| *P.* Exchequer Bills funded, amount - - - | L.3,755,700 |
| Capital funded at L.139 in 4 per cents. - - | L.5,220,423 |
| Interest at 4 per cent. - - - - | L.208,817 |
| Management at L.300, - - - - | 1,566 |
| Total charge, - - - - - | L.210,383 |

*Q.* Joint loan for Britain and Ireland, at L.110 in the 3 per cent. reduced, L.60 in the three per cent cons., and a long annuity of 8s. 6d. for 46¾ years.

| | Britain. | Ireland. | Total. |
|---|---|---|---|
| Sums raised, - - | 21,000,000 | 6,000,000 | 27,000,000 |
| Capital fund, in 3 per cent. reduced, - - | 23,100,000 | 6,600,000 | 29,700,000 |
| in 3 per cent cons. | 12,600,000 | 3,600,000 | 16,200,000 |
| Total funded, - - | 35,700,000 | 10,200,000 | 45,900,000 |
| Interest, - - - | 1,071,000 | 306,000 | 1,377,000 |
| Long annuity - - | 89,250 | 25,500 | 114,750 |
| Management at L.300 - | 11,379 | 3,251 | 14,630 |
| Total charge, - - | 1,171,629 | 334,751 | 1,506,380 |

*R.* November, for service of 1814. Loan at L.110 in the 3 per cent. reduced, and L.67 in the 3 per cent. cons.

| | |
|---|---|
| Sum raised, - - - - - | L.22,000,000 |
| Capital funded in 3 per cent. reduced, - - | L.24,200,000 |
| and in 3 per cent. cons. - - - | 14,740,000 |
| | L.38,940,000 |
| Interest, - - - - - - | L.1,168,200 |
| Management at L.300, - - - - | 11,682 |
| Total charge, - - - - - | L.1,179,882 |

1814.

*S.* Joint loan for Britain and Ireland, funded at L.80 in the 3 per cent. reduced, L.23½ in the 3 per cent. cons., and L.30 in the 5 per cent. navy.

| | Britain. | Ireland. | Total. |
|---|---|---|---|
| Sums raised, - | 18,500,000 | 5,500,000 | 24,000,000 |
| Capital funded in 3 p. ct. red. | 14,800,000 | 4,400,000 | 19,200,000 |
| in 3 per cent. navy, | 4,347,500 | 1,292,500 | 5,640,000 |
| | 19,147,500 | 5,692,500 | 24,840,000 |
| Deduct deficiency by non-payment, - - - | 2,070 | - - | 2,070 |
| Amount fund. in 3 p. cents. | 19,145,430 | 5,692,500 | 24,837,930 |
| in 5 per cents. | 5,550,000 | 1,650,000 | 7,200,000 |
| Deduct deficiency by non-payment, - - - | 600 | - - | 600 |
| | 5,549,400 | 1,650,000 | 7,199,400 |
| Total funded, deducting deficiency, - - - | 24,694,830 | 7,342,500 | 32,037,330 |
| Interest of 3 per cents. - | 574,363 | 170,775 | 745,138 |
| of 5 per cents. - | 277,470 | 82,500 | 359,970 |
| Amount interest - - | 851,833 | 253,275 | 1,105,108 |
| Management at L.300 - | 7,409 | 2,203 | 9,612 |
| | 859,242 | 255,478 | 1,114,720 |

L.7,400 of debentures, issued in 1813, were funded this year in the 3 per cent. reduced. Capital funded, L.11,100. Interest, L.333.

1815.

| | |
|---|---|
| *T.* Exchequer Bills funded, amount - - | L.10,313,000 |
| Capital funded at L.117 in 5 per cent. navy, - | L.12,066,210 |
| Interest at 5 per cent. - - - - | L.603,310 |
| Management at L.300, - - - - | 3,620 |
| Total charge, - - - - - | L.606,930 |

*U.* Exchequer Bills and Loan, funded in 5 per cent. navy.

| | | |
|---|---|---|
| Bills, L.814,500, funded at L.117, | - - | L.952,965 |
| Loan, 7,008,089, funded for* | - - - | 8,189,227 |
| L.7,822,589 | Capital funded - | L.9,142,192 |
| Interest at 5 per cent. | - - - - | L.457,109 |
| Management at L.300, | - - - - | 2,742 |
| Total charge | - - - - - | L.459,851 |

*V.* Joint loan for Britain and Ireland, funded at L.130 in 3 per cent. reduced, L.44 in 3 per cent. cons., and L.10 in 4 per cent. cons.

| | Britain. | Ireland. | Total. |
|---|---|---|---|
| Sums raised, - - | 27,000,000 | 9,000,000 | 36,000,000 |
| Capital fund. in 3 p. ct. red. | 35,100,000 | 11,700,000 | 46,800,000 |
| in 3 per cents. cons. | 11,880,000 | 3,960,000 | 15,840,000 |
| Capital funded in 3 p. cents. | 46,980,000 | 15,660,000 | 62,640,000 |
| in 4 per cents. | 2,700,000 | 900,000 | 3,600,000 |
| Total funded, - - | 49,680,000 | 16,560,000 | 66,240,000 |
| Interest of 3 per cents. - | 1,409,400 | 469,800 | 1,879,200 |
| of 4 per cents. - | 108,000 | 36,000 | 144,000 |
| Total interest, - - | 1,517,400 | 505,800 | 2,023,200 |
| Management at L.300 - | 14,904 | 4,968 | 19,872 |
| Total charge, - - | 1,532,304 | 510,768 | 2,043,072 |

1816.

*W.* Loan from Bank of England, at par.

| | | |
|---|---|---|
| Sum borrowed, | - - - - - | L.3,000,000 |
| Capital funded, | - - - - - | 3,000,000 |
| Interest at 3 per cent | - - - - | L.90,000 |

The loan in 1811 marked *I*, and that in 1812 marked *M*, were partly made in Exchequer Bills.

In 1809, an option was given to the holders of the 3 per cent. stock,



* This sum, at L.117, the terms granted for the loan, would amount to L.8,199,464 ; but the sum stated in the official account, 1st February, 1816, is only L.8,189,227.

stock, and of the long annuities, to convert their interest into life annuities, at certain rates, according to the age of the annuitant. In consequence of this, L.3,449,955 of the 3 per cent. stock, and L.4,420 long annuities, was converted into life annuities before 1st February, 1817, amounting, after deduction of what had fallen in by death, to L.225,255. These annuities were charged on the sinking fund, and the dividend, discharged by the extinction of the capital, amounting to L.107,918, applied to that fund.

An abstract of all these operations, together with the amount of the public debt, and the charge on the same at the commencement of the war, 1793; at the peace of Amiens, 1802; and on the 1st February, 1817, is exhibited in Table II.

It appears that the amount of the funded debt of Britain at the peace of Amiens, was,

| | |
|---|---|
| In the 3 per cents. - - | L.467,105,854 |
| In the 4 per cents. - - | 49,425,085 |
| In the 5 per cents. - - | 50,478,039 |
| Amount of funded capital - - | L.567,008,978 |
| Interest on above, - - | L.18,466,040 |
| Annuities for years or lives, - | 1,604,915 |
| Charges of management - - | 266,870 |
| Amount of annual charge, - | L.20,337,825 |

And on the 1st February, 1817, the amount of funded debt was,

| | | |
|---|---|---|
| In the 3 per cents. - - | | L.789,657,140 |
| In the 4 per cents. - - | | 76,777,744 |
| In the 5 per cents. - - | | 133,883,855 |
| Amount of funded capital, - | | L.1,000,318,739 |
| Interest on above, - - | | L.33,455,017 |
| Long annuities which terminate in 1860, - - - - | L.1,224,961 | |
| Annuities for lives,* - | 73,398 | |
| Ditto for capital converted, | 225,255 | |
| | | 1,523,614 |
| Charges of management,† - - | | 245,350 |
| Amount of annual charge - | | L.35,223,981 |



* See Note XXI. † See Note XXII.

## IRISH FUNDED DEBT.

We have already noticed, that part of most of the loans made in Britain since 1797, has been for the use of Ireland; and several separate loans have also been made in Britain for Ireland. The interest and other charges on these loans have been annually remitted from the treasury of Ireland to the British treasury.

Table IV. contains a state of the sums raised by these loans, and the capitals funded in the 3 per cents. 4 per cents. and 5 per cents.; the total capital funded each year; the amount of the Irish debt payable in Britain at the end of each year: also, the interest, annuities, and charges of management, contracted by each loan.

| | |
|---|---|
| It appears that the whole sum raised in Britain for Ireland, and guaranteed, to 1st February, 1817, is - - | L.64,750,000 |
| The capital funded in the 3 per cents, - | L.94,856,375 |
| in the 4 per cents. - | 5,954,375 |
| in the 5 per cents. - | 2,222,000 |
| Amount of capital funded and guaranteed in Britain for Ireland, - - - | L.103,032,750 |
| Interest of the above Irish debt, - - | L.3,194,966 |
| Annuities which terminate in 1860, - - | 129,583 |
| Charges of management, - - - | 28,826 |
| | L.3,353,375 |

Besides this, L.4,500,000, part of the loan raised in Britain in 1811 was for the use of Ireland; for which there was funded L.5,400,000, in the 3 per cents.; L.900,000 in the 4 per cents.; and a long annuity granted of L.15,562; but the interest of this being paid by Britain, is not stated in the account of the Irish debt.

But this is only part of the Irish funded debt. Another part has been funded in Ireland, the interest of which is payable, and the capital redeemable there.

The first operations in that kingdom were by tontine annuities. In the years 1773, 1775, and 1777, L.740,000 was raised in that manner, and annuities granted to the extent of L.48,900.



The

The method generally followed of late is that of granting a funded capital in the $3\frac{1}{2}$ per cents, equal to the sum borrowed, and an additional funded capital in the 5 per cents. such as the lender would accept of. Sometimes a *Douceur* in Irish treasury bills has been also granted.

The progress of the whole Irish funded debt is exhibited in Table V.

The sums raised for Ireland from 1773, when the public debt of that country commenced, to 5th January, 1817, were,

| | | Irish Currency.* |
|---|---|---|
| Sums raised in Britain for Ireland, including L.1,900,000 not guaranteed, L.66,650,000 British currency, - - - - | | L.72,204,166 |
| Sums raised in Ireland, - - - | | 28,435,667 |
| Total raised, - - - - - | | L.100,639,833 |
| Capital funded in Britain, the interest payable in London and guaranteed, | L.103,032,750 | |
| and a further sum, the interest of which is also payable in London but not guaranteed, - - - | 1,900,000 | |
| | L.104,932,750 | |
| equal in Irish currency to - - | | L.113,677,146 |
| Capital funded in Ireland, and the interest payable in Dublin. | | |
| $3\frac{1}{2}$ per cents. - | L.17,380,972 | |
| 4 per cents. - | 1,150,100 | |
| 5 per cents. - | 13,611,448 | |
| | | 32,142,520 |
| Total Irish funded debt, payable in London and Dublin, - - - - | | L.145,819,666 |
| Interest on above, - - - - - | | L.4,899,040 |
| Annuities, - - - - - | | 188,049 |
| | | L.5,087,089 |
| Management (5th January 1817,) | | 30,305 |
| | | L.5,117,395 |

By the articles of Union between Britain and Ireland, which took effect 1st January 1801, the debts of each country, existing at that time



* L.12 of British currency at par, is equal to L.13 Irish: But in the actual rate of exchange, the difference is often greater.

time, and their interest, were to continue as separate charges on the revenues of the respective countries; and such future expenses as were for the special service of either country, were to be charged on the revenue of the same: But the general charges for the army, navy, &c. being alike for the defence or advantage of each country. were appointed to be charged in the proportion of 15-17ths to Britain, and 2-17ths to Ireland.

But these arrangements are now done away. By an act passed in 1816, all the public revenues of Great Britain and Ireland are consolidated and applied to the service of the United Kingdom; and from the 5th January, 1817, the whole of the national debts of both kingdoms, and the interest and sinking funds, compose one consolidated national debt, interest and sinking fund.

When the Union between England and Scotland was accomplished in 1707, as Scotland was subjected, by the articles, to the payment of certain duties of customs and excise, then payable in England, and applicable to the debt of England contracted before the Union, it was agreed that the sum of L.398,085 should be granted by the Parliament of England as an equivalent for the same; and this sum was applied to the payment of the small public debt then due by Scotland, the indemnification of the losses sustained by the Darien Company, the improvement of fisheries and manufactures in Scotland, and some other public purposes.

The public debt of Scotland amounted at the Union to L.248,550; and the creditors were incorporated in 1724, under the name of the *Equivalent Company*, with a stock to that extent, and an annual payment of L.10,000 till redeemed.—L.111,348 of this sum was subscribed in 1727 into the Royal Bank of Scotland, and forms the original stock of that Company, and the remainder forms the present stock of the Equivalent Company.

---

## IMPERIAL LOANS.

Two loans have been raised in Britain for the Emperor of Germany, and guaranteed by the British government. The interest, if not provided by the Emperor, (and he has never made any provision) to be paid from the consolidated fund. The money for these loans was advanced by the subscribers to the British loans, in proportion to their subscriptions. The particulars are,

Loan of 1795, contracted at a capital of L.83. 6s. 8d. in a fund at 3 per cents. for each L.100 advanced, and an annuity of L.5 for 25 years.

 Loan

Loan of 1797, at a capital of L.226. 10s. in a 3 per cent. fund, for each L.100 advanced.

| Year. | Sum raised. | Funded at 3 per cent. | Interest. | Annuity. | Management. | Total charge. |
|---|---|---|---|---|---|---|
| 1795 | 4,600,000 | 3,833,333 | 115,000 | 230,000 | 4,312 | 349,312 |
| 1797 | 1,620,000 | 3,669,300 | 110,079 | | 1,651 | 111,730 |
| | 6,220,000 | 7,502,633 | 225,079 | 230,000 | 5,963 | 461,042 |
| | | Reduction in management, | | | 2,111 | 2,111 |
| | | | | | 3,852 | 458,931 |

## LOAN TO PORTUGAL.

A Loan of L.600,000 for the service of Portugal, was raised and guaranteed by Britain in 1809, and connected with the loan of that year, in the manner explained in Note XIX.

| | |
|---|---|
| The sum funded in the 3 per cent. reduced, was, - | L.895,522 |
| Interest, - - - - - - | L.26,865 |
| Management, - - - - - - | 314 |
| Annual charge, (besides sinking fund of L.30,000,) - | L.27,179 |

## MANAGEMENT OF THE NATIONAL DEBT.

The management of the national debt is conducted by the Bank of England, except a small part which is in the hands of the South Sea Company. The expense of management, in most articles, previous to 1786, was at the rate of L.562. 10s. per million of capital, whether of a three, four, or five per cent. annuity, reckoning L.40,000 of terminable annuities, equal to a million of capital.

In 1786, the rate of management was reduced to L.450 per million; and this was confirmed by an act of parliament in 1791.

In 1808, the rate of management was further reduced, and settled on the following terms:

L.450 per million, if the capital exceeded 300 millions, but fell below 400 millions.

L.340 per million, if the capital exceeded 400 millions, but fell below 600 millions.

L.300 per million, on such part of the public debt as exceeded 600 millions.

No agreement was made for the case of the public debt falling below 300 millions.

Besides these allowances for management, the bank receives considerable sums for conducting loans and lotteries. The sum at present allowed for receiving contributions to the loans, is L.800 per million, and for transacting the business of the lotteries, at the rate of L.1000 for each contract of 20,000 tickets.

---

# CHAPTER II.

## *Plans adopted for the Reduction of the Funded Debt, and their Operation.*

### SECTION I.

### SIR ROBERT WALPOLE'S SINKING FUND.*

THE first plan for the discharge of the national debt, formed on a regular system, and conducted for some time with a considerable degree of firmness, was that of the Sinking Fund established in 1716. The author of this plan was the Earl of Stanhope; but as it was adopted under the administration of Sir Robert Walpole, it is commonly denominated from him. The taxes which had been laid on before for limited periods, being rendered perpetual, and distributed among the *South Sea*, *Aggregate*, and *General Funds*, as has been mentioned already, and the produce of these funds being greater than the charges



upon

---

* This account of Sir Robert Walpole's sinking fund, is chiefly taken from Dr. Price's writings.

upon them, the surplusses, together with such farther surplusses as might afterwards accrue, were united under the name of the *Sinking Fund*, being appropriated for the discharge of the national debt, and expressly ordained to be applicable to no other purpose whatever. The legal interest had been reduced from six to five per cent. about two years before, and as that reduction was conformable to the commercial state of the country, Government was now able to obtain the same reduction on the interest of the public debt, and apply the savings in aid of the sinking fund. In 1727, a further reduction of the interest of the public debt, from five to four per cent. was obtained, by which nearly L.400,000 was added to the sinking fund. And in the year 1749, the interest of part of the debt was again reduced to three and a half per cent. for seven years, and to three per cent. thereafter; and in 1750, the interest of the remainder was reduced to three and a half per cent. for five years, and to three per cent. thereafter, by which a further saving of about L.600,000 was added to the sinking fund.

The opinion, strongly urged since by Dr. Price, seems to have been entertained at that time, of the importance of applying the produce of the sinking fund invariably to the discharge of the national debt, and borrowing by new loans, when the public exigencies required it. Accordingly, about eight millions were borrowed towards the supplies between 1718 and 1732, being a period of peace.* The sums applied from the sinking fund to the discharge of the national debt, from 1716 to 1728, amounted to

 L.6,648,000

* The particulars were given in our former editions, from Dr. Price's appeal to the public, amounting to L.6,168,732 before 1729, and to L.8,418,732 before 1732. If, instead of these sums, we take the loans as stated above, pages 82, 83, and 84, the difference is not important.

L.6,648,000, being nearly equal to the additional debt contracted in that time. About five millions more were paid between 1728 and 1733. The interest of several loans contracted between 1727 and 1732, was charged upon surplus duties, which, according to the original plan, ought to have been appropriated to the sinking fund.

Soon after, the principle of preserving the sinking fund inviolable was abandoned. In 1733, L.500,000 was taken from that fund, and applied to the services of the year. The reason for adopting that measure was to keep the land-tax, the burthen of which was then much complained of by the landed interest, at the low rate of a shilling in the pound. In 1734, L.1,200,000 was taken from the sinking fund, for current services; and in 1735 it was anticipated and mortgaged.

In the loans contracted after the establishment of the sinking fund, and charged upon special duties, that fund was made a collateral security. By this arrangement, when a tax produced less than was charged on it, the sinking fund supplied the deficiency; but when it produced more, the overplus, instead of being applied to the sinking fund, was carried to the service of the year. By an act passed in 1752, another regulation was introduced: All the new taxes were appointed to be carried directly to the sinking fund, which was charged with the interest on the loans. At first, the sinking fund lost more than it gained by this arrangement, as most of the new taxes proved deficient; but this loss was afterwards more than recompensed.

The only deviation from this plan was the additional tax upon houses and windows, granted in 1758, and applied directly to the payment of the interest of the loan contracted that year, without being carried to the sinking fund. This tax proving deficient, the deficiency was made good from the sinking fund, and afterwards replaced from the supplies.

The produce of the sinking fund, at its commencement in 1717, was, - - - L.323,437

| | |
|---|---|
| Medium annual produce, from 1717 to 1726, both inclusive, - - | 577,614 |
| From 1727 to 1736, - - | 1,132,251 |
| — 1737 to 1746, - - | 1,062,170 |
| — 1747 to 1756, - - | 1,356,758 |
| — 1757 to 1766, - - | 2,059,406 |
| — 1765 to 1769, - - | 2,234,780 |
| — 1770 to 1774, - - | 2,610,759 |

| | |
|---|---|
| In 1775, - - - | L.2,917,869 |
| 1776, - - - | 3,166,517 |
| 1777, - - - | 2,685,669 |
| 1778, - - - | 2,442,063 |
| 1779, - - - | 2,267,399 |
| 1780, - - - | 2,403,017 |

The sinking fund would have risen higher, had it not been depressed, especially in the later period, by various incroachments. It was charged with the interest of several loans, for which no provision was made; and in 1772, it was charged, with an annuity of L.100,000, granted in addition to the civil list. During the three wars which were waged while it subsisted, the whole of its produce was applied to the expense of the war; and even in time of peace, large sums were abstracted from it for current services. According to Dr. Price, the amount of public debt paid off by the sinking fund, since its first alienation in 1733, was only

Three millions paid off in 1736 and 1737.

Three millions in the peace between 1748 and 1756.

Two millions and a half in the peace between 1763 and 1775.

In all, eight millions and a half.

The additional debt discharged during these periods of



peace

peace was effected, not by the sinking fund, but from other sources.

On the whole, this fund did little in time of peace, and nothing in time of war, to the discharge of the national debt. The purpose of its inviolable application was abandoned, and the hopes entertained of its powerful efficacy entirely disappointed. At this time, the nation had no other free revenue except the land and malt tax, granted annually; and as the land tax during peace was then granted at a low rate, their produce was inadequate to the expense of a peace establishment, on the most moderate scale. This gave occasion to the incroachments on the sinking fund. Had the land tax been always continued at four shillings in the pound, it would have gone far to keep the sinking fund, during peace, inviolate.

This fund terminated in 1786, when the arrangements detailed in the following section, were adopted.

---

## SECTION II.

### MR. PITT'S SINKING FUNDS.

### 1786.

THE present sinking fund was established under Mr. Pitt's administration, in 1786. The various branches of revenue then existing were united under the name of the consolidated fund.* One million taken from that fund, was vested annually in the hands of Commissioners for the redemption of the national debt, to be applied for purchasing capital in such stocks as they should judge expedient, at the market prices. To this fund was to be added, the interest of the debt redeemed, and annuities



* See Note XXIII.

fallen in by the failure of lives, or the expiry of the terms for which they were granted, and life annuities unclaimed for three years were considered as expired, and added to the sinking fund. When this fund amounted to four millions, it was enacted, that the interest of the redeemed debt, and annuities fallen in, were no longer to be applied to it, but remain at the disposal of Parliament.

1792.

Another sinking fund was established this year, of one per cent. on the nominal capital of each loan, to which the dividends on the capital redeemed by this fund were to be added. When annuities for a longer term than forty-five years, or for lives, were granted, the value which would remain after forty-five years, was appointed to be estimated, and one per cent. on that value set aside for their redemption. This fund was appointed to be kept separate, and applied for the redemption of the debts contracted subsequent to its institution, by which means it was estimated that every loan would be redeemed in forty-five years* at furthest from its contraction.

In the same year, L.400,000 was granted in aid of the former sinking fund, and L.200,000 was granted by annual acts for the same purpose, till 1802, when the grant was rendered perpetual. Savings by reduction of the rate of interest of the national debt, were appointed to be added to that sinking fund; but no savings of this kind have taken place since its commencement.

1798.

This year, the application of one per cent. on the capital of the loans to the sinking fund, was deviated from. A



* See Note XXIV.

part of the loan, (16 millions capital,) was charged on a tax then imposed, called the aid and contribution tax; for which the income tax was substituted the following year. In like manner, a part, or the whole of the loans for several years, was charged on the income tax, and no sinking fund of one per cent. provided for their redemption. The amount of capital for which no sinking fund of one per cent. was provided, is L.86,796,375. This system was abandoned in 1802, when all the loans were united, and the interest of these loans charged on the consolidated fund.

1802.

The two sinking funds were united, applicable to the discharge of debts existing in 1802; and the system of a sinking fund of one per cent. on loans subsequent to 1802, was revived, and has been followed in all the subsequent loans till 1813, except that of 1807, when Lord Henry Petty's system was adopted. The limitation of the sinking fund to four millions, enacted at its commencement, and a similar limitation in 1792, were repealed; and the application of annuities whose term was expired, and of savings by the reduction of the rate of interest, to the sinking fund, was repealed.

Table VI. contains a state of the loans from 1793, distinguishing those that were charged and those that were not charged with the sinking fund of one per cent. and the present amount of that fund.

---

## SECTION III.

### LORD HENRY PETTY'S PLAN OF FINANCE.

A NEW plan of finance was proposed to Parliament in 1807, by Lord Henry Petty, (now Marquis of Lansdowne,) Chancellor

Chancellor of the Exchequer, and adopted in the arrangement of the loan for that year.

The annual expenditure during war, was estimated at L.32,000,000 beyond what the surplus of the consolidated fund, and the annual taxes, could supply. The war taxes were estimated at 21 millions, viz. property tax, L.11,500,000, and other articles, L.9,500,000. The annual deficiency to be supplied by loan was therefore 11 millions, which were proposed to be raised by mortgaging the war taxes to the extent of ten per cent. on the sum borrowed; the surplus of which sum mortgaged, after paying for interest and management, was to form a sinking fund for redeeming the debt, and thereby disengaging the part of the war taxes mortgaged, in a certain number of years, according to the rate of interest at which the loan was transacted. Thus, if the interest and management was five per cent. there would remain five per cent. as a sinking fund, and this would pay off the debt in fourteen years. The sums proposed to be borrowed in this manner were 12 millions for the first three years, 14 millions for the fourth, and 16 millions for each of the succeeding ten years, amounting altogether to 210 millions, for which, at the rate of ten per cent. the whole of the war taxes would be mortgaged: But the debt contracted the first year being now paid off by the sinking fund appropriated to it, the portion of the war taxes mortgaged for it would be set free, and be applicable to the loan of the following year; and another portion being set free the following and each succeeding year, these loans might be continued on this system without limitation of time.

But as the sums mortgaged for these loans were withdrawn from the war taxes, it was necessary to replace the same; and this was proposed to be done by raising supplementary loans, the annual amount of which would be equal to the sum mortgaged, deducting the excess of the war tax loan for the year, above the sum of L.11,000,000 wanted.

| | |
|---|---|
| Thus, the first year, the sum borrowed is, | L.12,000,000 |
| Of which required, - - - | 11,000,000 |
| Excess, - - - - | L1,000,000 |
| Portion of war taxes mortgaged, - | L.1,200,000 |
| Deduct above excess - - - | 1,000,000 |
| Sum to be raised by supplementary loan, first year, - - - - | L.200,000 |
| The second year an equal portion of the war taxes was proposed to be mortgaged, amounting together with the former, to | L.2,400,000 |
| Deduct excess of loan as before, - | 1,000,000 |
| Sum to be raised by supplementary loan, second year, - - - - | L.1,400,000 |

In this manner, the supplementary loan of the fourteenth year, would amount to 16 millions, and the amount of these loans for fourteen years, to L.94,200,000. In the fifteenth year, it would amount to 20 millions, which sum it would never exceed, and never fall below 16 millions. In twenty years, the amount of these loans would be L.204,200,000; and in each period of fourteen years after the first, the amount of supplementary loans would be 238 millions.

A sinking fund of one per cent. on the nominal capital, supposed funded in the three per cents. at 60, and therefore equal to 1-60th of the sum borrowed, was, agreeably to the system of 1792, to be added to the interest of these supplementary loans; and this charge to be provided for



by

by imposing new taxes. It was proposed to diminish the amount of these taxes, or to supersede them altogether, by taking aid from the falling in of annuities, and from the surplus of the present sinking fund, after the amount of the same should exceed the interest of the debt remaining unredeemed. This surplus was expected to become available in the year 1817.

If a larger sum than 11 millions was required for the service of any year, it was to be raised by other arrangements.

As the ministry who planned this system did not continue long in office, it was never followed out after the first year. Its merits will be considered afterwards.

---

## SECTION IV.

### MR. VANSITTART'S PLAN OF FINANCE.

THE plan of finance proposed in 1813 by Mr. Vansittart, and adopted by Parliament, is a modification of Mr. Pitt's sinking funds; and, among other objects, is intended to rescind the alterations, which have been made in these funds, as originally established in 1786 and 1792, by subsequent acts of Parliament, and restore them, as far as practicable, to the state in which they would have stood if no such alterations had taken place. It will be proper, therefore, to recapitulate the original enactments and alterations, in order to render the new system more clearly intelligible.

The original sinking fund of 1786, consisting of an annual grant of L.1,000,000 from the consolidated fund, (increased in 1792 to L.1,200,000) together with the interest of the debt redeemed, and annuities for lives or years which might expire, but limited not to exceed four millions, was appropriated for the redemption of the debt then existing,

 of

of L.238,231,248 ; and therefore when a sum of redeemed debt, to that amount, should be vested in the hands of the Commissioners, that debt was to be considered as discharged.

In 1792, when the war with France commenced, and new loans became necessary, a sinking fund of one per cent. was created on the nominal sum of each loan, which, it was estimated, would redeem it within 45 years at farthest from its contraction. In the succeeding years this system was so far deviated from, that loans to the amount of L.86,796,375 were contracted, without any sinking fund being provided for their discharge.

Had the original system of 1786 and 1792 been adhered to, so soon as the debt of 1786 was redeemed, the nation would have been eased of taxes to the amount of the interest of that debt, and of the sum appropriated to the first sinking fund; or these sums, or any part of them, might have been reserved for the charge of such loans as the exigencies of the times should require.

Also, after 45 years, or perhaps a shorter period, from the contraction of each loan, the nation would have been eased of taxes to the amount of the interest and sinking fund of that loan, or these sums reserved to bear the charge of future loans, as above-mentioned.

In 1802, the two sinking funds were united and appropriated to the discharge of the debt existing at that time, amounting to L.567,008,978, or, deducting the part then redeemed, to L.499,753,063, besides annuities for lives or years. The limitation of the sinking fund to four millions was repealed; and loans contracted in future were to be accompanied with a sinking fund of one per cent.; each sinking fund of this kind being applied, agreeably to the enactment of 1792, to the separate discharge of the loan to which it was attached, until that loan was completely discharged; and then to terminate, or be released for future exigencies.

 The

The effects produced by these alterations in the sinking funds were,

1st. The prospect of any relief from existing burthens, or the release of any funds at present appropriated, for future exigencies, was protracted by the union of the sinking funds to a more distant period. By the original plan, such relief would have taken place when the debt of 1786, (amount L.238,231,248,) was redeemed, which was expected about 1813. By the union of the sinking funds, no relief could be obtained till the debt of 1802 (amount L.499,753,063) should be relieved, which was not expected till 1830.

2d. By repealing the limitation of the sinking fund to four millions, the united amount has been increased far beyond what was originally intended.

3d. The amount of taxes for supplying this enlarged sinking fund has been much increased, at the same time that no relief is obtained from the repeal of the taxes appropriated to the redeemed debt, until the whole debt existing in 1802 shall be redeemed.

The design of Mr. Vansittart's plan is to counteract these effects; to provide at present that relief which the public would have obtained from the original plan; to restrain the excessive increase of the sinking fund; and, at the same time, to afford equal security to the public creditors as they were entitled to by the act of 1792, by securing the redemption of each loan in some way or other, within a period not exceeding 45 years at farthest from its contraction.

For these purposes it was proposed, 1st. That whereas a sum equal to the debt of 1786, and bearing an interest nearly equal to the interest of that debt, is now vested in the hands of the Commissioners; that so soon as the interest of the debt redeemed shall become fully equal to that of the debt of 1786, that debt should be declared discharged, and the sums hitherto appropriated for the

 interest

interest and sinking fund of the same shall be appropriated, so soon as required, to bear the charge of future loans; and therefore no new taxes should be imposed for the interest or sinking fund of the new loans, till the same amount to a sum equal to the interest of that considered as released. By this means the supposed loans of 1813, 1814, 1815, 1816, and part of that of 1817, were expected to be defrayed without any additional taxes.

2d. Whereas loans to the extent of L.86,796,375 were charged on the consolidated fund in 1802, without any sinking fund attached to them, in consideration that the advantages abovementioned, given to the general sinking fund by the enactments of that year, enabled it to bear that burthen; it was proposed, now that these enactments are partially repealed by the new system, in order to place the public creditors in a situation equally favourable to what they held by the establishment of 1792, that the one per cent. sinking fund on the abovementioned sum, amounting to L.867,963, should be replaced to it.

3d. That as the amount of exchequer bills in circulation, and not redeemed within the year, has much increased, and was then about L.26,000,000, that a sinking fund of one per cent. on that sum, or L.260,000, should be provided; and that taxes to the amount of L.1,127,963 should be imposed the first year, to meet that sum, together with the sum mentioned in the last article; and that, in like manner, a sinking fund of one per cent. should be annually provided for any addition to the amount of exchequer bills in circulation, for the discharge of which, within the year, no funds are provided.

4th. That, in future, instead of allocating the sinking fund of one per cent. for the discharge of each separate loan, the whole funds of this kind should be united, and applied to the discharge of the first contracted loan; and so soon as a sum equal to that loan shall be redeemed, the charge on the same should be considered as released for

 the

the public service; and in like manner each successive loan should be redeemed, and its charge released, in the order of their contraction, by the united produce of the sinking funds appropriated for the redemption of all the loans contracted since 1792: But the whole sinking fund created by the act of 1786, or by any subsequent acts, should be continued and applied, until the total redemption of all the debt now existing; or to be created during the present war.

5th. As, by this arrangement, the discharge of successive loans, instead of commencing from their contraction, is postponed till all prior loans be discharged; in order more effectually to secure the payment of each loan within forty-five years, a sinking fund, for the excess of the loan above the sum applicable in the same year to the reduction of the public debt, should be provided, equal to one-half of the interest, and a sinking fund of one per cent. on the nominal capital of the remainder, agreeably to the act of 1792.*

6th. That the amount of taxes imposed each year should be determined as follows:—The timeof the discharge of each loan, according to article 4th, being estimated, and the charge on the loan for the year, according to article 5th: Then, if no loan falls in within the year, new taxes should be imposed equal to the interest and sinking fund of the loan contracted; but, if one or more loans fall in, the interest on these loans, being released, shall be appropriated to the charge of the new one, and taxes imposed for the surplus only; and if the interest on the loans released exceed the charge on the loans contracted, no taxes shall be imposed that year; and the surplus of interest released shall be reserved in aid of the charge of the loan of the subsequent year.



* See Note XXV. Also Table XI.

## SECTION V.

### REDEMPTION OF THE NATIONAL DEBT BY THE PURCHASE OF THE LAND TAX.

Taxes in various forms have been frequently but not permanently imposed on land in England, from a very remote time. The present land tax commenced at the Revolution, and was brought to its present form in 1692, when a valuation of the land was made, and although considerably below the real value at the time, it afforded a revenue of about L.500,000, at one shilling per pound, including a like tax upon personal property, estimated at a very low rate. The valuation made at that time has never been altered; and the tax has been imposed annually till 1798, sometimes at one shilling, sometimes at two shillings, sometimes at three shillings, most frequently at four shillings, which rate it has never exceeded. This tax was long considered as a heavy burthen, and much resisted by the landed interest. Of late years it has been less regarded, partly from the increasing influence of the mercantile interest, and partly from its becoming, in consequence of the increase of the rent of land, the deterioration of the value of money, and the general magnitude of our taxes, comparatively an inferior object.

In 1798, the land tax was rendered perpetual at four shillings per pound, and the proprietors were empowered to purchase the sums charged on their estates for capital in the three per cents. affording an equal dividend. If they did not accept this offer within a limited time, it might be sold to others for capital affording a dividend of one-fifth more than the tax purchased. The term for purchase has been since repeatedly extended, and various regulations enacted. In consequence of these enactments, the purchases of land tax amounted the first year to L.13,059,586 in the 3 per cents., and the second year to L.3,034,216, but afterwards the purchases went on languidly; and after eighteen years the amount of capital transferred for this purpose, on the 1st February, 1817, was L.25,290,994, the interest of which, L.758,730, was deducted from the national charge; but nearly an equal sum of land tax being redeemed, was deducted from the national revenue, being somewhat more than one-third of the whole. In order to encourage the completion of this scheme, an act was passed, session 1813, in which terms more advantageous to the purchaser were offered.*

This plan is, in effect, no other than a transfer of part of the capital of the funded debt from the former stockholders to the landed proprietors. These last pay a value for the capital with which they redeem their land tax, and their relief from that tax is equivalent to their receiving a dividend to the same extent. The landholders may still be considered as subjected to the land tax at its highest rate; though some of them pay it by drawing a dividend for capital in the funds, which they have purchased for value, and have thereby become stockholders to that extent. The public revenue may still be considered as drawing the whole of the land tax, and paying the whole of the dividends. Could the portions of other taxes payable by particular classes of men be ascertained, it might as well be proposed to them to purchase an exemption from these taxes. Such of them as were able might embrace the offer, and after they had paid the value and received their exemption, they would be exactly in the same circumstances as if they had purchased capital in the funds,



* See Note XXVI.

funds, drawn their dividends, and applied them in payment of taxes. The public, in like manner, would lose in taxes what they saved in dividends. We cannot, therefore, consider the part of the national debt redeemed by the purchase of the land tax as affording any relief to the public burthens.

It has always been considered as necessary, upon the principles of the British constitution, that part of the taxes should be granted annually by Parliament as a restraint on the power of the Crown. The land and malt taxes, producing about L.2,700,000 annually, were formerly reserved for this purpose. Since the land tax was rendered perpetual, certain duties on sugar and tobacco, and on offices, pensions, and salaries, have been granted annually, together with the malt tax. The average net annual amount of these taxes for three years preceding 5th January, 1817, was L.5,040,195.

---

## SECTION VI.

### OPERATION OF THE SINKING FUNDS.

THE amount of money applied for the redemption of the national funded debt, and of capital and interest redeemed since the commencement of the sinking fund in 1786, to 1st February, 1817, and the produce of the sinking fund at that time, are as follows:



3 per

| | Sums expended. | Capital redeemed. | Interest redeemed. |
|---|---|---|---|
| 3 per cents. - - - | 176,652,174 | 283,777,272 | 8,513,319 |
| 4 per cents. - - - | 6,586,934 | 7,796,400 | 311,856 |
| 5 per cents. - - - | 130,113 | 145,500 | 7,275 |
| | 183,369,223 | 291,719,172 | 8,832,450 |
| Unclaimed for 10 years, 3 per cents. - | | 176,441 | 5,293 |
| 4 per cents. - | | 16,313 | 652 |
| 5 per cents. - | | 19,503 | 975 |
| 3 per cent. reduced stock, purchased with unclaimed dividends, - - - | | 327,000 | 9,810 |
| | | 292,258,430 | 8,849,181 |
| Converted into life annuities, - - - | | 3,449,955 | 103,498 |
| Long annuities converted into life annuities, | | - - | 4,420 |
| Transferred to purchase land tax, - - | | 25,290,994 | |
| | | 320,999,379 | 8,957,100 |
| Permanent annual grant, 26 Geo. III. - | | - - | 1,000,000 |
| Additional annual grant, 42 Geo. III. - | | - - | 200,000 |
| Amount of 1 per cent. on loans preceding 1st February, 1813, - - - - - | | 4,683,542 | |
| On loans 1798, 1799, 1800, and 1802, not formerly charged, - - - - - | | 867,963 | |
| Sinking fund on long annuities, - - | | 49,548 | |
| | | | 5,601,053 |
| Sinking Fund on Exchequer Bills. - - - - - | | | 200,000 |
| Sinking fund on Lord Henry Petty's plan, - - - | | | 626,255 |
| Sinking fund on loans 1813, 14, and 1815, on Mr. Vansittart's plan, - - - - - - - | | | 2,756,518 |
| Annuities of which the term is expired, - - - | | | 79,880 |
| Annuities of which the nominees died prior to 5th July 1802, - - - - - - - - - | | | 21,481 |
| Annuities unclaimed for 3 years, - - - - - | | | 28,838 |
| Long annuities unclaimed for 10 years, - - - | | | 471 |
| | | | 19,531,598 |
| Deduct charge on loans 1813 and 1814, on Mr. Vansittart's plan, - - - - - - - - | | L.5,782,969 | |
| Part of charge on loan 1815, - - - - | | 1,850,000 | 7,632,969 |
| | | | 11,898,629 |
| Also life annuities charged on this fund, - - - - | | | 225,255 |
| Sinking fund, 1st February, 1817, - - - - - | | | 11,673,374 |

| | | |
|---|---|---|
| The sum payable to the Commissioners for the Reduction of the National Debt, by official account, 5th January, 1817, was, - - - - - | | L.11,869,790 |
| Add unclaimed annuities, - - - | | 28,838 |
| | | L.11,898,629 |

The 3 per cents. were redeemed, at an average, nearly at $62\frac{1}{4}$ per cent.

The 4 per cents. at $84\frac{1}{2}$.

The 5 per cents. at $89\frac{3}{8}$.

| | | |
|---|---|---|
| The debt funded before 1st February, 1817, was | | L.1,003,768,694 |
| Of which transferred for life annuities, - | | 3,449,955 |
| | | L.1,000,318,739 |
| Transferred for land tax, - - - | | 25,290,994 |
| Transferred to Commissioners, - - | | L.975,027,745 |
| For stock purchased by sinking fund, - | L.291,719,172 | |
| Unclaimed for 10 years, - | 212,258 | |
| Stock purchased with unclaimed dividends, - - | 327,000 | |
| | | 292,258,430 |
| Unredeemed debt of Britain, 1st February 1817, | | L.682,769,315 |

Which debt was invested in the following funds:

| | | |
|---|---|---|
| Bank annuities, - - - | | L.14,686,338 |
| Loan of 1726, - - - | | 1,000,000 |
| South Sea annuities, including loan of 1751, - | | 14,345,685 |
| 3 per cent. consolidated, - - | | 345,305,810 |
| 3 per cent. reduced, - - - | | 104,747,599 |
| | | L.480,085,432 |
| 4 per cents. - - - | | 68,965,030 |
| 5 per cent. navy, - | L.132,660,349 | |
| Ditto loyalty, - | 1,058,503 | |
| | | 133,718,852 |
| | | L.682,769,315 |
| Debt cancelled, - - - | | L.251,738,858 |
| Redeemed debt standing in the name of the Commissioners, - - - | | 40,519,572 |
| | | L.292,258,430 |

Table III. contains the amount of the capital funded debt each year,* the



* See Note XXVII.

the amount redeemed each year, and the balance, or difference, between the capital funded and the capital redeemed; also the whole funded debt existing each year, without regard to redemption; the whole debt redeemed, and the whole debt unredeemed. But this gives an imperfect view of the progress of the public debt; for the loan of the year is perhaps made in the five per cents., and the redemption in the 3 per cents.; and therefore, if the capitals only be exhibited, the debt redeemed will appear more in proportion to the debt contracted than it really is. Therefore other columns are inserted, exhibiting the value of the capital funded, the capital redeemed, and the balance, reduced to 3 per cents.; the reduction of the capital being made in proportion to the rate of interest, when the loan is wholly or partially funded at a higher rate than 3 per cent.

If the whole of the present funded debts were reduced to three per cents. the amount would stand as follows:

| | |
|---|---|
| 3 per cents. - - - | L.480,085,432 |
| Value of L.68,965,030—4 per cents. - | 91,953,373 |
| of 133,718,852—5 per cents. - | 222,864,753 |
| | L.794,903,558 |

And if this be reduced to 5 per cents. or the sum for which it might be redeemed when the 3 per cents. are at 60, it comes to L.476,942,135.

---

## SECTION VII.

### IRISH, IMPERIAL, AND PORTUGUEZE SINKING FUNDS.

A SINKING fund for the redemption of the IRISH DEBT payable in Britain, was established in 1797, similar to the British one per cent. sinking fund of 1792.

| | |
|---|---|
| The amount of this sinking fund, 1st February, 1817, was L.1 per cent. on L.103,032,750, being the amount of the Irish debt payable in Britain, and guaranteed, - | L.1,030,327 |
| Sinking fund on long annuities, - | 9,258 |
| Interest of L.19,087,846, redeemed at 3 per cent. | 572,635 |
| Amount of sinking fund for Irish debt, payable in Britain, and guaranteed, - - . | L.1,612,220 |

| | |
|---|---|
| The capital of Irish debt funded in Britain, and guaranteed, 1st February, 1817, was - | L.103,032,750 |
| Of which redeemed in 3 per cents. - | 19,087,846 |
| Unredeemed debt - - - | L.83,944,904 |



This

This capital is invested in the following funds:

| | |
|---|---|
| 3 per cent. cons. - - - | L.32,819,955 |
| 3 per cent. reduced, - - | 42,948,574 |
| 4 per cents. - - - | 5,954,375 |
| 5 per cent. navy, - - - | 2,222,000 |
| | L.83,944,904 |

| | |
|---|---|
| Which, reduced to 3 per cent., amount to - | L.87,411,028 |
| And to 5 per cents. - - - | 54,446,617 |

Besides this capital, L.129,583 of long annuities have been contracted, which expire in 1860.

The sum paid for redeeming the above capital of L.19,087,846, was L.11,873,490, being about 62 3-16ths at an average.

Table IV contains, besides the particulars above mentioned, the Irish debt, payable in London, redeemed each year, the total redeemed, and the balances unredeemed.

There was also a sinking fund established at the same time for the redemption of the Irish debt payable in Ireland, which consists of a permanent grant of L.67,649, of a charge of one per cent. on the loans payable in Ireland, contracted since, of dividends on stock redeemed, and of annuities fallen in. The sum appropriated annually to the sinking fund was L.100,000 Irish currency; of which L.32,351 was appropriated for the reduction of the debt borrowed in Britain, for Ireland, in 1797; and the remainder, L.67,649, together with the expired annuities, to the reduction of the remainder of the Irish debt existing before 1797:* and since 1813, an allowance of one per cent. on Irish treasury bills has been added to this fund.

The amount of capital debt payable in Ireland, redeemed on the 5th January, 1817, was,

| | Irish currency. |
|---|---|
| In the 3½ per cents. - - | L.6,478,739 |
| In the 4 per cents. - - | 471,450 |
| In the 5 per cents. - - | 1,862,472 |
| | L.8,812,662 |
| Which was redeemed for - - • | L.6,976,521 |
| And there was redeemed between the 5th January, and 1st February, 1817, in the 3½ per cents. | L.106,700 |



Making

* There have been some small variations in the distribution of this sum since its commencement.

| | | |
|---|---|---|
| Making the whole sum redeemed, 1st February, 1817, - - - | | L.8,919,362 |
| Of which cancelled, | | |
| 3½ per cents. - | L.2,231,914 | |
| 4 per cents. - | 294,500 | |
| 5 per cents. - | 1,852,072 | |
| | | L.4,378,486 |
| Uncancelled, | | |
| 3½ per cents. - | L.4,353,525 | |
| 4 per cents. - | 176,950 | |
| 5 per cents. - | 10,400 | |
| | | 4,540,876 |
| | | L.8,919,362 |

The interest on debt redeemed, 5th January, 1817, was,

| | |
|---|---|
| On L.6,478,739, at 3½ per cent. - | L.226,755 |
| On 471,450, at 4 per cent. - | 18,858 |
| On 1,862,472, at 5 per cent. - | 93,123 |
| | L.338,738 |
| On L.106,700, at 3½ per cent. redeemed before 1st February, 1817 - | 3,734 |
| | L.342,472 |

The debt remaining unredeemed, 1st February, 1817, was,

| | |
|---|---|
| 3½ per cents. - - | L.10,795,534 |
| 4 per cents. - - | 678,650 |
| 5 per cents. - - | 13,807,309 |
| | L.25,281,493 |
| Which, in British currency, is - - | L.23,336,763 |

The interest on the unredeemed debt, 5th January, 1817, was,

| | Irish currency. |
|---|---|
| On L.10,795,534, at 3½ per cent. - | L.377,843 |
| On 678,650, at 4 per cent. - | 27,146 |
| On 13,807,309, at 5 per cent. - | 690,365 |
| | L.1,095,355 |
| Which, in British currency, is - | L.1,001,097 |

 Tontine

| | |
|---|---|
| Tontine annuities of 1773, 1774, and 1775, | |
| Irish currency, - - | L.47,668 |
| British currency - - | 44,001 |

The amount of the sinking fund in Ireland, 5th January, 1817, was,

| | |
|---|---|
| Part of annual grant as above, - | L.67,649 |
| Expired annuities, - - | 72,167 |
| L.1 per cent. on loans, - - | 282,187 |
| L.1 per cent. on treasury bills, - | 27,050 |
| Interest on debt redeemed as above, - | 338,738 |
| | L.787,791 |
| Deduct interest on L.3,041,666 treasury bills, charged on this fund, at 5 per cent. - | 152,084 |
| | L.635,707 |

This fund was united to the British sinking fund, 5th Jan. 1817, and their amount is,

| | British currency. |
|---|---|
| Sinking fund in Ireland, L.635,707, - | L.586,806 |
| Sinking fund in Britain for Ireland, - | 1,612,220 |
| Amount sinking funds for Irish debt, - | L.2,199,026 |
| Sinking fund for British debt, - | 11,673,374 |
| Sinking fund of United Kingdoms, - | L.13,872,400 |

A sinking fund of one per cent. was charged on the Imperial loan, of 1797, being L.36,693 annually. There was no sinking fund for the loan of 1795. Now the amount of the two imperial loans

| | |
|---|---|
| was, - - - | L.7,502,633 |
| And the capital redeemed by the above sinking fund, or unclaimed, 1st February, 1817, | 1,920,716 |
| Imperial debt, 1st February, 1817, - | L.5,581,917 |

The above debt was redeemed for L.1,160,976, being about 60½ per cent. at an average.

The present imperial sinking fund consists of the above mentioned charge of 1 per cent. - L.36,693

| | |
|---|---|
| Dividend on L.1,920,716, redeemed or unclaimed, at 3 per cent. - - | 57,659 |
| | L.94,352 |



The

The LOAN for PORTUGAL in 1809, was charged with an annual payment of L.30,000, in addition to the interest and charges of management, for its redemption.

| | |
|---|---|
| The capital funded for that loan in the 3 per cent. reduced, was, - - - | L.895,522 |
| Of which redeemed, 1st Feb., 1817, - | 426,721 |
| And remaining unredeemed, - | L.468,801 |
| The above debt was redeemed for - | L.266,292 |

being about 63⅜ per cent.

The present sinking fund is,

| | |
|---|---|
| Annual appropriation, - - | L.30,000 |
| Dividend on L.426,721, redeemed, at 3 per cent. | 12,801 |
| | L.42,801 |

## RECAPITULATION.

By collecting the particulars above detailed, the state of the funded debt, due or guaranteed by Britain, on the 1st February, 1817, appears to be as follows :

| | 3 per cents. | 4 per cents. | 5 per cents. | Total. |
|---|---|---|---|---|
| Amount British funded debt, | 793,107,095 | 76,777,744 | 133,883,855 | 1,003,768,694 |
| Of which transferred for land tax, - | 25,290,994 | - - | - - | 25,290,994 |
| | 767,816,101 | 76,777,744 | 133,883,855 | 978,477,700 |
| Transferred for life annuities, - | 3,449,955 | - - | - - | 3,449,955 |
| | 764,366,146 | 76,777,744 | 133,883,855 | 975,027,745 |
| Irish debt, funded and guaranteed by Britain, - | 94,856,375 | 5,954,375 | 2,222,000 | 103,032,750 |
| Imperial debt, | 7,502,633 | - - | - - | 7,502,633 |
| Portuguese debt, | 895,522 | - - | - - | 895,522 |
| | 867,620,676 | 82,732,119 | 136,105,855 | 1,086,458,650 |
| Of which redeemed by sinking funds, or unclaimed. | | | | |
| British debt cancelled, - | 243,800,458 | 7,796,400 | 142,000 | 251,738,858 |
| Standing in name of Commissioners | 40,480,255 | 16,314 | 23,003 | 40,519,572 |
| Amount British debt redeemed or unclaimed | 284,280,713 | 7,812,714 | 165,003 | 292,258,430 |
| Irish, - | 19,087,846 | - - | - - | 19,087,846 |
| Imperial, - | 1,920,716 | - - | - - | 1,920,716 |
| Portuguese, - | 426,721 | - - | - - | 426,721 |
| | 305,715,996 | 7,812,714 | 165,003 | 313,693,713 |
| Leaving unredeemed, | | | | |
| British, - | 480,085,433 | 68,965,030 | 133,718,852 | 682,769,315 |
| Irish, - | 75,768,529 | 5,954,375 | 2,222,000 | 83,944,904 |
| Imperial - | 5,581,917 | - - | - - | 5,581,917 |
| Portuguese - | 468,801 | - - | - - | 468,801 |
| | 561,904,680 | 74,919,405 | 135,940,852 | 772,764,937 |

 IRISH

## IRISH DEBT.

| | $3\frac{1}{2}$ p. cents. Irish curr. | 4 per cents. Irish curr. | 5 per cents. Irish curr. | Total Irish curr. |
|---|---|---|---|---|
| Capital fund in Ireland, - | 17,380,973 | 1,150,100 | 13,611,448 | 32,142,522 |
| In Britain, for Ireland, not guaranteed, | - - | - - | 2,058,333 | 2,058,333 |
| | 17,380,973 | 1,150,100 | 15,669,781 | 34,200,855 |
| Of which redeemed by sinking fund, cancelled, - | 2,231,914 | 294,500 | 1,852,072 | 4,378,486 |
| Uncancelled, - | 4,353,525 | 176,950 | 10,400 | 4,540,876 |
| Amount redeemed, | 6,585,439 | 471,450 | 1,862,472 | 8,919,362 |
| Unredeemed, Irish currency, - | 10,795,534 | 678,650 | 13,807,309 | 25,281,493 |
| In British currency, | - - | - - | - - | 23,336,763 |

| | Existing capitals. | Reduced to 3 per cents. | Reduced to 5 per cents. |
|---|---|---|---|
| Irish, funded in Britain, and guaranteed, British currency, | 83,944,904 | 87,411,028 | 52,446,617 |
| Funded in Ireland, &c. - | 23,336,763 | 33,703,234 | 20,221,940 |
| Total Irish debt, - - | 107,281,667 | 121,114,262 | 72,668,557 |
| British debt, - - | 682,769,315 | 794,903,558 | 476,942,135 |
| Debt of United Kingdoms - | 790,050,982 | 916,017,820 | 549,610,692 |
| Imperial debt, - - | 5,581,917 | 5,581,917 | 3,349,150 |
| Portuguese debt, - - | 468,801 | 468,801 | 281,281 |
| | 796,101,700 | 922,068,538 | 553,241,123 |

And the charge for interest, annuities, management, and sinking fund, is as follows :

| | Interest. | Annuit. | Managt. | Sink. fund. | Total. |
|---|---|---|---|---|---|
| On British debt - | 33,558,516 | 1,298,830 | 407,257 | - - | 35,264,603 |
| Deduct interest of stock, transferred for land tax, | 758,730 | - - | - - | - - | 758,730 |
| | 32,799,786 | - - | - - | - - | 34,505.873 |
| And for life annuities, - | 103,499 | - - | - - | - - | 103,499 |
| | | | | | 34,402,374 |
| And add to life annuities, | - - | 225,255 | - - | - - | 225,255 |
| On Irish debt, pay in Lon. | 32,696,287 | 1,524,085 | 407,257 | - - | 34,627,629 |
| On Imperial debt, - | 3,194,966 | 129,583 | 36,956 | - - | 3,361,505 |
| On Portuguese debt, - | 225,079 | 230,000 | 5,963 | - - | 461,042 |
| | 26,865 | - - | 305 | - - | 27,170 |
| | 36,143,197 | 1,883,668 | 450,481 | - - | 38,477,346 |
| Of which redeemed or unclaimed. | | | | | |
| British, - - | 8,849,181 | 471 | 161.907 | - - | 9,011,559 |
| Irish, - - | 572,635 | - - | 8,130 | - - | 580,765 |
| Imperial, - - | 57,621 | 38 | 2,111 | - - | 59,770 |
| Portuguese, - - | 12,801 | - - | 146 | - - | 12,947 |
| | 9,492,238 | 509 | 172,294 | - - | 9,665,041 |
| Unredeemed. | | | | | |
| British, - - | 23,847,106 | 1,523,614 | 245,350 | 11,869,790 | 37,485,862 |
| Irish, - - - | 2,622,331 | 129,583 | 28,826 | 1,612,220 | 4,392,961 |
| Imperial, - - | 167,458 | 229,962 | 3,852 | 94,353 | 495,625 |
| Portuguese, - - | 14,064 | - - | 159 | 42,801 | 57,024 |
| | 26,650,959 | 1,883,159 | 278,188 | 13,619,165 | 42,431,473 |
| Deduct from sinking fund for life annuities, - | - - | - - | - - | 225,255 | 225,255 |
| Annuit. for years or lives, | 1,883,159 | - - | - - | 13,393,910 | 42,206,218 |
| Management, - - | 278,188 | | | | |
| Amount int. ann. and mant. | 28,812,307 | | | | |
| Sinking fund, - | 13,393,910 | | | | |
| Total charge on British treasury, - - | 42,206,218 | | | | |
| On debt contd. in Ireland, | 1,437,826 | 47,688 | * | - - | 1,485,514 |
| Of which redeemed, - | 342,472 | - - | - - | - - | 342,472 |
| Remaining, Irish currency, | 1,095.354 | 47,688 | | 635,707 | 1,778,749 |
| In British currency, - | 1,001,096 | 44.020 | | 586,806 | 1,641,922 |
| To which add the charge on Britain as above, - - - | | | | | 42,206,218 |
| Total annual charge on united treasuries of Britain and Ireland, | | | | | 43,648,140 |

* See Note next page.

Such is the extent of the funded debt, due, or guaranteed by Britain, and the annual charge attending the same. It cannot now be doubted that the Imperial and Portuguese debt are as much a charge upon Britain as any part of its proper debt; and the suspicions formerly entertained that the Irish debt might terminate in the same manner, are now fully verified.

---

## CHAPTER III.

### UNFUNDED DEBT.

THERE is always a large sum, besides the funded debt, due by the British government. This may arise from any national expense for which no provision has been made, or the provision has proved insufficient, or not forthcoming at the time wanted. The forms of the unfunded debt are various; but the following are the principal branches.

I. EXCHEQUER BILLS. These are issued from the exchequer, in consequence of acts of Parliament, several of which are passed every session. The first were issued in 1696, to the amount of L.2,700,000, and being intended as a temporary substitute for money during the recoinage at that period, some of them were then so low as L.10 and L.5. There are none issued now under L.100, and many of them are for L.500 and L.1000.—They bear

 interest

* We have not stated the expense of management of the debt in Ireland. The management of the whole Irish debt is stated in the official account at L.30,305; but that of the Irish debt funded in Britain alone, when reduced to Irish currency, exceeds this sum.

interest at various rates, from 2d. to 3½d. per day for L.100; and being distributed among those who are willing to advance their value, they form a kind of circulating medium. After a certain time, they are received in payment of taxes, or other monies due to government; and the interest due on them at the time is allowed in the payment. They cease to bear interest when in the hands of the revenue collectors, or other public officers, and when called in by Government. The Bank of England often engages to receive them to a certain extent, and thereby promote their circulation; and the daily transactions between the bank and the exchequer are chiefly carried on by bills of L.1000, deposited in the exchequer by the bank, to the amount of the sums received by them on account of Government.

These bills are sometimes granted on the credit of the supplies for the present or the subsequent year; and in this way the produce of the annual taxes is generally anticipated; and a large sum is generally authorized to be raised on them in time of war, to answer exigencies, by an act, proceeding upon what is called a vote of credit, passed near the conclusion of each session of Parliament. New exchequer bills are frequently issued in discharge of former ones; and they are often converted into funded debt, by granting capital in some of the stocks, on certain terms, to such holders as are willing to accept them.—The operations of this kind since 1791, have been already detailed.

II. Navy Bills. These are issued from the navy office, to answer any purpose in that important branch of national expenditure; and they bear interest after a certain date, if not discharged. A practice had long prevailed, when the number of seamen for the service of the year was voted, to grant a sum estimated at the rate of L.4 per month for each man, allowing 13 months to the



year

year, for the whole naval expense; wages, victualling, wear of shipping, and ordnance, included. In consequence of the deterioration of the value of money, this allowance became insufficient; and navy bills, to a large amount, were issued to supply the deficiency; and these were often funded afterwards in the same manner as exchequer bills. Since 1797, this practice has been discontinued; and sums, considered as adequate in the present circumstances, voted at once for the service of the navy; since which, the amount of the navy bills has not been so great as formerly; and they have been paid from the money granted for the navy, without recurring to the system of funding. By an act, 37 Geo. III. all navy bills were to be made payable at a period not later than 90 days from the time when issued, with interest not exceeding 3½ per cent. from their date: but by an act passed last session (1817), the restriction to 90 days was repealed.

III. Ordnance Bills, or Debentures, are issued in like manner from the ordnance office, for supplying the exigencies in that branch of expenditure.

Victualling and transport bills are issued from the respective offices in the same manner. There is also always a large amount of floating debt at the navy, victualling, transport, and ordnance offices, for which no bills have been issued.

Table XII. exhibits the amount of exchequer bills, navy bills, and ordnance bills, and other debts at these offices, and the whole amount of unfunded debt, in these three branches, on the 5th January of each year, from 1793 to 1817; also the increase or decrease during the preceding year; and the interest on exchequer bills since 1799. The fluctuation of the unfunded debt explains in part the cause of the great inequality of the addition to the funded debt in different years, and must be taken into consideration along with the increase of the funded debt,

 after

after reducing both to the same rate of interest, in order to form a judgment of the whole increase of the public debt in any year.*

A singular kind of debt was contracted in the financial arrangements of the year 1813. The holders of exchequer bills proposed to be funded, and who were willing to contribute a further sum, payable by instalments, to the extent of one half of the bills funded, on the terms proposed, received assignable debentures, bearing interest at 5 per cent. and payable half yearly at the same terms as the 3 per cent. reduced stock; the holders of which were entitled to demand payment in money, on the 5th April 1815, or the 5th April of any succeeding year, upon three months previous notice; or, in place of money, to receive for each L.100 in said debentures, L.100 in the 5 per cent. cons., L.120 in the 4 per cent. cons., or L.150 in the 3 per cent. reduced, in option of the holder; and those remaining unfunded to be finally paid off 12 months after the conclusion of peace. The sum raised in this manner was L.799,300; of which, L.7,400 was funded in the 3 per cent. reduced, in 1814, for L.11,100, and money was provided for paying off the remainder in 1816. This part of the public debt seems not to have been included in the accounts presented to Parliament.

Besides these principal branches of the unfunded debt, there are always a number of demands on the public, for bills accepted by the treasury; army charges, and miscellaneous services of various kinds. These are daily fluctuating, and their amount at any particular time cannot be easily ascertained.

The amount of these debts on the 5th January each year since 1811, together with the whole amount of the unfunded debt as reported to Parliament these years, and the annual increase, are subjoined to the Table.

 The

* See Note XXVII.

| | |
|---|---|
| The amount of the three great branches, 5th January, 1817, was - - - | L.46,777,672 |
| Miscellaneous articles, - - | 3,269,416 |
| Amount reported to Parliament, - | L.50,047,088 |
| Increase of funded debt in 1816, - | L.1,321,729 |

To these sums a large addition may be made, for demands due by the public, not brought to account.

The outstanding taxes, due to the public, may be placed against the unfunded debt. While the property tax subsisted, a large arrear was generally due, sometimes amounting to eight millions; but since the repeal of that tax, and the collection of its arrears, the sums of this kind due to the public are inconsiderable.

The imprest monies, or sums in the hands of the treasurers of the army and navy, and other public accountants, and which, so far as not expended, are refunded to the public at clearance, may also be stated against the unfunded debt. The amount of these cannot be ascertained.

The unfunded debt of Ireland, on the 5th January, 1817, was L.5,774,883 Irish currency.

# PART III.

---

## EXAMINATION OF PLANS FOR THE REDEMPTION OF THE NATIONAL DEBT, AND OTHER FINANCIAL OPERATIONS.

---

## CHAPTER I.

### *Examination of Dr. Price's Views of Finance.*

DR. PRICE'S views of the national debt were first announced in his Treatise on Reversionary Annuities, in the year 1771; and more fully unfolded in an appeal to the public on that subject, published the following year; and in some subsequent publications.

His plan for the redemption of the national debt, is the application of a certain sum of money annually, set apart from the rest of our annual revenue, and appropriated for the purchase of stock at the current prices; the interest of the part of the debt thus redeemed being always added to the original sum, to increase the operation of the fund. This system to be inviolably followed, in time of war as well as in time of peace; and money, when wanted, to be raised by new loans, as if no such fund existed. To secure the steady execution of this plan, the management of the fund to be committed to special Commissioners; acting under penalties in such a manner as would take it out of the hands of the treasury, and form a check upon the House of Commons itself.

The efficacy of this plan depends upon the operation of compound interest, which he considers as omnipotent. Money, he says, bearing compound interest, increases at first slowly; but the rate being continually accelerated, it becomes in some time so rapid as to mock all the powers of imagination.

He proceeds to illustrate and enforce his plan in the following manner.

There are three ways in which a nation may apply a sinking fund:

1st, The interests disengaged by it from time to time may be applied in redeeming the public debt.

2d, They may be applied to current services.

3d, They may be immediately annihilated by abolishing the taxes charged with them.

In the first way of employing a sinking fund, it always increases, and that with a force which is continually accelerated; and which, therefore, however small at first, becomes at length equal to any effect. In the second way, it admits of no increase; because it always acts with the same force. In the first way it resembles a grain of corn sown, and the produce sown again, and so on; which will soon afford an increase sufficient to support a kingdom. In the second way, it resembles a seed, the produce of which is consumed. What has been said of the second way, is true in a higher degree of the third. A fund of the first sort is money bearing compound interest; a fund of the second sort is money bearing simple interest; and a fund of the third sort is money bearing no interest at all.

In illustration of this, the Doctor supposes an annual sum of L.200,000, set aside as a fund for keeping the debt, *which the nation is continually incurring*, in a state of redemption. If applied the first way, a debt of L.200,000 is discharged the first year, which, supposing interest at five per cent, disengages an annuity of L.10,000. If this annuity, instead of being spent on services, is added to the fund, and both employed in paying debts, an annuity of L.10,500 will be disengaged the second year,

 or

or L.20,500 in both years. Computing in this manner, the amount of annuities disengaged increases faster each succeeding year, and in 86 years, becomes L.13,083,000, which, being added to the original sinking fund, amounts to L.13,283,000. The full value, therefore, of an annuity of L.13,083,000, will have been paid off in eighty-six years, that is, nearly 262 millions of debt; and consequently, though the state had been adding three millions to its debt every year, or 258 millions altogether, it would have been more than discharged, and that at no greater expense than the annual saving of L.200,000.

In the second way, the sum of annuities disengaged by it would have been eighty-six times L.10,000, or L.860,000, and the discharged debt would have been L.17,200,000; but besides this, there would be a debt saved, in consequence of applying every year the disengaged annuities to current services; for which, otherwise, equivalent sums must have been borrowed. L.10,000 will be saved at the beginning of the second year; L.20,000 at the beginning of the third year; and L.850,000 at the beginning of the eighty-sixth year; and altogether, L.36,550,000, which, added to the L.17,200,000 of debt discharged, makes the advantage to the public, from this plan, in eighty-six years, L.53,750,000; and as it was 262 millions by the first one, the difference to the public in its favour, is L.208,250,000.

In the third way, the whole advantage derived from it is the discharge of a debt of L.200,000 annually, or L.17,200,000 in all.

Such is the substance of Dr. Price's views. He goes on to illustrate them by other suppositions, which, as his method of arguing is the same, it is unnecessary to recapitulate. His work is written in a very intemperate style, and contains, among others, the following assertions:

 1st.

1st, That no benefit is derived from applying a fund in the second of the abovementioned ways, rather than the first. In both cases the taxes are continued during the operation of the fund, and the national burthens are the same. The difference in favour of the former, already stated, is gained *without any kind of loss or expense.* By following the latter, we subject the nation to a loss of 208 millions, from a circumstance absolutely frivolous.

2d, War would increase the efficacy of the sinking fund: and any suspension of it then would be the *madness of giving it a mortal blow,* at the very time it was making the quickest progress.

3d, A state may, without difficulty, redeem its debts, by borrowing money at an equal, or even a higher interest than the funds bear, and without providing any other funds than such small ones as are necessary to pay the interest of the sums borrowed. In private life, such a measure would be justly deemed absurd. But, in a state, it would be the effect of the soundest policy. It is borrowing money at simple interest, in order to improve it at compound interest.

4th, The sinking fund proposed would render it of little or no consequence what interest a nation paid for its loans. Reduction of interest has not been attended with the advantages commonly imagined, and, as hitherto managed, has only been an expedient to postpone public bankruptcy, by lessening the possibility of avoiding it.

The arguments already adduced in support of our twelfth general proposition, are perhaps sufficient to point out the judgment which ought to be formed of this plan, and of these assertions. For several reasons, however, they demand a more particular discussion.

1st, The excellent character and high reputation of the author. A pious divine,—a respectable scholar,—an

 expert

expert calculator, a virtuous man, and an upright patriot.*

2d, The effects which his plan has produced upon our system of national finance. It has not shared the common fate of the projects of private individuals, and vanished in neglect and oblivion. It is the basis of Mr. Pitt's sinking fund, adopted fifteen years after its first publication, and now followed out for upwards of 30 years; and although with some deviations, yet, on the whole, with a steadiness seldom experienced in public measures for so great a length of time, and under a succession of different administrations.

It will be proper, before proceeding, to state distinctly the points in which all agree, and the points at issue.

It is universally admitted, that every productive additional taxation tends to prevent the progress of the national debt, if it be in a state of accumulation; and to accelerate its discharge, if it be in a state of redemption.

That every increase of expenditure, whether arising from necessity or profusion, tends to increase its accumulation, or retard its discharge.

That any sum of money, however small, improved by compound interest, will amount, in length of time, to an indefinite magnitude; and therefore,

That any surplus of national revenue above national expenditure, will be sufficient, if it continue for a long time, and be faithfully applied, to discharge any national debt, however great.

The doctrine maintained by Dr. Price is, that the formation and inviolable appropriation of a sinking fund,



operating

* We respect highly the integrity of the man, and believe that, in all his writings, he was actuated by the purest motives for the public welfare ; but we do not mean to insinuate any opinion in regard to his principles of civil liberty.

operating by compound interest, ***in war as well as in peace,*** is a measure of the utmost consequence, and that the effects of this system are greatly superior to those of any other application of a surplus, *the expenditure and taxation being equal.* That this is his opinion, appears from the passages above quoted, and many others to the same purpose. His work means this, or it means nothing: for it was never called in question, that saving of expenditure, or increase of taxation, have a powerful effect on the state of national finance.

In opposition to Dr. Price's doctrine, it is maintained, that the separation of a sinking fund from the general revenue, is a measure of no efficacy whatever; that the first and second methods of applying a surplus abovementioned, are merely different modes of official arrangement, leading to the same result;—that in time of war, when the expenditure exceeds the revenue, the preservation of the sinking fund, and consequent increase of loans, is a system from which no advantage can arise;—if it could be conducted without expense, it would be nugatory; as it is necessarily attended with expense, it is pernicious;—that at the conclusion of a war, any surplus revenue applied for the discharge of debt during the subsequent peace, operates by compound interest, during the continuance of peace: But the notion of uniting that period to another period of peace, or to a still longer period of alternate war and peace, in order to obtain the powerful effect of compound interest acting for a great length of time, is illusory.

We return to the case supposed by Dr. Price, abovementioned, and compare the effects of the first and second methods of applying the surplus, either in time of peace or war.

In time of peace, when the second method is followed, L.10,000, being the interest of the debt discharged the first year, is applied to the current services of the second

 year;

year; L.20,000, the third year; and these sums are supposed requisite to complete what the service of each year requires; and, as Dr. Price observes, they must have been borrowed, if the first method had been followed. If loans be made for this purpose, either taxes must be imposed for the payment of the interest, or the sums borrowed accumulate by compound interest. In the former case, the nation is subjected to the burthen of taxes for payment of the interest of L.10,000 the first year; of L.20,000 more, or L.30,000 altogether, the second year; and of L.36,550,000 the eighty-sixth year; none of which would have been imposed according to the second method. It is this gradually increasing, and ultimately large additional taxation, that occasions the difference of L.208,250,000 stated by Dr. Price, as the loss arising from the second method. If the same taxes be imposed when the second method is followed, their produce is not wanted for the services of the year, and must accumulate, at the end of the period, to the abovementioned sum in favour of the public.

If taxes be not imposed to pay the interest of these loans, then to the L.20,000 borrowed the second year, there must be added a sum sufficient to pay the interest of the loan of the former year; and, in like manner, a sum must be borrowed each succeeding year, equal to the interest of all the former loans, by which means the amount of these loans would accumulate by compound interest against the public.

The disengaged annuities under the second method, may be dissipated by profusion, and then there will be a difference between the methods equal to what Dr. Price states; but it is the profusion, and not the mode of application, that is the cause of that difference. They may be applied to the construction of canals, harbours, and other objects of national utility; and the benefits accruing from these to the public, may repay the expense of their

 execution

execution or otherwise; but the propriety of this mode of application of surplus revenue, does not belong to our present inquiry.

In war, let us adopt Dr. Price's supposition of three millions being required annually in addition to the sums raised within the year, and of continuing the application of L.200,000 as a sinking fund; which sum is comprehended in the loan of three millions. The debt contracted in three years, is nine millions; and the additional taxes for payment of interest at five per cent. come to L.450,000. The national debt redeemed by a sinking fund of L.200,000, operating by compound interest in three years, is L.630,500, and therefore the additional unredeemed debt is L.8,369,500.

If no sinking fund be continued during the war, a loan of L.2,800,000 only will be required the first year, the interest of which is L.140,000. But the taxes imposed that year amount to L.150,000, (for we suppose the extent of taxation in both methods equal,) therefore there is a surplus of L.10,000 applicable to the service of the second year. The loan required for the second year will therefore be L.2,790,000; the two loans together, L.5,590,000; and the interest upon them L.279,500. The additional taxes imposed the two first years amount to L.300,000, leaving a surplus of L.20,500 applicable to the service of the third year. The loan required the third, is therefore L.2,779,500, and the amount of the three loans L.8,369,500, exactly the same as the unredeemed debt when a sinking fund is continued; and it is obvious the same equality will hold for any number of years.

When Dr. Price says that a debt of 258 millions might be discharged in eighty-six years, at no greater expense than an annual saving of L.200,000, he overlooks the taxes imposed year after year, for the payment of interest; a great part of which would not have been needed, if that annual sum had not been separated from the public revenue.

revenue. The reasoning used above is equally applicable to any other supposition of war expenditure, whatever be the annual deficiency, whether uniform or varying,—whether continued for three, or thirty, or an hundred years, still the taxation and expenditure of each year being the same, the finances of the nation will be found in the same condition at the end of the period, whether the sinking fund be preserved inviolate, or entirely laid aside.

If no sinking fund be kept up for thirty years, a little alteration on the arrangement of public accounts would bring them exactly to the same state as if it had been uniformly adhered to; and conversely, the present form of our financial accounts, arising from a sinking fund, may be brought, by a like alteration of arrangement, to the form in which they would have stood, if no sinking fund had ever been thought of. It is impossible that a mere change of order in the public accounts, capable of being reversed at any time, can be attended with advantage to the public.

At the termination of a war, the nation remains charged with a certain debt, and it possesses, or ought to possess, a certain surplus revenue. The efficacy of this surplus to discharge the debt, depends upon its proportion to the debt, and the length of time during which it is applied to that purpose, and upon these alone. It operates by compound interest. But the manner in which the debt was contracted, or the surplus obtained, has no relation to the progress and period of its discharge. It is of no avail that a sinking fund had been operating by compound interest during a former peace. When war breaks out again, the operation of compound interest is at an end. In place of continuing to discharge debt, an additional debt is contracted. When peace returns, the operation of discharge re-commences from a new basis, according to the state of finance at the time. The public debt is certainly increased;—the proportion of surplus revenue to that

 debt

debt, and therefore the time requisite for its complete discharge, may be greater or less than at the former peace; but the two periods of peace cannot be united to obtain a powerful effect from the long continuance of compound interest.

The Doctor's plan for discharging the national debt by borrowing money at simple interest, in order to improve it at compound interest, is, we apprehend, completely delusive. He admits the absurdity of such a measure in private life,—and its absurdity in national finance is exactly the same. The cases differ only in extent of sum, and duration of time, which no ways alter the general tendency of the measure. Suppose a million borrowed for this purpose, and assigned to Commissioners for the redemption of the national debt, in whose hands it operates by compound interest. The interest of this loan is L.50,000, which must either be provided for by some additional tax, or saved by some measure of public economy: or if neither of these be adopted, an additional loan must be made next year to pay the interest. In the former case, it is the tax or the economy, and not the operation described, that benefits the revenue; and they would have produced the same effect by affording an additional surplus improved at compound interest, without any loan. In the latter case, an additional sum of L.50,000 is borrowed the second year; and a sum equal to the interest of both loans, or L.102,500, the third year: and thus the debt accumulates by compound interest against the public, exactly to the same extent that the money vested in the hands of the Commissioners accumulates in its favour.

Dr. Price's assertion, that it is of little consequence what interest a nation paid for its loans, is untenable. In time of war, additional interest must be met by additional taxes, or accumulate by compound interest against the public. In time of peace, reduction of interest produces or increases a surplus, upon the application of which the redemption of national debt entirely depends.

The Doctor remarks, that a debt bearing a high rate of interest, with a sinking fund attached, is redeemed in less time than the same debt with the same sinking fund at a low rate of interest; and he considers this circumstance as a recompense for the burthen of the high interest. He overlooks that, as a much larger sum is annually raised from the public when the interest is high, a great part of this additional burthen being paid to the national creditors, is entirely lost to the public; and a part only being added to the sinking fund as the redemption of the debt advances, accelerates the course of its discharge. A debt of ten millions, bearing interest at six per cent. is redeemed by a sinking fund of L.100,000, in about 33½ years. If the rate of interest be only three per cent. it will require 47 years. But in the former case, the annual burthen on the public is L.700,000, and the whole burthen L.23,450,000; and in the latter case, the annual burthen is L.400,000, and the whole burthen L.18,800,000. If the sum of L.700,000 had been raised annually while the debt bore interest at three per cent. it would have been discharged in 19 years for L.13,300,000. Or if L.477,000 had been raised annually, it would have been discharged in 33½ years, for L.15,979,500.

Dr. Price supposes the case of a state burthened with debt, bearing five millions of interest, and able, by its utmost exertions, to raise a million more as a sinking fund. "This, if the debts bear interest at six per cent. will pay " off three-fifths of them in twenty-three years, and the " state may be saved; but if the interest be no more than " 3 per cent, it will not give the same relief in less than " double that time, and a public bankruptcy may prove " unavoidable."* He does not mention that, in the

 former

* Observations on Reversionary Annuities, 4th edit. vol. i. p. 189.

former case, the debt supposed to exist, and to be partially discharged, is L.83,333,333, and in the latter case, L.166,666,666. The same national exigencies must have required the contraction of an equal debt. What he proves is only that a debt of half the amount, but bearing interest at a double rate, will be discharged in less time by the same sinking fund.

Dr. Price, in comparing the different ways of applying the disengaged annuities, says, that if they be not applied the first way, they might, for ought he knows, be best employed in the last way, that is, in the abolition of taxes; for a kingdom will then be sure of receiving some relief. We have endeavoured to evince that the first and second methods are the same in substance, and differ only in form. We esteem them greatly superior to the third. It is by continuing the taxes, and thus supporting the surplus during a period of peace, that any thing effectual can be done for discharging the national debt.

Dr. Price communicated to Mr. Pitt, in 1786, three plans for the redemption of the national debt.*

One of these, No. III. is the application of a million surplus, exactly the same as was adopted in the sinking fund established that year, which will be examined in the following chapter.

Another, No. II. proposed that the sinking fund should be raised from a million to L.1,600,000, by additional taxes imposed at the following periods.

| | |
|---|---|
| First year, - - | L.60,000 |
| Second year, - - | 180,000 |
| Third year, - - | 120,000 |
| Fourth year, - - | 120,000 |
| Fifth year, - - | 120,000 |
| | L.600,000 |

 This

* Morgan's Review of Dr. Price's writings on the Finances of Great Britain.

This plan is the more efficacious than the former, as the sum appropriated is greater; but of the same general tendency.

In the other plan, No. I. it is proposed to impose the same additional taxes, but apply their produce as follows:—A part of the three per cent. stocks to be converted into four per cents., and the additional interest to be paid by these taxes. The holders of the three per cent. stock converted to advance an adequate sum for the increase of interest, and this sum to be applied in addition to the million for the redemption of the national debt.

We entirely agree with Dr. Price in the disadvantage of borrowing at a low rate of interest, with an increase of nominal capital; and the last mentioned plan, so far as it tends to counteract that system, appears beneficial.

The Doctor, in a subsequent publication,* presuming that the sinking fund would strengthen the public credit, and raise the three per cents. considerably above par in intervals of peace, lays down a plan, founded upon that supposition, for reducing the national debt. Instead of a reduction of interest, which, he says, would retard the extinction of the public debt, he proposes a reduction of capital; and, supposing the three per cents. at 110, he assumes, that the public creditors would agree to have their capital reduced from L.100 to L.80, if secured of the present interest for fifteen years. At the end of that period, the reduced capital, bearing interest at $3\frac{3}{4}$ per cent. would sell much above par, and a similar operation might be repeated upon terms still more advantageous, and by this scheme, the operation of compound interest itself would be aided.

Admitting the price of stocks, and consent of the creditors, as supposed, this appears to us one of the best parts of the Doctor's plans. The methods he proposes to

 improve

* Preface to the third edition of Observations on Reversionary Annuities, p. 13, &c. This article is omitted in the following edition.

improve the surplus value of the stock for the public emolument, is, perhaps, the most effective that could be taken.

The advantages expected by Dr. Price and his friend, Mr. Morgan, from the execution of his plans, depend in a considerable degree upon the confidence which they suppose these measures would give in government security, and the rise of the price of stocks which that confidence would produce. All this is so hypothetical as to render a more minute examination of these plans, so far as they rest upon that expectation, unnecessary.

Much has been said by Dr. Price and others, of the advantage which a sinking fund produces in supporting the price of stock. We apprehend it is incapable of producing any such effect. The price of stock, like that of any commodity, depends on the proportion of supply and demand. Whatever sums are brought into the money market, and applied by the Commissioners for the purchase of stock; equal sums are withdrawn from the money market, by the additional loans required to replace what is invested in the hands of the Commissioners. Dr. Price justly observes,* that whatever effect borrowing every year has in sinking the funds, paying every year would have an equal contrary effect. He has not attended to the obvious consequence, that, if the payment be made by means of borrowing, it can produce no alteration in the price of the funds at all. He supposes ten millions borrowed every year to defray the expenses of war, nine millions only of which would have been wanted had not the surplus million been locked up; and further, that this scheme, by keeping up public credit, and throwing money every year into the hands of the lenders, enables Government to borrow at four instead of five per cent. and

151 thereby

* Preface to third edition of Observations on Reversionary Annuities, page 13.

thereby save L.50,000 of interest. He overlooks that the effect of throwing a million into the hands of the lenders, is compensated by demanding from them an additional million in the loan.

The purchases made by the Commissioners, no doubt, support the funds at a higher rate than they would stand, if there were no such purchasers in the field, and the loan for the year the same; and this advance takes place at a time when a high price is disadvantageous to the public; But the additional loan which the sinking fund requires, must have as great an effect in depressing the funds, and that depression takes place at a time when a low price is disadvantageous to the public.

---

## CHAPTER II.

### *Examination of Mr. Pitt's Sinking Funds.*

THE system of finance recommended by Dr. Price, is the same as that carried into execution under the administration of Mr. Pitt, and continued since. In the former chapter, we considered its merit and tendency on general principles. In this, we are to consider the effects it has actually produced.

The result of the foregoing reasoning is, that a sinking fund connected with an increasing debt, providing the loans be obtained on the same terms the debts were redeemed, and the additional operations conducted without expense, is attended with no consequence, good or evil. But in every loan, the contractors have a profit at the expense of the public: and when the system of a sinking fund is followed, the public, besides expense, sustains a loss equal to the *bonus* attending the additional loans.

It is of importance to ascertain whether the nation has

sustained a loss of this kind, and to what extent. If the fact be ascertained, it corroborates the foregoing reasoning; if it be considerable, it leads us to enquire for what reason the system is persevered in.

The whole sum raised by loans, from 1793, (when the first loan was made after the establishment of the sinking fund) to 1st February 1817, after deducting the part of the loyalty loan repaid, is, - L.420,307,425
Exchequer and navy bills funded, - 89,148,773

Amount loans and bills funded, - L.509,456,198

And the capitals funded for these were,

| | |
|---|---|
| In the 3 per cents. - - | L.605,495,840 |
| In the 4 per cents. - - | 44,027,744 |
| In the 5 per cents. - - | 116,013,861 |
| | L.765,537,445 |

And long annuities have been granted, at a medium for $58\frac{3}{4}$ years, - - L.525,111

Now these may be reduced to 3 per cents. by allowing a capital in proportion to the rate of interest, which is the natural value, and, although there be some fluctuation in the market price, comes near enough to the actual value.

| | |
|---|---|
| Sum funded in 3 per cents. - | L.605,495,840 |
| Value of L.44,027,744 in 4 per cents. | 58,703,658 |
| of 116,013,861 in 5 per cents. | 193,356,435 |
| | L.857,555,933 |
| Value of L.525,111 annuities for $58\frac{3}{4}$ years, at 18.86 years purchase, L.9,903,593, in 5 per cents. and in 3 per cents. - - | 16,505,988 |
| Whole value of funded capital and annuities, reduced to 3 per cents. - | L.874,061,921 |



The

The sums expended by the Commissioners for the reduction of the national debt, and capital redeemed, are as follows:

| | *Sums expended.* | *Capital redeemed* |
|---|---|---|
| 3 per cents. - | L.176,652,174 | L.283,777,272 |
| Of which redeemed before 1793, - | 8,147,630 | 10,242,100 |
| | L.168,504,544 | L.273,535,172 |
| 4 per cents. - - | 6,586,934 | 7,796,400 |
| 5 per cents. - - | 130,113 | 145,500 |
| Amount redeemed, from 1st Feb. 1793, to 1st February, 1817, - | L.175,221,593 | L.281,477,072 |

And the capital redeemed, reduced to 3 per cents., is

| | | |
|---|---|---|
| L.273,535,172, | 3 per cents. | L.273,535,172 |
| 7,796,400, | 4 per cents. | 10,395,200 |
| 145,500, | 5 per cents. | 242,500 |
| | | L.284,172,872 |

During the continuance of the war, the national debt increased annually; the sums borrowed, by loans or otherwise, exceeding the debt redeemed. Now, if no system for redeeming the national debt had been adopted, the amount of taxes and expenses remaining the same, the requisite money raised by loans or funded bills would have been less by the last mentioned sum made over to, and expended by, the Commissioners.

Now, as L.509,456,198 (the sum raised) is to L.874,061,921, (the capital required to be funded in the 3 per cents. in order to raise that sum) so is L.175,221,593 (the sum delivered to, and expended by, the Commissioners for the reduction of the national debt, and which might have been deducted from the loans, if no such commission had existed), to L.300,623,533, the sum which would have been saved from the funded capital, (3 per cents.) by lessening the loans.

| | | |
|---|---|---|
| Debts contracted from 1793 to 1817, reduced to 3 per cents. | - | L,874,061,921 |
| If no sinking fund had existed, it would have been less by | - | 300,623,533 |
| And would have amounted only to | - | L.573,438,388 |
| From above sum of L.874,061,921 | | |
| Deduct debt redeemed 284,172,872 | | |
| Unredeemed debt, | - | L.589,889,049 |
| Loss to the public by sinking fund,* | - | L.16,450,661 |

But the present excess of national debt occasioned by the sinking fund is much higher. A portion of this loss has occurred each year for a period of twenty-four years; and the whole effect ought to be estimated by accumulated computation of interest. If the last mentioned sum be equally divided, the annual loss is L.685,444, and this, in twenty-four years, at compound interest, amounts to about 30 millions. Something, however, may be deducted from this statement, because the loss was not equally diffused through the period; the portions appertaining to the early part being considerably smaller.

Neither has any thing been charged for the expense of the commission for the redemption of the public debt. This branch of public expense, indeed, has been very moderate; but its amount, with compound interest, ought to be added to the other loss, in order to ascertain the whole.

We are next to examine that part of Mr. Pitt's plan which attaches a sinking fund of one per cent. to the nominal capital of every loan, imposing taxes to that extent beyond what are required for the payment of the interest. This plan was also suggested by Dr. Price;† whose



* See Note XXVIII. † Appeal to the Public, p. 40, 41.

whose proposal, however, was one per cent. on the sum borrowed, and not on the capital funded.

There is an inequality in the extent of this fund from its being applied to the nominal capital. If the loan be made in the 3 per cents. valued at 60, it amounts to 1-60th of the sum borrowed. If it be made in the 5 per cents. valued at par, it amounts to 1-100th.

Like the other parts of the plan, it occasions a loss to the public by borrowing upon higher terms, in order to redeem a part of the debt upon lower ones. It is equally destitute of all real efficacy for the discharge of debt, under equal circumstances of taxation and expenditure.

The ultimate effects of adherence to this system, during a long period of continued warfare, remains to be ascertained. Suppose the annual deficiency to be supplied by loan is 11 millions: this funded in the 3 per cents. creates a capital of L.18,333,333, the interest of which is L.550,000, and the sinking fund, L.183,333; for both which additional taxes are imposed.

It is obvious that if no more taxes be imposed than are required to pay the interest, the annual deficiency of 11 millions remains the same. A loan to that extent must be made annually, and taxes imposed for the payment of the interest; and our debt, interest, and taxes, increase annually by equal sums, without the most distant prospect of relief.

But if taxes be imposed to a greater amount than the interest of the loan, the surplus fills up some part of the deficiency. On the foregoing supposition, L.183,333 is deducted from the 11 millions, leaving a deficiency of L.10,816,666, and if an equal amount of taxes be imposed the second and each succeeding year, the part of the deficiency supplied will increase by compound interest; and in a course of years, the whole 11 millions will be supplied, and no further loans or additional taxes will be



needed,

needed, provided the expenditure remain the same as at the beginning of the period.

Now, as an annuity of L.1, at five per cent. compound interest, amounts to L.60 in about twenty-nine years, that length of time is required before the deficiency of 11 millions be supplied. During that time, L.733,333 of additional taxes are imposed annually, or L.21,266,666 altogether. The result is, that if the nation, which cannot at present raise 11 millions more, to equalize its taxes to its expenditure, shall increase them gradually for twenty-nine years, till the addition amount to 21 millions, the point of equalization will be obtained; or, to use the language of the sinking fund, the debt annually redeemed, will then become equal to the debt contracted.

If the loan of 11 millions be made in a five per cent. fund, the sinking fund is L.110,000, which, added to the interest, gives an annual charge of L.660,000. Upon this supposition, thirty-seven years are required before the deficiency is supplied; and the additional taxes imposed, amount to L.24,420,000.

A sinking fund of this kind is preferable in ultimate efficacy, to one founded on the appropriation and accumulation of a fixed annual sum. It increases with the increase of the funded debt; and, in a long time, will be equal to the discharge of any debt, however great, provided the nation bear the taxes which it requires. An annual sum, esteemed large at first, is likely to become inadequate to the discharge of a debt which increases beyond expectation. A sinking fund of L.1,200,000 would require forty-seven years and a half to fill up a deficiency of 11 millions; and the additional taxes imposed, would amount to above 28 millions.

We have stated the case of continued warfare, as being more simple in calculation. In the case of alternate war and peace, the periods would be different, but the relative merits of the different systems the same.

But the chief point to be attended to is, that none of these plans, nor any possible plan, has any intrinsic power to discharge, or aid the discharge of our national burthens. An opinion prevails that the minister who instituted the sinking fund has put a powerful machine in action, which, although its first operations were feeble, has now become of great efficacy, and that the efficacy will continue to increase without any further exertion on our part, like the acceleration of falling bodies by the power of gravity, till it amount to an indefinite magnitude.

When a minister establishes a sinking fund connected with a system of borrowing, he acknowledges the inability of the nation to bear at present the expense which his system of administration requires; and his plan, whatever it be, does no more than inform the public, that if posterity be able and willing to raise such sums, by extended taxation, at certain periods which his plan points out, as will make up for our deficiencies, with interest, and furnish besides what is wanted for the exigencies and contests of their own time, the public debt which he contracts will then be discharged.

That minister would have reason to doubt whether posterity would submit to all this. Yet, the plan of our sinking fund established in 1786 and 1792, have been adhered to with great steadiness, and our taxes raised to an amount beyond precedent or expectation.

The sums annually raised by taxes, since the commencement of the war, are as follows:*

Year ending 5th January.

| | | | |
|---|---|---|---|
| 1793 | L.17,656,418 | 1796 | L.17,858,454 |
| 1794 | 17,170,400 | 1797 | 18,737,760 |
| 1795 | 17,308,811 | 1798 | 20,654,650 |



* See Note XXIX.

| | | | |
|---|---|---|---|
| 1799 | L.30,202,915 | 1809 | L.61,538,207 |
| 1800 | 35,229,968 | 1810 | 63,405,294 |
| 1801 | 33,896,464 | 1811 | 66,681,366 |
| 1802 | 35,415,096 | 1812 | 64,763,870 |
| 1803 | 37,240,213 | 1813 | 63,169,845 |
| 1804 | 37,677,063 | 1814 | 66,925,835 |
| 1805 | 45,359,442 | 1815 | 69,684,192 |
| 1806 | 49,659,281 | 1816 | 70,421,788 |
| 1807 | 53,304,254 | 1817 | 59,437,259 |
| 1808 | 58,390,255 | | |

From this statement, it appears that the amount of our taxes, which was nearly stationary for some years after the commencement of the war, has increased progressively, (with one or two slight exceptions) since the year 1795; that the increase was most rapid some years after the recommencement of the war, when heavy war taxes were imposed, and that the amount of taxes at the end of the war was about four times what it was at the commencement.

The whole amount of taxes, upon the average of the last three years of war, after deduction, was about 69 millions; a sum more than sufficient to defray the expense of the war, enormous as it was: but not sufficient to provide at the time for the interest of debt formerly contracted.

Our present national revenue would therefore have been sufficient to support, without limitation of time, the expense of the late war on the scale it was conducted, if the taxation during former wars, and the early period of the present one, had been equal to the expenditure.

The cause of this is, not that certain sinking funds were established twenty or thirty years ago, but that we submitted to a taxation of 69 millions, and to the privations occasioned thereby. The same amount of taxation would have produced the same effect, although none of these funds had ever been established.

Convinced that the sinking fund has contributed nothing to the discharge of the public debt, and that it has occasioned a large addition to our public burthens, we next enquire whether any, and what advantages have been derived from it.

The means, and the only means, of restraining the progress of national debt, are, saving of expenditure, and increase of revenue. Neither of these have a necessary connection with a sinking fund. But if they have an eventual connection: and if the nation, impressed with a conviction of the importance of a system established by a popular minister, has, in order to adhere to it, adopted measures, either of frugality in expenditure, or exertion in raising taxes, which it would not otherwise have done, the sinking fund ought not to be considered as inefficient; and its effects may be of great importance.

We are not of opinion that the sinking fund has contributed in any degree to frugality in expenditure. The time during which it has operated, has not been a time of national frugality. Ministers have had the full power of raising what loans they pleased, to supply the means of any expenditure, however lavish; and it will not be said they have used this power with a sparing hand.

In regard to increase of taxes, we are of opinion, that the sinking fund has had a real effect in calling forth exertions, which, although they might have been made as well and as effectually, would not have been made, unless to follow out the line which that system required. A loan is made, and the revenue is considered as charged, not only with the interest, but a certain proportion of the capital, annually. Taxes are imposed to meet the one as well as the other. If the sinking fund had not been in view, it is likely taxes would have been imposed for the interest only.

 If

If the sinking fund could be conducted without loss to the public, it would not be wise to propose an alteration of a system which has gained the confidence of the public, and which points out a rule of taxation that has the advantage at least of being steady. If that rule be laid aside, our measures of taxation might become entirely loose.

But if the sinking fund be attended with a heavy loss, it seems proper to inquire whether a plan might be followed that would deliver us from this loss, and at the same time carry on the necessary measure of increased taxation. The present proportion of one per cent. on the nominal capital might be continued. If a loan of twenty millions be transacted in the 3 per cents. valued at 60, the sinking fund attached to it on the present system is L.333,333. Now taxes may be imposed to that extent, besides what are required for interest; and that sum, instead of being made over to Commissioners, may be deducted from the loan. Thus the nation would save the loss it at present sustains, of borrowing on lower, and paying on higher terms; and the imposition of L.333,333 additional taxes, which is the only measure of real efficacy, would be the same as before.*

---

## CHAPTER III.

### *Examination of Lord Henry Petty's Plan of Finance.*

We have already given an account of Lord Henry Petty's plan of finance. It was proposed to Parliament and the public, in the year 1807, accompanied with an elaborate set of tables. Being very complex, it was not



* See Note XXX.

generally understood. As it promised to raise the necessary loans with little or no increase of taxes, it was favourably received, and probably would have been continued for some years, if the ministry who brought it forward had remained in office.

The scheme, as proposed, though sufficiently complex in itself, is blended with many circumstances extraneous to its general merit. Advantage is taken of the falling in of annuities at different periods, by the expiry of their term, and of the reduction of the rate of management, and of an expected surplus from the present sinking fund. The savings by annuities and management, must give the same relief to the national annual burthens, under any system of finance; and if it be a beneficial measure to call in the aid of the surplus of the present sinking fund, when it attains a certain magnitude, the advantage resulting from it will be the same, with whatever other measures it be connected. The proper way to judge of the new scheme, is to lay these extraneous circumstances aside; to leave the old debt to combat with the sinking funds already provided for its redemption, aided by any other means which existing circumstances supply; and to consider the operation of the new scheme, in regard to the new debt, contracted during the time it is in force, compared with the effects of the continuance of the former system. This will render our view of the subject simpler; and if the new scheme will not bear the test of examination when applied in this manner, it will not bear it all.

The first point which presents itself to our view, is, that the sums proposed to be raised by new taxes, during the first years of the scheme, are much less than the interest of the debts contracted; and therefore money must be borrowed, not only to supply the excess of the war expenditure above the sum raised within the year, but also to pay the interest of a great part of the loan, and thus subject the nation to the heavy and increasing expense of compound interest.

The sums borrowed the first year were,

| | |
|---|---|
| On war taxes, - - - - | L.12,000,000 |
| By supplementary loan, - - - | 200,000 |
| | L.12,200,000 |
| But there was applied to the redemption of the war tax loan from the mortgaged taxes, - - - - - | 600,000 |
| Nett loan, deducting part redeemed, - | L.11,600,000 |
| The sum required to complete the expenditure is - - - - | 11,000,000 |
| And the remainder, applied to pay the interest of the war loan, is - - | L.600,000 |

The only additional taxes imposed, are L.10,000 for interest of the supplementary loan, and L.3,333 for a sinking fund on the same; and as the former of these is appropriated, the latter only is to be stated against the interest of L.11,400,000, added to the funded debt, exclusive of the supplementary loan, of which additional debt, only 11 millions were applied to the public service.

In the second year, the sums proposed to be borrowed were,

| | |
|---|---|
| On war taxes, - - - - | L.12,000,000 |
| By supplementary loan, - - - | 1,400,000 |
| | L.13,400,000 |
| Of which applied to the redemption of war tax loans, by taxes mortgaged this and former year, - - - | 1,200,000 |
| Nett loan, deducting part redeemed, - | L.12,200,000 |
| Sum required for expenditure, - - | 11,000,000 |

 Remainder

| | |
|---|---|
| Remainder applied to pay the interest of the war loans for two years, - - | L.1,200,000 |

Against which there is to be stated,

| | |
|---|---|
| Sinking fund of supplementary loan of first year, with interest, - - | L.3,500 |
| Sinking fund of supplementary loan, second year, - - - - - | 23,333 |
| Interest of war tax loan redeemed first year, - - - - - | 30,000 |
| | L.56,833 |

Leaving an additional interest, for which no taxes are laid on, of L.1,143,667.

If we trace the proposed operations of this scheme further, we will find that the same pernicious mode of borrowing, for payment of the interest as well as the principal, continues for a course of years, though at a rate gradually diminishing, because the interest on the loans annually raised on the credit of the war taxes, for which no new provision is made, becomes less, owing to the redemption of part of that debt; and the interest on the supplementary loans, for which, together with a sinking fund, provision is made, increases, together with these loans themselves.

In order to shew what the progress and effects of this system, if continued, would have been in a period of twenty years, unincumbered with extraneous matter, Table IX. is inserted in the Appendix, divided into several parts.

Part I. relates to the loans on the war taxes; Part II. relates to the supplementary loans; and Part III. exhibits a general view of the effects of both loans combined.

The debts contracted and redeemed, inserted in this table, are according to their real value. If invested in a

 three

three per cent. fund, as was proposed, the nominal sum will be greater, (supposing the 3 per cents. at 60,) in the proportion of five to three.

By comparing the two last columns of Part III. it will appear how far the sums raised annually by taxes imposed since the commencement of the scheme, would fall short of the interest on additional debt contracted, for which taxes ought to have been provided. At the commencement, the difference is very great; and although they come near to an equality towards the end of the period, yet, taking in the whole, the difference is great. The necessary effect of this deficiency of taxation, is to subject the public to the loss incurred by compound interest.

Part IV. is added to assist us in forming a judgment of the effects of this system compared with others. It exhibits the amount of debt existing, and taxes paid, each year, for twenty years: first, upon the supposition of no sinking fund being established, and taxes imposed annually for the payment of the interest of the loans only; secondly upon the supposition of a sinking fund of 1-100th of the sum borrowed; thirdly, of a sinking fund of 1-60th of the same. The first of these was the old system; and, though not a good one, may be taken as a standard of comparison, whereby to judge of the merit of the others; the second is, the present system, when the loan is made in a five per cent. fund at par; and the third, when it is made in a three per cent. fund at 60.

It appears from this Table, that, at the end of fourteen years, the period at which the whole war taxes are mortgaged, the amount of unredeemed debt, by Lord Henry Petty's system, is L.202,784,803, and the amount of taxes paid during these fourteen years, is L.28,413,333. When no sinking fund is established, the amount of existing debt at the same period is L.154,000,000, and the taxes paid, L.57,750,000. The additional debt contracted by the former, is L.48,784,803, and the saving in taxes,

L.29,336,667. The excess of the additional debt above the saving in taxes, is L.19,448,136. At the end of twenty years, the amount of unredeemed debt, by Lord Henry Petty's system, is L.285,519,205, and the amount of taxes paid during these twenty years, is L92,893,333. The amount of debt on the old system is 220 millions, and of taxes, 115 millions. The additional debt contracted by the former, is L.65,519,205 ; and the saving in taxes, L.22,106,667 ; the excess of additional debt above the saving in taxes, L.43,412,538.

In the system where a sinking fund of 1-100th is established, the unredeemed debt at the end of fourteen years, is L.139,527,162 ; and the amount of taxes, L.69,300,000. The debt is less by L.14,472,838 than according to the old system; and to obtain this saving, there is paid, in additional taxes, L.11,550,000. The debt saved exceeds the additional taxes by L.2,922,838. At the end of twenty years, the unredeemed debt is L.187,617,650; the taxes, L.138,600,000. The saving in debt is L.32,382,350; the additional taxes, L.23,600,000. The excess in the saving of debt above the additional taxes, L.8,782,350.

In the system where a sinking fund of 1-60th is established, the unredeemed debt at the end of fourteen years, is L.129,878,604, and the amount of taxes, L.77,000,000. The debt is less by L.24,121,396, than according to the old system, and the additional taxes amount to L.19,250,000, and the debt saved exceeds the additional taxes by L.4,871,396. At the end of twenty years, the unredeemed debt is L.166,029,417, and the amount of taxes, L.154,000,000. The saving in debt is L.53,970,583; the additional taxes, L.39,000,000; and the debt saved exceeds the additional taxes by L.14,970,583.

Thus it appears that Lord Henry Petty's system is by far the worst, and in twenty years brings on an addition of funded debt, (five per cents.) besides what is applied to the public service, of - - - L.65,519,205



By

| | |
|---|---|
| By the old system, the debt contracted is equal to the sums applied to the public service. | |
| By the system of a sinking fund of 1-100th, the debt contracted is less than the sums applied to the public service, by - - - - - - | 32,382,350 |
| By the system of a sinking fund of 1-60th, the debt contracted is less than the sums applied to the public service, by - | 53,970,583 |

The general result might have been known without calculation. In Lord Henry Petty's system, taxes are only imposed for a part of the interest of the loan, and, in the first years, only for a small part; and the interest, not provided for, must accumulate in the manner of compound interest, to augment the capital debt. In the system where a sinking fund of 1-100th is established, a part of the loan is annually paid, and its interest of course cancelled; and as taxes were imposed for the full interest, the part thus saved, operates in depressing the capital debt: and this effect takes place in a higher degree when a sinking fund of 1-60th is established.

In comparing the merit of different systems, the only points necessary to be attended to are, the amount of the loans contracted,—the part of these loans redeemed,—the interest incurred,—and the sums raised by taxes. The arrangement of the loans under different branches, and the appropriation of particular funds for payment of their respective interests, are matters of official regulation; and the state of the public finance is neither the better nor the worse whether they be conducted one way or other. A complicated system may perplex and mislead, but it can never ameliorate.

It is frivolous to maintain that a part of the public debt is charged on the war taxes, and, being in a course of

 discharge,

discharge, ought to be separated from the remainder, in forming an estimate of the whole. That part, as much as any other, is a burthen on the nation. It must be discharged, if it be so, by taxes levied in future on the nation; and until it be paid, its interest must be provided for by such taxes; otherwise compound interest accumulates against the public. It is of no consequence whether these taxes be of the kind originally imposed under the name of war taxes, and afterwards rendered permanent, at least for a period, by such appropriation; or new taxes of a different kind, imposed when the war taxes are discontinued.*

As well might a land steward, when required by his employer to lay before him a state of his rents and debts, reply, that it was unnecessary to bring the whole into view at once; that he had allocated a part of the rents of such a manor for the gradual discharge of a certain bonded debt, and those of another manor for the discharge of another bond; that, if the remaining rents, after these defalcations, were insufficient to support his lordship's expenses, he could easily borrow what money might be wanted; and if a growing deficiency should be the result of these operations, it might perhaps be made up at some future time, when the present leases on the estate expired, and the rents might rise.

We have heard it maintained, that a system may be so constructed, that, although it does harm in the first years of its operation, the result, after a long continuance, will be beneficial. From its effects after a few years, we may judge with certainty of its ultimate tendency. Suppose, after a trial of ten years, it has rendered the state of our national finance so many millions worse than it would have been under a different system, but after that period it takes a beneficial turn. Were this possible, it would

 be

* See Note XXXI.

be better to follow the measures of that other system for these ten years, and then commence, upon a better basis, the measures of the former. But the supposition of a change of tendency is absurd. If it do harm in the beginning, it will do more harm the longer it is persevered in.

We have stated the loss to the public by Lord Henry Petty's system in twenty years, at L.65,519,205, or, deducting the saving in taxes, at L.43,412,538. But it may be justly estimated at a sum considerably higher. The above is the sum which the public must pay to the national creditors, or remain under the burthen of; in addition to the sums raised by loan, and applied to the national service. It arises from the operation of compound interest against the public, and is incurred for the sake of postponing the payment of interest, which should commence when the debt is contracted, to a distant time. But besides this, another loss is incurred by the system of borrowing larger sums than are wanted, in order to maintain a sinking fund, the consequences of which were considered in the last chapter: and a further loss is incurred by borrowing in a three per cent. fund during war, when the price is low, to be repaid during peace when the price is high, the consequences of which will be further considered in a following chapter. These two sources of loss indeed attach to other systems, where similar measures are followed, as well as to Lord Henry Petty's; but they take place in his system to a greater degree, because the measures from which they arise, are carried there to a greater extent.

The distinction of war tax loans and supplementary loans, is in itself entirely futile: But occasion is taken from it to ascertain the portions of debt for which the interest shall be levied in taxes, and the portions, for the interest of which no provision shall be made at present. The proportion of these, like the scheme from which they arise, is altogether arbitrary, and very irregular,—the taxes imposed in the early part of the system being much smaller than those imposed afterwards.

After a continuance of twenty years, the sum raised in taxes within the year, is L.13,613,333, being L.2,613,333, more than it would have been under the old system, though less by L.662,627 than it ought to be, in order to cover the interest of the debt. This, and an additional capital of L.65,519,205, is incurred, for the sake of saving L.22,106,677 in taxes during these twenty years, chiefly in the early part of them. In the 16th and following years, the taxes raised within each year are greater than those required by the old system.

---

## CHAPTER IV.

### *Examination of Mr. Vansittart's Plan of Finance.*

I. THIS plan has been assailed as trenching on the sinking funds formerly established, and thereby diminishing the security of the public creditors, to whom the national faith is pledged on the terms of these funds. It does not seem liable to any just censure upon this ground. It is justly observed, that "the separation kept up for the " purposes of account between the original sinking fund " of 1786, and the additions subsequently made to it, is " only nominal; it neither has been nor can be attended " to in practice, because the whole of the debt contracted " since the establishment of the sinking fund having been " borrowed upon the old stocks, and no distinction made " between the old and new proprietors, the whole debt is " now considered as *one indiscriminate mass*, to which the " purchases made by the sinking fund are equally applic- " able. No right of priority of redemption can exist in " any particular class of stockholders, nor any conditions " of repayment be claimed (except in the instance of the



5 per

"5 per cent. loan of 1797) beyond those laid down in the "act of 1792, under the faith of which all subsequent "loans may be considered as contracted. By that act, "provision is made for the redemption, within forty-five "years, of all the debts subsequently created; and within "this limit, Parliament has the power to regulate the "mode of redemption at its discretion."*

The advantages given to the public creditors by the regulations of Mr. Vansittart's plan, appear to place them in a situation equally favourable to that which they held under the enactments of 1792.

After all, the security of the public creditors, is not so much affected by any regulations adopted in the management of our finance, as by the magnitude and increase of the national debt. If the amount of the loans be greater than what the capitalists can easily supply, the consequence is a depression of the funds; and this, at the same time, that it occasions the loans to be contracted on unfavourable terms, induces a loss upon those stockholders who are obliged to sell. The largeness of the loans, and the high amount of funded capital, are the real causes of the depression of the funds; and no security ever was or could be given to the public creditors, at the contraction of any loan, that could limit the contraction of such debts in future as the exigencies of the time might require; and if the amount of debt seem to approach to its utmost limit, while the public expense is still increasing, the dread of a national bankruptcy will depress the funds in a still higher degree.

A private creditor attends to the amount of the debts, and the comparative state of the income and expenses of his debtor. If he finds his debts increasing beyond the measure of his estate, his alarms will be excited, and they will not be much relieved by any detail of the arrange- ment



* Outlines of a Plan of Finance, 1813, pages 6 and 7.

ment of his affairs which the steward may communicate to him.

II. It is observed, that "nothing more can be expected "in a permanent war system than to provide for such a "scale of expense as must necessarily arise out of the "war, without including that great increase which has "been occasioned by our extraordinary exertions abroad "in the four last years,—which must be considered as "only of an occasional nature,—that the equalization of "the public income and expenditure may be considered "as a primary advantage of the sinking fund; and this "object, so far as is requisite to meet that part of the "expenses of the war, which may be considered as neces-"sarily permanent, appears to have been already accom-"plished."*

The doctrine here laid down cannot be admitted without considerable limitation. If the situation of a nation, as connected with surrounding nations, and the system of conduct observed towards them, be such as to promise alternate periods of war and peace at no long intervals, the proportion of revenue and expenditure may be regulated with a view to such a prospect. When there is a probability of a long continued war, (and the outlines appear to be drawn with a view to that case) the public revenue must be raised to the average of war expenditure, in order to prevent the risk of our finances being overwhelmed. If, during the continuance of war, the expense of one year, or of a few years, should, from special circumstances not likely to recur, much exceed the average war expenditure, it is consistent with safety, and proper, that the revenue should equal the average expenditure, and not the increased expenditure of these years. There is the same reason for this, as for regulating the revenue under



* Outlines, 1813, pages 4 and 5.

a system of alternate peace and war, to the average expenditure of a period which comprehends both. So far the doctrine is admitted. But the application to existing circumstances should be made with caution. We ought to enquire what reason there is to believe, on the supposition of the continuance of war, that the expense of the following years will be less than that of the present and immediately preceding ones. Shall we have fewer enemies? Do we propose to carry on our operations, by sea or land, on a less extensive scale? Can we support our armies and navy, or defray any branch of public expenditure, at a lower, or even an equal sum, as we did some years ago? Have we fewer foreign possessions to defend? Shall we be less lavish in bestowing subsidies at every quarter? We have often flattered ourselves, during the late war, that our expensive exertions would not be of long continuance, and these hopes were uniformly disappointed.

III. No observation is juster, or of more importance than that already quoted from the Outlines, of considering the whole public debt as one *indiscriminate mass.* We have had occasion to enlarge on this point in former parts of the present inquiry. By the system of frittering down the public debt into various portions, and allocating different funds for the discharge of each, and noticing the time when this and the other part would be discharged, the public has been misled, and even our financiers have not escaped embarrassment. In the Outlines, however clearly the above principle is laid down *in limine*, it seems to be lost sight of in the detail. In the tables annexed to the Outlines, the time when *each loan* will be discharged, according to the different systems and suppositions, is calculated with special care, and seems to be considered as an important circumstance.

IV. The system now under consideration is attended with the same palatable feature which accompanied that of Lord Henry Petty's, of promising an exemption from additional taxes for the three next years, and a smaller amount of them in the succeeding years. The manner of obtaining the former of these points is by declaring the debt of 1786 cancelled, and allocating the sinking fund, provided for it, to bear the charge of the new loans. This is merely a point of official regulation. The measure itself is attended with no injury to the national creditors; but it is not clear that it is salutary for the public. Whenever a nation does not tax to the amount of its expenditure, an increase of debt, to a higher amount than the sum saved in taxes, is inevitable; and in the comparison of different systems, those which impose the lightest taxes must always bring on an increase of debt in a still higher degree. This principle has been fully illustrated in former parts of this inquiry: We shall now state its application to the different suppositions considered in the Outlines.

The first hypothesis, contained in Table A. annexed to the Outlines, is that of an annual loan of 28 millions, at 5 per cent. which is reduced in the then existing system to 27 millions, in the year 1821, but continues without diminution in the new system. To exhibit the comparative effect of these systems on this hypothesis, Table X. is inserted in our Appendix,* from which it appears that the amount of additional taxes to be laid on from 1814, to 1821 inclusive, according to the existing system,

| | |
|---|---|
| is - - - - - - | L.14,933,328 |
| According to the new system, - | 7,099,110 |
| The whole amount of additional taxes levied these eight years, by the existing system, is - - | L.67,199,976 |
| By the new system, - - | 22,227,352 |
| Excess of taxes by existing system, - | L.44,972,624 |
| The debt created, by either system in these eight years, is - - | 224,000,000 |

 The

* See Note XXXII.

The amount of the sinking fund,
Existing system, - - - L.152,912,380
New system, - - - 99,278,439

L.53,633,941

Additional debt unredeemed,
Existing system, - - - L.71,087,620
New system, - - - - 124,721,561

The national debt (reduced to 5 per cents.) is greater, after eight years, in the new system, by - - L.53,633,941
Saving in taxes, new system, during that period, - - - - 44,972,624

Excess of additional debt, above saving in taxes, - - - - L.8,661,317

The amount of additional taxes to be imposed in sixteen years, from 1814 to 1829 inclusive, by the existing system, is - - - - L.29,333,328
By the new system - - - 16,524,392

The whole amount of additional taxes levied these sixteen years, by the existing system - - - L.251,466,600
By the new system, - - - 118,859,736

Excess of taxes by existing system, - L.132,606,864

Debt contracted in these sixteen years, existing system, - - - 440,000,000
New system, - - - 448,000,000

Amount sinking fund,
Existing system, - - - L.403,586,488
New system, - - - 226,114,350

 Additional

| Additional debt unredeemed, | |
|---|---|
| Existing system - - - | L.36,413,512 |
| New system, - - - | 221,885,650 |

| | |
|---|---|
| The national debt (reduced to 5 per cents.) is greater after sixteen years, in the existing system, by - | L.185,472,138 |
| Saving in taxes, new system, during that period, - - - | 132,606,864 |
| Excess of additional debt above saving in taxes - - - - | L.52,865,274 |

The hypothesis in Table B. annexed to the Outlines, is that of an annual loan of 25 millions, at 5 per cent. reduced in the existing system, in 1821, to 24 millions. According to this hypothesis, there is more additional debt contracted and unredeemed by the new system, in the first eight years, to the amount of L.51,543,153

| | |
|---|---|
| The saving in taxes is - - | 43,626,792 |
| Excess of additional debt above saving in taxes, - - - - | L.7,916,361 |

The unredeemed national debt (reduced to 5 per cents.) will be greater in the new system, after sixteen years, by - - - - - L.184,692,891

| | |
|---|---|
| Saving in taxes, - - - | 130,208,242 |
| Excess of additional debt above saving in taxes - - - - | L.54,484,649 |

The hypothesis in Table C. is that of an annual loan of 12 millions, at 3 per cent. reduced, in the existing system in 1826, to 11 millions. According to this hypothesis, the national debt, on the new system, is greater after sixteen



years

years, by - - - - L.53,566,359
Saving in taxes, - - - 46,992,592

Excess of additional debt above saving
in taxes - - - - L.6,573,767

The hypothesis in Table D. is that of the continuance of war until 1820, and afterwards alternate periods of ten years peace and war; annual loans of 25 millions, during war, but reduced in the existing system after 1821 to 24 millions; interest during war, 5 per cent., during peace, 4 per cent. According to this hypothesis, the national debt is greater by the new system, at the end of
7 years war, by - - - L.42,000,234
And the saving in taxes, - - 35,600,907

Excess increase of debt above saving in
taxes, - - - - L.6,399,327

During the next ten years of peace, the sum applicable to the discharge of the public debt, in the existing system,
is greater by - - - - L.114,435,708
And the aggregate of additional taxes
in that period is greater by - 81,383,850

Excess of sum applicable to discharge
of debt above additional taxes - L.33,051,858

V. The next circumstance which claims our attention is the periods at which additional taxes are proposed by the new system. All the late systems of finance have held forth a distant prospect, that, after a certain period, more or less remote, the national revenue would become equal to its expenditure, even in a state of continued warfare, and therefore no further taxes would be needed. If that period should ever arrive, it is obvious that the amount of taxes then levied must be much greater than what would at present cover our expense. For what reasons then do we not now raise them to that amount?

 We

We shall not ascribe this to our propensity to stave off the evil day at present, and leave posterity to provide for themselves as they can. In whatever degree this motive may operate, it is too unprincipled to be openly avowed. The only other reasons we remember to have heard adduced, are, that the nation is increasing in wealth, and will be better able to bear heavier taxes at a future time; and that a sudden increase of taxes would occasion so much discontent that a Minister dare not attempt it; whereas, taxes at first moderate, and increased at intervals, are submitted to with less reluctance, and do not become unproductive in an equal degree by occasioning the disuse of the articles taxed. We shall not at present enter into a discussion of these reasons. Whether we refer the deferred and gradual increase of taxation to either or both of them, or to any other that can be imagined, they concur in this point, that additional taxes should be imposed annually and equally, while the public necessities continue the same. By the new system, the amount of taxes imposed in different years is very unequal. According to the first hypothesis there are no additional taxes imposed in the years 1814, 1815, and 1816. In 1817, the additional taxes come near to L.1,300,000; in 1818, they fall below L.700,000; in each of the three following years they amount to about L.2,000,000; in 1822, there are no additional taxes; and in 1823, the additional taxes little exceed L.600,000. Like inequalities occur in the following years, and according to the other suppositions. The reason of this is, that the amount of taxes imposed is regulated by the periods at which the loans of former years are declared to have been redeemed. If several loans, or one large loan, fall in, no new taxes are imposed. If none fall in within the year, a large amount of additional taxes is had recourse to. Thus the amount of taxes to be imposed in future years is made to depend on the amount of loans contracted many years ago, and the period of the

 redemption

redemption of these loans, as ascertained by their terms, and the sinking funds appropriated to them at their contraction, under the regulations of the new system. There seems to be no good reason for regulating the periods of additional taxation in this manner. The several loans constitute the public debt, united into *one indiscriminate mass.* If the means adopted to meet the increase of this debt be a progressive increase of taxation, the progress ought to be uniform; or if otherwise, any diversity ought to arise from the circumstances and exigencies of the times when the taxes are imposed, and not from the discharge of former loans as estimated by an artificial system. In time of war, there is no real discharge of debt, but an annual contraction of debt, equal to the difference between the capitals created and the capitals redeemed.

VI. An advantage of a very extraordinary kind is affirmed to result from this system. "The principal "advantage of the proposed plan in time of peace, would "be the facility of keeping in reserve a large sum (sup-"pose L.100,000,000) as a resource in the case of the "renewal of hostilities. This fund, which would be "formed in a few years by the redeemed stock standing "in the name of the Commissioners, would be con-"tinually increasing, unless checked in the manner above-"mentioned; and in no case should be reduced below "such a sum as may be thought amply sufficient to sup-"port the confidence of the country at home, and maintain "its dignity abroad. It would indeed be *such a treasure "as no other country has ever possessed,* and the first "example of an immense accumulation of public property, "formed without the impoverishment of any individual, or "any embarrassment of the general circulation."*

We are altogether at a loss to form a distinct conception

 of

* Outlines, page 17.

of the nature of the *valuable treasure* here held forth. So soon as any stock is purchased by the Commissioners, and stands invested in their name, a like amount of the public debt is in fact discharged. Whether a Parliamentary declaration to that effect be made or not, is only a matter of form. If the money remain vested in the name of the Commissioners, no doubt it may be transferred again to purchasers, in the stock exchange, when war breaks out anew, and money may be raised for the public in this manner. But this is in every respect a new loan. It is an application to the public to invest their capital in the purchase of this dormant stock. The capitalists must be possest of the sum wanted; and they will not part with it, except upon terms from which they derive a profit. They would do this with equal readiness, if a loan was proposed to them in the ordinary form. We can discover no facility or advantage which the public could derive from a loan conducted in this manner, rather than any other. Indeed the inefficacy of this *reserved treasure* appears so clear, that we almost doubt whether we have rightly apprehended the nature of the resource held forth: But we are not able to affix any other meaning to it.

If it be said that the whole capital of funded debt was once in circulation, and although a part of it is for a time withdrawn, it may be brought into circulation again, this amounts to no more than that the nation, having once borne a greater amount of debt than at the time alluded to, may be expected to be able to bear a like amount again. This may be affirmed either of a nation or a private estate, if other circumstances remain the same; but it is not much to the purpose. The proprietor of the private estate, who has experienced the hardships that result from being in debt, will feel little solacement, after these are relieved, from the consideration that if he chooses to engage in a fresh career of extravagance, he

 will

will only be plunged again into the same difficulties; and if ever the public be partially delivered from that load of debt which cramps its national operations, and occasions privations to the individuals who compose the public, it will be no great source of rejoicing that it may engage in new wars for a season without undergoing greater hardships than those which it had experienced before.

It is true, that if the taxes imposed during war for the purpose of a sinking fund, be continued after peace is restored, till a large sum (suppose L.100,000,000) be vested in the hands of the Commissioners, the public, upon the renewal of war, may spend to that amount without imposing fresh taxes. This amounts to no more than that if we choose, during peace, to submit to the hardships of war taxation after our debt is partially discharged, we may engage again in war, without bearing heavier burthens than those from which we might have been delivered, if we had repealed the taxes as the debt was discharged.

VII. In examining this and the other systems of finance, we have chiefly confined ourselves to a view of the effects expected from them, during the first 16 years or thereby from their establishment. Such a period is fully sufficient to ascertain their merits. In the Tables annexed to the plan, their operation is traced for a much longer time. That of the sinking fund, Table C. 2. is extended as far as the year 1866; and we are informed, in a note, that the remaining debt will be redeemed according to the existing system in the year 1912, and according to the new system in the year 1875. It is altogether unnecessary to trace their operations to such distant periods. It is morally impossible any system can be adhered to so long. Sir Robert Walpole's sinking fund was never supported with efficacy. Mr. Pitt's sinking fund commenced in 1786, and was corroborated in 1792; considerably infringed on in 1798; underwent a great

 alteration

alteration in 1802; was laid aside for Lord Henry Petty's plan in 1807; revived in 1808; and is now superseded by Mr. Vansittart's plan in 1813; and it may be almost certainly foreseen that measures different from those now proposed will be had recourse to by succeeding financiers. This will arise, not only from the different views of different men, but from the change of circumstances which the fluctuation of human affairs always induces. The proper measures to be followed in that great department of national administration half a century hence, will depend on the exigencies and resources of the time, and cannot be foreseen at present.

---

## CHAPTER V.

*General Observations on Sinking Funds.*

I. In the resolutions frequently proposed by Ministry to Parliament, in order to exhibit a general and comparative view of the state of our finance at different periods, the proportion of the sum applicable to the discharge of debt to the debt itself, is introduced, and seems to be considered as an important circumstance. This proportion in 1788 was $\frac{1}{238}$, in 1793 it was $\frac{1}{160}$, in 1803, $\frac{1}{77}$, 1809, $\frac{1}{54}$, and in 1813, $\frac{1}{44}$. The inference drawn from this growing proportion is, that although the national debt has greatly increased, the means provided for its discharge have increased in a still higher degree, and therefore its present magnitude affords no cause of alarm.

The extent of the sinking fund is artificial, and may be brought, by a mere change in the arrangement of the public accounts, to bear any proportion to the amount of debt, without the slightest advantage, or any tendency to



promote

promote its discharge. In time of war, we raise a certain sum by taxes for the expense of the year, and borrow what further is wanted. If a sinking fund be maintained, the sums appropriated are deducted from what would have otherwise been expended on the war, and a greater loan is required. We may throw into the sinking fund any share of the revenue we please. We have only to add as much to the loan, and we shall raise a larger sum in the form of loan, with the same facility, by the effect of the sums thrown into the money market for the stock purchased by the Commissioners. In time of war, the sinking fund is nominal; in time of peace, a large sinking fund will discharge the debt more quickly; but this amounts to no more than that a continuance of the taxes, which we paid in war, after peace is restored, will be attended with a speedier reduction of debt, than what would take place if a larger part of these taxes were repealed.

II. A similar circumstance, held forth to ease the alarms arising from the magnitude of the national debt, is the progress already made in its discharge by the sinking fund, and the large sum redeemed. We are told that these operations have succeeded beyond expectation, and that the whole debt existing in 1786, amounting to 238 millions is already paid off. This is altogether fictitious and delusive. We may pay off as much debt as we please at any time by borrowing: But the only real alteration in the state of our finance is the difference between the debt contracted and the debt paid off; and while the former of these exceeds the latter, our situation is growing worse to the extent of that difference.

A private gentleman, whose estate is incumbered, may, if he have any credit, pay off all his debt every year, by borrowing from other hands; but if he spends more than his free income, his embarrassments will continually increase, and his affairs are so much the worse by being

 conducted

conducted in this manner, from the fees he pays to his agents. The absurdity of supposing any advantage derived from this annual discharge of his debts will appear still stronger, if we suppose him, instead of borrowing from other hands, only to renew the securities to the same creditors annually, paying a fee to the agents, and a *douceur* to the creditors themselves on the renewal. All these observations are equally applicable to the debt of a nation, conducted as ours is. It would not be impracticable, or very difficult, to redeem our whole debt in any year, if the measures we follow be redemption. It would only require a large loan every month, and the large sums we were thus enabled to pay would supply the funds for these loans. Our capitalists would be well pleased to promote these loans, as they would derive a *bonus* from each. Such a system would be ruinous in the extreme; and the system we follow is the same on a smaller scale, and is therefore only pernicious in a less degree.

In the year 1786, our funded debt was 238 millions. We had paid all this off in 1813, but we had contracted (exclusive of the loans of that year) a new debt of 574 millions. Does not this amount to the same, as that we had paid no debt at all, but contracted an additional debt of 336 millions?

III. The dangers arising from the magnitude and progressive increase of the national debt, ought to be laid before the public without exaggeration, but without palliation. Another source of alarm has been started of late years, of the evils to be apprehended from too great an increase of the sinking fund, and too rapid a discharge of the national debt, or too sudden a repeal of taxes. These fears were first announced (at least with any degree of energy) on the publication of Lord Henry Petty's Plan of Finance, in 1807; and they seem to have taken considerable possession of the public mind. "It [the "plan of 1802] would throw such large and dispropor-

" tioned sums into the public market, in the latter years " of its operation, as might produce a very dangerous " depreciation of the value of money. Many inconve- " niences might also arise from the sudden stop which " might be put to the application of these sums, when " the whole debt shall have been redeemed, and from the " no less sudden change in the price of all commodities, " which must follow from taking off, at one and the same " moment, taxes to an extent then probably much exceed- " ing 30 millions." *—" This successive redemption is, " indeed, a point of no small importance to the regulation " of the money market, as the rate of interest, and the " value of money might be very inconveniently affected " by the too rapid increase, or the too sudden reduction of " the sums brought into circulation by the sinking fund. " It should not, therefore, be suffered to accumulate for " too long a period, while, on the other hand, it should " not be too much diminished, by extinguishing at once " too large a proportion of the public debt."† We have seen the fears of these inconveniences urged, in some private publications, in still stronger terms.—They appear to us altogether groundless.

The operation of the sinking fund during war, when loans to a higher amount are annually contracted, we trust we have evinced to be altogether fictitious. It is not probable, that during the continuance of war, taxes will be raised to the measure of war expenditure; but they are likely to exceed much what is wanted for a peace establishment; and the excess is likely to be larger, the longer that war is continued. At the restoration of peace, the nation possesses a surplus revenue, which may be either diminished or annihilated altogether, by the repeal of taxes, or applied to the discharge of the public debt. We have already annihilated a great part of this surplus by

185 the

* Plan of Finance, 1807. p. 14. † Plan of Finance, 1813, p. 9.

the repeal of the property tax; and it is proper and probable that we shall continue to embrace both measures. The proportions of surplus revenue to be disposed of, the one way or the other, are completely at command, and ought to be determined from the state of affairs at the time, and not from the results of an artificial system, laid down many years before.

It was generally believed, during the war, that, when it terminated, prudence would require us to support a higher peace establishment than we ever did before. We have done so since the restoration of peace, and are likely to continue it. This prospect alone may allay our fear of bad consequences from too sudden a discharge of debt.

Those who believe, as we do, that the load of public debt is a great evil, and that its discharge would be a great deliverance, may at the same time admit, that a *sudden alteration*, however beneficial in its ultimate result, would be attended with serious inconveniences, and that every precaution should be employed to prevent or alleviate these.

The inconveniences apprehended, arise from the difficulty of employing the capital paid off, and the reduction of the rate of interest.

A low rate of interest is generally esteemed beneficial, and is said to have prevailed in the wealthiest and most flourishing nations, while the rate has been much higher in those that were in a semi-barbarous state. We do not admit this doctrine without considerable qualification; but could not discuss the argument without a length of digression unsuitable to this place.

We have no doubt that the whole capital, at present invested in the funds, may be beneficially employed in agriculture, manufacture, and commerce, and thereby prove a source of increasing wealth to the country. But this cannot be done all at once. These objects must expand by degrees, and no more capital should be paid

 off

off in any year that can be otherwise disposed of to advantage. We have little apprehension that we should have more to offer; but, if the case should be otherwise, we can restrict it, in any degree, by the repeal of taxes.

Apprehensions of inconveniences from the sudden amelioration of the circumstances of the middling and lower ranks, arising from the repeal of taxes, have been insinuated. We cannot enter into these views. That numerous part of the community, which has for some time laboured under great privations, when they feel this relief, will afford themselves a greater share of the comforts of life; and, by their additional consumption, give encouragement to agriculture, manufacture, and trade. Excess, in a certain measure, will be the consequence of affluence in every rank; but it will not be maintained that, in order to avoid that evil, all ranks should be kept in a state of depression. The sudden dismission of many of the officers employed in collecting the revenue is surely too trivial an object, and admits of too obvious remedies to merit notice. One evil apprehended from the sudden repeal of taxes is the loss which dealers would sustain, by the fall in price of the commodities on hand, on which the taxes were repealed. This class of men gained by the rise in price of commodities on hand when the taxes were imposed. We would not, however, wish them to undergo a loss on their repeal. This might be greatly alleviated, if not altogether prevented by allowing a considerable time between the enactment and repeal, and by other regulations suited to that purpose.

A funded capital, transferable as ours, is considered to be beneficial, as affording an easy and secure way of investing small sums belonging to persons in the lower ranks of life—the hard-earned savings of industry. There is something in this; but there is no reason to apprehend the amount of our funded debt will ever fall so low as to be insufficient for that purpose.

## CHAPTER VI.

### *Examination of the System of Funding by Increase of Capital.*

In the early part of the funding system, the capital assigned to the public creditor seldom exceeded the sum advanced by him. We find only two slight deviations from this rule during the seven years war, and one in the American war, before 1781. Annuities for years or lives were granted, as a bonus on many of the loans, during these periods. Afterwards, when the difficulty of raising loans increased, capitals were assigned to the creditors much higher than the sums advanced; and this practice has been continued since to a great extent.

It has been maintained in the House of Commons, on the part of Ministry, and, if we mistake not, even admitted by the Opposition, that it was the duty of a financier to raise the loan at the least annual expense it could be procured for, without regard to the amount of the nominal capital. We apprehend that this opinion is indefensible, except upon the supposition that all views of discharging the national debt, or any part of it, are for ever laid aside; and that the measures founded on it are very pernicious. The nation ought to pay no more in discharge of debt than the sum borrowed, together with the interest during the time the debt subsists. By the system now followed, it pays, besides, the excess of the capital assigned above the sum borrowed, in case the redemption be at par. Or, if the price of the funds enable the public to redeem the debt on lower terms, the nation pays, in addition to the sum borrowed, the difference between the price of stock at the times of borrowing and paying, which is always great.

The terms of the debt contracted during the American war, and since the commencement of the war in 1793, have been already given. The excess of the capital funded, above the money borrowed, is as follows:

| | Sums borrowed. | Capital funded. |
|---|---|---|
| Debt contracted during American war, | L.91,763,842 | L.115,267,993 |
| Loans from 1793 to 1816, inclusive, - | 420,307,425 | 658,506,728 |
| Bills funded in that period, - - | 89,148,773 | 107,030,717 |
| | L.601,220,040 | L.880,805,438 |
| Of which redeemed, - - | 183,369,223 | 291,719,172 |
| | L.417,851,817 | L.589,086,266 |
| | | 417,851,817 |
| Excess of capital above sum raised, - - - | | L.171,234,449 |

Thus it appears, that if the funded debt, contracted since the commencement of the American war, were paid off at par, the nation would pay above 171 millions more than it ever received, which is more than four-tenths of the sum borrowed, deducting that expended in redemption. The far greater part of this excess has arisen since the war of 1793, and almost the whole of it since the year 1780.

The national creditors are not obliged to accept of payment under par, that is, a sum equal to their nominal capital. But as they cannot, like private creditors, demand payment, and as the price of those funds which bear a low rate of interest is generally under par, it has been in the power of the public, in former intervals of peace, to pay off part of the national debt considerably under par, with the voluntary consent of the creditors; and the same end is now obtained, in a more constant manner, by the purchases made by the Commissioners.

Dr. Price was of opinion, at the time he wrote, that the three per cents. on the return of peace, would rise to par, or above it; and he considered that as a desirable event. Whether it would be so, we may hesitate to pronounce,

 when

when we attend to the variety of interests involved. It could not take place without a general reduction of the rate of interest; and this must be accompanied by a like reduction of the profits on trade and manufacture. It would obstruct the redemption of the national debt under par, and prevent its being accomplished, unless at the loss abovementioned.

But we do not consider the rising of the three per cents. to par as a probable event; and had Dr. Price lived to see the magnitude which our debt has now attained, it is likely he would have been of the same opinion. From the establishment of the sinking fund to the 1st of February, 1791, there was L.6,772,350 of the three per cents. redeemed for L.5,424,592, being at the rate of 80 nearly.

Now, if we suppose the three per cents. redeemed at 80,* and the four per cents. and five per cents. at par, the sum required for the redemption of the abovementioned debt would be,

| | | |
|---|---|---|
| L.386,366,568 | Capital in three per cents. at 80, - - - | L.309,093,254 |
| 202,719,698 | Capital in 4 and 5 per cents. at par, - - | 202,719,698 |
| L.589,086,266 | redeemed for - - | L.511,812,952 |
| | Sum borrowed, - - | 417,851,817 |
| | | L.94,961,135 |

Hence the loss incurred by the public on this favourable supposition would be 95 millions, in discharging the whole capital, and a like proportion for any part of it that might be discharged during a period of peace.

190 This

* See Note XXXIII.

This system was only in its infancy when Dr. Price wrote, and he censures it in the following terms:—" In
" 1758, the lenders of L.6,600,000 were entitled to a capital
" of L.115 for every L.100 subscribed, or L.7,590,000 in
" the stock of the three per cent. annuities: The conse-
" quence of which must be, that, in discharging this debt,
" 15 per cent. or near a million, must be paid, which was
" never received, and by which nothing has been gained.
" —Were a person in private life to borrow L.100, on con-
" dition it should be reckoned L.200 borrowed, at two
" and a half per cent. he would, by subjecting himself to
" the necessity (if he ever discharged the debt) of paying
" *double* the sum he received, gain somewhat of the air
" of borrowing at two and a half per cent. though he
" really borrowed at five per cent. But would such a
" person be thought in his senses? One cannot, indeed,
" without pain consider how needlessly the capital of our
" debts has been, in several instances, increased.—Thus
" do spendthrifts go on, loading their estates with debt,
" careless what difficulties they throw on the discharge of
" the principal, leaving that to their successors, and satis-
" fied with any expedients that will make things do their
" time."*

This censure, severe as it is, appears in a great measure deserved. We ought, however, to pay attention to any saving of interest, which is the inducement for contracting the public debt in the manner that has been followed.

The natural proportion of the price of capital in the three per cent. four per cent. and five per cent. funds, is the same as that of the respective rates of interest. Thus, if the five per cents. be at par, the four per cents. should



* Preface to 3d edition of Observations on Reversionary Annuities, page 14.

be at 80, and the three per cents. at 60; and this proportion, except some slight deviations from transient causes, would continue to hold when the prices rose, if it were certain the debt would never be redeemed. The only object, in that case, in which the national creditors are interested, is to draw an annuity for the money they advance; and it would be to them a matter of indifference what denomination be given to the fund from which the dividends were drawn. If the three per cents. rose to 75, the four per cents. should rise to 100, and the five per cents. to 125. But as all the funds are redeemable at par,* the actual price can never much exceed it. So soon as the five per cents. rise above par, the financier will offer payment, and by doing so, induce the creditors to submit to a reduction of interest.—The holders of stock in a three per cent. or four per cent. fund, have thus a prospect of gain by the rise of value, in which the five per cent. stockholders do not participate; and, in like manner, when the three per cents. rise above 75, the holders have a further gain in which the four per cent. stockholders do not participate. In consequence of these expectations, the price of four per cents. is higher, compared with that of the five per cents.; and the price of the three per cents. higher than that of either of the others, than the proportion of the rates of interest; and loans are transacted in the three per cents. on easier terms. The lender expects to gain by the rise of stock; and what he gains, the public loses, at re-payment or redemption.

In order to estimate the extent of the difference of interest occasioned by funding in capitals of different sorts, we may consider the rates of interest paid by the public on those loans, and the sums funded, where the contract

 was

* See Note XXXIV.

was made at one rate only, and not incumbered with a long annuity.

There have been eleven loans of this sort, in the three per cents. since the commencement of the war in 1793, the amount borrowed being L.157,650,000, and the sum funded L.267,804,500, the interest of which is L.8,034,135 being at the rate of L.5 2s. per cent. at an average on the sum borrowed; the particulars being as follows:

| | Sums raised. | Capital funded. | Interest. |
|---|---|---|---|
| 1793, | 4,500,000 | 6,250,000 | 187,500 |
| 1798, | 3,000,000 | 5,624,250 | 168,727 |
| 1799, | 12,500,000 | 21,875,000 | 656,250 |
| 1800, | 18,500,000 | 29,045,000 | 871,350 |
| 1801, | 25,500,000 | 44,816,250 | 1,344,488 |
| 1804, | 10,000,000 | 18,200,000 | 546,000 |
| 1805, | 20,000,000 | 34,400,000 | 1,032,000 |
| 1806, | 18,000,000 | 29,880,000 | 896,400 |
| 1810, | 8,000,000 | 11,230,000 | 336,900 |
| 1812, | 15,650,000 | 27,544,000 | 826,320 |
| 1814, | 22,000,000 | 38,940,000 | 1,168,200 |
| | 157,650,000 | 267,804,500 | 8,034,135 |

There was only one loan, and one operation of funding bills, at 4 per cent. viz.

| | Sums raised. | Capital funded. | Interest. |
|---|---|---|---|
| 1808, Loan, - | L.8,000,000 | L.9,454,000 | L.378,160 |
| 1813, Bill funded, | 3,755,700 | 5,220,423 | 208,817 |
| | L.11,755,700 | L.14,674,423 | L.586,977 |

The interest being at the rate of L.4. 19s. 10d. at an average.

There have been twelve loans, and operations of funding bills, in the 5 per cents., viz.

| | Sums raised. | Capital fund. | Interest. |
|---|---|---|---|
| 1794, Bills funded, | 1,907,451 | 1,926,526 | 96,326 |
| 1795, Bills funded, | 1,490,647 | 1,609,898 | 80,495 |
| 1796, Bills funded, | 4,226,727 | 4,414,074 | 220,703 |
| —— Loyalty loan, | 18,000,000 | 20,124,843 | 1,006,243 |
| 1810, Bills funded, | 8,311,000 | 8,581,108 | 429,055 |
| 1811, Bills funded, | 7,018,700 | 7,278,392 | 363,919 |
| —— Loan& bills, | 4,981,300 | 5,166,319 | 258,316 |
| 1812, Bills funded, | 5,431,700 | 5,866,236 | 293,312 |
| —— Loan & bills, | 6,789,625 | 7,332,795 | 366,639 |
| 1813, Bills funded, | 12,000,000 | 13,860,000 | 693,000 |
| 1815, Bills funded | 10,313,000 | 12,066,210 | 603,310 |
| —— Loan & bills, | 7,822,598 | 9,142,192 | 457,109 |
| | 88,292,748 | 97,368,593 | 4,868,427 |

The interest being at the rate of L.5 10s. 3d. at an average.

Another consideration considerably reduces this difference in the interest. In the loans, the public pays the whole interest for the year that the loan is transacted, although the money be advanced by instalments, or discount allowed if the whole be paid up at once. If the lender did not obtain this advantage, he would demand an additional capital at least equivalent to L.2 10s. in the five per cents. and yielding an interest of 2s. 6d. Nothing similar to this occurs in the transactions of funding bills, from which the greater part of the 5 per cent. stock arises.

Thus, for a difference not exceeding six shillings or, at most, eight shillings per cent. on the interest, the public, by borrowing in the three per cents. incurs almost a certainty of paying L.133 for every L.100 borrowed, and a risk of paying L.166, when the debt comes to be discharged.

This view of the result is unfavourable to the system of borrowing on an advance of capital, and a low nominal interest.

If the debts were never to be paid, it would be proper to borrow in the manner in which money could be raised at the least interest, as the capital, in that case, would be

 merely

merely nominal: But, under such a view, the lenders would not accept of less interest in one fund than another. If there be a prospect of paying the debt, but at a very distant time, the public may gain more by saving of interest, than it loses by the additional sum ultimately paid. If the difference of interest be 8 shillings on L.100 borrowed, and the additional capital L.33, it would require 33 years before the accumulation of what was saved on the interest, at 5 per cent. compound interest, would become equal to the additional capital. But this is stating the saving too high, and the additional capital too low. If the saving of interest be 7 shillings, and the additional capital L.50, it would require 43 years for that purpose.

The only inducement which the lender can have for preferring a 3 per cent. capital, yielding a less interest, is the prospect of ultimate gain by the rise of the funds. This, he expects, will more than recompense the present loss he sustains by accepting an inferior interest. If he be right in his expectation, the public is a loser; and the lender, in this case, is more likely to conjecture right than the financier.

On the whole, we are of opinion, that the capital funded should never exceed the sum raised; and such a rate of interest should be allowed on this capital as the lender will accept of.

During a continued war, money often cannot be obtained for five per cent. interest; and it seems to be thought improper to give, in direct terms, a higher rate than can be legally taken in private transactions; though there is a necessity of doing so in an indirect manner.

For this purpose, it has been proposed to grant a long annuity, in addition to a capital equal to the sum borrowed at 5 per cent. This measure, however, is liable to one considerable objection—annuities being irredeemable, the public have it not in their power to take advantage of a fall in that rate of interest during peace, so far as the debt is constituted in that manner. This was heavily felt in the reign of George I. A large part of the debt contracted in the two former reigns was upon annuities; and when a general reduction of interest took place, a large additional capital was granted to the holders of these annuities, above the sum originally advanced, to induce them to convert their annuities into redeemable stock. There is not so much in the objection now, as the existing annuities form only a small part of the charge of our debt; and as we have enough to redeem besides, we may leave them to expire by the course of time, without seeking to redeem them. Still there is some weight in it. That part of the national charge cannot be diminished without the consent of the annuitants, whatever alteration may take place in the current rate of interest.

The objection against granting more than 5 per cent. interest, in direct terms, when necessary, is perhaps founded more in prejudice than reason. We affix an immorality to what is deemed usury; and, as we reprobate it in private life, we revolt at its admission into public transactions.

Many intelligent men are of opinion, that our usury laws originated in narrow views of political economy; and ought to be repealed, now that the advantage of leaving commerce free, in all its branches, is understood. Should these opinions gain ground so far as to influence legislative measures, every objection against contracting loans at a higher rate of interest would be removed.

We have lately heard of a proposal for borrowing in the 3 per cent., or, (what comes to the same purpose) selling out 3 per cent. stock in the hands of the Commissioners, in order to pay off the 5 per cents. at par. This does not appear to us so exceptionable as funding in the 3 per cents. The loans in the 3 per cents. were generally contracted when these funds were very low. In that of 1804, L.182 capital was granted for L.100 raised. In the imperial



loan

loan of 1797, a capital of L.226 10s. was granted; and on an average of all the 3 per cent. loans, since the commencement of the war, about L.170 has been granted. The public incurs the risk of paying all the additional capital and a certainty of paying the greater part of it when the debt is discharged. At the present price of the funds, (Dec. 1817,) L.100 may be procured for about L.120 in the 3 per cents; and if this were applied to pay off L.100, 5 per cents., the public would be freed from L.5 of interest, while it only incurred L.3 12s. and thereby save L.1 8s. annually; while the ultimate loss by increase of capital could not exceed L.20, and might probably not be so much. There are, however, various other ways by which the public may gain advantage from the present state of the funds; and we give the preference to those which may be effected without increase of capital, though the present saving were smaller.

We have seen a claim brought forward in the public papers, in favour of the stockholders, to whom payment might be offered, with an option of conversion; as if they should receive more than an equivalent in the 3 per cents. to recompense the diminution their incomes would sustain by the fall of interest. We consider such a claim as deserving the most decided reprobation. The capitalists have gained by that financial system, which has loaded the public with very heavy burthens; and it would be unjust and oppressive to the community, to pay them on more favourable terms than they have any claim to, or were ever held out to them. What would be thought of a private creditor, who, when offered payment of all that was due him, with interest, should demand from his debtor an additional sum, on the ground that he could not employ his money now in a manner that yielded so large a return as formerly?

It is impossible to go over this subject without remarking the great variety of modes that have been had recourse

 to

to in raising money. From 1793 to 1816, inclusive, there have been thirty-one loans, of which eighteen have been in the three per cents., and five of these have been aided by a long annuity. One has been funded in the four per cents. and four in the five per cents., three of which were blended with the funding of Exchequer Bills. Six have been funded partly in the three per cents. and partly in the four per cents.; five of which were accompanied by a long annuity: and two partly in the three per cents., and partly in the five per cents.

In the same period there have been thirteen operations of funding bills, besides those connected with the loans abovementioned; of which eight have been altogether in the five per cents., one altogether in the four per cents.; two partly in the four per cents., and partly in the five per cents.; and two, jointly in the three, four, and five per cents.; and to one of these a long annuity is attached.

# NOTES

### Note I.—Page 442.

The increase of circulating medium, of whatever kind, by deteriorating the value of money, enhances the money price of manufactures and native produce, and thereby obstructs, *cæteris paribus*, their sale in foreign markets. In this respect, paper money is always disadvantageous. It may give encouragement to industry by extending private credit, and thereby prove beneficial; but its application in this way is apt to be carried too far. The consideration of its influence upon the rate of exchange with foreign countries, and the other effects it produces, would lead us beyond the bounds of our present subject.

### Note II.—Page 447.

Since the imposition of war taxes in 1798, the permanent revenue was divided during the war into two great branches:

1st, The consolidated fund, consisting of all the branches existing in 1786, when Mr. Pitt's sinking fund was established, and many taxes which have been imposed since; and charged with the interest of the public debt, the sums payable to the Commissioners for its redemption, the allowance to the civil list, and pensions and other grants by Parliament. The surplus, which is always considerable, is applied to the current services of the year.

2d, The war taxes, consisting of the property-tax, and additional articles of customs and excise, appropriated thereto, and charged with the interest, &c. of the loans of 1807, 1809, and 1811, the amount of which is transferred from that branch of the revenue to the consolidated fund.

To these may be added,

3d, The duties granted annually. These were formerly the land and malt-tax: Since the land-tax was rendered perpetual, certain duties on sugar and tobacco, and the tax on offices, pensions, and salaries, formerly joined to the land-tax, besides the malt-tax, have been granted annually. These annual duties have of late years been charged with three millions to the supplies, and the overplus is transferred to the consolidated fund.

## Note III.—Page 453.

The amount of foreign property in the British funds, as ascertained by the claims of exemption from property tax in 1806, was L.18,598,666, besides L.17,147 per annum of terminable annuities. This account does not include the bank stock, the duty on the dividends of which are paid by the company. The whole amount at that time, may be estimated at about 22 millions, being about 1-25th of the funded debt then existing, besides a considerable sum belonging to foreigners, who did not claim the exemption. The foreign property in the British funds, in 1762, has been estimated at 18 millions, being about 1-7th of the funded debt at that time. In a late anonymous, but seemingly authentic statement, the capital held by foreigners is estimated at L.16,599,421, besides L.6,363 of terminable annuities.

## Note IV.—Page 460.

Paradoxical effects are ascribed to the increase of money by compound interest.

One penny put out at the Christian era, at five per cent. compound interest, would, before this time, have increased to a greater sum than could be contained in *five hundred millions of Earths*, all of solid gold.

Mr. Ricard appointed by his will, that the sum of 500 livres should be divided into five portions. The first, at the end of a hundred years, amounting to 13,100 livres, to be laid out in prizes for dissertations proving the lawfulness of putting out money to interest. The second, at the end of two centuries, amounting to 1,700,000 livres, to be employed in establishing a perpetual fund for prizes in literature and arts, and for virtuous actions. The third, at the end of three centuries, amounting to more than 226 millions of livres, to be employed for establishing patriotic banks, and founding museums with ample establishments. The fourth, at the end of four centuries, amounting to 30,000 millions, to be employed in building a hundred towns in France, containing each 150,000 inhabitants. The fifth, at the end of five centuries, amounting to four millions of millions of livres, to be appropriated for the payment of the national debt of Britain and France,—for producing an annual revenue to be divided among all the powers of Europe, for buying up useless offices, purchasing a royal domain, increasing the income of the clergy, and abolishing fees for masses,—for maintaining all children born in France till they be three years of age,—for improving waste lands, and bestowing them on married peasants,—for purchasing manors and exempting the vassals from all servitude, for founding houses of education, workhouses, houses of health, and asylums for females,—for portioning young women,—for conferring honorary rewards on merit;—besides a large surplus to be appropriated at the discretion of his executors.

Dr. Franklin is somewhat more moderate in his views. He leaves L.1000 to the city of Boston, and a like sum to Philadelphia, to be lent out at interest to young artificers, upon proper security, in sums not less than L.15, nor more than L.60. This plan, he says, if executed without interruption for an hundred years, will raise the capital to L.131,000 for each place, of which L.100,000 is to be applied for public works, such as fortifications, bridges, aqueducts, public buildings, baths, pavements, &c. The remaining L.31,000 to be lent out at interest for another hundred years, as before, when, if no unfortunate accident has intervened, it will amount to L.4,061,000; of which, L.1,061,000 to be given to the towns for such purposes as abovementioned; and the remaining L.3,000,000 to the Government of the State,—"not presuming," says the Doctor, "to carry my views any farther."

It is theoretically true that compound interest may accomplish all these things; but such extravagancies rather tend to throw ridicule on the subject, than increase our confidence in its operations.

### Note V.—Page 470.

In early times, all interest for money, or *usury*, as it was then called, was unlawful. Yet, in defiance of heavy penalties, necessity enforced the payment of interest, often upon exorbitant terms. The first statute authorising and limiting the rate of interest in England was in the reign of Henry VIII. in the year 1546, when it was fixed at ten per cent. In the reign of his successor, Edward VI. all interest was again prohibited. In the year 1572, in the reign of Elizabeth, interest was permitted at the rate of ten per cent In 1624, in the reign of James I. the rate was reduced to eight per cent.

cent. In 1651, during the usurpation of Cromwell, it was reduced to six per cent.; and this was confirmed at the Restoration. In 1714, it was reduced to five per cent.; at which, as the legal rate, it has continued since.

All these reductions by law seem rather to have followed than anticipated the actual rate of interest, arising from the commercial state of the nation. To compel the lending of money at a lower rate of interest than that which naturally results from existing circumstances, is equally impracticable as to prohibit interest altogether. But when the actual rate of interest fell below the legal standard, that rate was reduced, to prevent particular acts of oppression.

In Italy and other states where commerce was earlier established, interest was reduced sooner and lower than in England. In Scotland, the reduction took place a little later. Interest there was reduced to eight per cent. in the year 1633, being nine years later than in England; and it was reduced to six per cent. in 1661, ten years later than in England.

NOTE VI.—Page 471.

THE terms of this tontine were, That the subscribers of L.100. 5s. being distributed into six classes according to their ages, should receive the undermentioned annuities, with benefit of survivorship in their respective classes, till the annuity on the original share amounted to L.1000, after which the surplus is to fall to the public.

| | L. | s. | d. |
|---|---|---|---|
| 1st Class, under 20 years of age, - - - | L.4 | 3 | 0 |
| 2d Class, from 20 to 30, - - - - | 4 | 5 | 6 |
| 3d Class, from 30 to 40, - - - - - | 4 | 8 | 6 |
| 4th Class, from 40 to 50, - - - - | 4 | 13 | 6 |
| 5th Class, from 50 to 60, - - - - - | 5 | 1 | 6 |
| 6th Class, above 60, - - - - - - | 5 | 12 | 0 |

The amount of annuities granted on these terms (including a subsequent addition) was - - - - - L.18,847

And for the remainder, annuities for 69¼ years were allowed at the rate of L.4 5s. for each subscription, as above, amounting to - - - - - - L.24,365

And in order to place those persons who retained their shares in the tontine on the same footing as if the whole had been filled up, the treasury was empowered to nominate lives among persons in public station, to be distributed in the several classes in the same proportion as the nominees appointed by the subscribers; by whose death, as well as that of the actual holders of the tontine, the benefit of survivorship should be regulated. The amount of annuities



entered

entered in these names was L.24,681. Thus the sum payable by the public is variable, according as a greater proportion of deaths happen among the real or fictitious nominees.

NOTE VII.—Page 475.

THE cause of the difference of the interest of money in this and several other loans was, that the orders for repayment were discharged according to their dates, and those who subscribed late were obliged to wait longer for repayment; and if the fund prove deficient, the whole inconvenience fell on them, for which reason they were allowed a higher rate of interest.

NOTE VIII.—Page 480.

THE sum appointed to be raised on annuities by 3d Anne, chap. 3, is L.300,000; but there appears to have been raised,

| | | *Annuity.* | | |
|---|---|---|---|---|
| L.200,820 on single lives, at 9 years purchase, | - | L.22,313 | 6 | 8 |
| 115,808 on two lives, at 11 years purchase, | - | 10,528 | | |
| 47,756 on three lives, at 12 years purchase, | - | 3,979 | 13 | 4 |
| L.364,384 | | L.36,821 | | |

And, by an act of the following year, the holders of these annuities were entitled to extend them to the term of 99 years from their commencement, on payment of six years purchase for annuities on a single life; four years purchase for annuities on two lives; and three years purchase on annuities for three lives; and a like right was given to strangers when the holder of the annuity declined it. L.187,930 was raised by this conversion.

NOTE IX.—Page 483.

THE revenue appropriated to the civil list is charged not only with the personal expenses of the Sovereign and his household, but with part of the salaries of the judges, foreign Ambassadors, and officers of state, and other expenses of civil government. The separation of these from the other branches of public expenditure took place after the revolution. In king William's reign, they amounted to about L.680,000 per annum. At the beginning of queen Anne's, certain branches of the revenue were granted during her life, to defray the expenses of civil government, which were estimated at L.700,000, but are supposed to have fallen short of that sum. Of this, L.100,000 was annually appropriated by that Sovereign in aid of the expenses of the war. The same revenue, with some alterations,

alterations, was granted at the accession of George I.; but this, notwithstanding some casual accessions, being insufficient, L.1,000,000 was borrowed in 1721, charged on a duty on pensions, and still forms a separate article of our funded debt. At the accession of George II. the civil list was raised to L.800,000. The branches then appropriated to it were certain articles of the excise and customs, the profits of the post-office, part of the duty on wine licences, the revenue of the crown lands, and other remains of the ancient hereditary revenue, and L.120,000 charged on the aggregate fund. If these funds fell short of the stipulated sum, the deficiency was to be supplied by Parliament; but if they exceeded it, the Sovereign was to retain the advantage. At first, they proved deficient, and grants were made, at different times, of upwards of L.500,000, to make up the sum; but in the latter part of the reign, they considerably exceeded it.

At the beginning of the present reign, these branches were transferred to the aggregate fund; and that fund was charged with L.800,000, as a full and permanent allowance for the civil list. This list was subject at that time to payments of L.50,000 to the princess dowager of Wales; L.25,000 to the duke of Cumberland, and L.12,000 to the princess Amelia; and soon after, L.58,000 to the queen. In progress of time, these burthens on the civil list were much augmented, by allowances to different members of the royal family.

| | |
|---|---|
| To the abovementioned grant of - - | L.800,000 |
| there was added in 1777, - - | 98,000 |
| in 1802, - - | 60,000 |
| | L.958,000 |
| And in 1812, at the commencement of the regency, there was granted during its continuance, - | 70,000 |
| And transferred from the allowance formerly settled on the prince of Wales, - - - | 50,000 |
| | L.1,078,000 |
| And there is deducted L.100,000 for his majesty's expenses, L.60,000 for his privy purse, and L.10,000 additional to her majesty—in all, - | 170,000 |
| Leaving for the prince regent's civil list, - | L.908,000 |

Besides these sums, charged on the consolidated fund, an allowance from surplus fees is transferred to the civil list, and now fixed at L.48,000



The

The following sums have been granted in the present reign, in aid of the civil list.

| | |
|---|---|
| In 1769, - - - | L.513,581 |
| in 1777, - - - | 620,000 |
| in 1784, - - - | 60,000 |
| in 1786, - - - | 30,000 |
| | L.1,223,581 |
| And to the prince regent, for extra expenses, on his assuming the functions of government, | 100,000 |
| | L.1,323,581 |

Besides these, large sums have been granted for expenses on the royal palaces, portions to the princesses at their marriage, and annuities to the several branches of the royal family. The amount of these annuities in 1817 was L.355,500.

Notwithstanding these augmentations and additional grants, the whole money appropriated to it during the present reign is inferior to the produce of the branches which formerly belonged to it; and the augmentations are by no means adequate to the deterioration of the value of money during the period.

The revenue of the civil list being still found inadequate to defray the charges, an act was passed in 1816, by which, among other regulations, pensions to different branches of the royal family, amounting to L.30,500, formerly paid from the civil list, are transferred to the consolidated fund. By a schedule, annexed to this act, the future probable annual charge is classed, and estimated as follows:

| | |
|---|---|
| Class 1. Pensions and allowances to the royal family, | L.298,000 |
| 2. Allowances to the chancellor, judges, &c. - | 32,955 |
| 3. Allowances to foreign ministers, &c. - | 226,950 |
| 4. Bills of his majesty's tradesmen, - | 209,000 |
| 5. Departments of lord chamberlain, lord steward, master of the horse, master of the robes, and surveyor of the works, - | 140,700 |
| 6. Pensions, limited by 22 Geo. III. cap. 82. to | 95,000 |
| 7. Salaries and allowances to certain officers and persons, - - - | 41,300 |
| 8. Salaries to commissioners of the treasury, and chancellor of the exchequer, - | 13,822 |
| Occasional payments, - - | 26,000 |
| | L.1,083,727 |



Note X.

NOTE X.—Page 489.

L.500,000 was authorized to be raised in 1726, by Exchequer bills bearing interest at 2d. per day, charged on the victuallers' act, and L.481,400 thereof was raised. In 1743, a farther sum of L.518,600 was authorized to be raised, to complete a million; and, as the victuallers' act was repealed, the interest at 3 per cent. was charged on a duty on spirit licences. In 1746, the Exchequer bills issued upon these acts, amounting to L.986,800, were taken in by the Bank, and cancelled. The Bank were allowed 4 per cent. on that sum, which was then added to, and still forms a part of their permanent capital.

NOTE XI.—Page 493.

ALL the loans contracted in the American war were connected with lotteries. The subscribers to the loan of 1776 received for every L.100 subscribed, stock in the 3 per cents. L.77. 10 0
And three lottery tickets (in all 60,000) valued at L.10. The prizes being funded, the holders of the fortunate tickets received a capital, in the same fund, of - - - 30 0 0

L.107 10 0

This arrangement was intended to afford a profit on the lottery tickets to the subscribers, and a plan still more beneficial was adopted in the loans of the following years.

The subscribers to the loan of 1777 received 50,000 tickets, being one ticket for every L.100 subscribed.

The subscribers to the loan of 1778 received 48,000 tickets, being eight tickets for every L.1000 subscribed.

The subscribers to the loan of 1779 received 49,000 tickets, being seven tickets for every L.1000 subscribed.

The subscribers to the loan of 1780 received 48,000 tickets, being four tickets for every L.1000 subscribed.

The subscribers to the loan of 1781 received 48,000 tickets, being four tickets for every L.1000 subscribed.

The subscribers to the loan of 1782 received 40,500 tickets, being three tickets for every L.1000 subscribed.

The subscribers to the loan of 1783 received 48,000 tickets, being four tickets for every L.1000 subscribed.



The

The subscribers to the loan of 1784 received 36,000 tickets, being six tickets for every L.1000 subscribed.

The subscribers to the loans subsequent to 1776 paid for their tickets at the rate of L.10, in addition to the sum advanced by them for the loans ; and the prizes were not funded, as they had been in the seven years war, and in the lottery of 1776, but were paid to the holders of the fortunate tickets, to the extent of L.10 per ticket, in the spring of the following year.

## Note XII.—Page 494.

A more particular account of the progress of the national debt, previous to the war of the French revolution, is now given than in our former editions, and the sums stated as due at different periods are not all the same. The original documents at the earlier periods are not now easily accessible ; and those who have treated on the subject before us do not always agree in their statements. We shall not detain our readers with a detail of the labour we have undergone in endeavouring to reconcile their differences, and obtain an exact statement. We have not always succeeded, and cannot warrant every sum now given, previous to the commencement of the late war, as exact ; but are confident, that no error is committed that can materially affect the general view of the subject, and the reasonings founded on it. We have not followed any one writer implicitly, but have endeavoured to state every article in the way that appeared nearest the truth.

We have distinguished the permanent funded debt, the capital raised upon annuities, and the unfunded debt. The first of these is easily traced, and we trust little or no error on that head is committed. In regard to the second, a large part of the debt, contracted in the reigns of king William and queen Anne, was raised on annuities, without any permanent capital ; and, in the accounts of the national debt published by authority, the sum originally advanced, deducting only so much as corresponded to what had fallen in by the death of the annuitants, was stated as part of the debt, and added to the permanent capital. These amounted, at the peace of Utrecht, to upwards of twelve millions : A great part of which was subscribed into the South Sea Company, in the year 1720, and thereby converted into permanent stock. When these transactions were completed, the following sums remained, for many years charged as part of the national debt.

 Annuities,

| | *Principal.* | *Annuities.* |
|---|---|---|
| Annuities for long terms, granted in the reigns of king William and queen Anne, not subscribed into the South Sea stock, - - | L.1,836,275 | L.136,453 |
| Tontine annuities, 1692, - | 108,100 | 7,567 |
| Annuities for two or three lives, granted in 1693, decreasing annually, but originally, - - | 192,152 | 22,633 |
| | L.2,136,427 | L.166,653 |

The terms of the first of these expired in the years 1792, 1805, 1806, and 1807. The tontine annuities expired, by the death of the last nominee, in 1783. The other annuities for lives are, no doubt, all expired ; but a remnant of L.8,195 still stands in the books of the Exchequer, the deaths of the annuitants not having been reported. In the statements we have given previous to 1793, we have followed the mode used in the official accounts, though it obviously over-rates the value of the annuities. By this arrangement, a sum of more than two millions is subtracted from the amount of the public debt, in the statements subsequent to 1786, not by payment, but by the operation of time ; and, consequently, the debts paid in certain periods are represented greater, or those contracted less, than they ought to be.

The annuities granted at later periods (except the tontine of 1789,) are all in addition to a permanent capital equal at least to the sum advanced, and no capital is charged for them in the official statements. The first of these were life annuities, to the extent of L.22,500, granted on a loan during the rebellion, 1745, in addition to the permanent capital, at a time when public credit was low. Various other annuities have been granted for lives or years in the same manner.* In some private statements of the national debt,† a value is put upon these, equal to the supposed sum for which they might be bought off at the time : But as no such permanent capital existed, and there is little doubt of their being left to expire with the course of time, it seems more proper to view them in the light of an additional interest granted for a limited term, and state their amount and duration accordingly, in the enumeration of our public burthens.

We could not avoid some inaccuracy in stating the amount of

 subsisting

* See Note XXI.

† By Dr. Price and others.

subsisting life annuities, at some of the periods, not having met with a return of those which had fallen in by death since the former period; but any error of this kind must be very inconsiderable. Errors of greater magnitude are probably committed in regard to the unfunded debt, which we have not always accurate means of ascertaining. In regard to this, we must remark, that, in the statements previous to the American war, Exchequer bills, which were then circulated to a comparatively small extent, were classed along with the permanent debt; and what is stated as unfunded, consists of the debt of the navy, and other similar articles. In the later statements, the Exchequer bills are always classed as part, and generally the greatest part of the unfunded debt.

The statements of the unfunded debt since the commencement of the late war, are correct, so far as the returns to Parliament are complete. We have estimated the interest on the unfunded debt, since 1748, at 3 per cent. It ought to have been higher at some of the periods.

One observation more is necessary. The total sums of debt assigned at the different periods, comprehend the funded and unfunded. The latter of these cannot be discharged without payment of the full sum stated. The former may be redeemed for a less sum; and, as the proportions vary at different periods, the totals do not exhibit an exact comparative view of the amount of our burthens. There was no way of avoiding this, unless we had fixed a value on the funded debt, according to our views of what it might have been redeemed for. But as the prices of stock are continually fluctuating, an attempt to do so would have been liable to more exception than the statements we have given.

We may offer an apology for the acknowledged imperfection of this part of our work, from the inability of those who had every means of official information at command, to present a complete statement of the progress of our debts. In a Note, annexed to the account of the public debt presented to the House of Commons, in 1799, it is said, "It has been found impracticable to ascertain the amount of the sums raised at different periods, which created the capitals composing the several funds existing prior to 33 Geo. III. anno 1793."

The Note intended as XIII. being considered as unnecessary, is omitted.

### Note XIV.—Page 503.

The following annuities, expired before 1793, were transferred to the Commissioners for the redemption of the national debt.

| | |
|---|---|
| Old long annuities, William and Mary, - | L.54,881 |
| Annuities, 17 Geo. III. - - | 25,000 |
| | L.79,881 |
| Which added to the annuities existing in 1792, - | 1,293,870 |
| Makes up the sum stated by the select committee of finance, in 1797, - - - | L.1,373,751 |

### Note XV.—Page 506.

In funding the navy bills, 1797, option was given to the holders to receive capital either in the three per cents. the four per cents. or the five per cents. at different rates, according to the dates of the bills, as exhibited in the following table.

Bills dated before

| | 3 per cent. | 4 per cent. | 5 per cent. |
|---|---|---|---|
| 1st January 1796, | L.178 11 5 | L.138 17 9¼ | L.119 0 11¼ |
| 30th April, | 176 19 9¾ | 137 18 7¼ | 118 6 10¼ |
| 31st July, | 175 8 9 | 136 19 8½ | 117 12 11¼ |
| 27th October, | 173 18 3 | 136 1 1 | 116 19 2 |

If all the navy bills then funded, had been at the second of these rates, (which were the rates allowed for the Exchequer bills funded at the same time,) the amount would have stood as follows :—

| | | |
|---|---|---|
| L.9,293,483 | in 3 per cents. at L.176 19 9¾ | L.16,438,175 |
| 544,982 | in 4 per cents. at 137 18 7¼ | 765,428 |
| 1,728,617 | in 5 per cents. at 118 6 10¼ | 2,034,890 |
| L.11,567,082 | | L.19,238,493 |

But the amount of navy bills actually funded, was L.11,595,529 ; therefore the average rates must have been lower than those of the second class.

### Note XVI.—Page 506.

The loan of L.18,000,000 in the year 1796, (commonly called the *Loyalty Loan*,) was contracted on the following terms : The subscribers of L.100, received a capital of L.112 10s. in a separate fund



at

at five per cent. ; and it was agreed that the holders, two years after the ratification of a definitive treaty of peace, should be entitled either to receive payment, or to have their stock converted into three per cents. at the rate of L.133 6s. 8d. for L.100 capital. But this loan is not redeemable on the part of Government, till three years after the other five per cents. be paid. The subscription was filled up in a few days, the sum funded being L.20,124,843.

This agreement came to be implemented in 1804. The consequent operations were continued for several years ; but these are all introduced in Table II. in the year 1805 ; and some portion of this loan has been paid every year since, which payments are all deducted together at the end of the Table.

In consequence of the renewal of the war, the price of the funds was so low, that the holders of the loyalty would have been losers by accepting of L.133 6s. 8d. in the three per cents. It was necessary, therefore, either to pay them, or offer them more advantageous terms.

By act 44 Geo. III. cap. 99. the holders of the loyalty loan were entitled to receive L.100 in the five per cent. consols ; and so much additional in the three per cent. reduced, as would make up the value of L.100, at the current price.

By act 45 Geo. III. cap. 8. the holders of L.4,448,817 were to receive so much capital in the five per cent. consols, or the three per cent. reduced, as would be equal in value to L.100 ; and so much additional capital in the three per cents. reduced, as would be equal to ten shillings more ; and these terms were accepted by the holders of about three fourths of that sum.

By act 45 Geo. III. cap. 73. the same terms were granted to other holders of the loyalty loan, to the extent of L.1,254,629.

The money required to pay such as did not accept of these terms was obtained by allowing the same terms in the way of loan ; and the capital granted in the five per cents. for every L.100 advanced, as settled by the average price of stock for the ten preceding days, was L.113 13s. 4d.

The holders of the five per cent. annuities, 1802, amount, L.2,227,612, which was joined to the loyalty loan, were entitled to the same terms.

The result of the operations on the Loyalty Loan is as follows :

| | Sums transfd. from loyalty loan. | Sums added to 3 p. cent. red. | Sums added to 5 per cent. cons. |
|---|---|---|---|
| 1804. | | | |
| Subscribed into 5 p. ct. cons. - | 13,263,553 | - - | 13,263,553 |
| And an additional capital granted in 3 p. cent. red. of - | - - | 2,716,815 | |
| 1805. | | | |
| Subscribed into 3 p. ct. red. - | 2,678,561 | 2,678,561 | |
| And an additional capital of - | - - | 1,785,707 | |
| And afterwards a further capital of - - - | - - | 245,149 | |
| Subscribed into 5 p. ct. cons. - | 2,019,661 | - - | 2,019,661 |
| And an additional capital granted of - - - | - - | - - | 265,018 |
| Borrowed in 5 p. cent. cons. to pay off loyalty loan, - - | 1,005,290 | - - | 1,005,290 |
| And an additional capital granted of - - - | - - | - - | 130,434 |
| | 18,967,067 | 7,426,233 | 16,683,958 |
| Sum transferred from loyalty loan, - - | | | 18,967,067 |
| Sum deducted from 5 per cents. by these operations, - | | | 2,283,109 |
| Sum added to 3 per cents. - - - | | | 7,426,233 |
| Addition to funded capital, - - - | | | 5,143,124 |
| Addition to interest on 3 per cents. - | | L.222,788 | |
| Deduction from interest on 5 per cents. - | | 114,155 | |
| Addition to interest on funded debt by these operations, | | | 108,633 |
| And to management, about - - - - | | | 2,314 |

The present state of the loyalty loan is as follows:

| | | |
|---|---|---|
| Amount loyalty loan, - - | | L.20,124,843 |
| 5 per cents. 1802, - - - | | 2,227,612 |
| | | L.22,352,455 |
| Sums transferred or paid, before 1806, - | | 18,967,067 |
| Amount loyalty loan remaining 1st Feb. 1806, - | | L.3,385,388 |
| And the payments since that time are, | | |
| In 1806, - - | L.979,257 | |
| 1807, - - | 336,088 | |
| 1808, - - | 153,697 | |
| 1809, - - | 60,867 | |
| 1810, - - | 18,776 | |
| 1811, - - | 113,416 | |
| 1812, - - | 100,292 | |
| 1813, - - | 184,056 | |
| 1814, - - | 71,323 | |
| 1815, - - | 85,985 | |
| 1816, - - | 217,832 | |
| | L.2,321,590 | |
| Unclaimed, - - | 5,295 | |
| | | 2,326,885 |
| Loyalty loan remaining 1st February, 1817, | | L.1,058,503 |
| The interest on loyalty loan paid off, - - | | L.116,079 |
| And the interest added by the operations of 1804, and 1805, was, - - - | | 108,633 |
| Balance deducted from interest, - - | | L.7,446 |

NOTE XVII.—Pages 510 and 513.

A METHOD was had recourse to in adjusting the terms of the loan 1802, which indicated considerable pressure on our resources: L.125 was granted in the three per cents.; and as part of the annuities for terms of years expired in 1808, an additional capital was granted to complete the necessary emolument, the interest of which was deferred till these annuities should expire. Thus the relief in view by the falling in of these annuities, was disappointed to a certain extent. The bidding for the loan was on this deferred stock, and it was taken at L.6 19s. 3d.

NOTE XVIII.—Page 512.

THE loan of 1807 was raised on Lord Henry Petty's plan, an account of which is given, page 143, &c. L.12,000,000 was charged on the war taxes, and L.1,200,000 of these taxes mortgaged for interest and redemption. The remaining L.200,000 was raised as a supplementary loan in the common manner, with a sinking fund of one per cent. A separate accompt is kept of this loan: But this plan, though intended to be perpetual, was never followed out afterwards.

### NOTE XIX.—Page 514.

THE loan of 1809 was raised at L.60 in the three per cent. reduced, L.60 in the four per cent. cons. and a long annuity of 8s. 10d. L.600,000 of this loan was for Portugal; and instead of distributing that sum among the different funds charged with the general loan, L.895,522 was set aside in the three per cent. reduced, as an equivalent, and a sinking fund of L.30,000 provided for its redemption.

### NOTE XX.—Page 514.

AN option was given this year to the holders of the Exchequer bills proposed to be funded, that they might receive either L.103 5s. in the five per cent. cons. or L.81 8s. in the five per cents. and L.26 5s. in the four per cents. A similar option was given next year.

### NOTE XXI.—Pages 503 and 521.

ANNUITIES for lives have been granted at various times, to the amount of L.151,437, exclusive of those which were converted, or entirely fallen in before 1786; generally on single lives; sometimes on two or three lives; and sometimes with the benefit of survivorship. They were reduced by death in 1786, to L.94,878; at which time the present sinking fund was established, and the sums saved by their farther reduction, appointed to be carried to that fund. They were reduced in 1798 to L.87,380; in 1802, to L.81,891; and in 1816, to L.73,397; of which L.8,195, granted in king William's reign, and probably a considerable sum besides, may be considered as expired. The particulars of the original amount of these annuities; their state at the commencement of the sinking fund; and their present state, are exhibited in the following table.

| ACTS. | Original amount. | Expired before 1786. | Remaining 1786 | Exp. from 1786 to 1817. | Remaining Feb. 1, 1817 |
|---|---|---|---|---|---|
| 5 Will. and Mary, | 22,633 | 14,438 | 8,195 | - - | 8,195 |
| 18 Geo. II. | 22,500 | 10,182 | 12,318 | 4,039 | 8,279 |
| 19 Geo. II. | 45,000 | 22,533 | 22,467 | 7,552 | 14,915 |
| 30 Geo II. | 33,750 | 9,183 | 24,567 | 8,406 | 16,161 |
| 6 Geo. III. tontine, | 540 | - - | 540 | - - | 540 |
| 18 Geo. III. | 2,849 | 80 | 2,769 | 356 | 2,413 |
| 19 Geo. III. | 5,318 | 143 | 5,175 | 1,128 | 4,047 |
| 29 Geo. III. tontine, | 18,847 | - - | 18,847 | - - | 18,847 |
| | 151,437 | 56,559 | 94,878 | 21,481 | 73,397 |

| | | |
|---|---|---|
| The amount of annuities, granted for years or lives, to 1st February, 1817, as in Table II. - - | | L.1,818,981 |
| Addition to tontine of 1789, - - | | 405 |
| | | L.1,819,386 |
| Deduct annuities, fallen in by expiry of the term in 1805, 6, 7, and 8, | L.494,656 | |
| — By death of annuitants, from 1786 to 1817, - - | 21,481 | |
| Long annuities, converted into life annuities, - - | 4,420 | |
| Ditto, unclaimed, - - | 471 | |
| | | 521,028 |
| | | L.1,298,358 |
| Life annuities, for stock and long annuities converted, | | 225,255 |
| Amount annuities, 1st February, 1817 - | | L.1,523,614 |
| Annuities expired by term, - - | | L.494,656 |
| by death, - - | | 21,481 |
| Long annuities unclaimed, - - | | 471 |
| | | L.516,608 |
| Deduct addition to tontine of 1789, - - | | 405 |
| Deduction from annuities, Table II. - - | | L.516,202 |

### Note XXII.—Page 521.

An account of the allowances for the management of the national debt is given, page 525 and 526. It has been diminished by the reduction of the rate,—by the falling in of annuities,—the redemption of the capital by the sinking fund,—and the transference for



land

land tax. It was thought unnecessary to introduce the portions of abatement in the statement of each year's charge, and the whole is deducted at the end of Table II.

Note XXIII.—Page 530.

The interest, &c. of all the debt, whether existing at the establishment of the consolidated fund, or contracted since, as well as the civil list, and other parliamentary grants, are charged on the consolidated fund; and it is credited with all the taxes in force at its commencement, or imposed since, applicable to these purposes. But in the accounts of the consolidated fund lately reported to Parliament, the charges on the loans for ten years, or thereby, preceding, are placed against the branches of revenue appropriated to each. In the earlier parts of the accounts, they are placed promiscuously.

The interest, &c. of the loan 1803, is charged on L.250,000 reserved out of the consolidated customs; L.59,965 from the consolidated stamp duties; and a variable sum from the assessed taxes.

The interest. &c. of the loan 1804, is charged on the consolidated stamp duties, which were augmented by a duty on the transfer of property according to its value.

The interest, &c. of the loans 1805, is charged on consolidated stamp duties and customs, to which certain additions were made; on additional postage; additional duty on horses; and additional excise on salt, auctions, bricks, coffee, cyder, glass, vinegar, and wine.

The interest, &c. of the loan 1806, is charged on additional duties on wine and spirits: an addition of ten per cent. on assessed taxes; and a small charge on the stamp duties.

The interest, &c. of the loan 1807, is charged on the war taxes, agreeably to Lord Henry Petty's system.

The interest, &c. of the loans 1808, is charged on additional assessed taxes and stamp duties. The short annuities now fallen in, and savings by the reduction of the rate of management, were brought in aid of this year's charge.

The interest, &c. of the loans 1809, was charged on the war taxes, except an allowance of L.105,000 from the consolidated customs.

The interest, &c. of the loans 1810, was charged on the surplus of stamp duties, produced by their increase and consolidation.

The interest, &c. of the exchequer bills funded in 1811, was charged on additional duties on spirits; and that of the loan, on the war taxes: to replace which, additional duties were imposed on timber, ashes, and foreign linen, and added to the war taxes.

The interest, &c. of the debt contracted 1812, was charged on additional assessed taxes; additional duties on glass, hides, tobacco, and snuff; and additional postage.

The system of finance adopted in 1813, held forth an exemption from additional taxes for several years, the charge of the loans being compensated by cancelling part of the redeemed stock: But, as a sum was required to be added to the sinking fund at the commencement of that system, additional permanent customs were imposed that year to a considerable extent. No taxes were imposed in 1814. In 1815, the surplus arising from additional stamp duties, and excise duties on tobacco and licences, then imposed, were appropriated to defray part of the charge of the loan of that year; and in 1816, additional duties on soap, foreign butter and cheese, and the saving by the diminution of the drawback on sugar, and interest on exchequer bills, were appropriated for the charge of the money borrowed from the Bank, that year.

### NOTE XXIV.—Page 531.

THE term of forty-five years was mentioned when the one per cent. sinking fund was announced, as that in which each loan would be repaid at furthest. The actual term depends upon the rate of interest, and the comparative prices of stock when the debt is contracted, and during the period of its redemption.

Supposing the sinking fund 1-100th of the sum borrowed, the periods required for redemption are,

| | |
|---|---|
| At 3 per cent. interest, - - | 47 years. |
| At 3½ per cent. - - - | 44 years. |
| At 4 per cent. - - - | 41 years. |
| At 5 per cent. - - - | 37 years. |

If the loan be funded in the 3 per cents. at a capital proportionable to the rate of interest, and with a sinking fund of 1 per cent. on the capital funded, the periods required for redemption are,

| | |
|---|---|
| At 3 per cent. - - - | 47 years. |
| At 3½ per cent. - - - | 40 years. |
| At 4 per cent. - - - | 35½ years. |
| At 5 per cent. - - - | 29 years. |

### NOTE XXV.—Page 539.

To place the sinking fund proposed on the loans, upon Mr.

 Vansittart's

Vansittart's plan, in a clear point of view, we shall detail its application to the financial operations of the year 1813.*

| | Sums borrowed. | Capitals funded. |
|---|---|---|
| Exchequer bills funded at L.115 10s. in 5 per cents. - - - - - - - - | 12,000,000 | 13,860,000 |
| Ditto funded at L.139 in 4 per cents. - - | 3,755,700 | 5,220,423 |
| Loan funded at L.170 in 3 per cents. - - | 21,000,000 | 35,700,000 |
| | 36,755,700 | 54,780,423 |
| Estimated sum applicable to the discharge of national debt, 1st February, 1813, - - | 13,013,914 | |
| Additional debt contracted - - - - | 23,741,786 | |

The sinking fund to be provided on the former is 1 per cent. on the funded capital, and on the latter, one half of the interest.

The charge on the former part is,

| | | funded for | | |
|---|---|---|---|---|
| Ex. Bills, | L.12,000,000 | L.13,860,000 | Interest, | L.693,000 |
| Ditto, | 1,013,914 | 1,409,340 | Interest, | 56,374 |
| | L.13,013,914 | L.15,269,340 | Interest, | L.749,374 |
| | | | Managmt. | 4,580 |
| | | | 1 per cent. | 152,693 |
| Amount charge on former part, - - - | | | | L.906,647 |

The charge on the latter part is,

| | | | | |
|---|---|---|---|---|
| Ex. Bills, | L.2,741,786 | L.3,811,083 | Interest, | L.152,443 |
| | | | One half, | 76,221 |
| | | | Managmt. | 1,144 |
| Amount charge on latter part of Exchequer bills, | | | | L.229,808 |
| E.B. as above, | L.2,741,786 | L.3,811,083 | | |
| Loan, | 21,000,000 | 35,700,000 | Interest, | L.1,071,000 |
| | | | One half, | 535,500 |
| 2d part, | L.23,741,786 | L.39,511,083 | Long ann. | 89,250 |
| 1st part, | 13,013,914 | 15,269,340 | S.F. on do. | 1,499 |
| | | | Managmt. | 11,379 |
| | L.36,755,700 | L.54,780,423 | | |



Amount

* See Act 53, Geo. III. cap. 95.

| | | |
|---|---|---|
| Amount charge on loan, - - - | | L.1,708,628 |
| on Exchequer bills, - | | 229,808 |
| Amount charge on latter part - - - | | L.1,938,436 |
| on former part, - - - | | 906,647 |
| Whole charge, - - - - - | | L.2,845,084 |
| And the sinking fund is, | | |
| One per cent. on former part, - - - | | L.152,693 |
| And on long annuities, - - - - | | 1,499 |
| Half interest on latter part, - | L.76,221 | |
| and - | 535,500 | |
| | | 611,721 |
| Whole sinking fund on debt of 1813, - - | | L.765,913 |

Now, to meet the above charge of - - L.2,845,084

the following capitals are ordered to be cancelled.

| | | |
|---|---|---|
| 3 per cent. cons. | L.46,884,600 | |
| 3 per cent. reduced, | 47,892,500 | |
| | L.94,777,100 | Interest, L.2,843,313 |

Difference not accounted for, - - - L.1,771

(For the progress of this system afterwards, see Appendix II. Table XI.)

### Note XXVI.—Page 541.

The terms for the purchase of the land tax, now offered, are the following, in option of the purchaser.

1st. Transfer of stock at one time, or by four instalments in two years.

2d. Payment of money at like periods, the amount being regulated by the current price of stock.

3rd. Transfer of stock in sixteen years, by two instalments each year.

4th. Payment of money at the like periods, and to the like amount.

5th. Land tax on houses may be redeemed at 18 years purchase, to be paid within three months.

6th. Land tax on lands not exceeding L.10, may be redeemed by a double assessment of land-tax for 18 years.

7th. By a double assessment of land-tax, until the quantity of stock purchased therewith, and the dividends and interest accruing thereon, be be sufficient for the redemption of the land tax; giving the proprietor the benefit of accumulation at compound interest. This mode, at the present price of stock, will redeem the land tax in 14 years.

NOTE XXVII.—Page 544.

THE inequality of the funded debt contracted in different years is remarkable. The expense was much greater in some years than others; but the inequality is partly to be accounted for from the loans having sometimes been made near the end of the year, and applied to the service of the following year; and also, from the increase or diminution of the unfunded debt.—The debt contracted annually, after the renewal of the war in 1803, was less than in the former war, owing to the large sums raised by war taxes and otherwise, within the year. It is remarkable that the debt redeemed in 1808, before reduction to three per cent. is greater than the debt contracted. But part of the debt was contracted in the 4 and 5 per cent. stocks, and that redeemed was all in the 3 per cents.; so that a less sum of money was laid out in the redemption than the amount of the loans and funded bills.

The increase of the public debt for Britain, in 1812, may be thus estimated.

| | | Reduced to three per cents. |
|---|---|---|
| *L.* Funded in 5 per cents. - | L.5,866,236 | L.9,777,060 |
| *M.* Funded in ditto, - | 7,332,795 | 12,231,325 |
| *N.* Funded in 3 per cents. - | - | 27,544,000 |
| | | L.49,552,385 |
| Increase of unfunded debt, - | 3,800,637 - | 6,334,395 |
| Redeemed by sinking fund in 3 per cents. | | 20,922,876 |
| Addition to public debt, estimated in 3 per cents. | | L.34,963,904 |
| and estimated in 5 per cents. - - | | 20,978,342 |

And the increase in other years may be estimated in the same manner.

 NOTE XXVIII.

NOTE XXVIII.—Page 575.

WE have repeated this calculation at each of our editions, according to the state of finance at the time. On the 1st February 1812, the loss by the sinking fund appeared to be L.10,861,688 ; on the 1st February 1813, L.12,585,580 ; and now, on the 1st February 1817, L.16,450,661. In this last calculation, we have deducted the sums expended, and capital redeemed, before the war, from the whole sums expended and redeemed since the commencement of the sinking fund. This was not done in our former editions.

NOTE XXIX.—Page 578.

THE sums inserted in our last edition were taken from a return to the House of Commons, in which the hereditary revenue, and some other articles, were included with the taxes ; and the expense of management deducted, as mentioned in a note annexed to that passage. The sums of taxes now given, from 1803 to 1814, inclusive, are taken from an accurate statement compiled by Charles Stokes, Esq., from accounts presented to the House of Commons, in which nothing extraneous is blended with the taxes, and nothing deducted except drawbacks, and bounties in the nature of drawbacks. The sums for the two last years are compiled in the same manner.

NOTE XXX.—Page 581.

THE high encomiums bestowed upon Mr. Pitt's sinking funds, rendered it necessary to enter into a full discussion of their merits.

" To the consolidated fund the country has looked for the interest " of its debt ; and for its extinction, to the sinking fund. The best " eulogium that could be made on the sinking fund, was the plain " statement he had made. *There could be but one opinion in the* " *House on the subject. It was owing to the institution of the sinking* " *fund that the country was not charged with a much larger amount of* " *debt.* IT WAS AN ADVANTAGE GAINED BY NOTHING, and a system " likely to be attended with still greater advantages. Therefore, " independent of considerations of good faith, which should induce " the House to hold and cling to a system once adopted, it was " pledged to support it, having positive trial and experience of its " utility"—(*From Lord Henry Petty's Speech at opening the Budget, 29th March*, 1806, *as reported in the Newspapers at the time.*)

"On the same principle which guided the determination of Par-
"liament in 1786, another act was passed in 1792, which provided,
"that on all future loans, a surplus of one per cent. per annum on
"the capital, should be raised for the redemption of the capital.
"*This was an idea conceived in the spirit of inflexible integrity and*
"*economy*, of which nations rarely afford an example, though, like
"the same virtues in private life, it is calculated to promote, in the
"highest degree, their prosperity."—(*Examination into the Increase of the Revenue, from* 1792 *to* 1799, *by George Rose, Esq.*)

Quotations of a like kind might be adduced to a large extent.

NOTE XXXI.—Page 588.

IN Mr. Rose's Examination into the Increase of the Revenue, &c. 1799, a table is given of the money borrowed, and capital debt contracted since the commencement of the war, in which the loan of 1798 is stated at nine millions, with a corresponding capital, and the columns summed accordingly. He adds, indeed, in a note, that, "the loan of 1798 was for 17 millions; but the charge on the
"consolidated fund was only for nine millions, as the remaining
"eight millions is to be supplied from the aid and contribution tax,
"in purchasing stock to the extent of the capital created by that
"sum."

Did he believe, or did he expect his readers to believe, that this part of the loan, which he endeavours to keep out of view, was less a burthen on the public, because it was then proposed to discharge it by a certain tax *to be levied* on the public;—an arrangement which was soon after relinquished?

NOTE XXXII.—Page 594.

IN the first part of Table X. which exhibits the progress of taxation, and of the sinking fund on Mr. Vansittart's plan, compared with that of the former system, the years marked on the margin are higher by one, than in the outlines, Table A. 1.; because the taxes imposed, suppose in 1813, can hardly become effectual before the 1st August of that year; and, therefore, their produce the first year, or from 1st August 1813, to 1st August, 1814, ought to be set in opposition to the produce of the sinking fund during the same time.

Note XXXIII.—Page 610.

In our former editions, we ventured a conjecture, founded on the abovementioned fact, that the 3 per cents. on the restoration of peace, might rise to 80. They have now risen to a higher value, and are at present (January, 1818,) about 82. We shall not at present speculate upon the causes of their rise, or the height they may afterwards reach. As it does not affect the general reasoning, we did not think it necessary to alter the hypothetical rate we had used before in this calculation. It is obvious, that if we substitute a higher rate, the loss resulting will be greater.

Note XXXIV.—Page 612.

In order to support the value of the five per cent. stock, it was enacted in 1786, that it should not be redeemable till 25 millions of the three per cents. were paid off with money applicable to the redemption of the public debt. This restriction is now removed by the condition being fulfilled. The loyalty loan is not redeemable at par till the expiration of three years after the consolidated five per cents. are paid off.

# APPENDIX I.

## SECTION I.

### ACCOUNT OF THE STOCKS.

The term *Fund* properly signifies any sum of money, or annual revenue, appropriated to a particular purpose. Thus, the part of the revenue which is set aside for the payment of the national debt is called the *Sinking Fund.* But when we speak of the funds, we generally mean those large sums which have been lent to Government, and constitute the national debt, and for which the lenders or their assignees receive interest from the public revenue. These persons are said to invest their money in the funds. The term *Stock* is used nearly in the same sense, and is also applied to the sums which form the capital of the Bank of England, the East India and South Sea Company, and other public companies, the proprietors of which are entitled to a share of their respective profits.

The funds which at present constitute the public debt, or are connected with it, are,

*Bank Stock.* The Bank of England was incorporated in 1694. Their original stock, raised by subscriptions, not exceeding L.20,000 in one name, was L.1,200,000, which was lent to Government at 8 per cent. interest, and L.4000 allowed for the expense of the house, amounting together to L.100,000. In the year 1709, the Bank advanced L.400,000 more to Government, without additional interest, after the two first years, which reduced the interest received by them to 6 per cent. They afterwards advanced various sums to Government, by withdrawing Exchequer bills, or otherwise, until the permanent debt due to them amounted, in 1746, to L.11,686,800, at which it has remained till lately. The rate of interest has been



gradually

gradually reduced, and is now 3 per cent. Besides this permanent debt, the Bank has been long in the practice of assisting Government, by advancing money on Exchequer bills, in anticipation of the land and malt taxes, and now of the annual taxes substituted for the former; by payment of bills drawn on the treasury, and otherwise, to a great extent. The stock of the Bank has been enlarged, at a rate nearly keeping pace with their advances to Government, but not exactly the same: The sum upon which they divided, till lately, was L.11,642,400.

The first term of the charter of the Bank was only to the year 1705, and it has since been extended from time to time, being liable to dissolution at the term specified in each charter, upon twelve months notice, and repayment of the money advanced, by Government. It is also provided by the various loan acts, that the Bank shall remain an incorporation after the term specified in the charter, for the purpose of transacting the business of these loans, till they be redeemed.

In the year 1800, at which time their charter stood extended to 1812, it was agreed, upon the advance of L.3,000,000 by the Bank to Government for six years without interest, to prolong their charter till the end of twelve months notice, after 1st August, 1833; and, in 1806, it was agreed to continue this advance till six months after the conclusion of a definitive treaty of peace, at 3 per cent. interest. This debt was paid off in 1814.

In 1808, a further advance of L.3,000,000 was agreed to be made by the Bank, without interest during the war, in consideration of the large deposits of public money made in their hands, the average of which was estimated to exceed ten millions. Since the restoration of peace, this advance has been continued, and is at present extended to 5th April, 1818.

The practice of depositing money in the Bank, for payment of the dividends to the public creditors, is of long standing; and, after the establishment of Mr. Pitt's sinking fund, the money placed at the disposal of the Commissioners was deposited in the Bank at the commencement of each quarter. The amount of these deposits increased as our financial system expanded, and was much enlarged by the regulations established in 1806, of depositing all public money, so far as practicable, in the Bank, in consequence of malversations in office, detected at that time. The average amount of these deposits since 1806 has been estimated at eleven and a half millions, and supposed to yield a profit of 5 per cent. Admitting these suppositions, the profit accruing to the Bank, from the deposit of public money, will stand thus:

 From

| | |
|---|---|
| From 1806 to 1808, interest on eight millions and a half, at 5 per cent. - - - - - - | L.425,000 |
| And on three millions lent to Government, at 3 per cent. | 90,000 |
| Annual profit, - - - - - | L.515,000 |

| | |
|---|---|
| From 1808 (when three millions were advanced to Government, without interest,) to 1814, interest on five millions and a half, at 5 per cent. - - - | L.275,000 |
| And on three millions, at 3 per cent. - - | 90,000 |
| Annual profit, - - - - | L.365,000 |

| | |
|---|---|
| From 1814 (when the loan of three millions, at 3 per cent. was repaid,) interest on eight millions and a half, at 5 per cent. - - - - - - - | L.425,000 |

The last transaction between the Bank and Government was in 1816. The Bank agreed to continue the advance of three millions, without interest, to April, 1818; and to advance three millions, at 3 per cent. interest, to be repaid, at furthest, before August, 1833. They also agreed to advance six millions more, on Exchequer bills, at 4 per cent., for two years certain; and for three years more, subject to repayment during that period, upon six months notice, either by the Treasury or the Bank. In consideration of these stipulations, they were authorized to make an addition of one-fourth to their former capital; to be placed to the credit of the proprietors of Bank stock, from the undivided profits.

| | |
|---|---|
| Their former stock was - - - - | L.11,642,400 |
| Addition of one-fourth, - - - | 2,910,600 |
| Their present stock is - - - | L.14,553,000 |

In 1797, the unfavourable rate of foreign exchange occasioned such a demand for specie, as had nearly exhausted their treasure; and, upon application to Government, an act was obtained, restraining them from making payment in cash: at first for a limited time, afterwards continued during the war, and now prolonged to July, 1818, when the restriction is proposed to be removed.

The quantity of Bank notes in circulation has been much increased since the restriction. At that time, it amounted to between 11 and 12 millions, but went on afterwards gradually increasing, and in June. 1815, amounted to L.31,300,000; and the average amount for the two last years has been about L.27,000,000.

This great increase of circulation may be attributed to the following causes; first, the removal of the prudential restraint they were formerly under, from making large issues by discounting bills, or

 otherwise,

otherwise, arising from the risk of their being returned in demand for cash; secondly, the permission, granted at the same time the restriction was imposed, of issuing notes under L.5, which had been formerly prohibited. A circulation of such notes was then wanted, by reason of the scarcity of specie; and their amount for some years past has been about nine millions.

The Bank also advanced to Government L.376,739 in 1791, and afterwards L.500,000 more in 1808, without interest, in consideration of the large sum of unclaimed dividends on the public funds always remaining in their hands.

The dividend on the Bank stock at its establishment in 1694, was 8 per cent. In 1697, it rose to 9 per cent., but soon afterwards fell, and varied from 6 to 5½, and 5 per cent.; and in 1754 fell so low as 4½ per cent. In 1788, it rose to 7 per cent. and in 1807, to 10 per cent, at which rate it has continued since. The dividends are payable on the 5th April and 10th October.

In the interval between 1788 and 1807, the following *bonuses* were paid to the proprietors of Bank stock, over and above the usual dividend of 7 per cent. from the surplus profits.

| | | | | | | |
|---|---|---|---|---|---|---|
| Ladyday, | 1799, | L.10 | 0 | 0 | per cent. in the loyalty loan. | |
| Ladyday, | 1800, | 5 | 0 | 0 | in the navy 5 per cents. | |
| Michaelmas, | 1802, | 2 | 10 | 0 | in ditto. | |
| Michaelmas, | 1804, | 5 | 0 | 0 | in money. | Added to the half-year's dividend of 3½ per cent. |
| Michaelmas, | 1805, | 5 | 0 | 0 | in money. | |
| Michaelmas, | 1806, | 5 | 0 | 0 | in money. | |
| In all, | - - | L.32 | 10 | 0 | | |

The income of the Bank arises from the interest of the permanent debt, and temporary advances to Government; the allowance for the management of the public funds; for receiving contributions for loans, and transacting the business of lotteries; from the interest of stock held by the company, the discount of bills of exchange, and some smaller articles.*

228 South

* In a series of letters, addressed to the proprietors of Bank stock, by an old proprietor, in 1815, the income and outgoings of the Bank are stated as under.

*South Sea Stock.* We have already had occasion to notice (pages 478, 479,) the origin of the South Sea Company, and their first transactions with Government ; also, (pages 484, 485, 486,) their extensive undertakings in 1720, the failure of their expectations, and the arrangements which took place in consequence. The only branches of trade in which this Company ever engaged, were that of conveying slaves to the Spanish colonies, and the whale fishery ; and these being attended with loss, were abandoned. Since 1748 they have carried on no trade whatever. Their stock has since undergone various modifications, and has been considerably reduced by payments from Government, and the rate of interest has sustained the same reductions as in the other public funds. It is at present distributed into the following branches :—

A sum, considered as the trading capital of the Company, though



INCOME.

| | | |
|---|---|---|
| Interest on paper in circulation, 27 millions, - - | | L.1,350,000 |
| on public money deposited in Bank, - - | | 425,000 |
| Allowance for management of public debt, loans and lotteries, | | 325,746 |
| Interest on capital lent to Government, - | L.350,604 | |
| Deduct property tax, - - | 35,060 | |
| | | 315,544 |
| Allowance for house expenses, - - | L.4,000 | |
| Management of capital purchased from South Sea Company, - - - - | 1,898 | |
| | | 5,898 |
| Allowance for receiving property tax, - - | | 3,480 |
| Interest on accumulated profits, supposed 20 millions | | 1,000,000 |
| Total income - - - - | | L.3,425,668 |

OUTGOINGS.

| | |
|---|---|
| Salaries to 1000 Clerks, at L.160 each, - - | L.160,000 |
| Other expenses of the establishment, - - | 150,000 |
| Composition for stamps, - - - - | 87,500 |
| Property duty on gains, - - - - | 250,000 |
| Losses by forgeries, bankruptcies, &c. loss of interest on cash, and other unproductive effects, - - - | 500,000 |
| | L.1,147,500 |
| Leaving a balance of net profit, - - - | L.2,278,168 |
| Dividend on capital at 10 per cent. - - - | 1,164,240 |
| Undivided profits, - - - | L.1,113,928 |

Admitting the accuracy of this statement, some alterations have taken place since, in consequence of the repeal of the property tax, and the arrangements of 1816.

they have long ceased to trade. This was fixed, in 1733, at L.3,662,784, and has remained invariable since. The dividend received by the proprietors of the stock is 3½ per cent., of which 3 per cent. is paid by Government, and the remaining half per cent. by the Company. This they were enabled to make, from fines to which they are entitled from ships trading within the bounds of their charter, and the allowance received from Government for management. This article amounted, in 1786, to about L.15,000, but is since reduced, in consequence of the redemption of part of the capital under their management.

By act 55 Geo. III. cap. 57, the exclusive privileges of the South Sea Company are repealed; and, as a compensation, a guarantee fund of L.610,464 is appointed to be invested in some 3 per cent. stock; being raised from a duty of 2 per cent. on all goods imported from places within the limits of their charter, except the produce of the fisheries, and of 1s. 6d. tonnage duty on ships trading to these places. This fund, till completed, is under the management of the Commissioners for the reduction of the national debt; and is to be transferred, when completed, to the South Sea Company, when it will afford a dividend equal to one-half per cent. on their stock. In the mean time, a sum is annually allowed them from the consolidated fund, sufficient to enable them to make the accustomed dividend of one-half per cent.

*Old South Sea Annuities.* These were separated from the other funds of the Company in 1723, when they amounted to L.16,901,099 bearing interest at 5 per cent., reduced in 1727 to 4 per cent., in 1751 to 3½ per cent., and in 1757 to 3 per cent. Part of the capital being paid off at different times, it was reduced in 1775 to L.11,907,470, at which it remained till Mr. Pitt's sinking fund was established in 1786.

*New South Sea Annuities*, separated from the other funds of the Company in 1733, when they amounted to L.10,988,318, bearing interest at 4 per cent. The capital was reduced in 1775 to L.8,494,830, and the interest has undergone the same reductions as that of the old annuities.

*Three per cent. Annuities*, 1751, are also under the management of the South Sea Company. This fund consisted originally of L.2,100,000, borrowed for the purpose of paying off those holders of South Sea annuities who did not consent to the reduction of interest which took place at that time. It was reduced in 1775, by payments at various times, to L.1,919,600.

A considerable part of these three last mentioned funds has been redeemed since 1786.

The dividends on the South Sea stock, the new South Sea annuities, and the 3 per cents. 1751, are payable 5th January and 5th July; those on the old South Sea annuities, 5th April and 10th October.

*Three per cent. Reduced Annuities.* This fund commenced in 1749, and was then formed of various articles of public debt which formerly bore a higher rate of interest, from which circumstance it derived its name. But many additions have been made to it by subsequent loans, which never bore interest at any other rate. The dividends are payable 5th April and 10th October.

*Three per cent. Consolidated Annuities.* This is the largest of all the public funds. It commenced in 1731, but derived its present name from the consolidating act in 1751, being formed by the union of several capitals formerly kept separate. Many additions have since been made to it. The dividends are payable 5th January and 5th July.

*Three per cent. Annuities,* 1726. This fund consists of L.1,000,000 borrowed by lottery in that year, for the discharge of Exchequer bills issued for paying the arrears of the civil list. The interest was at first charged on a duty of 6d. per L.1 on pensions, but it is now paid from the consolidated fund; though the fund itself, for reasons which do not appear, is still kept separate. The dividends are payable at the same terms as those of the 3 per cent. cons.

A fund bearing interest at 3½ per cent., irredeemable for 15 years, was established in 1756, but it was paid off at the end of that term. A similar fund was established in 1758, irredeemable for 24 years; but at the end of that term it was united to the 3 per cent. consols.

*Four per cent. Consolidated Annuities.* This fund commenced in 1760; but L.23,500,000 borrowed on it, in that and the following years, being paid off, or the rate of interest reduced, the earliest article now belonging to it is a loan of L.5,000,000, in 1777, to which various other loans, or parts of loans, have since been added. The dividends are payable at the same terms as those of the 3 per cent. reduced.

*Navy five per cent. Consolidated Annuities.* This stock commenced in 1784, and was first applied for funding the navy, victualling, and transport bills, then in circulation, from which it derived its name. It has since received many additions, chiefly by funding Exchequer bills. The dividends are payable at the same terms as those of the 3 per cent. cons.

*Loyalty Loan, or five per cent. Annuities,* 1797 and 1802. An account of this fund is given in Note XVI. The dividends are payable at the same terms as those of the 3 per cent. reduced.

 *Imperial*

*Imperial three per cent. Annuities.* An account of this fund is given, pages 524, 525. The dividends, though due November 1st and May 1st are not paid till January and July.

*Irish five per cent. Annuities,* are not guaranteed by Britain, but transferable at the Bank of England, and the dividends payable there on the 25th March and 25th September.

And the terminable annuities are,

*Annuities on Lives.* The amount of these, standing in the books of the Exchequer, including tontines, on the 1st February, 1817, was L.73,397; but a considerable part had not been demanded for upwards of three years, and is probably expired. They are payable at the Exchequer, half yearly, on the 5th January and 5th July, and are transferable by assignment indorsed on the order, which must be registered at the Exchequer. Any person receiving an annuity, knowing the nominee to be dead, forfeits L.500, and treble the sum received. See Note XXI.

*Long Annuities.* These terminate on the 5th January, 1860, and are now payable half yearly, at the Bank, on the 5th April and 10th October. The amount on the 1st Feb. 1817, was,

| | |
|---|---|
| British, - - - - - | L.1,224,961 |
| Irish, - - - . - | 129,583 |
| | L.1,354,544 |

*Converted Life Annuities.* [See page 521.] The amount of stock converted on the 5th January, 1817, was,

| | |
|---|---|
| 3 per cent. cons. - - - - | L2,275,876 |
| 3 per cent. reduced - - - - | 1,174,079 |
| | L.3,449,955 |
| and the subsisting annuities amounted to - | L.225,254 |

| If either cons. or reduced stock be transferred between | The life annuity is payable on |
|---|---|
| 5th January and 4th April, | 5th July and 5th January. |
| 5th April and 4th July, | 10th October and 5th April. |
| 5th July and 9th October, | 5th January and 5th July. |
| 10th October and 4th January, | 5th April and 10th October. |

*Imperial Annuities,* granted along with the last imperial loan for 25 years, and payable at the same terms as the dividends on that loan. They expire in May 1819, amount L.230,000.

## SECTION II.

### OF THE EAST INDIA COMPANY.

THE affairs of the East India Company have been, and still are, so much blended with the public revenue, that some account of their progress and present state belongs to the subject of our inquiry.

This Company presents a singular example of a mercantile society commencing on slender funds, and gradually expanding, but not assuming for a century and a half any great political importance; and afterwards acquiring the sovereignty of a mighty empire, exceeding the British Isles in extent and population, perhaps in wealth; still remaining in complete subjection to the parent state, without contributing much, at least not directly, to the public revenue.

The first charter was granted by Queen Elizabeth, in 1600, and conferred the exclusive privilege of trade to all countries, from the Cape of Good Hope to the Streights of Magellan, for fifteen years. Their original capital was only L.72,000, in shares of L.50 each; and it was not formed into a joint stock for some years after, and for a long time their exertions were feeble. In the reign of James I. they received a new charter, and their stock was enlarged. The Company was dissolved during the usurpation of Cromwell in 1655, and the trade laid open to the public; but this being attended with inconveniences, it was re-established about three years after, at which time their nominal stock was L.739,782, whereof only one half, or L.369,891, was paid up, and was properly their trading capital. In the subsequent period, the renewals of their charter were frequent, there being no fewer than six between the Restoration and the Revolution, and three between the Revolution and 1698. These charters conferred sovereign power. The Company had been invested with criminal jurisdiction by the charter of James I. They were now authorized to possess all plantations, forts, and factories, in the East Indies, and erect new fortifications there, and at St. Helena, *and to make war or peace with any prince or people that were not Christians.* The other charters were chiefly granted for enlarging their powers to suppress interlopers. In 1693, a tax of 5 per cent. was imposed on their stock, which at that time amounted to L.744,000, and their charter was forfeited for nonpayment, but was immediately restored. These charters were not limited in point of time, but reserved a power of dissolving the Company upon three years intimation, if its privileges should be found prejudicial to the public.

A new East India Company was established by king William, in 1698, which advanced L.2,000,000 to Government, at 8 per cent. interest. Their right of trade was to continue till 1714, after which they might be dissolved upon three years notice, and repayment of the money due by the public ; and a similar clause was inserted in all the subsequent charters. In 1702, the two Companies were united, and, in 1708, the united Company lent a further sum of L.1,200,000 to Government without interest, which reduced the rate of interest to 5 per cent. upon which their charter was prolonged to 1729. In 1712, it was further prolonged to 1736, and again in 1730, to 1769, on which occasion the Company gave L.200,000 to the public revenue, and agreed to the reduction of the rate of interest on their debt to 4 per cent. The next prolongation of their charter took place in 1743, when they advanced L.1,000,000 to Government at 3 per cent. interest, and obtained an extension to 1783. When a general reduction of the interest on the public debt took place in 1749, the interest of the whole debt of L.4,200,000 due to the Company was reduced to 3 per cent. and they were empowered to borrow by the sale of annuities to that extent, and did borrow L.2,992,440 accordingly. The debt due them by the public remained in this state as a separate fund till 1793, when it was joined to the 3 per cent. reduced stock. The annuitants on the Company agreed to accept of 3 per cent. reduced stock in exchange for their annuities, and the Company themselves became holders in that stock, to the extent of L.1,207,560, being the residue of the debt of L.4,200,000. This is the only debt now due by the public to the Company.

The dividends of this Company, arising from the profits of trade have been variable, and the value of their stock exposed to greater fluctuation than that of any other of the other public funds. Previous to 1757, although invested, in some measure, with sovereign power, their possessions in India were limited to forts and factories, with a small contiguous territory : But soon after that time, in consequence of the conquests made by Lord Clive and others, they acquired extensive dominions, which they held at first by dependent Nabobs, whom they raised and removed at pleasure, but afterwards assumed into their immediate possession. From these dominions they drew, an ample revenue, which soon attracted the attention of Government, as an object in which the public had a right to participate. An agreement was made in 1767, that the Company should pay L.400,000 annually for two years, and in 1769 it was extended for five years more, as a consideration for being permitted to retain the revenue of their acquired territory. The Company, however, have



been

been so often engaged in expensive wars with the native powers, that the prospect of deriving a revenue to Britain from their possessions was never realized for any length of time. In 1773, they were not only unable to make the stipulated annual payment, but were obliged to apply to Government for a loan, and received one of L.1,400,000, their dividends being limited to 6 per cent. till it should be repaid. This debt was paid up in 1777, and the restriction on their dividends of course removed.

In 1781, a new agreement was made with the Company. A payment of L.400,000 made that year was accepted of, in discharge of all former claims; their exclusive privileges were extended to 1794; and, their dividends being at that time 8 per cent. it was stipulated that three-fourths of their surplus profits should be appropriated to the public service, and the other fourth retained by the Company for the enlargement of their dividends; which, however, were not to be increased above one per cent. in any year, and never to exceed 12½ per cent. The public never derived any revenue from this agreement; for, in the following years, the nett profits of the Company did not amount to 8 per cent., and their affairs fell under such embarrassment, that Government was induced to postpone the payment of customs due by them, and also to issue Exchequer bills to the amount of L.300,000, upon which the Bank advanced money, for their relief.

By an act passed in 1784, the Board of Commissioners for the affairs of India, generally called the Board of Controul, was established, to whose orders the Directors of the East India Company are subject, in all matters of civil and military government, and who have also the power of regulating the administration of their territorial revenue; and "*whereas schemes of conquest and extension of dominion* " *in India are measures repugnant to the wish, the honour, and the* " *interest of this nation*," the Governor-general was prohibited from commencing hostilities, or entering into any treaty for making war against any of the princes of the country, unless hostilities have been committed, or preparations made for hostilities against them or their allies. The history of the succeeding thirty years will shew how far the conduct of Britain to the native powers of India has been conformable to this excellent principle.

At the next renewal of their charter, in 1793, the exclusive privileges of the Company underwent some restrictions. Every British subject was permitted to export any goods, except military stores and copper, to India, but not to China; and the civil servants of the Company, and merchants residing in India under their protection, were permitted to import any goods, except piece goods of cotton and

 silk,

silk, on board the Company's ships to London; and for these exports and imports in private trade, the Company was obliged to appropriate 3000 tons of shipping, at L.5 per ton outwards, and L.15 inwards, of freight, in time of peace, with an addition in time of war. Under these limitations, their exclusive privileges were extended to 1st April, 1814. The full extent abovementioned of tonnage for private trade outwards has never been required.

The clear profits of the Company were directed to be applied as follows; 1st, in payment of 10 per cent. dividend on their stock, besides one half per cent. more, eventually, from a separate fund; 2d, in payment of L.500,000 annually of bills drawn from India for the liquidation of the debt due by the Company in that country; 3d, in payment of L.500,000 annually to the Exchequer for the public service. The surplus after these payments to be applied to the further discharge of the debts in India, till it should be reduced to two crores of rupees, or nearly two millions sterling; and of the bonded debt in England, till it should be reduced to L.1,500,000; after which one-sixth of the surplus profits was to be applied to the augmentation of the dividends, and the remaining five-sixths to be paid into the Bank of England, to be placed to the account of the Commissioners for the reduction of the national debt, till it should amount to 12 millions, (which sum was to be a guarantee fund for securing the stock and dividends of the Company); and when that fund was completed, the foresaid five-sixths of surplus profits was to be paid into the Exchequer, as the property of the public. The abovementioned payment of L.500,000 to the Exchequer, has not been made since April, 1794. It is unnecessary to add, that the guarantee fund has never been made up; and, consequently, that the public have never participated of any surplus profits. In 1812, the embarrassed state of the Company's affairs obliged them to apply again to Government for aid; and, accordingly, a loan of L.2,500,000 was granted to them, joined to the loan of that year.* The sum funded for this was L.4,400,000 in the 3 per cents.; and the Company was bound to pay into the Bank of England, besides the interest and charges of management, L.110,820 as a sinking fund for the discharge of the principal, being about 2½ per cent. on the funded capital. The sum redeemed, 1st February, 1817, was L.900,523.

The charter being on the eve of expiring in 1813, the object, so long contended for, of laying the trade to India open to the public, was at last, in a great measure, obtained. By act 53 Geo. III. cap. 155,



* See page 517, *N.*

155, permission is granted to every British subject to trade to India, but not to China, both in export and import, after 10th April, 1814. This trade, however, is subjected to various regulations, the most important of which are: That no vessel shall proceed on private trade, to India, without a licence from the Directors, which shall be granted, on application, of course, to the principal settlements of Fort-William, Fort-George, Bombay, or Prince of Wales Island; but no vessel may fit out to other places, unless specially authorized; and in case the Directors refuse to grant such special licence, the Board of Controul shall ultimately determine in regard to the same; That no vessel under 350 tons shall be employed: That goods imported in private trade shall be brought to some port in the United Kingdom, which shall have been declared fit for that purpose by order in Council: That the importation of articles of silk and cotton manufacture, for home consumption, shall be confined to the port of London, and the goods deposited in the Company's warehouses there: And the importation of tea, in private trade, is prohibited without licence from the Company.

The Company retain, till 10th April, 1834, the government and revenue of their territorial acquisitions, subject to the regulation of the Board of Controul, and the exclusive trade to China, and may trade as a corporation to India, in common with his Majesty's other subjects.

The same hopes of procuring a revenue to the public, which have so often before proved delusive, are still held forth. The enactments for the distribution of their territorial and commercial revenue are nearly the same as at the renewal of their charter in 1793. Their commercial profits are to be employed, 1st, in payment of bills of exchange; 2d, in paying debts, (the principal of the bond debt in England excepted,) and commercial charges; 3d, in payment of a dividend of 10½ per cent. on their capital; 4th, in the reduction of their bond debt. No annual payment to Government, except the interest and sinking fund of the loan of 1812, is required. The territorial revenue in India is applicable for the civil and military charges in that country, the payment of the interest, and liquidation of the Indian debt, and of the bond debt at home; and when the Indian debt is reduced to 10 millions, and the bond debt to 3 millions, then the surplus revenue, both territorial and commercial, shall be paid into the Exchequer, and applied, in the first place, for raising a guarantee fund of twelve millions; and when that fund is completed, one-sixth of the surplus shall belong to the Company, and the other five-sixths become the property of the public.

The progress and present state of the stock of the Company is as follows:

| | Capital. | | | Sums advanced. |
|---|---|---|---|---|
| 1708, | L.3,200,000 | at | 87½ per cent. | L.2,800,000 |
| 1786, | 800,000 | at | 155 per cent. | 1,240,000 |
| 1789, | 1,000,000 | at | 174 per cent. | 1,740,000 |
| 1793, | 1,000,000 | at | 200 per cent. | 2,000,000 |
| | L.6,000,000 | | | L.7,780,000 |

In 1797, an act was passed authorizing the Company to augment their capital by L.2,000,000; but this has not yet been carried into execution.

The dividends on India Stock have been as follows:—

| | | |
|---|---|---|
| Ladyday, | 1709, | 5 per cent. |
| Michaelmas, | 1709, | 8 per cent. |
| Michaelmas, | 1711, | 9 per cent. |
| Christmas, | 1716, | 10 per cent. |
| Midsummer, | 1722, | 8 per cent. |
| Christmas, | 1732, | 6 per cent. |
| Midsummer, | 1733, | 7 per cent. |
| Christmas, | 1755, | 8 per cent. |
| Christmas, | 1766, | 6 per cent. |
| Midsummer, | 1767, | 10 per cent. |
| Midsummer, | 1769, | 11 per cent. |
| Midsummer, | 1770, | 12 per cent. |
| Midsummer, | 1771, | 12½ per cent. |
| Christmas, | 1772, | 6 per cent. |
| Christmas, | 1776, | 7 per cent. |
| Midsummer, | 1778, | 8 per cent. |
| Midsummer, | 1798, | 10½ per cent. |

And they have continued at that rate since.

Additional regulations of the trade to the East Indies have been established by acts 54 Geo. III. cap. 34, 35, 36; and 55 Geo. III. cap. 10, 32, 93; and 57 Geo. III. cap. 36, 95, 120.

A grant of L.2,000,000 was made to the East India Company in 1813, and another of L.917,705 in 1816, to defray the expenses incurred by them in the public service.

*India Bonds.* The Company owes a large sum on transferable bonds, generally of L.100 each, the rate of interest on which has frequently varied, and is at present 5 per cent. payable twice a-year, on the 31st March and 30th Sept. Government have several times interfered to restrict the amount of this debt. In 1773, their dividend was limited to 7 per cent. till their bond debt was reduced to L.1,500,000; and this was effected in 1778. Being afterwards enlarged to L.3,200,000, they were again required to restrict it to

 L.1,500,000,

L.1,500,000, as a condition of the increase of their capital; but this reduction was not completed, and this debt has been enlarged since, with consent of the Board of Controul, occasioned partly by the transference of part of the debt due by the Company in India, to Britain. These bonds are received by the Company as cash, when there is six months interest due on them, and are a very marketable security, generally bearing a premium, being very convenient to be kept by merchants or public companies to answer exigencies. When sold, the interest to the day of sale, together with the premium, is added to the sum of the bond, and paid by the purchaser.

---

## SECTION III.

### MANNER OF TRANSACTING LOANS.

In the early part of the funding system, the subscription for loans was taken at the Exchequer; but, since 1714, they have been transacted at the Bank of England; and this was formerly done by open subscription. Terms were proposed to the public, and as these were calculated to afford a profit, the subscription was generally filled up in a short time. If the terms were not judged sufficient, and consequently the subscription not filled up, others more advantageous were offered afterwards.

For a considerable number of years, a mode of transacting loans still more favourable to the public has been adopted. The Chancellor of the Exchequer fixes upon the funds in which the loan is to be made. These are often of different kinds, and not unfrequently a long annuity forms part of the emolument. He then gives public intimation that he will be ready, on a certain day, to receive offers, and assign the loan to those who are willing to accept of the lowest terms. If a long annuity be a part of the proposed emolument, the other funds to be assigned to the lenders are fixed at a rate somewhat lower than the estimated value for each L.100 borrowed, and the bidding is on the long annuity, the loan being granted to those who will accept of the least annuity in addition to the capital offered If the loan be in different funds, but without an annuity, the capitals in all



the

the funds except one are previously fixed; and the bidding is on that fund, the loan being granted to those who will accept of the least capital. The Chancellor of the Exchequer is generally attended, at the time appointed, by several of the principal bankers in London, who deliver their offers, having previously made up a list of persons who are willing to share with them to a certain extent, in case their offer be accepted; and the loan is assigned to the offerer who proposes the lowest terms. This method, since its adoption, has been generally conducted with impartiality, and, being a fair and open competition for the public benefit, has been uniformly ratified by Parliament. The only deviation from it, since its first adoption, was in the loan of 1796, called the Loyalty Loan, when the method of open subscription at the Bank was had recourse to. In the loan of November, 1813, a preference was given to the contractors of the former loan; and, indeed, whenever a new loan has been contracted prior to the last instalment of the preceding loan, it has been usual to give the preference to the contractors of such preceding loan.

The loans are always payable by instalments at different periods of the year. But the dividends are payable on the whole from the first usual term of the funds in which the loan is made. Thus the lender receives dividends during the whole of the first year, although he only advances the money on the days appointed for payment of the instalments; or, if he advances the whole at first, he is allowed a suitable discount, and he derives part of his profit from these allowances; and, according to the terms of the loan, he is generally possest of several interests; so much perhaps in a 3 per cent. fund, so much in a 5 per cent. fund, so much in a long annuity, and formerly so much in lottery tickets. After the loan is completed, these interests are assignable separately; but when the loan is in progress, they may be either assigned separately or together. The separate parts, in this stage of the business, are called *scrip*, and their united amount is called *omnium*. In order to profit by a loan, it is necessary that the value of *omnium* at the time should be above par. This difference is called the *bonus* to the lenders. Instances, however, have occurred, in which the price of *omnium* fell below par, before the loan was completed. Lenders who do not pay their instalments at the appointed terms, forfeit their subscriptions. The Bank of England generally lends its aid in advancing some of the instalments.

The terms of the loan of 27 millions, contracted in June 1813 were,

| | | | |
|---|---|---|---|
| L.110 in 3 per cent. reduced, *scrip*, valued at $57\frac{3}{4}$, | L.63 | 10 | 6 |
| 60 in 3 per cent. cons. *scrip*, valued at $56\frac{1}{4}$, | 33 | 15 | 0 |
| Long annuity, *scrip*, of 8s. 6d. for $46\frac{3}{4}$ years, at 14 years purchase, - - - - - | 5 | 19 | 0 |
| Value of *omnium*, - - - - - | L.103 | 4 | 6 |
| *Bonus* to subscribers, besides discount for prompt payment, - - - - - - | 3 | 4 | 6 |

And the loan was payable by the following instalments.

| | | | | |
|---|---|---|---|---|
| | Deposit at subscription, - - | L.10 | 0 | 0 |
| | July 23d - - - | 10 | 0 | 0 |
| | August 20th, - - - | 15 | 0 | 0 |
| | September 17th, - - - | 10 | 0 | 0 |
| | October 22nd, - - - | 15 | 0 | 0 |
| | November 19th, - - - | 10 | 0 | 0 |
| | December 17th, - - - | 10 | 0 | 0 |
| 1814. | January 21st, - - - | 10 | 0 | 0 |
| | February 18th - - - | 10 | 0 | 0 |
| | | L.100 | 0 | 0 |

Upon payment of the first instalment, a separate sheet is delivered to the original holder, for the sums paid on each component part of the loan, containing, on one side, a receipt for the sum paid, and on the other, a form of assignment. When a sale takes place, the original holder puts his name to the assignment, without filling it up, and delivers it thus blank-indorsed to the purchaser; and, in this manner, *scrip* and *omnium* pass from hand to hand, like bank notes. These receipts are so made out, before delivery from the Bank, as to shew how much money must be paid upon the several *scrips*, at each instalment. Thus, in the abovementioned loan, there was paid for each L.1000 subscribed at the first instalment.

L.60 on the 3 per cent. reduced.
34 on the 3 per cent. cons.
6 on the long annuities.

---

L.100 being 10 per cent. on the loan; and like sums were payable at the instalments in July, September, November, and December, 1813; and in January and February, 1814; and one-half more, or 15 per cent. on the instalments in August and October, 1813. The holders of *scrip* must attend to the payment of these instalments at the Bank on the appointed days, under pain of forfeiture; and when the last instalment is paid at its term, or the whole paid up at an earlier time, with allowance of discount, the *scrip* is converted into stock, and consolidated with the mass of the stock of the same



name

name previously existing, from which it cannot afterwards be distinguished.

The value of *scrip*, after any given number of payments have been made thereon, is computed by deducting the amount of the remaining payments from the value of the stock at the market price.

---

## SECTION IV.

### MANNER OF TRANSFERRING STOCK.

AGREEMENTS for the sale of stock are generally made at the Stock Exchange, which is frequented by a set of middlemen called *Jobbers*, whose business is to accommodate buyers and sellers with the exact sums they want.* A Jobber must be possessed of considerable property in the funds ; and he declares a price, suppose 59½ or 59⅝ in the three per cent. cons. ; that is, he is willing to buy any sum from any person at 59½, or sell him at 59⅝. By this means, one who wishes to sell, suppose L.375 10s. and could hardly find a purchaser for that precise sum without the assistance of a Jobber, obtains his purpose, and the smallest sums are purchased and sold with the utmost facility. The Jobber's profit is generally ⅛ per cent. for which he transacts both a sale and a purchase; and these persons often engage in no other stock speculation, but go away when the business of the day is over, possessed of the exact sum of stock they had in the morning.

The bargain, being agreed on, is carried into execution at the transfer office, at the Bank, or the South Sea house. For this purpose, the seller makes out a note in writing, which contains the name and designation of the seller and purchaser, and the sum and description of the stock to be transferred. He delivers this to the proper clerk,† and then fills up a receipt, a printed form of which,

 with

* This is the proper acceptation of the term *Jobber*, in the language of the Stock Exchange. In common conversation, we generally understand by it, a speculator in the stocks.

† The letters of the alphabet are placed round the room, and the seller must apply to the clerk who has his station under the initial letter of his name. In all the offices, there are supervising clerks, who join in witnessing the transfer.

with blanks, is obtained at the office. The clerk, in the meantime, examines the seller's account, and if he find him possessed of the stock proposed to be sold, he makes out the transfer. This is signed in the book by the seller, who delivers the receipt to the clerk ; and upon the purchaser's signing his acceptance in the book, the clerk signs the receipt as witness. It is then delivered to the purchaser upon payment of the money, and thus the business is completed.

This business is generally transacted by brokers, who derive their authority from their employers by powers of attorney. Forms of these are obtained at the respective offices. Some authorize the broker to sell, others to accept a purchase, and others to receive the dividends. Some comprehend all these objects, and the two last are generally united. Powers of attorney, authorising to sell, must be deposited in the proper office for examination one day before selling. A stockholder acting personally, after granting a letter of attorney, revokes it by implication.*

The person in whose name the stock is invested when the books are shut, previous to the payment of the dividends, receives the dividend for the half year preceding ; and, therefore, a purchaser, during the currency of the half year, has the benefit of the interest on the stock he buys, from the last term of payment to the day of transfer. The price of stock, therefore, rises gradually, *cœteris paribus*, from term to term ; and when the dividend is paid, it undergoes a fall equal thereto. Thus the 3 per cent. cons. should be higher than the 3 per cent. reduced, by $\frac{3}{4}$ per cent. from 5th April to 5th July, and from 10th October to 5th January ; and should be as much lower from 5th January to 5th March, and from 5th July to 10th October ; and this is nearly the case. Accidental circumstances may occasion a slight deviation.

The dividends on the different stocks being payable at different terms, it is in the power of the stockholders to invest their property in such a manner as to draw their income quarterly.

The business of speculating in the stock is founded on the variation of the price of stock, which it probably tends, in some measure, to support. It consists in buying or selling stock, according to the views entertained by those who engage in this business of the probability of the value rising or falling.

 This

* The rate of brokerage is 2s. 6d. per L.100 for buying or selling. A letter of attorney costs L.1 1s. 6d. The registration of a will, 2s. 6d. The transfer of Bank stock under L.25, costs 9s., above it, 12s.; of South Sea stock under L.100, 10s., above it 12s.; of India stock, L.1. 4s. Government stock is transferred without any charge.

This business is partly conducted by persons who have property in the funds. But a practice also prevails among those who have no such property, of contracting for the sale of stock, on a future day, at a price now agreed on. For example, A. may agree to sell B. L.10,000 of three per cent. stock, to be transferred in twenty days, for L.6,000. A. has in fact no such stock ; but, if the price on the day appointed for the transfer, be only 58, he may purchase as much as will enable him to fulfil his bargain for L.5,800, and thus gain L.200 by the transaction : On the other hand, if the price of that stock should rise to 62, he will lose L.200. The business is generally settled without any actual purchase of stock, or transfer, by A. paying to B. or receiving from him, the difference between the price of the stock on the day of settlement, and the price agreed on.

This practice, which amounts to nothing else than a wager concerning the price of stock, is not sanctioned by law; yet it is carried on to a great extent: and as neither party can be compelled by law to implement these bargains, their sense of honour, and the disgrace attending a breach of contract, are the principles by which the business is supported. In the language of the Stock Exchange, the buyer is called a *Bull*, and the seller a *Bear*, and the person who refuses to pay his loss is called a *Lame Duck* ; and the names of these defaulters are exhibited in the Stock Exchange, where they dare not appear afterwards.

These bargains are usually made for certain days, fixed by a Committee of the Stock Exchange, called *settling days*, of which there are about eight in the year, viz. one in each of the months of January, February, April, May, July, August, October, and November ; and they are always on Tuesday, Wednesday, Thursday, or Friday, being the days on which the Commissioners for the reduction of the national debt make purchases. The settling days in January and July are always the first days of the opening of the Bank books for public transfer; and those days are notified at the Bank, when the consols are shut to prepare for the dividend. The price at which stock is sold, to be transferred on the next settling day, is called the price *on account*. Sometimes, instead of closing the account on the settling day, the stock is carried on to a future day, on such terms as the parties agree on. This is called a *continuation*.

All the business, however, which is done in the stocks *for time*, is not of a gambling nature. In a place of so extensive commerce as London, opulent merchants who possess property in the funds, and are unwilling to part with it, have frequently occasion to raise money for a short time. Their resource, in this case, is to sell for

 money,

money, and to buy for account ; and although the money raised in this manner costs more than the legal interest, it affords an important accommodation, and it may be rendered strictly legal and recoverable.

The following statement has been given of the highest and lowest prices of the stocks, since 1720.

HIGHEST PRICES.

| | | | |
|---|---|---|---|
| 3 per cents. | June | 1739, | L.107 |
| 4 per cents. | August | 1791, | 107⅛ |
| 5 per cents. | Ditto | — | 122¾ |
| Bank stock, | February | 1792, | 219* |
| South Sea stock, | May | 1768, | 111 |
| India stock, | December | 1768, | 276¾ |

LOWEST PRICES.

| | | | |
|---|---|---|---|
| 3 per cent. cons. | January | 1798, | L.47⅜ |
| 3 per cent. reduced, | June | 1797, | 47 |
| 4 per cents. | January | 1798, | 59¼ |
| 5 per cent. navy, | January | 1798, | 69⅜ |
| Bank stock, | January | 1782, | 91 |
| South Sea stock, | February | 1782, | 62 |
| India stock, | January | 1784, | 118½ |

In the time of the rebellion, 1745, the three per cents. fell to 75 ; but, during the war of that period, were generally above 80. After the peace of Aix-la-Chapelle, in 1748, they soon rose to par, and, in 1752, were at 106. In 1755, on the eve of the war, they fell to 90, and continued to fall during the war ; and in 1762, were at 63, which was their lowest depression that war. During the following peace, they generally fluctuated between 80 and 90. They fell rapidly during the American war, and were about 60 in the years 1779 and 80, and so low as 54 in 1782. They remained low for about two years after the peace, and afterwards rose gradually, and attained the height of 96 in March 1792 ; but fell rapidly after the commencement of the French revolution war, till they sunk to their lowest depression, 47, in January 1797. The other three per cent. stocks held nearly a similar course.

The four per cents., for some years after the American war, fluctuated between 70 and 80, and sometimes higher. In 1786, they rose to 96, and in August 1791, to 107⅛, their highest elevation. In January, 1798, they fell to 59¼, their lowest depression.

The five per cents. which commenced in 1784, rose to 110 in the beginning of 1789 ; attained their highest elevation, 122, in August 1791 ; and sunk to 68⅜, their lowest depression, in July 1798.



* The price of Bank stock here given is the highest price, previous to the late increase of dividend.

# APPENDIX II.*

## TABLE I.

Amount of the different Funds on the 5th January 1793, and 1st February 1817, with the sums redeemed, and balances unredeemed; including the debts for Ireland, Germany, and Portugal, guaranteed by Britain, and the loan for the East India Company in 1812.

| | Debt, Jan. 5, 1793. | Debt, 1st February, 1817. | | |
|---|---|---|---|---|
| | | Contracted. | Redeemed.† | Unredeemed. |
| 3 per cent. South Sea Stock, | 3,662,784 | 3,662,784 | - - | 3,662,784 |
| 3 per cent. old South Sea annuities, - - - | 11,907,470 | 11,907,470 | 6,119,000 | 5,788,470 |
| 3 per cent. new South Sea annuities, - - - | 8,494,830 | 8,494,830 | 4,481,000 | 4,013,830 |
| | 24,065,084 | 24,065,084 | 10,600,000 | 13,465,084 |
| 3 per cent. annuities, 1751, - | 1,919,600 | 1,919,600 | 1,039,000 | 880,600 |
| Amount transferable at the South Sea house, - - | 25,984,684 | 25,984,684 | 11,639,000 | 14,345,684 |
| Bank of England, - - | 11,686,800 | 14,686,800 | - - | 14,686,800 |
| 3 per cent. annuities, 1726, - | 1,000,000 | 1,000,000 | 462 | 999,538 |
| 3 per cent. cons. { British, - | 107,399,696 | 448,297,588 | 102,991,778 | 345,305,810 |
| 3 per cent. cons. { Irish, - | - - | 42,087,625 | 9,267,670 | 32,819,955 |
| 3 per cent. red. { British, - | 41,540,078 | 303,138,022 | 198,390,423 | 104,747,599 |
| 3 per cent. red. { Irish, - | - - | 52,768,750 | 9,820,176 | 42,948,574 |
| 3 per cent. red. { Portuguese, | - - | 895,522 | 426,721 | 468,801 |
| 3 per cent. Imperial loans, - | - - | 7,502,631 | 1,920,716 | 5,581,917 |
| Amount 3 per cents. - | 187,611,255 | 896,361,624 | 334,456,946 | 561,904,678 |
| Redeemed before 1793, - | 10,242,100 | | | |
| | 177,369,155 | | | |
| 4 per cent. cons. { British, - | 32,750,000 | 76,777,744 | 7,812,714 | 68,965,030 |
| 4 per cent. cons. { Irish, - | - - | 5,954,375 | - - | 5,954,375 |
| 5 per cent. navy, { British, - | 17,869,993 | 132,820,057 | 159,708 | 132,660,349 |
| 5 per cent. navy, { Irish, - | - - | 2,222,000 | - - | 2,222,000 |
| 5 per cent. loyalty loan - | - - | 1,063,798 | 5,295 | 1,058,503 |
| | 227,989,148 | 1,115,199,600 | 342,434,663 | 772,764,937 |
| 3 per cent. cons. as above, - - - | | 490,385,213 | 112,259,448 | 378,125,765 |
| Ditto, for East India Company, - - | | 1,400,000 | 451,227 | 948,773 |
| Total 3 per cent. cons. - - - - | | 491,785,213 | 112,710,675 | 379,074,538 |
| 3 per cent. reduced, as above, - - | | 356,802,294 | 208,637,320 | 148,164,974 |
| Ditto, for East India Company, - - | | 3,000,000 | 449,296 | 2,550,704 |
| Total, 3 per cent. reduced, - - - | | 359,802,294 | 209,086,616 | 150,715,678 |

* In the following tables, and also in the foregoing statements, the figure marked in the unit place of the sum of a column is often different from what it will be found on trial, owing to the omission of the shillings and pence.

† The capitals transferred for the purchase of land tax, and those converted into life annuities, and unclaimed, as well as those purchased by the Commissioners, are included in the statement of the redeemed debt here given.

TABLE II.

Progress of the Funded Debt of Britain from 1793 to 1817.

| | | Sums raised. | CAPITAL FUNDED. | | | |
|---|---|---|---|---|---|---|
| | | | 3 per cent. | 4 per cent. | 5 per cent. | Total. |
| Preceding 1793, | | Unknown. | 187,611,255 | 32,750,000 | 17,869,993 | 238,231,248 |
| 1793 Loan - | A | 4,500,000 | 6,250,000 | - - | - - | 6,250,000 |
| 1793 Loan - | B | 11,000,000 | 11,000,000 | 2,750,000 | - - | 13,750,000 |
| Navy Bills - | C | 1,907,451 | - .. | - - | 1,926,526 | 1,926,526 |
| 1795 Loan - | D | 18,000,000 | 18,000,000 | 6,000,000 | - - | 24,000,000 |
| Navy Bills - | E | 1,490,647 | - - | - - | 1,609,898 | 1,609,898 |
| Loan - | F | 18,000,000 | 26,095,800 | - - | - - | 26,095,800 |
| 1796 Loan - | G | 7,500,000 | 10,793,825 | - - | - - | 10,793,825 |
| Navy Bills - | H | 4,226,727 | - - | - - | 4,414,074 | 4,414,074 |
| N. and Ex. Bills | I | 13,029,399 | 18,437,874 | 869,860 | 2,305,092 | 21,612,826 |
| LOYALTY LOAN | K | 18,000,000 | - - | - - | 20,124,843 | 20,124,843 |
| 1797 Loan - | L | 13,000,000 | 22,750,000 | 2,600,000 | - - | 25,350,000 |
| 1798 Loan - | M | 15,000,000 | 30,000,000 | - - | - - | 30,000,000 |
| Loan - | N | 3,000,000 | 5,624,250 | - - | - - | 5,624,250 |
| 1799 Loan - | O | 12,500,000 | 21,875,000 | - - | - - | 21,875,000 |
| 1800 Loan - | P | 18,500,000 | 29,045,000 | - - | - - | 29,045,000 |
| 1801 Loan - | Q | 25,500,000 | 44,816,250 | - - | - - | 44,816,250 |
| 1802 Exchequer Bills | R | 8,910,450 | 4,455,225 | 4,455,225 | 2,227,612 | 11,138,063 |
| Loan - | S | 23,000,000 | 30,351,375 | - - | - - | 30,351,375 |
| | | 217,064,674 | 467,105,854 | 49,425,085 | 50,478,039 | 567,008,978 |
| 1803 Loan - | T | 10,000,000 | 16,000,000 | - - | - - | 16,000,000 |
| 1804 Loan - | U | 10,000,000 | 18,200,000 | - - | - - | 18,200,000 |
| 1805 Loan - | V | 20,000,000 | 34,400,000 | - - | - - | 34,400,000 |
| | | 257,064,674 | 535,705,854 | 49,425,085 | 50,478,039 | 635,608,978 |
| Operations LLTY. LOAN,* | | - - | +7,426,233 | - - | −2,283,109 | +5,143,124 |
| | | | 543,132,087 | 49,425,085 | 48,194,930 | 640,752,102 |
| 1806 Loan - | X | 18,000,000 | 29,880,000 | - - | - - | 29,880,000 |
| 1807 Loan - | Y | 12,200,000 | 17,080,000 | - - | 1,293,200 | 18,373,200 |
| 1808 Loan - | *A* | 8,000,000 | - - | 9,454,000 | - - | 9,454,000 |
| Exchequer Bills | *B* | 4,000,000 | - - | 237,900 | 4,001,354 | 4,239,254 |
| Interest deferred, 1802 | | - - | - - | - - | - - | - - |
| 1809 Loan - | *C* | 11,000,000 | 6,064,478 | 6,960,000 | - - | 13,024,478 |
| Exchequer Bills | *D* | 7,932,100 | - - | 380,336 | 7,873,308 | 8,253,644 |
| 1810 Exchequer Bills | *E* | 8,311,000 | - - | - - | 8,581,108 | 8,581,108 |
| Loan - | *F* | 8,000,000 | 11,230,000 | - - | - - | 11,230,000 |
| Carried forward | | 334,507,774 | 607,386,565 | 66,457,321 | 69,943,900 | 734,787,786 |



* See Note XVI.

With the Annual Charge on the same.

| | ANNUAL CHARGE ON EACH LOAN. | | | | Whole annual charge. |
|---|---|---|---|---|---|
| | Interest. | Annuities. | Managmt. | Total. | |
| | 7,831,837 | 1,293,870 | 116,127 | 9,241,834 | 9,241,834 |
| A | 187,500 | - - | 2,812 | 190,312 | 9,432,146 |
| B | 440,000 | 62,792 | 6,894 | 509,686 | 9,941,832 |
| C | 96,326 | - - | 867 | 97,193 | 10,039,025 |
| D | 780,000 | 85,500 | 11,762 | 877,262 | 10,916,928 |
| E | 80,495 | - - | 724 | 81,219 | 10,997,506 |
| F | 782,874 | 58,500 | 12,401 | 853,775 | 11,851,281 |
| G | 323,815 | 20,582 | 5,089 | 349,486 | 12,200,767 |
| H | 220,703 | - - | 1,986 | 222,689 | 12,423,456 |
| I | 703,185 | - - | 9,726 | 712,911 | 13,136,397 |
| K | 1,006,243 | - - | 9,056 | 1,015,299 | 14,051,666 |
| L | 786,500 | 39,000 | 11,864 | 837,364 | 14,989,030 |
| M | 900,000 | 36,875 | 13,915 | 950,790 | 15,939,820 |
| N | 168,727 | - - | 2,530 | 171,257 | 16,111,077 |
| O | 656,250 | - - | 9,843 | 666,093 | 16,777,170 |
| P | 871,350 | - - | 13,070 | 884,420 | 17,661,590 |
| Q | 1,344,488 | - - | 20,167 | 1,364,655 | 19,026,245 |
| R | 423,247 | 7,796 | 5,099 | 436,142 | 19,462,387 |
| S | 862,500 | - - | 12,937 | 875,437 | 20,337,825 |
| | 18,466,040 | 1,604,915 | 266,870 | 20,337,825 | |
| T | 480,000 | 32,083 | 5,713 | 517,796 | 20,855,621 |
| U | 546,000 | - - | 6,188 | 552,188 | 21,407,809 |
| V | 1,032,000 | - - | 11,696 | 1,043,696 | 22,451,505 |
| | 20,524,040 | 1,636,998 | 290,467 | 22,451,505 | |
| | + 108,633 | - - | + 2,314 | + 110,947 | |
| | 20,632,673 | 1,636,998 | 292,781 | 22,562,452 | 22,562,452 |
| X | 896,400 | - - | 10,159 | 906,559 | 23,469,011 |
| Y | 577,060 | - - | 6,247 | 583,307 | 24,052,318 |
| *A* | 378,160 | - - | 3,214 | 381,374 | 24,433,692 |
| *B* | 209,584 | - - | 1,441 | 211,025 | 24,644,717 |
| | 48,041 | - - | - - | 48,041 | 24,692,758 |
| *C* | 460,334 | 51,233 | 4,864 | 516,431 | 25,209,189 |
| *D* | 408,879 | - - | 2,806 | 411,685 | 25,620,874 |
| *E* | 429,055 | - - | 2,917 | 431,972 | 26,052,846 |
| *F* | 336,900 | - - | 3,818 | 340,718 | 26,393,564 |
| | 24,377,086 | 1,688,231 | 328,247 | 26,393,564 | |

 Continuation

Continuation of Table II.

| | | Sums raised. | CAPITAL FUNDED. | | | |
|---|---|---|---|---|---|---|
| | | | 3 per cent. | 4 per cent. | 5 per cent. | Total. |
| Brought forward | | 334,507,774 | 607,386,565 | 66,457,321 | 69,943,900 | 743,787,786 |
| 1811 Exchequer Bills | *H* | 7,018,700 | - - | - - | 7,278,392 | 7,278,392 |
| Loan - | *I* | 4,981,300 | - - | - - | 5,166,319 | 5,166,319 |
| Loan - | *K* | 12,000,000 | 14,400,000 | 2,400,000 | - - | 16,800,000 |
| 1812 Exchequer Bills | *L* | 5,431,700 | - - | - - | 5,866,236 | 5,866,236 |
| Loan - | *M* | 6,789,625 | - - | - - | 7,332,795 | 7,332,795 |
| Loan - | *N* | 15,650,000 | 27,544,000 | - - | - - | 27,544,000 |
| 1813 Exchequer Bills | *O* | 12,000,000 | - - | - - | 13,860,000 | 13,860,000 |
| Exchequer Bills | *P* | 3,755,700 | - - | 5,220,423 | - - | 5,220,423 |
| Loan - | *Q* | 21,000,000 | 35,700,000 | - - | - - | 35,700,000 |
| 1814 Loan - | *R* | 22,000,000 | 38,940,000 | - - | - - | 38,940,000 |
| Loan - | *S* | 18,500,000 | 19,145,430 | - - | 5,549,400 | 24,694,830 |
| Debentures | | 7,400 | 11,100 | - - | - - | 11,100 |
| 1815 Exchequer Bills | *T* | 10,313,000 | - - | - - | 12,066,210 | 12,066,210 |
| Ex. Bills and loan | *U* | 7,822,589 | - - | - - | 9,142,192 | 9,142,192 |
| Loan - | *V* | 27,000,000 | 46,980,000 | 2,700,000 | - - | 49,680,000 |
| 1816 Loan from Bank | *W* | 3,000,000 | 3,000,000 | - - | - - | 3,000,000 |
| | | 511,777,788 | 793,107,095 | 76,777,744 | 136,205,445 | 1,006,090,284 |
| Deduct annuities expired | a | - - | - - | - - | - - | - - |
| Loyalty Loan paid | b | —2,321,590 | - - | - - | —2,321,590 | —2,321,590 |
| | | | | | | 1,003,768,694 |
| Reduction in managmt. | c | - - | - - | - - | - - | - - |
| Transfd. to life annuities | d | - - | —3,449,955 | - - | - - | —3,449,955 |
| | | 509,456,198 | 789,657,140 | 76,777,744 | 133,883,855 | 1,000,318,739 |
| Add life annuities | e | - - | - - | - - | - - | - - |
| Debts contracted since 1793. | | 509,456,198 | 789,657,140 | 76,777,744 | 133,883,855 | 1,000,318,739 |
| By loans - | f | 420,307,425 | 582,591,641 | 32,864,000 | 43,051,087 | 658,506,728 |
| By funding bills - | g | 89,148,773 | 22,904,199 | 11,163,744 | 72,962,774 | 107,030,717 |
| | | 509,456,198 | 605,495,840 | 44,027,744 | 116,013,861 | 765,537,445 |
| Contracted before 1793 | h | unknown. | 187,611,255 | 32,750,000 | 17,869,993 | 238,231,248 |
| | | | 793,107,095 | 76,777,744 | 133,883,855 | 1,003,768,694 |



Continuation

Continuation of Table II.

| | ANNUAL CHARGE ON EACH LOAN. | | | | Whole annual charge. |
|---|---|---|---|---|---|
| | Interest. | Annuities. | Managmt. | Total. | |
| | 24,377,086 | 1,688,231 | 328,247 | 26,393,564 | |
| *H* | 363,919 | - - | 2,385 | 366,304 | 26,759,868 |
| *I* | 258,316 | - - | 1,550 | 259,866 | 27,019,734 |
| *K* | 528,000 | 41,500 | 5,392 | 574,892 | 27,594,626 |
| *L* | 293,312 | - - | 1,760 | 294,072 | 27,888,698 |
| *M* | 366,639 | - - | 2,200 | 368,839 | 28,257,537 |
| *N* | 826,320 | - - | 8,263 | 835,583 | 29,093,120 |
| *O* | 693,000 | - - | 4,158 | 697,158 | 29,790,278 |
| *P* | 208,817 | - - | 1,566 | 210,383 | 30,000,661 |
| *Q* | 1,071,000 | 89,250 | 11,379 | 1,171,629 | 31,172,290 |
| *R* | 1,168,200 | - - | 11,682 | 1,179,882 | 32,352,172 |
| *S* | 851,833 | - - | 7,409 | 859,242 | 33,211,414 |
| | 333 | - - | - - | 333 | 33,211,747 |
| *T* | 603,310 | - - | 3,620 | 606,930 | 33,818,677 |
| *U* | 457,109 | - - | 2,742 | 459,851 | 34,278,528 |
| *V* | 1,517,400 | - - | 14,904 | 1,532,304 | 35,810,833 |
| *W* | 90,000 | - - | | 90,000 | 35,900,833 |
| | 33,674,595 | 1,818,981 | 407,257 | 35,900,833 | - - |
| a | - - | — 516,202 | - - | — 516,202 | 35,384,631 |
| b | — 116,079 | - - | - - | — 116,079 | 35,268,552 |
| | 33,558,516 | 1,302,779 | - - | - - | - - |
| c | - - | - - | — 161,907 | — 161,907 | 35,106,645 |
| d | — 103,499 | — 4,420 | - - | — 107,919 | 34,998,726 |
| | 33,455,017 | 1,298,359 | 245,350 | 34,998,726 | |
| e | - - | + 225,255 | - - | 225,255 | |
| | 33,455,017 | 1,523,614 | 245,350 | 35,223,981 | 35,223,981 |
| f | 20,944,866 | 525,266 } | 155,825 | 26,415,566 | |
| g | 4,781,813 | 7,796 } | | | |
| | 25,726,679 | 533,062 | - - | - . | |
| h | 7,831,837 | 769,717 | 89,525 | 8,691,079 | |
| | 33,558,516 | 1,302,779 | 245,350 | 35,106,645 | |

## TABLE III.

Progress and Redemption of the Funded Debt of Great Britain.

| Preced. | | Capital funded each year. | Capital redeemed each year. | Balance each year. | Total funded. | Total redeemed. | Debt unredeemed. |
|---|---|---|---|---|---|---|---|
| 1791 | | 238,231,248 | 6,772,350 | 231,458,898 | 238,231,248 | 6,772,350 | 231,458,898 |
| 1791-2 | | - - | 3,469,750 | 227,898,148 | 238,231,248 | 10,242,100 | 227,989,148 |
| 1793 | A, | 6,250,000 | 2,174,405 | 4,075,595 | 244,481,248 | 12,416,505 | 232,064,743 |
| 1794 | B, C, | 15,676,526 | 2,804,945 | 12,871,581 | 260,157,774 | 15,221,450 | 244,936,323 |
| 1795 | D, E, | 25,609,898 | 3,083,455 | 22,526,443 | 285,782,672 | 18,304,905 | 267,457,767 |
| 1796 | F, G, H, | 41,303,699 | 4,390,670 | 36,913,029 | 327,071,371 | 22,695,575 | 304,375,796 |
| 1797 | I, K, L, | 67,087,669 | 6,695,585 | 60,392,084 | 394,159,040 | 29,391,160 | 364,797,880 |
| 1798 | M, | 30,000,000 | 7,779,807 | 22,220,193 | 424,159,040 | 37,170,976 | 386,889,073 |
| 1799 | N, O, | 27,499,250 | 7,151,984 | 20,347,266 | 451,658,290 | 44,322,951 | 407,355,339 |
| 1800 | P, | 29,045,000 | 7,247,560 | 21,797,440 | 480,703,290 | 51,571,111 | 429,132,799 |
| 1801 | Q, | 44,816,250 | 8,018,393 | 36,797,857 | 525,519,540 | 59,588,904 | 465,920,636 |
| 1802 | R, S, | 41,489,438 | 7,667,011 | 33,822,427 | 567,008,978 | 67,255,915 | 499,753,063 |
| | | 567,008,978 | 67,255,915 | 499,753,063 | | | |
| 1803 | T, | 16,000,000 | 10,442,552 | 5,557,448 | 583,008,978 | 77,698,915 | 505,310,511 |
| 1804 | U, | 18,200,000 | 11,305,292 | 6,894,708 | 601,208,978 | 89,003,759 | 512,205,219 |
| 1805 | V, | 34,400,000 | 12,142,043 | 22,257,957 | 635,608,978 | 101,145,802 | 434,463,176 |
| | | 635,608,978 | 101,145,802 | 534,463,176 | | | |
| | Operat. L. Loan. | 5,143,124 | - - | 5,143,124 | 640,752,102 | 101,145,802 | 539,606,300 |
| 1806 | X, | 29,880,000 | 12,714,715 | 17,165,285 | 670,632,102 | 113,860,517 | 556,771,585 |
| 1807 | Y. | 18,373,200 | 14,076,585 | 4.296,615 | 689,005,302 | 127,937,102 | 561,068,200 |
| 1808 | *A, B,* | 13,693,254 | 13,871,014 | — 177,760 | 702,698,556 | 141,808,116 | 560,890,440 |
| 1809 | *C, D,* | 21,278,122 | 14,234,820 | 7,043,302 | 723,976,678 | 156,042,936 | 567,933,742 |
| 1810 | *E, F,* | 19,811,108 | 15,512,087 | 4,299,021 | 743,797,786 | 171,555,023 | 572,232,763 |
| 1811 | *H, I, K,* | 29,244,711 | 17,983,457 | 11,261,254 | 773,032,497 | 189,538,480 | 583,494,017 |
| 1812 | *L, M, N,* | 40,743,031 | 20,922,876 | 19,820,155 | 813,775,528 | 210,461,356 | 603,314,172 |
| 1813 | *O, P, Q,* | 54,780,423 | 23,924,419 | 30,855,994 | 868,545,951 | 234,385,785 | 634,170,166 |
| 1814 | *R, S, & deb.* | 63,645,930 | 18,968,435 | 44,677,495 | 932,201,881 | 253,354,220 | 678,847,661 |
| 1815 | *T, U, V,* | 70,888,402 | 20,064,182 | 50,824,220 | 1,003,090,283 | 273,418,402 | 729,671,881 |
| 1816 | *W.* | 3,000,000 | 18,300,770 | -15,300,770 | 1,006,090,283 | 291,719,172 | 714,371,111 |
| | | 1,006,090,283 | 291,719,172 | 714,371,111 | | | |
| Loyalty Loan paid - | | | 2,321,590 | - - | - - | 294,040,762 | 712,049,521 |
| Unclaimed, or purchased with unclaimed dividends, | | | 539,258 | - - | - - | 294,580,020 | 711,510,263 |
| Transferred for life annuities, | | | 3,449,955 | - - | - - | 298,029,975 | 708,060,308 |
| Transferred for land tax, - | | | 25,290,994 | - - | - - | 323,320,969 | 682,769,314 |
| | | | 323,320,969 | | | | |



And

And Balances unredeemed.

| | REDUCED TO THREE PER CENTS. | | | | | |
|---|---|---|---|---|---|---|
| | Capital funded each year. | Capital redeemed each year. | Balance each year. | Total funded. | Total redeemed. | Debt unredeemed. |
| | 261,061,243 | 6,772,350 | 254,288,893 | 261,061,243 | 6,772,350 | 254,288,893 |
| | - - | 3,469,750 | 250,819,143 | 261,061,243 | 10,242,100 | 250,719,143 |
| A, | 6,250,000 | 2,174,405 | 4,075,595 | 267,311,243 | 12,416,505 | 254,894,738 |
| B, C, | 17,877,543 | 2,804,945 | 15,072,598 | 285,188,786 | 15,221,450 | 269,967,336 |
| D, E, | 28,683,163 | 3,252,455 | 25,430,708 | 313,871,949 | 18,473,005 | 295,398,044 |
| F, G, H, | 44,246,415 | 4,390,670 | 39,855,745 | 358,718,364 | 22,864,575 | 335,253,789 |
| I, K, L, | 83,197,579 | 6,695,585 | 76,501,994 | 441,315,943 | 29,560,160 | 411,755,783 |
| M, | 30,000,000 | 7,779,807 | 22,220,193 | 471,315,943 | 37,339,967 | 433,975,976 |
| N, O, | 27,499,250 | 7,151,984 | 20,347,266 | 498,815,193 | 44,491,951 | 454,323,242 |
| P, | 29,045,000 | 7,247,560 | 21,797,440 | 527,860,193 | 51,739,511 | 476,120,682 |
| Q, | 44,816,250 | 8,246,726 | 36,569,524 | 572,676,443 | 59,986,237 | 512,690,206 |
| R, S, | 44,459,587 | 8,142,144 | 36,317,443 | 617,136,030 | 68,128,381 | 549,007,649 |
| | 617,136,030 | 68,128,381 | 549,007,649 | | | |
| T, | 16,000,000 | 10,442,552 | 5,557,448 | 633,136,030 | 78,570,933 | 554,565,097 |
| U, | 18,200,000 | 11,399,958 | 6,800,042 | 651,336,030 | 89,970,891 | 561,365,139 |
| V, | 34,400,000 | 12,142,043 | 22,257,957 | 685,736,030 | 102,112,934 | 583,623,096 |
| | 685,736,030 | 102,112,934 | 583,623,096 | | | |
| L. Loan, | 3,621,051 | - - | 3,621,051 | 689,357,081 | 102,112,934 | 587,244,147 |
| X, | 29,880,000 | 12,714,715 | 17,165,285 | 719,237,081 | 114,827,839 | 604,409,432 |
| Y. | 19,235,333 | 14,076,585 | 5,158,748 | 738,472,414 | 128,904,234 | 609,568,180 |
| *A, B,* | 19,591,456 | 14,430,447 | 5,161,009 | 758,063,870 | 143,334,681 | 614,729,189 |
| *C, D,* | 28,973,773 | 15,012,820 | 13,960,953 | 787,037,643 | 158,347,501 | 628,690,142 |
| *E, F,* | 25,531,846 | 15,900,987 | 9,630,859 | 812,569,489 | 174,248,488 | 638,321,001 |
| *H, I, K,* | 38,341,185 | 17,983,457 | 20,357,728 | 850,910,674 | 192,231,945 | 658,678,729 |
| *L, M, N,* | 49,542,385 | 20,922,876 | 28,619,509 | 900,453,059 | 213,154,821 | 687,298,238 |
| *O, P, Q,* | 65,760,564 | 23,924,429 | 41,836,135 | 966,213,623 | 237,079,250 | 729,134,373 |
| *R, S, & deb.* | 67,345,530 | 18,986,435 | 48,377,095 | 1,033,559,153 | 256,047,685 | 777,511,468 |
| *T, U, V,* | 85,927,336 | 20,064,182 | 65,863,154 | 1,119,486,489 | 276,111,867 | 843,374,622 |
| *W.* | 3,000,000 | 18,303,103 | -15,303,103 | 1,122,486,489 | 294,414,970 | 828,071,519 |
| | 1,122,486,489 | 294,414,970 | 828,072,519 | | | |
| | - - | 3,869,316 | - - | - - | 298,284,286 | 824,202,203 |
| | - - | 557,697 | - - | - - | 298,841,983 | 823,644,506 |
| | - - | 3,449,955 | - - | - - | 302,291,938 | 820,194,551 |
| | - - | 25,290,994 | - - | - - | 327,582,932 | 794,903,557 |
| | | 327,582,932 | | | | |

## TABLE IV.

Loans for Ireland, guaranteed by Britain, with the annual Charges;

| Preced. | | Sums raised. | Funded at 3 per cent. | Funded at 4 per cent. | Funded at 5 per cent. | Total funded each year. | Amount funded debt. |
|---|---|---|---|---|---|---|---|
| 1797 | K | 1,500,000 | 2,625,000 | 300,000 | - - | 2,925,000 | 2,925,000 |
| 1798 | M | 2,000,000 | 4,000,000 | - - | - - | 4,000,000 | 6,925,000 |
| 1799 | O | 3,000,000 | 5,250,000 | - - | - - | 5,250,000 | 12,175,000 |
| 1800 | P | 2,000,000 | 3,140,000 | - - | - - | 3,140,000 | 15,315,000 |
| 1801 | R | 2,500,000 | 4,393,750 | - - | - - | 4,393,750 | 19,708,750 |
| 1802 | S | 2,000,000 | 2,639,250 | - - | - - | 2,639,250 | 22,348,000 |
| | | 13,000,000 | 22,048,000 | 300,000 | - - | 22,348,000 | |
| 1803 | T | 2,000,000 | 3,200,000 | - - | - - | 3,200,000 | 25,548,000 |
| 1804 | U | 4,500,000 | 8,190,000 | - - | - - | 8,190,000 | 33,738,000 |
| 1805 | V | 2,500,000 | 4,300,000 | - - | - - | 4,300,000 | 38,038,000 |
| Sep. loan | W | 1,500,000 | - - | - - | 360,000 | 360,000 | 38,398,000 |
| 1806 | X | 2,000,000 | 3,320,000 | - - | - - | 3,320,000 | 41,718,000 |
| 1807 | Y | 2,000,000 | 2,800,000 | - - | 212,000 | 3,012,000 | 44,730,000 |
| Sep. loan | Z | 1,500,000 | 2,409,625 | - - | - - | 2,409,625 | 47,139,625 |
| 1808 | *A* | 2,500,000 | - - | 2,954,375 | - - | 2,954,375 | 50,094,000 |
| Int. def. | | | - - | - - | - - | - - | - - |
| 1809 | *C* | 3,000,000 | 1,800,000 | 1,800,000 | - - | 3,600,000 | 53,694,000 |
| 1810 | *F* | 4,000,000 | 5,615,000 | - - | - - | 5,615,000 | 59,309,000 |
| Sep. loan | *G* | 1,400,000 | 1,965,250 | - - | - - | 1,965,250 | 61,274,250 |
| 1811 | | - - | - - | - - | - - | - - | - - |
| 1812 | *N* | 4,350,000 | 7,656,000 | - - | - - | 7,656,000 | 68,930,250 |
| 1813 | *Q* | 6,000,000 | 10,200,000 | - - | - - | 10,200,000 | 79,130,000 |
| 1814 | *S* | 5,500,000 | 5,692,500 | - - | 1,650,000 | 7,342,500 | 86,472,750 |
| | *T* | 9,000,000 | 15,660,000 | 900,000 | - - | 16,560,000 | 103,032,750 |
| 1816 | | - - | - - | - - | - - | - - | 103,032,750 |
| | | 64,750,000 | 94,856,375 | 5,954,375 | 2,222,000 | 103,032,750 | |

Also the Redemption of the same.

| | Sum redeemed each year. | Amount redeemed. | Amount unredeemed. | Interest. | Annuities. | Manage-ment. | Total charge each year. |
|---|---|---|---|---|---|---|---|
| K | 20,468 | 20,468 | 2,904,532 | 90,750 | 4,500 | 1,349 | 96,599 |
| M | 91,466 | 111,934 | 6,813,066 | 120,000 | 4,916 | 1,855 | 126,771 |
| O | 130,185 | 242,119 | 11,932,881 | 157,500 | - - | 2,362 | 159,862 |
| P | 233,360 | 475,479 | 14,839,521 | 94,200 | - - | 1,413 | 95,613 |
| R | 310,928 | 786,407 | 18,922,343 | 131,812 | - - | 1,977 | 133,789 |
| S | 337,008 | 1,123,415 | 21,224,585 | 75,000 | - - | 1,125 | 76,125 |
| | 1,123,415 | | | 669,262 | 9,416 | 10,081 | 888,759 |
| T | 472,256 | 1,595,671 | 23,952,329 | 96,000 | 6,417 | 1,142 | 103,559 |
| U | 579,338 | 2,175,009 | 31,562,901 | 245,700 | - - | 2,785 | 248,485 |
| V } | 738,939 | 2,013,048 | 35,484,052 { | 129,000 | - - | 1,462 | 130,462 |
| W } | | | | 18,000 | 75,000 | 700 | 93,760 |
| X | 807,393 | 3,721,341 | 37,996,659 | 99,600 | - - | 1,129 | 100,729 |
| Y } | 907,585 | 4,628,926 | 42,510,699 { | 94,600 | - - | 1,024 | 95,624 |
| Z } | | | | 72,289 | - - | 819 | 73,108 |
| *A* | 951,463 | 5,580,389 | 44,513,611 | 118,175 | - - | 1,004 | 119,179 |
| | - - | - - | - - | 4,178 | - - | - - | 4,178 |
| *C* | 1,013,577 | 6,593,966 | 47,100,034 | 126,000 | 18,250 | 1,337 | 140,587 |
| *F* } | 1,135,716 | 7,729,682 | 53,544,568 { | 168,450 | - - | 1,909 | 170,359 |
| *G* } | | | | 58,957 | - - | 667 | 59,624 |
| | 1,356,276 | 9,085,958 | 52,188,292 | - - | - - | - - | - - |
| *N* | 1,567,541 | 10,653,499 | 58,276,751 | 229,680 | - - | 2,414 | 232,094 |
| *Q* | 1,798,434 | 12,451,933 | 66,678,317 | 306,000 | - - | 3,251 | 334,751 |
| *S* | 1,812,122 | 14,264,055 | 72,208,695 | 253,275 | 25,500 | 2,203 | 255,478 |
| *T* | 2,316,690 | 16,580,745 | 86,452,005 | 505,800 | - - | 4,968 | 510,768 |
| | 2,507,101 | 19,087,846 | 83,944,904 | - - | - - | - - | - - |
| | 19,087,846 | | | 3,194,966 | 129,583 | 36,956 | 3,361,505 |
| | Deduct reduction in management, | | | - - | - - | —8,130 | 3,353,375 |
| | and interest on debt redeemed, | | | —572,635 | - - | - - | - - |
| | | | | 2,622,331 | 129,583 | 28,826 | 2,780,740 |



TABLE

TABLE V.

Progress of the Irish Debt, payable in Dublin

| Years. | Sums raised. Irish currency. | Capital funded in Dublin, Irish currency. | | | |
|---|---|---|---|---|---|
| | | $3\frac{1}{2}$ per cent. | 4 per cent. | 5 per cent. | Total. |
| 1773-5-7 | 740,000 | - - | - - | - - | - - |
| 1787 | 200,000 | 200,000 | - - | - - | 200,000 |
| 1788 | 918,240 | 918,240 | - - | - - | 918,240 |
| 1791, &c. | 174,600 | - - | 174,600 | - - | 174,600 |
| 1793 | 200,000 | - - | - - | 200,000 | 200,000 |
| Vote Cr. | 150,000 | - - | - - | 150,000 | 150,000 |
| 1794 | 1,029,650 | - - | - - | 487,983 | 487,983 |
| 1795 | 1,591,666 | - - | - - | 400,000 | 400,000 |
| 1796 | 640,000 | - - | - - | 640,000 | 640,000 |
| Vote Cr. | 325,000 | - - | - - | - - | - - |
| 1797 | 2,025,050 | - - | - - | 635,000 | 635,000 |
| 1798 | 3,413,476 | - - | - - | 2,043,950 | 2,043,950 |
| 1799 | 5,261,000 | - - | - - | 2,011,000 | 2,011,000 |
| 1800 | 4,666,666 | - - | - - | 2,500,000 | 2,500,000 |
| 1801 | 2,750,319 | - - | - - | 41,985 | 41,985 |
| 1802 | 3,791,666 | 1,770,232 | - - | - - | 1,770,232 |
| | 27,877,355 | 2,888,472 | 174,600 | 9,109,919 | 12,172,991 |
| 1803 | 2,177,666 | - - | - - | 11,000 | 11,000 |
| 1804 | 6,125,000 | - - | - - | 1,404,531 | 1,404,531 |
| 1805 | 4,333,333 | - - | - - | - - | - - |
| 1806 | 4,166,666 | 2,780,000 | - - | - - | 2,780,000 |
| 1807 | 3,844,666 | - - | 53,000 | - - | 53,000 |
| 1808 | 3,458,333 | 1,012,500 | - - | - - | 1,012,500 |
| 1809 | 4,500,000 | 1,500,000 | - - | - - | 1,500,000 |
| 1810 | 5,856,198 | - - | - - | 6,198 | 6,198 |
| 1811 | 2,501,000 | 3,000,000 | - - | 1,000 | 3,001,000 |
| 1812 | 6,225,500 | 1,500,000 | - - | 313,000 | 1,813,000 |
| 1813 | 8,500,000 | 2,000,000 | - - | 400,000 | 2,400,000 |
| 1814 | 8,959,533 | 2,700,000 | 922,500 | 1,200 | 3,623,700 |
| 1815 | 9,758,000 | - - | - - | 8,000 | 8,000 |
| 1816 | 6,600 | - - | - - | 6,600 | 6,600 |
| Bank of Ireland, prec. 1797 | 600,000 | - - | - - | 600,000 | 600,000 |
| 1797 | 500,000 | - - | - - | 500,000 | 500,000 |
| 1808 | 1,250,000 | - - | - - | 1,250,000 | 1,250,000 |
| | 100,639,833 | 17,380,972 | 1,150,100 | 13,611,448 | 32,142,521 |



and

and London, with the Annual Charge.

| Years. | Capital Funded in London, British currency. | | | Annual Charge, Irish currency. | |
|---|---|---|---|---|---|
| | 3 per cent. | 4 per cent. | 5 per cent. | Interest. | Annuities. |
| 1773-5-7 | - - | - - | - - | - - | 47,668 |
| 1787 | - - | - - | - - | 7,000 | |
| 1788 | - - | - - | - - | 32,138 | |
| 1792, &c. | - - | - - | - - | 6,984 | |
| 1793 | - - | - - | - - | 10,000 | |
| Vote Cr. | - - | - - | - - | 7,500 | |
| 1794 | - - | - - | * 500,000 | 51,482 | |
| 1795 | - - | - - | *1,100,000 | 79,583 | |
| 1796 | - - | - - | - - | 32,000 | |
| Vote Cr. | - - | - - | * 300,000 | 16,250 | |
| 1797 | 2,625,000 | 300,000 | - - | 130,062 | 4,875 |
| 1798 | 4,000,000 | - - | - - | 232,197 | 5,326 |
| 1799 | 5,250,000 | - - | - - | 271,175 | |
| 1800 | 3,140,000 | - - | - - | 227,050 | |
| 1801 | 4,393,750 | - - | - - | 144,896 | |
| 1802 | 2,639,250 | - - | - - | 147,733 | |
| | 22,048,000 | 300,000 | 1,900,000 | 1,396,054 | 57,869 |
| 1803 | 3,200,000 | - - | - - | 104,550 | 6,951 |
| 1804 | 8,190,000 | - - | - - | 336,401 | |
| 1805 | 4,300,000 | - - | 360,000 | 159,250 | 81,250 |
| 1806 | 3,320,000 | - - | - - | 205,200 | |
| 1807 | 5,209,625 | - - | 212,000 | 182,916 | |
| 1808 | - - | 2,954,375 | - - | 163,460 | |
| 1809 | 1,800,000 | 1,800,000 | - - | 189,000 | 14,354 |
| 1810 | 7,580,250 | - - | - - | 246,668 | |
| 1811 | - - | - - | - - | 105,050 | |
| 1812 | 7,656,000 | - - | - - | 316,970 | |
| 1813 | 10,200,000 | - - | - - | 421,500 | 27,625 |
| 1814 | 5,692,500 | - - | 1,650,000 | 405,841 | |
| 1815 | 15,660,000 | 900,000 | - - | 548,350 | |
| 1816 | - - | - - | - - | 330 | |
| Bank of Ireland, prec. 1797 | - - | - - | - - | 30,000 | |
| 1797 | - - | - - | - - | 25,000 | |
| 1808 | - - | - - | - - | 62,500 | |
| | 94,856,375 | 5,954,375 | 4,122,000 | 4,899,040 | 188,049 |
| | Annuities, - | - | - | 188,049 | |
| | Management, | - | - | 30,305 | |
| | | | | 5,117,395 | |



* The sums marked with an asterisk, amounting to L.1,900,000, though the dividends be payable at the Bank of England, are not guaranteed by Britain; and do not enter into the accompt of British debt annually reported to Parliament.

TABLE VI.—Sinking Fund of 1 per cent. on Loans.

| Years. | | Loans and Bills funded. | | Long annuities. | Sinking Fund of 1 per cent. | |
|---|---|---|---|---|---|---|
| | | Charged with 1 per cent. | Not charged with 1 p. cent. | | On loans. | On annuit. |
| 1793 | A | 6,250,000 | - - | - - | 62,500 | - - |
| 1794 | B | 13,750,000 | - - | 62,792 | 137,500 | 9,680 |
| | C | 1,926,526 | - - | - - | 19,265 | - - |
| 1795 | D | 24,000,000 | | 85,500 | 240,000 | 12,835 |
| | E | 1,609,898 | - - | - - | 16,099 | - - |
| 1796 | F | 26,095,800 | - - | 58,500 | 260,958 | 8,460 |
| | G | 10,793,825 | - - | 20,582 | 107,938 | 2,925 |
| | H | 4,414,074 | - - | - - | 44,140 | - - |
| 1797 | I | 21,612,826 | - - | - - | 216,127 | - - |
| | K | 20,124,843 | - - | - - | 201,248 | - - |
| | L | 25,350,000 | - - | 39,000 | 253,500 | 5,308 |
| 1798 | M | 14,000,000 | 16,000,000 | 17,209 | 140,000 | 2,240 |
| | N | 5,624,250 | - - | - - | 56,242 | - - |
| 1799 | O | 2,625,000 | 19,250,000 | - - | 26,250 | - - |
| 1800 | P | 7,850,000 | 21,195,000 | - - | 78,500 | - - |
| 1801 | Q | 44,816,250 | - - | - - | 448,162 | - - |
| | R | 11,138,063 | - - | 7,796 | 111,380 | 841 |
| 1802 | S | - - | 30,351,375 | - - | - - | - - |
| | | 241,981,355 | 86,796,375 | 291,379 | 2,419,813 | 42,289 |
| 1803 | T | 16,000,000 | - - | 32,083 | 160,000 | 3,138 |
| 1804 | U | 18,200,000 | - - | - - | 182,000 | - - |
| 1805 | V | 34,400,000 | - - | - - | 344,000 | - - |
| Operat. L. L. | | 5,143,124 | - - | - - | 51,431 | - - |
| 1806 | X | 29,880,000 | - - | - - | 298,800 | - - |
| 1807 | Y | 301,200 | 18,072,000 | - - | 3,012 | - - |
| 1808 | *A* | 9,454,000 | - - | - - | 94,540 | - - |
| | *B* | 4,239,254 | - - | - - | 42,392 | - - |
| 1809 | *C* | 13,024,478 | - - | 51,233 | 130,244 | 2,669 |
| | *D* | 8,253,644 | - - | - - | 82,536 | - - |
| 1810 | *E* | 8,581,108 | - - | - - | 85,811 | - - |
| | *F* | 11,230,000 | - - | - - | 112,300 | - - |
| 1811 | *H* | 7,178,392 | - - | - - | 72,783 | - - |
| | *I* | 5,166,319 | - - | - - | 51,663 | - - |
| | *K* | 16,800,000 | - - | 41,500 | 168,000 | 1,451 |
| 1812 | *L* | 5,866,236 | - - | - - | 58,662 | - |
| | *M* | 7,332,795 | - - | - - | 73,327 | - - |
| | *N* | 27,544,000 | - - | - - | 275,440 | - - |
| | | 470,675,905 | 18,072,000 | 416,195 | 4,706,759 | 49,548 |
| charged in 1813 | | 86,796,375 | - - | - - | 867,963 | - - |
| Deduct | | 557,472,280 | - - | - - | 5,574,722 | - - |
| L. L. pd. | | 2,321,590 | - - | - - | 23,216 | - - |
| | | 555,150,690 | - - | - - | 5,551,506 | - - |
| S. F. on annuit. | | - - | - - | - - | 49,548 | - - |
| | | Amount 1 per cent. sinking fund, 1st February, 1812 - - - - | | | 5,601,054 | - - |

For continuation of this sinking fund, under Mr. Vansittart's plan, see Table XI.

 TABLE

## TABLE VII.

Amount of British Funded Debt redeemed and transferred.

| Years. | 3 per cents. redeemed. | 4 per cents. redeemed. | 5 per cents. redeemed. | Total redeemed. | 3 per cents. transferred for land tax. | 3 per cents. converted into life annuities. | Total. |
|---|---|---|---|---|---|---|---|
| Prec. 1791 | 6,772,350 | - - | - - | 6,772,350 | - - | - - | 6,772,350 |
| 1791 | 1,507,100 | - - | - - | 1,507,100 | - - | - - | 1,507,100 |
| 1792 | 1,962,650 | - - | - - | 1,962,650 | - - | - - | 1,962,650 |
| 1793 | 2,174,405 | - - | - - | 2,174,405 | - - | - - | 2,174,405 |
| 1794 | 2,804,945 | - - | - - | 2,804,945 | - - | - - | 2,804,945 |
| 1795 | 2,576,455 | 507,000 | - - | 3,083,455 | - - | - - | 3,083,455 |
| 1796 | 4,390,670 | - - | - - | 4,390,670 | - - | - - | 4,390,670 |
| 1797 | 6,695,585 | - - | - - | 6,695,585 | - - | - - | 6,695,585 |
| 1798 | 7,779,807 | - - | - - | 7,779,807 | - - | - - | 7,779,807 |
| 1799 | 7,151,984 | - - | - - | 7,151,984 | 13,059,586 | - - | 20,211,570 |
| 1800 | 7,247,560 | - - | - - | 7,247,560 | 3,034,210 | - - | 10,281,776 |
| 1801 | 7,333,393 | 685,000 | - - | 8,018,393 | 1,907,346 | - - | 9,925,739 |
| 1802 | 6,241,611 | 1,425,400 | - - | 7,667,011 | 1,179,439 | - - | 8,846,450 |
| 1803 | 10,442,552 | - - | - - | 10,442,552 | 1,967,301 | - - | 12,409,853 |
| 1804 | 11,163,292 | - - | 142,000 | 11,305,292 | 646,419 | - - | 11,951,711 |
| 1805 | 12,142,043 | - - | - - | 12,142,043 | 531,433 | - - | 12,673,476 |
| 1806 | 12,714,715 | - - | - - | 12,714,715 | 390,465 | - - | 13,105,180 |
| 1807 | 14,076,585 | - - | - - | 14,076,585 | 260,624 | - - | 14,337,209 |
| 1808 | 12,192,714 | 1,678,300 | - - | 13,871,014 | 237,569 | 465,951 | 14,574,534 |
| 1809 | 11,900,820 | 2,334,000 | - - | 14,234,820 | 207,070 | 558,561 | 15,000,451 |
| 1810 | 14,345,387 | 1,166,700 | - - | 15,512,087 | 284,623 | 290,777 | 16,087,487 |
| 1811 | 17,983,457 | - - | - - | 17,983,457 | 234,966 | 290,751 | 18,509,174 |
| 1812 | 20,922,876 | - - | - - | 20,922,876 | 437,747 | 355,542 | 21,716,165 |
| 1813 | 23,924,429 | - - | - - | 23,924,429 | 255,077 | 400,085 | 24,579,591 |
| 1814 | 18,968,435 | - - | - - | 14,968,435 | 326,432 | 433,673 | 19,728,540 |
| 1815 | 20,064,182 | - - | - - | 20,064,182 | 194,743 | 302,211 | 20,561,136 |
| 1816 | 18,293,270 | - - | 3,500 | 18,300,770 | 135,937 | 352,404 | 18,789,111 |
| | 283,773,271 | 7,796,400 | 145,500 | 291,719,172 | 25,290,994 | 3,449,955 | 320,460,121 |

| | |
|---|---|
| Irish debt redeemed, 3 per cents. - - - | 19,087,846 |
| Imperial debt redeemed, ditto - - - - | 1,920,316 |
| Portuguese debt redeemed, ditto - - - - | 426,721 |
| Total capital redeemed - - - - - | 341,895,004 |

## TABLE VIII.

Rates of Interest and Annuities on Loans and Funded Bills.

| | Years. | Sums borrowed. | Interest. | | | Terminable annuities. | | | Duration of annuity. | Total. | | |
|---|---|---|---|---|---|---|---|---|---|---|---|---|
| | | | L. | S. | D. | L. | S. | D. | | L. | S. | D. |
| Seven years' war. | *1755 | 900,000 | 3 | 0 | 0 | - | | - | - - | 3 | 0 | 0 |
| | *1756 | 1,500,000 | 3 | 10 | 0 | - | | - | - - | 3 | 10 | 0 |
| | and by lottery, | 500,000 | 3 | 0 | 0 | - | | - | - - | 3 | 0 | 0 |
| | 1757 | 3,000,000 | 3 | 0 | 0 | 1 | 2 | 6 | life | 4 | 2 | 6 |
| | *1758 | 4,500,000 | 3 | 0 | 0 | 0 | 10 | 0 | 24 years | 3 | 10 | 0 |
| | and by lottery, | 500,000 | 3 | 0 | 0 | - | | - | - - | 3 | 0 | 0 |
| | *1759 | 6,600,000 | 3 | 9 | 0 | - | | - | - - | 3 | 9 | 0 |
| | *1760 | 8,000,000 | 3 | 1 | 9 | 1 | 0 | 7 | 21 years | 4 | 2 | 4 |
| | *1761 | 11,400,000 | 3 | 0 | 0 | 1 | 2 | 6 | 99 years | 4 | 2 | 6 |
| | and by lottery, | 600,000 | 3 | 0 | 0 | - | | - | - - | 3 | 0 | 0 |
| | 1762 | 12,000,000 | 3 | 0 | 0 | 1<br>1 | 0<br>0 | 0<br>0 | 19 years<br>98 years | 5 | 0 | 0 |
| | *1763 | 3,500,000 | 4 | 0 | 0 | - | | - | - - | 4 | 0 | 0 |
| Peace. | *1766 | 1,500,000 | 3 | 0 | 0 | - | | - | - - | 3 | 0 | 0 |
| | *1767 | 1,500,000 | 3 | 0 | 0 | - | | - | - - | 3 | 0 | 0 |
| | *1768 | 1,900,000 | 3 | 0 | 0 | - | | - | - - | 3 | 0 | 0 |
| American war. | *1776 | 2,000,000 | 3 | 4 | 6 | - | | - | - - | 3 | 4 | 6 |
| | †1778 | 5,000,000 | 4 | 0 | 0 | 0 | 10 | 0 | 10 years | 4 | 10 | 0 |
| | †1778 | 6,000,000 | 3 | 0 | 0 | 2 | 10 | 0 | life, or 30 yrs. | 5 | 10 | 0 |
| | †1779 | 5,000,000 | 3 | 0 | 0 | 3 | 15 | 0 | life, or 29 yrs. | 6 | 15 | 0 |
| | †1780 | 12,000,000 | 4 | 0 | 0 | 1 | 16 | 3 | 80 years | 5 | 16 | 3 |
| | †1781 | 12,000,000 | 5 | 10 | 0 | - | | - | - - | 5 | 10 | 0 |
| | †1782 | 13,500,000 | 5 | 0 | 0 | 0 | 17 | 6 | 78 years | 5 | 17 | 6 |
| | †1783 | 12,000,000 | 4 | 0 | 0 | 0 | 13 | 4 | 77 years | 4 | 13 | 4 |
| | †1784 | 6,000,000 | 5 | 0 | 0 | 0 | 5 | 6 | 75½ years | 5 | 7 | 6 |
| Bills funded. | 1764 | 1,482,000 | 3 | 0 | 0 | - | | - | - - | 3 | 0 | 0 |
| | 1784 | 6,397,900 | 5 | 7 | 6 | - | | - | - - | 5 | 7 | 6 |
| | 1785 | 9,865,942 | 5 | 11 | 4 | - | | - | - - | 5 | 11 | 4 |
| French revolution war. | 1793 | 4,500,000 | 4 | 3 | 4 | - | | - | - - | 4 | 3 | 4 |
| | 1794 | 11,000,000 | 4 | 0 | 0 | 0 | 11 | 5 | 66¼ years | 4 | 11 | 5 |
| | 1795 | 18,000,000 | 4 | 6 | 8 | 0 | 9 | 6 | 65¼ years | 4 | 16 | 2 |
| | 1796 | 18,000,000 | 4 | 7 | 0 | 0 | 6 | 6 | 64¼ years | 4 | 13 | 6 |
| | | 7,500,000 | 4 | 7 | 0 | 0 | 5 | 6 | 63¾ years | 4 | 12 | 6 |
| | 1797 | 18,000,000 | 5 | 12 | 6 | - | | - | - - | 5 | 12 | 6 |
| | | 14,500,000 | 6 | 1 | 0 | 0 | 6 | 0 | 62¾ years | 6 | 7 | 0 |
| | 1798 | 17,000,000 | 6 | 0 | 0 | 0 | 4 | 11 | 61¾ years | 6 | 4 | 11 |
| | 1799 | 3,000,000 | 5 | 12 | 5 | - | | - | - - | 5 | 12 | 5 |
| | | 15,500,000 | 5 | 5 | 0 | - | | - | - - | 5 | 5 | 0 |
| | 1800 | 20,500,000 | 4 | 14 | 2 | - | | - | - - | 4 | 14 | 2 |
| | 1801 | 28,000,000 | 5 | 5 | 5 | - | | - | - - | 5 | 5 | 5 |

Continuation of Table VIII.

| | Years. | Sums borrowed | Interest. | | | Terminable annuities. | | | Duration of annuities. | Total. | | |
|---|---|---|---|---|---|---|---|---|---|---|---|---|
| | | | L. | S. | D. | L. | S. | D. | Years. | L. | S. | D. |
| Peace. | 1802 | 25,000,000 | 3 | 19 | 2 | - | | - | - | 3 | 19 | 2 |
| Renewed war, 1803. | 1803 | 12,000,000 | 4 | 16 | 0 | 0 | 6 | 5 | 56¾ | 5 | 2 | 5 |
| | 1804 | 14,500,000 | 5 | 9 | 2 | - | | - | - | 5 | 9 | 2 |
| | 1805 | 22,500,000 | 5 | 3 | 2 | - | | - | - | 5 | 3 | 2 |
| | for Ireland, | 1,500,000 | 1 | 4 | 0 | 5 | 0 | 0 | 54¾ | 6 | 4 | 0 |
| | 1806 | 20,000,000 | 4 | 19 | 7 | - | | - | - | 4 | 19 | 7 |
| | 1807 | 14,200,000 | 4 | 14 | 7 | - | | - | - | 4 | 14 | 7 |
| | for Ireland, | 1,500,000 | 4 | 16 | 4 | - | | - | - | 4 | 16 | 4 |
| | 1808 | 10,500,000 | 4 | 14 | 0 | - | | - | - | 4 | 14 | 6 |
| | 1809 | 14,600,000 | 4 | 4 | 0 | 0 | 8 | 10 | 50¾ | 4 | 12 | 10 |
| | 1810 | 12,000,000 | 4 | 4 | 2 | - | | - | - | 4 | 4 | 2 |
| | for Ireland, | 1,400,000 | 4 | 4 | 2 | - | | - | - | 4 | 4 | 2 |
| | 1811 | 4,981,300 | 5 | 2 | 10 | - | | - | - | 5 | 2 | 10 |
| | | 12,000,000 | 4 | 8 | 0 | 0 | 6 | 11 | 48¾ | 4 | 14 | 11 |
| | 1812 | 6,789,625 | 5 | 8 | 0 | - | | - | - | 5 | 8 | 0 |
| | | 22,500,000 | 5 | 5 | 7 | - | | - | - | 5 | 5 | 7 |
| | 1813 | 27,000,000 | 5 | 2 | 0 | 0 | 8 | 6 | 46⅜ | 5 | 10 | 6 |
| | | 22,000,000 | 5 | 6 | 2 | - | | - | - | 5 | 6 | 2 |
| Peace, | 1814 | 24,000,000 | 4 | 12 | 2 | - | | - | - | 4 | 12 | 2 |
| War, | 1815 | 7,008,089 | 5 | 17 | 0 | - | | - | - | 5 | 17 | 0 |
| | | 36,000,000 | 5 | 12 | 0 | - | | - | - | 5 | 12 | 0 |
| Peace, | 1816 | 3,000,000 | 3 | 0 | 0 | - | | - | - | 3 | 0 | 0 |
| Bills funded during French Revolution wars. | 1794 | 1,907,451 | 5 | 1 | 0 | - | | - | - | 5 | 1 | 0 |
| | 1795 | 1,490,647 | 5 | 8 | 0 | - | | - | - | 5 | 8 | 0 |
| | 1796 | 4,226,727 | 5 | 4 | 2 | - | | - | - | 5 | 4 | 2 |
| | | 13,029,399 | 5 | 7 | 11 | - | | - | - | 5 | 7 | 11 |
| | 1802 | 8,910,450 | 4 | 15 | 0 | 10 | 9 | 9 | 58¾ | 5 | 5 | 9 |
| | 1808 | 4,000,000 | 5 | 4 | 9 | - | | - | - | 5 | 4 | 9 |
| | 1809 | 7,932,100 | 5 | 3 | 1 | - | | - | - | 5 | 3 | 1 |
| | 1810 | 8,311,000 | 5 | 3 | 3 | - | | - | - | 5 | 3 | 3 |
| | 1811 | 7,018,700 | 5 | 3 | 8 | - | | - | - | 5 | 3 | 8 |
| | 1812 | 5,431,700 | 5 | 8 | 0 | - | | - | - | 5 | 8 | 0 |
| | 1813 | 12,000,000 | 5 | 15 | 6 | - | | - | - | 5 | 15 | 6 |
| | | 3,755,700 | 5 | 11 | 2 | - | | - | - | 5 | 11 | 2 |
| | 1815 | 11,127,500 | 5 | 17 | 0 | - | | - | - | 5 | 17 | 0 |

The subscribers to the loans marked thus * had also the profits of lotteries, the prizes in which were funded.

The subscribers to the loans marked thus † had also the profits of lotteries, the prizes in which were paid.

Fractions under a penny in the rate of interest are omitted.

 TABLE

**TABLE IX.—Lord Henry Petty's Plan of Finance.**

PART I.—*Loans on War Taxes.*

| Yrs. | 1<br>Loans on war taxes. | 2<br>War taxes mortgaged each year. | 3<br>½ Amount war taxes mortgaged. | 4<br>Sum redeemed each year. | 5<br>Whole sum redeemed. | 6<br>Interest on amount redeemed. |
|---|---|---|---|---|---|---|
| 1807 | 12,000,000 | 1,200,000 | 600,000 | 600,000 | 600,000 | 30,000 |
| 1808 | 12,000,000 | 1,200,000 | 1,200,000 | 1,230,000 | 1,830,000 | 91,500 |
| 1809 | 12,000,000 | 1,200,000 | 1,800,000 | 1,891,500 | 3,721,500 | 186,075 |
| 1810 | 14,000,000 | 1,400,000 | 2,500,000 | 2,686,073 | 6,407,575 | 320,378 |
| 1811 | 16,000,000 | 1,600,000 | 3,300,000 | 3,620,378 | 10,027,953 | 501,398 |
| 1812 | 16,000,000 | 1,600,000 | 4,100,000 | 4,601,398 | 14,629,351 | 731,467 |
| 1813 | 16,000,000 | 1,600,000 | 4,900,000 | 5,631,467 | 20,260,818 | 1,013,041 |
| 1814 | 16,000,000 | 1,600,000 | 5,700,000 | 6,713,041 | 26,973,859 | 1,348,693 |
| 1815 | 16,000,000 | 1,600,000 | 6,500,000 | 7,848,693 | 34,822,552 | 1,741,127 |
| 1816 | 16,000,000 | 1,600,000 | 7,300,000 | 9,041,128 | 43,863,680 | 2,193,184 |
| 1817 | 16,000,000 | 1,600,000 | 8,100,000 | 10,293,184 | 54,156,864 | 2,707,843 |
| 1818 | 16,000,000 | 1,600,000 | 8,900,000 | 11,607,843 | 65,764,707 | 3,288,235 |
| 1819 | 16,000,000 | 1,600,000 | 9,700,000 | 12,988,235 | 78,752,942 | 3,937,647 |
| 1820 | 16,000,000 | 1,600,000 | 10,500,000 | 14,437,647 | 93,190,589 | 4,659,529 |
| | 210,000,000 | 21,000,000 | 75,100,000 | 93,190,589 | | |
| 1821 | 12,000,000 | 1,200,000 | 10,500,000 | 14,559,529 | 107,750,118 | 5,387,505 |
| 1822 | 12,000,000 | 1,200,000 | 10,500,000 | 14,687,505 | 122,437,623 | 6,121,880 |
| 1823 | 12,000,000 | 1,200,000 | 10,500,000 | 14,821,880 | 137,259,503 | 6,862,974 |
| 1824 | 14,000,000 | 1,400,000 | 10,500,000 | 14,862,974 | 152,122,477 | 7,606,123 |
| 1825 | 16,000,000 | 1,600,000 | 10,500,000 | 14,806,123 | 166,928,600 | 8,346,429 |
| 1826 | 16,000,000 | 1,600,000 | 10,500,000 | 14,746,429 | 181,675,029 | 9,083,751 |
| | 292,000,000 | 29,200,000 | | 181,675,029 | | |

PART II.—*Supplementary Loans.*

| Yrs. | 7<br>Supplementary loans. | 8<br>Interest. | 9<br>Sinking fund. | 10<br>Sum redeemed each year. | 11<br>Whole sum redeemed. | 12<br>Interest on amount redeemed. |
|---|---|---|---|---|---|---|
| 1807 | 200,000 | 10,000 | 3,333 | 3,333 | 3,333 | 166 |
| 1808 | 1,400,000 | 70,000 | 23,333 | 26,833 | 30,166 | 1,508 |
| 1809 | 2,600,000 | 130,000 | 43,333 | 71,508 | 101,674 | 5,083 |
| 1810 | 2,000,000 | 100,000 | 33,333 | 108,416 | 210,090 | 10,504 |
| 1811 | 1,600,000 | 80,000 | 26,666 | 140,504 | 350,594 | 17,530 |
| 1812 | 3,200,000 | 160,000 | 53,333 | 200,863 | 551,457 | 27,573 |
| 1813 | 4,800,000 | 240,000 | 80,000 | 290,906 | 842,363 | 42,118 |
| 1814 | 6,400,000 | 320,000 | 106,666 | 412,118 | 1,254,481 | 62,724 |
| 1815 | 8,000,000 | 400,000 | 133,333 | 566,057 | 1,820,538 | 91,027 |
| 1816 | 9,600,000 | 480,000 | 160,000 | 754,360 | 2,574,898 | 128,744 |
| 1817 | 11,200,000 | 560,000 | 186,666 | 978,744 | 3,553,642 | 177,682 |
| 1818 | 12,800,000 | 640,000 | 213,333 | 1,241,015 | 4,794,657 | 239,732 |
| 1819 | 14,400,000 | 720,000 | 240,000 | 1,543,065 | 6,337,722 | 316,886 |
| 1820 | 16,000,000 | 800,000 | 266,666 | 1,886,886 | 8,224,608 | 411,230 |
| | 94,200,000 | 4,710,000 | 1,570,000 | 8,224,608 | | |
| 1821 | 20,000,000 | 1,000,000 | 333,333 | 2,314,563 | 10,539,171 | 526,958 |
| 1822 | 20,000,000 | 1,000,000 | 333,333 | 2,763,624 | 13,302,795 | 665,139 |
| 1823 | 20,000,000 | 1,000,000 | 333,333 | 3,235,139 | 16,537,934 | 826,896 |
| 1824 | 18,000,000 | 900,000 | 300,000 | 3,696,896 | 20,234,830 | 1,011,741 |
| 1825 | 16,000,000 | 800,000 | 266,666 | 4,148,407 | 24,383,237 | 1,219,161 |
| 1826 | 16,000,000 | 800,000 | 266,666 | 4,622,494 | 29,005,731 | 1,450,286 |
| | 204,200,000 | 10,210,000 | 3,403,338 | 29,005,731 | | |



Lord

## Lord Henry Petty's plan of Finance continued.

### Part III.—*Joint View of both Loans.*

| Yrs. | 13 Amount war tax loan. | 14 Amount supplementary loans. | 15 War tax loans unredeemed. | 16 Supplementary loans unredeemed. | 17 Total loans unredeemed. | 18 Interest on loans unredeemed. | 19 Amount taxes raised each year. |
|---|---|---|---|---|---|---|---|
| 1807 | 12,000,000 | 200,000 | 11,400,000 | 196,666 | 11,596,666 | 579,833 | 13,333 |
| 1808 | 24,000,000 | 1,600,000 | 22,170,000 | 1,596,833 | 23,739,833 | 1,186,991 | 106,666 |
| 1809 | 36,000,000 | 4,200,000 | 32,278,500 | 4,098,326 | 36,377,126 | 1,818,856 | 280,000 |
| 1810 | 50,000,000 | 6,200,000 | 43,595,425 | 5,989,910 | 49,585,335 | 2,479,266 | 413,333 |
| 1811 | 66,000,000 | 7,800,000 | 55,972,047 | 7,449,406 | 63,421,453 | 3,171,072 | 520,000 |
| 1812 | 82,000,000 | 11,000,000 | 67,370,649 | 10,448,543 | 77,819,192 | 3,890,959 | 733,333 |
| 1813 | 98,000,000 | 15,800,000 | 77,739,182 | 14,957,637 | 92,696,819 | 4,634,841 | 1,053,333 |
| 1814 | 114,000,000 | 22,200,000 | 87,026,141 | 20,945,519 | 107,971,660 | 5,398,583 | 1,480,000 |
| 1815 | 130,000,000 | 30,200,000 | 95,177,448 | 28,379,462 | 123,556,910 | 6,177,845 | 2,013,333 |
| 1816 | 146,000,000 | 39,800,000 | 102,136,320 | 37,225,102 | 139,361,427 | 6,968,071 | 2,653,333 |
| 1817 | 162,000,000 | 51,000,000 | 107,843,136 | 47,446,358 | 155,289,494 | 7,764,474 | 3,400,000 |
| 1818 | 178,000,000 | 63,800,000 | 112,235,293 | 59,005,343 | 171,240,636 | 8,562,031 | 4,253,333 |
| 1819 | 194,000,000 | 78,200,000 | 115,247,058 | 71,862,278 | 187,109,336 | 9,355,466 | 5,213,333 |
| 1820 | 210,000,000 | 94,200,000 | 116,809,411 | 85,975,392 | 202,784,803 | 10,139,411 | 6,280,000 |
| | | | | | | 72,127,353 | 28,413,333 |
| 1821 | 222,000,000 | 114,200,000 | 114,429,882 | 103,660,829 | 218,090,711 | 10,904,535 | 7,613,333 |
| 1822 | 234,000,000 | 134,200,000 | 111,562,382 | 120,897,205 | 232,459,587 | 11,622,979 | 8,946,666 |
| 1823 | 246,000,000 | 154,200,000 | 108,740,502 | 137,662,066 | 246,402,568 | 12,320,128 | 10,280,000 |
| 1824 | 260,000,000 | 172,200,000 | 107,877,528 | 151,965,170 | 259,842,698 | 12,992,135 | 11,480,000 |
| 1825 | 276,000,000 | 188,200,000 | 109,071,405 | 163,816,763 | 272,888,168 | 13,644,408 | 12,546,666 |
| 1826 | 292,000,000 | 204,200,000 | 110,324,976 | 175,194,229 | 285,519,205 | 14,275,960 | 13,613,333 |
| | | | | | | 147,887,498 | 92,893,333 |

### Part IV.—*Comparison with other Systems.*

| Yrs. | 20 No sinking fund. Debt. | 21 Taxes. | 22 Sinking fund of 1-100. Debt unred. | 23 Taxes. | 24 Sinking fund of 1-60. Debt unred. | 25 Taxes. |
|---|---|---|---|---|---|---|
| 1807 | 11,000,000 | 550,000 | 10,890,000 | 660,000 | 10,816,666 | 733,333 |
| 1808 | 22,000,000 | 1,110,000 | 21,664,500 | 1,320,000 | 21,440,833 | 1,466,666 |
| 1809 | 33,000,000 | 1,650,000 | 32,317,725 | 1,980,000 | 31,862,875 | 2,200,000 |
| 1810 | 44,000,000 | 2,200,000 | 42,843,611 | 2,640,000 | 42,072,685 | 2,933,333 |
| 1811 | 55,000,000 | 2,750,000 | 53,235,792 | 3,300,000 | 52,059,653 | 3,666,666 |
| 1812 | 66,000,000 | 3,300,000 | 63,487,582 | 3,960,000 | 61,812,636 | 4,400,000 |
| 1813 | 77,000,000 | 3,850,000 | 73,591,961 | 4,620,000 | 71,319,935 | 5,133,333 |
| 1814 | 88,000,000 | 4,400,000 | 83,541,559 | 5,280,000 | 80,569,265 | 5,866,666 |
| 1815 | 99,000,000 | 4,950,000 | 93,328,627 | 5,940,000 | 89,547,729 | 6,600,000 |
| 1816 | 110,000,000 | 5,500,000 | 102,945,069 | 6,600,000 | 98,241,782 | 7,333,333 |
| 1817 | 121,000,000 | 6,050,000 | 112,382,323 | 7,260,000 | 106,737,206 | 8,066,666 |
| 1818 | 132,000,000 | 6,600,000 | 121,631,439 | 7,920,000 | 114,719,067 | 8,800,000 |
| 1819 | 143,000,000 | 7,150,000 | 130,683,011 | 8,580,000 | 122,471,687 | 9,533,333 |
| 1820 | 154,000,000 | 7,750,000 | 139,527,162 | 9,240,000 | 129,878,604 | 10,266,666 |
| | | 57,700,000 | | 69,300,000 | | 77,000,000 |
| 1821 | 165,000,000 | 8,250,000 | 148,153,520 | 9,900,000 | 136,922,535 | 11,000,000 |
| 1822 | 176,000,000 | 8,800,000 | 156,551,196 | 10,560,000 | 143,585,328 | 11,733,333 |
| 1823 | 187,000,000 | 9,350,000 | 164,708,756 | 11,220,000 | 149,847,928 | 12,466,666 |
| 1824 | 198,000,000 | 9,900,000 | 172,614,194 | 11,880,000 | 155,690,324 | 13,200,000 |
| 1825 | 209,000,000 | 10,450,000 | 180,254,904 | 12,540,000 | 161,091,507 | 13,933,333 |
| 1826 | 220,000,000 | 11,000,000 | 187,617,650 | 13,200,000 | 166,029,417 | 14,666,666 |
| | | 115,000,000 | | 138,600,000 | | 154,000,000 |

TABLE X.

Comparison of Mr. Vansittart's plan of Finance with the former system.

PART I.—*Comparison of Taxes Levied.*

| Year ending 1st Aug. | Former System. | | New System. | | Excess of taxes by former system. |
|---|---|---|---|---|---|
| | Taxes imposed ann. | Taxes levied annually. | Taxes imposed ann. | Taxes levied annually. | |
| 1814 | 1,866,666 | 1,866,666 | 1,127,963 | 1,127,963 | 738,703 |
| 1815 | 1,866,666 | 3,733,332 | - - | 1,127,963 | 2,605,369 |
| 1816 | 1,866,666 | 5,599,998 | - - | 1,127,963 | 4,472,035 |
| 1817 | 1,866,666 | 7,466,664 | - - | 1,127,963 | 6,338,701 |
| 1818 | 1,866,666 | 9,333,330 | 1,290,206 | 2,418,169 | 6,915,161 |
| 1819 | 1,866,666 | 11,199,996 | 676,775 | 3,094,944 | 8,105,052 |
| 1820 | 1,866,666 | 13,066,662 | 2,008,333 | 5,103,277 | 7,963,385 |
| 1821 | 1,866,666 | 14,933,328 | 1,995,833 | 7,099,110 | 7,834,218 |
| | 14,933,328 | 67,199,976 | 7,099,110 | 22,227,352 | 44,972,624 |
| 1822 | 1,800,000 | 16,733,328 | 1,987,500 | 9,086,610 | 7,646,718 |
| 1823 | 1,800,000 | 18,533,328 | - - | 9,086,610 | 9,446,718 |
| 1824 | 1,800,000 | 20,333,328 | 624,431 | 9,711,041 | 10,622,327 |
| 1825 | 1,800,000 | 22,133,328 | 1,158,356 | 10,869,397 | 11,263,931 |
| 1826 | 1,800,000 | 23,933,328 | 1,979,166 | 12,848,563 | 11,084,765 |
| 1827 | 1,800,000 | 25,733,328 | 1,095,316 | 13,943,879 | 11,789,449 |
| 1828 | 1,800,000 | 27,533,328 | 618,013 | 14,561,892 | 12,971,436 |
| 1829 | 1,800,000 | 29,333,328 | 1,962,500 | 16,524,392 | 12,808,936 |
| | 29,333,328 | 251,466,600 | 16,524,392 | 118,859,736 | 132,606,864 |

PART II.—*Comparison of Sinking Funds.*

| Years. | Sinking fund, former system. | Sinking fund, new system. | Excess of sinking fund, old system. | Excess of sinking fund o. s. above add. taxes. |
|---|---|---|---|---|
| 1814 | 14,423,455 | 13,647,817 | 775,638 | 36,935 |
| 1815 | 15,634,627 | 12,860,207 | 2,774,420 | 169,051 |
| 1816 | 16,906,357 | 12,033,217 | 4,873,140 | 401,105 |
| 1817 | 18,241,674 | 11,164,877 | 7,076,797 | 738,096 |
| 1818 | 19,643,757 | 11,607,837 | 8,035,920 | 1,120,759 |
| 1819 | 21,115,944 | 11,428,842 | 9,687,102 | 1,582,050 |
| 1820 | 22,661,740 | 12,639,033 | 10,022,707 | 2,059,322 |
| 1821 | 24,284,826 | 13,896,609 | 10,388,217 | 2,553,999 |
| | 152,912,380 | 99,278,439 | 53,633,941 | 8,661,317 |
| 1822 | 34,718,019 | 15,208,314 | 9,509,705 | 1,862,987 |
| 1823 | 26,426,419 | 14,498,729 | 11,927,690 | 2,480,972 |
| 1824 | 28,220,239 | 14,409,318 | 13,810,921 | 3,188,634 |
| 1825 | 30,103,750 | 14,876,057 | 15,227,693 | 3,963,762 |
| 1826 | 32,081,437 | 16,227,984 | 15,853,453 | 4,768,688 |
| 1827 | 34,158,008 | 16,719,465 | 17,438,543 | 5,649,094 |
| 1828 | 36,338,408 | 16,734,351 | 19,604,057 | 6,632,621 |
| 1829 | 38,627,828 | 18,161,693 | 20,466,135 | 7,657,199 |
| | 403,586,488 | 226,114,350 | 177,472,138 | 44,865,274 |



TABLE

TABLE XI.

Operations on Mr. Vansittart's Sinking Fund.

| | | Sums borrowed, or bills funded. | Capital funded. | Capital charged with 1 p. ct. S.F. | Cap. charg. with half int. S.F. |
|---|---|---|---|---|---|
| 1813 Ex. Bills, | *O* | 12,000,000 | 13,860,000 | 13,860,000 | |
| Ditto, | *P* | 3,755,700 | 5,220,423 | 1,409,340 | 3,811,083 |
| Loan, | *Q* | 21,000,000 | 35,700,000 | - - | 35,700,000 |
| Loan, | *R* | 22,000,000 | 38,940,000 | - - | 38,940,000 |
| 1814 Loan, | *S* | 18,500,000 | 24,694,830 | 15,126,153 | 9,568,677 |
| 1815 Ex. Bills, | *T* | 10,313,000 | 12,066,210 | 12,066,210 | - - |
| E. B. & loan, | *U* | 7,822,589 | 9,142,192 | 1,183,471 | 7,958,721 |
| Loan, | *V* | 27,000,000 | 49,680,000 | - - | 49,680,000 |
| | | 122,391,289 | 189,303,655 | 43,645,174 | 145,658,481 |

| | Sinking fund at 1 per cent. | Sink. fund at half interest. | Whole sinking fund. | Interest, annuit. and managemt. | Total charge. |
|---|---|---|---|---|---|
| *O* | 138,600 | - - | 138,600 | 697,158 | 835,758 |
| *P* | 14,093 | 76,221 | 90,314 | 210,383 | 300,697 |
| *Q* | * 1,499 | 535,500 | 536,999 | † 1,169,858 | 1,706,858 |
| *R* | - - | 584,100 | 584,100 | 1,179,882 | 1,763,982 |
| *S* | 151,261 | 165,079 | 316,340 | 859,334 | 1,175,674 |
| *T* | 120,662 | - - | 120,662 | 606,930 | 727,592 |
| *U* | 11,834 | 198,968 | 210,802 | 459,851 | 670,653 |
| *V* | - - | 758,700 | 758,700 | 1,532,406 | 2,291,106 |
| | 437,949 | 2,318,569 | 2,756,518 | 6,715,802 | 9,472,320 |
| Charged on consolidated fund, | | | 543,494 | 1,295,857 | 1,839,351 |
| On sinking fund, - - - | | | 2,213,024 | 5,419,945 | 7,632,969 |

Capitals Cancelled.

| | | 3 per cent. consols. | 3 per cent. reduced. | South Sea stock. | 4 per cent. | 5 per cent. navy. | Total. |
|---|---|---|---|---|---|---|---|
| | *O, P, Q,* | 46,884,600 | 47,892,500 | - - | - - | - - | 94,777,100 |
| | *R,* | 22,257,400 | 36,542,000 | - - | - - | - - | 58,799,400 |
| | *S,* | 10,272,392 | 23,733,099 | 4,947,000 | - - | 142,000 | 39,094,491 |
| Part of | *T, U, V,* | - - | 51,271,467 | - - | 7,796,400 | - - | 59,067,867 |
| | | 79,414,392 | 159,439,066 | 4,947,000 | 7,796,400 | 142,000 | 251,738,858 |

* For long annuities, attached to this loan.

† This is less by L.1,771, than stated in article *Q*. See Note XXV.

## TABLE XII.

### Unfunded Debt.

| Year ending 5th January | Exchequer Bills. | Navy debt. | Ordnance debt. | Total. | Increase or decrease. | Interest on Ex. Bills. |
|---|---|---|---|---|---|---|
| 1793 | 11,361,000 | 3,450,134 | 91,501 | 14,902,635 | | |
| 1794 | 11,849,000 | 6,709,748 | 303,458 | 18,862,206 | + 3,859,571 | |
| 1795 | 10,111,300 | 10,413,164 | 755,564 | 21,280,028 | + 2,417,822 | |
| 1796 | 13,781,000 | 12,321,828 | 1,235,631 | 27,338,459 | + 6,058,431 | |
| 1797 | 13,218,600 | 4,485,799 | 763,153 | 18,467,552 | — 8,870,907 | |
| 1798 | 13,368,400 | 6,150,588 | 548,233 | 20,067,221 | + 1,599,699 | |
| 1799 | 14,310,400 | 5,556,033 | 983,249 | 20,849,682 | + 782,461 | 356,847 |
| 1800 | 20,360,700 | 5,992,228 | 631,831 | 26,984,819 | + 6,135,137 | 1,021,620 |
| 1801 | 26,080,100 | 8,705,819 | 832,113 | 35,618,099 | + 8,633,280 | 766,480 |
| 1802 | 20,588,100 | 7,100,800 | 701,428 | 28,400,408 | — 7,217,691 | 1,121,890 |
| 1803 | 16,456,000 | 3,105,648 | 399,760 | 19,961,408 | — 8,439,000 | 1,105,935 |
| 1804 | 19,067,600 | 4,037,307 | 682,343 | 23,787,250 | + 3,825,842 | 801,874 |
| 1805 | 25,253,500 | 5,011,567 | 1,260,480 | 31,515,548 | + 7,718,297 | 624,859 |
| 1806 | 27,180,400 | 5,911,588 | 1,104,512 | 34,196,500 | + 2,680,971 | 1,478,316 |
| 1807 | 27,207,500 | 5,885,819 | 1,255,071 | 34,348,391 | + 151,981 | 1,310,686 |
| 1808 | 34,942,400 | 6,561,237 | 1,165,822 | 39,669,960 | + 5,331,569 | 1,574,361 |
| 1809 | 39,301,200 | 7,221,167 | 861,364 | 47,383,632 | + 7,713,672 | 1,610,562 |
| 1810 | 39,164,100 | 8,263,175 | 1,015,360 | 48,442,635 | + 1,059,003 | 1,862,943 |
| 1811 | 38,286,300 | 7,595,838 | 1,089,441 | 46,971,579 | — 1,471,056 | 1,815,105 |
| 1812 | 41,491,800 | 7,883,890 | 1,078,476 | 50,454,166 | + 3,482,587 | 1,556,755 |
| 1813 | 45,406,400 | 7,748,872 | 900,360 | 54,055,632 | + 3,601,466 | 1,019,238 |
| 1814 | 47,516,800 | 8,561,290 | 671,093 | 56,749,183 | + 2,693,551 | 2,081,529 |
| 1815 | 57,941,700 | 6,361,076 | 793,919 | 65,096,695 | + 8,347,512 | 2,256,907 |
| 1816 | 41,441,900 | 3,694,821 | 876,857 | 46,013,578 | —19,083,117 | 3,014,003 |
| 1817 | 44,650,300 | 1,735,731 | 391,641 | 46,777,672 | + 764,094 | 2,196,777 |

### Whole Unfunded Debt reported to Parliament.

| | Exch. Bills, Navy and Ordnance debt. | Miscellaneous articles. | Total. | Increase or decrease. |
|---|---|---|---|---|
| 1811 | 46,971,579 | 3,648,368 | 50,619,947 | |
| 1812 | 50,454,166 | 3,583,893 | 54,038,059 | + 3,418,122 |
| 1813 | 54,055,632 | * 3,783,064 | 57,838,696 | + 3,800,637 |
| 1814 | 56,749,183 | 4,219,783 | 60,968,966 | + 3,130,270 |
| 1815 | 65,096,695 | 3,483,829 | 68,580,524 | + 7,611,558 |
| 1816 | 46,031,578 | 2,711,601 | 48,725,359 | —19,865,165 |
| 1817 | 46,777,672 | 3,269,416 | 50,047,088 | + 1,321,729 |

* Besides this debt, L.799,300 was raised by debentures, (see page 518.)

## POSTSCRIPT.—February, 1818.

There was no loan in the year 1817. We have not yet materials for exhibiting a detailed account of the financial operations of that year: But, as was stated by the Chancellor of the Exchequer, in the House of Commons, that the increase of Exchequer Bills in circulation was little more than 12 millions, when about 15 millions* had been applied to the reduction of the national debt; being three millions more than the additional debt contracted. Most of the Exchequer Bills lately issued only bear interest at the rate of 2½d. on L.100 per day; and they are now issued at the low rate of 2d. per day.

The amount redeemed in the several stocks, payable in Britain, from 1st February to 1st October, 1817, was,

| | |
|---|---|
| 3 per cent. reduced, - - - - - | L.9,351,796 |
| 3 per cent. consols, - - - - - | 3,451,012 |
| Old South Sea annuities, - - - - | 240,000 |
| New South Sea annuities, - - - - | 255,500 |
| 3 per cents. 1751, - - - - - | 45,000 |
| Imperial annuities, - - - - - | 116,277 |
| | L.13,459,585 |
| And on various funds, from 1st Nov. 1817, to 5th January, 1818 - - - - - | 4,371,733 |
| | L.17,831,318 |
| The interest of which affords an addition to the sinking fund of - - - - - - | L.534,940 |

267 Corrigenda

* This seems to include a sum granted for the reduction of the debt of the navy, as the sinking fund that year was only about 13½ millions.

## *CORRIGENDA ET ADDENDA.*

Page 501.—The war in Queen Anne's reign is stated as commencing in 1701; and, therefore, to have been of 12 years' duration. The declaration of war was not made till May 1702; but preparations for it were begun the year before, in King William's reign. An alteration of the year would require the alteration of some figures, but would not much affect the general result.

---

Page 523.—Add

| | | | *Irish Currency.* |
|---|---|---|---|
| Interest on | L.17,380,972, | 3½ per cents. | L.608,334 |
| on | 1,150,100, | 4 per cents. | 46,004 |
| on | L.13,611,148, | | |
| and | 2,058,333—L.1,900,000 British. | | |
| | L.15,669,481, | 5 per cents. | 783,474 |
| | | | L.1,437,812 |
| Tontine annuities, - | - | - - - - | 47,668 |

# INDEX.

D.



E.

F.

G.



H.

## L.



## M.

O.



P.

## R.

U.



V.